### ISDN AND BROADBAND ISDN, with FRAME RELAY AND ATM, THIRD EDITION

An in-depth presentation of the technology and architecture of integrated services digital networks (ISDN). Covers the integrated digital network (IDN), ISDN services, architecture, Signaling System No. 7 (SS7) and provides detailed coverage of the ITU-T standards. This new edition also provides detailed coverage of protocols and congestion control strategies for both frame relay and ATM.

### BUSINESS DATA COMMUNICATIONS, SECOND EDITION

A comprehensive presentation of data communications and telecommunications from a business perspective. Covers voice, data, image, and video communications and applications technology and includes a number of case studies.

### OPERATING SYSTEMS, SECOND EDITION

A state-of-the-art survey of operating system principles. Covers fundamental technology as well as contemporary design issues, such as threads, real-time systems, multiprocessor scheduling, distributed systems, security, and object-oriented design.

### PROTECT YOUR PRIVACY: A GUIDE FOR PGP USERS

Provides detailed step-by-step instructions on the use of PGP on the most important computer platforms. It explains the fundamentals of encryption and digital signatures so that the reader will know what PGP can do for him or her. Also provides explicit instructions on solving the all-important problem of obtaining trusted public keys of other users.

# COMPUTER ORGANIZATION AND ARCHITECTURE

# COMPUTER ORGANIZATION AND ARCHITECTURE

## Designing for Performance

**FOURTH EDITION**

## William Stallings

**PRENTICE HALL**
Upper Saddle River, New Jersey 07458

*Library of Congress Cataloging-in-Publication Data*

Stallings, William
Computer organization and architecture : designing for performance /
    William Stallings. — 4th ed.
        p.     cm.
    Includes bibliographical references and index.
    ISBN 0–13–359985–X
    1. Computer organization. 2. Computer architecture. I. Title.
QA76.9.C643S73 1996
004.2'2—dc20                                            96–9115
                                                           CIP

Acquisitions editor: Alan Apt
Editorial-production service: Electronic Publishing Services Inc.
Manufacturing buyer: Donna Sullivan
Cover design: Amy Rosen
Cover photograph: Jon Churchman
Production coordinator: Rick DeLorenzo
Editorial assistant: Shirley McGuire

Printed in the United States of America

10 9 8 7

ISBN 0-13-359985-X

Prentice-Hall International (UK) Limited, *London*
Prentice-Hall of Austria Pty. Limited, *Sydney*
Prentice-Hall Canada Inc., *Toronto*
Prentice-Hall Hispanoamericana, S.A., *Mexico*
Prentice-Hall of India Private Limited, *New Delhi*
Prentice-Hall of Japan, Inc., *Tokyo*
Simon & Schuster Asia Pte. Ltd., *Singapore*
Editora Prentice-Hall do Brasil Ltda., *Rio de Janeiro*

To my loving wife, Tricia

# CONTENTS

PREFACE     xi


PART I   OVERVIEW                                                         1


CHAPTER 1    Introduction      3
1.1   Organization and Architecture      3
1.2   Structure and Function      4
1.3   Outline of the Book      9

CHAPTER 2    Computer Evolution and Performance      15
2.1   A Brief History of Computers      15
2.2   Designing for Performance      36
2.3   Pentium and PowerPC Evolution      40
2.4   Recommended Reading      44
2.5   Problems      45


PART II   THE COMPUTER SYSTEM                                             47


CHAPTER 3    System Buses      49
3.1   Computer Components      49
3.2   Computer Function      52
3.3   Interconnection Structures      65
3.4   Bus Interconnection      65
3.5   PCI      75
3.6   Futurebus+      84
3.7   Recommended Reading      94
3.8   Problems      94
APPENDIX 3A   Timing Diagrams      97

CHAPTER 4    Internal Memory      100
4.1    Computer Memory System Overview      100
4.2    Semiconductor Main Memory      108
4.3    Cache Memory      121
4.4    Advanced DRAM Organization      140
4.5    Recommended Reading      146
4.6    Problems      147
Appendix 4A    Performance Characteristics of Two-Level Memories      149

CHAPTER 5    External Memory      155
5.1    Magnetic Disk      155
5.2    RAID      161
5.3    Optical Memory      169
5.4    Magnetic Tape      174
5.5    Recommended Reading      175
5.6    Problems      175

CHAPTER 6    Input/Output      178
6.1    External Devices      178
6.2    I/O Modules      182
6.3    Programmed I/O      186
6.4    Interrupt-Driven I/O      190
6.5    Direct Memory Access      199
6.6    I/O Channels and Processors      202
6.7    The External Interface      204
6.8    Recommended Reading      218
6.9    Problems      219

CHAPTER 7    Operating System Support      222
7.1    Operating System Overview      222
7.2    Scheduling      234
7.3    Memory Management      240
7.4    Recommended Reading      262
7.5    Problems      263

PART III    THE CENTRAL PROCESSING UNIT                                        267

CHAPTER 8    Computer Arithmetic      269
8.1    The Arithmetic and Logic Unit (ALU)      269
8.2    Integer Representation      270
8.3    Integer Arithmetic      275
8.4    Floating-Point Representation      289
8.5    Floating-Point Arithmetic      295
8.6    Recommended Reading      304
8.7    Problems      305
APPENDIX 8A    Number Systems      306

CHAPTER 9    Instruction Sets: Characteristics and Functions    313
9.1    Machine Instruction Characteristics    313
9.2    Types of Operands    320
9.3    Types of Operations    325
9.4    Assembly Language    344
9.5    Recommended Reading    346
9.6    Problems    346
APPENDIX 9A    Stacks    351
APPENDIX 9B    Little-, Big-, and Bi-Endian    356

CHAPTER 10    Instruction Sets: Addressing Modes and Formats    361
10.1    Addressing    361
10.2    Instruction Formats    374
10.3    Recommended Reading    386
10.4    Problems    386

CHAPTER 11    CPU Structure and Function    388
11.1    Processor Organization    388
11.2    Register Organization    389
11.3    The Instruction Cycle    396
11.4    Instruction Pipelining    400
11.5    The Pentium Processor    412
11.6    The PowerPC Processor    418
11.7    Recommended Reading    425
11.8    Problems    425

CHAPTER 12    Reduced Instruction Set Computers (RISCs)    428
12.1    Instruction Execution Characteristics    429
12.2    The Use of a Large Register File    434
12.3    Compiler-Based Register Optimization    439
12.4    Reduced Instruction Set Architecture    440
12.5    RISC Pipelining    447
12.6    Motorola 88510    451
12.7    MIPS R4650    458
12.8    The RISC versus CISC Controversy    465
12.9    Recommended Reading    466
12.10 Problems    467

CHAPTER 13    Superscalar Processors    472
13.1    Overview    472
13.2    Design Issues    477
13.3    PowerPC    485
13.4    Pentium    492
13.5    Recommended Reading    497
13.6    Problems    498

# PART IV   THE CONTROL UNIT                                                       501

CHAPTER 14   Control Unit Operation      503
14.1   Micro-operations      503
14.2   Control of the CPU      510
14.3   Hardwired Implementation      520
14.4   Recommended Reading      524
14.5   Problems      524

CHAPTER 15   Microprogrammed Control      526
15.1   Basic Concepts      526
15.2   Microinstruction Sequencing      535
15.3   Microinstruction Execution      541
15.4   TI 8800      551
15.5   Applications of Microprogramming      560
15.6   Recommended Reading      563
15.7   Problems      564

# PART V   PARALLEL ORGANIZATION                                              567

CHAPTER 16   Parallel Processing      569
16.1   Multiprocessing      569
16.2   Cache Coherence and the MESI Protocol      578
16.3   Vector Computation      584
16.4   Parallel Processors      597
16.5   Recommended Reading      603
16.6   Problems      603

APPENDIX   Digital Logic      606
A.1   Boolean Algebra      606
A.2   Gates      608
A.3   Combinational Circuits      610
A.4   Sequential Circuits      632
A.6   Problems      643

Glossary      646

References      655

Index      669

# PREFACE

## Objectives

This book is about the structure and function of computers. Its purpose is to present, as clearly and completely as possible, the nature and characteristics of modern-day computer systems.

This task is challenging for several reasons.

First, there is a tremendous variety of products that can rightly claim the name of computer, from single-chip microprocessors costing a few dollars to supercomputers costing tens of millions of dollars. Variety is exhibited not only in cost, but in size, performance, and application. Second, the rapid pace of change that has always characterized computer technology continues with no letup. These changes cover all aspects of computer technology, from the underlying integrated circuit technology used to construct computer components to the increasing use of parallel organization concepts in combining those components.

In spite of the variety and pace of change in the computer field, certain fundamental concepts apply consistently throughout. To be sure, the application of these concepts depends on the current state of the technology and the price/performance objectives of the designer. The intent of this book is to provide a thorough discussion of the fundamentals of computer organization and architecture, and to relate these to contemporary design issues.

The subtitle suggests the theme and the approach taken in this book. It has always been important to design computer systems to achieve high performance, but never has this requirement been stronger or more difficult to satisfy than today. All of the basic performance characteristics of computer systems, including processor speed, memory speed, memory capacity, and interconnection data rates, are increasing rapidly. Moreover, they are increasing at different rates. This makes it difficult to design a balanced system that maximizes the performance and utilization of all elements. Thus, computer design increasingly becomes a game of changing the structure or function in one area to compensate for a performance mismatch in another area. We will see this game played out in numerous design areas throughout the book.

A computer system, like any system, consists of an interrelated set of components. The system is best characterized in terms of structure—the way in which components are interconnected—and function—the operation of the individual components. Furthermore, a computer's organization is hierarchic. Each major component can be further described by decomposing it into its major subcomponents and describing their structure and function. For clarity and ease of understanding, this hierarchical organization is described in this book from the top down:

- *Computer System:* Major components are processor, memory, I/O.
- *Processor:* Major components are control unit, registers, ALU, and instruction execution unit.
- *Control Unit:* Major components are control memory, microinstruction sequencing logic, and registers.

The objective is to present the material in a fashion that keeps new material in a clear context. This should minimize the chance that the reader will get lost and should provide better motivation than a bottom-up approach.

Throughout the discussion, aspects of the system are viewed from the points of view of both architecture (those attributes of a system visible to a machine language programmer) and organization (the operational units and their interconnections that realize the architecture).

## Example Systems

Throughout this book, examples from dozens of different machines are used to clarify and reinforce the concepts being presented. Many, but by no means all, of the examples are drawn from two computer families: the Intel Pentium and the PowerPC. These two computer designs together encompass most of the current computer design trends. The Pentium is essentially a complex instruction set computer (CISC), while the PowerPC is essentially a reduced instruction set computer (RISC). Both systems make use of superscalar design principles and both support multiple-processor configurations.

## Plan of the Text

The book is organized into five parts:

I. Overview: This part provides a preview and context for the remainder of the book.

II. The Computer System: A computer system consists of processor, memory, and I/O modules, plus the interconnections among these major components. With the exception of the processor, which is sufficiently complex to be explored by itself in Part III, this part examines each of these aspects in turn.

III. The Central Processing Unit: The CPU consists of a control unit, registers, the arithmetic and logic unit, the instruction execution unit, and the interconnections among these components. Architectural issues, such as instruction-set design and data types, are covered. The part also looks at organizational issues, such as pipelining.

IV. The Control Unit: The control unit is that part of the processor that activates its various components. This part looks at the functioning of the control unit and its implementation using microprogramming.

V. Parallel Organization: This final part looks at some of the issues involved in multiple processor and vector processing organizations.

A more detailed, chapter-by-chapter summary appears at the end of Chapter 1.

## Internet Services

There is a web page for this book that provides support for students and instructors. The page includes links to relevant sites, transparancy masters of figures in the book in PDF (Adobe Acrobat) format, and sign-up information for the book's internet mailing list. The mailing list has been set up so that instructors using this book can exchange information, suggestions, and questions with each other and with the author. The web page is at: http://www.shore.net/~ws/COA4e.html.

An errata list for the book is available at my web site at: http://www.shore.net/~ws/welcome.html.

## What's New in the Fourth Edition

In the three years since the third edition of this book was published, the field has seen continued innovations and improvements. In this new edition, I try to capture these changes, while maintaining a broad and comprehensive coverage of the entire field. In addition, many users of the third edition have made constructive comments that have resulted in a substantial reorganization of the material.

The most obvious changes in the fourth edition are the increased emphasis on performance (as reflected by the new subtitle) and the increased focus on microprocessors. With performance parameters of all aspects of computer systems improving rapidly but at different rates, the challenge of designing a system with balanced, optimized performance grows with each passing year. This challenge affects the design of buses, cache memory organization and protocols, instruction set architecture, I/O architecture, and more; and it has led to increased emphasis on instruction pipeline enhancements, innovative bus interconnection structures, and multiple-processor systems. All of these areas are examined in this book.

With respect to the focus in this book on microprocessors, this reflects the increasing dominance of microprocessors in the computer industry and the involvement of microprocessors in virtually all the innovative work on computer system design. Two systems that encompass many of the contemporary design initiatives are the Pentium and the PowerPC. Accordingly, these two systems are used as running examples throughout the book.

Roughly the same chapter organization has been retained, but much of the material has been revised and new material has been added. As an indication of the scope of the revision, 35 of the tables and 66 of the figures are new, 78 references have been added, and 25 new homework problems have been included. Some of the most noteworthy changes are the following:

- Two recent system bus specifications are used as examples: PCI and Futurebus+. These are perhaps the two most important system bus standards, and because they are quite different from each other, they encompass most of the important bus design concepts.
- The material on cache memory has been expanded to include consideration of separate instruction and data caches and the use of two levels of caches. The important new developments in DRAM organization are also covered.
- RAID technology is now covered.
- The important SCSI parallel and P1394 serial bus specifications are examined in detail.

- The material on integer arithmetic has been rewritten to provide a clearer, better-motivated treatment. The coverage of the IEEE 754 floating-point standard has been expanded.
- The issue of cache coherency in multiple-processor systems is explored, and the widely used MESI protocol is described.
- Parallel organizations involving many microprocessors are discussed.

## Acknowledgments

This new edition has benefited from review by a number of people, who gave generously of their time and expertise. A number of people reviewed the previous edition and made constructive comments for the new edition, including: Richard King of Oregon Institute of Technology; Ata Elahi of Southern Connecticut State University; and J. Rotherman, R. Berrsford, and L. Thornhill, all of the University of Portsmouth in England. G. Dattatreya at the University of Texas at Dallas provided some useful insights in presenting the concepts of integer arithmetic. Marie Sullivan, Marvin Denman, and Henry Warren, all of IBM, reviewed the PowerPC material. Doug Carmean and Theodore Omtzigt of Intel and Mike Schmit of Quantasm reviewed the Pentium material. Rodney Van Meter supplied several interesting problems. Finally, I would like to thank Nikitas Alexandridis for permission to borrow some of the problems from his book, *Design of Microprocessor-Based Systems*.

*William Stallings*

# PART I

# OVERVIEW

**P**art I provides an overview and a context for the remainder of the book.

First, Chapter 1 introduces the concept of the computer as a hierarchical system. A computer can be viewed as a structure of components and its function described in terms of the collective function of its cooperating components. Each component, in turn, can be described in terms of its internal structure and function. The major levels of this hierarchical view are introduced. The remainder of the book is organized, top down, using these levels.

Second, Chapter 2 provides a brief history of the development of computers from their mechanical ancestors to present-day systems. This history serves to highlight some important computer design features and to provide a top-level view of computer structure. The chapter then introduces a key theme of this book: designing for performance. The importance of achieving balance in the utilization of components with widely different performance characteristics is also addressed.

# CHAPTER 1

# Introduction

This book is about the structure and function of computers. Its purpose is to present, as clearly and completely as possible, the nature and characteristics of modern-day computer systems. This task is a challenging one for two reasons.

First, there is a tremendous variety of products, from single-chip microcomputers costing a few dollars to supercomputers costing tens of millions of dollars, that can rightly claim the name computer. Variety is exhibited not only in cost, but in size, performance, and application. Second, the rapid pace of change that has always characterized computer technology continues with no letup. These changes cover all aspects of computer technology, from the underlying integrated circuit technology used to construct computer components to the increasing use of parallel organization concepts in combining those components.

In spite of the variety and pace of change in the computer field, certain fundamental concepts apply consistently throughout. To be sure, the application of these concepts depends on the current state of technology and the price/performance objectives of the designer. The intent of this book is to provide a thorough discussion of the fundamentals of computer organization and architecture and to relate these to contemporary computer design issues. This introductory chapter discusses briefly the descriptive approach to be taken and provides an overview of the remainder of the book.

## 1.1

## ORGANIZATION AND ARCHITECTURE

In describing computer systems, a distinction is often made between *computer architecture* and *computer organization*. Although it is difficult to give precise definitions for these terms, a consensus exists about the general areas covered by each (e.g., see [VRAN80], [SIEW82], and [BELL78a]).

Computer architecture refers to those attributes of a system visible to a programmer, or put another way, those attributes that have a direct impact on the logical execution of a program. Computer organization refers to the operational units and their interconnections that realize the architectural specifications. Examples of architectural attributes include the instruction set, the number of bits used to represent various data types (e.g., numbers, characters), I/O mechanisms, and techniques for addressing memory. Organizational attributes include those hardware details transparent to the programmer, such as control signals, interfaces between the computer and peripherals, and the memory technology used.

As an example, it is an architectural design issue whether a computer will have a multiply instruction. It is an organizational issue whether that instruction will be implemented by a special multiply unit or by a mechanism that makes repeated use of the add unit of the system. The organizational decision may be based on the anticipated frequency of use of the multiply instruction, the relative speed of the two approaches, and the cost and physical size of a special multiply unit.

Historically, and still today, the distinction between architecture and organization has been an important one. Many computer manufacturers offer a family of computer models, all with the same architecture but with differences in organization. Consequently, the different models in the family have different price and performance characteristics. Furthermore, an architecture may survive many years, but its organization changes with changing technology. A prominent example of both these phenomena is the IBM System/370 architecture. This architecture was first introduced in 1970 and included a number of models. The customer with modest requirements could buy a cheaper, slower model and, if demand increased, later upgrade to a more expensive, faster model without having to abandon software that had already been developed. Over the years, IBM has introduced many new models with improved technology to replace older models, offering the customer greater speed, lower cost, or both. These newer models retained the same architecture so that the customer's software investment was protected. Remarkably, the System/370 architecture, with a few enhancements, has survived to this day and continues as the flagship of IBM's product line.

In a class of systems called microcomputers, the relationship between architecture and organization is very close. Changes in technology not only influence organization but also result in the introduction of more powerful and richer architectures. Generally, there is less of a requirement for generation-to-generation compatibility for these smaller machines. Thus, there is more of an interplay between organizational and architectural design decisions. An intriguing example of this is the reduced instruction set computer (RISC), which we examine in Chapter 12.

This book examines both computer organization and computer architecture. The emphasis is perhaps more on the side of organization. However, because a computer organization must be designed to implement a particular architectural specification, a thorough treatment of organization requires a detailed examination of architecture as well.

## 1.2

## STRUCTURE AND FUNCTION

A computer is a complex system; contemporary computers contain millions of elementary electronic components. How, then, can one clearly describe them? The key is to recognize the hierarchic nature of most complex systems, including the computer [SIMO69]. A hierarchic system is a set of interrelated subsystems, each of the latter, in turn, hierarchic in structure until we reach some lowest level of elementary subsystem.

The hierarchic nature of complex systems is essential to both their design and their description. The designer need only deal with a particular level of the system at a time. At each level, the system consists of a set of components and their interrelationships. The behavior at each level depends only on a simplified, abstracted characterization of the system at the next lower level. At each level, the designer is concerned with structure and function [KOES78]:

- *Structure:* The way in which the components are interrelated.
- *Function:* The operation of each individual component as part of the structure.

In terms of description, we have two choices: starting at the bottom and building up to a complete description, or beginning with a top view and decomposing the system into its subparts. Evidence from a number of fields suggests that the top-down approach is the clearest and most effective [WEIN75].

The approach taken in this book follows from this viewpoint. The computer system will be described from the top down. We begin with the major components of the system, describing their structure and function, and proceed to successively lower layers of the hierarchy. The remainder of this section provides a very brief overview of this plan of attack.

## Function

Both the structure and functioning of a computer are, in essence, simple. Figure 1.1 depicts the basic functions that a computer can perform. In general terms, there are only four:

- Data Processing
- Data Storage
- Data Movement
- Control

The computer, of course, must be able to *process data.* The data may take a wide variety of forms, and the range of processing requirements is broad. However, we shall see that there are only a few fundamental methods or types of data processing.

It is also essential that a computer *store data.* Even if the computer is processing data on the fly (i.e., data come in and get processed, and the results go right out), the computer must temporarily store at least those pieces of data that are being worked on at any given moment. Thus, there is at least a short-term data storage function. Equally important, the computer performs a long-term data storage function. Files of data are stored on the computer for subsequent retrieval and update.

The computer must be able to *move data* between itself and the outside world. The computer's operating environment consists of devices that serve as either sources or destinations of data. When data are received from or delivered to a device that is directly connected to the computer, the process is known as *input–output* (I/O), and the device is referred to as a *peripheral.* When data are moved

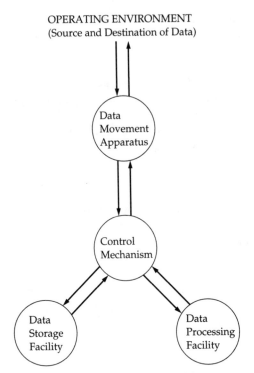

OPERATING ENVIRONMENT
(Source and Destination of Data)

**FIGURE 1.1. A functional view of the computer**

over longer distances, to or from a remote device, the process is known as *data communications*.

Finally, there must be *control* of these three functions. Ultimately, this control is exercised by the individual(s) who provides the computer with instructions. Within the computer system, a control unit manages the computer's resources and orchestrates the performance of its functional parts in response to those instructions.

At this general level of discussion, the number of possible operations that can be performed is few. Figure 1.2 depicts the four possible types of operations. The computer can function as a data movement device (Figure 1.2a), simply transferring data from one peripheral or communications line to another. It can also function as a data storage device (Figure 1.2b), with data transferred from the external environment to computer storage (read) and vice versa (write). The final two diagrams show operations involving data processing, on data either in storage (Figure 1.2c) or en route between storage and the external environment.

The preceding discussion may seem absurdly generalized. It is certainly possible, even at a top level of computer structure, to differentiate a variety of functions, but, to quote [SIEW82]:

> There is remarkably little shaping of computer structure to fit the function to be performed. At the root of this lies the general-purpose nature of computers, in which all

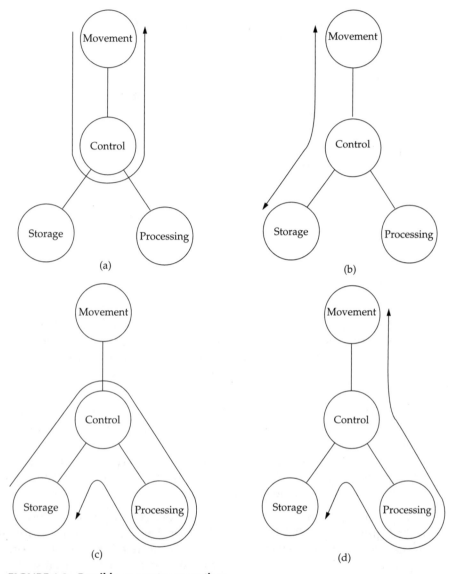

**FIGURE 1.2. Possible computer operations**

the functional specialization occurs at the time of programming and not at the time of design.

## Structure

Figure 1.3 is the simplest possible depiction of a computer. The computer is an entity that interacts in some fashion with its external environment. In general, all of

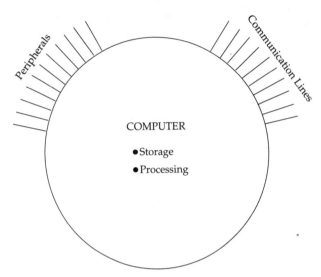

**FIGURE 1.3. The computer**

its linkages to the external environment can be classified as peripheral devices or communication lines. We will have something to say about both types of linkages.

But of greater concern in this book is the internal structure of the computer itself, which is shown at a top level in Figure 1.4. There are four main structural components:

- *Central Processing Unit (CPU):* Controls the operation of the computer and performs its data processing functions. Often simply referred to as *processor.*
- *Main Memory:* Stores data.
- *I/O:* Moves data between the computer and its external environment.
- *System Interconnection:* Some mechanism that provides for communication among CPU, main memory, and I/O.

There may be one or more of each of the above components. Traditionally, there has been just a single CPU. In recent years, there has been increasing use of multiple processors in a single system. Some design issues relating to multiple processors crop up and are discussed as the text proceeds; Chapter 16 focuses on such systems.

Each of these components will be examined in some detail in Part II. However, for our purposes, the most interesting and in some ways the most complex component is the CPU; its structure is depicted in Figure 1.5. Its major structural components are

- *Control Unit:* Controls the operation of the CPU and hence the computer.
- *Arithmetic and Logic Unit (ALU):* Performs the computer's data processing functions.
- *Registers:* Provides storage internal to the CPU.
- *CPU Interconnection:* Some mechanism that provides for communication among the control unit, ALU, and registers.

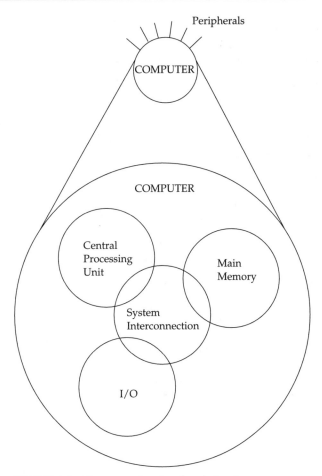

**FIGURE 1.4.  The computer: top-level structure**

Each of these components will be examined in some detail in Part III. Again, for our purposes, the most interesting component is the control unit. Now, there are several approaches to the implementation of the control unit, but the most common by far is a *microprogrammed* implementation. With this approach, the structure of the control unit can be depicted as in Figure 1.6. This structure will be examined in Part IV.

## 1.3

## OUTLINE OF THE BOOK

This chapter serves as an introduction to the entire book. A brief synopsis of the remaining chapters follows.

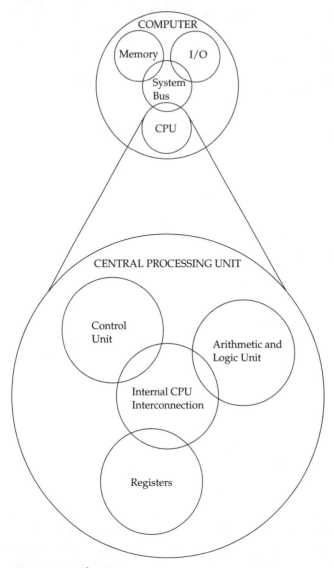

**FIGURE 1.5. The CPU**

## Computer Evolution and Performance

Chapter 2 serves two purposes. First, a discussion of the history of computer technology is an easy and interesting way of being introduced to the basic concepts of computer organization and architecture. The chapter also addresses the technology trends that have made performance the focus of computer system design and previews the various techniques and strategies that are used to achieve balanced, efficient performance.

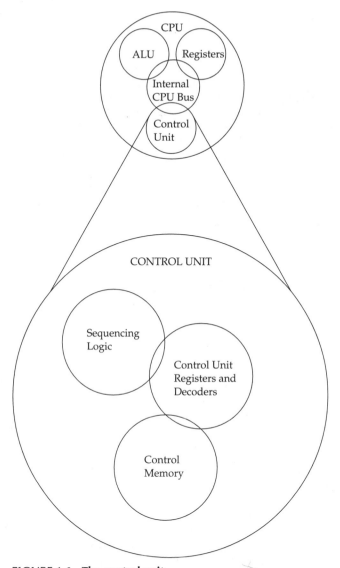

**FIGURE 1.6. The control unit**

## Computer Interconnection Structures

At a top level, a computer consists of a processor, memory, and I/O components. The functional behavior of the system consists of the exchange of data and control signals among these components. To support this exchange, these components must be interconnected. Chapter 3 begins with a brief examination of the computer's components and their input–output requirements. The chapter then looks at key issues that affect interconnection design, especially the need to support interrupts. The bulk of the chapter is devoted to a study of the most common approach to interconnection: the use of a structure of buses.

## Internal Memory

Computer memory exhibits a wide range of type, technology, organization, performance, and cost. The typical computer system is equipped with a hierarchy of memory subsystems, some internal (directly accessible by the processor) and some external (accessible by the processor via an I/O module). Chapter 4 begins with an overview of this hierarchy and then focuses on design issues related to internal memory. First, the nature and organization of semiconductor main memory is examined. Next, the chapter deals in detail with the design of cache memory, including separate code and data caches and two-level caches. Finally, recent advanced DRAM memory organizations are explored.

## External Memory

Chapter 5 examines the various design and performance parameters associated with disk memory. Next, RAID schemes, which are becoming increasingly common, are examined. Finally, optical memory and magnetic tape systems are examined.

## Input/Output

I/O modules are interconnected with the processor and main memory, and each controls one or more external devices. Chapter 6 examines the mechanisms by which an I/O module interacts with the rest of the computer system, using the techniques of programmed I/O, interrupt I/O, and direct memory access (DMA). The interface between an I/O module and external devices is also described.

## Operating System Support

At this point, it is appropriate to look at the operating system, to explain how basic computer components are managed to perform useful work, and how computer hardware is organized to provide operating system support. Chapter 7 begins with a brief history, which serves to identify the major types of operating systems and to motivate their use. Next, multiprogramming is explained by examining the long-term and short-term scheduling functions. Finally, an examination of memory management includes a discussion of segmentation, paging, and virtual memory.

## Computer Arithmetic

Chapter 8 begins a detailed examination of the processor with a discussion of computer arithmetic. Processors typically support two types of arithmetic: integer, or fixed point, and floating point. For both cases, the chapter first examines the representation of numbers and then discusses arithmetic operations. The important IEEE 754 floating-point standard is examined in detail.

## Instruction Sets

From a programmer's point of view, the best way to understand the operation of a processor is to learn the machine instruction set that it executes. Chapter 9 examines the key characteristics of machine instruction sets. It covers various data types and operation types commonly found in an instruction set. Then, the relationship of processor instructions to assembly language is briefly explained. In Chapter 10, the possible addressing modes are examined. Finally, the issue of instruction format is explored, including a discussion of trade-offs.

## CPU Structure and Function

Chapter 11 is devoted to a discussion of the internal structure and function of the processor. The overall organization (ALU, control unit, register file) is reviewed. Then, the organization of the register file is discussed. The remainder of the chapter describes the functioning of the processor in executing machine instructions. The instruction cycle is examined to show the function and interrelationship of fetch, indirect, execute, and interrupt cycles. Finally, the use of pipelining to improve performance is explored in depth.

## Reduced Instruction Set Computers (RISCs)

One of the most significant innovations in computer organization and architecture in recent years is the reduced instruction set computer (RISC). RISC architecture is a dramatic departure from the historical trend in processor architecture. An analysis of this approach brings into focus many of the important issues in computer organization and architecture. Chapter 12 presents the RISC approach and compares it with the complex instruction set computer (CISC) approach.

## Superscalar Processors

Chapter 13 examines an even more recent and equally important design innovation: the superscalar processor. Although superscalar technology can be used on any processor, it is especially well suited to a RISC architecture.

## Control Unit Operation

Chapter 14 turns to a discussion of how processor functions are performed or, more specifically, how the various elements of the processor are controlled to provide these functions, by means of the control unit. It is shown that each instruction cycle is made up of a set of micro-operations that generate control signals. Execution is accomplished by the effect of these control signals, emanating from the control unit to the ALU, registers, and system interconnection structure. Finally, an approach to the implementation of the control unit, referred to as hardwired implementation, is presented.

## Microprogrammed Control

Chapter 15 shows how the control unit can be implemented using the technique of microprogramming. First, micro-operations are mapped into microinstructions. Then, the layout of a control memory containing a microprogram for each machine instruction is described. The structure and function of the microprogrammed control unit can then be explained.

## Multiprocessors and Vector Processing

Traditionally, the computer has been viewed as a sequential machine. As computer technology has evolved and the cost of computer hardware has dropped, computer designers have increasingly sought opportunities for parallelism, usually to improve performance and, in some cases, to improve reliability. Chapter 16 looks at two of the most prominent and successful applications of parallel organization: multiple processor systems and vector organization. For multiple processors, the chapter examines the key design issue of cache coherence.

## Parallel Processors

Chapter 16 surveys the increasingly important area of parallel processors, which refers to the use of many processors in a multiple-processor configuration. This organization presents new problems not associated with traditional multiple-processor configuration simply because of the scale of the organization, which may include hundreds or even thousands of processors.

## Digital Logic

The body of the text treats binary storage elements and digital functions as the fundamental building blocks of computer systems. The appendix to the text describes how these storage elements and functions can be implemented in digital logic. The appendix begins with a brief review of Boolean algebra. Next, the concept of a gate is introduced. Finally, combinational and sequential circuits, which can be constructed from gates, are discussed.

# CHAPTER 2

# Computer Evolution and Performance

We begin our study of computers with a brief history. This history is interesting in itself and also serves the purpose of providing an overview of computer structure and function. Next, the issue of performance is addressed. A consideration of the need for balanced utilization of computer resources provides a context that is useful throughout the book. Finally, we look briefly at the evolution of the two systems that serve as key examples throughout the book: Pentium and PowerPC.

## 2.1

### A BRIEF HISTORY OF COMPUTERS

### The First Generation: Vacuum Tubes

#### *ENIAC*

The ENIAC (Electronic Numerical Integrator And Computer), designed by and constructed under the supervision of John Mauchly and John Presper Eckert at the University of Pennsylvania, was the world's first general-purpose electronic digital computer.

The project was a response to U.S. wartime needs. The Army's Ballistics Research Laboratory (BRL), an agency responsible for developing range and trajectory tables for new weapons, was having difficulty supplying these tables accurately and within a reasonable time frame. Without these firing tables, the new weapons and artillery were useless to gunners. The BRL employed more than 200 people, mostly women, who, using desktop calculators, solved the necessary ballistics equations. Preparation of the tables for a single weapon would take one person many hours, even days.

Mauchly, a professor of electrical engineering at the University of Pennsylvania, and Eckert, one of his graduate students, proposed to build a general-purpose computer using vacuum tubes to be used for the BRL's application. In 1943, this proposal was accepted by the Army, and work began on the ENIAC. The resulting machine was enormous, weighing 30 tons, occupying 15,000 square feet of floor space, and containing more than 18,000 vacuum tubes. When operating, it consumed 140 kilowatts of power. It was also substantially faster than any electro-mechanical computer, being capable of 5000 additions per second.

The ENIAC was a decimal rather than a binary machine. That is, numbers were represented in decimal form and arithmetic was performed in the decimal system. Its memory consisted of 20 "accumulators," each capable of holding a 10-digit decimal number. Each digit was represented by a ring of 10 vacuum tubes. At any time, only one vacuum tube was in the ON state, representing one of the 10 digits. The major drawback of the ENIAC was that it had to be programmed manually by setting switches and plugging and unplugging cables.

The ENIAC was completed in 1946, too late to be used in the war effort. Instead, its first task was to perform a series of complex calculations that were used to help determine the feasibility of the H-bomb. The use of the ENIAC for a purpose other than that for which it was built demonstrated its general-purpose nature. Thus, 1946 ushered in the new era of the electronic computer, culminating years of effort. The ENIAC continued to operate under BRL management until 1955, when it was disassembled.

### *The von Neumann Machine*

As was mentioned, the task of entering and altering programs for the ENIAC was extremely tedious. The programming process could be facilitated if the program could be represented in a form suitable for storing in memory alongside the data. Then, a computer could get its instructions by reading them from memory, and a program could be set or altered by setting the values of a portion of memory.

This idea, known as the *stored-program concept*, is usually attributed to the ENIAC designers, most notably the mathematician John von Neumann, who was a consultant on the ENIAC project. The idea was also developed at about the same time by Turing. The first publication of the idea was in a 1945 proposal by von Neumann for a new computer, the EDVAC (Electronic Discrete Variable Computer).

In 1946, von Neumann and his colleagues began the design of a new stored-program computer, referred to as the IAS computer, at the Princeton Institute for Advanced Studies. The IAS computer, although not completed until 1952, is the prototype of all subsequent general-purpose computers.

Figure 2.1 shows the general structure of the IAS computer. It consists of

- A main memory, which stores both data and instructions.
- An arithmetic–logical unit (ALU) capable of operating on binary data.
- A control unit, which interprets the instructions in memory and causes them to be executed.
- Input and output (I/O) equipment operated by the control unit.

This structure was outlined in von Neumann's earlier proposal, which is worth quoting at this point [VONM45]:

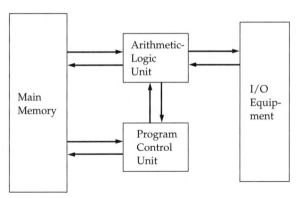

**FIGURE 2.1. Structure of the IAS computer**

2.2 First: Since the device is primarily a computer, it will have to perform the elementary operations of arithmetics most frequently. These are addition, subtraction, multiplication and division: +, −, ×, ÷. It is therefore reasonable that it should contain specialized organs for just these operations.

It must be observed, however, that while this principle as such is probably sound, the specific way in which it is realized requires close scrutiny . . . At any rate a *central arithmetical* part of the device will probably have to exist and this constitutes *the first specific part: CA.*

2.3 Second: The logical control of the device, that is, the proper sequencing of its operations, can be most efficiently carried out by a central control organ. If the device is to be *elastic,* that is, as nearly as possible *all purpose,* then a distinction must be made between the specific instructions given for and defining a particular problem, and the general control organs which see to it that these instructions—no matter what they are—are carried out. The former must be stored in some way; the latter are represented by definite operating parts of the device. By the *central control* we mean this latter function only, and the organs which perform it form *the second specific part: CC.*

2.4 Third: Any device which is to carry out long and complicated sequences of operations (specifically of calculations) must have a considerable memory. . .

(b) The instructions which govern a complicated problem may constitute considerable material, particularly so, if the code is circumstantial (which it is in most arrangements). This material must be remembered. . .

At any rate, the total *memory* constitutes *the third specific part of the device: M.*

2.6 The three specific parts CA, CC (together C), and M correspond to the *associative* neurons in the human nervous system. It remains to discuss the equivalents of the *sensory* or *afferent* and the *motor* or *efferent* neurons. These are the *input* and *output* organs of the device. . .

The device must be endowed with the ability to maintain input and output (sensory and motor) contact with some specific medium of this type (cf. 1.2): The medium will be called the *outside recording medium of the device: R.* . .

2.7 Fourth: The device must have organs to transfer . . . information from R into its specific parts C and M. These organs form its *input,* the *fourth specific part: I.* It will be seen that it is best to make all transfers from R (by I) into M and never directly from C. . .

2.8 Fifth: The device must have organs to transfer . . . from its specific parts C and M into R. These organs form its *output, the fifth specific part: O.* It will be seen that it is again best to make all transfers from M (by O) into R, and never directly from C. . .

With rare exceptions, all of today's computers have this same general structure and function and are thus referred to as von Neumann machines. Thus, it is worthwhile at this point to briefly describe the operation of the IAS computer [BURK46]. Following [HAYE88], the terminology and notation of von Neumann are changed in the following to conform more closely to modern usage; the examples and illustrations accompanying this discussion are based on that latter text.

The memory of the IAS consists of 1000 storage locations, called *words,* of 40 binary digits (bits) each. Both data and instructions are stored there. Hence, numbers must be represented in binary form, and each instruction also has to be a binary code. Figure 2.2 illustrates these formats. Each number is represented by a sign bit and a 39-bit value. A word may also contain two 20-bit instructions, with each instruction consisting of an 8-bit operation code (op code) specifying the operation to be performed and a 12-bit address designating one of the words in memory (numbered from 0 to 999).

The control unit operates the IAS by fetching instructions from memory and executing them one at a time. To explain this, a more detailed structure diagram is needed, as indicated in Figure 2.3. This figure reveals that both the control unit and the ALU contain storage locations, called *registers,* defined as follows:

- *Memory Buffer Register (MBR):* Contains a word to be stored in memory, or is used to receive a word from memory.
- *Memory Address Register (MAR):* Specifies the address in memory of the word to be written from or read into the MBR.
- *Instruction Register (IR):* Contains the 8-bit op code instruction being executed.
- *Instruction Buffer Register (IBR):* Employed to temporarily hold the right-hand instruction from a word in memory.
- *Program Counter (PC):* Contains the address of the next instruction-pair to be fetched from memory.

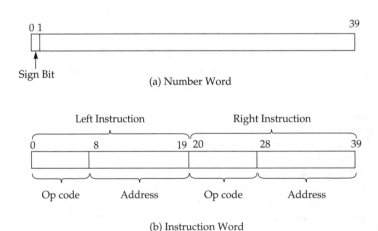

FIGURE 2.2. IAS memory formats

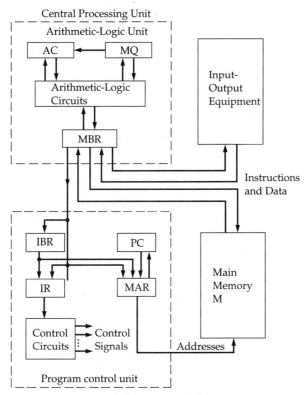

**FIGURE 2.3. Expanded structure of the IAS computer**

- *Accumulator (AC) and Multiplier-Quotient (MQ):* Employed to temporarily hold operands and results of ALU operations. For example, the result of multiplying two 40-bit numbers is an 80-bit number; the most significant 40 bits are stored in the AC and the least significant in the MQ.

The IAS operates by repetitively performing an *instruction cycle,* as shown in Figure 2.4. Each instruction cycle consists of two subcycles. During the *fetch cycle,* the op code of the next instruction is loaded into the IR and the address portion is loaded into the MAR. This instruction may be taken from the IBR, or it can be obtained from memory by loading a word into the MBR, and then down to the IBR, IR, and MAR.

Why the indirection? Well, all of these operations are controlled by electronic circuitry and result in the use of data paths. To simplify the electronics, there is only one register that is used to specify the address in memory for a read or write, and only one register to be used for the source or destination.

Once the op code is in the IR, the *execute cycle* is performed. Control circuitry interprets the op code and executes the instruction by sending out the appropriate control signals to cause data to be moved or an operation to be performed by the ALU.

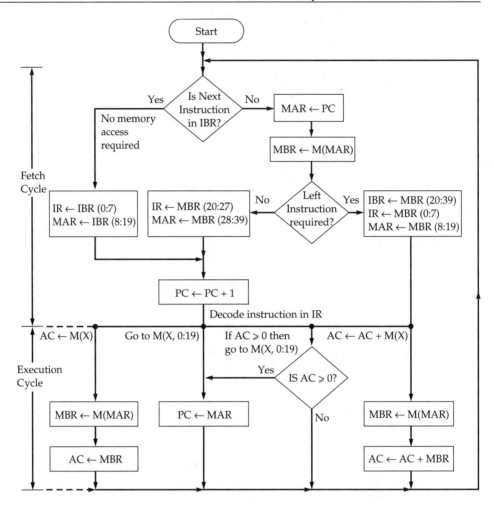

M(X) = contents of memory location whose address is X
(X : Y) = bits X through Y

**FIGURE 2.4.  Partial flowchart of IAS operation**

The IAS computer had a total of 21 instructions, which are listed in Table 2.1. These can be grouped as follows:

- *Data Transfer:* Move data between memory and ALU registers or between two ALU registers.
- *Unconditional Branch:* Normally, the control unit executes instructions in sequence from memory. This sequence can be changed by a branch instruction. This facilitates repetitive operations.
- *Conditional Branch:* The branch can be made dependent on a condition, thus allowing decision points.
- *Arithmetic:* Operations performed by the ALU.

- *Address Modify:* Permits addresses to be computed in the ALU and then inserted into instructions stored in memory. This allows a program considerable addressing flexibility.

Table 2.1 presents instructions in a symbolic, easy-to-read form. Actually, each instruction must conform to the format of Figure 2.2b. The op code portion (first 8 bits) specifies which of the 21 instructions is to be executed. The address portion (remaining 12 bits) specifies which of the 1000 memory locations is to be involved in the execution of the instruction.

Figure 2.4 shows several examples of instruction execution by the control unit. Note that each operation requires several steps. Some of these are quite elaborate. The multiplication operation requires 39 suboperations, one for each bit position except that of the sign bit!

## Commercial Computers

The 1950s saw the birth of the computer industry with two companies, Sperry and IBM, dominating the marketplace.

In 1947, Eckert and Mauchly formed the Eckert-Mauchly Computer Corporation to manufacture computers commercially. Their first successful machine was the UNIVAC I (Universal Automatic Computer), which was commissioned by the Bureau of the Census for the 1950 calculations. The Eckert-Mauchly Computer Corporation became part of the UNIVAC division of Sperry-Rand Corporation, which went on to build a series of successor machines.

The UNIVAC I was the first successful commercial computer. It was intended, as the name implies, for both scientific and commercial applications. The first paper describing the system listed matrix algebraic computations, statistical problems, premium billings for a life insurance company, and logistical problems as a sample of the tasks it could perform.

The UNIVAC II, which had greater memory capacity and higher performance than the UNIVAC I, was delivered in the late 1950s and illustrates several trends that have remained characteristic of the computer industry. First, advances in technology allow companies to continue to build larger, more powerful computers. Second, each company tries to make its new machines *upward compatible* with the older machines. This means that the programs written for the older machines can be executed on the new machine. This strategy is adopted in the hopes of retaining the customer base; that is, when a customer decides to buy a newer machine, he is likely to get it from the same company to avoid losing the investment in programs.

The UNIVAC division also began development of the 1100 series of computers, which was to be its bread and butter. This series illustrates a distinction that existed at one time. The first model, the UNIVAC 1103, and its successors for many years were primarily intended for scientific applications, involving long and complex calculations. Other companies concentrated on business applications, which involved processing large amounts of text data. This split has largely disappeared, but it was evident for a number of years.

**TABLE 2.1   The IAS Instruction Set**

| Instruction Type | Opcode | Symbolic Representation | Description |
|---|---|---|---|
| Data transfer | 00001010 | LOAD MQ | Transfer contents of register MQ to the accumulator AC |
| | 00001001 | LOAD MQ,M(X) | Transfer contents of memory location X to MQ |
| | 00100001 | STOR M(X) | Transfer contents of accumulator to memory location X |
| | 00000001 | LOAD M(X) | Transfer M(X) to the accumulator |
| | 00000010 | LOAD −M(X) | Transfer −M(X) to the accumulator |
| | 00000011 | LOAD \|M(X)\| | Transfer absolute value of M(X) to the accumulator |
| | 00000100 | LOAD −\|M(X)\| | Transfer −\|M(X)\| to the accumulator |
| Unconditional branch | 00001101 | JUMP M(X,0:19) | Take next instruction from left half of M(X) |
| | 00001110 | JUMP M(X,20:39) | Take next instruction from right half of M(X) |
| Conditional branch | 00001111 | JUMP+ M(X,0:19) | If number in the accumulator is nonnegative, take next instruction from left half of M(X) |
| | 00010000 | JUMP+ M(X,20:39) | If number in the accumulator is nonnegative, take next instruction from right half of M(X) |

IBM, which had helped build the Mark I and was then the major manufacturer of punched-card processing equipment, delivered its first electronic stored-program computer, the 701, in 1953. The 701 was intended primarily for scientific applications [BASH81]. In 1955, IBM introduced the companion 702 product, which had a number of hardware features that suited it to business applications. These were the first of a long series of 700/7000 computers that established IBM as the overwhelmingly dominant computer manufacturer.

## The Second Generation: Transistors

The first major change in the electronic computer came with the replacement of the vacuum tube by the transistor. The transistor is smaller, cheaper, and dissipates less

**TABLE 2.1   (continued)**

| Instruction Type | Opcode | Symbolic Representation | Description |
|---|---|---|---|
| Arithmetic | 00000101 | ADD M(X) | Add M(X) to AC; put the result in AC |
| | 00000111 | ADD \|M(X)\| | Add \|M(X)\| to AC; put the result in AC |
| | 00000110 | SUB M(X) | Subtract M(X) from AC; put the result in AC |
| | 00001000 | SUB \|M(X)\| | Subtract \|M(X)\| from AC; put the remainder in AC |
| | 00001011 | MUL M(X) | Multiply M(X) by MQ; put most significant bits of result in AC, put least significant bits in MQ |
| | 00001100 | DIV M(X) | Divide AC by M(X); put the quotient in MQ and the remainder in AC |
| | 00010100 | LSH | Multiply accumulator by 2, i.e., shift left one bit position |
| | 00010101 | RSH | Divide accumulator by 2, i.e., shift right one position |
| Address modify | 00010010 | STOR M(X,8:19) | Replace left address field at M(X) by 12 rightmost bits of AC |
| | 00010011 | STOR M(X,28:39) | Replace right address field at M(X) by 12 rightmost bits of AC |

heat than a vacuum tube but can be used in the same way as a vacuum tube to construct computers. Unlike the vacuum tube, which requires wires, metal plates, a glass capsule, and a vacuum, the transistor is a *solid-state device,* made from silicon.

The transistor was invented at Bell Labs in 1947 and by the 1950s had launched an electronic revolution. It was not until the late 1950s, however, that fully transistorized computers were commercially available. IBM again was not the first company to deliver the new technology. NCR and, more successfully, RCA were the front-runners with some small transistor machines. IBM followed shortly with the 7000 series.

The use of the transistor defines the *second generation* of computers. It has become widely accepted to classify computers into generations based on the fundamental hardware technology employed (Table 2.2). Each new generation is characterized by greater speed, larger memory capacity, and smaller size than the previous one.

**TABLE 2.2    Computer Generations**

| Generation | Approximate Dates | Technology | Typical Speed (operations per second) |
|---|---|---|---|
| 1 | 1946–1957 | Vacuum tube | 40,000 |
| 2 | 1958–1964 | Transistor | 200,000 |
| 3 | 1965–1971 | Small and medium scale integration | 1,000,000 |
| 4 | 1972–1977 | Large scale integration | 10,000,000 |
| 5 | 1978– | Very large scale integration | 100,000,000 |

But there are other changes as well. The second generation saw the introduction of more complex arithmetic and logic units and control units, the use of high-level programming languages, and the provision of *system software* with the computer.

The second generation is noteworthy also for the appearance of the Digital Equipment Corporation (DEC). DEC was founded in 1957 and, in that year, delivered its first computer, the PDP-1. This computer and this company began the minicomputer phenomenon that would become so prominent in the third generation.

### The IBM 7094

From the introduction of the 700 series in 1952 to the introduction of the last member of the 7000 series in 1964, this IBM product line underwent an evolution that is typical of computer products. Successive members of the product line show increased performance, increased capacity, and/or lower cost.

Table 2.3 illustrates this trend. The size of main memory, in multiples of $2^{10}$ 36-bit words, grew from 2K (1K = $2^{10}$) to 32K words, while the time to access one word of memory, the *memory cycle time,* fell from 30 μs to 1.4 μs. The number of op codes grew from a modest 24 to 185.

The final column indicates the relative execution speed of the CPU. Speed improvements are achieved by improved electronics (e.g., a transistor implementation is faster than a vacuum tube implementation) and more complex circuitry. For example, the IBM 7094 includes an Instruction Backup Register (IBR), used to buffer the next instruction. The control unit fetches two adjacent words from memory for an instruction fetch. Except for the occurrence of a branching instruction, which is typically infrequent, this means that the control unit has to access memory for an instruction on only half the instruction cycles. This prefetching significantly reduces the average instruction cycle time.

The remainder of the columns of Table 2.3 will become clear as the text proceeds.

Figure 2.5 shows a large (many peripherals) configuration for an IBM 7094, which is representative of second-generation computers [BELL71a]. Several differences from the IAS computer are worth noting. The most important of these is the use of *data channels*. A data channel is an independent I/O module with its own processor and its own instruction set. In a computer system with such devices, the CPU does not execute detailed I/O instructions. Such instructions are stored in a main memory to be executed by a special-purpose processor in the data

**TABLE 2.3  Example members of the IBM 700/7000 Series**

| Model Number | First Delivery | CPU Technology | Memory Technology | Cycle Time (μs) | Memory Size (K) | Number of Opcodes | Number of Index Registers | Hardwired Floating-Point | I/O Overlap (Channels) | Instruction Fetch Overlap | Speed (Approximate) |
|---|---|---|---|---|---|---|---|---|---|---|---|
| 701 | 1952 | Vacuum tubes | Electrostatic tubes | 30 | 2–4 | 24 | 0 | no | no | no | 1 |
| 704 | 1955 | Vacuum tubes | Core | 12 | 4–32 | 80 | 3 | yes | no | no | 2.5 |
| 709 | 1958 | Vacuum tubes | Core | 12 | 32 | 140 | 3 | yes | yes | no | 4 |
| 7090 | 1960 | Transistor | Core | 2.18 | 32 | 169 | 3 | yes | yes | no | 25 |
| 7094 I | 1962 | Transistor | Core | 2 | 32 | 185 | 7 | yes (double precision) | yes | yes | 30 |
| 7094 II | 1964 | Transistor | Core | 1.4 | 32 | 185 | 7 | yes (double precision) | yes | yes | 50 |

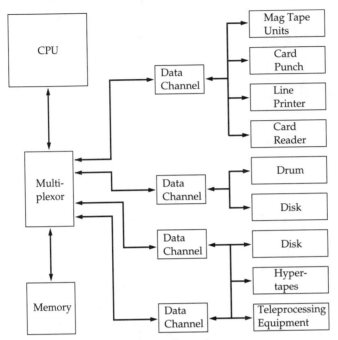

**FIGURE 2.5. An IBM 7094 configuration**

channel itself. The CPU initiates an I/O transfer by sending a control signal to the data channel, instructing it to execute a sequence of instructions in memory. The data channel performs its task independently of the CPU and signals the CPU when the operation is complete. This arrangement relieves the CPU of a considerable processing burden.

Another new feature is the *multiplexor*, which is the central termination point for data channels, the CPU, and memory. The multiplexor schedules access to the memory from the CPU and data channels, allowing these devices to act independently.

## The Third Generation: Integrated Circuits

A single, self-contained transistor is called a *discrete component*. Throughout the 1950s and early 1960s, electronic equipment was composed largely of discrete components—transistors, resistors, capacitors, and so on. Discrete components were manufactured separately, packaged in their own containers, and soldered or wired together onto masonite-like circuit boards, which were then installed in computers, oscilloscopes, and other electronic equipment. Whenever an electronic device called for a transistor, a little tube of metal containing a pinhead-sized piece of silicon had to be soldered to a circuit board. The entire manufacturing process, from transistor to circuit board, was expensive and cumbersome.

These facts of life were beginning to create problems in the computer industry. Early second-generation computers contained about 10,000 transistors. This figure grew to the hundreds of thousands, making the manufacture of newer, more powerful machines increasingly difficult.

In 1958 came the achievement that revolutionized electronics and started the era of microelectronics: the invention of the integrated circuit. It is the integrated circuit that defines the third generation of computers. In this section we provide a brief introduction to the technology of integrated circuits. Then, we look at perhaps the two most important members of the third generation, both of which were introduced at the beginning of that era: the IBM System/360 and the DEC PDP-8.

## Microelectronics

Microelectronics means, literally, "small electronics." Since the beginnings of digital electronics and the computer industry, there has been a persistent and consistent trend toward the reduction in size of digital electronic circuits. Before examining the implications and benefits of this trend, we need to say something about the nature of digital electronics. A more detailed discussion is found in Appendix A.

The basic elements of a digital computer, as we know, must perform storage, movement, processing, and control functions. Only two fundamental types of components are required (Figure 2.6): gates and memory cells. A gate is a device that implements a simple Boolean or logical function, such as IF *A* AND *B* ARE TRUE THEN *C* IS TRUE (AND gate). Such devices are called gates because they control data flow in much the same way that canal gates do. The memory cell is a device that can store one bit of data; that is, the device can be in one of two stable states at any time. By interconnecting large numbers of these fundamental

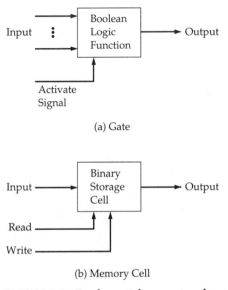

FIGURE 2.6. **Fundamental computer elements**

devices, we can construct a computer. We can relate this to our four basic functions as follows:

- *Data Storage:* Provided by memory cells.
- *Data Processing:* Provided by gates.
- *Data Movement:* The paths between components are used to move data from memory to memory and from memory through gates to memory.
- *Control:* The paths between components can carry control signals. For example, a gate will have one or two data inputs plus a control signal input that activates the gate. When the control signal is ON, the gate performs its function on the data inputs and produces a data output. Similarly, the memory cell will store the bit on its input lead when the WRITE control signal is ON and will place that bit on its output lead when the READ control signal is ON.

Thus, a computer consists of gates, memory cells, and interconnections among these elements. The gates and memory cells are, in turn, constructed of simple digital electronic components.

Although the transistor technology introduced in the second computer generation was a major improvement over vacuum tubes, problems remained. The transistors were individually mounted in separate packages and interconnected on printed circuit boards by separate wires. This was a complex, time-consuming, and error-prone process.

The integrated circuit exploits the fact that such components as transistors, resistors, and conductors can be fabricated from a semiconductor such as silicon. It is merely an extension of the solid-state art to fabricate an entire circuit in a tiny piece of silicon rather than assemble discrete components made from separate pieces of silicon into the same circuit. Hundreds and even thousands of transistors can be produced at the same time on a single wafer of silicon. Equally important, these transistors can be connected with a process of metallization to form circuits.

Figure 2.7 depicts the key concepts in an integrated circuit. A thin *wafer* of silicon is divided into a matrix of small areas, each a few millimeters square. The identical circuit pattern is fabricated in each area, and the wafer is broken up into *chips.* Each chip consists of many gates plus a number of input and output attachment points. This chip is then packaged in housing that protects it and provides pins for attachment to devices beyond the chip. A number of these packages can then be interconnected on a printed-circuit board to produce larger and more complex circuits.

Initially, only a few gates or memory cells could be reliably manufactured and packaged together. These early integrated circuits are referred to as *small-scale integration* (SSI). As time went on, it became possible to pack more and more components on the same chip. This growth in density is illustrated in Figure 2.8; it is one of the most remarkable technological trends ever recorded. Beginning at unity in 1959, the number of devices per chip doubled annually in the 1960s. In the 1970s, the rate declined, but only to the still remarkable level of quadrupling every three years. That level should persist through the early 1990s, when the effects of physical limits will probably slow the rate of growth again. Nevertheless, according to the more optimistic prediction, gigascale integration (GSI)—a one-billion-

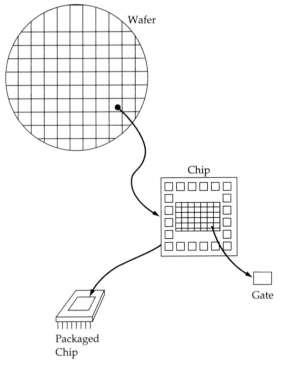

**FIGURE 2.7. Relationship between wafer, chip, and gate**

component chip—will be achieved by the end of the century. (The projections differ in assumptions about limits imposed by chip-fabrication processes.)

For the computer manufacturer, the use of ever more densely packed ICs provides many benefits:

1. The cost of a chip has remained virtually unchanged during this period of rapid growth in density. This means that the cost of computer logic and memory circuitry has fallen at a dramatic rate.
2. Because logic and memory elements are placed closer together on more densely packed chips, the electrical path length is shortened, increasing operating speed.
3. The computer becomes smaller, making it more convenient to place in a variety of environments.
4. There is a reduction in power and cooling requirements.
5. The interconnections on the integrated circuit are much more reliable than solder connections. With more circuitry on each chip, there are fewer interchip connections.

### IBM System/360

By 1964, IBM had a firm grip on the computer market with its 7000 series of machines. In that year, IBM announced the System/360, a new family of computer

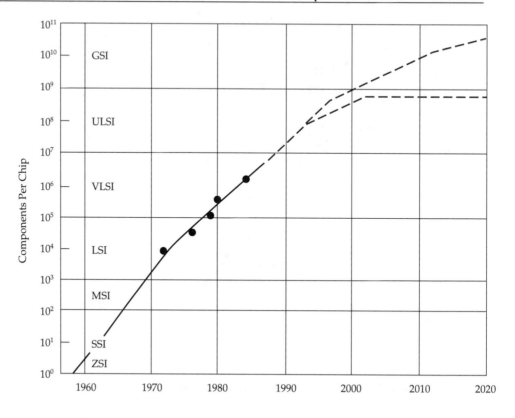

ZSI = Zero-Scale Integration (Discrete Components)
SSI = Small-Scale Integration
MSI = Medium-Scale Integration
LSI = Large-Scale Integration
VLSI = Very-Large-Scale Integration
ULSI = Ultra-Large-Scale Integration
GSI = Giga-Scale Integration

**FIGURE 2.8.  Growth in chip density [MEIN87]**

products. Although the announcement itself was no surprise, it contained some unpleasant news for current IBM customers: the 360 product line was incompatible with older IBM machines. Thus, the transition to the 360 would be difficult for the current customer base. This was a bold step by IBM, but one they felt was necessary to break out of some of the constraints of the 7000 architecture and to produce a system capable of evolving with the new integrated circuit technology [PADE81, GIFF87]. The strategy paid off both financially and technically. The 360 was the success of the decade and cemented IBM as the overwhelmingly dominant computer vendor, with a market share above 70%. And, with some modifications and extensions, the architecture of the 360 remains to this day the architecture of IBM's large computers. Examples using this architecture can be found throughout this text.

The System/360 was the industry's first planned family of computers. The family covered a wide range of performance and cost. Table 2.4 indicates some of the key characteristics of the various models in 1965 (each member of the family is distinguished by a model number). The various models were compatible in that a program written for one model should be capable of being executed by another model in the series, with only a difference in the time it takes to execute.

The concept of a family of compatible computers was both novel and extremely successful. A customer with modest requirements and a budget to match could start with the relatively inexpensive Model 30. Later, if the customer's needs grew, it was possible to upgrade to a faster machine with more memory without sacrificing the investment in already-developed software. The characteristics of a family are

- *Similar or Identical Instruction Set:* In many cases, the exact same set of machine instructions obtains on all members of the family. Thus, a program that executes on one machine will also execute on any other. In some cases, the lower end of the family has an instruction set that is a subset of that of the top end of the family. This means that programs can move up but not down.
- *Similar or Identical Operating System:* The same basic operating system is available for all family members. In some cases, additional features are added to the higher-end members.
- *Increasing Speed:* The rate of instruction execution increases in going from lower to higher family members.
- *Increasing Number of I/O Ports:* In going from lower to higher family members.
- *Increasing Memory Size:* In going from lower to higher family members.
- *Increasing Cost:* In going from lower to higher family members.

How could such a family concept be implemented? Differences were achieved based on three factors: basic speed, size, and degree of simultaneity [STEV64]. For example, greater speed in the execution of a given instruction could be gained by the use of more complex circuitry in the ALU, allowing suboperations to be carried out in parallel. Another way of increasing speed was to increase the width of the data path between main memory and the CPU. On the Model 30, only 1 byte (8 bits) could be fetched from main memory at a time, whereas 8 bytes could be fetched at a time on the Model 70.

The System/360 not only dictated the future course of IBM but also had a profound impact on the entire industry. Many of its features have become standard on other large computers.

**TABLE 2.4   Key Characteristics of the System/360 Family**

| Characteristic | Model 30 | Model 40 | Model 50 | Model 65 | Model 75 |
|---|---|---|---|---|---|
| Maximum memory size (bytes) | 64K | 256K | 256K | 512K | 512K |
| Data rate from memory (Mbytes/sec) | 0.5 | 0.8 | 2.0 | 8.0 | 16.0 |
| Processor cycle time (μsec) | 1.0 | 0.625 | 0.5 | 0.25 | 0.2 |
| Relative speed | 1 | 3.5 | 10 | 21 | 50 |
| Maximum number of data channels | 3 | 3 | 4 | 6 | 6 |
| Maximum data rate on one channel (Kbytes/sec) | 250 | 400 | 800 | 1250 | 1250 |

## DEC PDP-8

In the same year that IBM shipped its first System/360, another momentous first shipment occurred: DEC's PDP-8. At a time when the average computer required an air-conditioned room, the PDP-8 (dubbed a minicomputer by the industry, after the miniskirt of the day) was small enough that it could be placed on top of a lab bench or be built into other equipment. It could not do everything the mainframe could, but at $16,000, it was cheap enough for each lab technician to have one. In contrast, the System/360 series of mainframe computers introduced just a few months before cost hundreds of thousands of dollars.

The low cost and small size of the PDP-8 enabled another manufacturer to purchase a PDP-8 and integrate it into a total system for resale. These other manufacturers came to be known as original equipment manufacturers (OEMs), and the OEM market became and remains a major segment of the computer marketplace.

The PDP-8 was an immediate hit and made DEC's fortune. This machine and other members of the PDP-8 family that followed it (see Table 2.5) achieved a production status formerly reserved for IBM computers, with about 50,000 machines sold over the next dozen years. As DEC's official history puts it, the PDP-8 "established the concept of minicomputers, leading the way to a multibillion dollar industry." It also established DEC as the number one minicomputer vendor, and, by the time the PDP-8 had reached the end of its useful life, DEC was the number two computer manufacturer, behind IBM.

In contrast to the central-switched architecture (Figure 2.5) used by IBM on its 700/7000 and 360 systems, later models of the PDP-8 used a structure that is now

**TABLE 2.5    Evolution of the PDP-8 [VOEL88]**

| Model | First Shipped | Cost of Processor + 4K 12-bit Words of Memory ($1000s) | Data Rate from Memory (words/μsec) | Volume (cubic feet) | Innovations and Improvements |
|-------|---------------|--------------------------------------------------------|------------------------------------|---------------------|------------------------------|
| PDP-8 | 4/65 | 16.2 | 1.26 | 8.0 | Automatic wire-wrapping production |
| PDP-8/5 | 9/66 | 8.79 | 0.08 | 3.2 | Serial instruction implementation |
| PDP-8/1 | 4/68 | 11.6 | 1.34 | 8.0 | Medium scale integrated circuits |
| PDP-8/L | 11/68 | 7.0 | 1.26 | 2.0 | Smaller cabinet |
| PDP-8/E | 3/71 | 4.99 | 1.52 | 2.2 | Omnibus |
| PDP-8/M | 6/72 | 3.69 | 1.52 | 1.8 | Half-size cabinet with fewer slots than 8/E |
| PDP-8/A | 1/75 | 2.6 | 1.34 | 1.2 | Semiconductor memory; floating-point processor |

virtually universal for minicomputers and microcomputers: the bus structure. This is illustrated in Figure 2.9. The PDP-8 bus, called the Omnibus, consists of 96 separate signal paths, used to carry control, address, and data signals. Since all system components share a common set of signal paths, their use must be controlled by the CPU. This architecture is highly flexible, allowing modules to be plugged into the bus to create various configurations. Figure 2.10 shows a large PDP-8/E configuration.

## Later Generations

Beyond the third generation there is less general agreement on defining generations of computers. Table 2.2 suggests that there have been a fourth and a fifth generation, based on advances in integrated-circuit technology. With the introduction of large-scale integration (LSI), more than 1000 components can be placed on a single integrated-circuit chip. Very-large-scale integration (VLSI) achieved more than 10,000 components per chip, and current VLSI chips can contain more than 100,000 components.

With the rapid pace of technology, the high rate of introduction of new products, and the importance of software and communications as well as hardware, the classification by generation becomes less clear and less meaningful. It could be said that the commercial application of new developments resulted in a major change in the early 1970s and that the results of these changes are still being worked out. In this section, we mention two of the most important of these results.

### *Semiconductor Memory*

The first application of integrated-circuit technology to computers was construction of the processor (the control unit and the arithmetic and logic unit) out of integrated-circuit chips. But it was also found that this same technology could be used to construct memories.

In the 1950s and 1960s, most computer memory was constructed from tiny rings of ferromagnetic material, each about a sixteenth of an inch in diameter. These rings were strung up on grids of fine wires suspended on small screens inside the computer. Magnetized one way, a ring (called a *core*) represented a one; magnetized the other way, it stood for a zero. Magnetic-core memory was rather fast; it took as little as a millionth of a second to read a bit stored in memory. But it was expensive, bulky, and used destructive readout: the simple act of reading a core

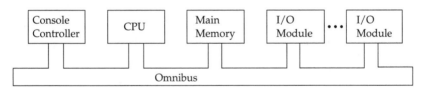

**FIGURE 2.9.  PDP-8 bus structure**

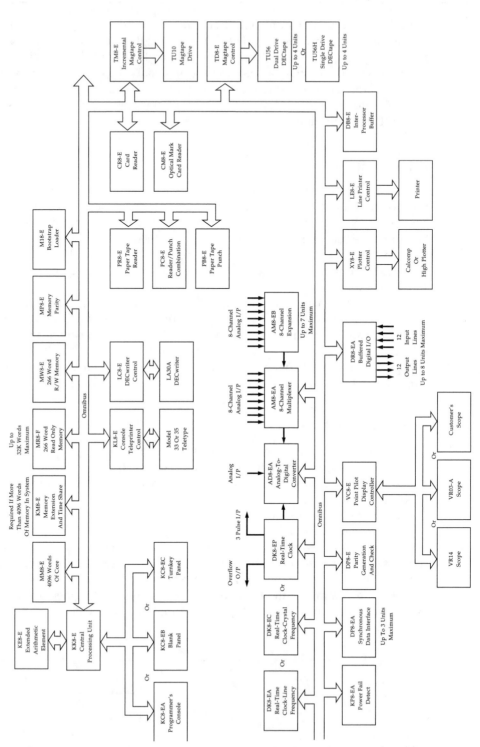

**FIGURE 2.10. PDP-8/E system block diagram**

erased the data stored in it. It was therefore necessary to install circuits to restore the data as soon as it had been extracted.

Then, in 1970, Fairchild produced the first relatively capacious semiconductor memory. This chip, about the size of a single core, could hold 256 bits of memory. It was nondestructive and much faster than core. It took only 70 billionths of a second to read a bit. However, the cost per bit was higher than for that of core.

In 1974, a seminal event occurred: the price per bit of semiconductor memory dropped below the price per bit of core memory. Following this, there has been a continuing and rapid decline in memory cost accompanied by a corresponding increase in physical memory density. This has led the way to smaller, faster machines with memory sizes of larger and more expensive machines with a time lag of just a few years. Developments in memory technology, together with developments in processor technology to be discussed next, changed the nature of computers in less than a decade. Although bulky, expensive computers remain a part of the landscape, the computer has also been brought out to the "end user," with office machines and personal computers.

Since 1970, semiconductor memory has been through eight generations: 1K, 4K, 16K, 64K, 256K, 1M, 4M, and now 16M bits on a single chip ($1K = 2^{10}$, $1M = 2^{20}$). Each generation has provided four times the storage density of the previous generation, accompanied by declining cost per bit and declining access time.

## Microprocessors

Just as the density of elements on memory chips has continued to rise, so has the density of elements on processor chips. As time went on, more and more elements were placed on each chip, so that fewer and fewer chips were needed to construct a single computer processor.

A breakthrough was achieved in 1971, when Intel developed its 4004. The 4004 was the first chip to contain *all* of the components of a CPU on a single chip: the microprocessor was born.

The 4004 can add two 4-bit numbers and can multiply only by repeated addition. By today's standards, the 4004 is hopelessly primitive, but it marked the beginning of a continuing evolution of microprocessor capability and power.

This evolution can be seen most easily in the number of bits that the processor deals with at a time. There is no clear-cut measure of this, but perhaps the best measure is the data bus width: the number of bits of data that can be brought into or sent out of the processor at a time. Another measure is the number of bits in the accumulator or in the set of general-purpose registers. Often, these measures coincide, but not always. For example, there are a number of microprocessors that operate on 16-bit numbers in registers but can only read and write 8 bits at a time.

The next major step in the evolution of the microprocessor was the introduction in 1972 of the Intel 8008. This was the first 8-bit microprocessor and was almost twice as complex as the 4004.

Neither of these steps was to have the impact of the next major event: the introduction in 1974 of the Intel 8080. This was the first general-purpose microprocessor. Whereas the 4004 and the 8008 had been designed for specific applications, the 8080 was designed to be the CPU of a general-purpose microcomputer. Like the 8008, the 8080 is an 8-bit microprocessor. The 8080, however, is faster, has a richer instruction set, and has a large addressing capability.

About the same time, 16-bit microprocessors began to be developed. However, it was not until the end of the 1970s that powerful, general-purpose 16-bit microprocessors appeared. One of these was the 8086. The next step in this trend occurred in 1981, when both Bell Labs and Hewlett-Packard developed 32-bit, single-chip microprocessors. Intel introduced its own 32-bit microprocessor, the 80386, in 1985 (Table 2.6).

## 2.2

## DESIGNING FOR PERFORMANCE

Year by year, the cost of computer systems continues to drop dramatically, while the performance and capacity of those systems continue to rise equally dramatically. At a local warehouse club, you can pick up a personal computer for less than $1000 that packs the wallop of an IBM mainframe from 10 years ago. Inside that personal computer, including the microprocessor and memory and other chips, you get roughly 100 million transistors. You cannot buy 100 million of anything else for so little. That many sheets of toilet paper would run more than $100,000.

Thus, we have virtually "free" computer power. And this continuing technological revolution has enabled the development of applications of astounding complexity and power. For example, desktop applications that require the great power of today's microprocessor-based systems include

- Image processing
- Speech recognition
- Videoconferencing
- Multimedia authoring
- Voice and video annotation of files

**TABLE 2.6   Evolution of Intel Microprocessors**

| Feature | 8008 | 8080 | 8086 | 80386 | 80486 |
|---|---|---|---|---|---|
| Year introduced | 1972 | 1974 | 1978 | 1985 | 1989 |
| Number of instructions | 66 | 111 | 133 | 154 | 235 |
| Address bus width | 8 | 16 | 20 | 32 | 32 |
| Data bus width | 8 | 8 | 16 | 32 | 32 |
| Number of flags | 4 | 5 | 9 | 14 | 14 |
| Number of registers | 8 | 8 | 16 | 8 | 8 |
| Memory addressability | 16 KB | 64 KB | 1 MB | 4 GB | 4 GB |
| I/O ports | 24 | 256 | 64K | 64K | 64K |
| Bus bandwidth | — | 0.75 MB/sec | 5 MB/sec | 32 MB/sec | 32 MB/sec |
| Register-to-register add time | — | 1.3 μsec | 0.3 μsec | 0.125 μsec | 0.06 μsec |

Workstation systems now support highly sophisticated engineering and scientific applications, as well as simulation systems, and the ability to apply workgroup principles to image and video applications. In addition, businesses are relying on increasingly powerful servers to handle transaction and database processing and to support massive client–server networks that have replaced the huge mainframe computer centers of yesteryear.

What is fascinating about all this from the perspective of computer organization and architecture is that, on the one hand, the basic building blocks for today's computer miracles are virtually the same as those of the IAS computer from nearly 50 years ago, while on the other hand, the techniques for squeezing the last iota of performance out of the materials at hand have become increasingly sophisticated.

This observation serves as a guiding principle for the presentation in this book. As we progress through the various elements and components of a computer, two objectives are pursued. First, the book explains the fundamental functionality in each area under consideration, and second, the book explores those techniques required to achieve maximum performance. In the remainder of this section, we highlight some of the driving factors behind the need to design for performance.

## Microprocessor Speed

What gives the Pentium or the PowerPC such mind-boggling power is the relentless pursuit of speed by processor chip manufacturers. The evolution of these machines continues to bear out what is known as Moore's law. Intel Chairman Gordon Moore observed in the mid-1960s that, by shrinking the size of the tiny lines that form transistor circuits in silicon roughly 10% a year, chipmakers could unleash a new generation of chips every three years—with four times as many transistors. In memory chips, this has quadrupled the capacity of dynamic random-access memory (DRAM), still the basic technology for computer main memory, every three years. In microprocessors, the addition of new circuits, and the speed boost that comes from reducing the distances between them, has improved performance four- or fivefold every three years since Intel launched its X86 family in 1979.

But the raw speed of the microprocessor will not achieve its potential unless it is fed a constant stream of work to do in the form of computer instructions. Anything that gets in the way of that smooth flow undermines the power of the processor. Accordingly, while the chipmakers have been busy learning how to fabricate chips of greater and greater density, the processor designers must come up with ever more elaborate techniques for feeding the monster. Among the techniques built into contemporary processors are

- *Branch Prediction:* The processor looks ahead in the software and predicts which branches, or groups of instructions, are likely to be processed next. If the processor guesses right most of the time, it can prefetch the correct instructions and buffer them so that the processor is kept busy. The more sophisticated examples of this strategy predict not just the next branch but multiple branches ahead. Thus, branch prediction increases the amount of work available for the processor to execute.

- *Data Flow Analysis:* The processor analyzes which instructions are dependent on each other's results, or data, to create an optimized schedule of instructions. In fact, instructions are scheduled to be executed when ready, independent of the original program order. This prevents unnecessary delay.
- *Speculative Execution:* Using branch prediction and data flow analysis, some processors speculatively execute instructions ahead of their actual appearance in the program execution, holding the results in temporary locations. This enables the processor to keep its execution engines as busy as possible by executing instructions that are likely to be needed.

These and other sophisticated techniques are made necessary by the sheer power of the processor. They make it possible to exploit the raw speed of the processor.

## Performance Balance

While processor power has raced ahead at breakneck speed, other critical components of the computer have not kept up. The result is a need to look for performance balance: an adjusting of the organization and architecture to compensate for the mismatch among the capabilities of the various components.

Nowhere is the problem created by such mismatches more critical than in the interface between processor and main memory. Consider the history depicted in Figure 2.11. While processor speed and memory capacity have grown rapidly, the speed with which data can be transferred between main memory and the processor

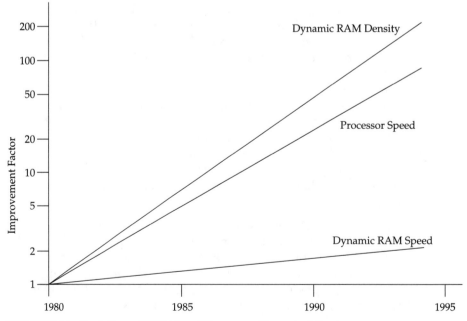

**FIGURE 2.11. Evolution of DRAM and Processor Characteristics**

has lagged badly. The interface between processor and main memory is the most crucial pathway in the entire computer, because it is responsible for carrying a constant flow of program instructions and data between memory chips and the processor. If memory or the pathway fails to keep pace with the processor's insistent demands, the processor stalls in a wait state, and valuable processing time is lost.

The effects of these trends are shown vividly in Figure 2.12. The amount of main memory needed is going up, but DRAM density is going up faster. The net result is that, on average, the number of DRAMS per system is going down. The solid black lines in the figure show that, for a fixed-size memory, the number of DRAMs needed is declining. But this has an effect on transfer rates, because with fewer DRAMs, there is less opportunity for parallel transfer of data. The shaded bands show that for a particular type of system, main memory size has slowly increased while the number of DRAMs has declined.

There are a number of ways that a system architect can attack this problem, all of which are reflected in contemporary computer designs. Some examples:

- Increase the number of bits that are retrieved at one time by making DRAMs "wider" rather than "deeper" and by using wide bus data paths.
- Changing the DRAM interface to make it more efficient, by including a cache or other buffering scheme on the DRAM chip.
- Reduce the frequency of memory access by incorporating increasingly complex and efficient cache structures between the processor and main memory. This includes the incorporation of one or more caches on the processor chip as well as on an off-chip cache close to the processor chip.

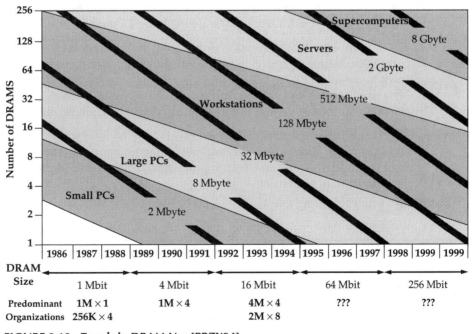

**FIGURE 2.12. Trends in DRAM Use [PRZY94]**

TABLE 2.7    Typical Bandwidth Requirements for Various Peripheral Technologies

| Peripheral | Technology | Required Bandwidth |
|---|---|---|
| Graphics | 24-bit color | 30 MBytes/sec |
| Local area network | 100BASEX or FDDI | 12 MBytes/sec |
| Disk controller | SCSI or P1394 | 10 MBytes/sec |
| Full-motion video | 1024 × 768@30fps | 67+ MBytes/sec |
| I/O Peripherals | Other miscellaneous | 5+ MBytes/sec |

- Increase the interconnect bandwidth between processors and memory by using higher-speed buses and by using a hierarchy of buses to buffer and structure data flow.

Another area of design focus is the handling of I/O devices. As computers become faster and more capable, more sophisticated applications are developed that support the use of peripherals with intensive I/O demands. Table 2.7 gives some examples of typical peripheral devices in use on personal computers and workstations. These devices create tremendous data throughput demands. While the current generation of processors can handle the data pumped out by these devices, there remains the problem of getting that data moved between processor and peripheral. Strategies here include caching and buffering schemes plus the use of higher-speed interconnection buses and more elaborate structures of buses. In addition, the use of multiple-processor configurations can aid in satisfying I/O demands.

The key in all this is balance. Designers all constantly strive to balance the throughput and processing demands of the processor components, main memory, I/O devices, and the interconnection structures. And this design must constantly be rethought to cope with two constantly evolving factors:

1. The rate at which performance is changing in the various technology areas (processor, buses, memory, peripherals) differs greatly from one type of element to another.
2. New applications and new peripheral devices constantly change the nature of the demand on the system in terms of typical instruction profile and the data access patterns.

Thus, computer design is a constantly evolving art form. This book attempts to present the fundamentals on which this art form is based and to present a survey of the current state of that art.

## 2.3

## PENTIUM AND POWERPC EVOLUTION

Throughout this book, we rely on many concrete examples of computer design and implementation to illustrate concepts and to illuminate trade-offs. Most of the time, the book relies on examples from two computer families: the Intel Pentium and the PowerPC. The Pentium represents the results of decades of design effort on complex instruction set computers (CISCs). It incorporates the sophisticated design principles once found only on mainframes and supercomputers and serves as an excellent example of CISC design. The PowerPC is a direct descendant of the first RISC system, the IBM 801, and is one of the most powerful and best-designed RISC-based systems on the market.

In this section, we provide a brief overview of both systems.

## Pentium

Intel has ranked as the number one maker of microprocessors for decades, a position it seems unlikely to yield. The evolution of its flagship microprocessor product serves as a good indicator of the evolution of computer technology in general.

Table 2.8 shows that evolution. Although the Pentium is now the star performer in Intel's product line, they already have two more processors in the pipeline: the P6, introduced in 1995, and the P7, still under development. Interestingly, as microprocessors have grown faster and much more complex, Intel has actually picked up the pace. Intel used to develop microprocessors one after another, every four years. But for the Pentium, the generation gap shrank to three years. And for its P6 and P7 chips, Intel hopes to keep rivals at bay by trimming another year off.

It is worthwhile to list some of the highlights of the evolution of the Intel product line:

- *8080:* The world's first general-purpose microprocessor. This was an 8-bit machine, with an 8-bit data path to memory.
- *8086:* A far more powerful, 16-bit machine. In addition to a wider data path and larger registers, the 8086 sported an instruction cache, or queue, that prefetches a few instructions before they are executed.
- *80286:* This extension of the 8086 enabled addressing a 16 MByte memory instead of just 1 MByte.
- *80386:* Intel's first 32-bit machine, and a major overhaul of the product. With a 32-bit architecture, the 80386 rivaled the complexity and power of minicomputers and mainframes introduced just a few years earlier.
- *80486:* The 80486 introduces the use of much more sophisticated and powerful cache technology and sophisticated instruction pipelining.

**TABLE 2.8  Intel Microprocessors [HOF95]**

| Characteristic | 286 | 386 | 486 | Pentium | P6 | P7 |
|---|---|---|---|---|---|---|
| Start of design work | 1978 | 1982 | 1986 | 1989 | 1990 | 1993 |
| Formal introduction | Feb. 1982 | Oct. 1985 | Apr. 1989 | Mar. 1993 | Q3 1995 | 1997 or 1998[b] |
| Volume shipments | 1983 | 1986 | 1990 | 1994 | 1996 | 1998 or 1999[b] |
| Number of transistors | 130,000 | 275,000 | 1.2 million | 3.1 million | 5.5 million | 10+ million[b] |
| Initial speed in MIPS[a] | 1 | 5 | 20 | 100 | 250[b] | 500[b] |
| Peak sales year | 1989 | 1992 | 1995[b] | 1997[b] | 1999[b] | 2000[b] |
| Installed units | 9.7 million | 44.2 million | 75 million | 4.5 million | none | none |

[a]Millions of instructions per second.
[b]Estimated.

- *Pentium:* With the Pentium, Intel introduces the use of superscalar techniques, which allow multiple instructions to execute in parallel.
- *P6:* The P6 continues the move into superscalar organization begun with the Pentium, with aggressive use of branch prediction, data flow analysis, and speculative execution.
- *P7:* Will see the introduction of some RISC-based technology into the product line.

## PowerPC

In 1975, the 801 minicomputer project at IBM pioneered many of the architecture concepts used in RISC systems. The 801, together with the Berkeley RISC I proces-

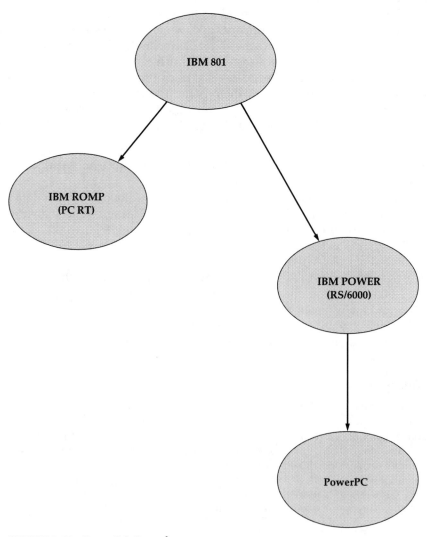

**FIGURE 2.13.  PowerPC Genealogy**

sor, launched the RISC movement. The 801, however, was simply a prototype intended to demonstrate design concepts. The success of the 801 project led IBM to develop a commercial RISC workstation product, the RT PC. The RT PC, introduced in 1986, adapted the architectural concepts of the 801 to an actual product. The RT PC was not a commercial success, and it had many rivals with comparable or better performance. In 1990, IBM produced a third system, which built on the lessons of the 801 and the RT PC. The IBM RISC System/6000 was a RISC-like superscalar machine marketed as a high-performance workstation; shortly after its introduction, IBM began to refer to this as the POWER architecture.

For its next step, IBM entered into an alliance with Motorola, developer of the 68000 series of microprocessors, and Apple, which used the Motorola chip in its Macintosh computers. The result is a series of machines that implement the PowerPC architecture. This architecture is derived from the POWER architecture (Figure 2.13). Changes were made to add key missing features and to enable more efficient implementation by eliminating some instructions and relaxing the specification to eliminate some troublesome special cases. The resulting PowerPC architecture is a superscalar RISC system.

So far, four members of the PowerPC family have been introduced (Figure 2.14):

- *601:* The purpose of the 601 was to bring the PowerPC architecture to the marketplace as quickly as possible. The 601 is a 32-bit machine.

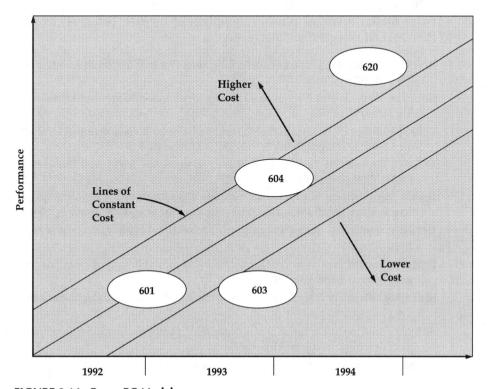

**FIGURE 2.14. PowerPC Models**

- *603:* Intended for low-end desktop and portable computers. It is also a 32-bit machine, comparable in performance with the 601, but with lower cost and a more efficient implementation.
- *604:* Intended for desktop computers and low-end servers. Again, this is a 32-bit machine, but it uses much more advanced superscalar design techniques to achieve greater performance.
- *620:* Intended for high-end servers. The first member of the PowerPC family to implement a full 64-bit architecture, including 64-bit registers and data paths.

## 2.4

## RECOMMENDED READING

A description of the IBM 7000 series can be found in [BELL71a]. There is good coverage of the IBM 360 in [SIEW82] and of the PDP-8 and other DEC machines in [BELL78a]. These three books also contain numerous detailed examples of other computers spanning the history of computers through the early 1980s.

One of the best treatments of the Pentium is [ANDE93]. The Intel documentation itself is also good [INTE94a, INTE94b]. [BREY95] provides a good survey of the Intel microprocessor line, with emphasis on the 32-bit machines.

[IBM94] is a thorough treatment of the PowerPC architecture. [SHAN94b] provides similar coverage plus a description of the 601. [WEIS94] treats both the POWER and PowerPC architectures.

ANDE93   Anderson, D., and Shanley, T. *Pentium Processor System Architecture.* Richardson, TX: Mindshare Press, 1993.

BELL71a   Bell, C., and Newell, A. *Computer Structures: Readings and Examples.* New York: McGraw-Hill, 1971.

BELL78a   Bell, C.; Mudge, J.; and McNamara, J. *Computer Engineering: A DEC View of Hardware Systems Design.* Bedford, MA: Digital Press, 1978.

BREY95   Brey, B. *The Intel 32-Bit Microprocessors: 80386, 80486, and Pentium.* Englewood Cliffs, NJ: Prentice-Hall, 1995.

IBM94   International Business Machines, Inc. *The PowerPC Architecture: A Specification for a New Family of RISC Processors.* San Francisco, CA: Morgan-Kaufmann, 1994.

INTE94a   Intel Corp. *Pentium Family User's Manual, Volume 1: Data Book.* Santa Clara, CA, 1994.

INTE94b   Intel Corp. *Pentium Family User's Manual, Volume 3: Architecture and Programming Manual.* Santa Clara, CA, 1994.

SHAN94b   Shanley, T. *PowerPC 601 System Architecture.* Richardson, TX: Mindshare Press, 1994.

SIEW82   Siewiorek, D.; Bell, C.; and Newell, A. *Computer Structures: Principles and Examples.* New York: McGraw-Hill, 1982.

WEIS94   Weiss, S., and Smith, J. *POWER and PowerPC.* San Francisco: Morgan Kaufmann, 1994.

2.5

## PROBLEMS

2.1. Let A = A(1), A(2), . . ., A(1,000) and B = B(1), B(2) . . . B(1000) be two vectors (one-dimensional arrays) comprising 1000 numbers each that are to be added to form an array C such that C(I) = A(I) + B(I) for I = 1, 2, . . ., 1000. Using the IAS instruction set, write a program for this problem.

2.2 For the flowchart of Figure 2.4, add the logic for the remaining IAS instructions, except for those involving a multiply or a divide.

2.3 In the IBM 360 Models 65 and 75, addresses are staggered in two separate main memory units (e.g., all even-numbered words in one unit and all odd-numbered words in another). What might be the purpose of this technique?

2.4 Discuss the advantages and disadvantages of storing programs and data in the same memory.

2.5 List those instructions in Table 2.1 that are redundant. An instruction is redundant if the identical function can be performed by some combination of other instructions from the instruction set. In each case, demonstrate the redundancy by showing an alternative sequence of instructions.

2.6 Discuss the relative merits of the central switch and bus architectures.

# PART II

# THE COMPUTER SYSTEM

A computer system consists of a processor, memory, I/O, and the interconnections among these major components. With the exception of the processor, which is sufficiently complex to devote Part III to its study, Part II examines each of these components in detail.

At the highest level, we can understand the function of each of the major components by describing the structure of their interconnection and the type of signals exchanged among them. This is done in Chapter 3. The next two chapters examine internal and external memory, respectively. Chapter 4 looks at the organization of main memory and the use of a cache strategy to enhance performance. Chapter 5 surveys the main types of external memory and looks at the use of RAID organization to improve disk memory performance. Chapter 6 is devoted to the various aspects of I/O organization. Finally, Chapter 7 describes the basic principles of operating systems, and it discusses the specific design features in the computer hardware intended to provide support for the operating system.

# CHAPTER 3

# System Buses

At a top level, a computer consists of CPU, memory, and I/O components, with one or more modules of each type. These components are interconnected in some fashion to achieve the basic function of the computer, which is to execute programs. Thus, at a top level, we can describe a computer system by (1) describing the external behavior of each component, that is, the data and control signals that it exchanges with other components, and (2) describing the interconnection structure and the controls required to manage the use of the interconnection structure.

This top-level view of structure and function is important because of its explanatory power in understanding the nature of a computer. Equally important is its use to understand the increasingly complex issues of performance evaluation. A grasp of the top-level structure and function offers insight into system bottlenecks, alternate pathways, the magnitude of system failures if a component fails, and the ease of adding performance enhancements. In many cases, requirements for greater system power and fail-safe capabilities are being met by changing the design rather than merely increasing the speed and reliability of individual components.

This chapter focuses on the basic structures used for computer component interconnection. As background, the chapter begins with a brief examination of the basic components and their interface requirements. Then, a functional overview is provided.

We are then prepared to examine the use of buses to interconnect system components.

## 3.1

## COMPUTER COMPONENTS

As discussed in Chapter 2, virtually all contemporary computer designs are based on concepts developed by John von Neumann at the Institute for Advanced Studies, Princeton. Such a design is referred to as the *von Neumann architecture* and is based on three key concepts:

- Data and instructions are stored in a single read–write memory.

- The contents of this memory are addressable by location, without regard to the type of data contained there.
- Execution occurs in a sequential fashion (unless explicitly modified) from one instruction to the next.

The reasoning behind these concepts was discussed in Chapter 1 but is worth summarizing here. There is a small set of basic logic components that can be combined in various ways to store binary data and to perform arithmetic and logical operations on that data. If there is a particular computation to be performed, a configuration of logic components designed specifically for that computation can be constructed. We can think of the process of connecting together the various components in the desired configuration as a form of programming. The resulting "program" is in the form of hardware and is termed a *hardwired program.*

If all programming were done in this fashion, very little use would be made of this type of hardware. But now consider this alternative. Suppose we construct a general-purpose configuration of arithmetic and logic functions. This set of hardware will perform various functions on data depending on control signals applied to the hardware. In the original case of customized hardware, the system accepts data and produces results (Figure 3.1a). With general-purpose hardware, the system accepts data and control signals and produces results. Thus, instead of

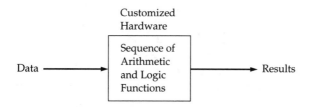

(a) Programming in Hardware

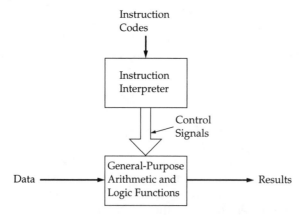

(b) Programming in Software

**FIGURE 3.1. Hardware and software approaches**

rewiring the hardware for each new program, the programmer merely needs to supply a new set of control signals.

How shall control signals be supplied? The answer is simple but subtle. The entire program is actually a sequence of steps. At each step, some arithmetic or logical operation is performed on some data. For each step, a new set of control signals is needed. Let us provide a unique code for each possible set of control signals, and let us add to the general-purpose hardware a segment that can accept a code and generate control signals (Figure 3.1b).

Programming is now much easier. Instead of rewiring the hardware for each new program, all we need to do is provide a new sequence of codes. Each code is, in effect, an instruction, and part of the hardware interprets each instruction and generates control signals. To distinguish this new method of programming, a sequence of codes or instructions is called *software*.

Figure 3.1b indicates two major components of the system: an instruction interpreter and a module of general-purpose arithmetic and logic functions. These two constitute the CPU. Several other components are needed to yield a functioning computer. Data and instructions must be put into the system. For this we need some sort of input module. This module contains basic components for accepting data and instructions in some form and converting them into an internal form of signals usable by the system. A means of reporting results is needed, and this is in the form of an output module. Taken together, these are referred to as *I/O components*.

One more component is needed. An input device will bring instructions and data in sequentially. But a program is not invariably executed sequentially; it may jump around (e.g., the IAS jump instruction). Similarly, operations on data may require access to more than just one element at a time in a predetermined sequence. Thus, there must be a place to temporarily store both instructions and data. That module is called *memory*, or *main memory* to distinguish it from external storage or peripheral devices. Von Neumann pointed out that the same memory could be used to store both instructions and data. Data would be treated as data upon which computations were performed. Instructions would be treated as data to be interpreted as codes for generating control signals.

Figure 3.2 illustrates these top-level components and suggests the interactions among them. The CPU is typically in control. It exchanges data with memory. For this purpose, it typically makes use of two internal (to the CPU) registers: a memory address register (MAR), which specifies the address in memory for the next read or write, and a memory buffer register (MBR), which contains the data to be written into memory or receives the data read from memory. Similarly, an I/O address register (I/OAR) specifies a particular I/O device. An I/O buffer register is used for the exchange of data between an I/O module and the CPU.

A memory module consists of a set of locations, defined by sequentially numbered addresses. Each location contains a binary number that can be interpreted as either an instruction or data. An I/O module transfers data from external devices to CPU and memory, and vice versa. It contains internal buffers for temporarily holding this data until it can be sent on.

Having looked briefly at these major components, we now turn to an overview of how these components function together to execute programs.

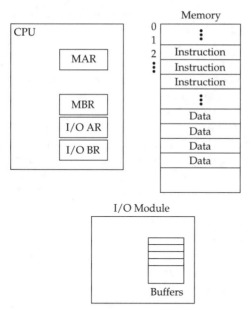

**FIGURE 3.2.  Computer components: top-level view**

## 3.2

### COMPUTER FUNCTION

The basic function performed by a computer is program execution. The program to be executed consists of a set of instructions stored in memory. The central processing unit (CPU) does the actual work by executing instructions specified in the program.

In order to gain a greater understanding of this function and of the way in which the major components of the computer interact to execute a program, we need to look in more detail at the process of program execution. The simplest point of view is to consider instruction processing as consisting of two steps: The CPU reads (*fetches*) instructions from memory one at a time, and it executes each instruction. Program execution consists of repeating the process of instruction fetch and instruction execution. Of course, the execution of an instruction may itself involve a number of steps (see, for example, the lower portion of Figure 2.4). At this stage, we can justify the breakdown of instruction processing into the two stages of fetch and execution as follows: The instruction fetch is a common operation for each instruction, and consists of reading an instruction from a location in memory. The instruction execution may involve several operations and depends on the nature of the instruction.

The processing required for a single instruction is called an *instruction cycle.* Using the simplified two-step description explained above, the instruction cycle is depicted in Figure 3.3. The two steps are referred to as the *fetch cycle* and the *exe-*

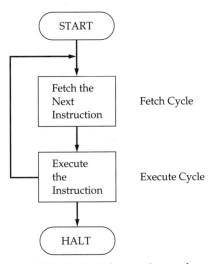

**FIGURE 3.3.  Basic instruction cycle**

*cute cycle.* Program execution halts only if the machine is turned off, some sort of unrecoverable error occurs, or a program instruction that halts the computer is encountered.

## The Fetch and Execute Cycles

At the beginning of each instruction cycle, the CPU fetches an instruction from memory. In a typical CPU, a register called the program counter (PC) is used to keep track of which instruction is to be fetched next. Unless told otherwise, the CPU always increments the PC after each instruction fetch so that it will fetch the next instruction in sequence (i.e., the instruction located at the next higher memory address). So, for example, consider a computer in which each instruction occupies one 16-bit word of memory. Assume that the program counter is set to location 300. The CPU will next fetch the instruction at location 300. On succeeding instruction cycles, it will fetch instructions from locations 301, 302, 303, and so on. This sequence may be altered, as explained presently.

The fetched instruction is loaded into a register in the CPU known as the instruction register (IR). The instruction is in the form of a binary code that specifies what action the CPU is to take. The CPU interprets the instruction and performs the required action. In general, these actions fall into four categories:

- *CPU–Memory:* Data may be transferred from the CPU to memory or from memory to CPU.
- *CPU–I/O:* Data may be transferred to or from the outside world by transferring between the CPU and an I/O module.
- *Data Processing:* The CPU may perform some arithmetic or logic operation on data.

```
0        3 4                                    15
  ┌──────────┬──────────────────────────────────┐
  │ Op Code  │    Address                        │
  └──────────┴──────────────────────────────────┘
```

(a) Instruction Format

```
0   1                                           15
  ┌───┬──────────────────────────────────────────┐
  │ S │ Magnitude                                 │
  └───┴──────────────────────────────────────────┘
```

(b) Integer Format

Program Counter (PC) = Address of Instruction
Instruction Register (IR) = Instruction Being Executed
Accumulator (AC) = Temporary Storage

(c) Internal CPU Registers

0001 = Load AC from Memory
0010 = Store AC to Memory
0101 = Add to AC from Memory

(d) Partial List of Opcodes

**FIGURE 3.4. Characteristics of a hypothetical machine**

- *Control:* An instruction may specify that the sequence of execution be altered (e.g., the IAS jump instruction, Table 2.1). For example, the CPU may fetch an instruction from location 149, which specifies that the next instruction be fetched from location 182. The CPU will remember this fact by setting the program counter to 182. Thus, on the next fetch cycle, the instruction will be fetched from location 182 rather than 150.

Of course, an instruction's execution may involve a combination of these actions.

Let us consider a simple example using a hypothetical machine that includes the characteristics listed in Figure 3.4. The CPU contains an accumulator (AC) to temporarily store data. Both instructions and data are 16 bits long. Thus, it is convenient to organize memory using 16-bit locations, or words. The instruction format indicates that there can be as many as $2^4 = 16$ different op codes, and up to $2^{12} = 4096$ (4K) words of memory can be directly addressed.

Figure 3.5 illustrates a partial program execution, showing the relevant portions of memory and CPU registers. The notation used is hexadecimal.[1] The program fragment shown adds the contents of the memory word at address $940_{16}$ to the contents of the memory word at address $941_{16}$ and stores the result in the latter location. Three instructions, which can be described as three fetch and three execute cycles, are required:

1. The program counter (PC) contains 300, the address of the first instruction. This address is loaded into the instruction register (IR). Note that this process would involve the use of a memory address register (MAR) and a memory buffer register (MBR). For simplicity, these intermediate registers are ignored.

---

[1] In hexadecimal notation, each digit represents four bits. This is the most convenient notation for representing the contents of memory and registers when the word length is a multiple of 4 (e.g., 8, 16, or 32). For the reader unfamiliar with this notation, it is reviewed in the appendix to Chapter 8.

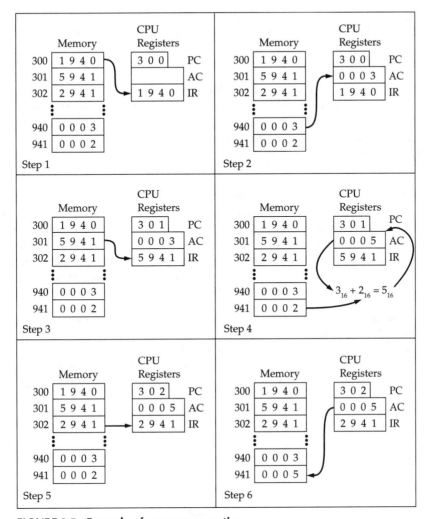

**FIGURE 3.5. Example of program execution**

2. The first 4 bits in the IR indicate that the accumulator (AC) is to be loaded. The remaining 12 bits specify the address, which is 940.
3. The PC is incremented, and the next instruction is fetched.
4. The old contents of the AC and the contents of location 941 are added, and the result is stored in the AC.
5. The PC is incremented, and the next instruction is fetched.
6. The contents of the AC are stored in location 941.

In this example, three instruction cycles, each consisting of a fetch cycle and an execute cycle, are needed to add the contents of location 940 to the contents of 941. With a more complex set of instructions, fewer cycles would be needed. Most modern CPUs include instructions that contain more than one address. The PDP-

11 instruction expressed symbolically as ADD B,A stores the sum of the contents of memory locations B and A into memory location A. A single instruction cycle with the following steps occurs:

1. Fetch the ADD instruction.
2. Read the contents of memory location A into the CPU.
3. Read the contents of memory location B into the CPU. In order that the contents of A are not lost, the CPU must have at least two registers for storing memory values, rather than a single accumulator.
4. Add the two values.
5. Write the result from the CPU to memory location A.

Thus, the execution cycle for a particular instruction may involve more than one reference to memory. Also, instead of memory references, an instruction may specify an I/O operation. With these additional considerations in mind, Figure 3.6 provides a more detailed look at the basic instruction cycle of Figure 3.3. The figure is in the form of a state diagram. For any given instruction cycle, some states may be null and others may be visited more than once. The states can be described as follows:

- *Instruction Address Calculation (iac):* Determine the address of the next instruction to be executed. Usually, this involves adding a fixed number to the address of the previous instruction. For example, if each instruction is 16 bits long and memory is organized into 16-bit words, then add 1 to the previous address. If, instead, memory is organized as individually addressable 8-bit bytes, then add 2 to the previous address.
- *Instruction Fetch (if):* Read instruction from its memory location into the CPU.
- *Instruction Operation Decoding (iod):* Analyze instruction to determine type of operation to be performed and operand(s) to be used.

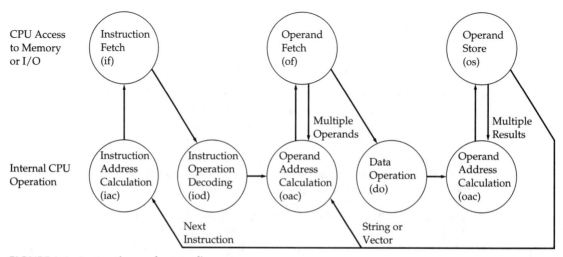

**FIGURE 3.6. Instruction cycle state diagram**

- *Operand Address Calculation (oac):* If the operation involves reference to an operand in memory or available via I/O, then determine the address of the operand.
- *Operand Fetch (of):* Fetch the operand from memory or read it in from I/O.
- *Data Operation (do):* Perform the operation indicated in the instruction.
- *Operand Store (os):* Write the result into memory or out to I/O.

States in the upper part of Figure 3.6 involve an exchange between the CPU and either memory or an I/O module. States in the lower part of the diagram involve only internal CPU operations. The oac state appears twice, since an instruction may involve a read, a write, or both. However, the action performed during that state is fundamentally the same in both cases, and so only a single-state identifier is needed.

Also note that the diagram allows for multiple operands and multiple results, since some instructions on some machines require this. For example, the PDP-11 instruction ADD A,B results in the following sequence of states: iac, if, iod, oac, of, oac, of, do, oac, os.

Finally, on some machines, a single instruction can specify an operation to be performed on a vector (one-dimensional array) of numbers or a string (one-dimensional array) of characters. As Figure 3.6 indicates, this would involve repetitive operand fetch and/or store operations.

### Interrupts

Virtually all computers provide a mechanism by which other modules (I/O, memory) may interrupt the normal processing of the CPU. Table 3.1 lists the most common classes of interrupts. The specific nature of these interrupts is examined later in this book, especially in Chapters 6 and 11. However, we need to introduce the concept now in order to understand more clearly the nature of the instruction cycle and the implications of interrupts on the interconnection structure. The reader need not be concerned at this stage about the details of the generation and processing of interrupts, but only focus on the communication between modules that results from interrupts.

Interrupts are provided primarily as a way to improve processing efficiency. For example, most external devices are much slower than the processor. Suppose that

**TABLE 3.1    Classes of Interrupts**

| | |
|---|---|
| **Program** | Generated by some condition that occurs as a result of an instruction execution, such as arithmetic overflow, division by zero, attempt to execute an illegal machine instruction, and reference outside a user's allowed memory space. |
| **Timer** | Generated by a timer within the processor. This allows the operating system to perform certain functions on a regular basis. |
| **I/O** | Generated by an I/O controller, to signal normal completion of an operation or to signal a variety of error conditions. |
| **Hardware failure** | Generated by a failure such as power failure or memory parity error. |

the processor is transferring data to a printer using the instruction cycle scheme of Figure 3.3. After each write operation, the processor will have to pause and remain idle until the printer catches up. The length of this pause can be on the order of many hundreds or even thousands of instruction cycles that do not involve memory. Clearly, this is a very wasteful use of the processor. With interrupts, the processor can be engaged in executing other instructions while an I/O operation is in progress.

Figure 3.7a illustrates this state of affairs for the application referred to in the preceding paragraph. The user program performs a series of WRITE calls interleaved with processing. Code segments 1, 2, and 3 refer to sequences of instructions that do not involve I/O. The WRITE calls are calls to an I/O program that is a system utility and that will perform the actual I/O operation. The I/O program consists of three sections:

- A sequence of instructions, labeled 4 in the figure, to prepare for the actual I/O operation. This may include copying the data to be output into a special buffer, and preparing the parameters for a device command.
- The actual I/O command. Without the use of interrupts, once this command is issued, the program must wait for the I/O device to perform the requested function. The program might wait by simply repeatedly performing a test operation to determine if the I/O operation is done.
- A sequence of instructions, labeled 5 in the figure, to complete the operation. This may include setting a flag indicating the success or failure of the operation.

Because the I/O operation may take a relatively long time to complete, the I/O program is hung up waiting for the operation to complete; hence, the user program is stopped at the point of the WRITE call for some considerable period of time.

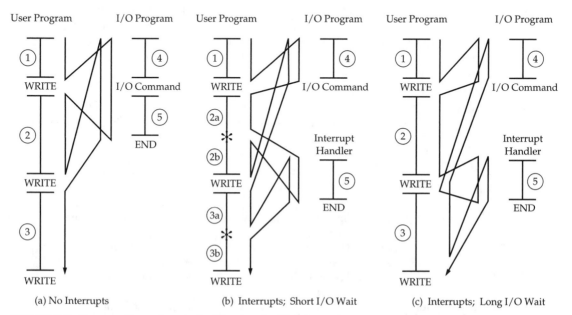

(a) No Interrupts          (b) Interrupts;  Short I/O Wait          (c) Interrupts;  Long I/O Wait

FIGURE 3.7.  Program flow of control without and with interrupts

*Interrupts and the Instruction Cycle*

With interrupts, the processor can be engaged in executing other instructions while an I/O operation is in progress. Consider the flow of control in Figure 3.7b. As before, the user program reaches a point at which it makes a system call in the form of a WRITE call. The I/O program that is invoked in this case consists only of the preparation code and the actual I/O command. After these few instructions have been executed, control returns to the user program. Meanwhile, the external device is busy accepting data from computer memory and printing it. This I/O operation is conducted concurrently with the execution of instructions in the user program.

When the external device becomes ready to be serviced, that is, when it is ready to accept more data from the processor, the I/O module for that external device sends an *interrupt request* signal to the processor. The processor responds by suspending operation of the current program, branching off to a program to service that particular I/O device, known as an interrupt handler, and resuming the original execution after the device is serviced. The points at which such interrupts occur are indicated by an asterisk (*) in Figure 3.7b.

From the point of view of the user program, an interrupt is just that: an interruption of the normal sequence of execution. When the interrupt processing is completed, execution resumes (Figure 3.8). Thus, the user program does not have to contain any special code to accommodate interrupts; the processor and the operating system are responsible for suspending the user program and then resuming it at the same point.

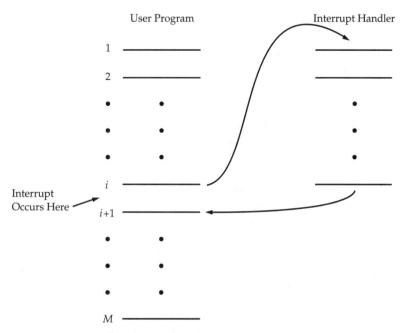

**FIGURE 3.8. Transfer of control via interrupts**

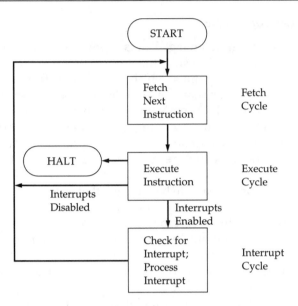

**FIGURE 3.9. Instruction cycle with interrupts**

To accommodate interrupts, an *interrupt cycle* is added to the instruction cycle, as shown in Figure 3.9. In the interrupt cycle, the processor checks to see if any interrupts have occurred, indicated by the presence of an interrupt signal. If no interrupts are pending, the processor proceeds to the fetch cycle and fetches the next instruction of the current program. If an interrupt is pending, the processor does the following:

1. It suspends execution of the current program being executed and saves its context. This means saving the address of the next instruction to be executed (current contents of the program counter) and any other data relevant to the processor's current activity.
2. It sets the program counter to the starting address of an *interrupt handler* routine.

The processor now proceeds to the fetch cycle and fetches the first instruction in the interrupt handler program, which will service the interrupt. The interrupt handler program is generally part of the operating system. Typically, this program determines the nature of the interrupt and performs whatever actions are needed. For example, in the example we have been using, the handler determines which I/O module generated the interrupt, and may branch to a program that will write more data out to that I/O module. When the interrupt handler routine is completed, the processor can resume execution of the user program at the point of interruption.

It is clear that there is some overhead involved in this process. Extra instructions must be executed (in the interrupt handler) to determine the nature of the interrupt and to decide on the appropriate action. Nevertheless, because of the relatively large amount of time that would be wasted by simply waiting on an I/O operation, the processor can be employed much more efficiently with the use of interrupts.

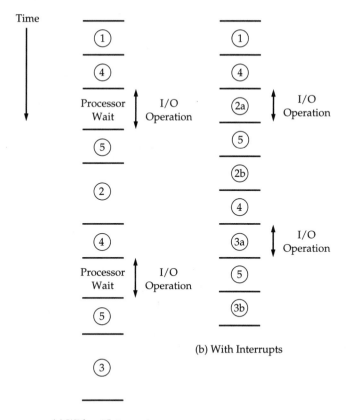

Time

(b) With Interrupts

(a) Without Interrupts

**FIGURE 3.10.  Program timing; short I/O wait**

To appreciate the gain in efficiency, consider Figure 3.10 which is a timing diagram based on the flow of control in Figures 3.7a and 3.7b.

Figure 3.7b and 3.10 assume that the time required for the I/O operation is relatively short: less than the time to complete the execution of instructions between write operations in the user program. The more typical case, especially for a slow device such as a printer, is that the I/O operation will take much more time than executing a sequence of user instructions. Figure 3.7c indicates this state of affairs. In this case, the user program reaches the second WRITE call before the I/O operation spawned by the first call is complete. The result is that the user program is hung up at that point. When the preceding I/O operation is completed, this new WRITE call may be processed, and a new I/O operation may be started. Figure 3.11 shows the timing for this situation with and without the use of interrupts. We can see that there is still a gain in efficiency because part of the time during which the I/O operation is under way overlaps with the execution of user instructions.

Figure 3.12 shows a revised instruction cycle state diagram that includes interrupt cycle processing.

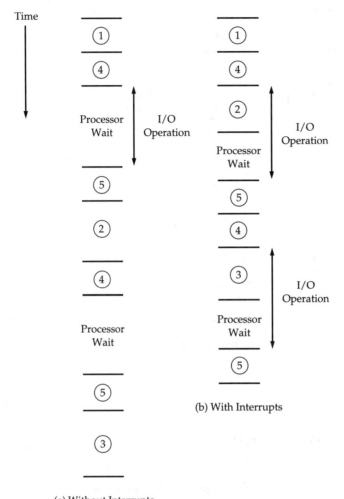

Time

Processor Wait | I/O Operation

Processor Wait

I/O Operation

Processor Wait

I/O Operation

Processor Wait

(a) Without Interrupts

(b) With Interrupts

**FIGURE 3.11.  Program timing; long I/O wait**

### Multiple Interrupts

The discussion so far has only discussed the occurrence of a single interrupt. Suppose, however, that multiple interrupts can occur. For example, a program may be receiving data from a communications line and printing results. The printer will generate an interrupt every time that it completes a print operation. The communication line controller will generate an interrupt every time a unit of data arrives. The unit could either be a single character or a block, depending on the nature of the communications discipline. In any case, it is possible for a communications interrupt to occur while a printer interrupt is being processed.

Two approaches can be taken to dealing with multiple interrupts. The first is to disable interrupts while an interrupt is being processed. A *disabled interrupt* simply

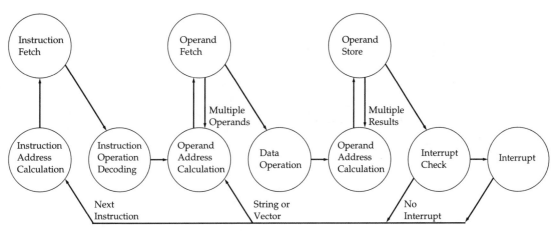

**FIGURE 3.12. Instruction cycle state diagram, with interrupts**

means that the processor can and will ignore that interrupt request signal. If an interrupt occurs during this time, it generally remains pending and will be checked by the processor after the processor has enabled interrupts. Thus, when a user program is executing and an interrupt occurs, interrupts are disabled immediately. After the interrupt handler routine completes, interrupts are enabled before resuming the user program, and the processor checks to see if additional interrupts have occurred. This approach is nice and simple, as interrupts are handled in strict sequential order (Figure 3.13a).

The drawback to the above approach is that it does not take into account relative priority or time-critical needs. For example, when input arrives from the communications line, it may need to be absorbed rapidly to make room for more input. If the first batch of input has not been processed before the second batch arrives, data may be lost.

A second approach is to define priorities for interrupts and to allow an interrupt of higher priority to cause a lower-priority interrupt handler to be itself interrupted (Figure 3.13b).

As an example of this second approach, consider a system with three I/O devices: a printer, a disk, and a communications line, with increasing priorities of 2, 4, and 5 respectively. Figure 3.14 illustrates a possible sequence. A user program begins at $t = 0$. At $t = 10$, a printer interrupt occurs; user information is placed on the system stack, and execution continues at the printer interrupt service routine (ISR). While this routine is still executing, at $t = 15$, a communications interrupt occurs. Since the communications line has higher priority than the printer, the interrupt is honored. The printer ISR is interrupted, its state is pushed onto the stack, and execution continues at the communications ISR. While this routine is executing, a disk interrupt occurs ($t = 20$). Since this interrupt is of lower priority, it is simply held, and the communications ISR runs to completion.

When the communications ISR is complete ($t = 25$), the previous processor state is restored, which is the execution of the printer ISR. However, before even a sin-

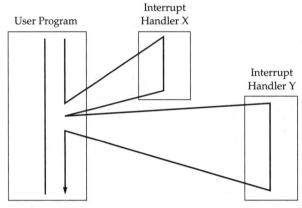

(a) Sequential Interrupt Processing

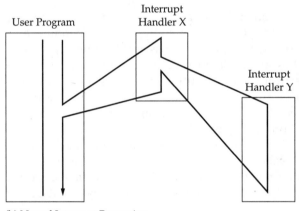

(b) Nested Interrupt Processing

**FIGURE 3.13.  Transfer of control with multiple interrupts**

gle instruction in that routine can be executed, the processor honors the higher-priority disk interrupt and control transfers to the disk ISR. Only when that routine is complete ($t = 35$) is the printer ISR resumed. When that routine completes ($t = 40$), control finally returns to the user program.

## I/O Function

Thus far, we have discussed the operation of the computer as controlled by the CPU, and we have looked primarily at the interaction of CPU and memory. The discussion has only alluded to the role of the I/O component. This role is discussed in detail in Chapter 6, but a brief summary is in order here.

An I/O module can exchange data directly with the CPU. Just as the CPU can initiate a read or write with memory, designating the address of a specific location, the CPU can also read data from or write data to an I/O module. In this latter case,

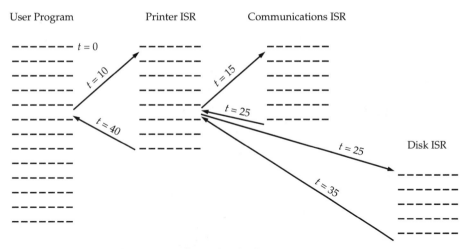

**FIGURE 3.14. Example time sequence of multiple interrupts**

the CPU identifies a specific device that is controlled by a particular I/O module. Thus, an instruction sequence similar in form to that of Figure 3.5 could occur, with I/O instructions rather than with memory-referencing instructions.

In some cases, it is desirable to allow I/O exchanges to occur directly with memory. In such a case, the CPU grants to an I/O module the authority to read from or write to memory, so that the I/O–memory transfer can occur without tying up the CPU. During such a transfer, the I/O module issues read or write commands to memory, relieving the CPU of responsibility for the exchange. This operation is known as *direct memory access* (DMA), and it will be examined in detail in Chapter 6. For now, all that we need to know is that the interconnection structure of the computer may need to allow for direct memory–I/O interaction.

## 3.3

## INTERCONNECTION STRUCTURES

A computer consists of a set of components or modules of three basic types (CPU, memory, I/O) that communicate with each other. In effect, a computer is a network of basic modules. Thus, there must be paths for connecting the modules together.

The collection of paths connecting the various modules is called the *interconnection structure*. The design of this structure will depend on the exchanges that must be made between modules.

Figure 3.15 suggests the types of exchanges that are needed by indicating the major forms of input and output for each module type:

- *Memory:* Typically, a memory module will consist of $N$ words of equal length. Each word is assigned a unique numerical address (0, 1, . . ., $N - 1$). A word of data can be read from or written into the memory. The nature of the operation is

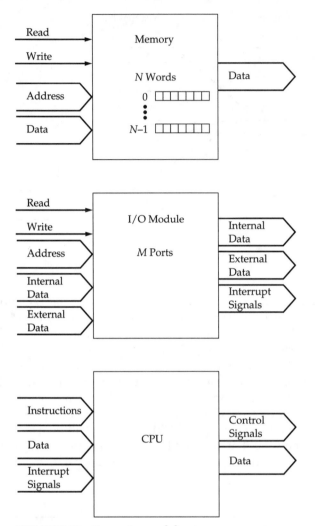

**FIGURE 3.15. Computer modules**

indicated by Read and Write control signals. The location for the operation is specified by an address.

- *I/O Module:* From an internal (to the computer system) point of view, I/O is functionally similar to memory. There are two operations, read and write. Further, an I/O module may control more than one external device. We can refer to each of the interfaces to an external device as a *port* and give each a unique address (e.g., 0, 1, . . ., $M - 1$). In addition, there are external data paths for the input and output of data with an external device. Finally, an I/O module may be able to send interrupt signals to the CPU.

- *CPU:* The CPU reads in instructions and data, writes out data after processing, and uses control signals to control the overall operation of the system. It also receives interrupt signals.

The preceding list defines the data to be exchanged. The interconnection structure must support the following types of transfers:

- *Memory to CPU:* The CPU reads an instruction or a unit of data from memory.
- *CPU to Memory:* The CPU writes a unit of data to memory.
- *I/O to CPU:* The CPU reads data from an I/O device via an I/O module.
- *CPU to I/O:* The CPU sends data to the I/O device.
- *I/O to or from Memory:* For these two cases, an I/O module is allowed to exchange data directly with memory, without going through the CPU, using direct memory access (DMA).

Over the years, a number of interconnection structures have been tried. By far the most common is the bus and various multiple-bus structures. The remainder of this chapter is devoted to an assessment of bus structures.

## 3.4

## BUS INTERCONNECTION

A bus is a communication pathway connecting two or more devices. A key characteristic of a bus is that it is a shared transmission medium. Multiple devices connect to the bus, and a signal transmitted by any one device is available for reception by all other devices attached to the bus. If two devices transmit during the same time period, their signals will overlap and become garbled. Thus, only one device at a time can successfully transmit.

In many cases, a bus actually consists of multiple communication pathways, or lines. Each line is capable of transmitting signals representing binary 1 and binary 0. Over time, a sequence of binary digits can be transmitted across a single line. Taken together, several lines of a bus can be used to transmit binary digits simultaneously (in parallel). For example, an 8-bit unit of data can be transmitted over eight bus lines.

Computer systems contain a number of different buses that provide pathways between components at various levels of the computer system hierarchy. A bus that connects major computer components (CPU, memory, I/O) is called a *system bus.* The most common computer interconnection structures are based on the use of one or more system buses.

### Bus Structure

A system bus consists, typically, of from 50 to 100 separate lines. Each line is assigned a particular meaning or function. Although there are many different bus designs, on any bus the lines can be classified into three functional groups (Figure 3.16): data, address, and control lines. In addition, there may be power distribution lines that supply power to the attached modules.

The *data lines* provide a path for moving data between system modules. These lines, collectively, are called the *data bus.* The data bus typically consists of 8, 16, or 32 separate lines, the number of lines being referred to as the *width* of the data bus.

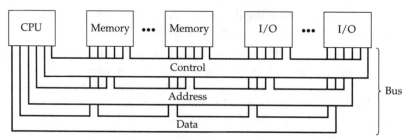

**FIGURE 3.16.  Bus interconnection scheme**

Since each line can carry only 1 bit at a time, the number of lines determines how many bits can be transferred at a time. The width of the data bus is a key factor in determining overall system performance. For example, if the data bus is 8 bits wide, and each instruction is 16 bits long, then the CPU must access the memory module twice during each instruction cycle.

The *address lines* are used to designate the source or destination of the data on the data bus. For example, if the CPU wishes to read a word (8, 16, or 32 bits) of data from memory, it puts the address of the desired word on the address lines. Clearly, the width of the address bus determines the maximum possible memory capacity of the system. Furthermore, the address lines are generally also used to address I/O ports. Typically, the higher-order bits are used to select a particular module on the bus, and the lower-order bits select a memory location or I/O port within the module. For example, on an 8-bit bus, address 01111111 and below might reference locations in a memory module (module 0) with 128 words of memory, and address 10000000 and above refer to devices attached to an I/O module (module 1).

The *control lines* are used to control the access to and the use of the data and address lines. Since the data and address lines are shared by all components, there must be a means of controlling their use. Control signals transmit both command and timing information between system modules. Timing signals indicate the validity of data and address information. Command signals specify operations to be performed. Typical control lines include

- *Memory Write:* Causes data on the bus to be written into the addressed location.
- *Memory Read:* Causes data from the addressed location to be placed on the bus.
- *I/O Write:* Causes data on the bus to be output to the addressed I/O port.
- *I/O Read:* Causes data from the addressed I/O port to be placed on the bus.
- *Transfer ACK:* Indicates that data have been accepted from or placed on the bus.
- *Bus Request:* Indicates that a module needs to gain control of the bus.
- *Bus Grant:* Indicates that a requesting module has been granted control of the bus.
- *Interrupt Request:* Indicates that an interrupt is pending.
- *Interrupt ACK:* Acknowledges that the pending interrupt has been recognized.
- *Clock:* Used to synchronize operations.
- *Reset:* Initializes all modules.

The operation of the bus is as follows. If one module wishes to send data to another, it must do two things: (1) obtain the use of the bus, and (2) transfer data via the bus. If one module wishes to request data from another module, it must (1) obtain the use of the bus, and (2) transfer a request to the other module over the appropriate control and address lines. It must then wait for that second module to send the data.

Physically, the system bus is actually a number of parallel electrical conductors. These conductors are metal lines etched in a card or board (printed-circuit board). The bus extends across all of the system components, each of which taps into some or all of the bus lines. A very common physical arrangement is depicted in Figure 3.17. In this example, the bus consists of two vertical columns of conductors. At regular intervals along the columns, there are attachment points in the form of slots that extend out horizontally to support a printed-circuit board. Each of the major system components occupies one or more boards and plugs into the bus at these slots. The entire arrangement is housed in a chassis.

This arrangement is most convenient. A small computer system may be acquired and then expanded later (more memory, more I/O) by adding more boards. If a component on a board fails, that board can easily be removed and replaced.

## Multiple-Bus Hierarchies

If a great number of devices are connected to the bus, performance will suffer. There are two main causes:

1. In general, the more devices attached to the bus, the greater the propagation delay. This delay determines the time it takes for devices to coordinate the use of the bus. When control of the bus passes from one device to another frequently, these propagation delays can noticeably affect performance.
2. The bus may become a bottleneck as the aggregate data transfer demand approaches the capacity of the bus. This problem can be countered to some extent by increasing the data rate that the bus can carry and by using wider buses (e.g.,

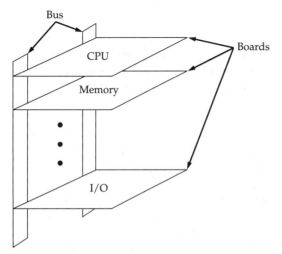

**FIGURE 3.17. Typical physical realization of a bus architecture**

increasing the data bus from 32 to 64 bits). However, since the data rates generated by attached devices (e.g., graphics and video controllers, network interfaces) are growing rapidly, this is a race that a single bus is ultimately destined to lose.

Accordingly, most computer systems enjoy the use of multiple buses, generally laid out in a hierarchy. A typical traditional structure is shown in Figure 3.18a. There is a local bus that connects the processor to a cache memory and that may support one or more local devices. The cache memory controller connects the cache not only to this local bus, but to a system bus to which is attached all of the main memory modules. As is discussed in Chapter 4, the use of a cache structure insulates the processor from a requirement to frequently access main memory. Hence, main memory can be moved off of the local bus onto a system bus. In this way, I/O transfers to and from the main memory across the system bus do not interfere with the processor's activity.

It is possible to connect I/O controllers directly onto the system bus. A more efficient solution is to make use of one or more expansion buses for this purpose. An expansion bus interface buffers data transfers between the system bus and the I/O controllers on the expansion bus. This arrangement allows the system to support a wide variety of I/O devices and at the same time insulate memory-to-processor traffic from I/O traffic.

Figure 3.18a shows some typical examples of I/O devices that might be attached to the expansion bus. Network connections include local area networks (LANs) such as a 10-Mbps Ethernet and connections to wide area networks such as a packet-switching network. SCSI (small computer system interface) is itself a type of bus used to support local disk drives and other peripherals. A serial port could be used to support a printer or scanner.

This traditional bus architecture is reasonably efficient but begins to break down as higher and higher performance is seen in the I/O devices. In response to these growing demands, a common approach taken by industry is to build a high-speed bus that is closely integrated with the rest of the system, requiring only a bridge between the processor's bus and the high-speed bus. This arrangement is sometimes known as a mezzanine architecture.

Figure 3.18b shows a typical realization of this approach. Again, there is a local bus that connects the processor to a cache controller, which is in turn connected to a system bus that supports main memory. The cache controller is integrated into a bridge, or buffering device, that connects to the high-speed bus. This bus supports connections to high-speed LANs, such as Fiber Distributed Data Interface (FDDI) at 100 Mbps, video and graphics workstation controllers, as well as interface controllers to local peripheral buses including SCSI and P1394. The latter is a high-speed bus arrangement specifically designed to support high-capacity I/O devices. Lower-speed devices are still supported off an expansion bus, with an interface buffering traffic between the expansion bus and the high-speed bus.

The advantage of this arrangement is that the high-speed bus brings high-demand devices into closer integration with the processor and at the same time is independent of the processor. Thus, differences in processor and high-speed bus speeds and signal line definitions are tolerated. Changes in processor architecture do not affect the high-speed bus, and vice versa.

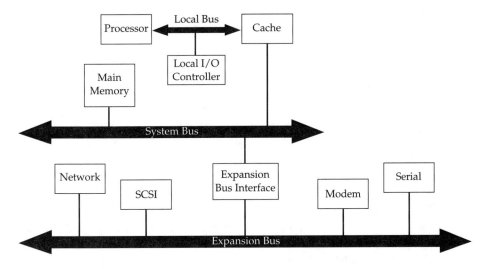

(a) Traditional Bus Architecture

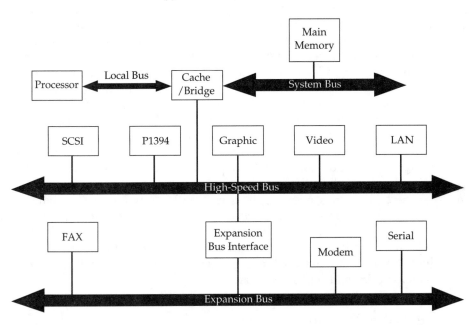

(b) High-Performance Architecture

**FIGURE 3.18.  Example Bus Configurations**

## Elements of Bus Design

Although a variety of different bus implementations exist, there are a few basic parameters or design elements that serve to classify and differentiate buses. Table 3.2 lists key elements.

**TABLE 3.2    Elements of Bus Design**

| Type | Bus Width |
|------|-----------|
| Dedicated | Address |
| Multiplexed | Data |
| **Method of Arbitration** | **Data Transfer Type** |
| Centralized | Read |
| Distributed | Write |
| **Timing** | Read-modify-write |
| Synchronous | Read-after-write |
| Asynchronous | Block |

## Bus Types

Bus lines can be separated into two generic types: dedicated and multiplexed. A dedicated bus line is permanently assigned either to one function or to a physical subset of computer components.

An example of functional dedication is the use of separate dedicated address and data lines, which is common to many buses. However, it is not essential. For example, address and data information may be transmitted over the same set of lines using an Address Valid control line. At the beginning of a data transfer, the address is placed on the bus and the Address Valid line is activated. At this point, each module has a specified period of time to copy the address and determine if it is the addressed module. The address is then removed from the bus, and the same bus connections are used for the subsequent read or write data transfer. This method of using the same lines for multiple purposes is known as *time multiplexing*.

The advantage of time multiplexing is the use of fewer lines, which saves space and, usually, cost. The disadvantage is that more complex circuitry is needed within each module. Also, there is a potential reduction in performance since certain events that share the same lines cannot take place in parallel.

*Physical dedication* refers to the use of multiple buses, each of which connects only a subset of modules. A typical example is the use of an I/O bus to interconnect all I/O modules; this bus is then connected to the main bus through some type of I/O adapter module. The potential advantage of physical dedication is high throughput, because there is less bus contention. A disadvantage is the increased size and cost of the system.

## Method of Arbitration

In all but the simplest systems, more than one module may need control of the bus. For example, an I/O module may need to read or write directly to memory, without sending the data to the CPU. Since only one unit at a time can successfully transmit over the bus, some method of arbitration is needed. The various methods can be roughly classified as being either centralized or distributed. In a centralized scheme, a single hardware device, referred to as a *bus controller* or *arbiter*, is responsible for allocating time on the bus. The device may be a separate module or part of the CPU. In a distributed scheme, there is no central controller. Rather, each module contains access control logic and the modules act together to share the bus. With both methods of arbitration, the purpose is to designate one device, either the CPU or an I/O module, as master. The master may then initiate a data transfer (e.g., read or write) with some other device, which acts as slave for this particular exchange. We will see examples of both methods of arbitration later in this section.

## Timing

Timing refers to the way in which events are coordinated on the bus. With synchronous timing, the occurrence of events on the bus is determined by a clock. The bus includes a clock line upon which a clock transmits a regular sequence of alternating 1s and 0s of equal duration. A single 1–0 transmission is referred to as a *clock cycle* or *bus cycle* and defines a time slot. All other devices on the bus can read the clock line, and all events start at the beginning of a clock cycle. Figure 3.19a shows the timing diagram for a synchronous read operation (see Appendix 3A for a description of timing diagrams). Other bus signals may change at the leading edge of the clock signal (with a slight reaction delay). Most events occupy a single

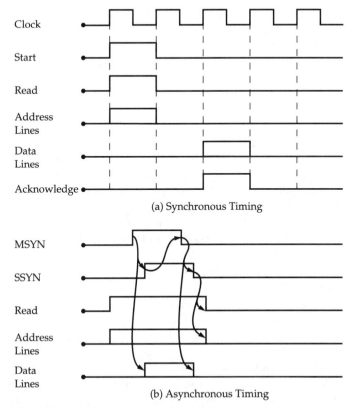

FIGURE 3.19. Timing of a read operation

clock cycle. In this simple example, the CPU issues a read signal and places a memory address on the address bus. It also issues a start signal to mark the presence of address and control information on the bus. A memory module recognizes the address and, after a delay of 1 cycle, places the data and an acknowledgment signal on the bus.

With asynchronous timing, the occurrence of one event on a bus follows and depends on the occurrence of a previous event. In the simple example of Figure 3.19b, the CPU places address and read signals on the bus. After pausing for these signals to stabilize, it issues an MSYN (master sync) signal, indicating the presence of valid address and control signals. The memory module responds with data and an SSYN (slave sync) signal, indicating the response.

Synchronous timing is simpler to implement and test. However, it is less flexible than asynchronous timing. Because all devices on a synchronous bus are tied to a fixed clock rate, the system cannot take advantage of advances in device performance. With asynchronous timing, a mixture of slow and fast devices, using older and newer technology, can share a bus. We will see examples of both synchronous and asynchronous timing.

### Bus Width

We have already addressed the concept of bus width. The width of the data bus has an impact on system performance: the wider the data bus, the greater the number of bits transferred at one time. The width of the address bus has an impact on system capacity: the wider the address bus, the greater the range of locations that can be referenced.

### Data Transfer Type

Finally, a bus supports various data transfer types, as illustrated in Figure 3.20. All buses support both write (master to slave) and read (slave to master) transfers. In the case of a multiplexed address/data bus, the bus is first used for specifying the address and then for transferring the data. For a read operation, there is typically a wait while the data is being fetched from the slave to be put on the bus. For either a read or a write, there may also be a delay if it is necessary to go through arbitration to gain control of the bus for the remainder of the operation (i.e., seize the bus to request a read or write, then seize the bus again to perform a read or write).

In the case of dedicated address and data buses, the address is put on the address bus and remains there while the data are put on the data bus. For a write operation, the master puts the data onto the data bus as soon as the address has stabilized and the slave has had the opportunity to recognize its address. For a read operation, the slave puts the data onto the data bus as soon as it has recognized its address and has fetched the data.

There are also several combination operations that some buses allow. A read–modify–write operation is simply a read followed immediately by a write to the same address. The address is only broadcast once at the beginning of the operation. The whole operation is typically indivisible in order to prevent any access to

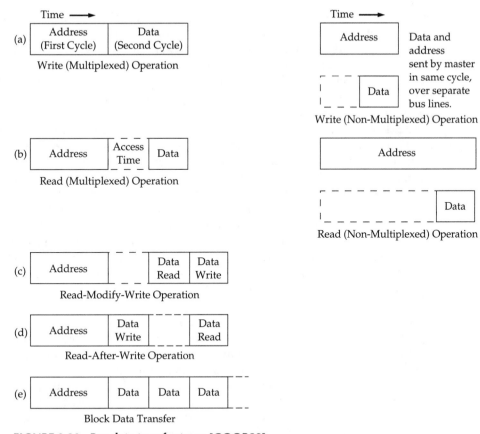

**FIGURE 3.20.  Bus data transfer types [GOOR89]**

the data element by other potential bus masters. The principal purpose of this capability is to protect shared memory resources in a multiprogramming system (see Chapter 7).

Read-after-write is an indivisible operation consisting of a write followed immediately by a read from the same address. The read operation may be performed for checking purposes.

Some bus systems also support a block data transfer. In this case, one address cycle is followed by $n$ data cycles. The first data item is transferred to or from the specified address; the remaining data items are transferred to or from subsequent addresses.

## 3.5

### PCI

The Peripheral Component Interconnect (PCI) is a recent high-bandwidth, processor-independent bus that can function as a mezzanine or peripheral bus. Compared with other common bus specifications, PCI delivers better system performance for high-speed I/O subsystems (e.g., graphic display adapters, network interface controllers, disk controllers, and so on). The current standard allows the use of up to 64 data lines at 33 MHz, for a raw transfer rate of 264 MBytes/sec, or 2.112 Gbps. But it is not just a high speed that makes PCI attractive. PCI is specifically designed to economically meet the I/O requirements of modern systems; it requires very few chips to implement and supports other buses attached to the PCI bus.

Intel began work on PCI in 1990 for its Pentium-based systems. Intel soon released all the patents to the public domain and promoted the creation of an industry association, the PCI SIG, to further develop and maintain the compatibility of the PCI specifications. The result is that PCI has been widely adopted and is finding increasing use in personal computer, workstation, and server systems. The current version, PCI 2.0, was released in 1993. Because the specification is in the public domain and is supported by a broad cross section of the microprocessor and peripheral industry, PCI products built by different vendors are compatible.

PCI is designed to support a variety of microprocessor-based configurations, including both single- and multiple-processor systems. Accordingly, it provides a general-purpose set of functions. It makes use of synchronous timing and a centralized arbitration scheme.

Figure 3.21a shows a typical use of PCI in a single-processor system. A combined DRAM controller and bridge to the PCI bus provides tight coupling with the processor and the ability to deliver data at high speeds. The bridge acts as a data buffer so that the speed of the PCI bus may differ from that of the processor's I/O capability. In a multiprocessor system (Figure 3.21b), one or more PCI configurations may be connected by bridges to the processor's system bus. The system bus supports only the processor/cache units, main memory, and the PCI bridges. Again, the use of bridges keeps the PCI independent of the processor speed yet provides the ability to receive and deliver data rapidly.

## Bus Structure

PCI may be configured as a 32- or 64-bit bus. Table 3.3 defines the 50 mandatory signal lines for PCI. These are divided into the following functional groups:

- *System Pins:* Include the clock and reset pins.
- *Address and Data Pins:* Include 32 lines that are time-multiplexed for addresses and data. The other lines in this group are used to interpret and validate the signal lines that carry the addresses and data.
- *Interface Control Pins:* Control the timing of transactions and provide coordination among initiators and targets.
- *Arbitration Pins:* Unlike the other PCI signal lines, these are not shared lines. Rather, each PCI master has its own pair of arbitration lines that connect it directly to the PCI bus arbiter.
- *Error Reporting Pins:* Used to report parity and other errors.

In addition, the PCI specification defines 50 optional signal lines (Table 3.4), divided into the following functional groups:

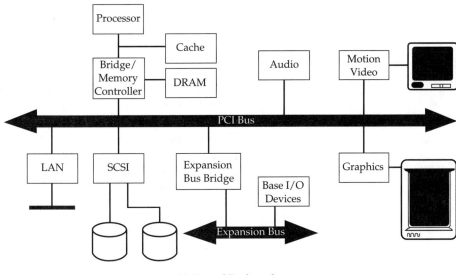

(a) Typical Desktop System

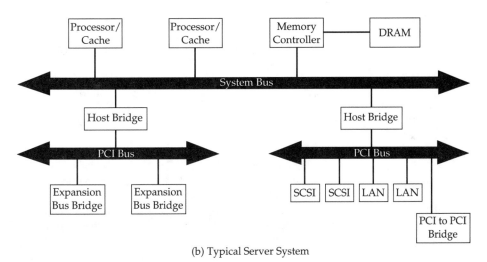

(b) Typical Server System

**FIGURE 3.21. Example PCI Configurations**

- *Interrupt Pins:* These are provided for PCI devices that must generate requests for service. As with the arbitration pins, these are not shared lines. Rather, each PCI device has its own interrupt line or lines to an interrupt controller.
- *Cache Support Pins:* These pins are needed to support a memory on PCI that can be cached in the processor or another device. These pins support snoopy cache protocols (see Chapter 16 for a discussion of such protocols).
- *64-bit Bus Extension Pins:* Include 32 lines that are time-multiplexed for addresses and data and that are combined with the mandatory address/data

## TABLE 3.3  Mandatory PCI Signal Lines

| Designation | Type | Description |
|---|---|---|
| | | *System Pins* |
| CLK | in | Provides timing for all transactions and is sampled by all inputs on the rising edge. Clock rates up to 33 MHz are supported. |
| RST# | in | Forces all PCI-specific registers, sequencers, and signals to an initialized state. |
| | | *Address and Data Pins* |
| AD[31::0] | t/s | Multiplexed lines used for address and data |
| C/BE[3::0]# | t/s | Multiplexed bus command and byte enable signals. During the data phase, the lines indicate which of the four byte lanes carry meaningful data. |
| PAR | t/s | Provides even parity across AD and C/BE lines one clock cycle later. The master drives PAR for address and write data phases; the target drive PAR for read data phases. |
| | | *Interface Control Pins* |
| FRAME# | s/t/s | Driven by current master to indicate the start and duration of a transaction. It is asserted at the start and deasserted when the initiator is ready to begin the final data phase. |
| IRDY# | s/t/s | Initiator Ready. Driven by current bus master (initiator of transaction). During a read, indicates that the master is prepared to accept data; during a write, indicates that valid data is present on AD. |
| TRDY# | s/t/s | Target Ready. Driven by the target (selected device). During a read, that valid data is present on AD; during a write, indicates that target is ready to accept data. |
| STOP# | s/t/s | Indicates that current target wishes the initiator to stop the current transaction. |
| LOCK# | s/t/s | Indicates an atomic operation that may require multiple transactions. |
| IDSEL | in | Initialization Device Select. Used as a chip select during configuration read and write transactions. |
| DEVSEL# | in | Device Select. Asserted by target when it has recognized its address. Indicates to current initiator whether any device has been selected. |
| | | *Arbitration Pins* |
| REQ# | t/s | Indicates to the arbiter that this device requires use of the bus. This is a device-specific point-to-point line. |
| GNT# | t/s | Indicates to the device that the arbiter has granted bus access. This is a device-specific point-to-point line. |
| | | *Error Reporting Pins* |
| PERR# | s/t/s | Parity Error. Indicates a data parity error is detected by a target during a write data phase or by an initiator during a read data phase. |
| SERR# | o/d | System Error. May be pulsed by any device to report address parity errors and critical errors other than parity. |

## TABLE 3.4  Optional PCI Signal Lines

| Designation | Type | Description |
| --- | --- | --- |
| | | *Interrupt Pins* |
| INTA# | o/d | Used to request an interrupt. |
| INTB# | o/d | Used to request an interrupt; only has meaning on a multifunction device. |
| INTC# | o/d | Used to request an interrupt; only has meaning on a multifunction device. |
| INTD# | o/d | Used to request an interrupt; only has meaning on a multifunction device. |
| | | *Cache Support Pins* |
| SBO# | in/out | Snoop Backoff. Indicates a hit to a modified line. |
| SDONE | in/out | Snoop Done. Indicates the status of the snoop for the current accent. Asserted when snoop has been completed. |
| | | *64-bit Bus Extension Pins* |
| AD[63::32] | t/s | Multiplexed lines used for address and data to extend bus to 64 bits. |
| C/BE[7::4]# | t/s | Multiplexed bus command and byte enable signals. During the address phase, the lines provide additional bus commands. During the data phase, the lines indicate which of the four extended byte lanes carry meaningful data. |
| REQ64# | s/t/s | Used to request 64-bit transfer. |
| ACK64# | s/t/s | Indicates target is willing to perform 64-bit transfer. |
| PAR64 | t/s | Provides even parity across extended AD and C/BE lines one clock cycle later. |
| | | *JTAG/Boundary Scan Pins* |
| TCK | in | Test Clock. Used to clock state information and test data into and out of the device during boundary scan. |
| TDI | in | Test Input. Used to serially shift test data and instructions into the device. |
| TDO | out | Test Output. Used to serially shift test data and instructions out of the device. |
| TMS | in | Test Mode Select. Used to control state of test access port controller. |
| TRST# | in | Test Reset. Used to initialize test access port controller. |

in    Input-only signal
out   Output-only signal
t/s   Bidirectional, tri-state, I/O signal
s/t/s Sustained tri-state signal driven by only one owner at a time
o/d   Open drain: allows multiple devices to share as a wire-OR
#     Signal's active state occurs at low voltage

lines to form a 64-bit address/data bus. Other lines in this group are used to interpret and validate the signal lines that carry the addresses and data. Finally, there are two lines that enable two PCI devices to agree to the use of the 64-bit capability.

- *JTAG/Boundary Scan Pins:* These signal lines support testing procedures defined in IEEE Standard 149.1.

## PCI Commands

Bus activity occurs in the form of transactions between an initiator, or master, and a target. When a bus master acquires control of the bus, it determines the type of transaction that will occur next. During the address phase of the transaction, the C/BE lines are used to signal the transaction type. The commands are

- Interrupt Acknowledge
- Special Cycle
- I/O Read
- I/O Write
- Memory Read
- Memory Read Line
- Memory Read Multiple
- Memory Write
- Memory Write and Invalidate
- Configuration Read
- Configuration Write
- Dual Address Cycle

Interrupt Acknowledge is a read command intended for the device that functions as an interrupt controller on the PCI bus. The address lines are not used during the address phase, and the byte enable lines indicate the size of the interrupt identifier to be returned.

The Special Cycle command is used by the initiator to broadcast a message to one or more targets.

The I/O Read and Write commands are used to transfer data between the initiator and an I/O controller. Each I/O device has its own address space, and the address lines are used to indicate a particular device and to specify the data to be transferred to or from that device. The concept of I/O addresses is explored in Chapter 6.

The memory read and write commands are used to specify the transfer of a burst of data, occupying one or more clock cycles. The interpretation of these commands depends on whether or not the memory controller on the PCI bus supports the PCI protocol for transfers between memory and cache. If so, the transfer of data to and from the memory is typically in terms of cache lines, or blocks.[2] The three memory read commands have the uses outlined in Table 3.5. The Memory Write command is used to transfer data in one or more data cycles to memory. The

---

[2]The fundamental principles of cache memory are described in Section 4.3; bus-based cache protocols are described in Section 16.2.

**TABLE 3.5    Interpretation of PCI Read Commands**

| Read Command Type | For Cachable Memory | For Noncachable Memory |
|---|---|---|
| Memory Read | Bursting one-half or less of a cache line | Bursting 2 data transfer cycles or less |
| Memory Read Line | Bursting more than one-half a cache line to three cache lines | Bursting 3 to 12 data transfers |
| Memory Read Multiple | Bursting more than three cache lines | Bursting more than 12 data transfers |

Memory Write and Invalidate command transfers data in one or more cycles to memory. In addition, it guarantees that at least one cache line is written. This command supports the cache function of writing back a line to memory.

The two configuration commands enable a master to read and update configuration parameters in a device connected to the PCI. Each PCI device may include up to 256 internal registers that are used during system initialization to configure that device.

The Dual Address Cycle command is used by an initiator to indicate that it is using 64-bit addressing.

## Data Transfers

Every data transfer on the PCI bus is a single transaction consisting of one address phase and one or more data phases. In this discussion, we illustrate a typical read operation; a write operation proceeds similarly.

Figure 3.22 shows the timing of the read transaction. All events are synchronized to the falling transitions of the clock, which occur in the middle of each clock cycle. Bus devices sample the bus lines on the rising edge at the beginning of a bus cycle. The following are the significant events, labeled on the diagram:

a. Once a bus master has gained control of the bus, it may begin the transaction by asserting FRAME. This line remains asserted until the initiator is ready to complete the last data phase. The initiator also puts the start address on the address bus, and the read command on the C/BE lines.

b. At the start of clock 2, the target device will recognize its address on the AD lines.

c. The initiator ceases driving the AD bus. A turnaround cycle (indicated by the two circular arrows) is required on all signal lines that may be driven by more than one device, so that the dropping of the address signal will prepare the bus for use by the target device. The initiator changes the information on the C/BE lines to designate which AD lines are to be used for transfer for the currently addressed data (from 1 to 4 bytes). The initiator also asserts IRDY to indicate that it is ready for the first data item.

d. The selected target asserts DEVSEL to indicate that it has recognized its address and will respond. It places the requested data on the AD lines and asserts TRDY to indicate that valid data is present on the bus.

e. The initiator reads the data at the beginning of clock 4 and changes the byte enable lines as needed in preparation for the next read.

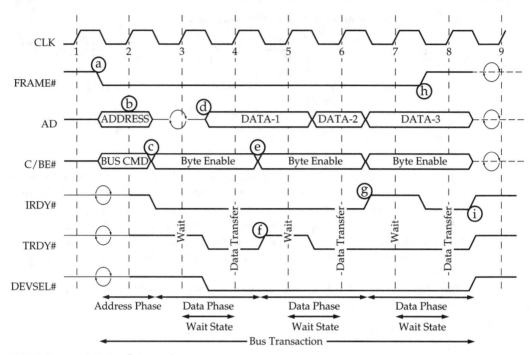

**FIGURE 3.22. PCI Read Operation**

    f. In this example, the target needs some time to prepare the second block of data for transmission. Therefore, it deasserts TRDY to signal the initiator that there will not be new data during the coming cycle. Accordingly, the initiator does not read the data lines at the beginning of the fifth clock cycle and does not change byte enable during that cycle. The block of data is read at beginning of clock 6.

    g. During clock 6, the target places the third data item on the bus. However, in this example, the initiator is not yet ready to read the data item (e.g., it has a temporary buffer full condition). It therefore deasserts IRDY. This will cause the target to maintain the third data item on the bus for an extra clock cycle.

    h. The initiator knows that the third data transfer is the last, and so it deasserts FRAME to signal the target that this is the last data transfer. It also asserts IRDY to signal that it is ready to complete that transfer.

    i. The initiator deasserts IRDY, returning the bus to the idle state, and the target deasserts TRDY and DEVSEL.

## Arbitration

PCI makes use of a centralized, synchronous arbitration scheme in which each master has a unique request (REQ) and grant (GNT) signal. These signal lines are attached to a central arbiter (Figure 3.23) and a simple request–grant handshake is used to grant access to the bus.

    The PCI specification does not dictate a particular arbitration algorithm. The arbiter can use a first-come-first-served approach, a round-robin approach, or

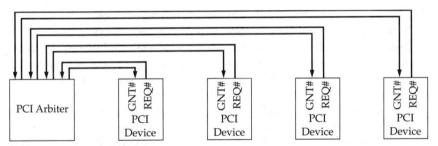

**FIGURE 3.23.  PCI Bus Arbiter**

some sort of priority scheme. A PCI master must arbitrate for each transaction that it wishes to perform, where a single transaction consists of an address phase followed by one or more contiguous data phases.

Figure 3.24 is an example in which devices A and B are arbitrating for the bus. The following sequence occurs:

a. At some point prior to the start of clock 1, A has asserted its REQ signal. The arbiter samples this signal at the beginning of clock cycle 1.
b. During clock cycle 1, B requests use of the bus by asserting its REQ signal.
c. At the same time, the arbiter asserts GNT-A to grant bus access to A.

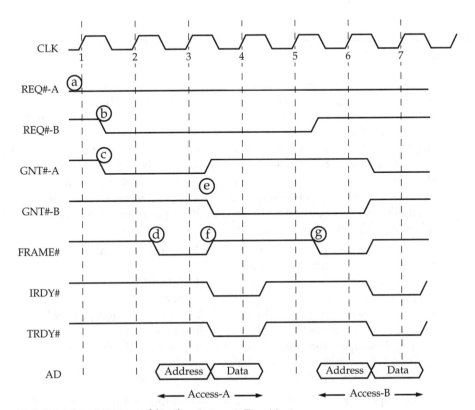

**FIGURE 3.24.  PCI Bus Arbitration Between Two Masters**

d. Bus master A samples GNT-A at the beginning of clock 2 and learns that it has been granted bus access. It also finds IRDY and TRDY deasserted, indicating that the bus is idle. Accordingly, it asserts FRAME and places the address information on the address bus and the command on the C/BE bus (not shown). It also continues to assert REQ-A, because it has a second transaction to perform after this one.

e. The bus arbiter samples all GNT lines at the beginning of clock 3 and makes an arbitration decision to grant the bus to B for the next transaction. It then asserts GNT-B and deasserts GNT-A. B will not be able to use the bus until it returns to an idle state.

f. A deasserts FRAME to indicate that the last (and only) data transfer is in progress. It puts the data on the data bus and signals the target with IRDY. The target reads the data at the beginning of the next clock cycle.

g. At the beginning of clock 5, B finds IRDY and FRAME deasserted and so is able to take control of the bus by asserting FRAME. It also deasserts its REQ line, because it only wants to perform one transaction.

Subsequently, master A is granted access to the bus for its next transaction.

Notice that arbitration can take place at the same time that the current bus master is performing a data transfer. Therefore, no bus cycles are lost in performing arbitration. This is referred to as *hidden arbitration*.

## 3.6

### FUTUREBUS+

Futurebus+ is a high-performance asynchronous bus standard developed by IEEE. An initial version, called Futurebus, was issued as ANSI/IEEE Std 896 in 1987. This initial version was for a 32-bit bus that was intended to be technology-independent. Since 1987, the initial Futurebus standard has been revised and expanded. To emphasize the difference, the standard is now known as Futurebus+. The plus sign refers to the extensible nature of the specification, and the hooks provided to allow further evolution to meet unanticipated needs of specific application architectures. This section is based on the current (1994) version of that standard.

The Futurebus+ committee defined eight requirements upon which the design is based [ANDR90]. The bus had to

- Be architecture-, processor-, and technology-independent.
- Have a basic asynchronous transfer protocol.
- Allow for optional source-synchronized protocol.
- Have no technology-based upper limit to performance.
- Be composed of fully distributed parallel and arbitration protocols, supporting both circuit-switched and split-transaction protocols.
- Provide support for fault-tolerant and high-reliability systems.
- Offer direct support for cache-based shared memory.
- Provide a compatible message transport definition.

The importance of Futurebus+ is the likelihood that it will supplant most current microprocessor bus schemes. Consider the following observation [ANDR91]:

The Futurebus+ committee has created the ultimate in bus enhancements. When it's through, there will probably be little left for future generations of bus designers to modify. When it's called up for its mandatory review five years after final acceptance, the committee may well look at the Futurebus+ spec and say, "there's nothing to add."

The key differences between the 1987 Futurebus standard and the current Futurebus+ specification are the following:

- Futurebus supports a 32-bit data bus; Futurebus+ supports data bus widths of 32, 64, 128, and 256 bits.
- Futurebus supports a distributed arbitration protocol. Futurebus+ supports both distributed and centralized models.
- Only Futurebus+ includes a 3-bit capability field to allow a module to declare its ability to accommodate major modes of bus transactions.

Futurebus+ is a complex bus specification. It introduces some innovative concepts in bus design. As a result, the standard includes a number of new and redefined terms that will become increasingly familiar in the next few years; Table 3.6 summarizes some of the most important. Table 3.7 lists the bus lines defined for Futurebus+.

### TABLE 3.6 Some Futurebus+ Terminology

**Arbitrated Message**

A number of broadcast on the arbitrated message lines to all modules on the bus.

**Beat**

An event that begins with the transition on a synchronization line by the master followed by the release of an acknowledge line by one or more slaves. Command and data information may be transferred from the master to one or more slaves in the first half of the beat. During the second half of the beat the slaves may transfer capability, status, and data information back to the master.

**Bus Tenure**

The duration of the master's control of the bus; i.e., the time during which a module has the right to initiate and execute bus transactions.

**Bus Transaction**

An event initiated with a connection phase and terminated with a disconnection phase. Data may or may not be transferred during a bus transaction.

**Compelled Data Transfer Protocol**

A technology-independent transfer mechanism in which the slave is compelled to provide a response before the master proceeds to the next transfer.

**Locking**

A facility whereby a module is requested to guarantee exclusive access to addressed data, blocking other modules from accessing the data. This allows indivisible operations to be performed on addressed resources.

**Parallel Contention Arbitration**

A process whereby modules assert their unique arbitration number on a parallel bus and release signals according to an algorithm such that after a period of time the winner's number appears on the bus.

**Split Transaction**

A system transaction in which the request is transmitted in one bus transaction and the response is transmitted in a separate subsequent bus transaction.

**Starvation**

A system condition that occurs when one or more modules perform no useful work for an indefinite period of time due to lack of access to the bus or other system resources.

**System Transaction**

A complete operation such as a memory read or write as viewed from the initiating unit. A system transaction can be translated into one or more bus transactions by the Futurebus+ interface to complete the operation.

**TABLE 3.7    Futurebus+ Signal Lines**

| Designation | Number of Lines | Description |
|---|---|---|
| | | *Information Lines* |
| AD(63...0) | 32, 64, 64, 64 | Carry address during transfer; carry data during data transfer. |
| D(255...64) | __, __, 64, 192 | Carry data during data transfer. |
| BP(31...0) | 4, 8, 16, 32 | One parity line for every eight address/data lines. |
| TG(7...0) | 8 | Carry additional information related to the address/data lines; standards does not prescribe specific use. |
| TP | 1 | Parity code for tag lines. |
| CM(7...0) | 8 | Carry command information from master to one or more slaves for the current transaction. |
| CP | 1 | Parity code for command lines |
| ST(7...0) | 8 | Carry information about the status of a slave and its disposition in regard to the requested transfer. |
| CA(2...0) | 3 | Activated by a module to declare its ability to accommodate major modes of bus transactions. |
| | | *Synchronization Lines* |
| AS, AK, AI | 3 | Address Synchronization. Asserted by master to inform slaves that the address and command information are valid. |
| | | Address Acknowledge. Released by all modules to indicate to master that their status information is valid. |
| | | Address Acknowledge Inverse. Released all modules to indicate a master that their status and capability information are valid. |
| DS, DK, DI | 3 | Data Synchronization. Asserted by master to inform slaves that the write data and command information are valid or that the master is ready to receive read data. |
| | | Data Acknowledge, Data Acknowledge Inverse. Released by participating slaves to indicate to master that status information and read data are valid or that write data has been received. |
| ET | 1 | Released by current master to notify master elect that it is the new master. |

## Addressing

Each module on the bus gets assigned a unique geographical address, which is hardwired into each slot of the backplane. When a board plugs into a slot, it senses the 5-bit number on lines GA(4 . . . 0) to determine which slot it resides in. This feature promotes high availability: Boards can be inserted and withdrawn without having to power down the system and without having to configure an address.

## Arbitration

The Futurebus+ arbitration process operates in parallel with data transfers on the bus. Futurebus+ supports both distributed and centralized arbitration schemes.

**TABLE 3.7    (continued)**

| Designation | Number of Lines | Description |
|---|---|---|
| | | *Arbitrated Message Lines* |
| AB(7...0) | 8 | Carry a number that signifies the precedence of competitors during the arbitrated message process and the distributed arbitration process. |
| ABP | 1 | Parity code for AB(7...0). |
| AP, AQ, AR | 3 | Handshake lines that perform a cyclic handshake sequence that controls the sequencing of the arbitrated message process and the distributed arbitration process. |
| AC(1...0) | 2 | Control the arbitration message process and the distributed arbitration process. |
| | | *Reset/Bus Initialize Line* |
| RE | 1 | Initializes the bus interface logic of all modules. |
| | | *Central Arbitration* |
| RQ(1...0) | 2 | One or both lines are asserted to request bus mastership. |
| GR | 1 | Asserted by central arbiter to grant bus mastership. |
| PE | 1 | Asserted by central arbiter to indicate to current master that a preemptive condition exists and the master should relinquish bus mastership. |
| GA(4...0) | 5 | A unique identifier assigned to each physical module slot on the bus and assumed by any module connected to that slot. |

The most powerful one, and the one most likely to be used on a given implementation, is the distributed arbitration scheme.

### Distributed Arbitration

Each module on the bus has a unique arbitration number that is used in a parallel contention algorithm during competition to become master. Before explaining the process for acquiring bus mastership, we need to look at the competition mechanism.

During parallel contention, any number of modules may compete using the 8-bit arbitrated message bus. The module that applies the largest number to the bus wins the competition. Each competitor applies its competition number, $cn(7 \ldots 0)$, to bus lines AB(7 . . . 0). The signal on any particular line is the OR of all the signals applied to that line; thus, the line has a logical 1 if any of the competing modules applies a 1. The arbitration logic in each module (Figure 3.25) senses the resulting bus values and modifies the number it is applying to the bus according to the following rule: If for any bit of a module's arbitration number that is 0, the corresponding arbitration bus line shows a 1, all lower-order bits of the number are withdrawn from the bus. Eventually, the module with the highest arbitration number will find that its number matches the number remaining on the bus and is therefore the winner.

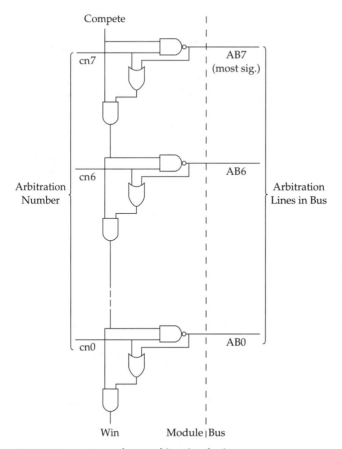

**FIGURE 3.25.  Futurebus+ arbitration logic**

To understand the logic diagram,[3] note that each of the module's bits is inverted prior to application to the bus, so that a logical 1 is a HIGH level in the module but a LOW level on the bus, and vice versa. The result is that the OR gate will produce a 0 (forcing a lose) only if the cn bit is a logical 0 and the corresponding AB bit is a logical 1.

The arbitration process requires that all competing modules (distributed arbiters) move through the same sequence of states together, at the speed of the slowest arbiter. To achieve this, a rather ingenious protocol involving three bus lines (AP, AQ, AR) has been developed. The protocol makes use of different bus lines than the data transfer protocol and can therefore take place concurrently with data transfer transactions driven by the current bus master.

The arbitration process consists of six phases (Figure 3.26). The beginning and end of each phase is defined by a transition on one of the arbitration synchronizing signals (AP, AQ, AR):

---

[3]See Appendix A for a discussion of digital logic.

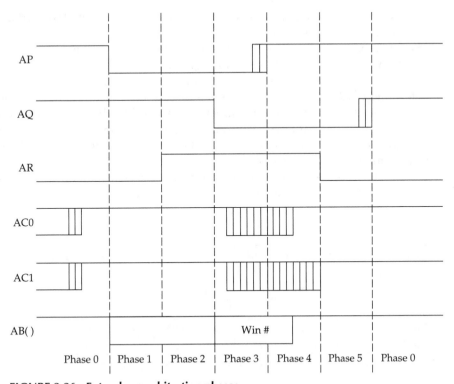

**FIGURE 3.26. Futurebus+ arbitration phases**

- *Phase 0—Idle:* Identified by AP and AQ released (HIGH) and AR asserted (LOW); no competition is in progress.
- *Phase 1—Decision:* Any arbiter requesting mastership asserts AP. Any arbiter that wishes to compete applies its competition number to AB(7 . . . 0). All modules synchronize with the arbitration process by releasing AR; only when all of the modules have released AR is it HIGH on the bus, signaling the end of phase 1.
- *Phase 2—Competition:* During this phase, competitors monitor their internal "win" signal for a time that allows for the competition logic (Figure 3.25) to settle to a final state. The winner asserts AQ and becomes "master-elect."
- *Phase 3—Error Check:* During this phase, all competition losers check that the winning competition number is greater than their own. Any modules detecting an error condition assert AC0 and AC1. This phase continues as long as the current master holds the bus. The current master signals the end of a transaction by releasing AS. Each module releases AP when it detects the release of AS.
- *Phase 4—Master Release:* The winning number is removed from AB(7 . . . 0). If the master wishes to retain the bus, it asserts AC1; otherwise it asserts AR.
- *Phase 5—Tenure:* All modules save the state of AC0 and AC1 to determine if tenure transfer is to take place or if some other action is appropriate. Once they have captured the status, they release AQ. When all modules have released AQ, the phase is over, and a new arbitration cycle may begin.

If the above sequence of steps occurs once and, at the end of phase 5, the master-elect assumes mastership, this is referred to as a single-pass arbitration. In other cases, two passes are required. In those cases, there is more than one winner at the end of the first pass, and phases 0 through 5 are repeated.

The values of the arbitration numbers used by modules in the competition determine whether one or two passes are required. Each pass of the arbitration cycle consists of an arbitration competition using the 8-bit competition numbers supplied by each module. An arbitration number consists of three fields as shown in Figure 3.27a: priority, round-robin, and geographical address. A module's arbitration number maps onto one or two competition numbers. The bit cn7 indicates whether the module requires another arbitration pass, so that a single-pass arbitration number defeats a two-pass arbitration number.

| Bit | cn7 | cn6 | cn6 | cn4 | cn3 | cn2 | cn1 | cn0 |
|-----|-----|-----|-----|-----|-----|-----|-----|-----|
| | | | | Single Pass | | | | |
| Pass 1 | 1 | PR0 | RR | GA4 | GA3 | GA2 | GA1 | GA0 |
| | | | | Two Pass | | | | |
| Pass 1 | 0 | PR7 | PR6 | PR5 | PR4 | PR3 | PR2 | PR1 |
| Pass 2 | 1 | PR0 | RR | GA4 | GA3 | GA2 | GA1 | GA0 |

(a) Distributed Arbitration Request Fields (Distributed Arbiter)

| Bit | cn7 | cn6 | cn6 | cn4 | cn3 | cn2 | cn1 | cn0 |
|-----|-----|-----|-----|-----|-----|-----|-----|-----|
| Pass 1 | 1 | 1 | 1 | 1 | 1 | 1 | 1 | 1 |
| Pass 2 | 1 | AM6 | AM5 | AM4 | AM3 | AM2 | AM1 | AM0 |

(b) Distributed Arbitration Message Fields (Distributed Arbiter)

| Bit | cn7 | cn6 | cn6 | cn4 | cn3 | cn2 | cn1 | cn0 |
|-----|-----|-----|-----|-----|-----|-----|-----|-----|
| Pass 1 | 1 | AM6 | AM5 | AM4 | AM3 | AM2 | AM1 | AM0 |

(c) General Arbitrated Message Fields (Central Arbiter)

| Bit | cn7 | cn6 | cn6 | cn4 | cn3 | cn2 | cn1 | cn0 |
|-----|-----|-----|-----|-----|-----|-----|-----|-----|
| Pass 1 | 0 | PR7 | PR6 | PR5 | PR4 | PR3 | PR2 | PR1 |
| Pass 2 | 1 | PR0 | RQ | GA4 | GA3 | GA2 | GA1 | GA0 |

(d) Central Arbitrated Message Fields (Central Arbiter)

**FIGURE 3.27. Futurebus+ arbitrated messages**

The 8-bit priority field PR(7 ... 0) selects one of 256 priority levels for the request (255 = highest, 0 = lowest). The highest two priority levels, with all but PRO set to 1, use the single-pass competition cycle.[4]

In a lightly loaded system, there may be several instances in which there are no bus requests pending. To save time, the current master retains control under such circumstances and may begin a new transaction without having to arbitrate. It is only when the master sees that an arbitration has taken place and that a master-elect exists that it may decide to release control to the master-elect. Even then, if the current master has higher priority than the master-elect, it may retain the bus.

The master-elect must wait for some period of time for the current master to finish using the bus. During that period, a module of higher priority may have need of the bus. If so, that module may force a new arbitration cycle and a new competition to establish a new master-elect. Thus, the cycle begins again at phase 1.

The round-robin feature ensures a fair and equitable allocation of bus tenure between competing modules of the same priority. The value of a module's round-robin bit is adjusted each time a transfer of tenure to another module in its priority class occurs. The bit is set when tenure is granted to a module in the same priority class but with a higher geographical address, and cleared for a module in the same priority class but with a lower geographical address. Thus, once the round-robin bit is cleared, the module will lose in any subsequent arbitration competition with modules in its priority class for which the bit is set. The effect of this feature is to assure a round-robin type of allocation under heavy load.

The arbitration number of the master-elect, since it is visible to all modules, can also be used to broadcast information to the entire system. This is referred to as an arbitration message. The arbitration message can be used to issue a system-wide interrupt or emergency message.

Arbitration messages look like any other priority request and follow the same sequence outlined above and illustrated in Figure 3.26. The arbitration message (Figure 3.27b) uses all 1s on the first pass to drive out any priority arbitration messages of priority less than 254. The actual message is conveyed on the second pass; it is up to the system to assign meaning to each message number.

The only change in the arbitration cycle is that the issuer of the arbitration message does not assume mastership after winning the arbitration.

### Centralized Arbitration

A Futurebus+ system can also be organized with a central arbiter (Figure 3.28). The central arbitration scheme makes use of the RQ1, RQ0, GR, and PE lines. The RQ and GR lines are not actually part of the common bus; rather, there are two separate request lines and one grant line from the central arbiter to each module on the bus. This configuration avoids the need for address resolution in dealing with multiple simultaneous requests.

---

[4]This is possible because when PR(7 ... 1) are all set to 1, the requestor would always win a first pass, and so it can be skipped in this case. For efficiency, in a system with only one or two priority levels, priorities 255 and 254 should be used.

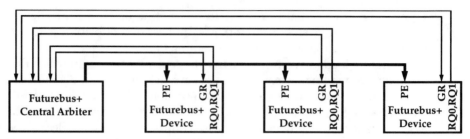

**FIGURE 3.28.  Futurebus+ central arbiter**

A module may assert RQ0 or RQ1 to request the bus at one of two priority levels. The actual priority of each module is determined by the arbiter based on the identity of the module and the priority level at which it is making its request. The arbiter indicates to a module that it is the new master-elect by asserting the GR line for that module. The module may then assume bus mastership when it detects that ET is released by the current bus master. The central arbiter may also assert PE to signal to the current bus master that it should relinquish control to the master-elect as soon as possible.

When the central arbiter is used, the arbitrated message lines are still available, and they are used solely for the transmission of arbitrated messages. Two types of messages are provided: general arbitrated messages and central arbitrated messages (Figures 3.27c and d). The numbering scheme used assures that general messages have precedence over central messages.

General messages are intended for broadcasting messages to other modules on the bus. As with distributed arbitration messages, they can be used to convey interrupts and other emergency messages.

Central messages are directed to the arbiter and are a means of sending priority information to the arbiter. The RQ field indicates whether RQ0 or RQ1 is the subject of this message. The priority field PR(7 . . . 0) selects the priority level to be assigned to the selected RQ line for this module.

## Data Transfer

Futurebus+ provides a wide variety of data transfer capabilities. In this subsection we present one example of a write, taken from [JONE91], as an illustration of the Futurebus+ approach.

In general, a Futurebus+ transaction consists of an address beat, followed by zero or more data beats. In this example, a block of four data words are being transferred. The sequence is as follows (Figure 3.29):

1. The sender gains control of the bus using one of the arbitration techniques described above.
2. The sender loads the address, as well as command information, onto the bus and asserts AS to indicate this.
3. All other modules read the address. Each module then asserts AK to indicate that it has read the address. Thus, AK on the bus will be asserted as soon as the fastest module responds.

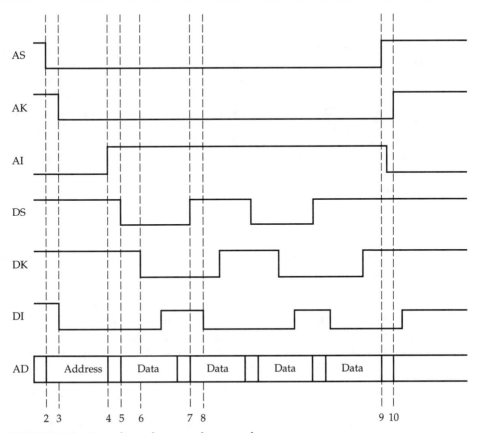

**FIGURE 3.29. Futurebus+ data transfer example**

4. Each module also releases AI at the time that it asserts AK. Thus, AI is not released until the slowest module responds. This signals the end of the address beat. The master can now safely remove the address from the bus.

5. The master now loads data onto the bus, signaled by asserting DS.

6. The recipient captures the data from the bus and asserts DK and then releases DI to signal successful capture.

7. The master loads the next data word onto the bus and releases DS to signal that the data is now valid.

8. The recipient captures the data from the bus and asserts DI, and then releases DK to signal successful capture.

9. Data transfer continues in this fashion, one word at a time, with each transition of DS and DK/DI, until the master has no more data to send. The master signals the end of the transaction by releasing AS.

10. The recipient, and all other slaves, acknowledge the release of AS by asserting AI and releasing AK. This completes the transaction.

This example illustrates the way in which Futurebus+ is independent of technology. Each event is causally related to the previous event only, with no other timing constraints.

## Summary

The Futurebus+ specification is one of the most technically complex bus standards ever produced. The standard covers the logical layer, the physical layer and profiles, recommended practices, plus references to several other standards documents. The result is a bus specification that can be used for the local processor–memory bus or that can compete with PCI for support of high-speed peripherals. Both PCI and Futurebus+ support very high data rates. The key distinction is that PCI is geared to provide a low-cost implementation that takes up minimal physical area, whereas Futurebus+ is intended to provide flexibility and broad functionality to meet the needs of a wide variety of high-performance systems, especially higher-cost systems.

## 3.7

## RECOMMENDED READING

The literature on buses and other interconnection structures is, surprisingly, not very extensive. [ALEX93] includes an in-depth treatment of bus structures and bus transfer issues, including accounts of several specific buses.

The clearest book-length description of PCI is [SHAN94a]. [SOLA94] also contains a lot of solid information on PCI.

ALEX93   Alexandridis, N. *Design of Microprocessor-Based Systems.* Englewood Cliffs, NJ: Prentice Hall, 1993.

SHAN94a   Shanley, T., and Anderson, D. *PCI Systems Architecture.* Richardson, TX: Mindshare Press, 1994.

SOLA94   Solari, E., and Willse, G. *PCI Hardware and Software: Architecture and Design.* San Diego, CA: Annabooks, 1994.

## 3.8

## PROBLEMS

3.1   For each of the IAS instructions (Table 2.1), specify the sequence of states (Figure 3.6) for the instruction cycle.

3.2   The hypothetical machine of Figure 3.4 also has two I/O instructions:
0011 = Load AC from I/O
0111 = Store AC to I/O
In these cases, the 12-bit address identifies a particular I/O device. Show the program execution (using format of Figure 3.5) for the following program:

1. Load AC from device 5.
2. Add contents of memory location 940.
3. Store AC to device 6.

3.3 Consider a computer system that contains an I/O module controlling a simple keyboard/printer teletype. The following registers are contained in the CPU and connected directly to the system bus:

INPR: Input Register—8 bits
OUTR: Output Register—8 bits
FGI: Input Flag—1 bit
FGO: Output Flag—1 bit
IEN: Interrupt Enable—1 bit

Keystroke input from the teletype and printer output to the teletype are controlled by the I/O module. The teletype is able to encode an alphanumeric symbol to an 8-bit word and decode an 8-bit word into an alphanumeric symbol.
**(a)** Describe how the CPU, using the first four registers listed in this problem, can achieve I/O with the teletype.
**(b)** Describe how the function can be performed more efficiently by also employing IEN.

3.4 Figure 3.30 indicates a distributed arbitration scheme that can be used with Multibus I. Agents are daisy-chained physically in priority order. The leftmost agent in the diagram receives a constant *bus priority in* (BPRN) signal indicating that no higher-priority agent desires the bus. If the agent does not wish the bus, it asserts its *bus priority out* (BPRO) line. At the beginning of a clock cycle, any agent can request control of the bus by lowering its BPRO line. This lowers the BPRN line of the next agent in the chain, which is in turn required to lower its BPRO line. Thus, the signal is propagated the length of the chain. At the end of this chain reaction, there should be only one agent whose BPRN is asserted and whose BPRO is not. This agent has priority. If, at the beginning of a bus cycle, the bus is not busy (BUSY inactive), the agent that has priority may seize control of the bus by asserting the BUSY line.

It takes a certain amount of time for the BPR signal to propagate from the highest-priority agent to the lowest. Must this time be less than the clock cycle? Explain.

3.5 A memory system consists of a number of memory modules connected together on a common memory bus. When a write request is made, the bus is occupied for 100 ns by the data, address, and control signals. During the

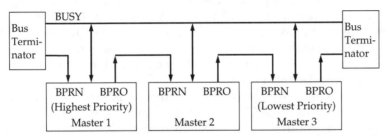

**FIGURE 3.30. Multibus I distributed arbitration**

same 100 ns, and for 500 ns thereafter, the addressed memory module executes 1 cycle accepting and storing the data. The operation of the memory
modules may overlap, but only one request can be on the bus at any time.

**(a)** Assume that there are eight such modules connected to the bus. What is
the maximum possible rate (in words/second) at which data can be
stored?

**(b)** Sketch a graph of the maximum write rate as a function of the module
cycle time, assuming eight memory modules and a bus busy time of
100 ns.

3.6  To save gates, buses are often time-multiplexed. Consider a machine with 48-
bit words, a $10^7$-bps disk, and a 600-ns main memory cycle time. Assume that
each bus transmission requires 750 ns for data bits and various control
"handshaking" operations. How many data bits would have to be sent in
each 750-ns period to stay ahead of the disk, and what bus format would you
choose? What fraction of the main memory bandwidth is consumed by a
disk I/O operation?

Sketch the sequence of timing events involved in a continuous input transmission from disk to main memory; that is, show how much of the bandwidth of the disk, bus, and main memory are used.

3.7  Regarding priorities on a daisy chain—assume that devices $d_1, \ldots, d_k$ are to be
put on a daisy chain and that each device, $d_i$, uses fraction $\alpha_i$ of the capacity
of the bus,

$$0 < a_i < 1; \quad \sum_{i=1}^{K} a_i < 1$$

and the capacity of the bus has a normalized value of 1.0. How should the
devices be attached to the daisy chain to obtain the maximum average
remaining capacity? The remaining capacity for a device on a daisy chain is 1
minus the sum of the capacities used by all the devices with higher priorities
on the daisy chain. Briefly comment on what your results mean and give an
example of when they may not be applicable.

3.8  The VAX SBI bus uses a distributed, synchronous arbitration scheme. Each
SBI device (i.e., processor, memory, Unibus adapter) has a unique priority
and is assigned a unique transfer request (TR) line. The SBI has 16 such lines
(TR0, TR1, . . ., TR15), with TR0 having the highest priority. When a device
wants to use the bus, it places a reservation for a future time slot by asserting
its TR line during the current time slot. At the end of the current time slot,
each device with a pending reservation examines the TR lines; the highest-
priority device with a reservation uses the next time slot.

A maximum of 17 devices can be attached to the bus. The device with priority 16 has no TR line. Why not?

3.9  Paradoxically, the lowest-priority device usually has the lowest average wait
time. For this reason, the CPU is usually given the lowest priority on the SBI.
Why does the priority 16 device usually have the lowest average wait time?
Under what circumstances would this not be true?

3.10 Consider a hypothetical 32-bit microprocessor having 32-bit instructions composed of two fields: the first byte contains the op code and the remainder the immediate operand or an operand address.
  (a) What is the maximum directly addressable memory capacity (in bytes)?
  (b) Discuss the impact on the system speed if the microprocessor bus has
      1. a 32-bit local address bus and a 16-bit local data bus, or
      2. a 16-bit local address bus and a 16-bit local data bus.
  (c) How many bits are needed for the program counter and the instruction register?
  Source: [ALEX93]

3.11 Consider a hypothetical microprocessor generating a 16-bit address (for example, assume that the program counter and the address registers are 16 bits wide) and having a 16-bit data bus.
  (a) What is the maximum memory address space that the processor can access directly if it is connected to a "16-bit memory"?
  (b) What is the maximum memory address space that the processor can access directly if it is connected to an "8-bit memory"?
  (c) What architectural features will allow this microprocessor to access a separate "I/O space"?
  (d) If an input and an output instruction can specify an 8-bit I/O port number, how many 8-bit I/O ports can the microprocessor support? How many 16-bit I/O ports? Explain.
  Source: [ALEX93]

3.12 Consider a 32-bit microprocessor, with a 16-bit external data bus, driven by an 8-MHz input clock. Assume that this microprocessor has a bus cycle whose minimum duration equals four input clock cycles. What is the maximum data transfer rate that this microprocessor can sustain? In order to increase its performance, would it be better to make its external data bus 32 bits or to double the external clock frequency supplied to the microprocessor? State any other assumptions you make, and explain.
  Source: [ALEX93]

3.13 Draw and explain a timing diagram for a PCI write operation (similar to Figure 3.22).

## APPENDIX 3A

### Timing Diagrams

In this chapter, timing diagrams are used to illustrate sequences of events and dependencies among events. For the reader unfamiliar with timing diagrams, this appendix provides a brief explanation.

Communication among devices connected to a bus takes place along a set of lines capable of carrying signals. Two different signal levels (voltage levels), representing binary 0 and binary 1, may be transmitted. A timing diagram shows the signal level on a line as a function of time (Figure 3.31a). By convention, the binary

1 signal level is depicted as a higher level than that of binary 0. Usually, binary 0 is the default value. That is, if no data or other signal is being transmitted, then the level on a line is that which represents binary 0. A signal transition from 0 to 1 is frequently referred to as the signal's *leading edge;* a transition from 1 to 0 is referred to as a *trailing edge.* For clarity, signal transitions are often depicted as occurring instantaneously. In fact, a transition takes a nonzero amount of time, but this transition time is usually small compared with the duration of a signal level. On a timing diagram, it may happen that a variable or at least irrelevant amount of time elapses between events of interest. This is depicted by a gap in the time line.

Signals are sometimes represented in groups (Figure 3.31b). For example, if data are transferred a byte at a time, then eight lines are required. Generally, it is not important to know the exact value being transferred on such a group, but rather whether signals are present or not.

A signal transition on one line may trigger an attached device to make signal changes on other lines. For example, if a memory module detects a read control

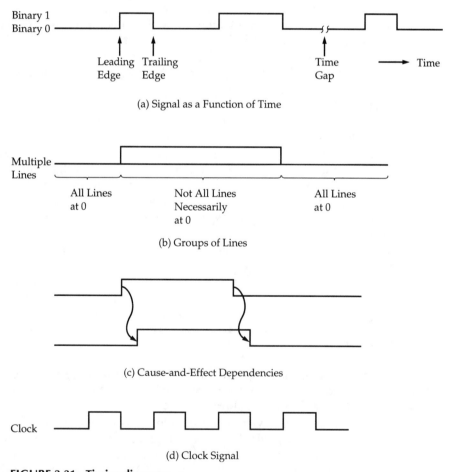

(a) Signal as a Function of Time

(b) Groups of Lines

(c) Cause-and-Effect Dependencies

(d) Clock Signal

**FIGURE 3.31. Timing diagrams**

signal (0 or 1 transition), it will place data signals on the data lines. Such cause-and-effect relationships produce sequences of events. Arrows are used on timing diagrams to show these dependencies (Figure 3.31c).

A clock line is often part of a system bus. An electronic clock is connected to the clock line and provides a repetitive, regular sequence of transitions (Figure 3.31d). Other events may be synchronized to the clock signal.

# CHAPTER 4

# Internal Memory

Although seemingly simple in concept, computer memory exhibits perhaps the widest range of type, technology, organization, performance, and cost of any feature of a computer system. No one technology is optimal in satisfying the memory requirements for a computer system. As a consequence, the typical computer system is equipped with a hierarchy of memory subsystems, some internal to the system (directly accessible by the processor), and some external (accessible by the processor via an I/O module).

This chapter focuses on internal memory elements, while Chapter 5 is devoted to external memory. To begin, the first section of this chapter examines key characteristics of computer memories. Then, we look at semiconductor main memory subsystems, including ROM, DRAM, and SRAM memories. Next, we examine an essential element of all modern computer systems: cache memory. Following this, we are in a position to return to DRAM memory and look at more advanced DRAM architectures.

## 4.1

### COMPUTER MEMORY SYSTEM OVERVIEW

### Characteristics of Memory Systems

The complex subject of computer memory is made more manageable if we classify memory systems according to their key characteristics. The most important of these are listed in Table 4.1.

We begin with the most visible aspect of memory: its *location.* As the title of this chapter and the next suggest, there is memory both internal and external to the computer. Internal memory is often equated with main memory. But there are other forms of internal memory. The CPU requires its own local memory, in the form of registers (e.g., see Figure 2.3). Further, as we shall see, the control unit portion of the CPU may also require its own internal memory. We will defer discussion of these latter two types of internal memory to later chapters. External memory consists of peripheral storage devices, such as disk and tape, that are accessible to the CPU via I/O controllers.

**TABLE 4.1   Key Characteristics of Computer Memory Systems**

| | |
|---|---|
| **Location** | **Performance** |
| CPU | Access time |
| Internal (main) | Cycle time |
| External (secondary) | Transfer rate |
| **Capacity** | **Physical Type** |
| Word size | Semiconductor |
| Number of words | Magnetic surface |
| **Unit of Transfer** | **Physical Characteristics** |
| Word | Volatile/nonvolatile |
| Block | Erasable/nonerasable |
| **Access Method** | **Organization** |
| Sequential access | |
| Direct access | |
| Random access | |
| Associative access | |

An obvious characteristic of memory is its *capacity*. For internal memory, this is typically expressed in terms of bytes (1 byte = 8 bits) or words. Common word lengths are 8, 16, and 32 bits. External memory capacity is typically expressed in terms of bytes.

A related concept is the *unit of transfer*. For internal memory, the unit of transfer is equal to the number of data lines into and out of the memory module. This is often equal to the word length, but it may not be. To clarify this point, consider three related concepts for internal memory:

- *Word:* The "natural" unit of organization of memory. The size of the word is typically equal to the number of bits used to represent a number and to the instruction length. Unfortunately, there are many exceptions. For example, the CRAY-1 has a 64-bit word length but uses a 24-bit integer representation. The VAX has a stupendous variety of instruction lengths, expressed as multiples of bytes, and a word size of 32 bits.
- *Addressable Units:* In many systems, the addressable unit is the word. However, some systems allow addressing at the byte level. In any case, the relationship between the length $A$ of an address and the number $N$ of addressable units is $2^A = N$.
- *Unit of Transfer:* For main memory, this is the number of bits read out of or written into memory at a time. The unit of transfer need not equal a word or an addressable unit. For external memory, data are often transferred in much larger units than a word, and these are referred to as blocks.

One of the sharpest distinctions among memory types is the *method of accessing* units of data. Four types may be distinguished:

- *Sequential Access:* Memory is organized into units of data, called records. Access must be made in a specific linear sequence. Stored addressing information is used to separate records and assist in the retrieval process. A shared read/write mechanism is used, and this must be moved from its current location to the desired location, passing and rejecting each intermediate record. Thus, the time to access an arbitrary record is highly variable. Tape units, discussed in Chapter 5, are sequential access.

- *Direct Access:* As with sequential access, direct access involves a shared read–write mechanism. However, individual blocks or records have a unique address based on physical location. Access is accomplished by direct access to reach a general vicinity plus sequential searching, counting, or waiting to reach the final location. Again, access time is variable. Disk units, discussed in Chapter 5, are direct access.
- *Random Access:* Each addressable location in memory has a unique, physically wired-in addressing mechanism. The time to access a given location is independent of the sequence of prior accesses and is constant. Thus, any location can be selected at random and directly addressed and accessed. Main memory systems are random access.
- *Associative:* This is a random-access type of memory that enables one to make a comparison of desired bit locations within a word for a specified match, and to do this for all words simultaneously. Thus, a word is retrieved based on a portion of its contents rather than its address. As with ordinary random-access memory, each location has its own addressing mechanism, and retrieval time is constant independent of location or prior access patterns. Cache memories, discussed in Section 4.3, may employ associative access.

From a user's point of view, the two most important characteristics of memory are capacity and *performance.* Three performance parameters are used:

- *Access Time:* For random-access memory, this is the time it takes to perform a read or write operation, that is, the time from the instant that an address is presented to the memory to the instant that data have been stored or made available for use. For nonrandom-access memory, access time is the time it takes to position the read–write mechanism at the desired location.
- *Memory Cycle Time:* This concept is primarily applied to random-access memory and consists of the access time plus any additional time required before a second access can commence. This additional time may be required for transients to die out on signal lines or to regenerate data if they are read destructively.
- *Transfer Rate:* This is the rate at which data can be transferred into or out of a memory unit. For random-access memory, it is equal to 1/(Cycle Time). For nonrandom-access memory, the following relationship holds:

$$T_N = T_A + \frac{N}{R}$$

where

$T_N$ = Average time to read or write $N$ bits
$T_A$ = Average access time
$N$ = Number of bits
$R$ = Transfer rate, in bits per second (bps)

A variety of *physical types* of memory have been employed. The two most common today are semiconductor memory, using LSI or VLSI technology, and magnetic surface memory, used for disk and tape.

Several *physical characteristics* of data storage are important. In a volatile memory, information decays naturally or is lost when electrical power is switched off. In a nonvolatile memory, information once recorded remains without deterioration until deliberately changed; no electrical power is needed to retain information. Magnetic-surface memories are nonvolatile. Semiconductor memory may be either volatile or nonvolatile. Nonerasable memory cannot be altered, except by destroying the storage unit. Semiconductor memory of this type is known as *read-only memory* (ROM). Of necessity, a practical nonerasable memory must also be nonvolatile.

For random-access memory, the organization is a key design issue. By *organization* is meant the physical arrangement of bits to form words. The obvious arrangement is not always used, as will be explained presently.

## The Memory Hierarchy

The design constraints on a computer's memory can be summed up by three questions: How much? How fast? How expensive?

The question of how much is somewhat open-ended. If the capacity is there, applications will likely be developed to use it. The question of how fast is, in a sense, easier to answer. To achieve greatest performance, the memory must be able to keep up with the CPU. That is, as the CPU is executing instructions, we would not want it to have to pause waiting for instructions or operands. The final question must also be considered. For a practical system, the cost of memory must be reasonable in relationship to other components.

As might be expected, there is a trade-off among the three key characteristics of memory, namely cost, capacity, and access time. At any given time, a variety of technologies are used to implement memory systems. Across this spectrum of technologies, the following relationships hold:

- Smaller access time, greater cost per bit
- Greater capacity, smaller cost per bit
- Greater capacity, greater access time

The dilemma facing the designer is clear. The designer would like to use memory technologies that provide for large-capacity memory, both because the capacity is needed and because the cost per bit is low. However, to meet performance requirements, the designer needs to use expensive, relatively lower-capacity memories with fast access times.

The way out of this dilemma is not to rely on a single memory component or technology, but to employ a *memory hierarchy*. A typical hierarchy is illustrated in Figure 4.1a. As one goes down the hierarchy, the following occur:

a. Decreasing cost/bit
b. Increasing capacity

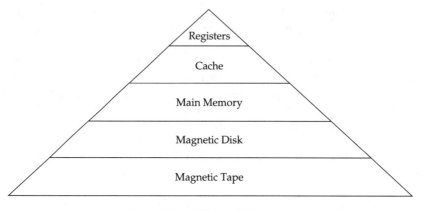

(a) Traditional Memory Hierarchy

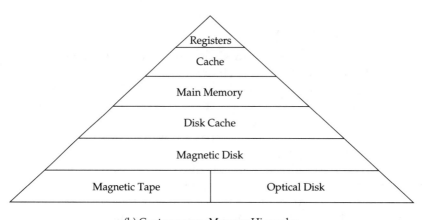

(b) Contemporary Memory Hierarchy

**FIGURE 4.1. The memory hierarchy**

c. Increasing access time
d. Decreasing frequency of access of the memory by the CPU

Thus, smaller, more expensive, faster memories are supplemented by larger, cheaper, slower memories. The key to the success of this organization is the last item, decreasing frequency of access. We will examine this concept in detail when we discuss the cache, later in this chapter, and virtual memory, in Chapter 7, but we give a brief explanation here.

If memory can be organized according to items (a) through (c) above, and if the data and instructions can be distributed across this memory according to (d), then it should be intuitively clear that this scheme will reduce overall costs while maintaining a given level of performance. We give a simple example to illustrate this point.

Suppose that the CPU has access to two levels of memory. Level 1 contains 1000 words and has an access time of 1 µs. Level 2 contains 100,000 words and has an access time of 10 μs. Assume that if a word to be accessed is in Level 1, then the CPU accesses it directly. If it is in Level 2, then the word is first transferred to Level 1 and then is accessed by the CPU. For simplicity, we ignore the time required for the CPU to determine whether the word is in Level 1 or Level 2. Figure 4.2 shows the average total access time as a function of the percentage of time that the desired word is already in Level 1. As can be seen, for high percentages of Level 1 access, the average total access time is much closer to that of Level 1 than that of Level 2.

This example illustrates that the strategy works in principle. It will work in practice if conditions (a) through (d) apply. Figures 4.3 and 4.4 show typical characteristics of contemporary alternative memory systems. Figure 4.3 shows that by employing a variety of technologies, a spectrum of memory systems exists that satisfy (b) and (c), and Figure 4.4 confirms that condition (a) is satisfied. Fortunately, condition (d) is also generally valid.

The basis for the validity of condition (d) is a principle known as *locality of reference* [DENN68]. During the course of execution of a program, memory references by the processor, for both instructions and data, tend to cluster. Programs typically contain a number of iterative loops and subroutines. Once a loop or subroutine is entered, there are repeated references to a small set of instructions. Similarly, operations on tables and arrays involve access to a clustered set of data words. Over a long period of time, the clusters in use change, but over a short period of time, the processor is primarily working with fixed clusters of memory references.

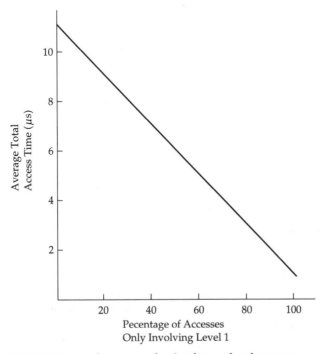

**FIGURE 4.2. Performance of a simple two-level memory**

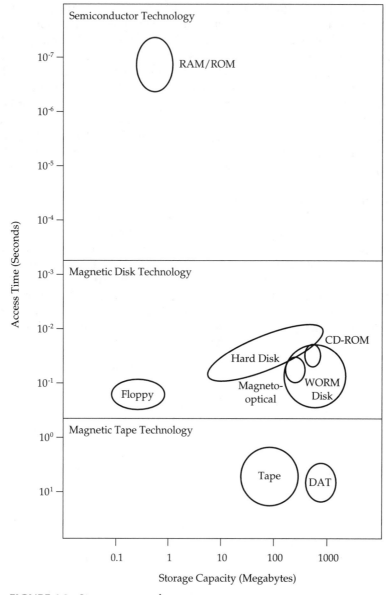

**FIGURE 4.3. Storage comparison**

Accordingly, it is possible to organize data across the hierarchy such that the percentage of accesses to each succeedingly lower level is substantially less than to the level above. Consider the two-level example already presented. Let Level 2 memory contain all program instructions and data. The current clusters can be temporarily placed in Level 1. From time to time, one of the clusters in Level 1 will have to be swapped back to Level 2 to make room for a new cluster coming into

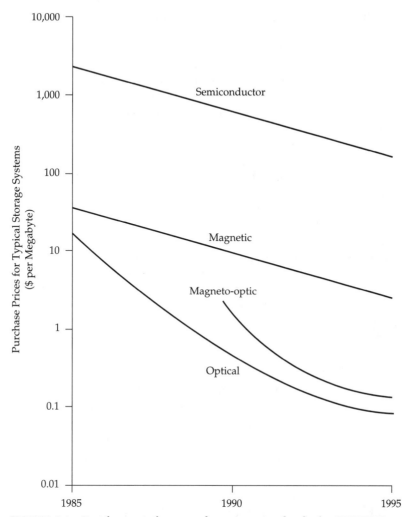

**FIGURE 4.4.  Cost forecasts for secondary storage technologies [WEIZ91]**

Level 1. On average, however, most references will be to instructions and data contained in Level 1.

This principle can be applied across more than two levels of memory. Consider the hierarchy shown in Figure 4.1a. The fastest, smallest, and most expensive type of memory consists of the registers internal to the processor. Typically, a processor will contain a few dozen such registers, although some machines contain hundreds of registers. Skipping down two levels, main memory, also referred to as real memory, is the principal internal memory system of the computer. Each location in main memory has a unique address, and most machine instructions refer to one or more main memory addresses. Main memory is usually extended with a higher-speed, smaller cache. The cache is not usually visible to the programmer or, indeed, to the processor. It is a device for staging the movement of data between main memory and processor registers to improve performance.

The three forms of memory just described are, typically, volatile and employ semiconductor technology. The use of three levels exploits the variety of types semiconductor memory comes in, which differ in speed and cost. Data are stored more permanently on external mass storage devices, of which the most common are magnetic disk and tape. External, nonvolatile memory is also referred to as secondary or auxiliary memory. These are used to store program and data files and are usually visible to the programmer only in terms of files and records, as opposed to individual bytes or words. Disk is also used to provide an extension to main memory known as virtual storage or virtual memory, which is discussed in Chapter 7.

Other forms of memory may be included in the hierarchy. For example, large IBM mainframes include a form of internal memory known as Expanded Storage. This uses a semiconductor technology that is slower and less expensive than that of main memory. Strictly speaking, this memory does not fit into the hierarchy but is a side branch: data can be moved between main memory and expanded storage but not between expanded storage and external memory. Other forms of secondary memory include optical disks and bubble memory devices. Finally, additional levels can be effectively added to the hierarchy in software. A portion of main memory can be used as a buffer to temporarily hold data that is to be read out to disk. Such a technique, sometimes referred to as a disk cache,[1] improves performance in two ways:

- Disk writes are clustered. Instead of many small transfers of data, we have a few large transfers of data. This improves disk performance and minimizes processor involvement.
- Some data destined for write-out may be referenced by a program before the next dump to disk. In that case, the data is retrieved rapidly from the software cache rather than slowly from the disk.

Figure 4.1b shows a contemporary memory hierarchy that includes a disk cache and optical disk as an additional type of secondary memory.

Appendix 4A examines the performance implications of multilevel memory structures.

4.2

## SEMICONDUCTOR MAIN MEMORY

In earlier computers, the most common form of random-access storage for computer main memory employed an array of doughnut-shaped ferromagnetic loops referred to as *cores*. Hence, main memory was often referred to as *core*, a term that persists to this day. The advent of, and advantages of, microelectronics has long

---

[1] Disk cache is generally a purely software technique, and it is not examined in this book. See [STAL95] for a discussion.

since vanquished the magnetic core memory. Today, the use of semiconductor chips for main memory is almost universal. Key aspects of this technology are explored in this section.

## Types of Random-Access Semiconductor Memory

All of the memory types that we will explore in this section are random access. That is, individual words of memory are directly accessed through wired-in addressing logic.

Table 4.2 lists the major types of semiconductor memory. The most common is referred to as *random-access memory* (RAM). This is, of course, a misuse of the term, since all of the types listed in the table are random access. One distinguishing characteristic of RAM is that it is possible both to read data from the memory and to easily and rapidly write new data into the memory. Both the reading and writing are accomplished through the use of electrical signals.

The other distinguishing characteristic of RAM is that it is volatile. A RAM must be provided with a constant power supply. If the power is interrupted, then the data are lost. Thus, RAM can be used only as temporary storage.

RAM technology has divided into two technologies: static and dynamic. A *dynamic RAM* is made with cells that store data as charge on capacitors. The presence or absence of charge in a capacitor is interpreted as a binary 1 or 0. Because capacitors have a natural tendency to discharge, dynamic RAMs require periodic charge refreshing to maintain data storage. In a *static RAM,* binary values are stored using traditional flip-flop logic-gate configurations (see Appendix A for a description of flip-flops). A static RAM will hold its data as long as power is supplied to it.

Both static and dynamic RAMs are volatile. A dynamic memory cell is simpler and hence smaller than a static memory cell. Thus, a dynamic RAM is more dense (smaller cells = more cells per unit area) and less expensive than a corresponding

**TABLE 4.2   Semiconductor Memory Types**

| Memory Type | Category | Erasure | Write Mechanism | Volatility |
|---|---|---|---|---|
| Random-access memory (RAM) | Read-write memory | Electrically, byte-level | Electrically | Volatile |
| Read-only memory (ROM) | Read-only memory | Not possible | Masks | Nonvolatile |
| Programmable ROM (PROM) | | | | |
| Erasable PROM (EPROM) | Read-mostly memory | UV light, chip-level | Electrically | |
| Flash memory | | Electrically, block-level | | |
| Electrically Erasable PROM (EEPROM) | | Electrically, byte-level | | |

static RAM. On the other hand, a dynamic RAM requires the supporting refresh circuitry. For larger memories, the fixed cost of the refresh circuitry is more than compensated for by the smaller variable cost of dynamic RAM cells. Thus, dynamic RAMs tend to be favored for large memory requirements. A final point is that static RAMs are generally somewhat faster than dynamic RAMs.

In sharp contrast to the RAM is the *read-only memory* (ROM). As the name suggests, a ROM contains a permanent pattern of data that cannot be changed. While it is possible to read a ROM, it is not possible to write new data into it. An important application of ROMs is microprogramming, discussed in Part IV. Other potential applications include

- Library subroutines for frequently wanted functions
- System programs
- Function tables

For a modest-sized requirement, the advantage of ROM is that the data or program is permanently in main memory and need never be loaded from a secondary storage device.

A ROM is created like any other integrated-circuit chip, with the data actually wired-in to the chip as part of the fabrication process. This presents two problems:

- The data insertion step includes a relatively large fixed cost, whether one or thousands of copies of a particular ROM are fabricated.
- There is no room for error. If one bit is wrong, the whole batch of ROMs must be thrown out.

When only a small number of ROMs with a particular memory content is needed, a less expensive alternative is the *programmable ROM* (PROM). Like the ROM, the PROM is nonvolatile and may be written into only once. For the PROM, the writing process is performed electrically and may be performed by a supplier or customer at a time later than the original chip fabrication. Special equipment is required for the writing or "programming" process. PROMs provide flexibility and convenience. The ROM remains attractive for high-volume production runs.

Another variation on read-only memory is the read-mostly memory, which is useful for applications in which read operations are far more frequent than write operations but for which nonvolatile storage is required. There are three common forms of read-mostly memory: EPROM, EEPROM, and flash memory.

The optically *erasable programmable read-only memory* (EPROM) is read and written electrically, as with PROM. However, before a write operation, all the storage cells must be erased to the same initial state by exposure of the packaged chip to ultraviolet radiation. This erasure process can be performed repeatedly; each erasure can take as much as 20 minutes to perform. Thus, the EPROM can be altered multiple times and, like the ROM and PROM, holds its data virtually indefinitely. For comparable amounts of storage, the EPROM is more expensive than PROM, but it has the advantage of the multiple update capability.

A more attractive form of read-mostly memory is *electrically erasable programmable read-only memory* (EEPROM). This is a read-mostly memory that can be written into at any time without erasing prior contents; only the byte or bytes addressed are updated. The write operation takes considerably longer than the read operation, on the order of several hundred microseconds per byte. The EEPROM combines the advantage of nonvolatility with the flexibility of being updatable in place, using ordinary bus control, address, and data lines. EEPROM is more expensive than EPROM and also is less dense, supporting fewer bits per chip.

The newest form of semiconductor memory is *flash memory* (so named because of the speed with which it can be reprogrammed). First introduced in the mid-1980s, flash memory is intermediate between EPROM and EEPROM in both cost and functionality. Like EEPROM, flash memory uses an electrical erasing technology. An entire flash memory can be erased in one or a few seconds, which is much faster than EPROM. In addition, it is possible to erase just blocks of memory rather than an entire chip. However, flash memory does not provide byte-level erasure. Like EPROM, flash memory uses only one transistor per bit, and so achieves the high density (compared with EEPROM) of EPROM.

## Organization

The basic element of a semiconductor memory is the memory cell. Although a variety of electronic technologies are used, all semiconductor memory cells share certain properties:

- They exhibit two stable (or semistable) states, which can be used to represent binary 1 and 0.
- They are capable of being written into (at least once), to set the state.
- They are capable of being read to sense the state.

Figure 4.5 depicts the operation of a memory cell. Most commonly, the cell has three functional terminals capable of carrying an electrical signal. The select terminal, as the name suggests, selects a memory cell for a read or write operation. The control terminal indicates read or write. For writing, the other terminal provides an electrical signal that sets the state of the cell to 1 or 0. For reading, that terminal is used for output of the cell's state. The details of the internal organization, functioning, and timing of the memory cell depend on the specific integrated-circuit technology used and are beyond the scope of this book. For our purposes, we will take it as given that individual cells can be selected for reading and writing operations.

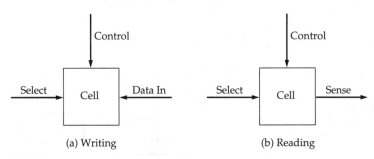

**FIGURE 4.5. Memory cell operation**

## Chip Logic

As with other integrated-circuit products, semiconductor memory comes in packaged chips (Figure 2.7). Each chip contains an array of memory cells. With current technology, 4-Mbit chips are common, with 16-Mbit chips coming into use.

In the memory hierarchy as a whole, we saw that there are trade-offs among speed, capacity, and cost. These trade-offs also exist when we consider the organization of memory cells and functional logic on a chip. For semiconductor memories, one of the key design issues is the number of bits of data that may be read/written at a time. At one extreme is an organization in which the physical arrangement of cells in the array is the same as the logical arrangement (as perceived by the processor) of words in memory. The array is organized into $W$ words of $B$ bits each. For example, a 16-Mbit chip could be organized as 1M 16-bit words. At the other extreme is the so-called one-bit-per-chip organization, in which data is read/written one bit at a time. We will illustrate memory chip organization with a DRAM; ROM organization is similar, though simpler.

Figure 4.6 shows a typical organization of a 16-Mbit DRAM. In this case, four bits are read or written at a time. Logically, the memory array is organized as four square arrays of 2048 by 2048 elements. Various physical arrangements are possible. In any case, the elements of the array are connected by both horizontal (row) and vertical (column) lines. Each horizontal line connects to the Select terminal of each cell in its row; each vertical line connects to the Data-In/Sense terminal of each cell in its column.

Address lines supply the address of the word to be selected. A total of $\log_2 W$ lines are needed. In our example, 11 address lines are needed to select one of 2048

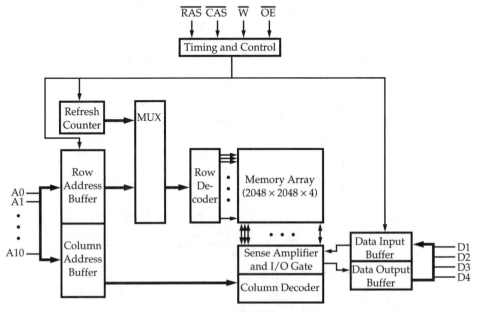

**FIGURE 4.6. Typical 16 megabit DRAM (4M x 4)**

rows. These 11 lines are fed into a row decoder, which has 11 lines of input and 2048 lines for output. The logic of the decoder activates a single one of the 2048 outputs depending on the bit pattern on the 11 input lines ($2^{11} = 2048$).

An additional 11 address lines select one of 2048 columns of four bits per column. Four data lines are used for the input and output of four bits to and from a data buffer. On input (write), the bit driver of each bit line is activated for a 1 or 0 according to the value of the corresponding data line. On output (read), the value of each bit line is passed through a sense amplifier and presented to the data lines. The row line selects which row of cells is used for reading or writing.

Since only four bits are read/written to this DRAM, there must be multiple DRAMs connected to the memory controller in order to read/write a word of data to the bus.

Note that there are only 11 address lines (A0–A10), half the number you would expect for a 2048 × 2048 array. This is done to save on the number of pins. The 22 required address lines are passed through select logic external to the chip and multiplexed onto the 11 address lines. First, 11 address signals are passed to the chip to define the row address of the array, and then the other 11 address signals are presented for the column address. These signals are accompanied by row address select (RAS) and column address select (CAS) signals to provide timing to the chip.

As an aside, multiplexed addressing plus the use of square arrays result in a quadrupling of memory size with each new generation of memory chips. One more pin devoted to addressing doubles the number of rows and columns, and so the size of the chip memory grows by a factor of 4. So far, we have gone through the following generations, at a rate of roughly one every three years: 1K, 4K, 16K, 64K, 256K, 1M, 4M, 16M.

Figure 4.6 also indicates the inclusion of refresh circuitry. All DRAMs require a refresh operation. A simple technique for refreshing is to in effect disable the DRAM chip while all data cells are refreshed. The refresh counter steps through all of the row values. For each row, the output lines from the refresh counter are supplied to the row decoder and the RAS line is activated. This causes each cell in the row to be refreshed.

## Chip Packaging

As was mentioned in Chapter 2, an integrated circuit is mounted on a package that contains pins for connection to the outside world.

Figure 4.7a shows an example EPROM package, which is an 8-Mbit chip organized as 1M × 8. In this case, the organization is treated as a one-word-per-chip package. The package includes 32 pins, which is one of the standard chip package sizes. The pins support the following signal lines:

- The address of the word being accessed. For 1M words, a total of 20 ($2^{20} = 1M$) pins are needed (A0–A19).
- The data to be read out, consisting of 8 lines (D0–D7).
- The power supply to the chip (Vcc).
- A ground pin (Vss).

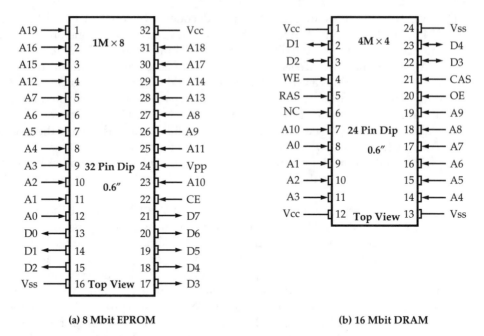

(a) 8 Mbit EPROM                              (b) 16 Mbit DRAM

**FIGURE 4.7.  Typical memory package pins and signals**

- A chip enable (CE) pin. Since there may be more than one memory chip, each of which is connected to the same address bus, the CE pin is used to indicate whether or not the address is valid for this chip. The CE pin is activated by logic connected to the higher-order bits of the address bus (i.e., address bits above A19). The use of this signal is illustrated presently.
- A program voltage (Vpp) that is supplied during programming (write operations)

A typical DRAM pin configuration is shown in Figure 4.7b, for a 16-Mbit chip organized as 4M × 4. There are several differences from a ROM chip. Since a RAM can be updated, the data pins are input/output. The write enable (WE) and output enable (OE) pins indicate whether this is a write or read operation. Because the DRAM is accessed by row and column, and the address is multiplexed, only 11 address pins are needed to specify the 4M row/column combinations ($2^{11} \times 2^{11} = 2^{22} = 4M$). The function of the row address select (RAS) and column address select (CAS) pins were discussed previously.

## Module Organization

If a RAM chip contains only 1 bit per word, then clearly we will need at least a number of chips equal to the number of bits per word. As an example, Figure 4.8 shows how a memory module consisting of 256K 8-bit words could be organized. For 256K words, an 18-bit address is needed and is supplied to the module from some external source (e.g., the address lines of a bus to which the module is

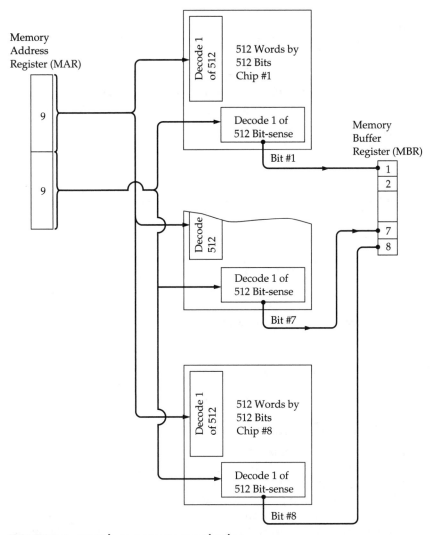

**FIGURE 4.8. 256K-byte memory organization**

attached). The address is presented to 8 256K × 1-bit chips, each of which provides the input/output of 1 bit.

This organization works as long as the size of memory equals the number of bits per chip. In the case in which larger memory is required, an array of chips is needed. Figure 4.9 shows the possible organization of a memory consisting of 1M word by 8 bits per word. In this case, we have four columns of chips, each column containing 256K words arranged as in Figure 4.8. For 1M word, 20 address lines are needed. The 18 least significant bits are routed to all 32 modules. The high-order 2 bits are input to a group select logic module that sends a chip enable signal to one of the four columns of modules.

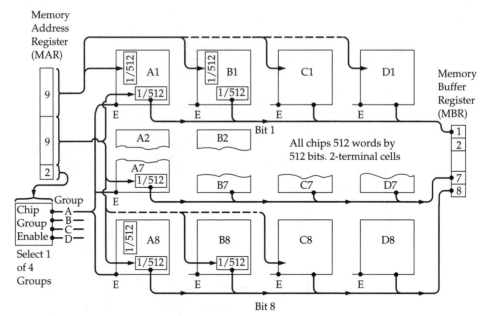

**FIGURE 4.9. 1M-byte memory organization**

## Error Correction

A semiconductor memory system is subject to errors. These can be categorized as hard failures and soft errors. A *hard failure* is a permanent physical defect so that the memory cell or cells affected cannot reliably store data, but become stuck at 0 or 1 or switch erratically between 0 and 1. Hard errors can be caused by harsh environmental abuse, manufacturing defects, and wear. A *soft error* is a random, nondestructive event that alters the contents of one or more memory cells, without damaging the memory. Soft errors can be caused by power supply problems or alpha particles. These particles result from radioactive decay and are distressingly common because radioactive nuclei are found in small quantities in nearly all materials. Both hard and soft errors are clearly undesirable, and most modern main memory systems include logic for both detecting and correcting errors.

Figure 4.10 illustrates in general terms how the process is carried out. When data are to be read into memory, a calculation, depicted as a function $f$, is performed on the data to produce a code. Both the code and the data are stored. Thus, if an $M$-bit word of data is to be stored, and the code is of length $K$ bits, then the actual size of the stored word is $M + K$ bits.

When the previously stored word is read out, the code is used to detect and possibly correct errors. A new set of $K$ code bits is generated from the $M$ data bits and compared with the fetched code bits. The comparison yields one of three results:

- No errors are detected. The fetched data bits are sent out.
- An error is detected, and it is possible to correct the error. The data bits plus error-correction bits are fed into a corrector, which produces a corrected set of $M$ bits to be sent out.

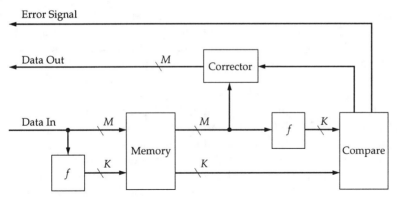

**FIGURE 4.10.  Error-correcting code function**

- An error is detected, but it is not possible to correct it. This condition is reported.

Codes that operate in this fashion are referred to as *error-correcting codes.* A code is characterized by the number of bit errors in a word that it can correct and detect.

The simplest of the error-correcting codes is the *Hamming code* devised by Richard Hamming at Bell Laboratories. Figure 4.11 uses Venn diagrams to illustrate the use of this code on 4-bit words ($M = 4$). With three intersecting circles, there are seven compartments. We assign the 4 data bits to the inner compartments (Figure 4.11a). The remaining compartments are filled with what are called

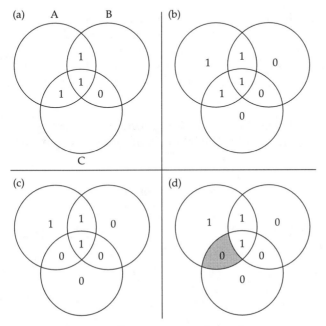

**FIGURE 4.11.  Hamming error-correcting code**

*parity bits*. Each parity bit is chosen so that the total number of 1s in its circle is even (Figure 4.11b). Thus, since circle A includes three data 1s, the parity bit in that circle is set to 1. Now, if an error changes one of the data bits (Figure 4.11c), it is easily found. By checking the parity bits, discrepancies are found in circle A and circle C but not in circle B. Only one of the seven compartments is in A and C but not B. The error can therefore be corrected by changing that bit.

To clarify the concepts involved, we will develop a code that can detect and correct single-bit errors in 8-bit words (example based on [ALTN79]).

To start, let us determine how long the code must be. Referring to Figure 4.10, the comparison logic receives as input two $K$-bit values. A bit-by-bit comparison is done by taking the exclusive-or of the two inputs. The result is called the *syndrome word*. Thus, each bit of the syndrome is 0 or 1 according to if there is or is not a match in that bit position for the two inputs.

The syndrome word is therefore $K$ bits wide and has a range of $2^K$ values between 0 and $2^K - 1$. The value 0 indicates that no error was detected, leaving $2^K - 1$ values to indicate, if there is an error, which bit was in error. Now, since an error could occur on any of the $M$ data bits or $K$ check bits, we must have

$$2^K - 1 \geq M + K$$

This equation gives the number of bits needed to correct a single bit error in a word containing $M$ data bits. Table 4.3 lists the number of check bits required for various data word lengths.

From this table, we see that a word of 8 data bits requires 4 check bits. For convenience, we would like to generate a 4-bit syndrome with the following characteristics:

- If the syndrome contains all 0s, no error has been detected.
- If the syndrome contains one and only one bit set to 1, then an error has occurred in one of the 4 check bits. No correction is needed.
- If the syndrome contains more than one bit set to 1, then the numerical value of the syndrome indicates the position of the data bit in error. This data bit is inverted for correction.

To achieve these characteristics, the data and check bits are arranged into a 12-bit word as depicted in Figure 4.12. The bit positions are numbered from 1 to 12.

**TABLE 4.3    Increase in Word Length with Error Correction**

| | *Single-Error Correction* | | *Single-Error Correction/ Double-Error Detection* | |
|---|---|---|---|---|
| *Data Bits* | *Check Bits* | *% Increase* | *Check Bits* | *% Increase* |
| 8 | 4 | 50 | 5 | 62.5 |
| 16 | 5 | 31.25 | 6 | 37.5 |
| 32 | 6 | 18.75 | 7 | 21.875 |
| 64 | 7 | 10.94 | 8 | 12.5 |
| 128 | 8 | 6.25 | 9 | 7.03 |
| 256 | 9 | 3.52 | 10 | 3.91 |

| Bit Position | Position Number | Check Bit | Data Bit |
|---|---|---|---|
| 12 | 1 1 0 0 | | M8 |
| 11 | 1 0 1 1 | | M7 |
| 10 | 1 0 1 0 | | M6 |
| 9 | 1 0 0 1 | | M5 |
| 8 | 1 0 0 0 | C8 | |
| 7 | 0 1 1 1 | | M4 |
| 6 | 0 1 1 0 | | M3 |
| 5 | 0 1 0 1 | | M2 |
| 4 | 0 1 0 0 | C4 | |
| 3 | 0 0 1 1 | | M1 |
| 2 | 0 0 1 0 | C2 | |
| 1 | 0 0 0 1 | C1 | |

**FIGURE 4.12. Layout of data bits and check bits**

Those bit positions whose position numbers are powers of 2 are designated as check bits. The check bits are calculated as follows, where the symbol $\oplus$ designates the exclusive-or operation:

$$C1 = M1 \oplus M2 \oplus \quad\quad M4 \oplus M5 \quad\quad \oplus M7$$
$$C2 = M1 \oplus \quad\quad M3 \oplus M4 \quad\quad \oplus M6 \oplus M7$$
$$C4 = \quad\quad M2 \oplus M3 \oplus M4 \quad\quad\quad\quad \oplus M8$$
$$C8 = \quad\quad\quad\quad\quad\quad M5 \oplus M6 \oplus M7 \oplus M8$$

Each check bit operates on every data bit position whose position number contains a 1 in the corresponding column position. Thus, data bit positions 3, 5, 7, 9, and 11 all contain the term $2^0$; bit positions 3, 6, 7, 10, and 11 all contain the term $2^1$; bit positions 5, 6, 7, and 12 all contain the term $2^2$; and bit positions 9, 10, 11, and 12 all contain the term $2^3$. Looked at another way, bit position $n$ is checked by those bits $C_i$ such that $\Sigma i = n$. For example, position 7 is checked by bits in position 4, 2, and 1; and $7 = 4 + 2 + 1$.

Let us verify that this scheme works with an example. Assume that the 8-bit input word is 00111001, with data bit M1 in the rightmost position. The calculations are as follows:

$$C1 = 1 \oplus 0 \oplus 1 \oplus 1 \oplus 0 = 1$$
$$C2 = 1 \oplus 0 \oplus 1 \oplus 1 \oplus 0 = 1$$
$$C4 = 0 \oplus 0 \oplus 1 \oplus 0 = 1$$
$$C8 = 1 \oplus 1 \oplus 0 \oplus 0 = 0$$

Suppose now that data bit 3 sustains an error and is changed from 0 to 1. When the check bits are recalculated, we have

$$C1 = 1 \oplus 0 \oplus 1 \oplus 1 \oplus 0 = 1$$
$$C2 = 1 \oplus 1 \oplus 1 \oplus 1 \oplus 0 = 0$$
$$C4 = 0 \oplus 1 \oplus 1 \oplus 0 = 0$$
$$C8 = 1 \oplus 1 \oplus 0 \oplus 0 = 0$$

When the new check bits are compared with the old check bits, the syndrome word is formed:

$$
\begin{array}{cccc}
\text{C8} & \text{C4} & \text{C2} & \text{C1} \\
0 & 1 & 1 & 1 \\
\oplus \quad 0 & 0 & 0 & 1 \\
\hline
0 & 1 & 1 & 0
\end{array}
$$

The result is 0110, indicating that bit position 6, which contains data bit 3, is in error.

Figure 4.13 illustrates the above calculation. The data and check bits are positioned properly in the 12-bit word. By laying out the position number of each data bit in columns, the 1s in each row indicate the data bits checked by the check bit for that row. Since the result is affected only by 1s, only the columns containing 1s are circled for identification. The check bits can then be calculated along the rows. The results are shown for the original data bits and for the data bits including the error.

The code just described is known as a *single-error-correcting* (SEC) code. More commonly, semiconductor memory is equipped with a single-error-correcting, double-error-detecting (SEC-DED) code. As Table 4.3 shows, such codes require 1 additional bit compared with SEC codes.

Figure 4.14 illustrates how such a code works, again with a 4-bit data word. The sequence shows that if two errors occur (Figure 4.14c), the checking procedure goes astray (d), and worsens the problem by creating a third error (e). To overcome the problem, an eighth bit is added that is set so that the total number of 1s in the diagram is even. The extra parity bit catches the error (f).

An error-correcting code enhances the reliability of the memory at the cost of added complexity. With a one-bit-per-chip organization, a SEC-DED code is generally considered adequate. For example, the IBM 30xx implementations use an 8-bit SEC-DED code for each 64 bits of data in main memory. Thus, the size of main memory is actually about 12% larger than is apparent to the user. The VAX computers use a 7-bit SEC-DED for each 32 bits of memory, for a 22% overhead.

| Bit Position | 12 | 11 | 10 | 9 | 8 | 7 | 6 | 5 | 4 | 3 | 2 | 1 | |
|---|---|---|---|---|---|---|---|---|---|---|---|---|---|
| Data Bit | M8 | M7 | M6 | M5 | | M4 | M3 | M2 | | M1 | | | |
| Check Bit | | | | | C8 | | | | C4 | | C2 | C1 | |
| | 1 | 1 | 1 | 1 | | 0 | 0 | 0 | 0 | | | | C8 0 |
| | 1 | 0 | 0 | 0 | | 1 | 1 | 1 | 0 | | | | C4 1 |
| | 0 | 1 | 1 | 0 | | 1 | 1 | 0 | 1 | | | | C2 1 |
| | 0 | 1 | 0 | 1 | | 1 | 0 | 1 | 1 | | | | C1 1 |
| Word Stored As: | 0 | 0 | 1 | 1 | 0 | 1 | 0 | 0 | 1 | 1 | 1 | 1 | |
| | | | | | | | | | | | | | |
| Word Fetched As: | 0 | 0 | 1 | 1 | 0 | 1 | 1 | 0 | 1 | 1 | 1 | 1 | |
| | 1 | 1 | 1 | 1 | | 0 | 0 | 0 | 0 | | | | C8 0 |
| | 1 | 0 | 0 | 0 | | 1 | 1 | 1 | 0 | | | | C4 0 |
| | 0 | 1 | 1 | 0 | | 1 | 1 | 0 | 1 | | | | C2 0 |
| | 0 | 1 | 0 | 1 | | 1 | 0 | 1 | 1 | | | | C1 1 |

**FIGURE 4.13. Check bit generation**

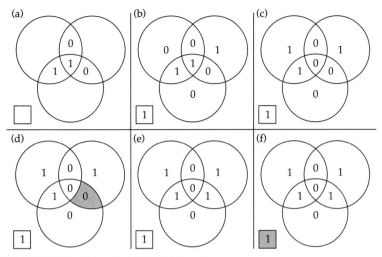

**FIGURE 4.14. Hamming SEC-DED code**

## CACHE MEMORY

### Principles

Cache memory is intended to give memory speed approaching that of the fastest memories available, and at the same time provide a large memory size at the price of less expensive types of semiconductor memories. The concept is illustrated in Figure 4.15. There is a relatively large and slower main memory together with a smaller, faster cache memory. The cache contains a copy of portions of main memory. When the CPU attempts to read a word of memory, a check is made to determine if the word is in the cache. If so, the word is delivered to the CPU. If not, a block of main memory, consisting of some fixed number of words, is read into the cache and then the word is delivered to the CPU. Because of the phenomenon of locality of reference, when a block of data is fetched into the cache to satisfy a single memory reference, it is likely that future references will be to other words in the block.

Figure 4.16 depicts the structure of a cache/main-memory system. Main memory consists of up to $2^n$ addressable words, with each word having a unique $n$-bit address. For mapping purposes, this memory is considered to consist of a number of fixed-length blocks of $K$ words each. That is, there are $M = 2^n/K$ blocks. Cache consists of $C$ slots of $K$ words each, and the number of slots, or *lines*, is considerably less than the number of main memory blocks ($C << M$). At any time, some subset of the blocks of memory resides in slots in the cache. If a word in a block of memory is read, that block is transferred to one of the slots of the cache. Since there are more blocks than slots, an individual slot cannot be uniquely and permanently dedicated to a particular block. Thus, each slot includes a tag that iden-

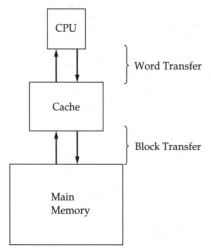

**FIGURE 4.15.  Cache and main memory**

tifies which particular block is currently being stored. The tag is usually a portion of the main memory address, as described later in this section.

Figure 4.17 illustrates the read operation. The CPU generates the address, RA, of a word to be read. If the word is contained in the cache, it is delivered to the CPU. Otherwise, the block containing that word is loaded into the cache, and the word is delivered to the CPU.

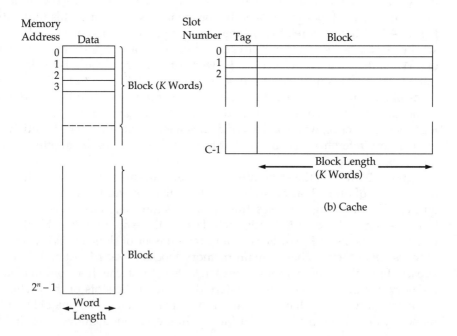

**FIGURE 4.16.  Cache/main memory structure**

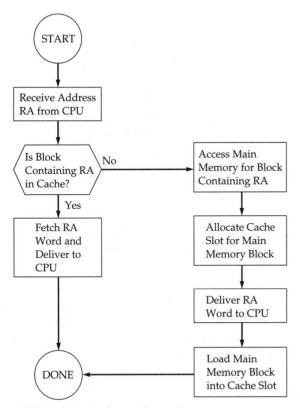

**FIGURE 4.17.  Cache read operation**

A discussion of the performance parameters related to cache use is contained in Appendix 4A.

## Elements of Cache Design

Although there are a large number of cache implementations, there are a few basic design elements that serve to classify and differentiate cache architectures. Table 4.4 lists key elements.

### *Cache Size*

The first element, cache size, has already been discussed. We would like the size of the cache to be small enough so that the overall average cost per bit is close to that of main memory alone and large enough so that the overall average access time is close to that of the cache alone. There are several other motivations for minimizing cache size. The larger the cache, the larger the number of gates involved in addressing the cache. The result is that large caches tend to be slightly slower than small ones—even when built with the same integrated-circuit technology and put in the same place on chip and circuit board. Cache size is also limited by the available chip and board area. In Appendix 4A, we point out that a number of studies

**TABLE 4.4    Elements of Cache Design**

| | |
|---|---|
| **Cache Size** | **Write Policy** |
| **Mapping Function** | Write through |
| Direct | Write back |
| Associative | Write once |
| Set associative | **Block Size** |
| **Replacement Algorithm** | **Number of Caches** |
| Least-recently used (LRU) | Single- or two-level |
| First-in-first-out (FIFO) | Unified or split |
| Least-frequently used (LFU) | |
| Random | |

have suggested that cache sizes of between 1K and 512K words would be optimum. Because the performance of the cache is very sensitive to the nature of the workload, it is impossible to arrive at an "optimum" cache size.

## Mapping Function

Since there are fewer cache lines than main memory blocks, an algorithm is needed for mapping main memory blocks into cache lines. Further, a means is needed for determining which main memory block currently occupies a cache line. The choice of the mapping function dictates how the cache is organized. Three techniques can be used: direct, associative, and set associative. We examine each of these in turn. In each case, we look at the general structure and then a specific example. For all three cases, the example includes the following elements:

1. The cache can hold 64 KBytes.
2. Data is transferred between main memory and the cache in blocks of 4 bytes each. This means that the cache is organized as 16K = $2^{14}$ lines of 4 bytes each.
3. The main memory consists of 16 Mbytes, with each byte directly addressable by a 24-bit address ($2^{24}$ = 16M). Thus, for mapping purposes, we can consider main memory to consist of 4M blocks of 4 bytes each.

### Direct Mapping

The simplest technique, known as direct mapping, maps each block of main memory into only one possible cache line. Figure 4.18 illustrates the general mechanism. The mapping is expressed as

$i = j$ modulo $m$

where

$i$ = cache line number
$j$ = main memory block number
$m$ = number of lines in the cache

The mapping function is easily implemented using the address. For purposes of cache access, each main memory address can be viewed as consisting of three fields.

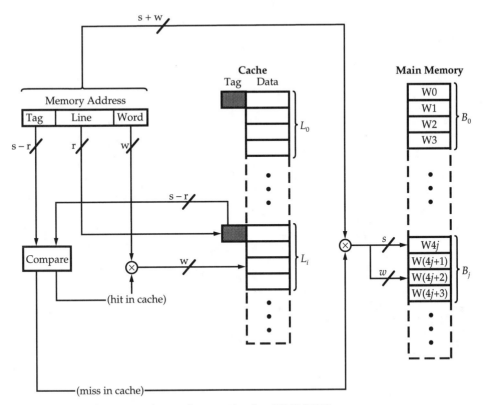

**FIGURE 4.18.  Direct-mapping cache organization [HWAN93]**

The least significant $w$ bits identify a unique word or byte within a block of main memory; in most contemporary machines, the address is at the byte level. The remaining $s$ bits specify one of the $2^s$ blocks of main memory. The cache logic interprets these $s$ bits as a tag of $s - r$ bits (most significant portion) and a line field of $r$ bits. This latter field identifies one of the $m = 2^r$ lines of the cache. The effect of this mapping is that blocks of main memory are assigned to lines of the cache as follows:

| Cache line | Main memory blocks assigned |
|:---:|:---:|
| 0 | $0, m, \ldots, 2^s - m$ |
| 1 | $1, m + 1, \ldots, 2^s - m + 1$ |
| . | . |
| . | . |
| . | . |
| $m - 1$ | $m - 1, 2m - 1, \ldots, 2^s - 1$ |

Thus, the use of a portion of the address as a line number provides a unique mapping of each block of main memory into the cache. When a block is actually read into its assigned line, it is necessary to tag the data to distinguish it from other blocks that can fit into that line. The most significant $s - r$ bits serve this purpose.

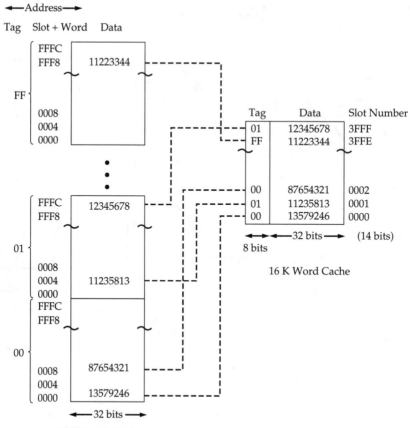

FIGURE 4.19.  Direct mapping example

Figure 4.19 shows our example system using direct mapping.[2] In the example, $m$ = $16K$ = $2^{14}$ and $i = j$ modulo $2^{14}$. The mapping becomes

| Cache line | Main memory blocks assigned |
|------------|-----------------------------|
| 0 | 000000, 010000, ..., FF0000 |
| 1 | 000001, 010001, ..., FF0001 |
| . | . |
| . | . |
| . | . |
| 3FFF | 00FFFC, 01FFFC, ..., FFFFFC |

[2]In the figure, addresses and memory values are represented in hexadecimal notation for convenience. For the reader unfamiliar with this notation, see the appendix to Chapter 8.

Note that no two blocks that map into the same line number have the same tag number. Thus, blocks 000000, 010000, . . ., FF0000 have tag numbers 00, 01, . . ., FF, respectively.

Referring back to Figure 4.17, a read operation works as follows. The cache system is presented with a 24-bit address. The 14-bit line number is used as an index into the cache to access a particular line. If the 8-bit tag number matches the tag number currently stored in that line, then the 2-bit word number is used to select one of the four bytes in that line. Otherwise, the 22-bit tag-plus-line field is used to fetch a block from main memory. The actual address that is used for the fetch is the 22-bit tag-plus-line concatenated with two 0 bits, so that four bytes are fetched starting on a block boundary.

The direct mapping technique is simple and inexpensive to implement. Its main disadvantage is that there is a fixed cache location for any given block. Thus, if a program happens to repeatedly reference words from two different blocks that map into the same line, then the blocks will be continually swapped in the cache, and the hit ratio will be low.

### Associative Mapping

Associative mapping overcomes the disadvantage of direct mapping by permitting each main memory block to be loaded into any line of the cache. In this case, the cache control logic interprets a memory address simply as a tag and a word field. The tag field uniquely identifies a block of main memory. To determine whether a block is in the cache, the cache control logic must simultaneously examine every line's tag for a match. Figure 4.20 illustrates the logic.

Figure 4.21 shows our example using associative mapping. A main memory address consists of a 22-bit tag and a 2-bit byte number. The 22-bit tag must be stored with the 32-bit block of data for each line in the cache.

With associative mapping, there is flexibility as to which block to replace when a new block is read into the cache. Replacement algorithms, discussed later in this section, are designed to maximize the hit ratio. The principal disadvantage of associative mapping is the complex circuitry required to examine the tags of all cache lines in parallel.

### Set Associative Mapping

Set associative mapping is a compromise that exhibits the strengths of both the direct and associative approaches without their disadvantages. In this case, the cache is divided into $v$ sets, each of which consists of $k$ lines. The relationships are

$$m = v \times k$$
$$i = j \text{ modulo } v$$

where

$i$ = cache set number
$j$ = main memory block number
$m$ = number of lines in the cache

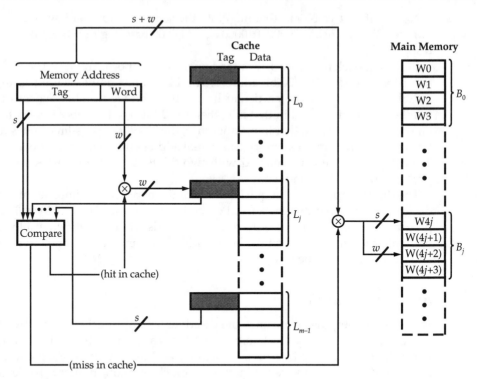

**FIGURE 4.20. Fully associative cache organization**

With the set associative mapping block $B_j$ can be mapped into any of the lines of set $i$. In this case, the cache control logic interprets a memory address simply as three fields: tag, set, and word. The $d$ set bits specify one of $v = 2^d$ sets. The $s$ bits of the tag and set fields specify one of the $2^s$ blocks of main memory. Figure 4.22 illustrates the cache control logic.

Figure 4.23 shows our example using set associative mapping with two lines in each set, referred to as two-way set associative. The 13-bit set number identifies a unique set of two lines within the cache. It also gives the number of the block in main memory, modulo $2^{13}$. This determines the mapping of blocks into lines. Thus, blocks 000000, 00A000, . . ., FF1000 of main memory map into cache set 0. Any of those blocks can be loaded into either of the two lines in the set. Note that no two blocks that map into the same cache set have the same tag number. For a read operation, the 13-bit set number is used to determine which set of two lines is to be examined. Both lines in the set are examined for a match with the tag number of the address to be accessed.

In the extreme case of $v = m, k = 1$, the set associative technique reduces to direct mapping, and for $v = 1, k = m$, it reduces to associative mapping. The use of two lines per set ($v = m/2, k = 2$) is the most common set associative organization. It significantly improves the hit ratio over direct mapping. Four-way set associative ($v = m/4, k = 4$) makes a modest additional improvement for a relatively small

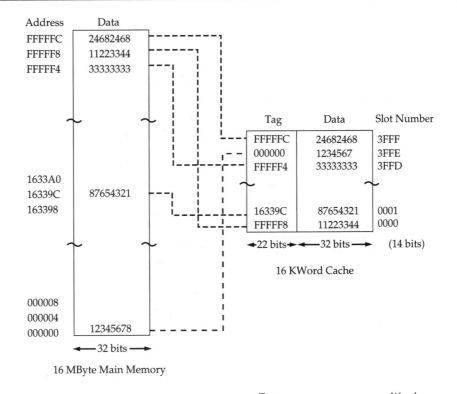

**FIGURE 4.21.** **Associative mapping example**

additional cost [MAYB84, HILL89]. Further increases in the number of lines per set have little effect.

### Replacement Algorithms

When a new block is brought into the cache, one of the existing blocks must be replaced. For direct mapping, there is only one possible slot for any particular block, and no choice is possible. For the associative and set associative techniques, a replacement algorithm is needed. To achieve high speed, such an algorithm must be implemented in hardware. A number of algorithms have been tried: we mention four of the most common. Probably the most effective is **least-recently used (LRU):** Replace that block in the set which has been in the cache longest with no reference to it. For two-way set associative, this is easily implemented. Each slot includes a USE bit. When a slot is referenced, its USE bit is set to 1 and the USE bit of the other slot in that set is set to 0. When a block is to be read into the set, the slot whose USE bit is 0 is used. Since we are assuming that more-recently used

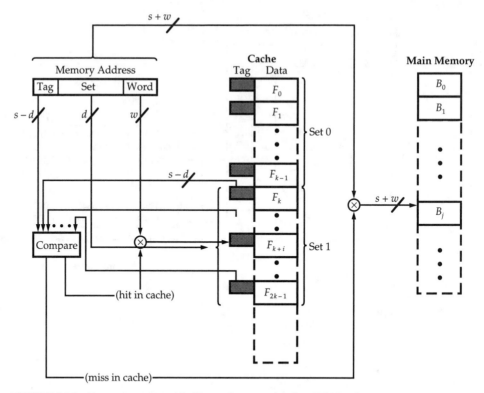

**FIGURE 4.22.  Two-way set associative cache organization [HWAN93]**

memory locations are more likely to be referenced, LRU should give the best hit ratio. Another possibility is **first-in-first-out (FIFO)**: Replace that block in the set which has been in the cache longest. FIFO is easily implemented as a round-robin or circular buffer technique. Still another possibility is **least-frequently used (LFU)**: replace that block in the set which has experienced the fewest references. LFU could be implemented by associating a counter with each slot. A technique not based on usage is to just pick a slot from among the candidate slots at **random.** Simulation studies have shown that random replacement provides only slightly inferior performance to an algorithm based on usage [SMIT82].

## *Write Policy*

Before a block that is resident in the cache can be replaced, it is necessary to consider whether it has been altered in the cache but not in main memory. If it has not, then the old block in the cache may be overwritten. If it has, that means that at least one write operation has been performed on a word in that slot of the cache, and main memory must be updated accordingly. A variety of write policies, with performance and economic trade-offs, are possible. There are two problems to contend with. First, more than one device may have access to main memory. For

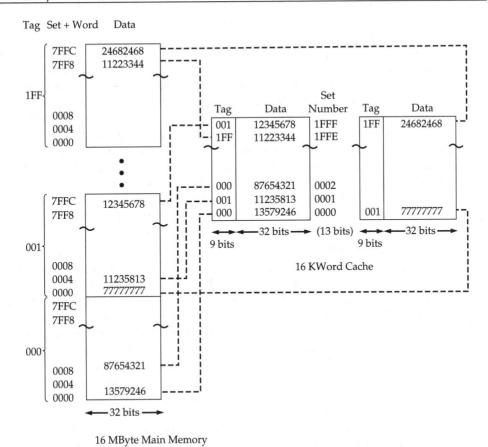

FIGURE 4.23. **Two-way set associative mapping**

example, an I/O module may be able to read/write directly to memory. If a word has been altered only in the cache, then the corresponding memory word is invalid. Further, if the I/O device has altered main memory, then the cache word is invalid. A more complex problem occurs when multiple CPUs are attached to the same bus and each CPU has its own local cache. Then, if a word is altered in one cache, it could conceivably invalidate a word in other caches.

The simplest technique is called **write through.** Using this technique, all write operations are made to main memory as well as to the cache, ensuring that main memory is always valid. Any other CPU–cache module can monitor traffic to main memory to maintain consistency within its own cache. The main disadvantage of this technique is that it generates substantial memory traffic and may create a bottleneck. An alternative technique, known as **write back,** minimizes memory writes.

With write back, updates are made only in the cache. When an update occurs, an UPDATE bit associated with the slot is set. Then, when a block is replaced, it is written back to main memory if and only if the UPDATE bit is set. The problem with write back is that portions of main memory are invalid, and hence accesses by I/O modules can be allowed only through the cache. This makes for complex circuitry and a potential bottleneck. Experience has shown that the percentage of memory references that are writes is on the order of 15 percent [SMIT82].

In a bus organization in which more than one device (typically a processor) has a cache and main memory is shared, a new problem is introduced. If data in one cache is altered, this invalidates not only the corresponding word in main memory, but also that same word in other caches (if any other cache happens to have that same word). Even if a write-through policy is used, the other caches may contain invalid data. A system that prevents this problem is said to maintain cache coherency. Possible approaches to cache coherency include

- *Bus Watching with Write Through:* Each cache controller monitors the address lines to detect write operations to memory by other bus masters. If another master writes to a location in shared memory that also resides in the cache memory, the cache controller invalidates that cache entry. This strategy depends on the use of a write-through policy by all cache controllers.
- *Hardware Transparency:* Additional hardware is used to ensure that all updates to main memory via cache are reflected in all caches. Thus, if one processor modifies a word in its cache, this update is written to main memory. In addition, any matching words in other caches are similarly updated.
- *Non-cachable Memory:* Only a portion of main memory is shared by more than one processor, and this is designated as non-cachable. In such a system, all accesses to shared memory are cache misses, because the shared memory is never copied into the cache. The non-cachable memory can be identified using chip-select logic or high-address bits.

Cache coherency is an active field of research, and it is likely that simpler and more effective ways of ensuring consistency will be developed in the next several years.

## Block Size

Another design element is the block, or line, size. When a block of data is retrieved and placed in the cache, not only the desired word but some number of adjacent words are retrieved. As the block size increases from very small to larger sizes, the hit ratio will at first increase because of the principle of locality: the high probability that data in the vicinity of a referenced word is likely to be referenced in the near future. As the block size increases, more useful data is brought into the cache. The hit ratio will begin to decrease, however, as the block becomes even bigger and the probability of using the newly fetched information becomes less than the probability of reusing the information that has to be replaced. Two specific effects come into play:

1. Larger blocks reduce the number of blocks that fit into a cache. Because each block fetch overwrites older cache contents, a small number of blocks results in data being overwritten shortly after it is fetched.

2. As a block becomes larger, each additional word is farther from the requested word, therefore less likely to be needed in the near future.

The relationship between block size and hit ratio is complex, depending on the locality characteristics of a particular program, and no definitive optimum value has been found. A size of from 4 to 8 addressable units (words or bytes) seems reasonably close to optimum [SMIT87a, PRZY88, PRZY90].

## Number of Caches

When caches were originally introduced, the typical system had a single cache. More recently, the use of multiple caches has become the norm. Two aspects of this design issue concern the number of levels of caches and the use of unified versus split caches.

### Single- Versus Two-Level Caches

As logic density has increased, it has become possible to have a cache on the same chip as the processor: the on-chip cache. Compared with a cache reachable via an external bus, the on-chip cache reduces the processor's external bus activity and therefore speeds up execution times and increases overall system performance. When the requested instruction or data is found in the on-chip cache, the bus access is eliminated. Because of the short data paths internal to the processor, compared with bus lengths, on-chip cache accesses will complete appreciably faster than would even zero-wait state bus cycles. Furthermore, during this period the bus is free to support other transfers.

The inclusion of an on-chip cache leaves open the question of whether an off-chip, or external, cache is still desirable. Typically, the answer is yes, and most contemporary designs include both on-chip and external caches. The resulting organization is known as a two-level cache, with the internal cache designated as level 1 (L1) and the external cache designated as level 2 (L2). The reason for including an L2 cache is the following. If there is no L2 cache and the processor makes an access request for a memory location not in the L1 cache, then the processor must access DRAM or ROM memory across the bus. Due to the typically slow bus speed and slow memory access time, this results in poor performance. On the other hand, if an L2 SRAM cache is used, then frequently the missing information can be quickly retrieved. If the SRAM is fast enough to match the bus speed, then the data can be accessed using a zero-wait state transaction, the fastest type of bus transfer.

The potential savings due to the use of an L2 cache depends on the hit rates in both the L1 and L2 caches. Several studies have shown that, in general, the use of a second-level cache does improve performance (e.g., see [AZIM92], [NOVI93]).

### Unified Versus Split Cache

When the on-chip cache first made an appearance, many of the designs consisted of a single cache used to store references to both data and instructions. More recently, it has become common to split the cache into two: one dedicated to instructions and one dedicated to data.

There are several potential advantages of a unified cache:

1. For a given cache size, a unified cache has a higher hit rate than split caches because it balances the load between instruction and data fetches automatically. That is, if an execution pattern involves many more instruction fetches than data fetches, then the cache will tend to fill up with instructions, and if an execution pattern involves relatively more data fetches, the opposite will occur.
2. Only one cache needs to be designed and implemented.

Despite these advantages, the trend is toward split caches, particularly for superscalar machines such as the Pentium and PowerPC, which emphasize parallel instruction execution and the prefetching of predicted future instructions. The key advantage of the split cache design is that it eliminates contention for the cache between the instruction processor and the execution unit. This is important in any design that relies on the pipelining of instructions. Typically, the processor will fetch instructions ahead of time and fill a buffer, or pipeline, with instructions to be executed. Suppose now that we have a unified instruction/data cache. When the execution unit performs a memory access to load and store data, the request is submitted to the unified cache. If, at the same time, the instruction prefetcher issues a read request to the cache for an instruction, that request will be temporarily blocked so that the cache can service the execution unit first, enabling it to complete the currently executing instruction. This cache contention can degrade performance by interfering with efficient use of the instruction pipeline. The split cache structure overcomes this difficulty.

## Pentium Cache Organization

The evolution of cache organization is seen clearly in the evolution of Intel microprocessors. The 80386 does not include an on-chip cache. The 80486 includes a single on-chip cache of 8 KBytes, using a line size of 16 bytes and a four-way set associative organization. The Pentium includes two on-chip caches, one for data and one for instructions. Each cache is 8 KBytes, using a line size of 32 bytes and a two-way set associative organization.

Figure 4.24 provides a simplified view of the Pentium organization, highlighting the placement of the two caches. The core execution units are two integer arithmetic and logic units, which can execute in parallel, and a floating-point unit with its own registers and its own multiply, add, and divide components. The data cache feeds both integer and floating-point operations. The data cache is dual-ported. The two 32-bit ports can be used to separately interface to the two integer ALU units and can be combined for a 64-bit interface to the floating-point unit. The code cache, which is read-only, feeds into a prefetch buffer; the operation of the instruction pipeline is discussed in Chapter 13.

Figure 4.25 depicts the key elements of the internal data cache. The data in the cache consist of 128 sets of two lines each. This is logically organized as two 4 KByte "ways." Associated with each line is a tag and two state bits; these are logi-

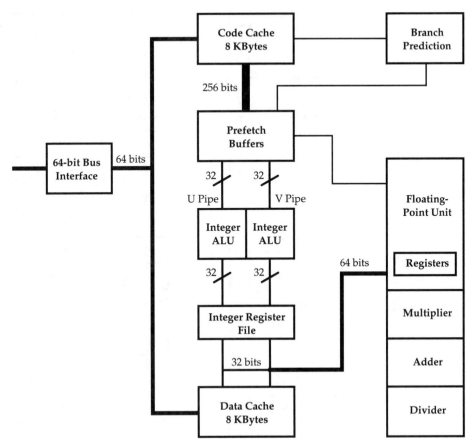

**FIGURE 4.24. Pentium processor block diagram**

cally organized into two directories, so that there is one directory entry for each line of the cache. The tag is the 20 most significant bits of the memory address of the data stored in the corresponding line. The cache controller uses a least-recently-used (LRU) replacement algorithm, and so a single LRU bit is associated with each set of two lines.

The data cache employs a write-back policy: data is written to main memory only when it is removed from the cache and there has been an update. The Pentium processor can be dynamically configured to support write-through caching.

The Pentium processor supports the use of an external level 2 cache. This cache may be 256 or 512 KBytes, using a 32-, 64-, or 128-byte line. The external cache is two-way set associative.

### Data Cache Consistency

To provide cache consistency, the data cache supports a protocol known as MESI (modified/exclusive/shared/invalid). MESI is designed to support the cache con-

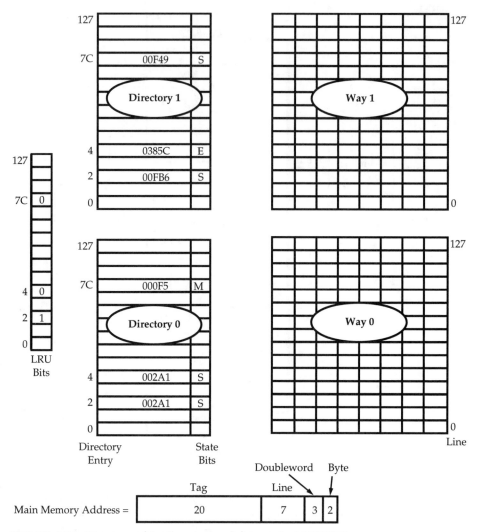

**FIGURE 4.25. Structure of Pentium internal data cache [ANDE93]**

sistency requirements of a multiprocessor system, but it is also useful in a single-processor Pentium organization.

The data cache includes two status bits per tag, so that each line can be in one of four states:

- *Modified:* The line in the cache has been modified (different from main memory) and is available only in this cache.
- *Exclusive:* The line in the cache is the same as that in main memory and is not present in any other cache.
- *Shared:* The line in the cache is the same as that in main memory and may be present in another cache.
- *Invalid:* The line in the cache does not contain valid data.

**TABLE 4.5    MESI Cache Line States**

|  | M<br>Modified | E<br>Exclusive | S<br>Shared | I<br>Invalid |
|---|---|---|---|---|
| This cache line valid? | Yes | Yes | Yes | No |
| The memory copy is... | out of date | valid | valid | — |
| Copies exist in other<br>   caches? | No | No | Maybe | Maybe |
| A write to this line... | does not go<br>to bus | does not go<br>to bus | goes to bus<br>and updates cache | goes directly<br>to bus |

Table 4.5 summarizes the meaning of the four states. Let us first consider the action in the single-processor case.[3] Here, the concern is the interaction between the level 1 and level 2 caches. A cache line begins in an initial state of invalid (I), after a reset. When new data is read into the invalid line, that data will be retrieved from main memory and stored first in the L2 cache and then into the L1 data cache. The state of the line in the L1 cache becomes shared (S). Subsequent reads do not affect the cache state.

Now suppose that one of the execution units writes to this line. The line in the L1 cache will be updated. At this point, the line in the L2 cache is obsolete. To avoid a cache inconsistency, the first time that the line is updated in L1, the write operation is written through to the L2 cache, and the state of the L1 line is changed to exclusive (E). After that, a subsequent update to the line in L1 moves it to the modified (M) state. For any further updates, the line remains in the M state, and for all of these subsequent updates, there is no transfer to L2. Thus, this is known as a write-once policy. Finally, when it is necessary to replace a line in the L1 cache, if it is in the S or E state, it need not be written out. If it is in the M state, the line is written back to the L2 cache and then flushed from the L1 cache. When new data is read into that L1 line, the line is marked in the S state, as before.

The operation from the point of view of the L2 cache is more complex. When a line is first read into the L1 and L2 caches, the line in the L2 cache is marked in the E state, indicating that the data is exclusive to the L2 cache and its associated processor and L1 cache. When a write-once occurs, the L2 updates the line and puts it in the M state. The L2 cache will not be notified of any subsequent updates to this line by the L1 cache. Accordingly, if another bus master attempts to read data stored in an L2 line that is in the M state, the L2 cache causes the bus master to back off and passes the requested address to the Pentium processor. The Pentium processor performs a write-back cycle to update main memory. The L2 cache then releases the bus master to perform its read operation.

If another bus master attempts to write data that is in an L2 line in the M state, then again, the L2 cache logic temporarily blocks the action. The L2 must assure that operations are performed in the proper sequence. The L2 cannot simply flush its line and let the operation proceed, because the other bus master may update a

---

[3]The discussion assumes that both the L1 and L2 caches are configured for the write-back policy, which is the typical state of affairs.

different portion of the line than was modified in the L2 line. Therefore, the L2 line must be written out to main memory before the other write takes place. But before that can take place, the L2 must determine if the corresponding line in the L1 cache has been updated since the write-once. So the correct sequence is the following:

1. The L2 cache detects and blocks the write operation.
2. The L2 signals the L1 cache with the address of the write operation. If the L1 has been updated since the write-once, it performs a write through to main memory. In any case, it declares the affected line invalid (I state).
3. If the L1 has not performed a write through, the L2 cache updates main memory. In any case, it declares the affected line invalid (I state).
4. The L2 releases the bus master, allowing it to complete the write operation.

We return to the MESI protocol in Chapter 16 and examine its operation in a multiprocessor configuration.

### Cache Control

The internal cache is controlled by two bits in one of the control registers, labeled the CD (cache disable) and NW (not writethrough) bits (Table 4.6). There are also two Pentium instructions that can be used to control the cache: INVD flushes the cache memory and signals the external cache (if any) to flush. WBINVD performs the same function and also signals an external write-back cache to write back modified blocks before flushing.

## PowerPC Cache Organization

The PowerPC cache organization has undergone a modification with each new model in the PowerPC family, reflecting the relentless pursuit of performance that is the driving force for all microprocessor designers.

Table 4.7 shows this evolution. The original model, the 601, includes a single code/data 32-KByte cache that is eight-way set associative. The 603 employs a more sophisticated RISC design but has a smaller cache: 16 KBytes divided into separate instruction and data caches, both using two-way set associative organization. The result is that the 603 gives approximately the same performance as the 601 at lower cost. The 604 and 620 each doubled the size of the caches from the preceding model.

**TABLE 4.6   Pentium Cache Operating Modes**

| Control Bits | | Operating Mode | | |
|---|---|---|---|---|
| CD | NW | Cache Fills | Write-Throughs | Invalidates |
| 0 | 0 | Enabled | Enabled | Enabled |
| 1 | 0 | Disabled | Enabled | Enabled |
| 1 | 1 | Disabled | Disabled | Disabled |

Note: CD=0; NW=1 is an invalid combination.

**TABLE 4.7    PowerPC Internal Caches**

| Model | Size | Bytes/Line | Organization |
|-------|------|------------|--------------|
| PowerPC 601 | 1 32-KByte | 32 | 8-way set associative |
| PowerPC 603 | 2 8-KByte | 32 | 2-way set associative |
| PowerPC 604 | 2 16-KByte | 32 | 4-way set associative |
| PowerPC 620 | 2 32-KByte | 64 | 8-way set associative |

Figure 4.26 provides a simplified view of the PowerPC 620 organization, high-lighting the placement of the two caches; the organization of the other members of the family is similar. The core execution units are three integer arithmetic and logic units, which can execute in parallel, and a floating-point unit with its own registers and its own multiply, add, and divide components. The data cache feeds both integer and floating-point operations via a load/store unit. The instruction cache, which is read-only, feeds into an instruction unit, whose operation is discussed in Chapter 12.

The internal caches are eight-way set associative and use the MESI cache coherency protocol. The protocol is extended to include a new state called Allocated (A). This state is used when a block of data in a line is swapped out and replaced. The state is A until the old data are written out and the new data written in. At that point, the state moves to S or E depending on circumstances (Figure 4.27).

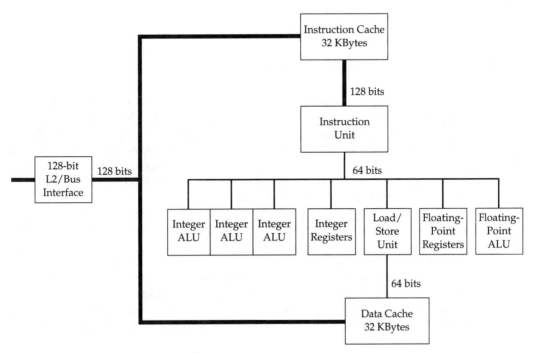

**FIGURE 4.26. PowerPC 620 block diagram**

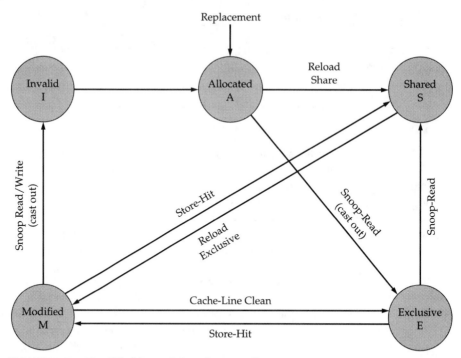

**FIGURE 4.27. Simplified PowerPC cache state diagram**

## ADVANCED DRAM ORGANIZATION

As was discussed in Chapter 2, one of the most critical system bottlenecks when using high-performance processors is the interface to main internal memory. This interface is the most important pathway in the entire computer system. The basic building block of main memory remains the DRAM chip, as it has for more than 20 years, and until recently, there had been no significant changes in DRAM architecture since the early 1970s. The traditional DRAM chip is constrained both by its internal architecture and by its interface to the processor's memory bus.

We have seen that one attack on the performance problem of DRAM main memory has been to insert one or more levels of high-speed SRAM cache between the DRAM main memory and the processor. But SRAM is much costlier than DRAM, and expanding cache size beyond a certain point yields diminishing returns.

In the past few years, a number of enhancements to the basic DRAM architecture have been explored, and some of these are now on the market. It is not clear at this point whether one of these will emerge as the unique DRAM standard or whether several will survive. This section provides a survey of these new DRAM technologies.

## Enhanced DRAM

Perhaps the simplest of the new DRAM architectures is the enhanced DRAM (EDRAM), developed by Ramtron [BOND94]. The EDRAM integrates a small SRAM cache onto a generic DRAM chip.

Figure 4.28 illustrates a 4-Mbit version of the EDRAM. The SRAM cache stores the entire contents of the last row read, which consists of 2048 bits, or 512 4-bit chunks. A comparator stores the 11-bit value of the most recent row address selection. If the next access is to the same row, then access need only be made to the fast SRAM cache.

The EDRAM includes several other features that improve performance. Refresh operations can be conducted in parallel with cache read operations, minimizing the time that the chip is unavailable due to refresh. Also note that the read path from the row cache to the output port is independent of the write path from the I/O module to the sense amplifiers. This enables a subsequent read access to the cache to be satisfied in parallel with the completion of the write operation.

Studies done by Ramtron indicate that the EDRAM performs as well as or better than an ordinary DRAM with an external (to the DRAM) but larger SRAM cache.

## Cache DRAM

The cache DRAM (CDRAM), developed by Mitsubishi [HIDA90], is similar to the EDRAM. The CDRAM includes a larger SRAM cache than the EDRAM (16 vs. 2 Kb).

The SRAM on the CDRAM can be used in two ways. First, it can be used as a true cache, consisting of a number of 64-bit lines. This is in contrast to the EDRAM, in which the SRAM cache only contains one block, namely the most recently accessed row. The cache mode of the CDRAM is effective for ordinary random access to memory.

The SRAM on the CDRAM can also be used as a buffer to support the serial access of a block of data. For example, to refresh a bit-mapped screen, the CDRAM can prefetch the data from the DRAM into the SRAM buffer. Subsequent accesses to the chip result in accesses solely to the SRAM.

## Synchronous DRAM

A quite different approach to improving DRAM performance is the synchronous DRAM (SDRAM), which is being jointly developed by a number of companies [VOGL94].

Unlike the typical DRAM, which is asynchronous, the SDRAM exchanges data with the processor synchronized to an external clock signal and running at the full speed of the processor/memory bus without imposing wait states.

In a typical DRAM, the processor presents addresses and control levels to the memory, indicating that a set of data at a particular location in memory should be either read from or written into the DRAM. After a delay, the access time, the DRAM either writes or reads the data. During the access-time delay, the DRAM

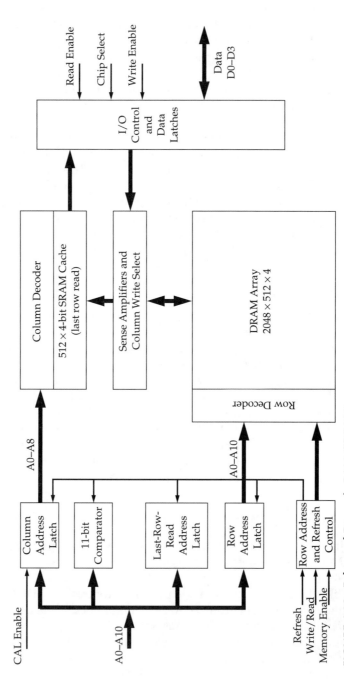

**FIGURE 4.28. Enhanced Dynamic RAM (EDRAM)**

performs various internal functions, such as activating the high capacitance of the row and column lines, sensing the data, and routing the data out through the output buffers. The processor must simply wait through this delay, slowing system performance.

With synchronous access, the DRAM moves data in and out under control of the system clock. The processor or other master issues the instruction and address information, which is latched by the DRAM. The DRAM then responds after a set number of clock cycles. Meanwhile, the master can safely do other tasks while the SDRAM is processing the request.

Figure 4.29 shows the internal logic of the SDRAM. The SDRAM employs a burst mode to eliminate the address setup time and row and column line

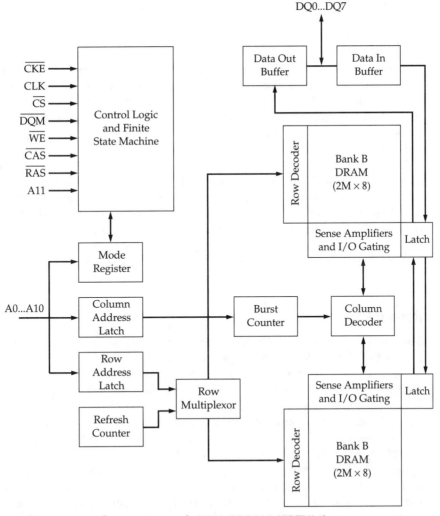

**FIGURE 4.29. Synchronous Dynamic RAM (SDRAM) [PRZY94]**

precharge time after the first access. In burst mode, a series of data bits can be clocked out rapidly after the first bit has been accessed. This mode is useful when all the bits to be accessed are in sequence and in the same row of the array as the initial access.

In addition, the SDRAM has a dual-bank internal architecture that improves opportunities for on-chip parallelism.

The mode register and associated control logic is another key feature differentiating SDRAMs from conventional DRAMs. It provides a mechanism to customize the SDRAM to suit specific system needs. The mode register specifies the burst length, which is the number of separate units of data synchronously fed onto the bus. The register also allows the programmer to adjust the latency between receipt of a read request and the beginning of data transfer.

The SDRAM performs best when it is transferring large blocks of data serially, such as for applications like word processing, spreadsheets, and multimedia.

## Rambus DRAM

RDRAM, developed by Rambus [GARR94], takes a more revolutionary approach to the memory-bandwidth problem. RDRAM chips are vertical packages, with all pins on one side. The chip exchanges data with the processor over 28 wires no more than 12 centimeters long. The bus can address up to 320 RDRAM chips and is rated at 500 Mbps. That compares with about 33 Mbps for asynchronous DRAMs.

The special RDRAM bus delivers address and control information using an asynchronous block-oriented protocol. After an initial 480 ns access time, this produces the 500 Mbps data rate. What makes this speed possible is the bus itself, which defines impedances, clocking, and signals very precisely. Rather than being controlled by the explicit RAS, CAS, R/W, and CE signals used in conventional DRAMs, an RDRAM gets a memory request over the high-speed bus. This request contains the desired address, the type of operation, and the number of bytes in the operation.

## RamLink

The most radical change from the traditional DRAM is found in the RamLink product [GJES92], developed as part of an IEEE working group effort called the Scalable Coherent Interface (SCI). The RamLink concentrates on the processor/memory interface rather than the internal architecture of the DRAM chips.

RamLink is a memory interface with point-to-point connections arranged in a ring (Figure 4.30a). Traffic on the ring is managed by a memory controller that sends messages to the DRAM chips, which act as nodes on the ring network. Data is exchanged in the form of packets (Figure 4.30b).

Request packets initiate memory transactions. They are sent by the controller and contain a command header, address, checksum, and in the case of write commands, the data to be written. The command header consists of type, size, and control information and contains either a specific response time or the maximum

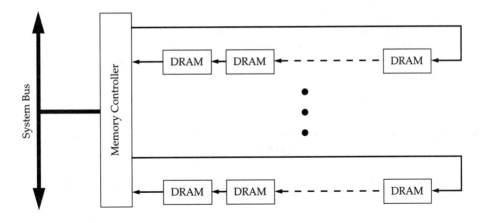

(a) RamLink Architecture

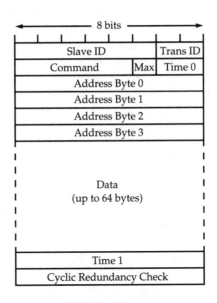

(b) Packet Format

**FIGURE 4.30. RamLink**

time allowed for the slave to respond. The control information includes a bit that indicates whether subsequent requests will be to sequential addresses. Up to four transactions per device can be active simultaneously; thus, all packets have a two-bit transaction ID to unambiguously match request and response packets.

For a successful read, the DRAM slave sends a response packet that includes the read data. For an unsuccessful request, the slave issues a retry packet that indicates how much additional time it needs to complete the transaction.

One of the strengths of the RamLink approach is that it provides a scalable architecture that supports a small or large number of DRAMs and does not dictate internal DRAM structure. The RamLink ring arrangement is designed to coordinate the activity of many DRAMs and provide an efficient interface to the memory controller.

## 4.5

## RECOMMENDED READING

[PRIN91] provides a comprehensive treatment of semiconductor memory technologies, including SRAM, DRAM, and flash memories.

A good explanation of error-correcting codes is contained in [MCEL85]; another good treatment is [HEGD92]. For a deeper study, worthwhile book-length treatments are [ADAM91] and [BLAH83].

A thorough treatment of cache design is to be found in [HAND93]. Many computer architecture texts also offer useful treatments of cache design; one of the more detailed and clearest accounts is in [ALEX93].

Detailed descriptions of Pentium cache organization can be found in [ANDE93] and [INTE94a], and of PowerPC cache organization in [SHAN94b] and [WEIS94]. A classic paper that is still well worth reading is [SMIT82]; it surveys the various elements of cache design and presents the results of an extensive set of analyses. A detailed examination of a variety of cache design issues related to multiprogramming and multiprocessing is presented in [AGAR89]. [HIGB90] provides a set of simple formulas that can be used to estimate cache performance as a function of various cache parameters.

ADAM91    Adamek, J. *Foundations of Coding.* New York: Wiley, 1991.

AGAR89    Agarwal, A. *Analysis of Cache Performance for Operating Systems and Multiprogramming.* Boston: Kluwer Academic Publishers, 1989.

ALEX93    Alexandridis, N. *Design of Microprocessor-Based Systems.* Englewood Cliffs, NJ: Prentice Hall, 1993.

ANDE93    Anderson, D., and Shanley, T. *Pentium Processor System Architecture.* Richardson, TX: Mindshare Press, 1993.

BLAH83    Blahut, R. *Theory and Practice of Error Control Codes.* Reading, MA: Addison-Wesley, 1983.

HAND93    Handy, J. *The Cache Memory Book.* San Diego: Academic Press, 1993.

HEGD92    Hedge, A. "Detect/Correct Errors to Improve Data Reliability." *Electronic Design,* June 11, 1992.

HIGB90    Higbie, L. "Quick and Easy Cache Performance Analysis." *Computer Architecture News,* June 1990.

INTE94a   Intel Corp. *Pentium Family User's Manual, Volume 1: Data Book.* Santa Clara, CA, 1994.

MCEL85    McEliece, R. "The Reliability of Computer Memories." *Scientific American,* January 1985.

PRIN91   Prince, B. *Semiconductor Memories.* New York: Wiley, 1991.

SHAN94b   Shanley, T. *PowerPC 601 System Architecture.* Richardson, TX: Mindshare Press, 1994.

SMIT82   Smith, A. "Cache Memories." *ACM Computing Surveys,* September 1982.

WEIS94   Weiss, S., and Smith, J. *POWER and PowerPC.* San Francisco: Morgan Kaufmann, 1994.

## 4.6

## PROBLEMS

4.1. Draw a configuration showing a processor, four 1K × 8-bit ROMs, and a bus containing 12 address lines and 8 data lines. Add a chip-select logic block that will select one of the four ROM modules for each of the 4K addresses.

4.2 Suggest reasons that RAMs traditionally have been organized as only one bit per chip whereas ROMs are usually organized with multiple bits per chip.

4.3 The address lines shown in Figure 4.7 are multiplexed so that only half as many lines are needed as for dedicated address lines. Would you expect that this arrangement results in a time penalty? If not, justify the assertion that there would be no time penalty.

4.4 Consider a dynamic RAM that must be given a refresh cycle 64 times per ms. Each refresh operation requires 150 ns; a memory cycle requires 250 ns. What percentage of the memory's total operating time must be given to refreshes?

4.5 Design a 16-bit memory of total capacity 8192 bits using SRAM chips of size 64 × 1 bit. Give the array configuration of the chips on the memory board, showing all required input and output signals for assigning this memory to the lowest address space. The design should allow for both byte and 16-bit word accesses.
Source: [ALEX93]

4.6 Develop an SEC code for a 16-bit data word. Generate the code for the data word 0101000000111001. Show that the code will correctly identify an error in data bit 4.

4.7 A set associative cache consists of 64 lines, or slots, divided into 4-slot sets. Main memory contains 4K blocks of 128 words each. Show the format of main memory addresses.

4.8 Consider a 32-bit microprocessor that has an on-chip 16 KByte four-way set associative cache. Assume that the cache has a line size of four 32-bit words. Draw a block diagram of this cache showing its organization and how the different address fields are used to determine a cache hit/miss. Where in the cache is the word from memory location ABCDE8F8 mapped?
Source: [ALEX93]

4.9 Given the following specifications for an external cache memory: four-way set associative; line size of two 16-bit words; able to accommodate a total of 4K 32-bit words from main memory; used with a 16-bit processor that issues

24-bit addresses. Design the cache structure with all pertinent information, and show how it interprets the processor's addresses.
Source: [ALEX93]

4.10 The Intel 80486 has an on-chip, unified cache. It contains 8 KBytes and has a four-way set associative organization and a block length of four 32-bit words. The cache is organized into 128 sets. There is a single "line valid bit" and three bits, B0, B1, and B2 (the "LRU" bits), per line. On a cache miss, the 80486 reads a 16-byte line from main memory in a bus memory read burst. Draw a simplified diagram of the cache, and show how the different fields of the address are interpreted.
Source: [ALEX93]

4.11 The replacement algorithm of the Intel 40486 is referred to as pseudo-least-recently-used. Associated with each of the 128 sets of four lines (labeled L1, L2, L3, L4) are three bits, B0, B1, and B2. The replacement algorithm works as follows: When a line must be replaced, the cache will first determine whether the most recent use was from L0 and L1 or L2 and L3. Then the cache will determine which of the pair of blocks was least recently used and mark it for replacement.

(a) Specify how the bits B0, B1, and B2 are set and how they are used in the replacement algorithm.

(b) Show that the 80486 algorithm approximates a true LRU algorithm.

(c) Demonstrate that a true LRU algorithm would require six bits per set.

4.12 A set associative cache has a block size of four 16-bit words and a set size of 2. The cache can accommodate a total of 4096 words. The main memory size that is cachable is 64K × 32 bits. Design the cache structure, and show how the processor's addresses are interpreted.
Source: [ALEX93]

4.13 Generalize Equations 4–1 and 4–2, in Appendix 4A, to N-level memory hierarchies.

4.14 A computer system contains a main memory of 32K 16-bit words. It also has a 4K-word cache divided into 4-slot sets with 64 words per slot. Assume that the cache is initially empty. The processor fetches words from locations 0, 1, 2, . . ., 4351 in that order. It then repeats this fetch sequence 9 more times. The cache is 10 times faster than main memory. Estimate the improvement resulting from the use of the cache. Assume an LRU policy for block replacement.

4.15 Describe a simple technique for implementing an LRU replacement algorithm in a four-way set associative cache.

4.16 Consider a memory system with the following parameters:

$$T_c = 100 \text{ ns} \quad C_c = 0.01 \text{ ¢/bit}$$
$$T_m = 1,200 \text{ ns} \quad C_m = 0.001 \text{ ¢/bit}$$

a. What is the cost of a 1-MByte main memory?
b. What is the cost of a 1-MByte main memory using cache technology?
c. If the effective access time is 10% greater than the cache access time, what is the hit ratio H?

APPENDIX 4A

*Performance Characteristics of Two-Level Memories*

In this chapter, reference is made to a cache that acts as a buffer between main memory and processor, creating a two-level internal memory. This two-level architecture provides improved performance over a comparable one-level memory, by exploiting a property known as locality, which is explored below.

The main memory cache mechanism is part of the computer architecture, implemented in hardware, and typically invisible to the operating system. In addition, there are two other instances of a two-level memory approach that also exploit locality and that are, at least partially, implemented in the operating system: virtual memory and the disk cache (Table 4.8). Virtual memory is explored in Chapter 7; disk cache is beyond the scope of this book but is examined in [STAL95]. In this appendix, we look at some of the performance characteristics of two-level memories that are common to all three approaches.

## 4A.1   Locality

The basis for the performance advantage of a two-level memory is a principle known as *locality of reference* [DENN68]. This principle states that memory references tend to cluster. Over a long period of time the clusters in use change, but over a short period of time, the processor is primarily working with fixed clusters of memory references.

From an intuitive point of view, the principle of locality makes sense. Consider the following line of reasoning:

1. Except for branch and call instructions, which constitute only a small fraction of all program instructions, program execution is sequential. Hence, in most cases, the next instruction to be fetched immediately follows the last instruction fetched.
2. It is rare to have a long uninterrupted sequence of procedure calls followed by the corresponding sequence of returns. Rather, a program remains confined to a rather narrow window of procedure-invocation depth. Thus, over a short period of time references to instructions tend to be localized to a few procedures.

**TABLE 4.8   Characteristics of Two-Level Memories**

|                                        | *Main Memory Cache* | *Virtual Memory (Paging)* | *Disk Cache*       |
|----------------------------------------|---------------------|---------------------------|--------------------|
| **Typical access time ratios**         | 5/1                 | 1000/1                    | 1000/1             |
| **Memory management system**           | Implemented by special hardware | Combination of hardware and system software | System software |
| **Typical block size**                 | 4 to 128 bytes      | 64 to 4096 bytes          | 64 to 4096 bytes   |
| **Access of processor to second level**| Direct access       | Indirect access           | Indirect access    |

3. Most iterative constructs consist of a relatively small number of instructions repeated many times. For the duration of the iteration, computation is therefore confined to a small contiguous portion of a program.
4. In many programs, much of the computation involves processing data structures, such as arrays or sequences of records. In many cases, successive references to these data structures will be to closely located data items.

This line of reasoning has been confirmed in many studies. For example, let us consider point 1. A variety of studies have been made to analyze the behavior of high-level language programs. Table 4.9 includes key results, measuring the appearance of various statement types during execution, from the following studies. The earliest study of programming language behavior, performed by Knuth [KNUT71], examined a collection of FORTRAN programs used as student exercises. Tanenbaum [TANE78] published measurements collected from more than 300 procedures used in operating-system programs and written in a language that supports structured programming (SAL). Patterson and Sequin [PATT82a] analyzed a set of measurements taken from compilers and programs for typesetting, CAD, sorting, and file comparison. The programming languages C and Pascal were studied. Huck [HUCK83] analyzed four programs intended to represent a mix of general-purpose scientific computing, including fast Fourier transform and the integration of systems of differential equations. There is quite good agreement in the results of this mixture of languages and applications that branching and call instructions represent only a fraction of statements executed during the lifetime of a program. Thus, these studies confirm assertion 1 above.

With respect to assertion 2, studies reported in [PATT85a] provide confirmation. This is illustrated in Figure 4.31, which shows call–return behavior. Each call is represented by the line moving down and to the right, and each return by the line moving up and to the right. In the figure, a *window* with depth equal to 5 is defined. Only a sequence of calls and returns with a net movement of 6 in either direction causes the window to move. As can be seen, the executing program can remain within a stationary window for quite long periods of time. A study by the same group of C and Pascal programs showed that a window of depth 8 will only need to shift on less than one percent of the calls or returns [TAMI83].

**TABLE 4.9    Relative Dynamic Frequency of High-Level Language Operations**

| Study | [HUCK83] | [KNUT71] | [PATT82a] | | [TANE78] |
|---|---|---|---|---|---|
| Language | Pascal | FORTRAN | Pascal | C | SAL |
| Workload | Scientific | Student | System | System | System |
| Assign | 74 | 67 | 45 | 38 | 42 |
| Loop | 4 | 3 | 5 | 3 | 4 |
| Call | 1 | 3 | 15 | 12 | 12 |
| IF | 20 | 11 | 29 | 43 | 36 |
| GOTO | 2 | 9 | — | 3 | — |
| Other | — | 7 | 6 | 1 | 6 |

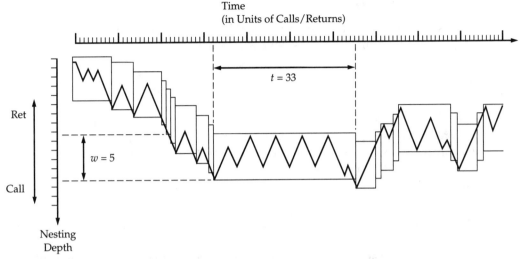

**FIGURE 4.31. The call/return behavior of programs**

### 4A.2 Operation of Two-Level Memory

The locality property can be exploited in the formation of a two-level memory. The upper-level memory (M1) is smaller, faster, and more expensive (per bit) than the lower-level memory (M2). M1 is used as a temporary store for part of the contents of the larger M2. When a memory reference is made, an attempt is made to access the item in M1. If this succeeds, then a quick access is made. If not, then a block of memory locations is copied from M2 to M1 and the access then takes place via M1. Because of locality, once a block is brought into M1, there should be a number of accesses to locations in that block, resulting in fast overall service.

To express the average time to access an item, we must consider not only the speeds of the two levels of memory, but also the probability that a given reference can be found in M1. This probability is known as the hit ratio. We have

$$T_s = H \times T_1 + (1 - H) \times (T_1 + T_2) \tag{4-1}$$
$$= T_1 + (1 - H) \times T_2$$

where

$T_s$ = average (system) access time
$T_1$ = access time of M1 (e.g., cache, disk cache)
$T_2$ = access time of M2 (e.g., main memory, disk)
$H$ = hit ratio (fraction of time reference is found in M1)

Figure 4.2 shows average access time as a function of hit ratio. As can be seen, for a high percentage of hits, the average total access time is much closer to that of M1 than M2.

### 4A.3 Performance

Let us look at some of the parameters relevant to an assessment of a two-level memory mechanism. First, consider cost. We have

$$C_s = \frac{C_1 S_1 + C_2 S_2}{S_1 + S_2}$$

where

$C_s$ = average cost per bit for the combined two-level memory
$C_1$ = average cost per bit of upper-level memory M1
$C_2$ = average cost per bit of lower-level memory M2
$S_1$ = size of M1
$S_2$ = size of M2

We would like $C_s \approx C_2$. Given that $C_1 \gg C_2$, this requires $S_1 \ll S_2$. Figure 4.32 shows the relationship.

Next, consider access time. For a two-level memory to provide a significant performance improvement, we need to have $T_s$ approximately equal to $T_1$ ($T_s \approx T_1$). Given that $T_1$ is much less than $T_2$ ($T_1 \ll T_2$), a hit ratio of close to 1 is needed.

So, we would like M1 to be small to hold down cost, and large to improve the hit ratio and therefore the performance. Is there a size of M1 that satisfies both requirements to a reasonable extent? We can answer this question with a series of sub-questions:

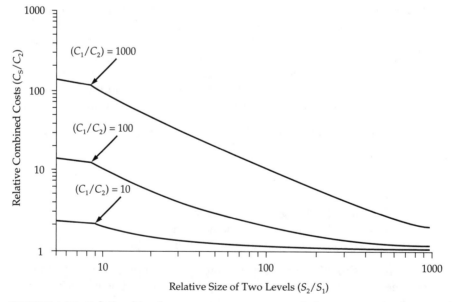

**FIGURE 4.32. Relationship of average memory cost to relative memory size for a two-level memory**

- What value of hit ratio is needed to satisfy the performance requirement?
- What size of M1 will assure the needed hit ratio?
- Does this size satisfy the cost requirement?

To get at this, consider the quantity $T_1/T_s$, referred to as the *access efficiency*. It is a measure of how close average access time ($T_s$) is to M1 access time ($T_1$). From Equation 4–1,

$$\frac{T_1}{T_s} = \frac{1}{H + (1 - H)\dfrac{T_2}{T_1}}$$

In Figure 4.33, we plot $T_1/T_s$ as a function of the hit ratio $H$, with the quantity $T_2/T_1$ as a parameter. Typically, cache access time is about five to ten times faster than main memory access time (i.e., $T_2/T_1$ is 5 to 10), and main memory access time is about 1000 times faster than disk access time ($T_2/T_1 = 1000$). Thus, a hit ratio in the range of 0.8 to 0.9 would seem to be needed to satisfy the performance requirement.

We can now phrase the question about relative memory size more exactly. Is a hit ratio of 0.8 or better reasonable for $S_1 \ll S_2$? This will depend on a number of factors, including the nature of the software being executed and the details of the design of the two-level memory. The main determinant is, of course, the degree of locality. Figure 4.34 suggests the effect that locality has on the hit ratio. Clearly, if M1 is the same size as M2, then the hit ratio will be 1.0: all of the items in M2 are always also stored in M1. Now, suppose that there is no locality; that is, references

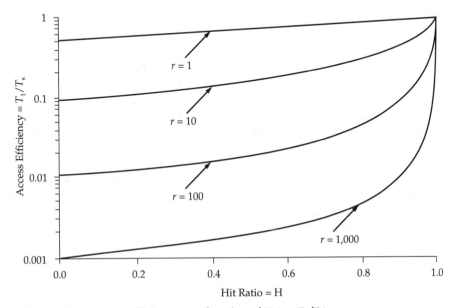

**FIGURE 4.33. Access efficiency as a function of H (r = T₂/T₁)**

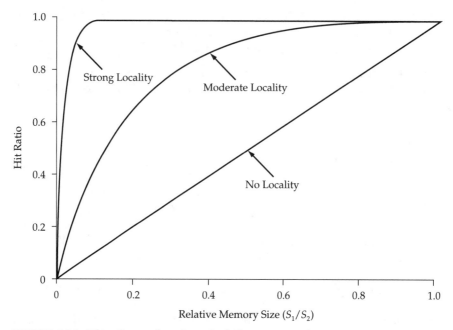

**FIGURE 4.34. Hit ratio as a function of relative memory size**

are completely random. In that case, the hit ratio should be a strictly linear function of the relative memory size. For example, if M1 is half the size of M2, then at any time half of the items from M2 are also in M1, and the hit ratio will be 0.5. In practice, however, there is some degree of locality in the references. The effects of moderate and strong locality are indicated in the figure.

So, if there is strong locality, it is possible to achieve high values of hit ratio even with relatively small upper-level memory size. For example, numerous studies have shown that rather small cache sizes will yield a hit ratio above 0.75, *regardless of the size of main memory* (e.g., [AGAR89], [PRZY88], [STRE83], and [SMIT82]). A cache in the range of 1K to 512K words is generally adequate, whereas main memory is now typically in the multiple-megabyte range. When we consider virtual memory and disk cache, we will cite other studies that confirm the same phenomenon, namely that a relatively small M1 yields a high value of hit ratio because of locality.

This brings us to the last question listed earlier: Does the relative size of the two memories satisfy the cost requirement? The answer is clearly yes. If we need only a relatively small upper-level memory to achieve good performance, then the average cost per bit of the two levels of memory will approach that of the cheaper lower-level memory.

# CHAPTER 5

# External Memory

This chapter examines a range of external memory devices and systems. We begin with the most important device, the magnetic disk. Magnetic disks are the foundation of external memory on virtually all computer systems. The next section examines the use of disk arrays to achieve greater performance, looking specifically at the family of systems known as RAID (Redundant Array of Independent Disks). An increasingly important component of many computer systems is external optical memory, and this is examined in the third section. Finally, magnetic tape is described.

## 5.1 MAGNETIC DISK

A disk is a circular platter constructed of metal or of plastic coated with a magnetizable material. Data are recorded on and later retrieved from the disk via a conducting coil, named the *head*. During a read or write operation, the head is stationary while the platter rotates beneath it.

The write mechanism is based on the magnetic field produced by electricity flowing through a coil. Pulses are sent to the head, and magnetic patterns are recorded on the surface below, with different patterns for positive and negative currents. The read mechanism is based on the electric current in a coil produced by a magnetic field moving relative to the coil. When the surface of the disk passes under the head, it generates a current of the same polarity as the one already recorded.

### Data Organization and Formatting

The head is a relatively small device capable of reading from or writing to a portion of the platter rotating beneath it. This gives rise to the organization of data on the platter in a concentric set of rings, called *tracks*. Each track is the same width as the head.

Figure 5.1 depicts this data layout. Adjacent tracks are separated by *gaps*. This prevents, or at least minimizes, errors due to misalignment of the head or simply interference of magnetic fields. To simplify the electronics, the same number of

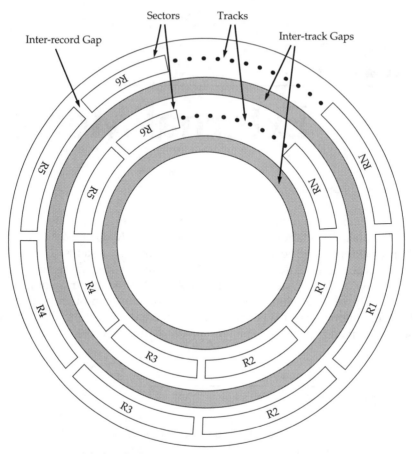

**FIGURE 5.1.  Disk data layout**

bits are typically stored on each track. Thus, the *density*, in bits per linear inch, increases as we move from the outermost track to the innermost track (this same phenomenon is present on a phonograph record).

As was mentioned earlier, data are transferred to and from the disk in blocks. Typically, the block is smaller than the capacity of a track. Accordingly, data are stored in block-size regions known as *sectors* (Figure 5.1). There are typically between 10 and 100 sectors per track, and these may be of either fixed or variable length. To avoid imposing unreasonable precision requirements on the system, adjacent sectors are separated by intra-track (inter-record) gaps.

How are sector positions within a track identified? Clearly, there must be some starting point on the track and a way of identifying the start and end of each sector. These requirements are handled by means of control data recorded on the disk. Thus, the disk is formatted with some extra data used only by the disk drive and not accessible to the user.

An example of disk formatting is shown in Figure 5.2. In this case, each track contains 30 fixed-length sectors of 600 bytes each. Each sector holds 512 bytes of

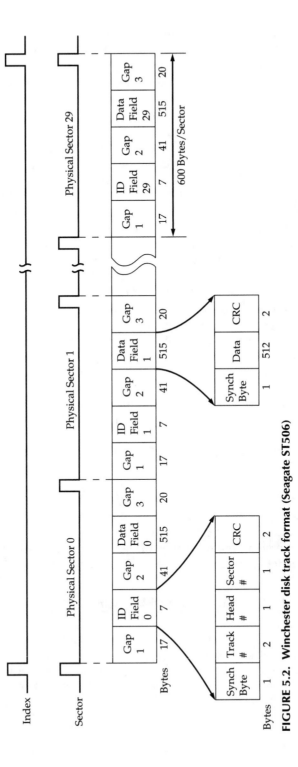

**FIGURE 5.2. Winchester disk track format (Seagate ST506)**

157

data plus control information useful to the disk controller. The ID field is a unique identifier or address used to locate a particular sector. The SYNCH byte is a special bit pattern that delimits the beginning of the field. The track number identifies a track on a surface. The head number identifies a head, since this disk has multiple surfaces (explained presently). The ID and data fields each contain an error-detecting code.

## Characteristics

Table 5.1 lists the major characteristics that differentiate among the various types of disks. First, the head may either be fixed or movable with respect to the radial direction of the platter. In a *fixed-head* disk, there is one read/write head per track. All the heads are mounted on a rigid arm that extends across all tracks (Figure 5.3a). In a movable-head disk, there is only one read/write head (Figure 5.3b). As before, the head is mounted on an arm. Since the head must be able to be positioned above any track, the arm can be extended or retracted for this purpose.

The disk itself is mounted in a disk drive, which consists of the arm, a shaft that rotates the disk, and the electronics needed for input and output of binary data. A *nonremovable disk* is permanently mounted in the disk drive. The *removable disk* can be removed and replaced with another disk. The advantage of the latter type is that unlimited amounts of data are available with a limited number of disk systems. Furthermore, a disk may be moved from one computer system to another.

For most disks, the magnetizable coating is applied to both sides of the platter, which is then referred to as *double-sided.* Some less expensive disk systems use *single-sided* disks.

Some disk drives accommodate *multiple platters* stacked vertically about an inch apart (Figure 5.4). Multiple arms are provided. The platters come as a unit known as a *disk pack.*

Finally, the head mechanism provides a clear classification of disks into three types. Traditionally, the read/write head has been positioned a fixed distance above the platter, allowing an air gap. At the other extreme is a head mechanism that actually comes into physical contact with the medium during a read or write operation. This mechanism is used with the *floppy disk,* which is a small, flexible platter and the least expensive type of disk.

To understand the third type of disk, we need to comment on the relationship between data density and the size of the air gap. The head must generate or sense

**TABLE 5.1    Characteristics of Disk Systems**

| **Head Motion** | **Platters** |
|---|---|
| Fixed head (one per track) | Single-platter |
| Movable head (one per surface) | Multiple-platter |
| **Disk Portability** | **Head Mechanism** |
| Nonremovable disk | Contact (floppy) |
| Removable disk | Fixed gap |
| **Sides** | Aerodynamic gap (Winchester) |
| Single-sided | |
| Double-sided | |

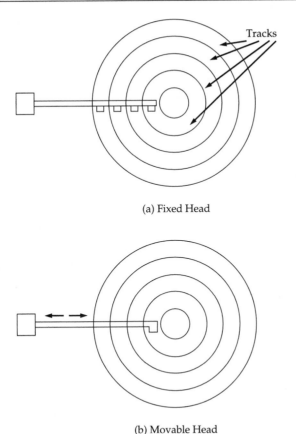

(a) Fixed Head

(b) Movable Head

**FIGURE 5.3. Fixed and movable head disks**

an electromagnetic field of sufficient magnitude to write and read properly. The narrower the head is, the closer it must be to the platter surface to function. Since a narrower head means narrower tracks and therefore greater data density, this is desirable. However, the closer the head is to the disk, the greater the risk of error from impurities or imperfections. To push the technology further, the Winchester disk was developed. Winchester heads are used in sealed drive assemblies that are almost free of contaminants. They are designed to operate closer to the disk's surface than conventional rigid disk heads, thus allowing greater data density. The head is in the shape of an aerodynamic foil that rests lightly on the platter's surface when the disk is motionless. The air pressure generated by the spinning disk is enough to make the foil rise above the surface. The resulting noncontact system can be engineered to use narrower heads that operate closer to the platter's surface than conventional rigid disk heads.

As a matter of historical interest, the term *Winchester* was originally used by IBM as a code name for their 3340 disk model prior to announcement. The 3340 was a removable disk pack with the heads sealed within the pack. The term is now applied to any sealed-unit disk drive with aerodynamic head design.

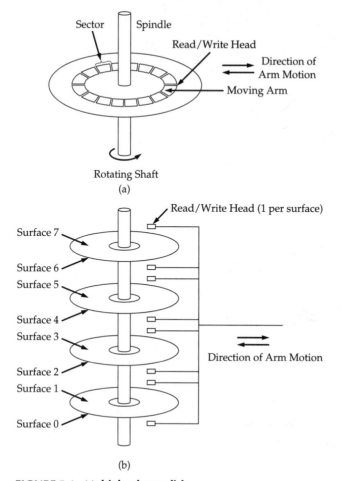

FIGURE 5.4. Multiple-platter disk

## Disk Access Time

When the disk drive is operating, the disk is rotating at constant speed. To read or write, the head must be positioned at the desired track and at the beginning of the desired sector on that track. Track selection involves moving the head in a movable-head system or electronically selecting one head on a fixed-head system. On a movable-head system, the time it takes to position the head at the track is known as *seek time*. In either case, once the track is selected, the system waits until the appropriate sector rotates to line up with the head. The time it takes for the sector to reach the head is known as *rotational latency*. The sum of the seek time, if any, and the rotational latency is the *access time*, the time it takes to get into position to read or write. Once the head is in position, the read or write operation is then performed as the sector moves under the head.

## RAID

As discussed earlier, the rate in improvement in secondary storage performance has been considerably less than the rate for processors and main memory. This mismatch has made the disk storage system perhaps the main focus of concern in improving overall computer system performance.

As in other areas of computer performance, disk storage designers recognize that if one component can only be pushed so far, additional gains in performance are to be had by using multiple components in parallel. In the case of disk storage, this leads to the development of arrays of disks that operate independently and in parallel. With multiple disks, separate I/O requests can be handled in parallel, so long as the data required reside on separate disks. Further, a single I/O request can be executed in parallel if the block of data to be accessed is distributed across multiple disks.

With the use of multiple disks, there is a wide variety of ways in which the data can be organized and in which redundancy can be added to improve reliability. This could make it difficult to develop database schemes that are usable on a number of platforms and operating systems. Fortunately, industry has agreed on a standardized scheme for multiple-disk database design, known as RAID (Redundant Array of Independent Disks). The RAID scheme consists of six levels,[1] zero through five. These levels do not imply a hierarchical relationship but designate different design architectures that share three common characteristics:

1. RAID is a set of physical disk drives viewed by the operating system as a single logical drive.
2. Data is distributed across the physical drives of an array.
3. Redundant disk capacity is used to store parity information, which guarantees data recoverability in case of a disk failure.

The details of the second and third characteristics differ for the different RAID levels. RAID 0 does not support the third characteristic.

The term RAID was originally coined in a paper by a group of researchers at the University of California at Berkeley.[2] The paper outlined various RAID configurations and applications and introduced the definitions of the RAID levels, which are still used. RAID is proposed to close the widening gap between processor speeds and relatively slow electromechanical disk drives. The strategy is to

---

[1] Additional levels have been defined by some researchers and some companies, but the six levels described in this section are the ones universally agreed upon.

[2] In that paper, the acronym RAID stood for Redundant Array of Inexpensive Disks. The term *inexpensive* was used to contrast the small relatively inexpensive disks in the RAID array to the alternative, a single large expensive disk (SLED). Today, the SLED is essentially a thing of the past, with similar disk technology being used for both RAID and non-RAID configurations. Accordingly, the industry has adopted the term *independent*, to emphasize that the RAID array creates significant performance and reliability gains.

replace a large capacity disk drive with multiple smaller capacity drives, and to distribute the data in such a way as to enable simultaneous access to data from multiple drives, thereby improving I/O performance and allowing easier incremental increases in capacity.

The unique contribution of the RAID proposal is to effectively address the need for redundancy. Although allowing multiple heads and actuators to operate simultaneously achieves higher I/O and transfer rates, the use of multiple devices increases the probability of failure. To compensate for this decreased reliability, RAID makes use of stored parity information that enables the recovery of data lost due to a disk failure.

We now examine each of the RAID levels. Table 5.2 summarizes the six levels. Of these, levels 2 and 4 are not commercially offered and are not likely to achieve industry acceptance. Nevertheless, a description of these levels helps to clarify the design choices in some of the other levels.

Figure 5.5 illustrates the six RAID schemes that support a data capacity requiring four disks with no redundancy. The figure highlights the layout of user data and redundant data and indicates the relative storage requirements of the various levels. We refer to this figure throughout the following discussion.

## RAID Level 0

RAID level 0 is not a true member of the RAID family, because it does not include redundancy to improve performance. However, there are a few applications, such as some run on supercomputers in which performance and capacity are primary concerns and low cost is more important than improved reliability.

For RAID 0, the user and system data are distributed across all the disks in the array. This has a notable advantage over the use of a single large disk: If two different I/O requests are pending for two different blocks of data, then there is a good chance that the requested blocks are on different disks. Thus, the two requests can be issued in parallel, reducing the I/O queuing time.

But RAID 0, as with all of the RAID levels, goes further than simply distributing the data across a disk array: the data are *striped* across the available disks. This is best understood by considering Figure 5.6. All the user and system data is viewed as being stored on a logical disk. The disk is divided into strips; these strips may be physical blocks, sectors, or some other unit. The strips are mapped round-robin to consecutive array members. A set of logically consecutive strips that maps exactly one strip to each array member is referred to as a stripe. In an $n$-disk array, the first $n$ logical strips are physically stored as the first strip on each of the $n$ disks, the second $n$ strips are distributed as the second strips on each disk, and so on. The advantage of this layout is that if a single I/O request consists of multiple logically contiguous strips, then up to $n$ strips for that request can be handled in parallel, greatly reducing the I/O transfer time.

Figure 5.6 indicates the use of array management software to map between logical and physical disk space. This software may execute either in the disk subsystem or in a host computer.

**TABLE 5.2  RAID Levels**

| Category | Level | Description | I/O Request Rate (Read/Write) | Data Transfer Rate (Read/Write) | Typical Application |
|---|---|---|---|---|---|
| Striping | 0 | Nonredundant | Large strips: Excellent | Small strips: Excellent | Applications requiring high performance for noncritical data |
| Mirroring | 1 | Mirrored | Good/Fair | Fair/Fair | System drives; critical files |
| Parallel access | 2 | Redundant via Hamming code | Poor | Excellent | |
| | 3 | Bit-interleaved parity | Poor | Excellent | Large I/O request size applications, such as imaging, CAD |
| Independent access | 4 | Block-interleaved parity | Excellent/Fair | Fair/Poor | |
| | 5 | Block-interleaved distributed parity | Excellent/Fair | Fair/Poor | High request rate, read-intensive, data lookup |

(a) RAID 0 (Non-redundant)

(b) RAID 1 (Mirrored)

(c) RAID 2 (Redundancy Through Hamming Code)

**FIGURE 5.5.  RAID Levels**

## RAID 0 for High Data Transfer Capacity

The performance of any of the RAID levels depends critically on the request patterns of the host system and on the layout of the data. These issues can be most clearly addressed in RAID 0, where the impact of redundancy does not interfere with the analysis. First, let us consider the use of RAID 0 to achieve a high data transfer rate. For applications to see a high transfer rate, two requirements must be met. First, a high transfer capacity must exist along the entire path between host memory and the individual disk drives. This includes internal controller buses, host system I/O buses, I/O adapters, and host memory buses.

The second requirement is that the application must make I/O requests that drive the disk array efficiently. This requirement is met if the typical request is for large amounts of logically contiguous data, compared with the size of a strip. In this case, a single I/O request involves the parallel transfer of data from multiple disks, increasing the effective transfer rate compared with a single-disk transfer.

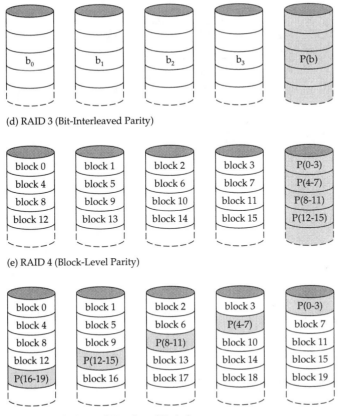

(d) RAID 3 (Bit-Interleaved Parity)

(e) RAID 4 (Block-Level Parity)

(f) RAID 5 (Block-Level Distributed Parity)

**FIGURE 5.5. (Continued)**

## RAID 0 for High I/O Request Rate

In a transaction-oriented environment, the user is typically more concerned with response time than with transfer rate. For an individual I/O request for a small amount of data, the I/O time is dominated by the motion of the disk heads (seek time) and the movement of the disk (rotational latency).

In a transaction environment, there may be hundreds of I/O requests per second. A disk array can provide high I/O execution rates by balancing the I/O load across multiple disks. Effective load balancing is achieved only if there are typically multiple I/O requests outstanding. This in turn implies that there are multiple independent applications or a single transaction-oriented application that is capable of multiple asynchronous I/O requests. The performance will also be influenced by the strip size. If the strip size is relatively large, so that a single I/O request only involves a single disk access, then multiple waiting I/O requests can be handled in parallel, reducing the queuing time for each request.

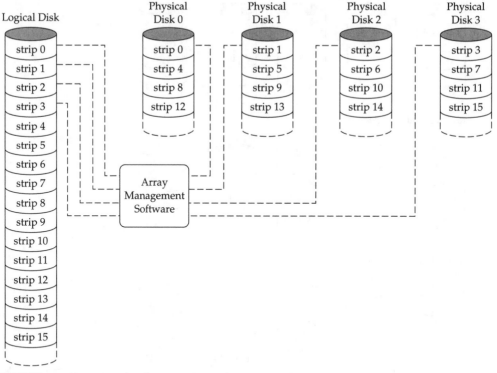

**FIGURE 5.6. Data Mapping for a RAID Level 0 Array [MASS94]**

## RAID Level 1

RAID 1 differs from RAID levels 2 through 5 in how redundancy is achieved. In these other RAID schemes, some form of parity calculation is used to introduce redundancy; in RAID 1, redundancy is achieved by the simple expedient of duplicating all the data. As Figure 5.5b shows, data striping is used, as in RAID 0. But in this case, each logical strip is mapped to two separate physical disks so that every disk in the array has a mirror disk that contains the same data.

There are a number of positive aspects to the RAID 1 organization:

1. A read request can be serviced by either of the two disks that contains the requested data, whichever one involves the minimum seek time plus rotational latency.
2. A write request requires that both corresponding strips be updated, but this can be done in parallel. Thus, the write performance is dictated by the slower of the two writes (i.e., the one that involves the larger seek time plus rotational latency). However, there is no "write penalty" with RAID 1. RAID levels 2 through 5 involve the use of parity bits. Therefore, when a single strip is updated, the array management software must first compute and update the parity bits as well as updating the actual strip in question.

3. Recovery from a failure is simple. When a drive fails, the data may still be accessed from the second drive.

The principal disadvantage of RAID 1 is the cost; it requires twice the disk space of the logical disk that it supports. Because of that, a RAID 1 configuration is likely to be limited to drives that store system software and data and other highly critical files. In these cases, RAID 1 provides real-time backup of all data so that in the event of a disk failure, all the critical data is still immediately available.

In a transaction-oriented environment, RAID 1 can achieve high I/O request rates if the bulk of the requests are reads. In this situation, the performance of RAID 1 can approach double that of RAID 0. However, if a substantial fraction of the I/O requests are write requests, then there may be no significant performance gain over RAID 0. RAID 1 may also provide improved performance over RAID 0 for data-transfer-intensive applications with a high percentage of reads. Improvement occurs if the application can split each read request so that both disk members participate.

## RAID Level 2

RAID levels 2 and 3 make use of a parallel access technique. In a parallel access array, all member disks participate in the execution of every I/O request. Typically, the spindles of the individual drives are synchronized so that each disk head is in the same position on each disk at any given time.

As in the other RAID schemes, data striping is used. In the case of RAID 2 and 3, the strips are very small, often as small as a single byte or word. With RAID 2, an error-correcting code is calculated across corresponding bits on each data disk, and the bits of the code are stored in the corresponding bit positions on multiple parity disks. Typically, a Hamming code is used (see Chapter 4), which is able to correct single-bit errors and detect double-bit errors.

Although RAID 2 requires fewer disks than RAID 1, it is still rather costly. The number of redundant disks is proportional to the log of the number of data disks. On a single read, all disks are simultaneously accessed. The requested data and the associated error-correcting code are delivered to the array controller. If there is a single-bit error, the controller can recognize and correct the error instantly, so that the read access time is not slowed. On a single write, all data disks and parity disks must be accessed for the write operation.

RAID 2 would only be an effective choice in an environment in which many disk errors occur. Given the high reliability of individual disks and disk drives, RAID 2 is overkill and is not implemented.

## RAID Level 3

RAID 3 is organized in a similar fashion to RAID 2. The difference is that RAID 3 requires only a single redundant disk, no matter how large the disk array. RAID 3 employs parallel access, with data distributed in small strips. Instead of an error-correcting code, a simple parity bit is computed for the set of individual bits in the same position on all of the data disks.

*Redundancy*

In the event of a drive failure, the parity drive is accessed and data is reconstructed from the remaining devices. Once the failed drive is replaced, the missing data can be restored on the new drive and operation resumed.

The data reconstruction is quite simple. Consider an array of five drives in which X0 through X3 contain data and X4 is the parity disk. The parity for the *i*th bit is calculated as follows:

$$X4(i) = X3(i) \oplus X2(i) \oplus X1(i) \oplus X0(i)$$

Suppose that drive X1 has failed. If we add $X4(i) \oplus X1(i)$ to both sides of the above equation, we get

$$X1(i) = X4(i) \oplus X3(i) \oplus X2(i) \oplus X0(i)$$

Thus, the contents of any strip of data on any one of the data disks in an array can be regenerated from the contents of the corresponding strips on the remaining disks in the array. This principle is true for RAID levels 3, 4, and 5.

In the event of a disk failure, all the data is still available in what is referred to as reduced mode. In this mode, for reads, the missing data is regenerated on the fly using the exclusive-or calculation. When data is written to a reduced RAID 3 array, consistency of the parity must be maintained for later regeneration. Return to full operation requires that the failed disk be replaced and the entire contents of the failed disk be regenerated on the new disk.

*Performance*

Because data is striped in very small strips, RAID 3 can achieve very high data transfer rates. Any I/O request will involve the parallel transfer of data from all the data disks. For large transfers, the performance improvement is especially noticeable.

On the other hand, only one I/O request can be executed at a time. Thus, in a transaction-oriented environment, performance suffers.

## RAID Level 4

RAID levels 4 and 5 make use of an independent access technique. In an independent access array, each member disk operates independently, so that separate I/O requests can be satisfied in parallel. Because of this, independent access arrays are more suitable for applications that require high I/O request rates and are relatively less suited for applications that require high data transfer rates.

As in the other RAID schemes, data striping is used. In the case of RAID 4 and 5, the strips are relatively large. With RAID 4, a bit-by-bit parity strip is calculated across corresponding strips on each data disk, and the parity bits are stored in the corresponding strip on the parity disk.

RAID 4 involves a write penalty when an I/O write request of small size is performed. Each time a write occurs, the array management software must update not only the user data but also the corresponding parity bits. Consider an array of five drives in which X0 through X3 contain data and X4 is the parity disk. Suppose that a write is performed that involves only a strip on disk X1. Initially, for each bit $i$, we have the following relationship:

$$X4(i) = X3(i) \oplus X2(i) \oplus X1(i) \oplus X0(i)$$

After the update, with potentially altered bits indicated by a prime,

$$\begin{aligned} X4'(i) &= X3(i) \oplus X2(i) \oplus X1'(i) \oplus X0(i) \\ &= X3(i) \oplus X2(i) \oplus X1'(i) \oplus X0(i) \oplus X1(i) \oplus X1(i) \\ &= X4(i) \oplus X1(i) \oplus X1'(i) \end{aligned}$$

To calculate the new parity, the array management software must read the old user strip and the old parity strip. Then it can update these two strips with the new data and the newly calculated parity. Thus, each strip write involves two reads and two writes.

In the case of a larger size I/O write that involves strips on all disk drives, parity is easily computed by calculation using only the new data bits. Thus, the parity drive can be updated in parallel with the data drives, and there are no extra reads or writes.

In any case, every write operation must involve the parity disk, which therefore can become a bottleneck.

## RAID Level 5

RAID 5 is organized in a similar fashion to RAID 4. The difference is that RAID 5 distributes the parity strips across all disks. A typical allocation is a round-robin scheme, as illustrated in Figure 5.5f. For an $n$-disk array, the parity strip is on a different disk for the first $n$ stripes, and the pattern then repeats.

The distribution of parity strips across all drives avoids the potential I/O bottleneck found in RAID 4.

## 5.3

## OPTICAL MEMORY

In 1983, one of the most successful consumer products of all time was introduced: the compact disk (CD) digital audio system [GUTE88]. The CD is a nonerasable disk that can store more than 60 minutes of audio information on one side. The huge commercial success of the CD enabled the development of low-cost optical-disk storage technology that now promises to revolutionize computer data storage. In the past few years, a variety of optical-disk systems have been introduced (Table 5.3). Three of these systems are increasingly coming to be used in computer applications: CD-ROM, WORM, and the erasable optical disk. We will briefly review each of these.

**TABLE 5.3    Optical Disk Products**

**CD**
Compact Disk. A nonerasable disk that stores digitized audio information. The standard system uses 12-cm disks and can record more than 60 minutes of uninterrupted playing time.
**CD-ROM**
Compact Disk Read-Only Memory. A nonerasable disk used for storing computer data. The standard system uses 12-cm disks and can hold more than 550 Mbytes.
**CD-I**
Compact Disk Interactive. A specification based on the use of CD-ROM. It describes methods for providing audio, video, graphics, text, and machine-executable code on CD-ROM.
**DVI**
Digital Video Interactive. A technology for producing digitized, compressed representation of video information. The representation can be stored on CD or other disk media. Current systems use CDs and can store about 20 minutes of video on one disk.
**WORM**
Write-Once Read-Many. A disk that is more easily written than CD-ROM, making single-copy disks commercially feasible. As with CD-ROM, after the write operation is performed, the disk is read-only. The most popular size is 5.25-inch, which can hold from 200 to 800 Mbytes of data.
**Erasable Optical Disk**
A disk that uses optical technology but that can be easily erased and rewritten. Both 3.25-inch and 5.25-inch disks are in use. A typical capacity is 650 Mbytes.

## CD-ROM

Both the audio CD and the CD-ROM (compact disk read-only memory) share a similar technology. The main difference is that CD-ROM players are more rugged and have error-correction devices to ensure that data are properly transferred from disk to computer. Both types of disk are also made the same way. The disk is formed from a resin, such as polycarbonate, and coated with a highly reflective surface, usually aluminum. Digitally recorded information (either music or computer data) is imprinted as a series of microscopic pits on the reflective surface. This is done, first of all, with a finely focused, high-intensity laser to create a master disk. The master is used in turn to make a die to stamp out copies. The pitted surface of the copies is protected against dust and scratches by a top coat of clear lacquer.

Information is retrieved from a CD or CD-ROM by a low-powered laser housed in an optical-disk player or drive unit. The laser shines through the clear protective coating while a motor spins the disk past it. The intensity of the reflected light of the laser changes as it encounters a pit. This change is detected by a photosensor and converted into a digital signal.

A pit near the center of a rotating disk travels past a fixed point (such as a laser beam) slower than a pit on the outside, and so some way must be found to compensate for the variation in speed so that the laser can read all the pits at the same rate. This can be done—as it is on magnetic disks—by increasing the spacing between bits of information recorded in segments of the disk. The information can then be scanned at the same rate by rotating the disk at a fixed speed, known as the **constant angular velocity (CAV)**. Figure 5.7 shows the layout of a disk using CAV. The disk is divided into a number of pie-shaped sectors and into a series of concentric tracks. The advantage of using CAV is that individual blocks of data can be directly addressed by track and sector. To move the head from its current location to a specific address, it only takes a short movement of the head to a specific track and a short wait for the proper sector to spin under the head. The disadvantage of CAV is that the amount of data that can be stored on the long outer tracks is the same as what can be stored on the short inner tracks.

Because putting less information on the outside of a disk wastes space, the CAV method is not used on CDs and CD-ROMs. Instead, information is packed evenly across the disk in segments of the same size, and these are scanned at the same rate by rotating the disk at a variable speed. The pits are then read by the laser at a **constant linear velocity (CLV)**. The disk rotates more slowly for accesses near the outer edge than for those near the center. Thus, the capacity of a track and the rotational delay both increase for track positions nearer the outer edge of the disk.

CD-ROMs of various densities have been produced. For a typical example, the track-to-track spacing is 1.6 microns ($1.6 \times 10^{-6}$ meters). The recordable width of a CD-ROM, along its radius, is 32.55 mm, so the total number of apparent tracks is 32,550 microns divided by the track spacing, or 20,344 tracks. In fact, there is a single spiral track, and we can work out the length of that track by multiplying the average circumference by the number of turns in the spiral; this works out to be approximately 5.27 kilometers. The constant linear velocity of the CD-ROM is 1.2 meters/second, which yields a total of 4391 seconds, or 73.2 minutes, which is about the standard maximum playing time of an audio compact disk. Since data is streamed from the disk at 176.4 KBytes/second, the storage capacity of the CD-ROM is 774.57 MBytes. This is equivalent to more than 550 3.25-inch diskettes.

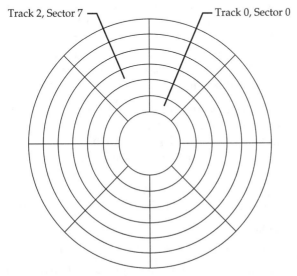

Track 2, Sector 7          Track 0, Sector 0

**FIGURE 5.7.  Disk layout using constant angular velocity**

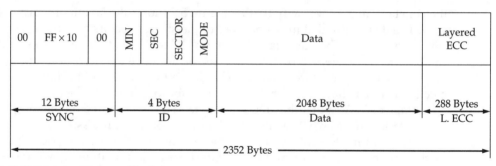

**FIGURE 5.8. CD-ROM block format**

Data on the CD-ROM is organized as a sequence of blocks. A typical block format is shown in Figure 5.8. It consists of the following fields:

- *Sync:* The sync field identifies the beginning of a block. It consists of a byte of all 0s, 10 bytes of all 1s, and a byte of all 0s.
- *Header:* The header contains the block address and the mode byte. Mode 0 specifies a blank data field; mode 1 specifies the use of an error-correcting code and 2048 bytes of data; mode 2 specifies 2336 bytes of user data with no error-correcting code.
- *Data:* User data.
- *Auxiliary:* Additional user data in mode 2. In mode 1, this is a 288-byte error-correcting code.

Figure 5.9 indicates the layout used for CDs and CD-ROMs. As mentioned, data are arranged sequentially along a spiral track. With the use of CLV, random access becomes more difficult. Locating a specific address involves moving the head to the general area, adjusting the rotation speed and reading the address, and then making minor adjustments to find and access the specific sector.

CD-ROM is appropriate for the distribution of large amounts of data to a large number of users. Because of the expense of the initial writing process, it is not appropriate for individualized applications. Compared with traditional magnetic disks, the CD-ROM has three major advantages:

- The information-storage capacity is much greater on the optical disk.
- The optical disk together with the information stored on it can be mass replicated inexpensively—unlike a magnetic disk. The database on a magnetic disk has to be reproduced by copying one disk at a time using two disk drives.
- The optical disk is removable, allowing the disk itself to be used for archival storage. Most magnetic disks are nonremovable. The information on it must first be copied to tape before the disk drive/disk can be used to store new information.

The disadvantages of CD-ROM:

- It is read-only and cannot be updated.
- It has an access time much longer than that of a magnetic disk drive, as much as half a second.

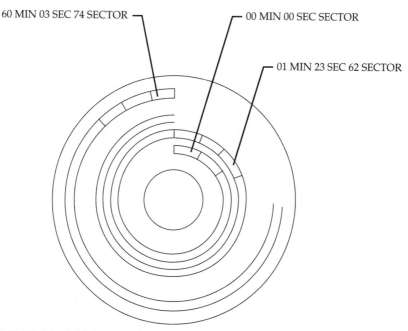

60 MIN 03 SEC 74 SECTOR

00 MIN 00 SEC SECTOR

01 MIN 23 SEC 62 SECTOR

**FIGURE 5.9.  Disk layout using constant linear velocity**

## WORM

To accommodate applications in which only one or a small number of copies of a set of data is needed, the write-once read-many CD has been developed. For WORM, a disk is prepared in such a way that it can be subsequently written once with a laser beam of modest intensity. Thus, with a somewhat more expensive disk controller than for CD-ROM, the customer can write once as well as read the disk. To provide for more rapid access, the WORM uses constant angular velocity, at the sacrifice of some capacity.

A typical technique for preparing the disk is to use a high-power laser to produce a series of blisters on the disk. When the preformatted medium is placed in a WORM drive, a low-powered laser can produce just enough heat to burst the prerecorded blisters. During a disk-read operation, a laser in the WORM drive illuminates the disk's surface. Since the burst blisters provide higher contrast than the surrounding area, these are easily recognized by simple electronics.

The WORM optical disk is attractive for archival storage of documents and files. It provides a permanent record of large volumes of user data.

## Erasable Optical Disk

The most recent development in computer optical disks is the erasable optical disk. This disk can be repeatedly written and overwritten, as with any magnetic disk. Although a number of approaches have been tried, the only technology that has proved commercially feasible is the magneto-optical system. In this system, the energy of a laser beam is used together with a magnetic field to record and erase information by reversing the magnetic poles in a small area of a disk coated with a magnetic material. The laser beam heats a specific spot on the medium, and a magnetic field can change the orientation of that spot while its temperature is elevated. As the polarization process does not cause a physical change in the disk, the process can be repeated many times. For reading, the direction of magnetism can be detected by polarized laser light. Polarized light reflected from a particular spot will change its degree of rotation depending on the magnetic field's orientation.

The erasable optical disk has the obvious advantage over CD-ROM and WORM that it can be rewritten and thus used as a true secondary storage. As such, it competes with the magnetic disk. The principal advantages of erasable optical disks compared with magnetic disks are

- *High Capacity:* A 5.25-inch optical disk can hold about 650 Mbytes of data. The most advanced Winchester disks can carry less than half that amount.
- *Portability:* The optical disk can be removed from the drive.
- *Reliability:* The engineering tolerances for optical disks are much less severe than for high-capacity magnetic disks. Thus, they exhibit higher reliability and longer life.

As with WORM, the erasable optical disk uses constant angular velocity.

## 5.4

### MAGNETIC TAPE

Tape systems use the same reading and recording techniques as disk systems. The medium is flexible mylar tape coated with magnetic oxide. The tape and the tape drive are analogous to a home tape recorder system.

The tape medium is structured as a small number of parallel tracks. Earlier tape systems typically used 9 tracks. This made it possible to store data one byte at a time, with an additional parity bit as the ninth track. Newer tape systems use 18 or 36 tracks, corresponding to a digital word or double word. As with the disk, data are read and written in contiguous blocks, called *physical records* on a tape. Blocks on the tape are separated by gaps referred to as *inter-record* gaps. Figure 5.10 suggests the structure for a 9-track tape. As with the disk, the tape is formatted to assist in locating physical records.

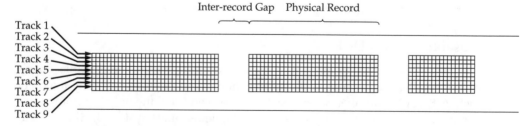

FIGURE 5.10. Nine-track magnetic tape format

A tape drive is a *sequential-access* device. If the tape head is positioned at record 1, then in order to read record $N$, it is necessary to read physical records 1 through $N - 1$, one at a time. If the head is currently positioned beyond the desired record, it is necessary to rewind the tape a certain distance and begin reading forward. Unlike the disk, the tape is in motion only during a read or write operation.

In contrast to the tape, the disk drive is referred to as a *direct-access* device. A disk drive need not read all the sectors on a disk sequentially to get to the desired one. It must only wait for the intervening sectors within one track and can make successive accesses to any track.

Magnetic tape was the first kind of secondary memory. It is still widely used as the lowest-cost, slowest-speed member of the memory hierarchy.

## 5.5

### RECOMMENDED READING

A good discussion of disk technology is [SIER90].

An excellent survey of RAID technology, written by the inventors of the RAID concept, is [CHEN94]. A more detailed discussion is published by the RAID Advisory Board, an association of suppliers and consumers of RAID-related products [MASS94].

[MARC90] gives an excellent overview of the optical storage field.

Finally, [ROSC94] provides a comprehensive overview of all types of external memory systems, with a modest amount of technical detail on each.

CHEN94   Chen, P.; Lee, E.; Gibson, G.; Katz, R.; and Patterson, D. "RAID: High-Performance, Reliable Secondary Storage." *ACM Computing Surveys,* June 1994.

MARC90   Marchant, A. *Optical Recording.* Reading, MA: Addison-Wesley, 1990.

MASS94   Massiglia, P. (editor). *The RAIDbook: A Sourcebook for Disk Array Technology.* St. Peter, MN: The Raid Advisory Board, 1994.

ROSC94   Rosch, W. *The Winn L. Rosch Hardware Bible.* Indianapolis, IN: Sams, 1994.

SIER90   Sierra, H. *An Introduction to Direct Access Storage Devices.* Boston, MA: Academic Press, 1990.

## 5.6

### PROBLEMS

5.1   Define the following for a disk system:

$t_s$ = seek time; average time to position head over track
$r$ = rotation speed of the disk, in revolutions per second
$n$ = number of bits per sector
$N$ = capacity of a track, in bits
$t_A$ = time to access a sector

Develop a formula for $t_A$ as a function of the other parameters.

5.2 Assume a 10-drive RAID configuration. Fill in the following matrix, which compares the various RAID levels:

| RAID Level | Storage density | Bandwidth performance | Transaction performance |
|---|---|---|---|
| 0 | 1 | | 1 |
| 1 | | | |
| 2 | | | |
| 3 | | 1 | |
| 4 | | | |
| 5 | | | |

Each parameter is normalized to the RAID level that delivers the best performance. Storage density refers to the fraction of disk storage available for user data. Bandwidth performance reflects how fast data can be transferred out of an array. Transaction performance measures how many I/O operations per second an array can perform.

5.3 It should be clear that disk striping can improve data transfer rate when the strip size is small compared with the I/O request size. It should also be clear that RAID 0 provides improved performance relative to a single large disk, because multiple I/O requests can be handled in parallel. However, in this latter case, is disk striping necessary? That is, does disk striping improve I/O request rate performance compared with a comparable disk array without striping?

5.4 What is the transfer rate for a 9-track magnetic tape unit whose tape speed is 120 inches per second and whose tape density is 1600 linear bits per inch?

5.5 Assume a 2400-foot tape reel; an inter-record gap of 0.6 inch where the tape stops midway, between reads; that the rate of tape speed increase/decrease during gaps is linear; and that other characteristics of the tape are the same as in Problem 5.4. Data on the tape are organized in physical records, where each physical record contains a fixed number of user-defined units, called logical records.

(a) How long will it take to read a full tape of 120-byte logical records blocked 10 per physical record?

(b) How long will it take to read a full tape of 120-byte logical records blocked 30 per physical record?

(c) How many logical records will the tape hold with each of the above blocking factors?

(d) What is the effective overall transfer rate for each of the two blocking factors above?

(e) What is the capacity of the tape?

5.6 Calculate how much disk space (in sectors, tracks, and surfaces) will be required to store the logical records read in Problem 5.5a if the disk is fixed-sector of 512 bytes/sector, with 96 sectors/track, 110 tracks per surface, and 8 usable surfaces. Ignore any file header record(s) and track indexes, and assume that records cannot span more than one sector.

5.7 Neglecting processor time, how long will it take to write the records in Problem 5.6 on the disk sequentially if average track-to-track time is 8 ms and the disk rotates at 360 rpm? Assume that the head is initially above the first track to be written.

5.8 Considering the combined problems of 5.5b and 5.7, and neglecting processor time, will the tape-to-disk copy be tape-bound (limited by tape performance) or disk-bound (limited by disk performance), assuming separate I/O modules?

5.9 For the tape unit described in Problem 5.4, what would be the effective transfer rate if the data were all numeric, packed 2 digits per byte?

5.10 In Problem 5.5a, if the tape did not slow down or stop in passing over the gaps (i.e., streaming tape), what would be the improvement in reading time for the same data?

# CHAPTER 6

# Input/Output

In addition to the CPU and a set of memory modules, the third key element of a computer system is a set of I/O modules. Each module interfaces to the system bus or central switch and controls one or more peripheral devices. An I/O module is not simply mechanical connectors that wire a device into the system bus. Rather, the I/O module contains some "intelligence," that is, it contains logic for performing a communication function between the peripheral and the bus.

The reader may wonder why one does not connect peripherals directly to the system bus. The reasons are

- There are a wide variety of peripherals with various methods of operation. It would be impractical to incorporate the necessary logic within the CPU to control a range of devices.
- The data transfer rate of peripherals is often much slower than that of the memory or CPU. Thus, it is impractical to use the high-speed system bus to communicate directly with a peripheral.
- Peripherals often use different data formats and word lengths than the computer to which they are attached.

Thus, an I/O module is required. This module has two major functions (Figure 6.1):

- Interface to the CPU and memory via the system bus or central switch.
- Interface to one or more peripheral devices by tailored data links.

We begin this chapter with a brief discussion of external devices, followed by an overview of the structure and function of an I/O module. Then, we look at the various ways in which the I/O function can be performed in cooperation with the CPU and memory: the internal I/O interface. Finally, the external I/O interface, between the I/O module and the outside world, is examined.

## 6.1

### EXTERNAL DEVICES

A computer system is of no use without some means of input and output. I/O operations are accomplished through a wide assortment of external devices that provide a means of exchanging data between the external environment and the computer. An external device attaches to the computer by a link to an I/O module

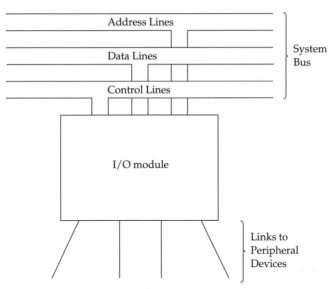

**FIGURE 6.1. Generic model of an I/O module**

(Figure 6.1). The link is used to exchange control, status, and data between the I/O module and the external device. An external device connected to an I/O module is often referred to as a *peripheral device* or, simply, a *peripheral.*

We can broadly classify external devices into three categories:

- *Human-Readable:* Suitable for communicating with the computer user.
- *Machine-Readable:* Suitable for communicating with equipment.
- *Communication:* Suitable for communicating with remote devices.

Examples of human-readable devices are video display terminals (VDTs) and printers. Examples of machine-readable devices are magnetic disk and tape systems, and sensors and actuators, such as are used in a robotics application. Note that we are viewing disk and tape systems as I/O devices in this chapter, whereas in Chapter 5 we viewed them as memory devices. From a functional point of view, these devices are part of the memory hierarchy, and their use is appropriately discussed in Chapter 5. From a structural point of view, these devices are controlled by I/O modules and are hence to be considered in this chapter.

Communication devices allow a computer to exchange data with a remote device, which may be a human-readable device, such as a terminal, a machine-readable device, or even another computer.

In very general terms, the nature of an external device is indicated in Figure 6.2. The interface to the I/O module is in the form of control, status, and data signals. *Data* are in the form of a set of bits to be sent to or received from the I/O module. *Control signals* determine the function that the device will perform, such as send data to the I/O module (INPUT or READ), accept data from the I/O module (OUTPUT or WRITE), report status, or perform some control function particular to the device (e.g., position a disk head). *Status signals* indicate the state of the device. Examples are READY/NOT-READY to show whether the device is ready for data transfer.

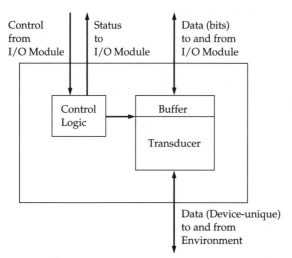

**FIGURE 6.2. An external device**

*Control logic* associated with the device controls the device's operation in response to direction from the I/O module. The *transducer* converts data from electrical to other forms of energy during output and from other forms to electrical during input. Typically, a buffer is associated with the transducer to temporarily hold data being transferred between the I/O module and the external environment; a buffer size of 8 to 16 bits is common.

The interface between the I/O module and the external device will be examined in Section 6.7. The interface between the external device and the environment is beyond the scope of this book, but several brief examples are given here.

## Keyboard/Monitor

The most common means of computer/user interaction is a keyboard/monitor arrangement. The user provides input through the keyboard. This input is then transmitted to the computer and may also be displayed on the monitor. In addition, the monitor displays data provided by the computer.

The basic unit of exchange is the character. Associated with each character is a code, typically 7 or 8 bits in length. The most commonly used code is a 7-bit code referred to as ASCII (American Standard Code for Information Interchange) in the United States and CCITT Alphabet Number 5 internationally. Each character in this code is represented by a unique 7-bit binary code; thus, 128 different characters can be represented.[1] Table 6.1 lists all of the code values. In the table, the bits of each character are labeled from $b_7$, which is the most significant bit, to $b_1$, the least significant bit. Characters are of two types: printable and control. Printable characters are the alphabetic, numeric, and special characters that can be printed on paper or displayed on a screen. For example, the bit representation of the char-

---

[1] ASCII-encoded characters are almost always stored and transmitted using 8 bits per character (a block of 8 bits is referred to as an *octet*, or *byte*). The eighth bit is a parity bit used for error detection. The parity bit is in the most-significant-bit position and therefore would be labeled $b_8$.

acter "K" is 1001011. Some of the control characters have to do with controlling the printing or displaying of characters; an example is carriage return. Other control characters are concerned with communications procedures.

For keyboard input, when a key is depressed by the user, this generates an electronic signal that is interpreted by the transducer in the keyboard and translated into the bit pattern of the corresponding ASCII code. This bit pattern is then transmitted to the I/O module in the computer. At the computer, the text can be stored in the same ASCII code. On output, ASCII code characters are transmitted to an external device from the I/O module. The transducer at the device interprets this code and sends the required electronic signals to the output device to either display the indicated character or perform the requested control function.

## Disk Drive

A disk drive contains electronics for exchanging data, control, and status signals with an I/O module plus the electronics for controlling the disk read/write mechanism. In a fixed-head disk, the transducer is capable of converting between the magnetic patterns on the moving disk surface and bits in the device's buffer (Figure 6.2). A moving-head disk must also be able to cause the disk arm to move radially in and out across the disk's surface.

**TABLE 6.1   The American Standard Code for Information Interchange (ASCII)**

bit position

| $b_7 b_6 b_5 b_4 b_3 b_2 b_1$ | 0 0 0 | 0 0 1 | 0 1 0 | 0 1 1 | 1 0 0 | 1 0 1 | 1 1 0 | 1 1 1 |
|---|---|---|---|---|---|---|---|---|
| 0 0 0 0 | NUL | DLE | SP | 0 | @ | P | ` | p |
| 0 0 0 1 | SOH | DC1 | ! | 1 | A | Q | a | q |
| 0 0 1 0 | STX | DC2 | " | 2 | B | R | b | r |
| 0 0 1 1 | ETX | DC3 | # | 3 | C | S | c | s |
| 0 1 0 0 | EOT | DC4 | $ | 4 | D | T | d | t |
| 0 1 0 1 | ENQ | NAK | % | 5 | E | U | e | u |
| 0 1 1 0 | ACK | SYN | & | 6 | F | V | f | v |
| 0 1 1 1 | BEL | ETB | ' | 7 | G | W | g | w |
| 1 0 0 0 | BS | CAN | ( | 8 | H | X | h | x |
| 1 0 0 1 | HT | EM | ) | 9 | I | Y | i | y |
| 1 0 1 0 | LF | SUB | * | : | J | Z | j | z |
| 1 0 1 1 | VT | ESC | + | ; | K | [ | k | { |
| 1 1 0 0 | FF | FS | , | < | L | \ | l | \| |
| 1 1 0 1 | CR | GS | - | = | M | ] | m | } |
| 1 1 1 0 | SO | RS | . | > | N | ^ | n | ~ |
| 1 1 1 1 | SI | US | / | ? | O | _ | o | DEL |

This is the U.S. national version of CCITT International Alphabet Number 5 (T.50). The control characters are explained on the following pages.

**TABLE 6.1    (continued)**

*Format Control*

**BS** (Backspace): Indicates movement of the printing mechanism or display cursor backward in one position.

**HT** (Horizontal Tab): Indicates movement of the printing mechanism or display cursor forward to the next preassigned "tab" or stopping position.

**LF** (Line Feed): Indicates movement of the printing mechanism or display cursor to the start of the next line.

**VT** (Vertical Tab): Indicates movement of the printing mechanism or display cursor to the next of a series of preassigned printing lines.

**FF** (Form Feed): Indicates movement of the printing mechanism or display cursor to the starting position of the next page, form, or screen.

**CR** (Carriage Return): Indicates movement of the printing mechanism or display cursor to the starting position of the same line.

*Transmission Control*

**SOH** (Start of Heading): Used to indicate the start of a heading, which may contain address or routing information.

**STX** (Start of Text): Used to indicate the start of the text and so also indicates the end of the heading.

**ETX** (End of Text): Used to terminate the text that was started with STX.

**EOT** (End of Transmission): Indicates the end of a transmission, which may have included one or more "texts" with their headings.

**ENQ** (Enquiry): A request for a response from a remote station. It may be used as a "WHO ARE YOU?" request for a station to identify itself.

**ACK** (Acknowledge): A character transmitted by a receiving device as an affirmation response to a sender. It is used as a positive response to polling messages.

**NAK** (Negative Acknowledgment): A character transmitted by a receiving device as a negative response to a sender. It is used as a negative response to polling messages.

**SYN** (Synchronous/Idle): Used by a synchronous transmission system to achieve synchronization. When no data is being sent a synchronous transmission system may send SYN characters continuously.

**ETB** (End of Transmission Block): Indicates the end of a block of data for communication purposes. It is used for blocking data where the block structure is not necessarily related to the processing format.

## 6.2

## I/O MODULES

### Module Function

An I/O module is the entity within a computer responsible for the control of one or more external devices and for the exchange of data between those devices and main memory and/or CPU registers. Thus, the I/O module must have an interface internal to the computer (to the CPU and main memory) and an interface external to the computer (to the external device).

The major functions or requirements for an I/O module fall into the following categories:

- Control and Timing
- CPU Communication
- Device Communication

**TABLE 6.1    (continued)**

*Information Separator*

**FS** (File Separator):
**GS** (Group Separator)
**RS** (Record Separator)
**US** (United Separator)

Information separators to be used in an optional manner except that their hierarchy shall be FS (the most inclusive) to the US (the least inclusive).

*Miscellaneous*

**NUL** (Null): No character. Used for filling in time or filling space on tape when there are no data.

**BEL** (Bell): Used when there is need to call human attention. It may control alarm or attention devices.

**SO** (Shift Out): Indicates that the code combinations that follow shall be interpreted as *outside* of the standard character set until a SHIFT IN character is reached.

**SI** (Shift In): Indicates that the code combinations that follow shall be interpreted according to the standard set.

**DEL** (Delete): Used to obliterate unwanted characters (for example, on paper tape by punching a hole in *every* bit position).

**SP** (Space): A nonprinting character used to separate words, or to move the printing mechanism or display cursor forward by one position.

**DLE** (Data Link Escape): A character that shall change the meaning of one or more contiguously following characters. It can provide supplementary controls, or permits the sending of data characters having any bit combination.

**DC1, DC2, DC3, and DC4** (Device Controls): Characters for the control of ancillary devices or special terminal features.

**CAN** (Cancel): Indicates that the data that precedes it in a message or block should be disregarded (usually because an error has been detected).

**EM** (End of Medium): Indicates the physical end of a card, tape, or other medium, or the end of the required or used portion of the medium.

**SUB** (Substitute): Substituted for a character that is found to be erroneous or invalid.

**ESC** (Escape): A character intended to provide code extension in that it gives a specified number of continuously following characters an alternate meaning.

- Data Buffering
- Error Detection

During any period of time, the CPU may communicate with one or more external devices in unpredictable patterns, depending on the program's need for I/O. The internal resources, such as main memory and the system bus, must be shared among a number of activities including data I/O. Thus, the I/O function includes a *control and timing* requirement, to coordinate the flow of traffic between internal resources and external devices. For example, the control of the transfer of data from an external device to the CPU might involve the following sequence of steps:

1. The CPU interrogates the I/O module to check the status of the attached device.
2. The I/O module returns the device status.
3. If the device is operational and ready to transmit, the CPU requests the transfer of data, by means of a command to the I/O module.
4. The I/O module obtains a unit of data (e.g., 8 or 16 bits) from the external device.
5. The data are transferred from the I/O module to the CPU.

If the system employs a bus, then each of the interactions between the CPU and the I/O module involves one or more bus arbitrations.

The preceding simplified scenario also illustrates that the I/O module must have the capability to engage in communication with the CPU and with the external device. *CPU communication* involves:

- *Command Decoding:* The I/O module accepts commands from the CPU. These commands are generally sent as signals on the control bus. For example, an I/O module for a disk drive might accept the following commands: READ SECTOR, WRITE SECTOR, SEEK track number, and SCAN record ID. The latter two commands each include a parameter that is sent on the data bus.
- *Data:* Data are exchanged between the CPU and the I/O module over the data bus.
- *Status Reporting:* Because peripherals are so slow, it is important to know the status of the I/O module. For example, if an I/O module is asked to send data to the CPU (read), it may not be ready to do so because it is still working on the previous I/O command. This fact can be reported with a status signal. Common status signals are BUSY and READY. There may also be signals to report various error conditions.
- *Address Recognition:* Just as each word of memory has an address, so does each I/O device. Thus, an I/O module must recognize one unique address for each peripheral it controls.

On the other side, the I/O module must be able to perform *device communication*. This communication involves commands, status information, and data (Figure 6.2).

An essential task of an I/O module is *data buffering*. The need for this function is apparent from Table 6.2. Whereas the transfer rate into and out of main memory or the CPU is quite high, the rate is orders of magnitude lower for most peripheral devices. Data coming from main memory are sent to an I/O module in a rapid

**TABLE 6.2   Examples of I/O Devices Categorized by Behavior, Partner, and Data Rate [HENN90]**

| Device | Behavior | Partner | Data Rate (KBytes/sec) |
|---|---|---|---|
| Keyboard | Input | Human | 0.01 |
| Mouse | Input | Human | 0.02 |
| Voice input | Input | Human | 0.02 |
| Scanner | Input | Human | 200 |
| Voice output | Output | Human | 0.6 |
| Line printer | Output | Human | 1 |
| Laser printer | Output | Human | 100 |
| Graphics display | Output | Human | 30,000 |
| CPU to frame buffer | Output | Human | 200 |
| Network-terminal | Input or output | Machine | 0.05 |
| Network-LAN | Input or output | Machine | 200 |
| Optical disk | Storage | Machine | 500 |
| Magnetic tape | Storage | Machine | 2,000 |
| Magnetic disk | Storage | Machine | 2,000 |

burst. The data are buffered in the I/O module and then sent to the peripheral device at its data rate. In the opposite direction, data are buffered so as not to tie up the memory in a slow transfer operation. Thus, the I/O module must be able to operate at both device and memory speeds.

Finally, an I/O module is often responsible for *error detection* and for subsequently reporting errors to the CPU. One class of errors includes mechanical and electrical malfunctions reported by the device (e.g., paper jam, bad disk track). Another class consists of unintentional changes to the bit pattern as it is transmitted from device to I/O module. Some form of error-detecting code is often used to detect transmission errors. A common example is the use of a parity bit on each character of data. For example, the ASCII character code occupies 7 bits of a byte. The eighth bit is set so that the total number of "one"s in the byte is even (even parity) or odd (odd parity). When a byte is received, the I/O module checks the parity to determine whether an error has occurred.

## I/O Module Structure

I/O modules vary considerably in complexity and the number of external devices that they control. We will attempt only a very general description here. (One specific device, the Intel 8255A, is described in Section 6.4.) Figure 6.3 provides a general block diagram of an I/O module. The module connects to the rest of the computer through a set of signal lines (e.g., system bus lines). Data transferred to and from the module are buffered in one or more data registers. There may also be one or more status registers that provide current status information. A status register may also function as a control register, to accept detailed control information from the CPU. The logic within the module interacts with the CPU via a set of control lines. These are used by the CPU to issue commands to the I/O module. Some of the control lines may be used by the I/O module (e.g., for arbitration and status

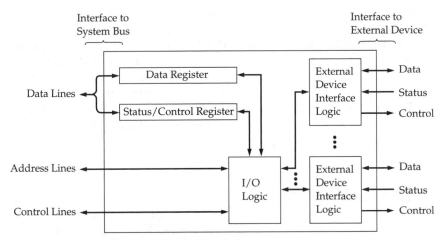

**FIGURE 6.3. Block diagram of an I/O module**

signals). The module must also be able to recognize and generate addresses associated with the devices it controls. Each I/O module has a unique address or, if it controls more than one external device, a unique set of addresses. Finally, the I/O module contains logic specific to the interface with each device that it controls.

An I/O module functions to allow the CPU to view a wide range of devices in a simple-minded way. There is a spectrum of capabilities that may be provided. The I/O module may hide the details of timing, formats, and the electromechanics of an external device so that the CPU can function in terms of simple read and write commands, and possibly open and close file commands. In its simplest form, the I/O module may still leave much of the work of controlling a device (e.g., rewind a tape) visible to the CPU.

An I/O module that takes on most of the detailed processing burden, presenting a high-level interface to the CPU, is usually referred to as an *I/O channel* or *I/O processor*. An I/O module that is quite primitive and requires detailed control is usually referred to as an *I/O controller* or *device controller*. I/O controllers are commonly seen on microcomputers, whereas I/O channels are used on mainframes, with minicomputers employing a mixture.

In what follows, we will use the generic term *I/O module* when no confusion results and will use more specific terms where necessary.

## 6.3

### PROGRAMMED I/O

Three techniques are possible for I/O operations. With *programmed I/O,* data are exchanged between the CPU and the I/O module. The CPU executes a program that gives it direct control of the I/O operation, including sensing device status, sending a read or write command, and transferring the data. When the CPU issues a command to the I/O module, it must wait until the I/O operation is complete. If the CPU is faster than the I/O module, this is wasteful of CPU time. With *interrupt-driven I/O*, the CPU issues an I/O command, continues to execute other instructions, and is interrupted by the I/O module when the latter has completed its work. With both programmed and interrupt I/O, the CPU is responsible for extracting data from main memory for output and storing data in main memory for input. The alternative is known as *direct memory access* (DMA). In this mode, the I/O module and main memory exchange data directly, without CPU involvement.

Table 6.3 indicates the relationship among these three techniques. In this section, we explore programmed I/O. Interrupt I/O and DMA are explored in the following two sections, respectively.

**TABLE 6.3    I/O Techniques**

|                                          | *No Interrupts*  | *Use of Interrupts*        |
| ---------------------------------------- | ---------------- | -------------------------- |
| I/O-to-memory transfer through CPU       | Programmed I/O   | Interrupt-driven I/O       |
| Direct I/O-to-memory transfer            |                  | Direct memory access (DMA) |

## Overview

When the CPU is executing a program and encounters an instruction relating to I/O, it executes that instruction by issuing a command to the appropriate I/O module. With programmed I/O, the I/O module will perform the requested action and then set the appropriate bits in the I/O status register (Figure 6.3). The I/O module takes no further action to alert the CPU. In particular, it does not interrupt the CPU. Thus, it is the responsibility of the CPU to periodically check the status of the I/O module until it finds that the operation is complete.

To explain the programmed I/O technique, we view it first from the point of view of the I/O commands issued by the CPU to the I/O module, and then from the point of view of the I/O instructions executed by the CPU.

## I/O Commands

To execute an I/O-related instruction, the CPU issues an address, specifying the particular I/O module and external device, and an I/O command. There are four types of I/O commands that an I/O module may receive when it is addressed by a CPU. They are classified as control, test, read, and write.

A *control* command is used to activate a peripheral and tell it what to do. For example, a magnetic-tape unit may be instructed to rewind or to move forward one record. These commands are tailored to the particular type of peripheral device.

A *test* command is used to test various status conditions associated with an I/O module and its peripherals. The CPU will want to know that the peripheral of interest is powered on and available for use. It will also want to know if the most recent I/O operation is completed and if any errors occurred.

A *read* command causes the I/O module to obtain an item of data from the peripheral and place it in an internal buffer (depicted as a data register in Figure 6.3). The CPU can then obtain the data item by requesting that the I/O module place it on the data bus. Conversely, a *write* command causes the I/O module to take an item of data (byte or word) from the data bus and subsequently transmit that data item to the peripheral.

Figure 6.4a gives an example of the use of programmed I/O to read in a block of data from a peripheral device (e.g., a record from tape) into memory. Data are read in one word (e.g., 16 bits) at a time. For each word that is read in, the CPU must remain in a status-checking cycle until it determines that the word is available in the I/O module's data register. This flowchart highlights the main disadvantage of this technique: it is a time-consuming process that keeps the processor busy needlessly.

## I/O Instructions

With programmed I/O, there is a close correspondence between the I/O-related instructions that the CPU fetches from memory and the I/O commands that the CPU issues to an I/O module to execute the instructions. That is, the instructions are easily mapped into I/O commands, and there is often a simple one-to-one relationship. The form of the instruction depends on the way in which external devices are addressed.

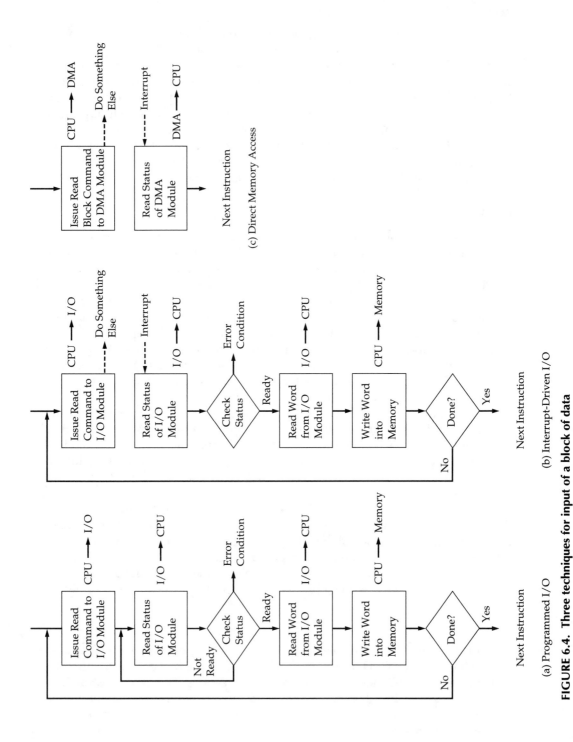

FIGURE 6.4.  **Three techniques for input of a block of data**

(a) Programmed I/O

(b) Interrupt-Driven I/O

(c) Direct Memory Access

Typically, there will be many I/O devices connected through I/O modules to the system. Each device is given a unique identifier or address. When the CPU issues an I/O command, the command contains the address of the desired device. Thus, each I/O module must interpret the address lines to determine if the command is for itself.

When the CPU, main memory, and I/O share a common bus, two modes of addressing are possible: memory-mapped and isolated. With *memory-mapped I/O*, there is a single address space for memory locations and I/O devices. The CPU treats the status and data registers of I/O modules as memory locations and uses the same machine instructions to access both memory and I/O devices. So, for example, with 10 address lines, a combined total of 1024 memory locations and I/O addresses can be supported, in any combination.

With memory-mapped I/O, a single read line and a single write line are needed on the bus. Alternatively, the bus may be equipped with memory read and write plus input and output command lines. Now, the command line specifies whether the address refers to a memory location or an I/O device. The full range of addresses may be available for both. Again, with 10 address lines, the system may now support both 1024 memory locations and 1024 I/O addresses. Since the address space for I/O is isolated from that for memory, this is referred to as *isolated I/O*.

Figure 6.5 contrasts these two programmed I/O techniques. Figure 6.5a shows how the interface for a simple input device such as a terminal keyboard might

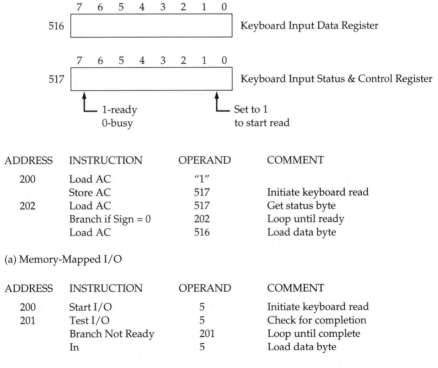

(a) Memory-Mapped I/O

| ADDRESS | INSTRUCTION | OPERAND | COMMENT |
|---|---|---|---|
| 200 | Load AC | "1" | |
| | Store AC | 517 | Initiate keyboard read |
| 202 | Load AC | 517 | Get status byte |
| | Branch if Sign = 0 | 202 | Loop until ready |
| | Load AC | 516 | Load data byte |

(b) Isolated I/O

| ADDRESS | INSTRUCTION | OPERAND | COMMENT |
|---|---|---|---|
| 200 | Start I/O | 5 | Initiate keyboard read |
| 201 | Test I/O | 5 | Check for completion |
| | Branch Not Ready | 201 | Loop until complete |
| | In | 5 | Load data byte |

FIGURE 6.5. **Memory-mapped and isolated I/O**

appear to a programmer using memory-mapped I/O. Assume a 10-bit address, with a 512-bit memory (locations 0–511) and up to 512 I/O addresses (locations 512–1023). Two addresses are dedicated to keyboard input from a particular terminal. Address 516 refers to the data register and address 517 refers to the status register, which also functions as a control register for receiving CPU commands. The program shown will read 1 byte of data from the keyboard into an accumulator register in the CPU. Note that the CPU loops until the data byte is available.

With isolated I/O (Figure 6.5b), the I/O ports are accessible only by special I/O commands, which activate the I/O command lines on the bus.

For most types of CPUs, there is a relatively large set of different instructions for referencing memory. If isolated I/O is used, there are only a few I/O instructions. Thus, an advantage of memory-mapped I/O is that this large repertoire of instructions can be used, allowing more efficient programming. A disadvantage is that valuable memory address space is used up. Both memory-mapped and isolated I/O are in common use.

## 6.4

### INTERRUPT-DRIVEN I/O

The problem with programmed I/O is that the CPU has to wait a long time for the I/O module of concern to be ready for either reception or transmission of data. The CPU, while waiting, must repeatedly interrogate the status of the I/O module. As a result, the level of the performance of the entire system is severely degraded.

An alternative is for the CPU to issue an I/O command to a module and then go on to do some other useful work. The I/O module will then interrupt the CPU to request service when it is ready to exchange data with the CPU. The CPU then executes the data transfer, as before, and then resumes its former processing.

Let us consider how this works, first from the point of view of the I/O module. For input, the I/O module receives a READ command from the CPU. The I/O module then proceeds to read data in from an associated peripheral. Once the data are in the module's data register, the module signals an interrupt to the CPU over a control line. The module then waits until its data are requested by the CPU. When the request is made, the module places its data on the data bus and is then ready for another I/O operation.

From the CPU's point of view, the action for input is as follows. The CPU issues a READ command. It then goes off and does something else (e.g., the CPU may be working on several different programs at the same time). At the end of each instruction cycle, the CPU checks for interrupts (Figure 3.9). When the interrupt from the I/O module occurs, the CPU saves the context (e.g., program counter and CPU registers) of the current program and processes the interrupt. In this case, the CPU reads the word of data from the I/O module and stores it in memory. It then restores the context of the program it was working on (or some other program) and resumes execution.

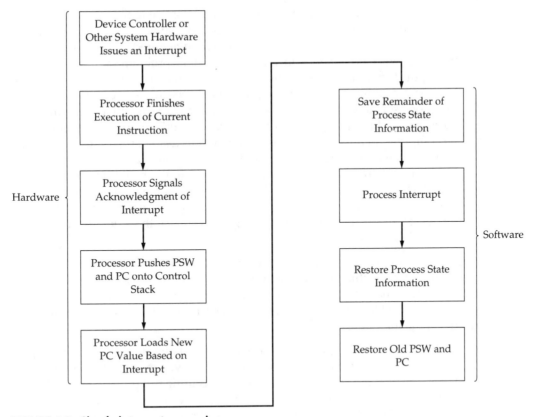

**FIGURE 6.6.  Simple interrupt processing**

Figure 6.4b shows the use of interrupt I/O for reading in a block of data. Compare this with Figure 6.4a. Interrupt I/O is more efficient than programmed I/O because it eliminates needless waiting. However, interrupt I/O still consumes a lot of CPU time, since every word of data that goes from memory to I/O module or from I/O module to memory must pass through the CPU.

## Interrupt Processing

Let us consider the role of the processor in I/O in more detail. The occurrence of an interrupt triggers a number of events, both in the processor hardware and in software. Figure 6.6 shows a typical sequence. When an I/O device completes an I/O operation, the following sequence of hardware events occurs:

1.  The device issues an interrupt signal to the processor.
2.  The processor finishes execution of the current instruction before responding to the interrupt, as indicated in Figure 3.9.
3.  The processor tests for an interrupt, determines that there is one, and sends an acknowledgment signal to the device that issued the interrupt. The acknowledgment allows the device to remove its interrupt signal.

4. The processor now needs to prepare to transfer control to the interrupt routine. To begin, it needs to save information needed to resume the current program at the point of interrupt. The minimum information required is (a) the status of the processor, which is contained in a register called the program status word (PSW), and (b) the location of the next instruction to be executed, which is contained in the program counter. These can be pushed onto the system control stack.[2]

5. The processor now loads the program counter with the entry location of the interrupt-handling program that will respond to this interrupt. Depending on the computer architecture and operating-system design, there may be a single program, one for each type of interrupt, or one for each device and each type of interrupt. If there is more than one interrupt-handling routine, the processor must determine which one to invoke. This information may have been included in the original interrupt signal, or the processor may have to issue a request to the device that issued the interrupt to get a response that contains the needed information.

Once the program counter has been loaded, the processor proceeds to the next instruction cycle, which begins with an instruction fetch. Since the instruction fetch is determined by the contents of the program counter, the result is that control is transferred to the interrupt-handler program. The execution of this program results in the following operations:

6. At this point, the program counter and PSW relating to the interrupted program have been saved on the system stack. However, there is other information that is considered part of the "state" of the executing program. In particular, the contents of the processor registers need to be saved, since these registers may be used by the interrupt handler. So, all of these values, plus any other state information, need to be saved. Typically, the interrupt handler will begin by saving the contents of all registers on the stack. Figure 6.7a shows a simple example. In this case, a user program is interrupted after the instruction at location $N$. The contents of all of the registers plus the address of the next instruction ($N + 1$) are pushed onto the stack. The stack pointer is updated to point to the new top of stack, and the program counter is updated to point to the beginning of the interrupt service routine.

7. The interrupt handler may now proceed to process the interrupt. This will include an examination of status information relating to the I/O operation or other event that caused an interrupt. It may also involve sending additional commands or acknowledgments to the I/O device.

8. When interrupt processing is complete, the saved register values are retrieved from the stack and restored to the registers (e.g., see Figure 6.7b).

9. The final act is to restore the PSW and program counter values from the stack. As a result, the next instruction to be executed will be from the previously interrupted program.

Note that it is important to save all the state information about the interrupted program for later resumption. This is because the interrupt is not a routine called

---

[2]See Appendix 9A for a discussion of stack operation.

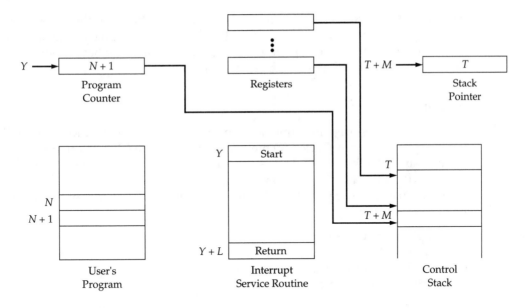

(a) Interrupt Occurs After Instruction at Location $N$

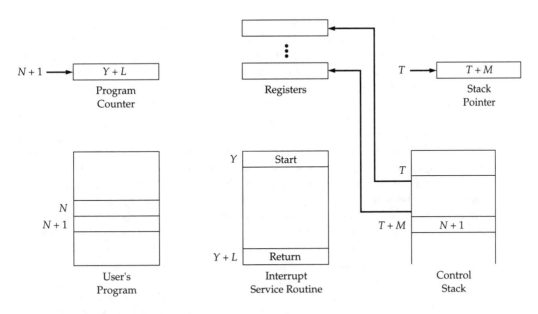

(b) Return from Interrupt

**FIGURE 6.7. Changes in memory and register for an interrupt**

from the program. Rather, the interrupt can occur at any time and therefore at any point in the execution of a user program. Its occurrence is unpredictable. Indeed, as we will see in the next chapter, the two programs may not have anything in common and may belong to two different users.

## Design Issues

Two design issues arise in implementing interrupt I/O. First, since there will almost invariably be multiple I/O modules, how does the CPU determine which device issued the interrupt? And second, if multiple interrupts have occurred, how does the CPU decide which one to process?

Let us consider device identification first. Four general categories of techniques are in common use:

- Multiple Interrupt Lines
- Software Poll
- Daisy Chain (hardware poll, vectored)
- Bus Arbitration (vectored)

The most straightforward approach to the problem is to provide *multiple interrupt lines* between the CPU and the I/O modules. However, it is impractical to dedicate more than a few bus lines or CPU pins to interrupt lines. Consequently, even if multiple lines are used, it is likely that each line will have multiple I/O modules attached to it. Thus, one of the other three techniques must be used on each line.

One alternative is the *software poll*. When the CPU detects an interrupt, it branches to an interrupt-service routine whose job it is to poll each I/O module to determine which module caused the interrupt. The poll could be in the form of a separate command line (e.g., TESTI/O). In this case, the CPU raises TESTI/O and places the address of a particular I/O module on the address lines. The I/O module responds positively if it set the interrupt. Alternatively, each I/O module could contain an addressable status register. The CPU then reads the status register of each I/O module to identify the interrupting module. Once the correct module is identified, the CPU branches to a device-service routine specific to that device.

The disadvantage of the software poll is that it is time consuming. A more efficient technique is to use a *daisy chain*, which provides, in effect, a hardware poll. An example of a daisy-chain configuration is shown in Figure 3.30. For interrupts, all I/O modules share a common interrupt request line. The interrupt acknowledge line is daisy-chained through the modules. When the CPU senses an interrupt, it sends out an interrupt acknowledge. This signal propagates through a series of I/O modules until it gets to a requesting module. The requesting module typically responds by placing a word on the data lines. This word is referred to as a *vector* and is either the address of the I/O module or some other unique identifier. In either case, the CPU uses the vector as a pointer to the appropriate device-service routine. This avoids the need to execute a general interrupt-service routine first. This technique is referred to as a *vectored interrupt*.

There is another technique that makes use of vectored interrupts, and that is *bus arbitration*. With bus arbitration, an I/O module must first gain control of the bus before it can raise the interrupt request line. Thus, only one module can raise the line at a time. When the CPU detects the interrupt, it responds on the interrupt acknowledge line. The requesting module then places its vector on the data lines.

The techniques listed above serve to identify the requesting I/O module. They also provide a way of assigning priorities when more than one device is requesting interrupt service. With multiple lines, the CPU just picks the interrupt line with the highest priority. With software polling, the order in which modules are polled determines their priority. Similarly, the order of modules on a daisy chain determines their priority. Finally, bus arbitration can employ a priority scheme, as discussed in Section 3.4.

We now turn to two examples of interrupt structures.

## Intel 8259A Interrupt Controller

The Intel 8086 provides a single Interrupt Request (INTR) and a single Interrupt Acknowledge (INTA) line. To allow the 8086 to flexibly handle a variety of devices and priority structures, it is usually configured with an external interrupt arbiter, the 8259A. External devices are connected to the 8259A, which in turn connects to the 8086.

Figure 6.8 shows the use of the 8259A to connect multiple I/O modules for the 8086. A single 8259A can handle up to 8 modules. If control for more than 8 modules is required, a cascade arrangement can be used to handle up to 64 modules.

The 8259A's sole responsibility is the management of interrupts. It accepts interrupt requests from attached modules, determines which interrupt has the highest priority, and then signals the CPU by raising the INTR line. The CPU acknowledges via the INTA line. This prompts the 8259A to place the appropriate vector information on the data bus. The CPU can then proceed to process the interrupt and to communicate directly with the I/O module to read or write data.

The 8259A is programmable. The 8086 determines the priority scheme to be used by setting a control word in the 8259A. The following interrupt modes are possible.

- *Fully Nested:* The interrupt requests are ordered in priority from 0 (IR0) through 7 (IR7).
- *Rotating:* In some applications a number of interrupting devices are of equal priority. In this mode a device, after being serviced, receives the lowest priority in the group.
- *Special Mask:* This allows the CPU to selectively inhibit interrupts from certain devices.

## The Intel 8255A Programmable Peripheral Interface

As an example of an I/O module used for programmed I/O and interrupt-driven I/O, we consider the Intel 8255A Programmable Peripheral Interface. The 8255A is a single-chip, general-purpose I/O module designed for use with the Intel 8086 CPU. Figure 6.9 shows a general block diagram plus the pin assignment for the 40-pin package in which it is housed.

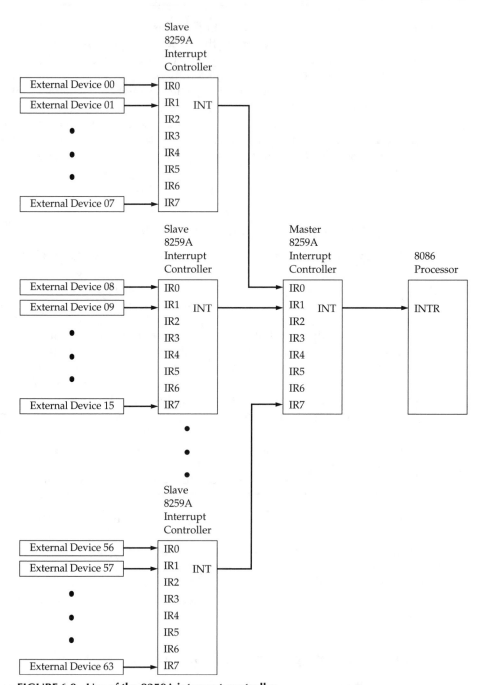

**FIGURE 6.8. Use of the 8259A interrupt controller**

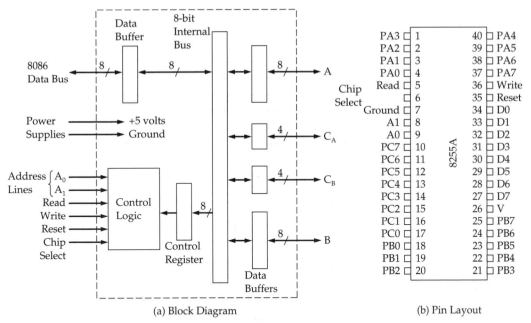

(a) Block Diagram

(b) Pin Layout

**FIGURE 6.9. The Intel 8255A programmable peripheral interface**

The right side of the block diagram is the external interface of the 8255A. The 24 I/O lines are programmable by the 8086 by means of the control register. The 8086 can set the value of the control register to specify a variety of operating modes and configurations. The 24 lines are divided into three 8-bit groups (A, B, C). Each group can function as an 8-bit I/O port. In addition, group C is subdivided into 4-bit groups ($C_A$ and $C_B$), which may be used in conjunction with the A and B I/O ports. Configured in this manner, they carry control and status signals.

The left side of the block diagram is the internal interface to the 8086 bus. It includes an 8-bit bidirectional data bus (D0 through D7), used to transfer data to and from the I/O ports and to transfer control information to the control register. The two address lines specify one of the three I/O ports or the control register. A transfer takes place when the CHIP SELECT line is enabled together with either READ or WRITE line. The RESET line is used to initialize the module.

The control register is loaded by the CPU to control the mode of operation and to define signals, if any. In Mode 0 operation, the three groups of 8 external lines function as three 8-bit I/O ports. Each port can be designated as input or output. Otherwise, group A and B function as I/O ports, and the lines of group C serve as control lines for A and B. The control signals serve two principal purposes: "hand-shaking" and interrupt request. Handshaking is a simple timing mechanism. One control line is used by the sender as a DATA READY line, to indicate when the data are present on the I/O data lines. Another line is used by the receiver as an ACKNOWLEDGE, indicating that the data have been read and the data lines may be cleared. Another line may be designated as an INTERRUPT REQUEST line and tied back to the system bus.

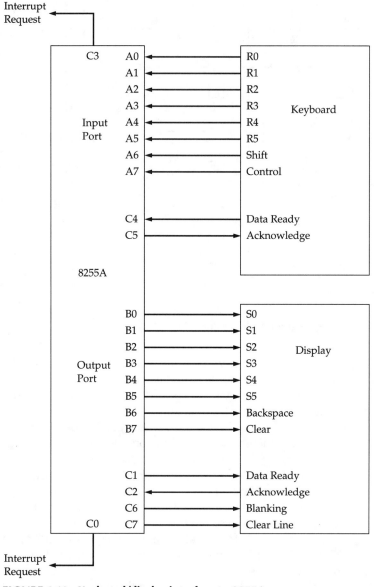

**FIGURE 6.10. Keyboard/display interface to 8255A**

Because the 8255A is programmable via the control register, it can be used to control a variety of simple peripheral devices. Figure 6.10 illustrates its use to control a keyboard/display terminal. The keyboard provides 8 bits of input. Two of these bits, SHIFT and CONTROL, have special meaning to the keyboard-handling program executing in the CPU. However, this interpretation is transparent to the 8255A, which simply accepts the 8 bits of data and presents them on the system data bus. Two handshaking control lines are provided for use with the keyboard.

The display is also linked by an 8-bit data port. Again, 2 of the bits have special meanings that are transparent to the 8255A. In addition to two handshaking lines, two lines provide additional control functions.

## 6.5

### DIRECT MEMORY ACCESS

### Drawbacks of Programmed and Interrupt-Driven I/O

Interrupt-driven I/O, though more efficient than simple programmed I/O, still requires the active intervention of the CPU to transfer data between memory and an I/O module, and any data transfer must traverse a path through the CPU. Thus, both these forms of I/O suffer from two inherent drawbacks:

1. The I/O transfer rate is limited by the speed with which the CPU can test and service a device.
2. The CPU is tied up in managing an I/O transfer; a number of instructions must be executed for each I/O transfer (e.g., Figure 6.4).

There is somewhat of a trade-off between these two drawbacks. Consider the transfer of a block of data. Using simple programmed I/O, the CPU is dedicated to the task of I/O and can move data at a rather high rate, at the cost of doing nothing else. Interrupt I/O frees up the CPU to some extent at the expense of I/O transfer rate. Nevertheless, both methods have an adverse impact on both CPU activity and I/O transfer rate.

When large volumes of data are to be moved, a more efficient technique is required: direct memory access (DMA).

### DMA Function

DMA involves an additional module on the system bus. The DMA module (Figure 6.11) is capable of mimicking the CPU and, indeed, of taking over control of the system from the CPU. The technique works as follows. When the CPU wishes to read or write a block of data, it issues a command to the DMA module, by sending to the DMA module the following information:

- Whether a read or write is requested.
- The address of the I/O device involved.
- The starting location in memory to read from or write to.
- The number of words to be read or written.

The CPU then continues with other work. It has delegated this I/O operation to the DMA module, and that module will take care of it. The DMA module transfers the entire block of data, one word at a time, directly to or from memory, without going through the CPU. When the transfer is complete, the DMA module sends an interrupt signal to the CPU. Thus, the CPU is involved only at the beginning and end of the transfer (Figure 6.4c).

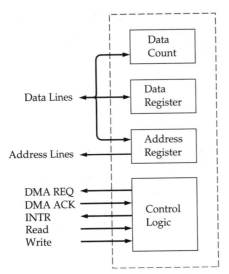

**FIGURE 6.11. Typical DMA block diagram**

The DMA module needs to take control of the bus in order to transfer data to and from memory. For this purpose, the DMA module must use the bus only when the CPU does not need it, or it must force the CPU to temporarily suspend operation. The latter technique is more common and is referred to as *cycle-stealing* since the DMA module in effect steals a bus cycle.

Figure 6.12 shows where in the instruction cycle the CPU may be suspended. In each case, the CPU is suspended just before it needs to use the bus. The DMA module then transfers one word and returns control to the CPU. Note that this is not an interrupt; the CPU does not save a context and do something else. Rather, the CPU pauses for one bus cycle. The overall effect is to cause the CPU to execute more slowly. Nevertheless, for a multiple-word I/O transfer, DMA is far more efficient than interrupt-driven or programmed I/O.

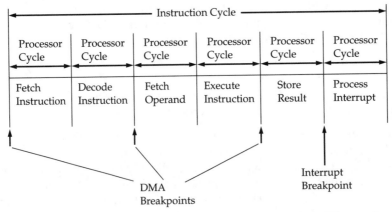

**FIGURE 6.12. DMA and interrupt breakpoints during an instruction cycle**

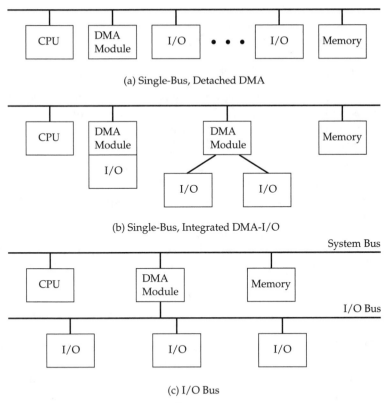

(a) Single-Bus, Detached DMA

(b) Single-Bus, Integrated DMA-I/O

(c) I/O Bus

**FIGURE 6.13.  Possible DMA configuration**

The DMA mechanism can be configured in a variety of ways. Some possibilities are shown in Figure 6.13. In the first example, all modules share the same system bus. The DMA module, acting as a surrogate CPU, uses programmed I/O to exchange data between memory and an I/O module through the DMA module. This configuration, while it may be inexpensive, is clearly inefficient. As with CPU-controlled programmed I/O, each transfer of a word consumes two bus cycles.

The number of required bus cycles can be cut substantially by integrating the DMA and I/O functions. As Figure 6.13b indicates, this means that there is a path between the DMA module and one or more I/O modules that does not include the system bus. The DMA logic may actually be a part of an I/O module, or it may be a separate module that controls one or more I/O modules. This concept can be taken one step further by connecting I/O modules to the DMA module using an I/O bus (Figure 6.13c). This reduces the number of I/O interfaces in the DMA module to one and provides for an easily expandable configuration. In all of these cases (Figures 6.13b and c), the system bus that the DMA module shares with the CPU and memory is used by the DMA module only to exchange data with memory. The exchange of data between the DMA and I/O modules takes place off the system bus.

## I/O CHANNELS AND PROCESSORS

### The Evolution of the I/O Function

As computer systems have evolved, there has been a pattern of increasing complexity and sophistication of individual components. Nowhere is this more evident than in the I/O function. We have already seen part of that evolution. The evolutionary steps can be summarized as follows:

1. The CPU directly controls a peripheral device. This is seen in simple microprocessor-controlled devices.
2. A controller or I/O module is added. The CPU uses programmed I/O without interrupts. With this step, the CPU becomes somewhat divorced from the specific details of external device interfaces.
3. The same configuration as in step 2 is used, but now interrupts are employed. The CPU need not spend time waiting for an I/O operation to be performed, increasing efficiency.
4. The I/O module is given direct access to memory via DMA. It can now move a block of data to or from memory without involving the CPU, except at the beginning and end of the transfer.
5. The I/O module is enhanced to become a processor in its own right, with a specialized instruction set tailored for I/O. The CPU directs the I/O processor to execute an I/O program in memory. The I/O processor fetches and executes these instructions without CPU intervention. This allows the CPU to specify a sequence of I/O activities and to be interrupted only when the entire sequence has been performed.
6. The I/O module has a local memory of its own and is, in fact, a computer in its own right. With this architecture, a large set of I/O devices can be controlled, with minimal CPU involvement. A common use for such an architecture has been to control communication with interactive terminals. The I/O processor takes care of most of the tasks involved in controlling the terminals.

As one proceeds along this evolutionary path, more and more of the I/O function is performed without CPU involvement. The CPU is increasingly relieved of I/O-related tasks, improving performance. With the last two steps (5–6), a major change occurs with the introduction of the concept of an I/O module capable of executing a program. For step 5, the I/O module is often referred to as an *I/O channel*. For step 6, the term *I/O processor* is often used. However, both terms are on occasion applied to both situations. In what follows, we will use the term I/O channel.

### Characteristics of I/O Channels

The I/O channel represents an extension of the DMA concept. An I/O channel has the ability to execute I/O instructions, which gives it complete control over I/O operations. In a computer system with such devices, the CPU does not execute I/O instructions. Such instructions are stored in main memory to be executed by a special-purpose processor in the I/O channel itself. Thus, the CPU initiates an I/O transfer by instructing the I/O channel to execute a program in memory. The program will specify the device or devices, the area or areas of memory for storage, priority, and actions to be taken for certain error conditions. The I/O channel follows these instructions and controls the data transfer.

Two types of I/O channels are common, as illustrated in Figure 6.14. A *selector channel* controls multiple high-speed devices and, at any one time, is dedicated to the transfer of data with one of those devices. Thus, the I/O channel selects one device and effects the data transfer. Each device, or a small set of devices, is handled by a *controller,* or I/O module, that is much like the I/O modules we have been

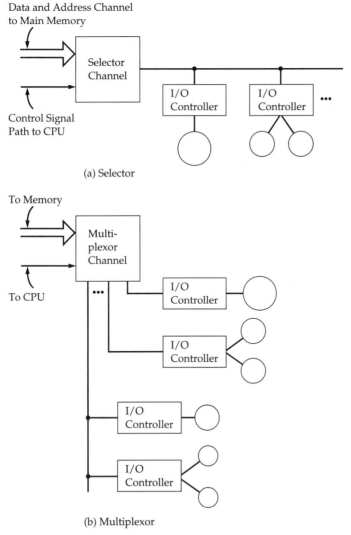

(a) Selector

(b) Multiplexor

**FIGURE 6.14. I/O channel architecture**

discussing. Thus, the I/O channel serves in place of the CPU in controlling these I/O controllers. A *multiplexor channel* can handle I/O with multiple devices at the same time. For low-speed devices, a *byte multiplexor* accepts or transmits characters as fast as possible to multiple devices. For example, the resultant character stream from three devices with different rates and individual streams $A_1A_2A_3A_4 \ldots$, $B_1B_2B_3B_4 \ldots$, and $C_1C_2C_3C_4 \ldots$ might be $A_1B_1C_1A_2C_2A_3B_2C_3A_4$, and so on. For high-speed devices, a *block multiplexor* interleaves blocks of data from several devices.

## 6.7

### THE EXTERNAL INTERFACE

### Types of Interfaces

The interface to a peripheral from an I/O module must be tailored to the nature and operation of the peripheral. One major characteristic of the interface is whether it is serial or parallel (Figure 6.15). In a *parallel interface,* there are multiple lines connecting the I/O module and the peripheral, and multiple bits are transferred simultaneously, just as all of the bits of a word are transferred simultaneously over the data bus. In a *serial interface,* there is only one line used to transmit data, and bits must be transmitted one at a time. A parallel interface is commonly used for higher-speed peripherals, such as tape and disk. The serial interface is more common for printers and terminals.

In either case, the I/O module must engage in a dialogue with the peripheral. In general terms, the dialogue for a write operation is as follows:

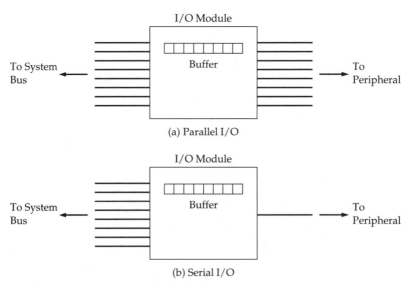

FIGURE 6.15.  **Parallel and serial I/O**

1. The I/O module sends a control signal requesting permission to send data.
2. The peripheral acknowledges the request.
3. The I/O module transfers data (one word or a block depending on the peripheral).
4. The peripheral acknowledges receipt of the data.

A read operation proceeds similarly.

Key to the operation of an I/O module is an internal buffer that can store data being passed between the peripheral and the rest of the system. This buffer allows the I/O module to compensate for the differences in speed between the system bus and its external lines.

## Point-to-Point and Multipoint Configurations

The connection between an I/O module in a computer system and external devices can be either point-to-point or multipoint. A point-to-point interface provides a dedicated line between the I/O module and the external device. On small systems (PCs, workstations), typical point-to-point links include those to the keyboard, printer, and external modem. A typical example of such an interface is the EIA-232 specification (see [STAL94] for a description).

Of increasing importance are multipoint external interfaces, used to support external mass storage devices (disk and tape drives) and multimedia devices (CD-ROMs, video, audio). These multipoint interfaces are in effect external buses, and they exhibit the same type of logic as the buses discussed in Chapter 3. In this section, we look at two key examples: SCSI and P1394.

## Small Computer System Interface (SCSI)

A good example of an interface for external peripheral devices is SCSI. First popularized on the Macintosh in 1984, SCSI is now widely used on both Macintosh and IBM PC-compatible systems, as well as on many workstations. SCSI is the standard interface for CD-ROM drives, audio equipment, and external mass storage devices. SCSI uses a parallel interface, with 8, 16, or 32 data lines.

The SCSI configuration is generally referred to as a bus, although in fact devices are daisy-chained together. Each SCSI device has two connectors: one for input and one for output. All the devices are chained together, and one end of the chain is hooked into the host computer. All devices function independently and can exchange data with each other as well as with the host system. For example, a hard disk may back itself up to a tape drive without involving the host processor. Data is transferred in message packets, as described below.

### SCSI Versions

The original SCSI specification, now called SCSI-1, was developed in the early 1980s. SCSI-1 provides for 8 data lines and operates at a clock speed of 5 MHz, or a data rate of 5 MBytes/sec. SCSI-1 allows up to seven devices to be daisy-chained and hooked to the host system.

In 1991, a revised specification, SCSI-2, was introduced. The most noteworthy changes were the optional expansion of the data lines to 16 or 32 and the increase of the clock speed to 10 Mhz. The result is a maximum data rate of 20 or 40 MBytes/sec.

Work is currently underway on an SCSI-3 specification, which will support greater speeds.

### Signals and Phases

All exchanges on the SCSI bus are between an initiator and a target. Typically, the host system is the initiator and a peripheral controller is the target, but some devices are able to assume either role. In any case, all activity on the bus occurs in a sequence of phases. The phases are

- *Bus Free:* Indicates that no device is using the bus and that the bus is available for use.
- *Arbitration:* Enables one device to gain control of the bus so that it can initiate or resume an I/O process.
- *Selection:* Enables an initiator to select a target to perform a function, such as a Read or Write command.
- *Reselection:* Enables a target to reconnect to an initiator to resume an operation previously started by the initiator but suspended by the target.
- *Command:* Enables the target to request command information from the initiator.
- *Data:* Enables the target to request the transfer of data either to the initiator from the target (Data In) or from the initiator to the target (Data Out).
- *Status:* Enables the target to request that status information be sent from the target to the initiator.
- *Message:* Enables the target to request the transfer of one or more messages either to the initiator from the target (Message In) or from the initiator to the target (Message Out).

Figure 6.16 illustrates the order in which SCSI bus phases occur. Following a reset or power up, the bus enters the Bus Free phase. This is followed by the Arbitration phase, which usually results in the acquisition of control by one device. If arbitration fails, the bus returns to the Bus Free phase. When arbitration succeeds, the bus enters a Selection or Reselection phase that results in the assignment of initiator and target devices for this exchange. After the two devices are determined, there will be one or more information transfer phases (Command, Data, Status, Message) involving the two devices. The final information transfer phase is normally the Message In phase, in which a Disconnect or Command Complete message is transferred to the initiator, followed by the Bus Free phase.

One important feature of SCSI is the reselection capability. If a command is issued that takes some time to complete, the target can release the bus and reconnect to the initiator later. For example, a host can issue a command to a disk drive to format a disk and the drive can carry out the operation without tying up the bus.

The SCSI-1 specification defines a cable consisting of 18 signal lines, 9 for control and 9 for data (8 data lines and 1 parity line). The control lines are

- *BSY:* Set by any initiator or target to indicate that the bus is busy.

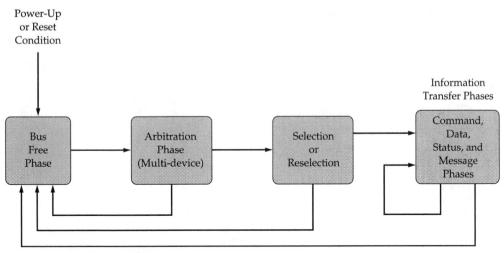

FIGURE 6.16.  SCSI Bus Phases

- *SEL:* Used by the initiator to select a target to perform a command, or by a target to reselect the initiator from which it is disconnected. The I/O signal distinguishes between selection and reselection.
- *C/D:* Used by the target to indicate whether data on the data bus is Control (Command, Status, or Message) or Data information.
- *I/O:* Used by the target to control the direction of data movement on the data bus.
- *MSG:* Used by the target to indicate to the initiator that the information being transferred is a message.
- *REQ:* Used by the target to request a data information transfer. In response to the REQ signal, the initiator accepts data from the bus during a Data In phase or places information on the bus during a Data Out phase.
- *ACK:* Used by the initiator to acknowledge a REQ from the target. The ACK signal indicates that the initiator has placed information on the bus during a Data Out phase or accepted data from the bus during a Data In phase.
- *ATN:* Used by the initiator to inform the target that it has a message available for transfer. The initiator may assert this signal during the Selection phase or at any time after the target assumes control of the bus.
- *RST:* Used to reset the bus.

Table 6.4 shows the relationship between the bus signals and the bus phases. For SCSI-2, there are additional data and parity lines plus an additional REQ/ACK pair of lines.

## SCSI Timing

Figure 6.17 illustrates a typical SCSI timing that can be used to explain the various bus phases and signals. This example is a Read command, which transfers data from the target to the initiator.

**TABLE 6.4    SCSI Bus Signals**

| Bus Phase | A Cable Signals | | | | | B Cable Signals | | |
|---|---|---|---|---|---|---|---|---|
| | BSY | SEL | C/D, I/O MSG, REQ | ACK, ATN | DB(7–0), DB(P) | REQP | ACKB | DB(31–8), DB(P1), DB(P2), DB(P3) |
| Bus Free | None | None | None | None | None | None | None | None |
| Arbitration | All | Win | None | None | S ID | None | None | None |
| Selection | I&T | Init | None | Init | Init | None | None | None |
| Reselection | I&T | Targ | Targ | Init | Targ | None | None | None |
| Command | Targ | None | Targ | Init | Init | None | None | None |
| Data In | Targ | None | Targ | Init | Targ | Targ | Init | Targ |
| Data Out | Targ | None | Targ | Init | Init | Targ | Init | Init |
| Status | Targ | None | Targ | Init | Targ | None | None | None |
| Message In | Targ | None | Targ | Init | Targ | None | None | None |
| Message Out | Targ | None | Targ | Init | Init | None | None | None |

All:    The signal is driven by all SCSI devices that are actively arbitrating.
S ID:   A unique data bit (the SCSI ID) is driven by each device that is actively arbitrating.
I&T:    The signal is driven by the initiator, target, or both, as specified in the Selection and Reselection phase.
Init:   If driven, the signal is driven only by the active initiator
None:   The signal is not driven.
Win:    The signal is driven by the winning device.
Targ:   If driven, the signal is driven only by the active target.

With all lines unasserted, the sequence begins in the Bus Free phase. Next, there is an Arbitration phase, in which one or more devices compete for control of the bus. Each of the devices asserts the BSY line and one of the data lines. Each of the eight devices (one host and up to seven other devices) has a unique ID from 0 through 7, and each device asserts one of the data lines corresponding to its own ID. The IDs are assigned a priority, with 7 being the highest and 0 the lowest. If more than one device asserts its ID during the arbitration phase, then the device with the highest priority wins. The other devices recognize this by observing the data lines and concede the arbitration.

Once a device has won arbitration it becomes the initiator. It enters the Selection phase by asserting the SEL signal. During this phase, it asserts both its own ID and the target ID on the two corresponding data lines. After a delay, it negates the BSY signal. When the intended target detects SEL asserted, BSY and I/O negated, and recognizes its ID, it asserts the BSY signal. When the initiator detects BSY, it releases the data bus and negates SEL.

Next, the target indicates that it has entered the Command phase by asserting the C/D line; this line will remain asserted throughout this phase. It then asserts REQ to request the first byte of the initiator's command. The initiator places the first byte of the command on the data bus and asserts ACK. After the target has read the byte, it negates REQ and then the initiator negates ACK. The first byte of the command contains the operation code of the command, which indicates how many bytes remain to be transferred. These additional bytes are transferred with the same REQ/ACK handshaking before and after each byte transfer.

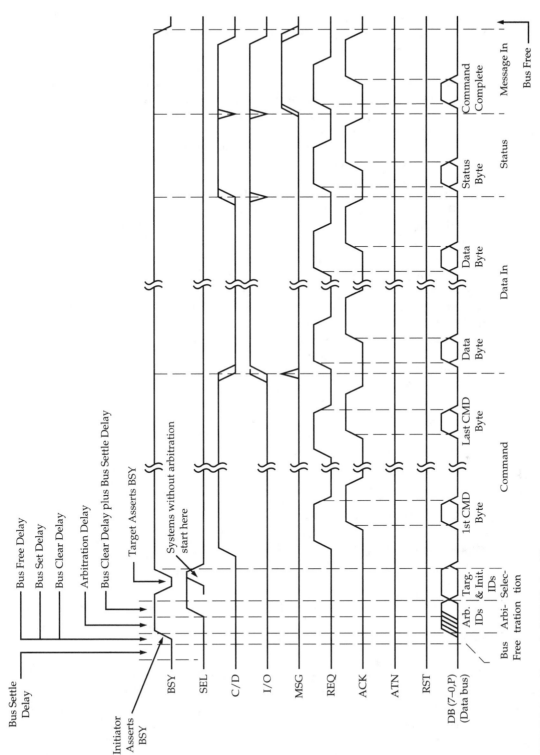

**FIGURE 6.17. Example SCSI Timing Diagram**

**209**

After the target has received and interpreted the command, it places the bus in the Data In phase by negating the C/D line (means data bus contains data) and asserts the I/O line (means direction of transfer is target to initiator). The target places the first byte of the requested data on the data bus and asserts the REQ line. The initiator asserts the ACK line after it has read the byte. Additional data bytes are transferred with the same REQ/ACK handshaking before and after each byte transfer.

After transferring all the requested data, the target places the bus in the Status phase and transfers a status byte to the initiator, indicating that it has successfully completed the transfer. In this case, the C/D line is again asserted and the I/O line remains asserted. The initiator and target use the REQ/ACK handshake to coordinate the transfer of the status byte.

Finally, the target places the bus in the Message In phase by asserting the MSG line and transferring a message byte containing the Command Complete message. Once this byte is received by the initiator, the target releases all bus signals to place the bus in the Bus Free phase.

The transaction depicted in Figure 6.17 is an example of an asynchronous transfer. With asynchronous transfer, a REQ/ACK handshake is required for every byte transferred. SCSI also supports synchronous transfer, which requires less overhead. The synchronous transfer mode is used only for the Data In and Data Out phases. Because the default mode of transfer is asynchronous, the synchronous mode must be negotiated. The target sends the initiator a Synchronous Data Transfer Request message that contains its minimum transfer period and its maximum offset allowed between a REQ and its corresponding ACK. The initiator responds with the same message indicating its own minimum transfer period and maximum REQ/ACK offset.

Once this exchange has taken place, the synchronous transfer mode has been established with the greater of the two minimum transfer periods and the lesser of the two maximum REQ/ACK offsets. Data transfer then proceeds as follows. The sending side will send bytes of data spaced at least by the minimum transfer period and signal each byte by pulsing the REQ signal. The receiver need not immediately ACK each received byte but must ACK a byte within the offset period. The sender can send a continuous stream of bytes so long as it receives the corresponding ACKs within the offset period. If an ACK is late, the sender must pause for acknowledgment.

## Messages

Messages are exchanged between initiators and targets for the purpose of managing the SCSI interface. There are three message formats: single-byte, two-byte, and extended messages of three or more bytes. Some examples of messages are

- *Command Complete:* Sent by the target to the initiator to indicate that a command has been terminated and that a valid status has been sent to the initiator.
- *Disconnect:* Sent from the target to inform an initiator that the present connection is going to be broken but that a later reconnect will be required to complete the current operation.
- *Initiator Detected Error:* Sent from the initiator to inform a target that an error (e.g., parity) has occurred that does not preclude the target from retrying the operation.

- *Abort:* Sent from the initiator to the target to clear the present operation.
- *Synchronous Data Transfer:* Exchanged between initiator and target to establish synchronous data transfer.

## Commands

The heart of the SCSI protocol is the command set. A command is issued by an initiator to cause some action at a target. The command may involve retrieving data from the target (reading), sending data to the target (writing), or some other action specific to a particular peripheral. In all cases, execution of the command involves some or all of the following steps:

- The target acquires and decodes command information.
- Data is transferred to or from the target [not performed for all commands].
- The target generates and returns status information.

The command is defined in a Command Descriptor Block (CDB) prepared by the initiator. Once a connection is established between an initiator and a target, the initiator transfers the CDB to the target over the data bus to begin command execution.

Figure 6.18 shows the general format of the CDB. It consists of the following fields:

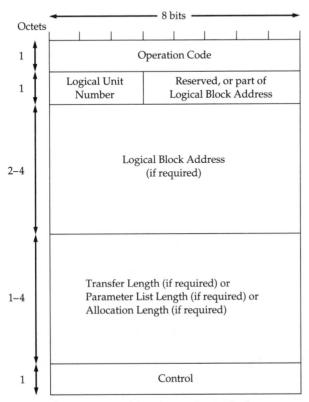

**FIGURE 6.18. SCSI Command Descriptor Block Format**

- *Operation Code:* This code specifies the particular command. The operation code also dictates the format of the remainder of the CDB.
- *Logical Unit Number:* Identifies a physical or virtual device attached to a target. Logical unit numbers can be used to address multiple peripheral devices that share a common controller, or multiple logical volumes on a disk.
- *Logical Block Address:* For read/write operations, the CDB includes the logical starting address for the transfer.
- *Transfer Length:* For read/write operations, this field specifies the number of contiguous logical blocks of data to be transferred.
- *Parameter List Length:* Specifies the number of bytes sent during the Data Out phase. This field is typically used for parameters that are sent to a target (e.g., mode, diagnostic, or log parameters).
- *Allocation Length:* Specifies the maximum number of bytes that an initiator has allocated for returned data.
- *Control:* This field includes the Link and Flag bits, which control the linked commands mechanism. If the Link bit is set, the current command does not end with the Bus Free phase but instead attaches the following command by starting its Command phase. If the Flag bit is set, the target sends the Linked Command Complete message if the command completes successfully and returns the same flag value as in the CDB. Typically, a Flag value of 1 is used by the initiator to cause an interrupt in the initiator between linked commands.

The SCSI specification defines a wide range of command types. Most of these are specific to a particular kind of device. The SCSI-2 standard includes commands for the following device types:

- Direct-access devices
- Sequential-access devices
- Printers
- Processors
- Write-once devices
- CD-ROMs
- Scanners
- Optical memory devices
- Medium-changer devices
- Communication devices

In addition, there is a set of 17 commands that apply to all device types. Of these, four are mandatory and must be implemented by all devices:

- *Inquiry:* Requests that parameters of the target and its attached peripheral devices be sent to the initiator.
- *Request Sense:* Requests that the target transfer sense data to the initiator. Sense data includes error conditions (e.g., out of paper), positioning information (e.g., end of medium), and logical status information (e.g., current command has reached a filemark).
- *Send Diagnostic:* Requests the target perform diagnostic tests on itself, on the attached peripheral devices, or on both.
- *Test Unit Ready:* Provides a means to check if a logical unit is ready.

The command repertoire of SCSI is a major strength of this specification. It provides a standardized way of dealing with the most common devices attached to personal computers and workstations, simplifying the task of writing I/O software in the host system.

## P1394 Serial Bus

With processor speeds reaching 100 MHz and storage devices holding multiple gigabits, the I/O demands for personal computers, workstations, and servers are formidable. Yet the high-speed I/O channel technologies that have been developed for mainframe and supercomputer systems are too expensive and bulky for use on these smaller systems. Accordingly, there has been great interest in developing a high-speed alternative to SCSI and other small-system I/O interfaces. The result is the proposed ANSI standard, P1394, for a High Performance Serial Bus.

P1394 has a number of advantages over SCSI and other I/O interfaces. It is very high speed, low cost, and easy to implement. In fact, P1394 is finding favor not only for computer systems, but also in consumer electronics products, such as digital cameras, VCRs, and televisions. In these products, P1394 is used to transport video images, which are increasingly coming from digitized sources.

One of the strengths of the P1394 interface is that it uses serial transmission (bit at a time) rather than parallel. Parallel interfaces, such as SCSI, require more wires, which means wider, more expensive cables and wider, more expensive connectors with more pins to bend or break. A cable with more wires requires shielding to prevent electrical interference between the wires. Also, with a parallel interface, synchronization between wires becomes a requirement, a problem that gets worse with increased cable length.

In addition, computers are getting physically smaller even as they expand in computing power and I/O needs. Handheld and pocket-size computers have little room for connectors, yet need high data rates to handle images and video.

The intent of P1394 is to provide a single I/O interface with a simple connector that can handle numerous devices through a single port, so that the mouse, laser printer, SCSI, external disk drive, sound, and local area network hookups can be replaced with this single connector. The connector is inspired by the one used in the Nintendo Gameboy. It is so convenient that the user can reach behind the machine and plug it in without looking.

### P1394 Configurations

P1394 uses a daisy-chain configuration, with up to 63 devices connected off a single port. Moreover, up to 1022 P1394 buses can be interconnected using bridges, enabling a system to support as many peripherals as required.

P1394 provides for what is known as hot plugging, which makes it possible to connect and disconnect peripherals without having to power the computer system down or reconfigure the system. Also, P1394 provides for automatic configuration; it is not necessary to manually set device IDs or to be concerned with the relative position of devices. Figure 6.19 compares the P1394 configuration with

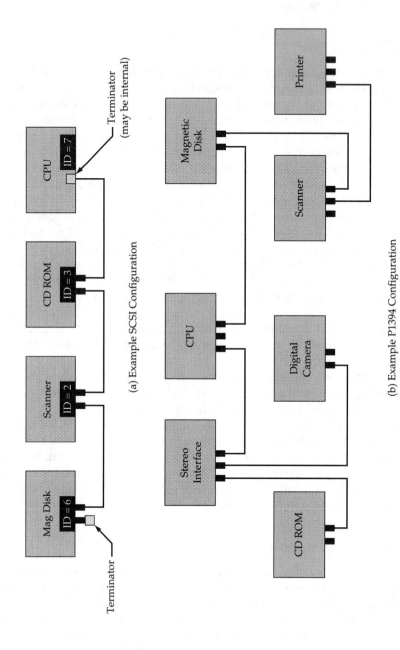

(a) Example SCSI Configuration

(b) Example P1394 Configuration

**FIGURE 6.19. Comparison of SCSI and P1394 Configurations (from P1394 Technical Summary, Apple Computer, 1994)**

that of SCSI. With SCSI, both ends of the bus must have terminators and each device must be assigned a unique address as part of the configuration. With P1394, there are no terminations, and the system automatically performs a configuration function to assign addresses. Also note that a P1394 bus need not be a strict daisy-chain. Rather, a tree-structured configuration is possible.

An important feature of the P1394 standard is that it specifies a set of three layers of protocols to standardize the way in which the host system interacts with the peripheral devices over the serial bus. Figure 6.20 illustrates this stack. The three layers of the stack are

- *Physical Layer:* Defines the transmission media that are permissible under P1394 and the electrical and signaling characteristics of each.
- *Link Layer:* Describes the transmission of data in the packets.
- *Transaction Layer:* Defines a request–response protocol that hides the lower-layer details of P1394 from applications.

### *Physical Layer*

The Physical Layer of P1394 specifies several alternative transmission media and their connectors, with different physical and data transmission properties. Data

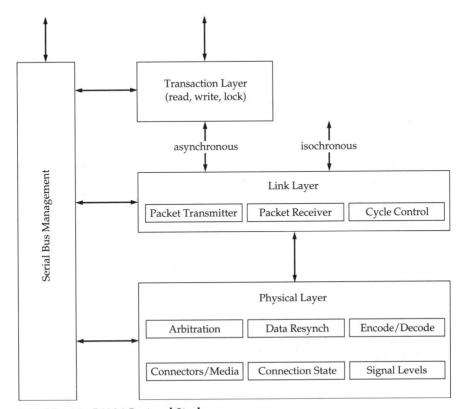

**FIGURE 6.20. P1394 Protocol Stack**

rates from 25 to 400 Mbps are defined. The Physical Layer converts binary data into electrical signals for various physical media. This layer also provides the arbitration service that guarantees that only one device at a time will transmit data.

Two forms of arbitration are provided by P1394. The simplest form is based on the tree-structured arrangement of the nodes on a P1394 bus, mentioned earlier. A special case of this structure is a linear daisy-chain. The Physical Layer contains logic that allows all the attached devices to configure themselves so that one node is designated as the root of the tree and other nodes are organized in a parent/child relationship forming the tree topology. Once this configuration is established, the root node acts as a central arbiter and processes requests for bus access in a first-come-first-served fashion. In the case of simultaneous requests, the node with the highest natural priority is granted access. The natural priority is determined by which competing node is closest to the root and among those of equal distance from the root, which one has the lower ID number.

The above arbitration method is supplemented by two additional functions: fair arbitration and urgent arbitration. With fairness arbitration, time on the bus is organized into *fairness intervals.* At the beginning of an interval, each node sets an arbitration_enable flag. During the interval, each node may compete for bus access. Once a node has gained access to the bus, it resets its arbitration_enable flag and may not again compete for fair access during this interval. This scheme makes the arbitration more fair, in that it prevents one or more busy high-priority devices from monopolizing the bus.

In addition to the fairness scheme, some devices may be configured as having *urgent* priority. Such nodes may gain control of the bus multiple times during a fairness interval. In essence, a counter is used at each high-priority node that enables the high-priority nodes to control 75% of the available bus time. For each packet that is transmitted as non-urgent, three packets may be transmitted as urgent.[3]

## Link Layer

The Link Layer defines the transmission of data in the form of packets. Two types of transmission are supported:

- *Asynchronous:* A variable amount of data and several bytes of Transaction Layer information are transferred as a packet to an explicit address and an acknowledgment is returned.
- *Isochronous:* A variable amount of data is transferred in a sequence of fixed-size packets transmitted at regular intervals. This form of transmission uses simplified addressing and no acknowledgment.

Asynchronous transmission is used by data that have no fixed data rate requirements. Both the fair arbitration and urgent arbitration schemes may be used for asynchronous transmission. The default method is fair arbitration. Devices that desire a substantial fraction of the bus capacity or have severe latency require-

---

[3]The arbitration protocol is discussed in detail in the standard and in [TEEN93]. Both documents are available via ftp at ftp.apple.com in directory/pub/standards/p1394.

ments use the urgent arbitration method. For example, a high-speed real-time data collection node may use urgent arbitration when critical data buffers are more than half full.

Figure 6.21a depicts a typical asynchronous transaction. The process of delivering a single packet is called a subaction. The subaction consists of five time periods:

- *Arbitration Sequence:* This is the exchange of signals required to give one device control of the bus.
- *Packet Transmission:* Every packet includes a header containing the source and destination IDs. The header also contains packet type information, a CRC checksum, and parameter information for the specific packet type. A packet may also include a data block consisting of user data and another CRC.
- *Acknowledgment Gap:* This is the time delay for the destination to receive and decode a packet and generate an acknowledgment.
- *Acknowledgment:* The recipient of the packet returns an acknowledgment packet with a code indicating the action taken by the recipient.
- *Subaction Gap:* This is an enforced idle period to ensure that other nodes on the bus do not begin arbitrating before the acknowledgment packet has been transmitted.

At the time that the acknowledgment is sent, the acknowledging node is in control of the bus. Therefore, if the exchange is a request/response interaction between

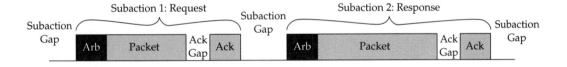

(a) Example Asynchronous Subactions

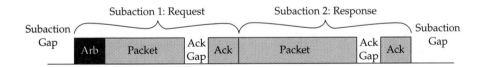

(b) Concatenated Asynchronous Subactions

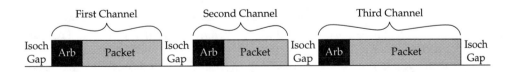

(c) Example Isochronous Subactions

**FIGURE 6.21. P1394 Subactions**

two nodes, then the responding node can immediately transmit the response packet without going through an arbitration sequence (Figure 6.21b).

For devices that regularly generate or consume data, such as digital sound or video, isochronous access is provided. This method guarantees that data can be delivered within a specified latency with a guaranteed data rate.

To accommodate a mixed traffic load of isochronous and asynchronous data sources, one node is designated as *cycle master*. Periodically, the cycle master issues a cycle_start packet. This signals all other nodes that an isochronous cycle has begun. During this cycle, only isochronous packets may be sent (Figure 6.21c). Each isochronous data source arbitrates for bus access. The winning node immediately transmits a packet. There is no acknowledgment to this packet, and so other isochronous data sources immediately arbitrate for the bus after the previous isochronous packet is transmitted. The result is that there is a small gap between the transmission of one packet and the arbitration period for the next packet, dictated by delays on the bus. This delay, referred to as the isochronous gap, is smaller than a subaction gap.

After all isochronous sources have transmitted, the bus will remain idle long enough for a subaction gap to occur. This is the signal to the asynchronous sources that they may now compete for bus access. Asynchronous sources may then use the bus until the beginning of the next isochronous cycle.

Isochronous packets are labeled with 8-bit channel numbers that are previously assigned by a dialogue between the two nodes that are to exchange isochronous data. The header, which is shorter than that for asynchronous packets, also includes a data length field and a header CRC.

## 6.8

### RECOMMENDED READING

The March 1994 issue of *Computer* is devoted to the I/O subsystem. Texts with good coverage of I/O include [PATT94], [FELD94], and [MANO93]. A good discussion of Intel I/O modules and architecture can be found in [BREY95].

Two small books that provide good introductions to SCSI are [DEDE94] and [NCR90].

BREY95 Brey, B. *The Intel 32-Bit Microprocessors: 80386, 80486, and Pentium.* Englewood Cliffs, NJ: Prentice Hall, 1995.

DEDE94 Dedek, J. *Basics of SCSI.* Menlo Park, CA: Ancot Corp., 1994.

FELD94 Feldman, J., and Retter, C. *Computer Architecture.* New York: McGraw-Hill, 1994.

MANO93 Mano, M. *Computer System Architecture.* Englewood Cliffs, NJ: Prentice Hall, 1993.

NCR90 NCR Corp. *SCSI: Understanding the Small Computer System Interface.* Englewood Cliffs, NJ: Prentice Hall, 1990.

PATT94 Patterson, D., and Hennessy, J. *Computer Organization and Design: The Hardware/Software Interface.* San Mateo, CA: Morgan Kaufmann, 1994.

6.9

## PROBLEMS

6.1 In Section 6.3, one advantage and one disadvantage of memory-mapped I/O, compared with isolated I/O, were listed. List two more advantages and two more disadvantages.

6.2 For vectored interrupts, why does the I/O module place the vector on the data lines rather than the address lines?

6.3 In virtually all systems that include DMA modules, DMA access to main memory is given higher priority than CPU access to main memory. Why?

6.4 Consider the disk system described in Problems 5.7 and 5.8. A CPU reads one sector from the disk using interrupt-driven I/O, with one interrupt per byte. If it takes 2.5 µs to process each interrupt, what percentage of the time will the CPU spend handling I/O (disregard seek time)?

6.5 Repeat Problem 6.4 using DMA, and assume one interrupt per sector.

6.6 A DMA module is transferring characters to memory using cycle-stealing, from a device transmitting at 9600 bps. The CPU is fetching instructions at the rate of 1 million instructions per second (1 MIPS). By how much will the processor be slowed down due to the DMA module?

6.7 A 32-bit computer has two selector channels and one multiplexor channel. Each selector channel supports two magnetic disk and two magnetic tape units. The multiplexor channel has two line printers, two card readers, and 10 VDT terminals connected to it. Assume the following transfer rates:

| | |
|---|---|
| Disk drive | 800 KBytes/sec |
| Magnetic tape drive | 200 KBytes/sec |
| Line printer | 6.6 KBytes/sec |
| Card reader | 1.2 KBytes/sec |
| VDT | 1 KBytes/sec |

Estimate the maximum aggregate I/O transfer rate in this system.

6.8 A computer consists of a CPU and an I/O device D connected to main memory M via a 1-word shared bus. The CPU can execute a maximum of $10^5$ instructions per second. An average instruction requires five machine cycles, three of which use the memory bus. A memory read or write operation uses one machine cycle. Suppose that the CPU is continuously executing "background" programs that require 95% of its instruction execution rate but not any I/O instructions. Now the I/O device is to be used to transfer very large blocks of data to and from main memory M.

(a) If programmed I/O is used and each 1-word I/O transfer requires the CPU to execute two instructions, estimate the maximum I/O data-transfer rate per second possible through D.

(b) Estimate the same rate if DMA is used.

6.9 A data source produces 7-bit ASCII characters, to each of which is appended a parity bit. Derive an expression for the maximum effective data rate (rate of ASCII data bits) over an $R$-bps line for the following:

(a) Asynchronous transmission, with a 1.5-unit stop bit.

(b) Bit-synchronous transmission, with a frame consisting of 48 control bits and 128 information bits.

(c) Same as (b), with a 1024-bit information field.

(d) Character-synchronous, with 9 control characters per frame and 16 information characters.

(e) Same as (d), with 128 information characters.

6.10 The following problem is based on a suggested illustration of I/O mechanisms in [ECKE90] (Figure 6.22):

Two boys are playing on either side of a high fence. One of the boys, named Apple-server, has a beautiful apple tree loaded with delicious apples growing on his side of the fence; he is happy to supply apples to the other boy whenever needed. The other boy, named Apple-eater, loves to eat apples but has none. In fact, he must eat his apples at a fixed rate (an apple a day keeps the doctor away). If he eats them faster than that rate, he will get sick. If he eats them slower, he'll suffer malnutrition. Neither boy can talk, and so the problem is to get apples from Apple-server to Apple-eater at the correct rate.

(a) Assume that there is an alarm clock sitting on top of the fence, and that the clock can have multiple alarm settings. How can the clock be used to solve the problem? Draw a timing diagram to illustrate the solution.

(b) Now assume that there is no alarm clock. Instead Apple-eater has a flag that he can wave whenever he needs an apple. Suggest a new solution. Would it be helpful for Apple-server to also have a flag? If so, incorporate this into the solution. Discuss the drawbacks of this approach.

(c) Now take away the flag and assume the existence of a long piece of string. Suggest a solution that is superior to that of (b) using the string.

6.11 Assume that one 16-bit and two 8-bit microprocessors are to be interfaced to a system bus. The following details are given:

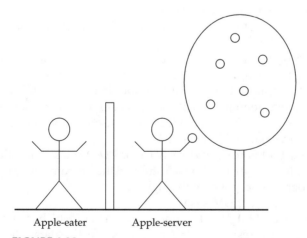

Apple-eater          Apple-server

**FIGURE 6.22.**

1. All microprocessors have the hardware features necessary for any type of data transfer: programmed I/O, interrupt-driven I/O, and DMA.
2. All microprocessors have a 16-bit address bus.
3. Two memory boards, each of 64 KBytes capacity, are interfaced with the bus. The designer wishes to use a shared memory that is as large as possible.
4. The system bus supports a maximum of four interrupt lines and one DMA line.

   Make any other assumptions necessary, and

   (a) Give the system bus specifications in terms of number and types of lines.
   (b) Describe a possible protocol for communicating on the bus, i.e., read/write, interrupt, and DMA sequences.
   (c) Explain how the above devices are interfaced to the system bus.
   Source: [ALEX93]

6.12 On an SCSI bus, each I/O device negotiates with the host computer to determine the burst transfer rate to use—usually the fastest mutually supported speed. Assume that the maximum burst transfer rate supported by the host computer is 20 MByte/sec. Assume that all devices have adequate buffering so that they can maintain their sustained transfer rate even when competing for bus time.

   (a) Assume a tape drive with a sustained transfer rate of 500 KB/sec and a burst rate of 4 MB/sec is attached to the SCSI. You want to attach disk drives to the same bus, each with a sustained transfer rate of 6 MB/sec and a burst rate of 20 MB/sec. How many disk drives can you attach to the bus and expect to be able to run all devices simultaneously at full speed? What will the bus utilization be in that case? *Hint:* Determine the percentage of time each device requires to transfer all its data. (Note: Use 1K = 1000 rather than 1024 and 1M = 1,000,000 rather than 1,048,576; the approximations are close enough for the purpose of this problem. Transfer rates are usually quoted using the decimal-based numbers, but numbers such as buffer sizes and transfer sizes are usually quoted using the binary-based values.)

   (b) Now refine the model slightly. Assume the tape drive requires 4 ms of bus overhead for each transfer, and the maximum transfer size is 64 KB. The disk drives also require 4 ms of bus overhead per transfer, but they can transfer up to 256 KB per request. Reevaluate the amount of bus utilization by each device, and the total utilization. Is the bus still adequate for the number of devices specified in your answer to (a)?

# CHAPTER 7

# Operating System Support

Although the focus of this text is computer hardware, there is one area of software that needs to be addressed: the computer's operating system. The operating system is a program that manages the computer's resources, provides services for programmers, and schedules the execution of other programs. Some understanding of operating systems is essential in following the mechanisms by which the CPU controls the computer system. In particular, explanations of the effect of interrupts and of the management of the memory hierarchy are best explained in this context.

The chapter begins with an overview, a brief history of operating systems, and a survey of the types of services provided to a programmer. The bulk of the chapter looks at the two operating-system functions that are most relevant to the study of computer organization and architecture: scheduling and memory management.

## 7.1

### OPERATING SYSTEM OVERVIEW

#### Operating System Objectives and Functions

An operating system is a program that controls the execution of application programs and acts as an interface between the user of a computer and the computer hardware. An operating system can be thought of as having two objectives or performing two functions:

- *Convenience:* An operating system makes a computer system more convenient to use.
- *Efficiency:* An operating system allows the computer system resources to be used in an efficient manner.

Let us examine these two aspects of an operating system in turn.

## The Operating System as a User/Computer Interface

In Chapter 1, we discussed the hierarchical nature of a computer system, referring to hardware. That view can be extended to the software that is executed on the computer, as depicted in Figure 7.1. In most cases, the ultimate use of the computer is to provide one or a set of applications. The user of those applications is called the *end user* and generally is not concerned with the computer's architecture. Thus, the end user views a computer system in terms of an application. That application can be expressed in a programming language and is developed by an *application programmer.* Now, it should soon become clear that if one were to develop an *application program* as a set of machine instructions that is completely responsible for controlling the computer hardware, one would be faced with an overwhelmingly complex task. To ease this task, a set of *system programs* is provided. Some of these programs are referred to as *utilities.* These implement frequently used functions that assist in program creation, the management of files, and the control of I/O devices. A programmer will make use of these facilities in developing an application, and the application, while it is running, will invoke the utilities to perform certain functions. The most important system program is the *operating system.* The operating system masks the details of the hardware from the programmer and provides the programmer with a convenient interface for using the system. It acts as a mediator, making it easier for the programmer and for application programs to access and use those facilities and services.

Briefly, the operating system typically provides services in the following areas:

- *Program Creation:* The operating system provides a variety of facilities and services to assist the programmer in creating programs. These are lumped under the generic name *utilities.*
- *Program Execution:* A number of tasks need to be performed to execute a program. Instructions and data must be loaded into main memory, I/O devices and files must be initialized, and other resources must be prepared. The operating system handles all of this for the user.

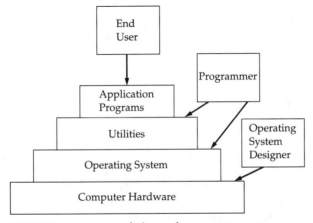

**FIGURE 7.1. Layers and views of a computer system**

- *Access to I/O Devices:* Each I/O device requires its own peculiar set of instructions or control signals for operation. The operating system takes care of the details so that the programmer can think in terms of simple reads and writes.
- *Controlled Access to Files:* In the case of files, control must include an understanding of not only the nature of the I/O device (disk drive, tape drive) but also the file format on the storage medium. Again, the operating system worries about the details. Further, in the case of a system with multiple simultaneous users, the operating system can provide protection mechanisms to control access to shared resources, such as files.
- *System Access:* In the case of a shared or public system, the operating system controls access to the system as a whole and to specific system resources.

We will not further pursue the subject of operating-system services. Our concern in this chapter is the resource-management function of the operating system, and its implications for computer organization and architecture.

### The Operating System as a Resource Manager

A computer is a set of resources for the movement, storage, and processing of data and for the control of these functions. The operating system is responsible for managing these resources.

Can we say that it is the operating system that controls the movement, storage, and processing of data? From one point of view, the answer is yes; by managing the computer's resources, the operating system is in control of the computer's basic functions. But this control is exercised in a curious way. Normally, we think of a control mechanism as something external to that which is controlled or, at least, as something that is a distinct and separate part of that which is controlled. (For example, a residential heating system is controlled by a thermostat, which is completely distinct from the heat-generation and heat-distribution apparatus.) This is not the case with the operating system, which as a control mechanism is unusual in two respects:

- The operating system functions in the same way as ordinary computer software; that is, it is a program executed by the CPU.
- The operating system frequently relinquishes control and must depend on the CPU to allow it to regain control.

The operating system is, in fact, nothing more than a computer program. Like other computer programs, it provides instructions for the CPU. The only difference is in the intent of the program. The operating system directs the CPU in the use of the other system resources and in the timing of its execution of other programs. But in order for the CPU to do any of these things, it must cease executing the operating system program and execute other programs. Thus, the operating system relinquishes control for the processor to do some "useful" work and then resumes control long enough to prepare the CPU to do the next piece of work. The mechanisms involved in all this should become clear as the chapter proceeds.

Figure 7.2 suggests the main resources that are managed by the operating system. A portion of the operating system is in main memory. This includes the

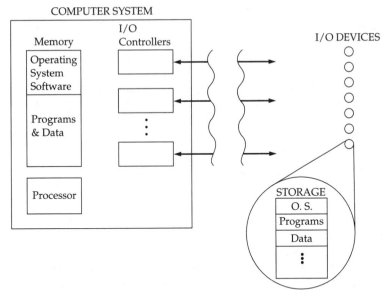

**FIGURE 7.2. The operating system as resource manager**

*nucleus,* which contains the most-frequently-used functions in the operating system and, at a given time, other portions of the operating system currently in use. The remainder of main memory contains other programs and data. The allocation of this resource (main memory) is controlled jointly by the operating system and memory-management hardware in the CPU, as we shall see. The operating system decides when an I/O device can be used by a program in execution and controls access to and use of files.

## Types of Operating Systems

Certain key characteristics serve to differentiate various types of operating systems. The characteristics fall along two independent dimensions. The first dimension specifies whether the system is batch or interactive. In an *interactive* system, the user/programmer interacts directly with the computer, usually through a keyboard/display terminal, to request the execution of a job or to perform a transaction. Furthermore, the user may, depending on the nature of the application, communicate with the computer during the execution of the job. A *batch* system is the opposite of interactive. The user's program is batched together with programs from other users and submitted by a computer operator. After the program is completed, results are printed out for the user. Pure batch systems are rare today. However, it will be useful to the description of contemporary operating systems to briefly examine batch systems.

An independent dimension specifies whether the system employs *multiprogramming* or not. With multiprogramming, the attempt is made to keep the processor as busy as possible by having it work on more than one program at a time.

Several programs are loaded into memory, and the processor switches rapidly among them. The alternative is a *uniprogramming* system that works only one program at a time.

Based on these two dimensions, we can describe four general types of operating systems, as shown in Table 7.1. The best way to describe these various types is to take a brief excursion into the history of operating systems.

### Early Systems

With the earliest computers, the programmer interacted directly with the computer hardware. These machines were run from a console, consisting of display lights, toggle switches, some form of input device, and a printer. Programs in machine code were loaded via the input device (e.g., card reader). If an error halted the program, the error condition was indicated by the lights.

As time went on, additional hardware and software were developed. The hardware additions included magnetic tape and high-speed line printers. The software additions included compilers, assemblers, and libraries of common functions. Common functions could be linked together with application programs without having to be written again.

These early systems presented two main problems:

- *Scheduling:* Most installations used a sign-up sheet to reserve machine time. A user could typically sign up for a block of time in multiples of a half hour or so. A user might sign up for an hour and finish in 45 minutes; this would result in wasted computer idle time. Alternatively, the user might run into problems, not finish in the allotted time, and be forced to stop before resolving the problem.
- *Setup Time:* A single program, called a *job*, could involve loading the compiler plus the high-level language program (source program) into memory, saving the compiled program (object program), and then loading and linking together the object program and common functions. Each of these steps could involve mounting or dismounting tapes or setting up card decks. Thus, a considerable amount of time was spent just in setting up the program to run.

### Simple Batch Systems

Early machines were very expensive, and therefore it was important to maximize machine utilization. The wasted time due to scheduling and setup time was unacceptable.

To improve utilization, simple batch operating systems were developed. With such a system, also called a *monitor*, the user no longer has direct access to the

**TABLE 7.1   Dimensions of an Operating System**

|                        | *Batch*            | *Interactive*    |
| ---------------------- | ------------------ | ---------------- |
| **One task at a time** | Simple batch       | Dedicated system |
| **Multiprogrammed**    | Sophisticated batch | Time sharing     |

machine. Rather, the user submits the job on cards or tape to a computer operator, who *batches* the jobs together sequentially and places the entire batch on an input device, for use by the monitor.

To understand how the scheme works, let us look at it from two points of view: that of the monitor and that of the CPU. From the point of view of the monitor, it is the monitor that controls the sequence of events. For this to be so, the monitor is always in main memory (hence is often called the *resident monitor*) and available for execution (Figure 7.3). The monitor reads in the jobs one at a time. As it is read in, the current job is placed in the user program area, and control is passed to this job. When the job is completed, an interrupt (internal to the CPU) occurs that returns control to the monitor, which immediately reads in the next job. The results of each job are printed out for delivery to the user.

Now let us consider this sequence from the point of view of the CPU. At a certain point in time, the CPU is executing instructions from the portion of main memory containing the monitor. These instructions cause the next job to be read in to another portion of main memory. Once a job has been read in, the CPU will encounter in the monitor a branch instruction that instructs the CPU to continue execution at another location in memory (the start of the user program). The CPU will then execute the instructions in the user's program until it encounters an ending or error condition. Either event causes the CPU to fetch its next instruction from the monitor program. Thus, the phrase, "control is passed to a job," simply means that the CPU is now fetching and executing instructions in a user program, and "control is returned to the monitor" means that the CPU is now fetching and executing instructions from the monitor program.

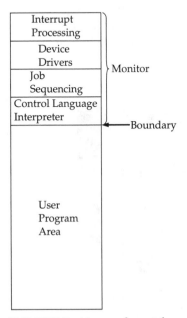

**FIGURE 7.3. Memory layout for a resident monitor**

It should be clear that the monitor handles the scheduling problem. A batch of jobs is queued up, and jobs are executed as rapidly as possible, with no intervening idle time.

How about the job setup problem? The monitor handles this as well. With each job, instructions are included in a *job control language.* This is just a special type of programming language used to provide instructions to the monitor. Figure 7.4 shows a simple example, with job input via cards. In this example, the user is submitting a program written in FORTRAN plus some data to be used by the program. In addition to FORTRAN and data cards, the deck includes job control instructions, which are denoted by the beginning "$."

We see that the monitor, or batch operating system, is simply a computer program. It relies on the ability of the CPU to fetch instructions from various portions of main memory in order to alternately seize and relinquish control. Certain other hardware features are also required:

- *Memory Protection:* While the user program is executing, it must not alter the memory area containing the monitor. If such an attempt is made, the CPU hardware detects an error and transfers control to the monitor. The monitor aborts the job, prints out an error message, and loads in the next job.
- *Timer:* A timer is used to prevent a single job from monopolizing the system. The timer is set at the beginning of each job. If the timer expires, an interrupt occurs, and control returns to the monitor.
- *Privileged Instructions:* Certain instructions are designated privileged and can be executed only by the monitor. These include I/O instructions, so that the monitor retains control of all I/O devices. This prevents, for example, a user program from accidentally reading job control instructions from the next job. If a user program wishes to perform I/O, it must request that the monitor perform the operation for it. If a privileged instruction is encountered by the CPU while it is executing a user program, the CPU hardware considers this an error and transfers control to the monitor.

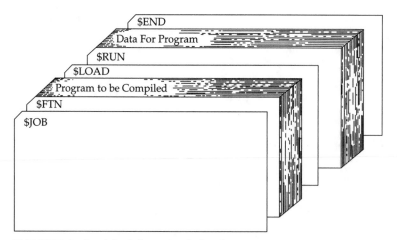

**FIGURE 7.4. Card deck for a simple batch system**

Machine time thus alternates between execution of user programs and execution of the monitor. There have been two sacrifices: some main memory is now given over to the monitor, and some machine time is consumed by the monitor. Both of these are forms of overhead. Even with this overhead, the simple batch system improves the utilization of the computer.

### Sophisticated Batch Systems

Even with the automatic job sequencing provided by a simple batch operating system, the processor is often idle. The problem is that I/O devices are slow compared with the processor. Figure 7.5 details a representative calculation. The calculation concerns a program that processes a file of records and performs, on average, 100 machine instructions per record. In this example the computer spends over 96% of its time waiting for I/O devices to finish transferring data! Figure 7.6a illustrates this situation. The processor spends a certain amount of time executing, until it reaches an I/O instruction. It must then wait until that I/O instruction concludes before proceeding.

This inefficiency is not necessary. We know that there must be enough memory to hold the operating system (resident monitor) and one user program. Suppose that there is room for the operating system and two user programs. Now, when one job needs to wait for I/O, the processor can switch to the other job, which likely is not waiting for I/O (Figure 7.6b). Furthermore, we might expand memory to hold three, four, or more programs and switch among all of them (Figure 7.6c). This process is known as *multiprogramming*. It is the central theme of modern operating systems.

To illustrate the benefit of multiprogramming, let us consider an example, based on one in [TURN86]. Consider a computer with 256K words of available memory (not used by the operating system), a disk, a terminal, and a printer. Three programs, JOB1, JOB2, and JOB3, are submitted for execution at the same time, with the attributes listed in Table 7.2. We assume minimal processor requirements for JOB2 and JOB3, and continuous disk and printer use by JOB3. For a uniprogramming environment, these jobs will be executed in sequence. Thus, JOB1 completes in 5 minutes. JOB2 must wait until the 5 minutes is over, and then completes 15 minutes after that. JOB3 begins after 20 minutes and completes at 30 minutes from the time it was initially submitted. The average resource utilization, throughput, and response times are shown in the uniprogramming column of Table 7.3. Device-by-device utilization is illustrated in Figure 7.7. It is evident that there is

| | |
|---|---|
| Read one record | 0.0015 seconds |
| Execute 100 instructions | 0.0001 seconds |
| Write one record | 0.0015 seconds |
| TOTAL | 0.0031 seconds |

$$\text{Percent CPU Utilization} = \frac{0.0001}{0.0031} = 0.032 = 3.2\%$$

**FIGURE 7.5. System utilization example**

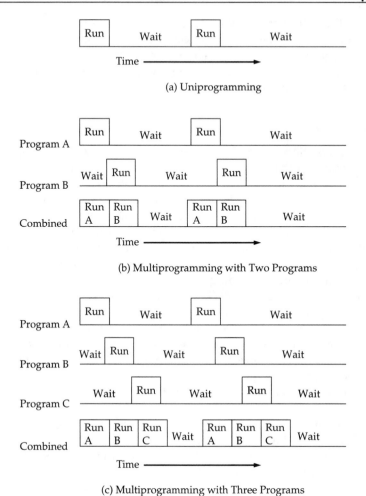

(a) Uniprogramming

(b) Multiprogramming with Two Programs

(c) Multiprogramming with Three Programs

**FIGURE 7.6. Multiprogramming**

gross under-utilization of all resources when averaged over the required 30-minute time period.

Now suppose that the jobs are run concurrently under a multiprogramming operating system. Since there is little resource contention between the jobs, all three can run in nearly minimum time while coexisting with the others in the computer (assuming that JOB2 and JOB3 are allotted enough processor time to keep their input and output operations active). JOB1 will still require 5 minutes to complete, but at the end of that time, JOB2 will be one-third finished and JOB3 half finished. All three jobs will have finished within 15 minutes. The improvement is evident when examining the multiprogramming column of Table 7.3, obtained from the histogram shown in Figure 7.8.

As with a simple batch system, a multiprogramming batch system is a program that must rely on certain computer hardware features. The most notable addi-

**TABLE 7.2   Sample Program Execution Attributes**

|                   | JOB1           | JOB2      | JOB3      |
|-------------------|----------------|-----------|-----------|
| Type of job:      | Heavy compute  | Heavy I/O | Heavy I/O |
| Duration:         | 5 min          | 15 min    | 10 min    |
| Memory required:  | 50K            | 100K      | 80K       |
| Need disk?        | No             | No        | Yes       |
| Need terminal?    | No             | Yes       | No        |
| Need printer?     | No             | No        | Yes       |

tional feature that is useful for multiprogramming is the hardware that supports I/O interrupts and DMA. With interrupt-driven I/O or DMA, the CPU can issue an I/O command for one job and proceed with the execution of another job. When the I/O operation is complete, the CPU is interrupted and control is passed to an interrupt-handling program in the operating system. The operating system will then pass control to another job.

Multiprogrammed operating systems are fairly sophisticated compared with single-program, or *uniprogramming,* systems. In order to have several jobs ready to run, they must be kept in memory, requiring some form of *memory management.* In addition, if several jobs are ready to run, the processor must decide which one to run, which requires some algorithm for *scheduling.* These concepts are discussed later in this chapter.

## Time Sharing

With the use of multiprogramming, batch processing can be quite efficient. However, for many jobs, it is desirable to provide a mode in which the user interacts directly with the computer. Indeed, for some jobs, such as transaction processing, an interactive mode is essential.

Today, the requirement for an interactive computing facility can be, and often is, met by the use of a dedicated microcomputer. That option was not available in the 1960s, when most computers were big and costly. Instead, time sharing was developed.

Just as multiprogramming allows the processor to handle multiple batch jobs at a time, it also can be used to handle multiple interactive jobs. In this latter case, the technique is referred to as *time sharing,* reflecting the fact that the processor's time

**TABLE 7.3   Effects of Multiprogramming on Resource Utilization**

|                        | Uniprogramming | Multiprogramming |
|------------------------|----------------|------------------|
| Processor utilization: | 17%            | 33%              |
| Memory utilization:    | 30%            | 67%              |
| Disk utilization:      | 33%            | 67%              |
| Printer utilization:   | 33%            | 67%              |
| Elapsed time:          | 30 min         | 15 min           |
| Throughput rate:       | 6 jobs/hour    | 12 jobs/hour     |
| Mean response time:    | 18 min         | 10 min           |

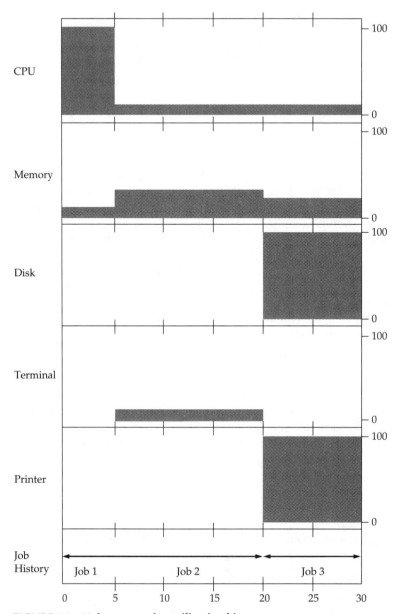

**FIGURE 7.7. Uniprogramming utilization histogram**

is shared among multiple users. Both batch multiprogramming and time sharing use multiprogramming. The key differences are listed in Table 7.4.

### Classes of Computers

Most operating system research and development has been done for mainframe computers. As first minicomputers and then microcomputers were developed, and

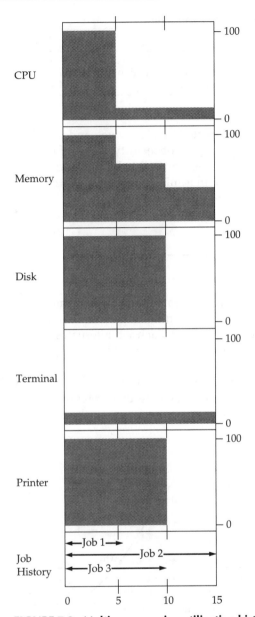

**FIGURE 7.8. Multiprogramming utilization histogram**

as these systems developed increasing hardware capability, the technology developed for mainframes has been transferred to these different classes of computers.

Figure 7.9 illustrates this phenomenon. A good example of the migration of concepts and features can be seen by considering the evolution of UNIX from Multics. Multics is a mainframe operating system developed jointly by M.I.T., Bell Laboratories, and a division of General Electric that subsequently became part of Honey-

**TABLE 7.4    Batch Programming Versus Time Sharing**

|                                          | Batch Multiprogramming                              | Time Sharing                      |
|------------------------------------------|-----------------------------------------------------|-----------------------------------|
| **Principal objective**                  | Maximize processor utilization                      | Minimize response time            |
| **Source of instructions to** <br> **operating system** | Job control language instructions <br> provided with the job | Commands entered <br> at the terminal |

well. This operating system is still marketed by Honeywell and is still considered an advanced system, particularly in the area of security. Many of the ideas developed for Multics were subsequently used at Bell Labs in the design of UNIX, which has become one of the most popular minicomputer operating systems and is now offered on many microcomputers.

## 7.2

### SCHEDULING

The central task of modern operating systems is multiprogramming (with the exception of single-user microcomputers). With multiprogramming, multiple jobs or user programs are maintained in memory. Each job alternates between using the central processor and waiting for I/O to be performed. The processor keeps busy by executing one job while the others wait.

The key to multiprogramming is scheduling. In fact, three types of scheduling are typically involved (Table 7.5). We will explore these presently. But first, we introduce the concept of *process*. This term was first used by the designers of Mul-

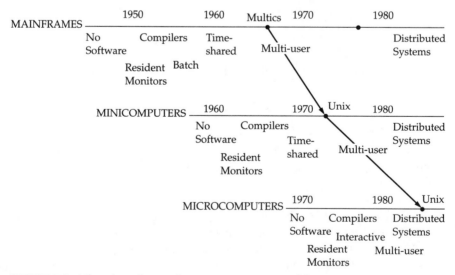

**FIGURE 7.9. Migration of operating system concepts and features**

**TABLE 7.5    Scheduling For Multiprogramming**

| | |
|---|---|
| High-level scheduling | The decision to add to the pool of programs to be executed. |
| Short-term scheduling | The decision as to which available process shall be executed by the processor. |
| I/O scheduling | The decision as to which process's pending I/O request shall be handled by an available I/O device. |

tics in the 1960s. It is a somewhat more general term than *job*. Many definitions have been given for the term *process*, including

- A program in execution.
- The "animated spirit" of a program.
- That entity to which a processor is assigned.

This concept should become clearer as we proceed.

## High-Level Scheduling

The high-level scheduler determines which programs are admitted to the system for processing. Thus, the high-level scheduler controls the *degree of multiprogramming* (number of processes in memory). Once admitted, a job or program becomes a process and is added to a queue for the short-term scheduler. The more processes that are created, the smaller is the percentage of time that each process can be executed. The long-term scheduler may limit the degree of multiprogramming to provide satisfactory service to its current set of processes.

In a batch system, newly submitted jobs are routed to disk and held in a queue or waiting line. The high-level scheduler adds jobs from that queue when it can. There are two decisions involved here. First, the scheduler must decide that it can take on one or more additional processes. This decision is generally made each time an existing process is completed. Second, the scheduler must decide which job or jobs to accept and turn into processes. The criteria used may include priority, expected execution time, and I/O requirements.

For time sharing, a process request is generated by the act of a user attempting to connect to the system. Time-sharing users are not simply queued up and kept waiting until the system can accept them. Rather, the operating system will accept all authorized comers until the system is saturated. At that point, a connection request is met with a message indicating that the system is full and the user should try again later.

## Short-Term Scheduling

The high-level scheduler executes relatively infrequently and makes the coarse-grained decision of whether or not to take on a new process, and which one to take. The short-term scheduler, also known as the *dispatcher*, executes frequently and makes the fine-grained decision of which job to execute next.

## Process States

To understand the operation of the short-term scheduler, we need to consider the concept of a process state. During the lifetime of a process, its status will change a number of times. Its status at any point in time is referred to as a *state*. The term *state* is used because it connotes that certain information exists that defines the status at that point. Typically, there are five defined states for a process (Figure 7.10):

- *New:* A program is admitted by the high-level scheduler but is not yet ready to execute. The operating system will initialize the process, moving it to the ready state.
- *Ready:* The process is ready to execute and is awaiting access to the processor.
- *Running:* The process is being executed by the processor.
- *Waiting:* The process is suspended from execution waiting for some system resource, such as I/O.
- *Halted:* The process has terminated and will be destroyed by the operating system.

For each process in the system, the operating system must maintain state information indicating the status of the process and other information necessary for process execution. For this purpose, each process is represented in the operating system by a *process control block* (Figure 7.11), which typically contains

- *Identifier:* Each current process has a unique identifier.
- *State:* The current state of the process (new, ready, and so on).
- *Priority:* Relative priority level.
- *Program Counter:* The address of the next instruction in the program to be executed.
- *Memory Pointers:* The starting and ending locations of the process in memory.
- *Context Data:* These are data that are present in registers in the processor while the process is executing, and they will be discussed in Part III. For now, it is enough to say that these data represent the "context" of the process. The context data plus the program counter are saved when the process leaves the ready state. They are retrieved by the processor when it resumes execution of the process.
- *I/O Status Information:* Includes outstanding I/O requests, I/O devices (e.g., tape drives) assigned to this process, a list of files assigned to the process, and so on.
- *Accounting Information:* May include the amount of processor time and clock time used, time limits, account numbers, and so on.

**FIGURE 7.10. Process states**

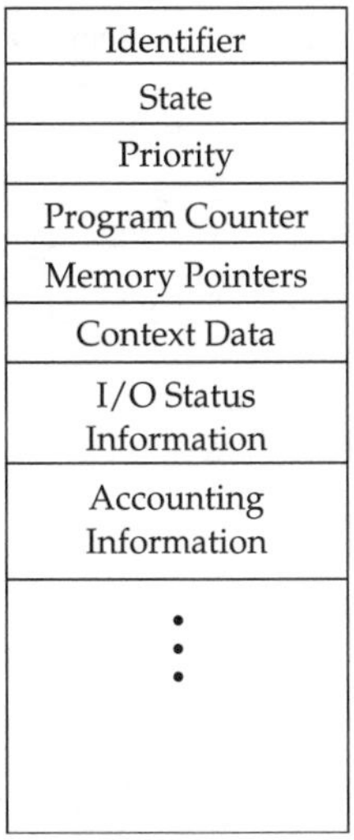

| Identifier |
| :---: |
| State |
| Priority |
| Program Counter |
| Memory Pointers |
| Context Data |
| I/O Status Information |
| Accounting Information |
| ⋮ |

**FIGURE 7.11. Process control block**

When the processor accepts a new job or user request for execution, it creates a blank process control block and places the associated process in the new state. After the system has properly filled in the process control block, the process is transferred to the ready state.

## Scheduling Techniques

To understand how the operating system manages the scheduling of the various jobs in memory, let us begin by considering the simple example in Figure 7.12. The figure shows how main memory is partitioned at a given point in time. The nucleus of the operating system is, of course, always resident. In addition, there are a number of active processes, including A and B, each of which is allocated a portion of memory.

We begin at a point in time (Figure 7.12a) when process A is running. The processor is executing instructions from the program contained in A's memory partition. At some later point in time (Figure 7.12b), the processor ceases to execute instructions in A and begins executing instructions in the operating system area. This will happen for one of three reasons:

1. Process A issues a service call (e.g., an I/O request) to the operating system. Execution of A is suspended until this call is satisfied by the operating system.
2. Process A causes an *interrupt*. An interrupt is a hardware-generated signal to the processor. When this signal is detected, the processor ceases to execute A and transfers to the interrupt handler in the operating system. A variety of events related to A will cause an interrupt. One example is an error, such as attempting to execute a privileged instruction. Another example is a timeout; to prevent any one process from monopolizing the processor, each process is only granted the processor for a short period at a time.

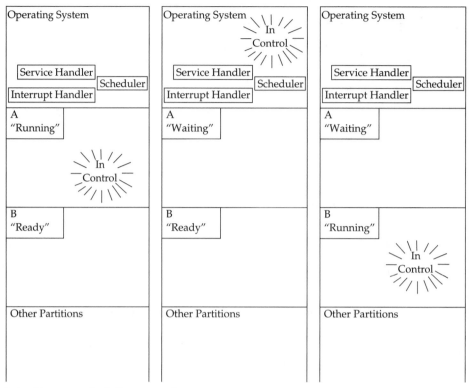

**FIGURE 7.12. Scheduling example**

3. Some event unrelated to process A that requires attention causes an interrupt. An example is the completion of an I/O operation.

In any case, the result is the following. The processor saves the current context data and the program counter for A in A's process control block and then begins executing in the operating system. The operating system may perform some work, such as initiating an I/O operation. Then the short-term-scheduler portion of the operating system decides which process should be executed next. In this example, B is chosen. The operating system instructs the processor to restore B's context data and proceed with the execution of B where it left off (Figure 7.12c).

This simple example highlights the basic functioning of the short-term scheduler. Figure 7.13 shows the major elements of the operating system involved in the multiprogramming and scheduling of processes. The operating system receives control of the processor at the interrupt handler if an interrupt occurs and at the service-call handler if a service call occurs. Once the interrupt or service call is handled, the short-term scheduler is invoked to pick a process for execution.

To do its job, the operating system maintains a number of queues. Each queue is simply a waiting list of processes waiting for some resource. The *long-term queue* is a list of jobs waiting to use the system. As conditions permit, the high-level scheduler will allocate memory and create a process for one of the waiting items. The

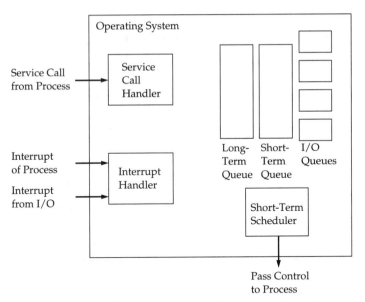

**FIGURE 7.13. Key elements of an operating system for multiprogramming**

*short-term queue* consists of all processes in the ready state. Any one of these processes could use the processor next. It is up to the short-term scheduler to pick one. Generally, this is done with a round-robin algorithm, giving each process some time in turn. Priority levels may also be used. Finally, there is an *I/O queue* for each I/O device. More than one process may request the use of the same I/O device. All processes waiting to use each device are lined up in that device's queue.

Figure 7.14 suggests how processes progress through the computer under the control of the operating system. Each process request (batch job, user-defined interactive job) is placed in the long-term queue. As resources become available, a process request becomes a process and is then placed in the ready state and put in the short-term queue. The processor alternates between executing operating system instructions and executing user processes. While the operating system is in control, it decides which process in the short-term queue should be executed next. When the operating system has finished its immediate tasks, it turns the processor over to the chosen process.

As was mentioned earlier, a process being executed may be suspended for a variety of reasons. If it is suspended because the process requests I/O, then it is placed in the appropriate I/O queue. If it is suspended because of a timeout or because the operating system must attend to pressing business, then it is placed in the ready state and put right back into the short-term queue.

Finally, we mention that the operating system also manages the I/O queues. When an I/O operation is completed, the operating system removes the satisfied process from that I/O queue and places it in the short-term queue. It then selects another waiting process (if any) and signals for the I/O device to satisfy that process's request.

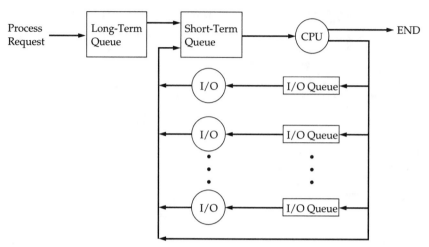

**FIGURE 7.14. Queuing diagram representation of processor scheduling**

We have said that the major task of the operating system is to manage the system's resources. The queuing technique depicted in Figure 7.14 illustrates how the operating system manages processor time and I/O devices. There is one remaining major resource to manage, namely memory, and we now turn to this topic.

## 7.3

### MEMORY MANAGEMENT

In a uniprogramming system, main memory is divided into two parts: one part for the operating system (resident monitor) and one part for the program currently being executed. In a multiprogramming system, the "user" part of memory must be further subdivided to accommodate multiple processes. The task of subdivision is carried out dynamically by the operating system and is known as *memory management*.

Effective memory management is vital in a multiprogramming system. If only a few processes are in memory, then for much of the time all of the processes will be waiting for I/O and the processor will be idle. Thus, memory needs to be allocated efficiently to pack as many processes into memory as possible.

### Swapping

Referring back to Figure 7.14, we have discussed three types of queues: the long-term queue of requests for new processes, the short-term queue of processes ready to use the processor, and the various I/O queues of processes that are not ready to use the processor. Recall that the reason for this elaborate machinery is that I/O activities are much slower than computation and therefore the processor in a uniprogramming system is idle most of the time.

But the arrangement in Figure 7.14 does not entirely solve the problem. It is true that, in this case, memory holds multiple processes and that the processor can move to another process when one process is waiting. But the processor is so much faster than I/O that it will be common for *all* the processes in memory to be waiting on I/O. Thus, even with multiprogramming, a processor could be idle most of the time.

What to do? Main memory could be expanded, and so be able to accommodate more processes. But there are two flaws in this approach. First, main memory is expensive, even today. Second, the appetite of programs for memory has grown as fast as the cost of memory has dropped. So larger memory results in larger processes, not more processes.

Another solution is *swapping,* depicted in Figure 7.15. We have a long-term queue of process requests, typically stored on disk. These are brought in, one at a time, as space becomes available. As processes are completed, they are moved out of main memory. Now, the situation will arise that none of the processes in memory are in the ready state. Rather than remain idle, the processor *swaps* one of these processes back out to disk into an *intermediate queue*. This is a queue of existing

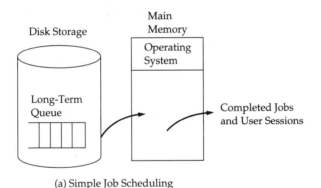

(a) Simple Job Scheduling

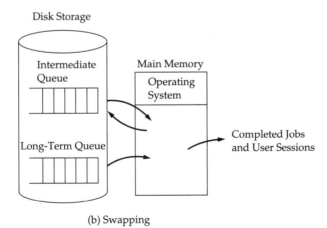

(b) Swapping

**FIGURE 7.15. The use of swapping**

processes that have been temporarily kicked out of memory. The operating system then brings in another process from the intermediate queue, or it honors a new process request from the long-term queue. Execution then continues with the newly arrived process.

Swapping, however, is an I/O operation, and therefore there is the potential for making the problem worse, not better. But, since disk I/O is generally the fastest I/O on a system (e.g., compared with tape or printer I/O), swapping will usually enhance performance. A more sophisticated scheme, involving virtual memory, improves performance over simple swapping. This will be discussed shortly. But first, we must prepare the ground by explaining partitioning and paging.

## Partitioning

The operating system occupies a fixed portion of main memory. The rest of memory is partitioned for use by multiple processes. The simplest scheme for partitioning available memory is to use *fixed-size partitions,* as shown in Figure 7.16. Note that, although the partitions are of fixed size, they are not of equal size. When a process is brought into memory, it is placed in the smallest available partition that will hold it.

Even with the use of unequal fixed-size partitions, there will be wasted memory. In most cases, a process will not require exactly as much memory as provided by the partition. For example, a process that requires 128K bytes of memory would be placed in the 192K partition of Figure 7.16, wasting 64K that could be used by another process.

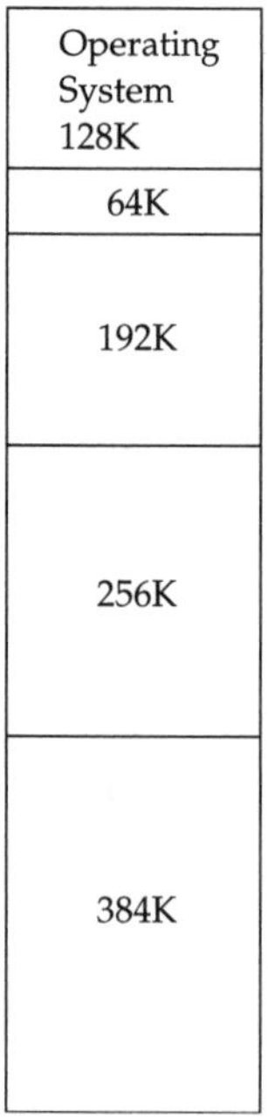

| Operating System 128K |
| 64K |
| 192K |
| 256K |
| 384K |

**FIGURE 7.16. Example of fixed partitioning**

A more efficient approach is to use *variable-size partitions*. When a process is brought into memory, it is allocated exactly as much memory as it requires and no more. An example is shown in Figure 7.17. Initially main memory is empty, except for the operating system. The first three processes are loaded in, starting where the operating system ends (a). This leaves a "hole" at the end of memory that is too small for a fourth process. When process 2 is swapped out (b), there is room for process 4. Since process 4 is smaller than process 2, another small hole is created. As this example shows, this method starts out well, but eventually it leads to a situation in which there are a lot of small holes in memory. As time goes on, memory becomes more and more fragmented, and memory utilization declines. One technique for overcoming this problem is *compaction:* From time to time, the operating system shifts the processes in memory to place all the free memory together in one block. This is a time-consuming procedure, wasteful of processor time.

Before we consider ways of dealing with the shortcomings of partitioning, we must clear up one loose end. If the reader will ponder Figure 7.17 for a moment, it should become obvious that a process is not likely to be loaded into the same place in main memory each time it is swapped in. Furthermore, if compaction is used, a process may be shifted while in main memory. Now, the process in memory consists of instructions plus data. The instructions will contain addresses for memory locations of two types:

- Addresses of data items.
- Addresses of instructions, used for branching instructions.

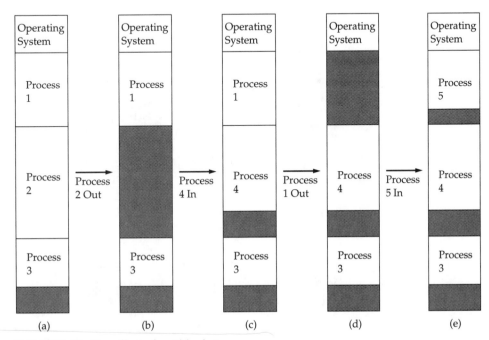

**FIGURE 7.17. The effect of partitioning**

But now we see that these addresses are not fixed! They will change each time a process is swapped in. To solve this problem, a distinction is made between logical addresses and physical addresses. A *logical address* is expressed as a location relative to the beginning of the program. Instructions in the program contain only logical addresses. A *physical address* is, of course, an actual location in main memory. When the processor executes a process, it automatically converts from logical to physical address by adding the current starting location of the process, called its *base address,* to each logical address. This is another example of a CPU hardware feature designed to meet an operating system requirement. The exact nature of this hardware feature depends on the memory management strategy in use. We will see several examples later in this section.

## Paging

Both unequal fixed-size and variable-size partitions are inefficient in the use of memory. Suppose, however, that memory is partitioned into equal fixed-size chunks that are relatively small, and that each process is also divided into small fixed-size chunks of some size. Then the chunks of a program, known as *pages,* could be assigned to available chunks of memory, known as *frames,* or page frames. At most, then, the wasted space in memory for that process is a fraction of the last page.

Figure 7.18 shows an example of the use of pages and frames. At a given point in time, some of the frames in memory are in use and some are free. The list of free

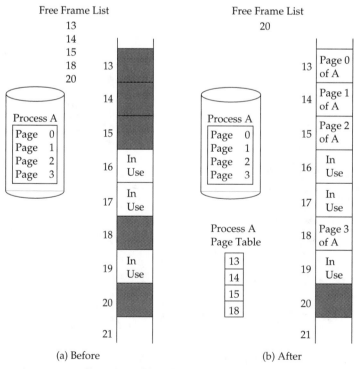

(a) Before                                    (b) After

**FIGURE 7.18.  Allocation of free frames**

frames is maintained by the operating system. Process A, stored on disk, consists of four pages. When it comes time to load this process, the operating system finds four free frames and loads the four pages of the process A into the four frames.

Now suppose, as in this example, that there are not sufficient unused contiguous frames to hold the process. Does this prevent the operating system from loading A? The answer is no, because we can once again use the concept of logical address. A simple base address will no longer suffice. Rather, the operating system maintains a *page table* for each process. The page table shows the frame location for each page of the process. Within the program, each logical address consists of a page number and a relative address within the page. Recall that in the case of simple partitioning, a logical address is the location of a word relative to the beginning of the program; the CPU translates that into a physical address. With paging, the logical-to-physical address translation is still done by CPU hardware. Now, the CPU must know how to access the page table of the current process. Presented with a logical address (page number, relative address), the CPU uses the page table to produce a physical address (frame number, relative address). An example is shown in Figure 7.19.

This approach solves the problems raised earlier. Main memory is divided into many small equal-size frames. Each process is divided into frame-size pages: smaller processes require fewer pages, larger processes require more. When a process is brought in, its pages are loaded into available frames, and a page table is set up.

## Virtual Memory

### Demand Paging

With the use of paging, truly effective multiprogramming systems came into being. Equally important, the simple tactic of breaking a process up into pages led to the development of another important concept: virtual memory.

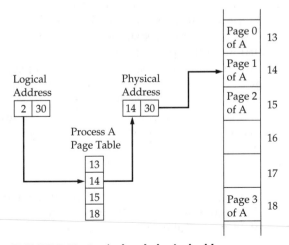

**FIGURE 7.19. Logical and physical addresses**

To understand virtual memory, we must add a refinement to the paging scheme just discussed. That refinement is *demand paging,* which simply means that each page of a process is brought in only when it is needed, that is, on demand.

Consider a large process, consisting of a long program plus a number of arrays of data. Over any short period of time, execution may be confined to a small section of the program (e.g., a subroutine), and perhaps only one or two arrays of data are being used. This is the principle of locality, which we introduced in Appendix 4A to Chapter 4. It would clearly be wasteful to load in dozens of pages for that process when only a few pages will be used before the program is suspended. We can make better use of memory by loading in just a few pages. Then, if the program branches to an instruction on a page not in main memory, or if the program references data on a page not in memory, a *page fault* is triggered. This tells the operating system to bring in the desired page.

Thus, at any one time, only a few pages of any given process are in memory, and therefore more processes can be maintained in memory. Furthermore, time is saved because unused pages are not swapped in and out of memory. However, the operating system must be clever about how it manages this scheme. When it brings one page in, it must throw another page out. If it throws out a page just before it is about to be used, then it will just have to go get that page again almost immediately. Too much of this leads to a condition known as *thrashing:* the processor spends most of its time swapping pages rather than executing instructions. The avoidance of thrashing was a major research area in the 1970s and led to a variety of complex but effective algorithms. In essence, the operating system tries to guess, based on recent history, which pages are least likely to be used in the near future.

With demand paging, it is not necessary to load an entire process into main memory. This fact has a remarkable consequence: *It is possible for a process to be larger than all of main memory.* One of the most fundamental restrictions in programming has been lifted. Without demand paging, a programmer must be acutely aware of how much memory is available. If the program being written is too large, the programmer must devise ways to structure the program into pieces that can be loaded one at a time. With demand paging, that job is left to the operating system and the hardware. As far as the programmer is concerned, he or she is dealing with a huge memory, the size associated with disk storage. The operating system uses demand paging to load portions of that process into main memory.

Because a process executes only in main memory, that memory is referred to as *real memory.* But a programmer or user perceives a much larger memory—that which is allocated on the disk. This latter is therefore referred to as *virtual memory* (Figure 7.20). Virtual memory allows for very effective multiprogramming and relieves the user of the unnecessarily tight constraints of main memory.

## Page Table Structure

Thus, the basic mechanism for reading a word from memory involves the translation of a virtual, or logical, address, consisting of page number and offset, into a physical address, consisting of frame number and offset, using a page table.

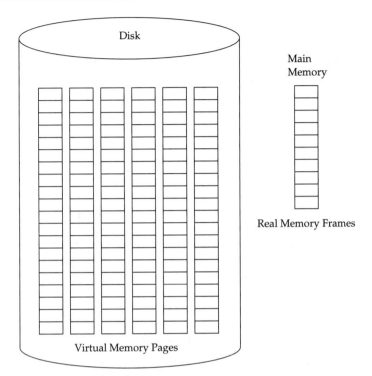

**FIGURE 7.20. Virtual memory**

Because the page table is of variable length, depending on the size of the process, we cannot expect to hold it in registers. Instead, it must be in main memory to be accessed. Figure 7.19 suggests a hardware implementation of this scheme. When a particular process is running, a register holds the starting address of the page table for that process. The page number of a virtual address is used to index that table and look up the corresponding frame number. This is combined with the offset portion of the virtual address to produce the desired real address.

Let us consider the number of page table entries required. In most systems, there is one page table per process. But each process can occupy huge amounts of virtual memory. For example, in the VAX architecture, each process can have up to $2^{31} = 2$ GBytes of virtual memory. Using $2^9 = 512$-byte pages, that means that as many as $2^{22}$ page table entries are required *per process*. Clearly, the amount of memory devoted to page tables alone could be unacceptably high. To overcome this problem, most virtual memory schemes store page tables in virtual memory rather than real memory. This means that page tables are subject to paging just as other pages are. When a process is running, at least a part of its page table must be in main memory, including the page table entry of the currently executing page. Some processors make use of a two-level scheme to organize large page tables. In this scheme, there is a page directory, in which each entry points to a page table.

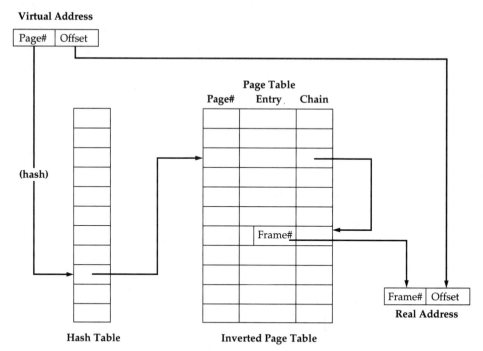

**FIGURE 7.21. Inverted Page Table Structure**

Thus, if the length of the page directory is $X$, and if the maximum length of a page table is $Y$, then a process can consist of up to $X \times Y$ pages. Typically, the maximum length of a page table is restricted to be equal to one page. We will see an example of this two-level approach when we consider the Pentium later in this chapter.

An alternative approach to the use of one- or two-level page tables is the use of an **inverted page table** structure (Figure 7.21). This approach is used on IBM's AS/400 and on all of their RISC products, including the PowerPC.

In this approach, the page number portion of a virtual address is mapped into a hash table using a simple hashing function.[1] The hash table contains a pointer to the inverted page table, which contains the page table entries. With this structure, there is one entry in the hash table and inverted page table for each real memory page rather than one per virtual page. Thus, a fixed proportion of real memory is required for the tables regardless of the number of processes or virtual pages supported. Since more than one virtual address may map into the same hash table entry, a chaining technique is used for managing the overflow. The hashing technique results in chains that are typically short—either one or two entries.

---

[1]A hash function maps numbers in the range 0 through $M$ into numbers in the range 0 through $N$, where $M > N$. The output of the hash function is used as an index into the hash table. Since more than one input maps to the same output, it is possible for an input item to map to a hash table entry that is already occupied. In that case, the new item must *overflow* into another hash table location. Typically, the new item is placed in the first succeeding empty space, and a pointer from the original location is provided to chain the entries together. See [STAL95] for a more detailed discussion of hash tables.

## Translation Lookaside Buffer

In principle, then, every virtual memory reference can cause two physical memory accesses: one to fetch the appropriate page table entry, and one to fetch the desired data. Thus, a straightforward virtual memory scheme would have the effect of doubling the memory access time. To overcome this problem, most virtual memory schemes make use of a special cache for page table entries, usually called a translation lookaside buffer (TLB). This cache functions in the same way as a memory cache and contains those page table entries that have been most recently used. Figure 7.22 is a flowchart that shows the use of the TLB. By the principle of locality, most virtual memory references will be to locations in recently used pages. Therefore, most references will involve page table entries in the cache. Studies of the VAX TLB have shown that this scheme can significantly improve performance [CLAR85, SATY81].

Note that the virtual memory mechanism must interact with the cache system (not the TLB cache, but the main memory cache). This is illustrated in Figure 7.23. A virtual address will generally be in the form of a page number, offset. First, the memory system consults the TLB to see if the matching page table entry is present. If it is, the real (physical) address is generated by combining the frame number with the offset. If not, the entry is accessed from a page table. Once the real address is generated, which is in the form of a tag and a remainder (see Figure 4.17), the cache is consulted to see if the block containing that word is present. If so, it is returned to the CPU. If not, the word is retrieved from main memory.

The reader should be able to appreciate the complexity of the CPU hardware involved in a single memory reference. The virtual address is translated into a real address. This involves reference to a page table, which may be in the TLB, in main memory, or on disk. The referenced word may be in cache, main memory, or on disk. In the latter case, the page containing the word must be loaded into main memory and its block loaded into the cache. In addition, the page table entry for that page must be updated.

## Segmentation

There is another way in which addressable memory can be subdivided, known as *segmentation*. Whereas paging is invisible to the programmer and serves the purpose of providing the programmer with a larger address space, segmentation is usually visible to the programmer and is provided as a convenience for organizing programs and data, and as a means for associating privilege and protection attributes with instructions and data.

Segmentation allows the programmer to view memory as consisting of multiple address spaces or segments. Segments are of variable, indeed dynamic, size. Typically, the programmer or the operating system will assign programs and data to different segments. There may be a number of program segments for various types of programs as well as a number of data segments. Each segment may be assigned access and usage rights. Memory references consist of a (segment number, offset) form of address.

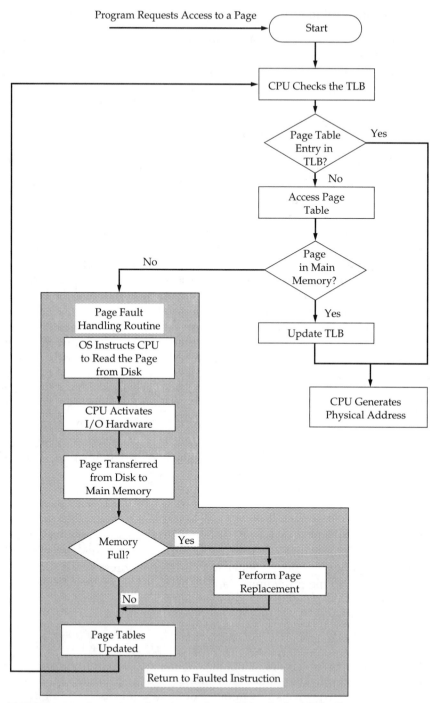

**FIGURE 7.22. Operation of paging and translation lookaside buffer (TLB) [FURH87]**

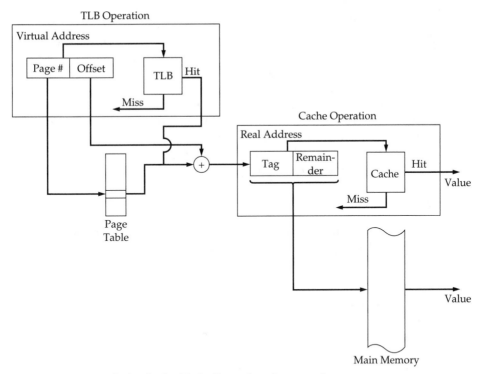

**FIGURE 7.23. Translation lookaside buffer and cache operation**

This organization has a number of advantages to the programmer over a non-segmented address space:

1. It simplifies the handling of growing data structures. If the programmer does not know ahead of time how large a particular data structure will become, it is not necessary to guess. The data structure can be assigned its own segment, and the operating system will expand or shrink the segment as needed.
2. It allows programs to be altered and recompiled independently, without requiring that an entire set of programs be relinked and reloaded. Again, this is accomplished using multiple segments.
3. It lends itself to sharing among processes. A programmer can place a utility program or a useful table of data in a segment that can be addressed by other processes.
4. It lends itself to protection. Since a segment can be constructed to contain a well-defined set of programs or data, the programmer or a system administrator can assign access privileges in a convenient fashion.

These advantages are not available with paging, which is invisible to the programmer. On the other hand, we have seen that paging provides for an efficient form of memory management. To combine the advantages of both, some systems are equipped with the hardware and operating-system software to provide both.

## Pentium Memory Management

Since the introduction of the 32-bit architecture, microprocessors have evolved sophisticated memory management schemes that build on the lessons learned with medium- and large-scale systems. In many cases, the microprocessor versions are superior to their larger-system antecedents. Since the schemes were developed by the microprocessor hardware vendor and may be employed with a variety of operating systems, they tend to be quite general-purpose. A representative example is the scheme used on the Pentium. The Pentium memory management hardware is essentially the same as that used in the Intel 80386 and 80486 processors, with some refinements.

### Address Spaces

The Pentium includes hardware for both segmentation and paging. Both mechanisms can be disabled, allowing the user to choose from four distinct views of memory:

- *Unsegmented Unpaged Memory:* In this case, the virtual address is the same as the physical address. This is useful, for example, in low-complexity, high-performance controller applications.
- *Unsegmented Paged Memory:* Here memory is viewed as a paged linear address space. Protection and management of memory is done via paging. This is favored by some operating systems—e.g., Berkeley UNIX.
- *Segmented Unpaged Memory:* Here memory is viewed as a collection of logical address spaces. The advantage of this view over a paged approach is that it affords protection down to the level of a single byte, if necessary. Furthermore, unlike paging, it guarantees that the translation table needed (the segment table) is on-chip when the segment is in memory. Hence, segmented unpaged memory results in predictable access times.
- *Segmented Paged Memory:* Segmentation is used to define logical memory partitions subject to access control, and paging is used to manage the allocation of memory within the partitions. Operating systems such as UNIX System V favor this view.

### Segmentation

When segmentation is used, each virtual address (called a logical address in the Pentium documentation) consists of a 16-bit segment reference and a 32-bit offset. Two bits of the segment reference deal with the protection mechanism, leaving 14 bits for specifying a particular segment. Thus, with unsegmented memory, the user's virtual memory is $2^{32}$ = 4 GBytes. With segmented memory, the total virtual memory space as seen by a user is $2^{46}$ = 64 terabytes (TBytes). The physical address space employs a 32-bit address for a maximum of 4 GBytes.

The amount of virtual memory can actually be larger than the 64 TBytes. This is because the processor's interpretation of a virtual address depends on which process is currently active. Virtual address space is divided into two parts. One-half of the virtual address space (8K segments × 4 GBytes) is global, shared by all processes; the remainder is local and is distinct for each process.

Associated with each segment are two forms of protection: privilege level and access attribute. There are four privilege levels from most protected (level 0) to least protected (level 3). The privilege level associated with a data segment is its "classification"; the privilege level associated with a program segment is its "clearance." An executing program may only access data segments for which its clearance level is lower than (more privileged) or equal to (same privilege) the privilege level of the data segment.

The hardware does not dictate how these privilege levels are to be used; this depends on the operating system design and implementation. It was intended that privilege level 1 would be used for most of the operating system, and level 0 would be used for that small portion of the operating system devoted to memory management, protection, and access control. This leaves two levels for applications. In many systems, applications will reside at level 3, with level 2 being unused. Specialized application subsystems that must be protected because they implement their own security mechanisms are good candidates for level 2. Some examples are database management systems, office automation systems, and software engineering environments.

In addition to regulating access to data segments, the privilege mechanism limits the use of certain instructions. Some instructions, such as those dealing with memory-management registers, can only be executed in level 0. I/O instructions can only be executed up to a certain level that is designated by the operating system; typically, this will be level 1.

The access attribute of a data segment specifies whether read/write or read-only accesses are permitted. For program segments, the access attribute specifies read/execute or read-only access.

The address translation mechanism for segmentation involves mapping a virtual address into what is referred to as a linear address (Figure 7.24b). A virtual address consists of the 32-bit offset and a 16-bit segment selector (Figure 7.24a). The segment selector consists of the following fields:

- *Table Indicator (TI):* Indicates whether the global segment table or a local segment table should be used for translation.
- *Segment Number:* The number of the segment. This serves as an index into the segment table.
- *Requested Privilege Level (RPL):* The privilege level requested for this access.

Each entry in a segment table consists of 64 bits, as shown in Figure 7.24c. The fields are defined in Table 7.6.

## Paging

Segmentation is an optional feature and may be disabled. When segmentation is in use, addresses used in programs are virtual addresses and are converted into

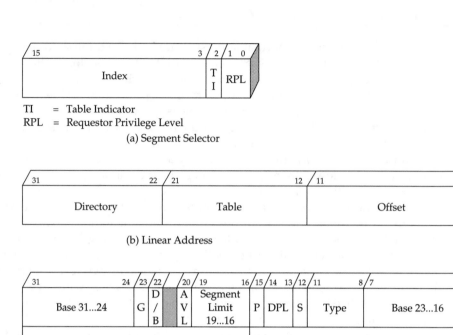

TI = Table Indicator
RPL = Requestor Privilege Level

(a) Segment Selector

(b) Linear Address

AVL = Available for Use by System Software    G = Granularity    ▨ = Reserved
Base = Segment Base Address    Limit = Segment Limit
D/B = Default Operation Size    P = Segment Present
DPL = Descriptor Privilege Size    Type = Segment Type
   S = Descriptor Type

(c) Segment Descriptor (segment table entry)

AVL = Available for Systems Programmer Use    PWT = Write Through
PS = Page Size    US = User/Supervisor
A = Accessed    RW = Read/Write
PCD = Cache Disable    P = Present

(d) Page Directory Entry

D = Dirty

(e) Page Table Entry

**FIGURE 7.24. Pentium Memory Management Formats**

### TABLE 7.6    Pentium Memory Management Parameters

*Segment Descriptor (Segment Table Entry)*

**Base**
 Defines the starting address of the segment within the 4-GByte linear address space.
**D/B bit**
 In a code segment, this is the D bit and indicates whether operands and addressing modes
 are 16 or 32 bits.
**Descriptor Privilege Level (DPL)**
 Specifies the privilege level of the segment referred to by this segment descriptor.
**Granularity bit (G)**
 Indicates whether the Limit field is to be interpreted in units by one byte or 4 KBytes.
**Limit**
 Defines the size of the segment. The processor interprets the limit field in one of two ways,
 depending on the granularity bit: in units of one byte, up to a segment size limit of 1 MByte,
 or in units of 4 KBytes, up to a segment size limit of 4 GBytes.
**S bit**
 Determines whether a given segment is a system segment or a code or data segment.
**Segment Present bit (P)**
 Used for nonpaged systems. It indicates whether the segment is present in main memory. For
 paged systems, this bit is always set to 1.
**Type**
 Distinguishes between various kinds of segments and indicates the access attributes.

linear addresses, as just described. When segmentation is not in use, linear addresses are used in programs. In either case, the following step is to convert that linear address into a real 32-bit address.

To understand the structure of the linear address, you need to know that the Pentium paging mechanism is actually a two-level table lookup operation. The first level is a page directory, which contains up to 1024 entries. This splits the 4-GByte linear memory space into 1024 page groups, each with its own page table, and each 4 MBytes in length. Each page table contains up to 1024 entries; each entry corresponds to a single 4-KByte page. Memory management has the option of using one page directory for all processes, one page directory for each process, or some combination of the two. The page directory for the current task is always in main memory. Page tables may be in virtual memory.

Figure 7.24 shows the formats of entries in page directories and page tables, and the fields are defined in Table 7.6. Note that access control mechanisms can be provided on a page or page group basis.

The Pentium also makes use of a translation lookaside buffer. The buffer can hold 32 page table entries. Each time that the page directory is changed, the buffer is cleared.

Figure 7.25 illustrates the combination of segmentation and paging mechanisms. For clarity, the translation lookaside buffer and memory cache mechanisms are not shown.

Finally, the Pentium includes a new extension not found on the 80386 or 80486, the provision for two page sizes. If the PSE (page size extension) bit in control reg-

**TABLE 7.6    (continued)**

*Page Directory Entry and Page Table Entry*

**Accessed bit (A)**
This bit is set to 1 by the processor in both levels of page tables when a read or write operation to the corresponding page occurs.

**Dirty bit (D)**
This bit is set to 1 by the processor when a write operation to the corresponding page occurs.

**Page Frame Address**
Provides the physical address of the page in memory if the present bit is set. Since page frames are aligned on 4K boundaries, the bottom 12 bits are 0, the only the top 20 bits are included in the entry. In a page directory, the address is that of a page table.

**Page Cache Disable bit (PCD)**
Indicates whether data from page may be cached.

**Page Size bit (PS)**
Indicates whether page size is 4 KByte or 4 MByte.

**Page Write Through bit (PWT)**
Indicates whether write-through or write-back caching policy will be used for data in the corresponding page.

**Present bit (P)**
Indicates whether the page table or page is in main memory.

**Read/Write bit (RW)**
For user-level pages, indicates whether the page is read-only access or read/write access for user-level programs.

**User/Supervisor bit (US)**
Indicates whether the page is available only to the operating system (supervisor level) or is available to both operating system and applications (user level).

ister 4 is set to 1, then the paging unit permits the operating-system programmer to define a page as either 4 KByte or 4 MByte in size.

When 4-MByte pages are used, there is only one level of table lookup for pages. When the hardware accesses the page directory, the page directory entry (Figure 7.24d) has the PS bit set to 1. In this case, bits 9 through 21 are ignored and bits 22 through 31 define the base address for a 4-MByte page in memory. Thus, there is a single page table.

The use of 4-MByte pages reduces the memory-management storage requirements for large main memories. With 4-KByte pages, a full 4-GByte main memory requires about 4 MBytes of memory just for the page tables. With 4-MByte pages, a single table, 4 KBytes in length, is sufficient for page memory management.

## PowerPC Memory Management

The PowerPC provides a comprehensive set of addressing mechanisms. For 32-bit implementations of the architecture, a paging scheme with a simple segmentation mechanism is implemented. For 64-bit implementations, paging and a more powerful segmentation mechanism are supported. In addition, for both 32-bit and 64-bit machines there is an alternative hardware mechanism, known as block address translation. Briefly, the block addressing scheme is designed to address one draw-

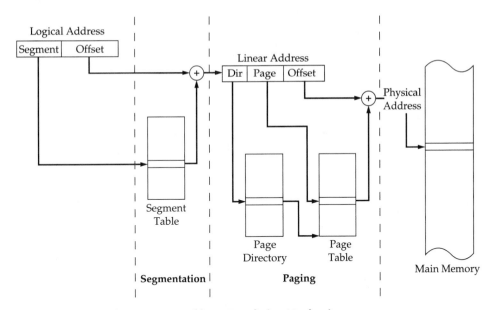

**FIGURE 7.25. Pentium Memory Address Translation Mechanisms**

back of paging mechanisms. With paging, a large number of pages may be frequently referenced by a program. For example, programs that use OS tables or graphics frame buffers may exhibit this behavior. The result may be that frequently used pages are constantly paged in and out. Block addressing enables the processor to map four large blocks of instruction memory and four large blocks of data memory in a way that bypasses the paging mechanism.

A discussion of block addressing is beyond the scope of this chapter. In this subsection, we concentrate on the paging and segmentation mechanisms of the PowerPC.

### 32-bit PowerPC Memory Management

The 32-bit PowerPC makes use of a 32-bit effective address (Figure 7.26a). The address includes a 16-bit page identifier and a 12-bit byte selector. Thus, $2^{12} = 4$ KByte pages are used. Up to $2^{16} = 64$K pages per segment are allowed. Four bits of the address are used to designate one of 16 segment registers. The contents of these registers are controlled by the operating system. Each segment register includes access control bits and a 24-bit identifier, so that the 32-bit effective address maps into a 52-bit virtual address (Figure 7.27).

The PowerPC makes use of a single inverted page table. The virtual address is used to index into the page table in the following manner. First, a hash code is computed as follows:

$$H(0 \dots 19) = SID(5 \dots 23) \oplus VPN(0 \dots 18)$$

The virtual page number in the virtual address is padded on the left (most significant end) with three binary zeros to form a 19-bit number. Then a bit-by-bit

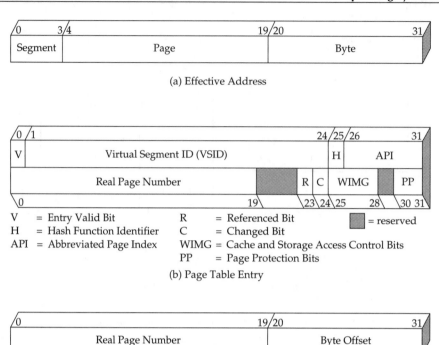

V = Entry Valid Bit    R = Referenced Bit    ▨ = reserved
H = Hash Function Identifier    C = Changed Bit
API = Abbreviated Page Index    WIMG = Cache and Storage Access Control Bits
                   PP = Page Protection Bits

(b) Page Table Entry

(c) Real Address

**FIGURE 7.26. PowerPC 32-bit Memory Management Formats**

exclusive-or is calculated of that number and the 19 rightmost bits of the virtual segment ID to form a 19-bit hash code. The table is organized as *n* groups of 8 entries. From 10 to 19 bits of the hash code (depending on the size of the page table) are used to select one of the groups in the table. The memory management hardware then scans the eight entries of the group to test for a match with the virtual address.

In order to do the match, each page table entry includes the virtual segment ID and the leftmost 6 bits of the virtual page number, called the abbreviated page index (since at least 10 bits of the 16-bit virtual page number always participate in the hash to select a page table entry group, only an abbreviated form of the virtual page number need be carried in the page table entry to uniquely match the virtual address). If there is a match, then the 20-bit real page number from the address is concatenated with the lower 12 bits of the effective address to form the 32-bit physical address to be accessed.

If there is no match, then the hash code is complemented to produce a new page table index that is in the same relative position at the opposite end of the table. This group is then scanned for a match. If no match is found, a page fault interrupt occurs.

Figure 7.28 shows the logic of the address translation mechanism, and Figure 7.27 shows the formats of the effective address, page table entry, and real address. Finally, Table 7.7 defines the parameters in the page table entry.

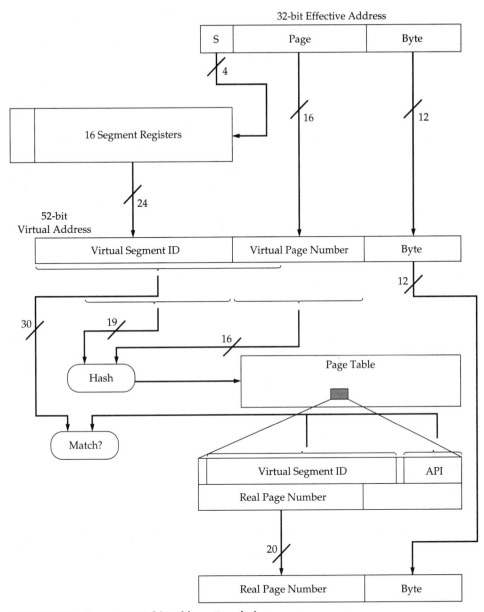

**FIGURE 7.27. PowerPC 32-bit Address Translation**

## 64-bit PowerPC Memory Management

The 64-bit memory management scheme is designed to be upwardly compatible with the 32-bit implementation. In essence, all effective addresses, general registers, and branch address registers are extended on the left to 64 bits. To accommodate the memory mapping requirement, the simple use of segment registers is replaced by a hashed segment table structure that is similar to the page table struc-

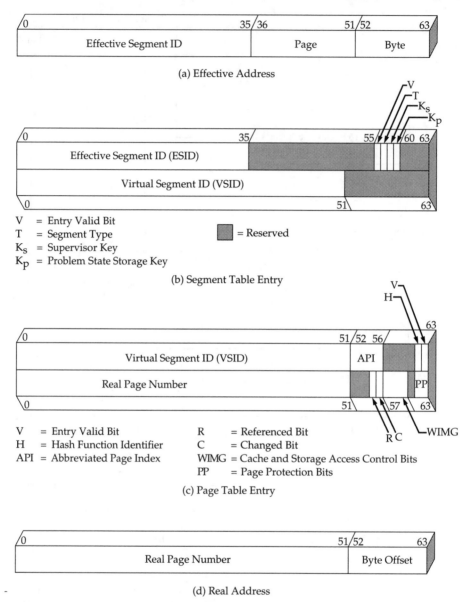

**FIGURE 7.28. PowerPC 64-bit Memory Management Formats**

ture described previously. In the segment table, segment table entry groups contain eight segment table entries; each entry contains a 36-bit effective segment identifier, a 52-bit virtual segment identifier, and the same access protection and I/O space selector bits as were contained in the segment registers of the 32-bit implementations (Figure 7.28).

Figure 7.29 illustrates the mapping of a 64-bit effective address into an 80-bit virtual address. As in the 32-bit implementation, the effective address includes a

### TABLE 7.7    PowerPC Memory Management Parameters

*Segment Table Entry*

**Effective Segment ID**
Indicates one of 64G effective segments; used to determine entry in segment table.
**Entry Valid (V) bit**
Indicates whether this is a memory or I/O segment
**Segment Type (T) bit**
Indicates whether this is a memory or I/O segment
**Supervisor Key ($K_s$)**
Used with the virtual page number to determine entry in page table.

*Page Table Entry*

**Entry Valid (V) bit**
Indicates whether there is valid data in this entry.
**Hash Function Identifier (H)**
Indicates whether this is a primary or secondary hash entry.
**Abbreviated Page Index (API)**
Used to uniquely match a virtual address.
**Referenced (R) bit**
This bit is set to 1 by the processor when a read or write operation to the corresponding page occurs.
**Changed (C) bit**
This bit is set to 1 by the processor when a write operation to the corresponding page occurs.
**WIMG bits**
W=0: use write-back policy; W=1: use write-through policy.
I=0: caching not inhibited; I=1: caching inhibited.
M=0: not shared memory; M=1: shared memory.
G=0: not guarded memory; G=1: guarded memory.
**Page Protection (PP) bits**
Access control bits used with K bits from segment register or segment table entry to define access rights.

12-bit byte selector and a 16-bit page number. The remaining 36 bits form an effective segment ID. Since it is not feasible to have $2^{36}$ segment registers, the hashed segment table is used.

The segment table consists of 256 entries organized as 32 groups of 8 entries. The memory management hardware uses the low-order 5 bits of the effective segment ID to index into the table to select one of the 32 groups. If a match is found in the group, by comparing segment IDs, then an 80-bit virtual address is formed. This consists of the 52-bit virtual segment ID from the segment table entry concatenated to the page and byte fields of the effective address. Again, if no match is found, the 5 index bits are complemented to index into the table a second time. If no match is found on the second search, a page fault interrupt occurs.

The remainder of the address translation, from virtual address to real address, follows the same structure as for the 32-bit case. In this case, the 16-bit virtual page number is hashed with the lower 39 bits of the virtual segment number to select a page table entry group. The 64-bit page table entry format has a 52-bit virtual seg-

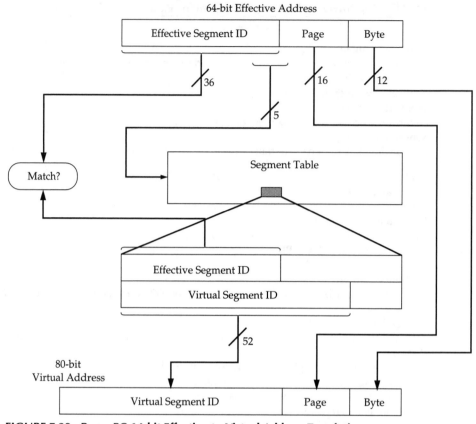

**FIGURE 7.29. PowerPC 64-bit Effective-to-Virtual Address Translation**

ment ID, a 5-bit abbreviated page index, and a 52-bit real page number. The result of the mapping is a 64-bit real address.

## RECOMMENDED READING

[STAL95] covers the topics of this chapter in detail. In addition, as in the area of computer architecture, there are many books on operating systems. [SILB94], [TANE92], [MILE92], and [DEIT90] cover the basic principles using a number of important operating systems as case studies. [SING94] and [NUTT92] treat OS topics at a more advanced level.

[INTE94b] describes the Pentium memory management architecture. Good descriptions of the PowerPC memory management architecture are found in [DIEF94a] and [MAY94].

DIEF94a   Diefendorff, K.; Oehler, R.; and Hochsprung, R. "Evolution of the PowerPC Architecture." *IEEE Micro*, April 1994.

DEIT90   Deitel, H. *An Introduction to Operating Systems.* Reading, MA: Addison-Wesley, 1990.

INTE94b   Intel Corp. *Pentium Family User's Manual, Volume 3: Architecture and Programming Manual.* Santa Clara, CA, 1994.

MAY94   May, C.; Silha, E.; Simpson, R.; and Warren, H., editors. *The PowerPC Architecture.* San Francisco: Morgan Kaufmann, 1994.

MILE92   Milenkovic, M. *Operating Systems: Concepts and Design.* New York: McGraw-Hill, 1992.

NUTT92   Nutt, G. *Centralized and Distributed Operating Systems.* Englewood Cliffs, NJ: Prentice-Hall, 1992.

SILB94   Silberschatz, A., and Galvin, P. *Operating System Concepts.* Reading, MA: Addison-Wesley, 1994.

SING94   Singhal, M., and Shivaratri, N. *Advanced Concepts in Operating Systems.* New York: McGraw-Hill, 1994.

STAL95   Stallings, W. *Operating Systems, Second Edition.* Englewood Cliffs, NJ: Prentice-Hall, 1995.

TANE92   Tanenbaum, A. *Modern Operating Systems.* Englewood Cliffs, NJ: Prentice-Hall, 1992.

## 7.5

## PROBLEMS

7.1   In a certain time-sharing system, each user spends an average of 20 seconds thinking and typing between interactions. The majority of interactions require 50 ms of CPU time, but 1 in 20 requires 2 seconds. In addition, each interaction involves swap-in and swap-out times of 100 ms each.

Describe the scheduling and swapping policies to be adopted in this system to achieve the fastest possible response time for the maximum number of users.

Indicate how much storage your system would require (in terms of the typical job size). Derive an expression for the response time $R$ for short interactions, in terms of the number of users $N$. What are the assumptions and inaccuracies of this?

7.2   Suppose we have a multiprogrammed computer in which each job has identical characteristics. In one computation period, $T$, for a job, half the time is spent in I/O and the other half in CPU activity. Each job runs for a total of $N$ periods. Assume a simple round-robin priooty is used. Define the following quantities:

- Turnaround time = actual time to complete a job.
- Throughput = average number of jobs completed per time period, $T$.
- CPU utilization = percentage of time that the CPU is active (not waiting).

Compute these quantities for one, two, and four simultaneous jobs, assuming that the period $T$ is distributed in each of the following ways:
**(a)** I/O first half, CPU second half.
**(b)** I/O first and fourth quarters, CPU second and third quarters.

7.3 Define waiting time as the amount of time that a job spends waiting in the short-term queue (Figure 7.14). Give an equation that relates turnaround time, CPU busy time, and waiting time.

7.4 An I/O-bound program is one that, if run alone, would spend more time waiting for I/O than using the CPU. A CPU-bound program is the opposite.

Suppose a short-term scheduling algorithm favors those programs that have used little CPU time in the recent past. Explain why this algorithm favors I/O-bound programs and yet does not permanently starve CPU-bound programs.

7.5 A program computes the row sums

$$C_i = \sum_{j=1}^{n} a_{ij}$$

of an array $A$ that is 100 by 100. Assume that the computer uses demand paging with a page size of 1000 words, and that the amount of main memory allotted for data is five page frames. Is there any difference in the page fault rate if $A$ were stored in virtual memory by rows or columns? Explain.

7.6 A virtual memory system has a page size of 1024 words, eight virtual pages, and four physical page frames. The page table is as follows:

| Virtual Page Number | Page Frame Number |
|:---:|:---:|
| 0 | 3 |
| 1 | 1 |
| 2 | — |
| 3 | — |
| 4 | 2 |
| 5 | — |
| 6 | 0 |
| 7 | — |

**(a)** Make a list of all virtual addresses that will cause page faults.

**(b)** What are the main memory addresses for the following virtual addresses: 0, 3728, 1023, 1024, 1025, 7800, 4096?

7.7 Give reasons that the page size in a virtual memory system should be neither very small nor very large.

7.8 The following sequence of virtual page numbers is encountered in the course of execution on a computer with virtual memory:

3 4 2 6 4 7 1 3 2 6 3 5 1 2 3

Assume that a least-recently-used page replacement policy is adopted. Plot a graph of page hit ratio (fraction of page references in which the page is in main memory) as a function of main-memory page capacity $n$ for $1 \leq n \leq 8$. Assume that main memory is initially empty.

7.9 In the VAX, user page tables are located at virtual addresses in the system space. What is the advantage of having user page tables in virtual rather than main memory?

7.10 Consider a computer system with both virtual memory and a cache. For an item that exists in main memory (and possibly in the cache), two steps are involved:

1. Translating from virtual address to main memory address.
2. Checking to see if the data in the main memory location are also in the cache.

To save time, we would like to overlap these two activities, that is, to perform them, at least partially, in parallel.

In the Amdahl 470, address translation always leaves the low-order 11 address bits (byte offset) unchanged. The cache is $N$-way set associative. If some of the 11 bits are used to select one of 64 cache columns, which of the following cache steps can be overlapped with the virtual-address translation of the high-order bits?

1. Column select.
2. Read $N$ cache-address tags in selected column.
3. Compare $N$ address tags with real address.
4. Select one of $N$ data lines.

7.11 Consider a computer system with both segmentation and paging. When a segment is in memory, some words are wasted on the last page. In addition, for a segment size $s$ and a page size $p$, there are $s/p$ page table entries. The smaller the page size, the less waste in the last page of the segment, but the larger the page table. What page size minimizes the total overhead?

7.12 A computer has a cache, main memory, and a disk used for virtual memory. If a word is in the cache, $A$ ns are required to access it. If it is in main memory but not in cache, $B$ ns are first needed to load it into the cache, and then the reference is started again. If the word is not in main memory, $C$ ns are required to fetch it from disk, followed by $B$ ns to get it to the cache. If the cache hit ratio is $(n-1)/n$ and the main memory hit ratio is $(m-1)/m$, what is the average access time?

7.13 Assume a task is divided into four equal-sized segments, and that the system builds an 8-entry page descriptor table for each segment. Thus, the system has a combination of segmentation and paging. Assume also that the page size is 2 KBytes.
   **(a)** What is the maximum size of each segment?
   **(b)** What is the maximum logical address space for the task?
   **(c)** Assume that an element in physical location 00021 ABC is accessed by this task. What is the format of the logical address that the task generates for it? What is the maximum physical address space for the system?
   Source: [ALEX93]

7.14 Assume a certain microprocessor is capable of accessing up to $2^{32}$ bytes of physical main memory. It implements one segmented logical address space of maximum size $2^{31}$ bytes. Each instruction contains the whole two-part address. External memory management units (MMUs) are used, whose management scheme assigns contiguous blocks of physical memory of fixed size

$2^{22}$ bytes to segments. The starting physical address of a segment is always divisible by 2048. Show the detailed interconnection of the external mapping mechanism that converts logical addresses to physical addresses using the appropriate number of MMUs, and show the detailed internal structure of an MMU (assuming that each MMU contains a 128-entry directly mapped segment descriptor cache) and how each MMU is selected.
Source: [ALEX93]

7.15 Consider a paged logical address space (composed of 32 pages of 2 KBytes each) mapped into a 1-MByte physical memory space.

(a) What is the format of the processor's logical address?

(b) What is the length and width of the page table (disregarding the "access rights" bits)?

(c) What is the effect on the page table if the physical memory space is reduced by half?

Source: [ALEX93]

# PART III

# THE CENTRAL PROCESSING UNIT

U p to this point, we have viewed the CPU essentially as a "black box" and have considered its interaction with I/O and memory. Part III examines the internal structure and function of the CPU.

Chapter 8 examines the functionality of the ALU, and it focuses on the representation of numbers and techniques for implementing arithmetic operations. The complex topic of instruction set design occupies Chapters 9 and 10. Chapter 11 describes the use of registers as the CPU's internal memory, and then it pulls together all the material so far covered to provide an overview of CPU structure and function. The remainder of Part III looks in more detail at the key trends in CPU design. Chapter 12 describes the approach associated with the concept of a reduced instruction set computer (RISC), while Chapter 13 looks at the use of superscalar techniques, an approach that is used in many of the more recent processor designs.

# CHAPTER 8

# Computer Arithmetic

We begin our examination of the CPU with the arithmetic and logic unit (ALU). After a brief introduction to the ALU, the chapter focuses on the most complex aspect of the ALU, computer arithmetic. The logic functions that are part of the ALU are described in Chapter 9, and implementations of simple logic and arithmetic functions in digital logic are described in the appendix of this book.

Computer arithmetic is commonly performed on two very different types of numbers: integer and floating point. In both cases, the representation chosen is a crucial design issue and is treated first, followed by a discussion of arithmetic operations.

A review of number systems is provided in an appendix to this chapter.

## 8.1

### THE ARITHMETIC AND LOGIC UNIT (ALU)

The arithmetic and logic unit (ALU) is that part of the computer that actually performs arithmetic and logical operations on data. All of the other elements of the computer system—control unit, registers, memory, I/O—are there mainly to bring data into the ALU for it to process and then to take the results back out. We have, in a sense, reached the core or essence of a computer when we consider the ALU.

An arithmetic and logic unit and, indeed, all electronic components in the computer are based on the use of simple digital logic devices that can store binary digits and perform simple Boolean logic operations. The appendix to this text explores digital logic implementation for the interested reader.

Figure 8.1 indicates, in very general terms, how the ALU is interconnected with the rest of the CPU. Data are presented to the ALU in registers, and the results of an operation are stored in registers. These registers are temporary storage locations within the CPU that are connected by signal paths to the ALU (e.g., see Figure 2.3). The ALU will also set flags as the result of an operation. For example, an overflow flag is set to 1 if the result of a computation exceeds the length of the register into which it is to be stored. The flag values are also stored in registers within the CPU. The control unit provides signals that control the operation of the ALU, and the movement of the data into and out of the ALU.

**FIGURE 8.1. ALU inputs and outputs**

## INTEGER REPRESENTATION

In the binary number system (see Appendix 8A), arbitrary numbers can be represented with just the digits 0 and 1, the minus sign, and the period. For example:

$-1101.0101_2 = -11.3125_{10}$

For purposes of computer storage and processing, however, we do not have the benefit of minus signs and periods. Only binary digits (0 and 1) may be used to represent numbers. If we only use nonnegative integers, the representation is straightforward. An 8-bit word could be used to represent the numbers from 0 to 255. For example:

00000000 = 0
00000001 = 1
00101001 = 41
10000000 = 128
11111111 = 255

In general, if an $n$-bit sequence of binary digits $a_n - 1a_n - 2 \ldots a_1a_0$ is interpreted as an unsigned integer $A$, its value is

$$A = \sum_{i=0}^{n-1} 2^i a_i$$

### Sign–Magnitude Representation

The use of unsigned integers is insufficient in the many cases when we need to represent negative as well as positive integers. There are several other conventions we could use for this. All of them involve treating the most significant (leftmost) bit in the word as a sign bit: If the leftmost bit is 0, the number is positive, and if the leftmost bit is 1, the number is negative.

The simplest form of representation that employs a sign bit is the sign–magnitude representation. In an $n$-bit word, the rightmost $n - 1$ bits hold the magnitude of the integer. For example:

+18 = 00010010
−18 = 10010010     (sign–magnitude)

The general case can be expressed as follows:

$$A = \begin{cases} \displaystyle\sum_{i=0}^{n-2} 2^i a_i & \text{if } a_{n-1} = 0 \\ \displaystyle -\sum_{i=0}^{n-2} 2^i a_i & \text{if } a_{n-1} = 1 \end{cases}$$

There are several drawbacks to sign–magnitude representation. One is that addition and subtraction require consideration of both the signs of the numbers and their relative magnitudes in order to carry out the required operation. This should become clear in the discussion in Section 8.3. Another drawback is that there are two representations of 0:

$$+0_{10} = 00000000$$
$$-0_{10} = 10000000 \qquad \text{(sign–magnitude)}$$

This is inconvenient, because it is slightly more difficult to test for 0 (an operation performed frequently by computers) than if there were a single representation.

## Two's Complement Representation[1]

The two's complement representation was developed to overcome the two principal drawbacks of the sign–magnitude representation: addition and subtraction in sign–magnitude are inefficient, and there are two representations for zero.

Like sign–magnitude, two's complement representation uses the most significant bit as a sign bit, making it easy to test whether an integer is positive or negative. It differs from sign–magnitude representation in the way that the other bits are interpreted.

Two's complement representation is best understood by defining it in terms of a weighted sum of bits, as we did above for unsigned and sign–magnitude representations. Consider an $n$-bit integer, $A$, in two's complement representation. If $A$ is positive, then the sign bit, $a_{n-1}$, is zero. The remaining bits represent the magnitude of the number in the same fashion as for sign–magnitude; thus,

$$A = \sum_{i=0}^{n-2} 2^i a_i \text{ for } A > 0.$$

The number zero is identified as positive and therefore has a 0 sign bit and a magnitude of all 0s. We can see that the range of positive integers that may be represented is from 0 (all of the magnitude bits are 0) through $2^{n-1} - 1$ (all of the magnitude bits are 1). Any larger number would require more bits.

Now, for a negative number $A$, the sign bit, $a_{n-1}$, is 1. The remaining $n - 1$ bits can take on any one of $2^{n-1}$ values. Therefore, the range of negative integers that can be

[1]The presentation of two's complement integers in this section and in Section 8.3 is based on an approach suggested by G. Dattatreya of the University of Texas (see [DATT93]).

represented is from $-1$ to $-2^{n-1}$. It turns out that a convenient assignment of values is to let the bits $a_{n-1}a_{n-2} \ldots a_1a_0$ be equal to the positive number $2^{n-1} + A$, as obtained by

$$2^{n-1} + A = \sum_{i=0}^{n-2} 2^i a_i, \quad \text{so that} \quad A = -2^{n-1} + \sum_{i=0}^{n-2} 2^i a_i$$

Since the sign bit is 1, we can write the expression for the negative number as

$$A = -2^{n-1}a_{n-1} + \sum_{i=0}^{n-2} 2^i a_i \tag{8-1}$$

In the case of positive integers, $a_{n-1} = 0$, and so the term $-2^{n-1}a_{n-1} = 0$. Therefore, Equation 8–1 defines the two's complement representation for both positive and negative numbers.

Table 8.1 compares the sign–magnitude and two's complement representations for 4-bit integers. Although two's complement is an awkward representation from the human point of view, we will see that it facilitates the most important arithmetic operations, addition and subtraction. For this reason, it is almost universally used as the processor representation for integers.

A useful illustration of the nature of two's complement representation is a value box, in which the value on the far right in the box is 1 ($2^0$) and each succeeding position to the left is double in value, until the leftmost position, which is negated. As you can see in Figure 8.2a, the most negative two's complement number that

**TABLE 8.1   Comparison of Sign–Magnitude and Two's-Complement Representation for 4-bit Integers**

| Decimal Representation | Sign–Magnitude Representation | Two's-Complement Representation |
|:---:|:---:|:---:|
| +7 | 0111 | 0111 |
| +6 | 0110 | 0110 |
| +5 | 0101 | 0101 |
| +4 | 0100 | 0100 |
| +3 | 0011 | 0011 |
| +2 | 0010 | 0010 |
| +1 | 0001 | 0001 |
| +0 | 0000 | 0000 |
| −0 | 1000 | — |
| −1 | 1001 | 1111 |
| −2 | 1010 | 1110 |
| −3 | 1011 | 1101 |
| −4 | 1100 | 1100 |
| −5 | 1101 | 1011 |
| −6 | 1110 | 1010 |
| −7 | 1111 | 1001 |
| −8 | — | 1000 |

| −128 | 64 | 32 | 16 | 8 | 4 | 2 | 1 |
|------|-----|-----|-----|-----|-----|-----|-----|
|      |     |     |     |     |     |     |     |

(a) An Eight-Position Two's Complement Value Box

| −128 | 64 | 32 | 16 | 8 | 4 | 2 | 1 |
|------|-----|-----|-----|-----|-----|-----|-----|
| 1    | 0   | 0   | 0   | 0   | 0   | 1   | 1   |

−128                                    +2    +1   = −125

(b) Convert Binary 10000011 to Decimal

| −128 | 64 | 32 | 16 | 8 | 4 | 2 | 1 |
|------|-----|-----|-----|-----|-----|-----|-----|
| 1    | 0   | 0   | 0   | 1   | 0   | 0   | 0   |

−120 =  −128                     +8

(c) Convert Decimal −120 to Binary

**FIGURE 8.2. Use of a Value Box for Conversion Between Two's Complement Binary and Decimal**

can be represented is $-2^{n-1}$; if any of the bits other than the sign bit is 1, it adds a positive amount to the number. Also, it is clear that a negative number must have a 1 at its leftmost position and a positive number must have a 0 in that position. Thus, the largest positive number is a 0 followed by all 1s, which equals $2^{n-1} - 1$.

The remainder of Figure 8.2 illustrates the use of the value box to convert from two's complement to decimal, and from decimal to two's complement.

## Converting Between Different Bit Lengths

It is sometimes desirable to take an $n$-bit integer and store it in $m$ bits, where $m > n$. In sign–magnitude notation, this is easily accomplished: simply move the sign bit to the new leftmost position and fill in with zeros. For example:

| | | |
|---|---|---|
| +18 = | 00010010 | (sign–magnitude, 8 bits) |
| +18 = | 0000000000010010 | (sign–magnitude, 16 bits) |
| −18 = | 10010010 | (sign–magnitude, 8 bits) |
| −18 = | 1000000000010010 | (sign–magnitude, 16 bits) |

This procedure will not work for two's complement negative integers. Using the same example:

| | | |
|---|---|---|
| +18 = | 00010010 | (two's complement, 8 bits) |
| +18 = | 0000000000010010 | (two's complement, 16 bits) |
| −18 = | 11101110 | (two's complement, 8 bits) |
| −32,658 = | 1000000001101110 | (two's complement, 16 bits) |

Instead, the rule for two's complement integers is to move the sign bit to the new leftmost position and fill in with copies of the sign bit. For positive numbers, fill in with 0s, and for negative numbers, fill in with 1s. Thus, we have

$-18 =$               11101110       (two's complement, 8 bits)
$-18 =$    1111111111101110       (two's complement, 16 bits)

To see why this rule works, let us again consider an $n$-bit sequence of binary digits $a_{n-1}a_{n-2} \ldots a_1a_0$ interpreted as a two's complement integer $A$, so that its value is

$$A = -2^{n-1}a_{n-1} + \sum_{i=0}^{n-2} 2^i a_i$$

If $A$ is a positive number, the rule clearly works. Now, suppose $A$ is negative and we want to construct an $m$-bit representation, with $m > n$. Then

$$A = -2^{m-1}a_{m-1} + \sum_{i=0}^{m-2} 2^i a_i$$

The two values must be equal:

$$-2^{m-1} + \sum_{i=0}^{m-2} 2^i a_i = -2^{n-1} + \sum_{i=0}^{n-2} 2^i a_i$$

$$-2^{m-1} + \sum_{i=n-1}^{m-2} 2^i a_i = -2^{n-1}$$

$$2^{n-1} + \sum_{i=n-1}^{m-2} 2^i a_i = 2^{m-1}$$

$$1 + \sum_{i=0}^{n-2} 2^i + \sum_{i=n-1}^{m-2} 2^i a_i = 1 + \sum_{i=0}^{m-2} 2^i$$

$$\sum_{i=n-1}^{m-2} 2^i a_i = \sum_{i=n-1}^{m-2} 2^i$$

In going from the first to the second equation, we require that the least significant $n - 1$ bits do not change between the two representations. Then, we get to the final equation, which is only true if all of the bits in positions $n - 1$ through $m - 2$ are 1. Thus, the rule works.

## Fixed-Point Representation

Finally, we mention that the representations discussed in this section are sometimes referred to as fixed point. This is because the radix point (binary point) is fixed and assumed to be to the right of the rightmost digit. The programmer can use the same representation for binary fractions by scaling the numbers so that the binary point is implicitly positioned at some other location.

## 8.3

### INTEGER ARITHMETIC

This section examines common arithmetic function on numbers in two's complement representation.

### Negation

In sign–magnitude representation, the rule for forming the negation of an integer is simple: invert the sign bit. In two's complement notation, the negation of an integer can be formed using the following rules:

1. Take the Boolean complement of each bit of the integer (including the sign bit).
2. Treating the result as an unsigned binary integer, add 1.

For example:

$$18 = 00010010 \text{ (two's complement)}$$
$$\text{bitwise complement} = 11101101$$
$$+ \qquad 1$$
$$\overline{\qquad\qquad}$$
$$11101110 = -18$$

As expected, the negative of the negative of that number is itself:

$$-18 = 11101110 \text{ (two's complement)}$$
$$\text{bitwise complement} = 00010001$$
$$+ \qquad 1$$
$$\overline{\qquad\qquad}$$
$$00010010 = 18$$

We can demonstrate the validity of the operation just described using the definition of the two's complement representation in Equation (8-1). Again, interpret an $n$-bit sequence of binary digits $a_{n-1}a_{n-2} \ldots a_1a_0$ as a two's-complement integer $A$, so that its value is

$$A = -2^{n-1}a_{n-1} + \sum_{i=0}^{n-2} 2^i a_i$$

Now form the bitwise complement, $\overline{a_{n-1}}\,\overline{a_{n-2}} \cdots \overline{a_0}$, and treating this as an unsigned integer, add 1. Finally, interpret the resulting $n$-bit sequence of binary digits as a two's complement integer $B$, so that its value is

$$B = -2^{n-1}\overline{a_{n-1}} + 1 + \sum_{i=0}^{n-2} 2^i \overline{a_i}$$

Now, we want $A = -B$, which means $A + B = 0$. This is easily shown to be true:

$$A + B = -(a_{n-1} + \overline{a_{n-1}})2^{n-1} + 1 + \sum_{i=0}^{n-2} 2^i (a_i + \overline{a_i})$$

$$= -2^{n-1} + 1 + \sum_{i=0}^{n-2} 2^i$$

$$= -2^{n-1} + 2^{n-1} = 0$$

The above derivation assumes that we can first treat the bitwise complement of A as an unsigned integer to add 1, and then treat the result as a two's complement integer. There are two special cases to consider. First, consider $A = 0$. In that case, for an 8-bit representation,

$$0 = 00000000 \text{ (two's complement)}$$
$$\text{bitwise complement} = 11111111$$
$$\underline{+\qquad 1}$$
$$1\ 00000000 = 0$$

There is an overflow, which is ignored. The result is that the negation of 0 is 0, as it should be.

The second special case is more of a problem. If we take the negation of the bit pattern of 1 followed by $n - 1$ zeros, we get back the same number. For example, for 8-bit words,

$$-128 = 10000000 \text{ (two's complement)}$$
$$\text{bitwise complement} = 01111111$$
$$\underline{+\qquad 1}$$
$$10000000 = -128$$

Some such anomaly is unavoidable. The number of different bit patterns in an $n$-bit word is $2^n$, which is an even number. We wish to represent positive and negative integers and 0. If an equal number of positive and negative integers are represented (sign–magnitude), then there are two representations for 0. If there is only one representation of 0 (two's complement), then there must be an unequal number of negative and positive numbers represented. In the case of two's complement, there is an $n$-bit representation for $-2^n$, but not for $2^n$.

Addition in two's complement is illustrated in Figure 8.3. The first four examples illustrate successful operation. If the result of the operation is positive, we get a positive number in ordinary binary notation. If the result of the operation is negative, we get a negative number in two's complement form. Note that, in some instances, there is a carry bit beyond the end of the word. This is ignored.

On any addition, the result may be larger than can be held in the word size being used. This condition is called *overflow*. When overflow occurs, the ALU must signal this fact so that no attempt is made to use the result. To detect overflow, the following rule is observed.

OVERFLOW RULE:
If two numbers are added, and they are both positive or both negative, then overflow occurs if and only if the result has the opposite sign.

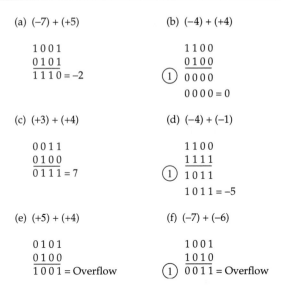

(a)  (−7) + (+5)

    1 0 0 1
    0 1 0 1
    ‾‾‾‾‾‾‾
    1 1 1 0 = −2

(b)  (−4) + (+4)

    1 1 0 0
    0 1 0 0
    ‾‾‾‾‾‾‾
  ① 0 0 0 0
    0 0 0 0 = 0

(c)  (+3) + (+4)

    0 0 1 1
    0 1 0 0
    ‾‾‾‾‾‾‾
    0 1 1 1 = 7

(d)  (−4) + (−1)

    1 1 0 0
    1 1 1 1
    ‾‾‾‾‾‾‾
  ① 1 0 1 1
    1 0 1 1 = −5

(e)  (+5) + (+4)

    0 1 0 1
    0 1 0 0
    ‾‾‾‾‾‾‾
    1 0 0 1 = Overflow

(f)  (−7) + (−6)

    1 0 0 1
    1 0 1 0
    ‾‾‾‾‾‾‾
  ① 0 0 1 1 = Overflow

**FIGURE 8.3.  Addition of numbers in two's complement representation**

Figures 8.3e and f show examples of overflow. Note that overflow can occur whether or not there is a carry. Subtraction is also easily handled:

SUBTRACTION RULE:
To subtract one number (subtrahend) from another (minuend), take the two's complement of the subtrahend and add it to the minuend.

Thus, subtraction is achieved using addition, as illustrated in Figure 8.4. The last two examples demonstrate that the overflow rule still applies.

Figure 8.5 suggests the data paths and hardware elements needed to accomplish addition and subtraction. The central element is a binary adder, which is presented two numbers for addition and produces a sum and an overflow indication. The binary adder treats the two numbers as unsigned integers. (A logic implementation of an adder is given in the appendix to this book). For addition, the two numbers are presented to the adder from two registers, designated in this case as A and B registers. The result is typically stored in one of these registers rather than a third. The overflow indication is stored in a 1-bit Overflow Flag (0 = no overflow; 1 = overflow). For subtraction, the subtrahend (B register) is passed through a complementer so that its two's complement is presented to the adder.

## Multiplication

Compared with addition and subtraction, multiplication is a complex operation, whether performed in hardware or software. A wide variety of algorithms have been used in various computers. The purpose of this subsection is to give the reader some feel for the type of approach typically taken. We begin with the simpler problem of multiplying two unsigned (nonnegative) integers, and then we look at one of the most common techniques for multiplication of numbers in two's complement representation.

(a) M = 2 = 0010
   S  = 7 = 0111
   S' =     1001

       0010
      +1001
      ‾‾‾‾
      1011 = −5

(d) M = 5 = 0101
   S  = −2 = 1110
   S' =     0010

       0101
      +0010
      ‾‾‾‾
      0111 = 7

(b) M = 5 = 0101
   S  = 2 = 0010
   S' =     1110

       0101
      +1110
      ‾‾‾‾
 ①   0011
      0011 = 3

(e) M =  7 = 0111
   S  = −7 = 1001
   S' =     0111

       0111
      +0111
      ‾‾‾‾
      1110 = Overflow

(c) M = −5 = 1011
   S  = 2  = 0010
   S' =     1110

       1011
     + 1110
      ‾‾‾‾
 ①   1001
      1001 = −7

(f) M = −6 = 1010
   S  = 4  = 0100
   S' =     1100

       1010
     + 1100
      ‾‾‾‾
 ①   0110 = Overflow

**FIGURE 8.4. Subtraction of numbers in two's complement notation (M—S)**

## Unsigned Integers

Figure 8.6 illustrates the multiplication of unsigned binary integers, as might be carried out using paper and pencil. Several important observations can be made:

1. Multiplication involves the generation of partial products, one for each digit in the multiplier. These partial products are then summed to produce the final product.
2. The partial products are easily defined. When the multiplier bit is 0, the partial product is 0. When the multiplier is 1, the partial product is the multiplicand.

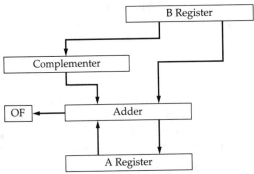

**FIGURE 8.5. Block diagram of hardware for addition and subtraction**

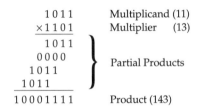

```
    1 0 1 1      Multiplicand (11)
  × 1 1 0 1      Multiplier     (13)
    1 0 1 1  ⎫
    0 0 0 0  ⎬   Partial Products
    1 0 1 1  ⎪
  1 0 1 1    ⎭
1 0 0 0 1 1 1 1   Product (143)
```

**FIGURE 8.6. Multiplication of unsigned binary integers**

3. The total product is produced by summing the partial products. For this operation, each successive partial product is shifted one position to the left relative to the preceding partial product.
4. The multiplication of two $n$-bit binary integers results in a product of up to $2n$ bits in length.

Compared with the pencil-and-paper approach, there are several things we can do to make the operation more efficient. First, we can perform a running addition on the partial products rather than waiting until the end. This eliminates the need for storage of all the partial products; fewer registers are needed. Second, we can save some time on the generation of partial products. For each 1 on the multiplier, an add and a shift operation are required; but for each 0, only a shift is required.

Figure 8.7a shows a possible implementation employing these measures. The multiplier and multiplicand are loaded into two registers (Q and M). A third register, the A register, is also needed and is initially set to 0. There is also a 1-bit C register, initialized to 0, which holds a potential carry bit resulting from addition.

The operation of the multiplier is as follows. Control logic reads the bits of the multiplier one at a time. If $Q_0$ is 1, then the multiplicand is added to the A register and the result is stored in the A register. Then, all of the bits of the C, A, and Q registers are shifted to the right one bit, so that the C bit goes into $A_{n-1}$, $A_0$ goes into $Q_{n-1}$, and $Q_0$ is lost. If $Q_0$ is 0, then no addition is performed, just the shift. This process is repeated for each bit of the original multiplier. The resulting $2n$-bit product is contained in the A and Q registers. A flowchart of the operation is shown in Figure 8.8, and an example is given in Figure 8.7b. Note that on the second cycle, when the multiplier bit is 0, there is no add operation.

### Two's Complement Multiplication

We have seen that addition and subtraction can be performed on numbers in two's complement notation by treating them as unsigned integers. Consider:

```
 1001
+0011
 1100
```

If these numbers are considered to be unsigned integers, then we are adding 9 (1001) plus 3 (0011) to get 12 (1100). As two's complement integers, we are adding −7 (1001) to 3 (0011) to get −4 (1100).

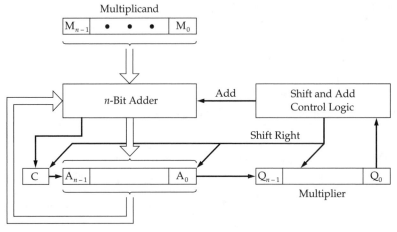

(a) Block Diagram

| C | A | Q | | |
|---|------|------|---|---|
| 0 | 0000 | 1101 | Initial Values | |
| 0 | 1011 | 1101 | Add | } First Cycle |
| 0 | 0101 | 1110 | Shift | |
| 0 | 0010 | 1111 | Shift } | Second Cycle |
| 0 | 1101 | 1111 | Add | } Third Cycle |
| 0 | 0110 | 1111 | Shift | |
| 1 | 0001 | 1111 | Add | } Fourth Cycle |
| 0 | 1000 | 1111 | Shift | (Product in A, Q) |

(b) Example (from Figure 8.6)

**FIGURE 8.7. Hardware implementation of unsigned binary multiplication (M contains 1011)**

Unfortunately, this simple scheme will not work for multiplication. To see this, consider again Figure 8.6. We multiplied 11 (1011) by 13 (1101) to get 143 (10001111). If we interpret these as two's complement numbers, we have –5 (1011) times –3 (1101) equals –113 (10001111). This example demonstrates that straightforward multiplication will not work if both the multiplicand and multiplier are negative. In fact, it will not work if either the multiplicand or the multiplier is negative. To explain this statement, we need to go back to Figure 8.6 and explain what is being done in terms of operations with powers of 2. Recall that any unsigned binary number can be expressed as a sum of powers of 2. Thus,

$$1101 = 1 * 2^3 + 1 * 2^2 + 0 * 2^1 + 1 * 2^0$$
$$= 2^3 + 2^2 + 2^0$$

Further, the multiplication of a binary number by $2^n$ is accomplished by shifting that number to the left $n$ bits. With this in mind, Figure 8.9 recasts Figure 8.6 to

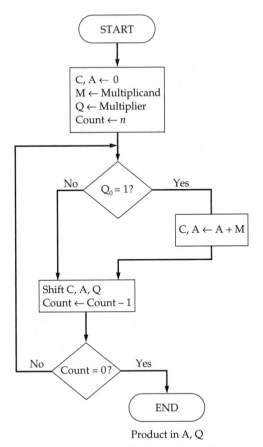

FIGURE 8.8.  **Flowchart for unsigned binary multiplication**

make the generation of partial products by multiplication explicit. The only difference in Figure 8.9 is that it recognizes that the partial products should be viewed as $2n$-bit numbers generated from the $n$-bit multiplicand.

Thus, as an unsigned integer, the 4-bit multiplicand 1011 is stored in an 8-bit word as 00001011. Each partial product (other than that for $2^0$) consists of this number shifted to the left, with the unoccupied positions on the right filled with zeros (e.g., a shift to the left of two places yields 00101100).

$$
\begin{array}{r}
1011 \\
\times 1101 \\
\hline
\end{array}
$$

| | |
|---|---|
| 00001011 | $1011 \times 1 \times 2^0$ |
| 00000000 | $1011 \times 0 \times 2^1$ |
| 00101100 | $1011 \times 1 \times 2^2$ |
| 01011000 | $1011 \times 1 \times 2^3$ |
| 10001111 | |

FIGURE 8.9.  **Multiplication of two unsigned 4-bit integers yielding an 8-bit result**

Now we can demonstrate that straightforward multiplication will not work if the multiplicand is negative. The problem is that each contribution of the negative multiplicand as a partial product must be a negative number on a $2n$-bit field; the sign bits of the partial products must line up. This is demonstrated in Figure 8.10, which shows that multiplication of 1001 by 0011. If these are treated as unsigned integers, the multiplication of 9 * 3 = 27 proceeds simply. However, if 1001 is interpreted as the two's complement $-7$, then each partial product must be a negative two's complement number of $2n$ (8) bits, as shown in Figure 8.10b. Note that this could be accomplished by padding out each partial product to the left with binary 1s.

It should also be clear that if the multiplier is negative, straightforward multiplication will not work. The reason is that the bits of the multiplier no longer correspond to the shifts or multiplications that must take place. For example:

$$-3 = 1101$$
$$= -(0 * 2^3 + 0 * 2^2 + 1 * 2^1 + 1 * 2^0)$$
$$= -2^1 - 2^0$$

So this multiplier cannot be used directly in the manner we have been describing.

There are a number of ways out of this dilemma. One would be to convert both multiplier and multiplicand to positive numbers, perform the multiplication, and then take the two's complement of the result if and only if the sign of the two original numbers differed. Implementers have preferred to use techniques that do not require this final transformation step. One of the most common of these is Booth's algorithm [BOOT51]. This algorithm also has the benefit of speeding up the multiplication process, relative to a more straightforward approach.

Booth's algorithm is depicted in Figure 8.11 and can be described as follows. As before, the multiplier and multiplicand are placed in the Q and M registers, respectively. There is also a 1-bit register placed logically to the right of the least significant bit ($Q_0$) of the Q register and designated $Q_{-1}$; its use is explained shortly. The results of the multiplication will appear in the A and Q registers. A and $Q_{-1}$ are initialized to 0. As before, control logic scans the bits of the multiplier one at a time. Now, as each bit is examined, the bit to its right is also examined. If the two bits are the same (1–1 or 0–0), then all of the bits of the A, Q, and $Q_{-1}$ registers are shifted to the right 1 bit. If the two bits differ, then the multiplicand is added to or subtracted from the A register, according as the two bits are 0–1 or 1–0. Following the addition or subtraction, the right shift occurs. In either case, the right shift is such that the leftmost bit of A, namely $A_{n-1}$, not only is shifted into $A_{n-2}$, but also remains in $A_{n-1}$. This is required to preserve the sign of the number in A and Q. It is known as an *arithmetic shift*, since it preserves the sign bit.

```
      1 0 0 1      (9)                    1 0 0 1      (–7)
    × 0 0 1 1      (3)                  × 0 0 1 1      (3)
  ─────────────                      ─────────────
  0 0 0 0 1 0 0 1  (1001) × 2⁰        1 1 1 1 1 0 0 1  (–7) × 2⁰ = (–7)
  0 0 0 1 0 0 1 0  (1001) × 2¹        1 1 1 1 0 0 1 0  (–7) × 2¹ = (–14)
  ─────────────                      ─────────────
  0 0 0 1 1 0 1 1  (27)               1 1 1 0 1 0 1 1  (–21)

    (a) Unsigned Integers               (b) Two's Complement Integers
```

**FIGURE 8.10. Comparison of multiplication of unsigned and two's complement integers**

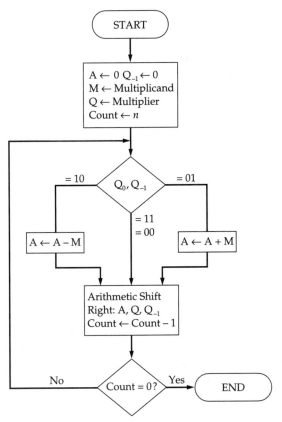

**FIGURE 8.11.  Booth's algorithm for two's complement multiplication**

Figure 8.12 shows the sequence of events in Booth's algorithm for the multiplication of 7 by 3. More compactly, the same operation is depicted in Figure 8.13a. The rest of Figure 8.13 gives other examples of the algorithm. As can be seen, it works with any combination of positive and negative numbers. Note also the efficiency of the algorithm. Blocks of 1s or 0s are skipped over, with an average of only one addition or subtraction per block.

| A | Q | $Q_{-1}$ | | |
|---|---|---|---|---|
| 0000 | 0011 | 0 | Initial | |
| 1001 | 0011 | 0 | $A \leftarrow A - M$ | First Cycle |
| 1100 | 1001 | 1 | Shift | |
| 1110 | 0100 | 1 | Shift | Second Cycle |
| 0101 | 0100 | 1 | $A \leftarrow A + M$ | Third Cycle |
| 0010 | 1010 | 0 | Shift | |
| 0001 | 0101 | 0 | Shift | Fourth Cycle (Product in A, Q) |

**FIGURE 8.12.  Example of Booth's algorithm (M contains 0111)**

```
        0111                                      0111
      ×0011 (0)                                 ×1101 (0)
    11111001         1 – 0                    11111001         1 – 0
    0000000          1 – 1                    0000111          0 – 1
    000111           0 – 1                    111001           1 – 0
    00010101         (21)                     11101011         (–21)
```

(a) (7) × (3) = (21)                          (b) (7) × (–3) = (–21)

```
        1001                                      1001
      ×0011 (0)                                 ×1101 (0)
    00000111         1 – 0                    00000111         1 – 0
    0000000          1 – 1                    1111001          0 – 1
    111001           0 – 1                    000111           1 – 0
    11101011         (–21)                    00010101         (21)
```

(c) (–7) × (3) = (–21)                        (d) (–7) × (–3) = (–21)

**FIGURE 8.13.  Examples using Booth's alogirithm**

Why does Booth's algorithm work? Consider first the case of a positive multiplier. In particular, consider a positive multiplier consisting of one block of 1s surrounded by 0s, for example, 00011110. As we know, multiplication can be achieved by adding appropriately shifted copies of the multiplicand:

$$M * (00011110) = M * (2^4 + 2^3 + 2^2 + 2^1)$$
$$= M * (16 + 8 + 4 + 2)$$
$$= M * 30$$

The number of such operations can be reduced to two if we observe that

$$2^n + 2^{n-1} + \ldots + 2^{n-K} = 2^{n+1} - 2^{n-K} \tag{8-2}$$

Thus,

$$M * (00011110) = M * (2^5 - 2^1)$$
$$= M * (32 - 2)$$
$$= M * 30$$

So the product can be generated by one addition and one subtraction of the multiplicand. This scheme extends to any number of blocks of 1s in a multiplier, including the case in which a single 1 is treated as a block. Thus,

$$M * (01111010) = M * (2^6 + 2^5 + 2^4 + 2^3 + 2^1)$$
$$= M * (2^7 - 2^3 + 2^2 - 2^1)$$

Booth's algorithm conforms to this scheme by performing a subtraction when the first 1 of the block is encountered (1–0) and an addition when the end of the block is encountered (0–1).

To show that the same scheme works for a negative multiplier, we need to observe the following. Let $X$ be a negative number in two's complement notation:

Representation of $X = \{1x_{n-2}x_{n-3} \ldots x_1x_0\}$

Then the value of $X$ can be expressed as follows:

$$X = -2^{n-1} + x_{n-2} * 2^{n-2} + x_{n-3} * 2^{n-3} + \ldots + x_1 * 2^1 + x_0 * 2^0 \qquad (8\text{-}3)$$

The reader can verify this by applying the algorithm to the numbers in Table 8.1.

Now, we know that the leftmost bit of $X$ is 1, since $X$ is negative. Assume that the leftmost 0 is in the $k^{th}$ position. Thus, $X$ is of the form

Representation of $X = \{111 \ldots 10x_{k-1}\, x_{k-2} \ldots x_1x_0\} \qquad (8\text{-}4)$

Then the value of $X$ is

$$X = -2^{n-1} + 2^{n-2} + \ldots + 2^{k+1} + x_{k-1} * 2^{k-1} + \ldots + x_0 * 2^0 \qquad (8\text{-}5)$$

Now, from Equation 8-2 we can say that

$$2^{n-2} + 2^{n-3} + \ldots + 2^{k+1} = 2^{n-1} - 2^{k+1}$$

Rearranging

$$-2^{n-1} + 2^{n-2} + 2^{n-3} + \ldots + 2^{k+1} = -2^{k+1} \qquad (8\text{-}6)$$

Substituting Equation 8-6 into Equation 8-5, we have

$$X = -2^{k+1} + x_{k-1} * 2^{k-1} + \ldots + x_0 * 2^0 \qquad (8\text{-}7)$$

At last we can return to Booth's algorithm. Remembering the representation of $X$ (Equation 8-4), it is clear that all of the bits from $X_0$ up to the leftmost 0 are handled properly, since they produce all of the terms in Equation 8-7 but $(-2^{k+1})$ and thus are in the proper form. As the algorithm scans over the leftmost 0 and encounters the next 1 $(2^{k+1})$, a 1–0 transition occurs and a subtraction takes place $(-2^{k+1})$. This is the remaining term in Equation 8-7.

As an example, consider the multiplication of some multiplicand by $(-6)$. In two's complement representation, using an 8-bit word, $(-6)$ is represented as 11111010. By Equation 8-3, we know that

$$-6 = -2^7 + 2^6 + 2^5 + 2^4 + 2^3 + 2^1$$

which the reader can easily verify. Thus,

$$M2 * (11111010) = M * (-2^7 + 2^6 + 2^5 + 2^4 + 2^3 + 2^1)$$

Using Equation 8-7,

$$M * (11111010) = M * (-2^3 + 2^1)$$

which the reader can verify is still $M * (-6)$. Finally, following our earlier line of reasoning,

$$M * (11111010) = M * (-2^3 + 2^2 - 2^1)$$

But now we can see that Booth's algorithm conforms to this scheme. It performs a subtraction when the first 1 is encountered (1–0), an addition when (0–1) is encountered, and finally another subtraction when the first 1 of the next block of 1s is encountered. Thus, Booth's algorithm performs fewer additions and subtractions than a more straightforward algorithm.

## Division

Division is somewhat more complex than multiplication but is based on the same general principles. As before, the basis for the algorithm is the paper-and-pencil approach, and the operation involves repetitive shifting and addition or subtraction.

Figure 8.14 shows an example of the long division of unsigned binary integers. It is instructive to describe the process in detail. First, the bits of the dividend are examined from left to right, until the set of bits examined represents a number greater than or equal to the divisor; this is referred to as the divisor being able to *divide* the number. Until this event occurs, 0s are placed in the quotient from left to right. When the event occurs, a 1 is placed in the quotient and the divisor is subtracted from the partial dividend. The result is referred to as a *partial remainder*. From this point on, the division follows a cyclic pattern. At each cycle, additional bits from the dividend are appended to the partial remainder until the result is greater than or equal to the divisor. As before, the divisor is subtracted from this number to produce a new partial remainder. The process continues until all the bits of the dividend are exhausted.

Figure 8.15 shows a machine algorithm that corresponds to the long division process. The divisor is placed in the M register, the dividend in the Q register. At each step, the A and Q registers together are shifted to the left 1 bit. M is subtracted from A to determine whether A divides the partial remainder. If it does, then $Q_0$ gets a 1 bit. Otherwise, $Q_0$ gets a 0 bit and M must be added back to A to restore the previous value. The count is then decremented, and the process continues for $n$ steps. At the end, the quotient is in the Q register and the remainder is in the A register.

This process can, with some difficulty, be extended to negative numbers. We give here one approach for two's complement numbers. Several examples of this approach are shown in Figure 8.16. The algorithm can be summarized as follows.

1. Load the divisor into the M register and the dividend into the A, Q registers. The dividend must be expressed as a $2n$-bit two's complement number. Thus, for example, the 4-bit 0111 becomes 00000111, and 1001 becomes 11111001.

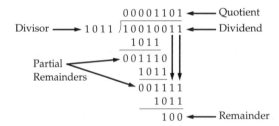

**FIGURE 8.14. Division of unsigned binary integers**

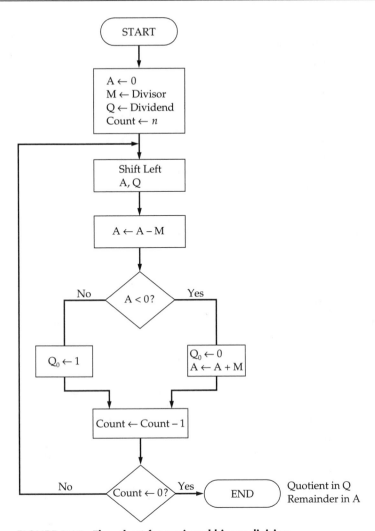

**FIGURE 8.15. Flowchart for unsigned binary division**

2. Shift A, Q left 1 bit position.
3. If M and A have the same signs, perform $A \leftarrow A - M$; otherwise, $A \leftarrow A + M$.
4. The above operation is successful if the sign of A is the same before and after the operation.
   a. If the operation is successful or $(A = 0$ AND $Q = 0)$, then set $Q_0 \leftarrow 1$.
   b. If the operation is unsuccessful and $(A \neq 0$ OR $Q \neq 0)$, then set $Q_0 \leftarrow 0$ and restore the previous value of A.
5. Repeat steps 2 through 4 as many times as there are bit positions in Q.
6. The remainder is in A. If the signs of the divisor and dividend were the same, then the quotient is in Q; otherwise, the correct quotient is the two's complement of Q.

| A | Q | M = 0011 |
|---|---|---|
| 0 0 0 0 | 0 1 1 1 | Initial Value |
| 0 0 0 0 | 1 1 1 0 | Shift |
| 1 1 0 1 | | Subtract |
| 0 0 0 0 | 1 1 1 0 | Restore |
| 0 0 0 1 | 1 1 0 0 | Shift |
| 1 1 1 0 | | Subtract |
| 0 0 0 1 | 1 1 0 0 | Restore |
| 0 0 1 1 | 1 0 0 0 | Shift |
| 0 0 0 0 | | Subtract |
| 0 0 0 0 | 1 0 0 1 | Set $Q_0 = 1$ |
| 0 0 0 1 | 0 0 1 0 | Shift |
| 1 1 1 0 | | Subtract |
| 0 0 0 1 | 0 0 1 0 | Restore |

(a) $(7) \div (3)$

| A | Q | M = 1101 |
|---|---|---|
| 0 0 0 0 | 0 1 1 1 | Initial Value |
| 0 0 0 0 | 1 1 1 0 | Shift |
| 1 1 0 1 | | Add |
| 0 0 0 0 | 1 1 1 0 | Restore |
| 0 0 0 1 | 1 1 0 0 | Shift |
| 1 1 1 0 | | Add |
| 0 0 0 1 | 1 1 0 0 | Restore |
| 0 0 1 1 | 1 0 0 0 | Shift |
| 0 0 0 0 | | Add |
| 0 0 0 0 | 1 0 0 1 | Set $Q_0 = 1$ |
| 0 0 0 1 | 0 0 1 0 | Shift |
| 1 1 1 0 | | Add |
| 0 0 0 1 | 0 0 1 0 | Restore |

(b) $(7) \div (-3)$

| A | Q | M = 0011 |
|---|---|---|
| 1 1 1 1 | 1 0 0 1 | Initial Value |
| 1 1 1 1 | 0 0 1 0 | Shift |
| 0 0 1 0 | | Add |
| 1 1 1 1 | 0 0 1 0 | Restore |
| 1 1 1 0 | 0 1 0 0 | Shift |
| 0 0 0 1 | | Add |
| 1 1 1 0 | 0 1 0 0 | Restore |
| 1 1 0 0 | 1 0 0 0 | Shift |
| 1 1 1 1 | | Add |
| 1 1 1 1 | 1 0 0 1 | Set $Q_0 = 1$ |
| 1 1 1 1 | 0 0 1 0 | Shift |
| 0 0 1 0 | | Add |
| 1 1 1 1 | 0 0 1 0 | Restore |

(c) $(-7) \div (3)$

| A | Q | M = 1101 |
|---|---|---|
| 1 1 1 1 | 1 0 0 1 | Initial Value |
| 1 1 1 1 | 0 0 1 0 | Shift |
| 0 0 1 0 | | Subtract |
| 1 1 1 1 | 0 0 1 0 | Restore |
| 1 1 1 0 | 0 1 0 0 | Shift |
| 0 0 0 1 | | Subtract |
| 1 1 1 0 | 0 1 0 0 | Restore |
| 1 1 0 0 | 1 0 0 0 | Shift |
| 1 1 1 1 | | Subtract |
| 1 1 1 1 | 1 0 0 1 | Set $Q_0 = 1$ |
| 1 1 1 1 | 0 0 1 0 | Shift |
| 0 0 1 0 | | Subtract |
| 1 1 1 1 | 0 0 1 0 | Restore |

(d) $(-7) \div (-3)$

**FIGURE 8.16. Examples of two's complement division**

The reader will note from Figure 8.16 that $(-7) \div (3)$ and $(7) \div (-3)$ produce different remainders. This is because the remainder is defined as

$$D = Q * V + R$$

where

D = dividend
Q = quotient
V = divisor
R = remainder

The results of Figure 8.16 are consistent with this formula.

## 8.4

## FLOATING-POINT REPRESENTATION

### Principles

With a fixed-point notation (e.g., two's complement) it is possible to represent a range of positive and negative integers centered on 0. By assuming a fixed binary or radix point, this format allows the representation of numbers with a fractional component as well.

This approach has limitations. Very large numbers cannot be represented, nor can very small fractions. Further, the fractional part of the quotient in a division of two large numbers could be lost.

For decimal numbers, one gets around this limitation by using scientific notation. Thus, 976,000,000,000,000 can be represented as $9.76 * 10^{14}$, and 0.0000000000000976 can be represented as $9.76 * 10^{-14}$. What we have done, in effect, is to dynamically slide the decimal point to a convenient location and use the exponent of 10 to keep track of that decimal point. This allows a range of very large and very small numbers to be represented with only a few digits.

This same approach can be taken with binary numbers. We can represent a number in the form

$$\pm S * B^{\pm E}$$

This number can be stored in a binary word with three fields:

- Sign: plus or minus
- Significand S
- Exponent E

The base B is implicit and need not be stored since it is the same for all numbers.

The principles used in representing binary floating-point numbers are best explained with an example. Figure 8.17a shows a typical 32-bit floating-point format. The leftmost bit stores the sign of the number (0 = positive, 1 = negative). The exponent value is stored in bits 1 through 8. The representation used is known as a *biased* representation. A fixed value, called the bias, is subtracted from the field to

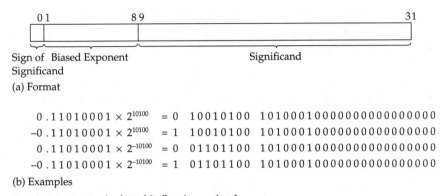

(a) Format

$$0.11010001 \times 2^{10100} = 0 \quad 10010100 \quad 10100010000000000000000$$
$$-0.11010001 \times 2^{10100} = 1 \quad 10010100 \quad 10100010000000000000000$$
$$0.11010001 \times 2^{-10100} = 0 \quad 01101100 \quad 10100010000000000000000$$
$$-0.11010001 \times 2^{-10100} = 1 \quad 01101100 \quad 10100010000000000000000$$

(b) Examples

**FIGURE 8.17. Typical 32-bit floating-point format**

get the true exponent value. In this case, the 8-bit field yields the numbers 0 through 255. With a bias of 128, the true exponent values are in the range –128 to +127. In this example, the base is assumed to be 2.

The final portion of the word is the *significand*, also called the *mantissa*. Now, any floating-point number can be expressed in many ways. Thus, the following are equivalent:

$0.110 * 2^5$
$110 * 2^2$
$0.0110 * 2^6$

and so on. To simplify operations on floating-point numbers, it is typically required that they be *normalized*. For our example, a normalized number is one in the form

$\pm 0.1 \, bbb \ldots b * 2^{\pm E}$

where b is either binary digit (0 or 1). This would imply that the leftmost bit of the significand would always be 1. Since it is obviously unnecessary to store this bit, it is implicit. Thus, the 23-bit field is used to store a 24-bit significand with a value between 0.5 and 1.0.

Figure 8.17b gives some examples of numbers stored in this format. Note the following features:

- The sign is stored in the first bit of the word.
- The first bit of the true significand is always 1 and need not be stored in the significand field.
- The value 128 is added to the true exponent to be stored in the exponent field.
- The base is 2.

With this representation, Figure 8.18 indicates the range of numbers that can be represented in a 32-bit word. Using two's complement integer representation, all of the integers from $-2^{31}$ to $2^{31} - 1$ can be represented, for a total of $2^{32}$ different numbers. With the example floating-point format of Figure 8.17, the following ranges of numbers are possible:

- Negative numbers between $-(1 - 2^{-24}) * 2^{127}$ and $-0.5 * 2^{-128}$
- Positive numbers between $0.5 * 2^{-128}$ and $(1 - 2^{-24}) * 2^{127}$

Five regions on the number line are not included in these ranges:

- Negative numbers less than $-(1 - 2^{-24}) * 2^{127}$, called *negative overflow*.
- Negative numbers greater than $-0.5 * 2^{-128}$, called *negative underflow*.
- Zero
- Positive numbers less than $0.5 * 2^{-128}$, called *positive underflow*.
- Positive numbers greater than $(1 - 2^{-24}) * 2^{127}$, called *positive overflow*.

The representation as presented will not accommodate a value of 0. However, as we shall see, actual floating-point representations include a special bit pattern to designate zero. Overflow occurs when an arithmetic operation results in a magnitude greater than can be expressed with an exponent of 127 (e.g., $2^{120} * 2^{100} = 2^{220}$). Underflow occurs when the fractional magnitude is too small (e.g., $2^{-120} * 2^{-100} = 2^{-220}$).

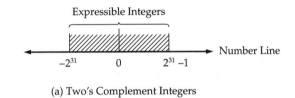

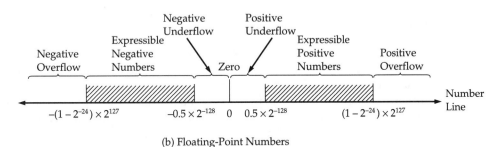

FIGURE 8.18. **Expressible numbers in typical 32-bit formats**

Underflow is a less serious problem because the result can generally be satisfactorily approximated by 0.

It is important to note that we are not representing more individual values with floating-point notation. The maximum number of different values that can be represented with 32 bits is still $2^{32}$. What we have done is to spread those numbers out in two ranges, one positive and one negative.

Also, note that the numbers represented in floating-point notation are not spaced evenly along the number line, as are fixed-point numbers. The possible values get closer together near the origin and farther apart as you move away, as shown in Figure 8.19. This is one of the trade-offs of floating-point math: Many calculations produce results that are not exact and have to be rounded to the nearest value that the notation can represent.

In the type of format depicted in Figure 8.17, there is a trade-off between range and precision. The example shows 8 bits devoted to the exponent and 23 to the significand. If we increase the number of bits in the exponent, we expand the range of expressible numbers. But, since only a fixed number of different values can be expressed, we have reduced the density of those numbers and therefore the precision. The only way to increase both range and precision is to use more bits.

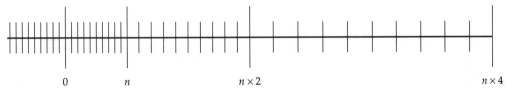

FIGURE 8.19. **Density of floating-point numbers**

Thus, most computers offer, at least, *single-precision* numbers and *double-precision* numbers. For example, a single-precision format might be 32 bits, and a double-precision format 64 bits.

So there is a trade-off between the number of bits in the exponent and the number of bits in the significand. But it is even more complicated than that. The implied base of the exponent need not be 2. The IBM S/370 architecture, for example, uses a base of 16. The format consists of a 7-bit exponent and a 24-bit significand. So, for example,

$$0.11010001 * 2^{10100} = 0.11010001 * 16^{101}$$

and the exponent is stored to represent 5 rather than 20.

The advantage of using a larger exponent is that a greater range can be achieved for the same number of exponent bits. But, remember, we have not increased the number of different values that can be represented. Thus, for a fixed format, a larger exponent base gives a greater range at the expense of less precision.

## IEEE Standard for Binary Floating-Point Arithmetic

The most important floating-point representation is defined in IEEE Standard 754 [IEEE85]. This standard was developed to facilitate the portability of programs from one processor to another and to encourage the development of sophisticated numerically oriented programs. The standard has been widely adopted and is used on virtually all contemporary processors and arithmetic coprocessors.

The IEEE standard defines both a 32-bit single and a 64-bit double format (Figure 8.20), with 8-bit and 11-bit exponents, respectively. The implied base is 2. In addition, the standard defines two extended formats, single and double, whose exact format is implementation-dependent. The extended formats include additional bits in the exponent (extended range) and in the significand (extended precision). The extended formats are to be used for intermediate calculations. With their greater precision, the extended formats lessen the chance of a final result that has been contaminated by excessive roundoff error; with their greater range, they

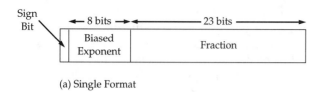

(a) Single Format

(b) Double Format

**FIGURE 8.20.  IEEE 754 Formats**

also lessen the chance of an intermediate overflow aborting a computation whose result would have been representable in a basic format. An additional motivation, for the single format, is that it affords some of the benefits of a double format without incurring the time penalty usually associated with higher precision. Table 8.2 summarizes the characteristics of the four formats.

Not all bit patterns in the IEEE formats are interpreted in the usual way; instead, some bit patterns are used to represent special values. Table 8.3 indicates the values assigned to various bit patterns. The extreme exponent values of all zeros (0) and all ones (255 in single format, 2047 in double format) define special values. The following classes of numbers are represented:

- For exponents values in the range of 1 through 254 for single format and 1 through 2046 for double format, normalized nonzero floating-point numbers are represented. The exponent is biased, so that the range of exponents is –126 through +127 for single format and –1022 through +1023 for double format. A normalized number requires a 1 bit to the left of the binary point; this bit is implied, giving an effective 24-bit or 53-bit significand (called fraction in the standard).
- An exponent of zero together with a fraction of zero represents positive or negative zero, depending on the sign bit. As was mentioned, it is useful to have an exact value of 0 represented.
- An exponent of all ones together with a fraction of zero represents positive or negative infinity, depending on the sign bit. It is also useful to have a representation of infinity. This leaves it up to the user to decide whether to treat overflow as an error condition or to carry the value $\infty$ and proceed with whatever program is being executed.
- An exponent of zero together with a nonzero fraction represents a denormalized number. In this case, the bit to the left of the binary point is zero and the true exponent is –126 or –1022. The number is positive or negative depending on the sign bit.
- An exponent of all ones together with a nonzero fraction is given the value NaN, which means *not a number,* and is used to signal various exception conditions.

The significance of denormalized numbers and NaNs is discussed in Section 8.5.

### TABLE 8.2    IEEE 754 Format Parameters

| Parameter | *Single* | *Single Extended* | *Double* | *Double Extended* |
|---|---|---|---|---|
| | | *Format* | | |
| Word width (bits) | 32 | ≥43 | 64 | ≥79 |
| Exponent width (bits) | 8 | ≥11 | 11 | ≥15 |
| Exponent bias | 127 | unspecified | 1023 | unspecified |
| Maximum exponent | 127 | ≥1023 | 1023 | ≥16,383 |
| Minimum exponent | –126 | ≤–1022 | –1022 | ≤–16,382 |
| Number range (base 10) | $10^{-38}$, $10^{+38}$ | unspecified | $10^{-308}$, $10^{+308}$ | unspecified |
| Significand width (bits) | 23 | ≥31 | 52 | ≥63 |
| Number of exponents | 254 | unspecified | 2046 | unspecified |
| Number of fractions | $2^{23}$ | unspecified | $2^{52}$ | unspecified |
| Number of values | $1.98 \times 2^{31}$ | unspecified | $1.99 \times 2^{63}$ | unspecified |

**TABLE 8.3** Interpretation of IEEE 754 Floating-Point Numbers

| | Single Precision (32 bits) | | | | Double Precision (64 bits) | | |
|---|---|---|---|---|---|---|---|
| | Sign | Biased Exponent | Fraction | Value | Sign | Biased Exponent | Fraction | Value |
| Positive zero | 0 | 0 | 0 | 0 | 0 | 0 | 0 | 0 |
| Negative zero | 1 | 0 | 0 | $-0$ | 1 | 0 | 0 | $-0$ |
| Plus infinity | 0 | 255 (all 1s) | 0 | $\infty$ | 0 | 2047 (all 1s) | 0 | $\infty$ |
| Minus infinity | 1 | 255 (all 1s) | 0 | $-\infty$ | 1 | 2047 (all 1s) | 0 | $-\infty$ |
| Quiet NaN | 0 or 1 | 255 (all 1s) | $\neq 0$ | NaN | 0 or 1 | 2047 (all 1s) | $\neq 0$ | NaN |
| Signaling NaN | 0 or 1 | 255 (all 1s) | $\neq 0$ | NaN | 0 or 1 | 2047 (all 1s) | $\neq 0$ | NaN |
| Positive normalized nonzero | 0 | 0<e<255 | f | $2^{e-127}(1.f)$ | 0 | 0<e<2047 | f | $2^{e-1023}(1.f)$ |
| Negative normalized nonzero | 1 | 0<e<255 | f | $-2^{e-127}(1.f)$ | 1 | 0<e<2047 | f | $-2^{e-1023}(1.f)$ |
| Positive denormalized | 0 | 0 | $f\neq 0$ | $2^{e-126}(0.f)$ | 0 | 0 | $f\neq 0$ | $2^{e-1022}(0.f)$ |
| Negative denormalized | 1 | 0 | $f\neq 0$ | $-2^{e-126}(0.f)$ | 1 | 0 | $f\neq 0$ | $-2^{e-1022}(0.f)$ |

## FLOATING-POINT ARITHMETIC

Table 8.4 summarizes the basic operations for floating-point arithmetic. For addition and subtraction, it is necessary to ensure that both operands have the same exponent. This may require shifting the radix point on one of the operands to achieve alignment. Multiplication and division are more straightforward.

Problems may arise as the result of these operations. These are

- *Exponent Overflow:* A positive exponent exceeds the maximum possible exponent value. In some systems, this may be designated as $+\infty$ or $-\infty$.
- *Exponent Underflow:* A negative exponent exceeds the maximum possible exponent value. This means that the number is too small to be represented, and it may be reported as 0.
- *Significand Underflow:* In the process of aligning significands, digits may flow off the right end of the significand. As we shall discuss, some form of rounding is required.
- *Significand Overflow:* The addition of two significands of the same sign may result in a carry out of the most significant bit. This can be fixed by realignment, as we shall explain.

### Addition and Subtraction

In floating-point arithmetic, addition and subtraction are more complex than multiplication and division. This is because of the need for alignment. There are four basic phases of the algorithm for addition and subtraction:

1. Check for zeros.
2. Align the significands.
3. Add or subtract the significands.
4. Normalize the result.

A typical flowchart is shown in Figure 8.21. A step-by-step narrative highlights the main functions required for floating-point addition and subtraction. We assume a format similar to those of Figure 8.20. For the addition or subtraction operation, the two operands must be transferred to registers that will be used by

---

**TABLE 8.4    Floating-Point Numbers and Arithmetic Operations**

Floating-Point Numbers

$x = x_s\ B^{X_E}$

$x = y_s\ B^{Y_E}$

Arithmetic Operations

$\left. \begin{aligned} x + y &= (x_s\ B^{X_E - Y_E} + y_s) \times B^{Y_E} \\ x - y &= (x_s\ B^{X_E - Y_E} - y_s) \times B^{Y_E} \end{aligned} \right\} X_E \le Y_E$

$x \times y = (x_s \times y_z) \times B^{X_E + Y_E}$

$x \div y = (x_s \div y_s) \times B^{X_E - Y_E}$

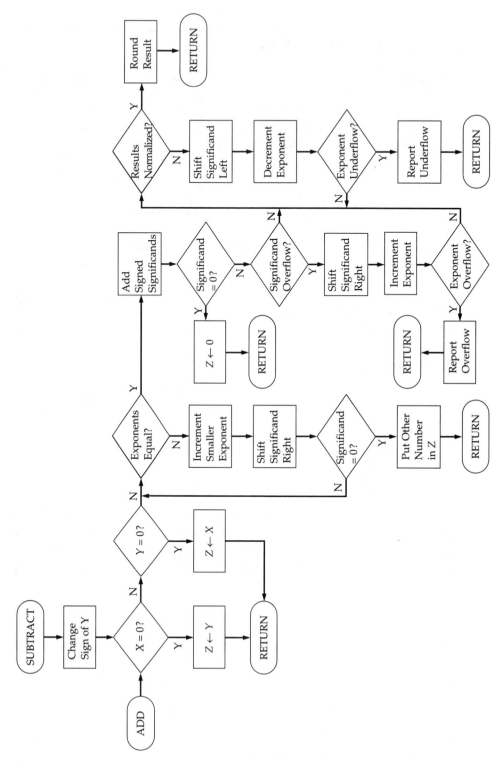

**FIGURE 8.21. Floating-point addition and subtraction (z ← x ± y)**

the ALU. If the floating-point format includes an implicit significand bit, that bit must be made explicit for the operation. Typically, the exponents and significands will be stored in separate registers, to be reunited when the result is produced.

Because addition and subtraction are identical except for a sign change, the process begins by changing the sign of the subtrahend if it is a subtract operation. Next, if either operand is 0, the other is reported as the result.

The next phase is to manipulate the numbers so that the two exponents are equal. To see the need for this, consider the following decimal addition:

$123 \times 10^0 + 456 \times 10^{-2}$

Clearly, we cannot just add the significands. The digits must first be set into equivalent positions, that is, the 4 of the second number must be *aligned* with the 3 of the first. Under these conditions, the two exponents will be equal, which is the mathematical condition under which two numbers in this form can be added. Thus:

$123 \times 10^0 + 456 \times 10^{-2} = 123 \times 10^0 + 4.56 \times 10^0 = 127.56 \times 10^0$

Alignment is achieved by shifting either the smaller number to the right (increasing its exponent) or shifting the larger number to the left. Since either operation may result in the loss of digits, it is the smaller number that is shifted; any digits that are lost are therefore of relatively small significance. The alignment is achieved by repeatedly shifting the magnitude portion of the significand right 1 digit and incrementing the exponent until the two exponents are equal. (Note that if the implied base is 16, a shift of 1 digit is a shift of 4 bits.) If this process results in a 0 value for the significand, then the other number is reported as the result. Thus, if two numbers have exponents that differ significantly, the lesser number is lost.

Next, the two significands are added together, taking into account their signs. Since the signs may differ, the result may be 0. There is also the possibility of significand overflow by 1 digit. If so, the significand of the result is shifted right and the exponent is incremented. An exponent overflow could occur as a result; this would be reported and the operation halted.

The next phase normalizes the result. Normalization consists of shifting significand digits left until the most significant digit (bit, or 4 bits for base-16 exponent) is nonzero. Each shift causes a decrement of the exponent and thus could cause an exponent underflow. Finally, the result must be rounded off and then reported. We defer a discussion of rounding until after a discussion of multiplication and division.

## Multiplication and Division

Floating-point multiplication and division are much simpler processes than addition and subtraction, as the following discussion indicates.

We first consider multiplication, illustrated in Figure 8.22. First, if either operand is 0, 0 is reported as the result. The next step is to add the exponents. If the exponents are stored in biased form, the exponent sum would have doubled the bias. Thus, the bias value must be subtracted from the sum. The result could be either an exponent overflow or underflow, which would be reported, ending the algorithm.

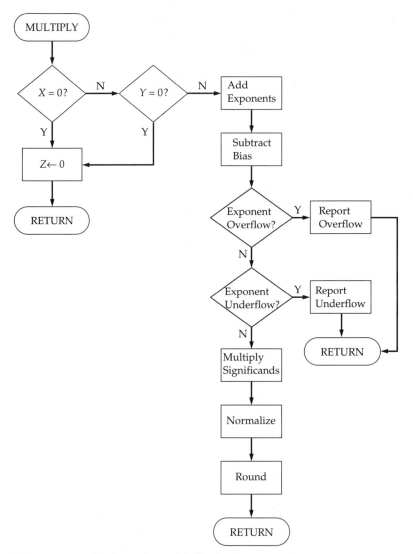

**FIGURE 8.22. Floating-point multiplication ($z \leftarrow x \times y$)**

If the exponent of the product is within the proper range, the next step is to multiply the significands, taking into account their signs. The multiplication is performed in the same way as for integers. In this case, we are dealing with a sign–magnitude representation, but the details are similar to those for two's complement representation. The product will be double the length of the multiplier and multiplicand. The extra bits will be lost during rounding.

After the product is calculated, the result is then normalized and rounded, as was done for addition and subtraction. Note that normalization could result in exponent underflow.

Finally, let us consider the flowchart for division depicted in Figure 8.23. Again, the first step is testing for 0. If the divisor is 0, an error report is issued, or the result is set to infinity, depending on the implementation. A dividend of 0 results in 0. Next, the divisor exponent is subtracted from the dividend exponent. This removes the bias, which must be added back in. Tests are then made for exponent underflow or overflow.

The next step is to divide the significands. This is followed with the usual normalization and rounding.

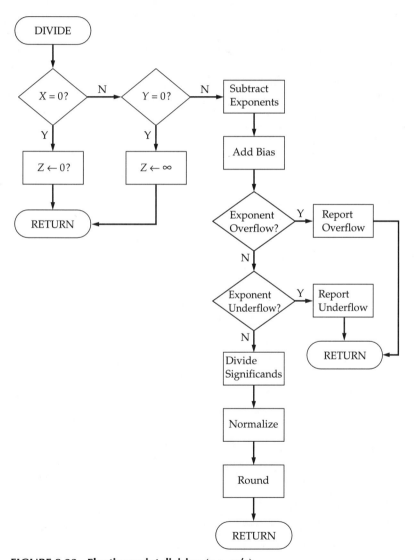

**FIGURE 8.23. Floating-point division (z ← x/y)**

## Precision Considerations

### Guard Bits

We mentioned that, prior to a floating-point operation, the exponent and significand of each operand are loaded into ALU registers. In the case of the significand, the length of the register is almost always greater than the length of the significand plus an implied bit, if used. The register contains additional bits, called *guard bits*, that are used to pad out the right end of the significand with 0s.

The reason for the use of guard bits is illustrated in Figure 8.24. Consider numbers in the IEEE format, which has a 24-bit significand, including an implied 1 bit to the left of the binary point. Two numbers that are very close in value are $X = 1.00 \ldots 00 * 2^1$ and $Y = 1.11 \ldots 11 * 2^0$. If the smaller number is to be subtracted from the larger, it must be shifted right 1 bit to align the exponents. This is shown in Figure 8.24a. In the process, $Y$ loses 1 bit of significance; the result is $2^{-23}$. The same operation is repeated in part b with the addition of guard bits. Now, the least significant bit is not lost due to alignment, and the result is $2^{-24}$, a difference of a factor of 2 from the previous answer. When the radix is 16, the loss of precision can be greater. As Figures 8.24c and d show, the difference can be a factor of 16.

$$
\begin{aligned}
x &= 1.000 \ldots 00 \times 2^1 \\
-y &= 0.111 \ldots 11 \times 2^1 \\
\hline
z &= 0.000 \ldots 01 \times 2^1 \\
&= 1.000 \ldots 00 \times 2^{-22}
\end{aligned}
$$

(a) Binary Example, Without Guard Bits

$$
\begin{aligned}
x &= 1.000 \ldots 00 \quad 0000 \times 2^1 \\
-y &= 0.111 \ldots 11 \quad 1000 \times 2^1 \\
\hline
z &= 0.000 \ldots 00 \quad 1000 \times 2^1 \\
&= 1.000 \ldots 00 \quad 0000 \times 2^{-23}
\end{aligned}
$$

(b) Binary Example, With Guard Bits

$$
\begin{aligned}
x &= .100000 \times 16^1 \\
-y &= .0FFFFF \times 16^1 \\
\hline
z &= .000001 \times 16^1 \\
&= .100000 \times 16^{-4}
\end{aligned}
$$

(c) Hexadecimal Example, Without Guard Bits

$$
\begin{aligned}
x &= .100000 \quad 00 \times 16^1 \\
-y &= .0FFFFF \quad F0 \times 16^1 \\
\hline
z &= .000000 \quad 10 \times 16^1 \\
&= .100000 \quad 00 \times 16^{-5}
\end{aligned}
$$

(d) Hexadecimal Example, With Guard Bits

**FIGURE 8.24. The use of guard bits**

## Rounding

Another detail that affects the precision of the result is the rounding policy. The result of any operation on the significands is generally stored in a longer register. When the result is put back into the floating-point format, the extra bits must be disposed of.

A number of techniques have been explored for performing rounding. In fact, the IEEE standard lists four alternative approaches:

- *Round to Nearest:* The result is rounded to the nearest representable number.
- *Round Toward +∞:* The result is rounded up toward plus infinity.
- *Round Toward −∞:* The result is rounded down toward negative infinity.
- *Round Toward 0:* The result is rounded toward zero.

Let us consider each of these policies in turn. **Round to nearest** is the default rounding mode listed in the standard and is defined as follows: The representable value nearest to the infinitely precise result shall be delivered; if the two nearest representable values are equally near, the one with its least significant bit 0 shall be delivered.

For example, if the extra bits, beyond the 23 bits that can be stored, are 10010, then the extra bits amount to more than one-half of the last representable bit position. In this case, the correct answer is to add binary 1 to the last representable bit, rounding up to the next representable number. Now consider that the extra bits are 01111. In this case, the extra bits amount to less than one-half of the last representable bit position. The correct answer is to simply drop the extra bits (truncate), which has the effect of rounding down to the next representable number.

The standard also addresses the special case of extra bits of the form 10000. . . . Here the result is exactly halfway between the two possible representable values. One possible technique here would be to always truncate, as this would be the simplest operation. However, the difficulty with this simple approach is that it introduces a small but cumulative bias into a sequence of computations. What is required is an unbiased method of rounding. One possible approach would be to round up or down on the basis of a random number so that, on average, the result would be unbiased. The argument against this approach is that it does not produce predictable, deterministic results. The approach taken by the IEEE standard is to force the result to be even: If the result of a computation is exactly midway between two representable numbers, the value is rounded up if the last representable bit is currently 1 and left alone if it is currently 0.

The next two options, **rounding to plus and minus infinity,** are useful in implementing a technique known as interval arithmetic. The idea behind interval arithmetic is the following: At the end of a sequence of floating-point operations, we cannot know the exact answer because of the limitations of the hardware, which introduces rounding. If we perform every calculation in the sequence twice: once rounding up and once rounding down, then the result is to maintain an upper and lower bound on the correct answer. If the range between the upper and lower bounds is sufficiently narrow, then a sufficiently accurate result has been obtained. If not, at least we know this and can perform additional analysis.

The final technique specified in the standard is **round toward zero.** This is in fact simple truncation: the extra bits are ignored. This is certainly the simplest technique. However, the result is that the magnitude of the truncated value is always less than or equal to the more precise original value, introducing a consistent downward bias in the operation. This is a more serious bias than was discussed earlier, since this bias affects *every* operation for which there are nonzero extra bits.

## IEEE Standard for Binary Floating-Point Arithmetic

IEEE 754 goes beyond the simple definition of a format to lay down specific practices and procedures so that floating-point arithmetic produces uniform, predictable results independent of the hardware platform. One aspect of this has already been discussed, namely rounding. This subsection looks at three other topics: infinity, NaNs, and denormalized numbers.

### Infinity

Infinity arithmetic is treated as the limiting case of real arithmetic, with the infinity values given the following interpretation:

$$-\infty < \text{(every finite number)} < +\infty$$

With the exception of the special cases discussed below, any arithmetic operation involving infinity yields the obvious result. For example:

$$5 + (+\infty) = +\infty$$
$$5 - (+\infty) = -\infty$$
$$5 + (-\infty) = -\infty$$
$$5 - (-\infty) = +\infty$$
$$(+\infty) + (+\infty) = +\infty$$
$$(-\infty) + (-\infty) = -\infty$$
$$(-\infty) - (+\infty) = -\infty$$
$$(+\infty) - (-\infty) = +\infty$$

### Quiet and Signaling NaNs

A NaN is a symbolic entity encoded in floating-point format, of which there are two types: signaling and quiet. A signaling NaN signals an invalid operation exception whenever it appears as an operand. Signaling NaNs afford values for uninitialized variables and arithmetic-like enhancements that are not the subject of the standard. A quiet NaN propagates through almost every arithmetic operation without signaling an exception. Table 8.5 indicates operations that will produce a quiet NaN.

Note that both types of NaNs have the same general format: an exponent of all ones and a nonzero fraction. The actual bit pattern of the nonzero fraction is implementation-dependent; the fraction values can be used to distinguish quiet NaNs from signaling NaNs and to specify particular exception conditions.

**TABLE 8.5    Operations that Produce a Quiet NaN**

| Operation | Quiet NaN Produced by |
|---|---|
| Any | Any operation on a signaling NaN |
| Add or Subtract | Magnitude subtraction of infinities: $(+\infty) + (-\infty)$ $(-\infty) + (+\infty)$ $(+\infty) - (+\infty)$ $(-\infty) - (-\infty)$ |
| Multiply | $0 \times \infty$ |
| Division | $\dfrac{0}{0}$ or $\dfrac{\infty}{\infty}$ |
| Remainder | $x$ REM $0$ or $\infty$ REM $y$ |
| Square root | $\sqrt{x}$ where $x < 0$ |

## Denormalized Numbers

Denormalized numbers are included in IEEE 754 to handle cases of exponent underflow. When the exponent of the result is too small (a negative exponent with too large a magnitude), the result is denormalized by right-shifting the fraction and incrementing the exponent for each shift, until the exponent is within a representable range.

Figure 8.25 illustrates the effect of the addition of denormalized numbers. The representable numbers can be grouped into intervals of the form $[2^n, 2^n + 1]$. Within each such interval, the exponent portion of the number remains constant

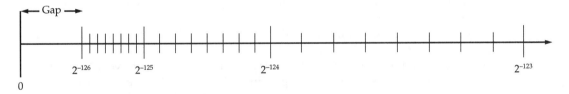

(a) 32-bit Format Without Denormalized Numbers

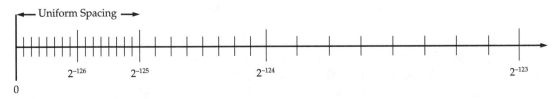

(b) 32-bit Format With Denormalized Numbers

**FIGURE 8.25.  The effect of IEEE 754 denormalized numbers**

while the fraction varies, producing a uniform spacing of representable numbers within the interval. As we get closer to zero, each successive interval is half the width of the preceding interval but contains the same number of representable numbers. Hence, the density of representable numbers increases as we approach zero. However, if only normalized numbers are used, there is a gap between the smallest normalized number and zero. In the case of the 32-bit IEEE 754 format, there are $2^{23}$ representable numbers in each interval, and the smallest representable positive number is $2^{-126}$. With the addition of denormalized numbers, an additional $2^{23}$ numbers are uniformly added between 0 and $2^{-126}$.

The use of denormalized numbers is referred to as *gradual underflow* [COON81]. Without denormalized numbers, the gap between the smallest representable nonzero number and zero is much wider than the gap between the smallest representable nonzero number and the next larger number. Gradual underflow fills in that gap and reduces the impact of exponent underflow to a level comparable with roundoff among the normalized numbers.

## 8.6

## RECOMMENDED READING

For the serious student of computer arithmetic, a *sine qua non* is the two-volume [SWAR90]. Volume I was originally published in 1980 and provides key papers (some very difficult to obtain otherwise) on computer arithmetic fundamentals. Volume II contains more recent papers, covering theoretical, design, and implementation aspects of computer arithmetic. Two other valuable collections of papers are the August 1990 and August 1994 issues of *IEEE Transactions on Computers*. Good books on computer arithmetic include [OMON94], [KORE93], and [MORG92].

For floating-point arithmetic, [GOLD91] is well-named: "What Every Computer Scientist Should Know About Floating-Point Arithmetic." A more advanced treatment is to be found in [WALL90]. Another excellent treatment of the topic is contained in [KNUT81].

GOLD91    Goldberg, D. "What Every Computer Scientist Should Know About Floating-Point Arithmetic." *ACM Computing Surveys*, March 1991.

KNUT81    Knuth, D. *The Art of Computer Programming, Volume 2: Seminumerical Algorithms.* Reading, MA: Addison-Wesley, 1981.

KORE93    Koren, I. *Computer Arithmetic Algorithms.* Englewood Cliffs, NJ: Prentice Hall, 1993.

MORG92    Morgan, D. *Numerical Methods.* San Mateo, CA: M&T Books, 1992.

OMON94 Omondi, A. *Computer Arithmetic Systems: Algorithms, Architecture, and Implementations.* Englewood Cliffs, NJ: Prentice Hall, 1994.

SWAR90    Swartzlander, E., editor. *Computer Arithmetic, Volumes I and II.* Los Alamitos, CA: IEEE Computer Society Press, 1990.

WALL90    Wallis, P. *Improving Floating-Point Programming.* New York: Wiley, 1992.

8.7

## PROBLEMS

8.1　Find the following differences using two's complements:

  **a.** 111000 **b.** 11001100 **c.** 111100001111 **d.** 11000011
   $-110011$  $-\ \ \ 101110$ $-110011110011$  $-11101000$

8.2　Is the following a valid alternative definition of overflow in two's complement arithmetic?

  If the exclusive-OR of the carry bits into and out of the leftmost column is 1, then there is an overflow condition. Otherwise, there is not.

8.3　Compare Figures 8.8 and 8.11. Why is the C bit not used in the latter?

8.4　Draw a block diagram similar to Figure 8.7 that illustrates the division process.

8.5　The division algorithm depicted in Figure 8.15 is known as the *restoral* method since the value in the A register must be restored following unsuccessful subtraction. A slightly more complex approach, known as *nonrestoral*, avoids the unnecessary subtraction and addition. Propose an algorithm for this latter approach.

8.6　Under integer arithmetic, the quotient $J/K$ of two integers $J$ and $K$ is less than or equal to the usual quotient. True or false?

8.7　Prove that the multiplication of two $n$-digit numbers in base B gives a product of no more than $2n$ digits.

8.8　Compare the biased representation to sign–magnitude and two's complement representation, in terms of strengths and weaknesses.

8.9　Divide –145 by 13 in binary two's complement notation, using 12-bit words. Use the algorithm described in Section 8.3.

8.10　Assume that the exponent $e$ is constrained to lie in the range $0 \le e \le X$, with a bias of $q$, that the base is $b$, and that the significand is $p$ digits in length.
  **(a)**　What are the largest and smallest positive values that can be written?
  **(b)**　What are the largest and smallest positive values that can be written as normalized floating-point numbers?

8.11　Express the following numbers in IEEE 32-bit floating-point format:
  **(a)**　–5
  **(b)**　–6
  **(c)**　–1.5
  **(d)**　384
  **(e)**　1/16
  **(f)**　–1/32

8.12　Express the following numbers in IBM's 32-bit floating-point format, which uses a 7-bit exponent with an implied base of 16:
  **(a)**　1.0
  **(b)**　0.5
  **(c)**　1/64
  **(d)**　0.0

    **(e)** –15.0

    **(f)** 5.4 * 10⁻⁷⁹

    **(g)** 7.2 * 10⁷⁵

8.13 What would be the bias value for

    **(a)** A base-2 exponent (B = 2) in a 6-bit field?

    **(b)** A base-8 exponent (B = 8) in a 7-bit field?

8.14 Draw a number line similar to that in Figure 8.18b for the floating-point formats of Figure 8.20.

8.15 When people speak about inaccuracy in floating-point arithmetic, they often ascribe errors to cancellation that occurs during the subtraction of nearly equal quantities. But when $X$ and $Y$ are approximately equal, the difference $X - Y$ is obtained exactly, with no error. What do these people really mean?

8.16 Any floating-point representation used in a computer can represent only certain real numbers exactly; all others must be approximated. If $A'$ is the stored value approximating the real value $A$, then the relative error, $r$, is expressed as

$$r = \frac{A - A'}{A}$$

Represent the decimal quantity +0.4 in the following floating-point format:

- Base: 2
- Exponent: biased, 4 bits
- Significand: 7 bits

What is the relative error?

8.17 Numerical values $A$ and $B$ are stored in the computer as approximations $A'$ and $B'$. Neglecting any further truncation or roundoff errors, show that the relative error of the product is approximately the sum of the relative errors in the factors.

8.18 If $A = 1.427$, find the relative error if $A$ is truncated to 1.42 and if it is rounded to 1.43.

8.19 One of the most serious errors in computer calculations occurs when two nearly equal numbers are subtracted. Consider $A = 0.22288$ and $B = 0.22211$. The computer truncates all values to four decimal digits. Thus $A' = 0.2228$ and $B' = 0.2221$.

    **(a)** What are the relative errors for $A'$ and $B'$?

    **(b)** What is the relative error for $C' = A' - B'$?

## APPENDIX 8A

### *Number Systems*

#### *8A.1   The Decimal System*

It may not have occurred to you, but in everyday life you use a system based on digits to represent numbers. In this case, we use decimal digits (0, 1, 2, 3, 4, 5, 6, 7, 8, 9) and refer to the system as the *decimal system.*

Consider what the number 83 means. It means eight tens plus three:

83 = 8 * 10 + 3

The number 4728 means four thousands, seven hundreds, two tens, plus eight:

4728 = 4 * 1000 + 7 * 100 + 2 * 10 + 8

The decimal system is said to have a *base*, or *radix*, of ten. This means that each digit in the number is multiplied by ten raised to a power corresponding to that digit's position. Thus,

$$83 = 8 * 10^1 + 3 * 10^0$$
$$4728 = 4 * 10^3 + 7 * 10^2 + 2 * 10^1 + 8 * 10^0$$

Fractional values are represented in the same fashion. Thus,

$$472.83 = 4 * 10^2 + 7 * 10^1 + 2 * 10^0 + 8 * 10^{-1} + 3 * 10^{-2}$$

In general, for

Decimal representation of $X = \{ \ldots x_2 x_1 x_0 \cdot x_{-1} x_{-2} x_{-3} \ldots \}$

the value of X is

$$X = \sum_i x_i 10^i$$

## 8A.2 The Binary System

In the decimal system, ten different digits are used to represent numbers with a base of ten. In the binary system, we have only two digits, 1 and 0. Thus, numbers in the binary system are represented to the base two.

To avoid confusion, we will sometimes put a subscript on a number to indicate its base. For example, $83_{10}$ and $4728_{10}$ are numbers represented in decimal notation, or more briefly, decimal numbers. Now, 1 and 0 in binary notation have the same meaning as in decimal notation:

$$0_2 = 0_{10}$$
$$1_2 = 1_{10}$$

How do we represent larger numbers? As with decimal notation, each digit in a binary number has a value depending on its position:

$$10_2 = 1 * 2^1 + 0 * 2^0 = 2_{10}$$
$$11_2 = 1 * 2^1 + 1 * 2^0 = 3_{10}$$
$$100_2 = 1 * 2^2 + 0 * 2^1 + 0 * 2^0 = 4_{10}$$

and so on. Table 8.6 shows the first 64 8-bit binary numbers, together with their decimal equivalents (the table also shows a hexadecimal notation, explained presently).

TABLE 8.6    Binary Numbers and Their Decimal and Hexadecimal Equivalents

| Binary | Decimal | Hexadecimal | Binary | Decimal | Hexadecimal |
|--------|---------|-------------|--------|---------|-------------|
| 00000000 | 0 | 0 | 00100000 | 32 | 20 |
| 00000001 | 1 | 1 | 00100001 | 33 | 21 |
| 00000010 | 2 | 2 | 00100010 | 34 | 22 |
| 00000011 | 3 | 3 | 00100011 | 35 | 23 |
| 00000100 | 4 | 4 | 00100100 | 36 | 24 |
| 00000101 | 5 | 5 | 00100101 | 37 | 25 |
| 00000110 | 6 | 6 | 00100110 | 38 | 26 |
| 00000111 | 7 | 7 | 00100111 | 39 | 27 |
| 00001000 | 8 | 8 | 00101000 | 40 | 28 |
| 00001001 | 9 | 9 | 00101001 | 41 | 29 |
| 00001010 | 10 | A | 00101010 | 42 | 2A |
| 00001011 | 11 | B | 00101011 | 43 | 2B |
| 00001100 | 12 | C | 00101100 | 44 | 2C |
| 00001101 | 13 | D | 00101101 | 45 | 2D |
| 00001110 | 14 | E | 00101110 | 46 | 2E |
| 00001111 | 15 | F | 00101111 | 47 | 2F |
| 00010000 | 16 | 10 | 00110000 | 48 | 30 |
| 00010001 | 17 | 11 | 00110001 | 49 | 31 |
| 00010010 | 18 | 12 | 00110010 | 50 | 32 |
| 00010011 | 19 | 13 | 00110011 | 51 | 33 |
| 00010100 | 20 | 14 | 00110100 | 52 | 34 |
| 00010101 | 21 | 15 | 00110101 | 53 | 35 |
| 00010110 | 22 | 16 | 00110110 | 54 | 36 |
| 00010111 | 23 | 17 | 00110111 | 55 | 37 |
| 00011000 | 24 | 18 | 00111000 | 56 | 38 |
| 00011001 | 25 | 19 | 00111001 | 57 | 39 |
| 00011010 | 26 | 1A | 00111010 | 58 | 3A |
| 00011011 | 27 | 1B | 00111011 | 59 | 3B |
| 00011100 | 28 | 1C | 00111100 | 60 | 3C |
| 00011101 | 29 | 1D | 00111101 | 61 | 3D |
| 00011110 | 30 | 1E | 00111110 | 62 | 3E |
| 00011111 | 31 | 1F | 00111111 | 63 | 3F |

Again, fractional values are represented with negative powers of the radix:

$$1001.101 = 2^3 + 2^0 + 2^{-1} + 2^{-3}$$

### 8A.3   Converting Between Binary and Decimal

It is a simple matter to convert a number from binary notation to decimal notation. In fact, we showed several examples in the previous subsection. All that is required is to multiply each binary digit by the appropriate power of 2 and add the results.

To convert from decimal to binary, the integer and fractional parts are handled separately. Suppose it is required to convert a decimal integer $N$ into binary form.

If we divide $N$ by 2, in the decimal system, and obtain a quotient $N_1$ and a remainder $r_1$, we may write

$$N = 2 * N_1 + r_1 \qquad r_1 = 0 \text{ or } 1$$

Next, we divide the quotient $N_1$ by 2. Assume that the new quotient is $N_2$ and the new remainder $r_2$. Then

$$N_1 = 2 * N_2 + r_2 \qquad r_2 = 0 \text{ or } 1$$

so that

$$N = 2(2N_2 + r_2) + r_1 = 2^2 N_2 + r_2 * 2^1 + r_1 * 2^0$$

If next

$$N_2 = 2N_3 + r_3$$

we have

$$N = 2^3 N_3 + r_3 * 2^2 + r_2 * 2^1 + r_1 * 2^0$$

Continuing thus, since $N > N_1 > N_2 \ldots$, we must eventually obtain a quotient $N_k = 1$ and a remainder $r_k$, which is 0 or 1. Then

$$N = 1 * 2^k + r_k * 2^{k-1} + \ldots + r_3 * 2^2 + r_2 * 2^1 + r_1 * 2^0$$

That is, we convert from base 10 to base 2 by repeated divisions by 2. The remainders and the final quotient, 1, give us, in order of increasing significance, the binary digits of $N$. Figure 8.26 shows two examples.

The fractional part involves repeated multiplication by 2, as illustrated in Figure 8.27. At each step, the fractional part of the decimal number is multiplied by 2. The digit to the left of the decimal point in the product will be 0 or 1 and contributes to the binary representation, starting with the most significant bit. The fractional part of the product is used as the multiplicand in the next step. To see that this works, let us take a positive decimal fraction $F < 1$. We can express $F$ as

$$F = a_{-1} * \frac{1}{2} + a_{-2} * \frac{1}{2^2} + a_{-3} * \frac{1}{2^3} + \cdots$$

where each $a_{-i}$ is 0 or 1. If we multiply this by 2, we obtain

$$2F = a_{-1} + a_{-2} * \frac{1}{2} + a_{-3} * \frac{1}{2^2} + \cdots$$

The integer parts of these two expressions must be equal. Hence the integer part of $2F$, which must be either 0 or 1 since $0 < F < 1$, is simply $a_{-1}$. Thus $2F = a_{-1} + F_1$, where $0 < F_1 < 1$ and where

$$F = a_{-2} * \frac{1}{2} + a_{-3} * \frac{1}{2^2} + \cdots$$

To find $a_{-2}$ we now repeat the process. This process is not necessarily exact; that is, a decimal fraction with a finite number of digits may require a binary fraction with

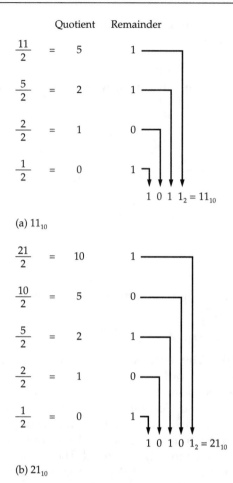

$$1\ 0\ 1\ 1_2 = 11_{10}$$

(a) $11_{10}$

$$1\ 0\ 1\ 0\ 1_2 = 21_{10}$$

(b) $21_{10}$

**FIGURE 8.26. Examples of converting from decimal notation to binary notation for integral numbers**

an infinite number of digits. In such cases, the conversion algorithm is usually halted after a prespecified number of steps, depending on the desired accuracy.

## 8A.4  Hexadecimal Notation

Because of the inherent binary nature of digital computer components, all forms of data within computers are represented by various binary codes. We have seen examples of binary codes for text and binary notation for integers. Later, we shall see examples of the use of binary codes for other types of data. However, no matter how convenient the binary system is for computers, it is exceedingly cumbersome for human beings. Consequently, most computer professionals who must

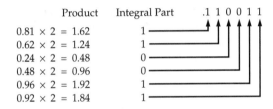

(a) $0.81_{10} = 0.110011_2$ (approximate)

```
                        .0 1
0.25 × 2 = 0.5      0
0.5  × 2 = 1.0      1
```

(b) $0.25_{10} = 0.01_2$ (exact)

**FIGURE 8.27. Eamples of converting from decimal notation to binary notation for fractional numbers**

spend time working with the actual raw data in the computer prefer a more compact notation.

What notation to use? One possibility is the decimal notation. We have seen, in Table 8.6, that every binary number has a decimal equivalent. This is certainly more compact than binary notation, but it is awkward because of the tediousness of converting between base 2 and base 10.

Instead, a notation known as *hexadecimal* has been adopted. Binary digits are grouped into sets of 4. Each possible combination of 4 binary digits is given a symbol, as follows:

| | |
|---|---|
| 0000 = 0 | 1000 = 8 |
| 0001 = 1 | 1001 = 9 |
| 0010 = 2 | 1010 = A |
| 0011 = 3 | 1011 = B |
| 0100 = 4 | 1100 = C |
| 0101 = 5 | 1101 = D |
| 0110 = 6 | 1110 = E |
| 0111 = 7 | 1111 = F |

Since 16 symbols are used, the notation is called *hexadecimal*, and the 16 symbols are the hexadecimal digits.

A sequence of hexadecimal digits can be thought of as representing an integer in base 16. Thus,

$$1A_{16} = 1_{16} * 16^1 + A_{16} * 16^0$$
$$= 1_{10} * 16^1 + 10_{10} * 16^0 = 26$$

But hexadecimal notation is not used just for representing integers. It is used as a concise notation for representing any sequence of binary digits, whether they represent text, numbers, or some other type of data. The reasons for using hexadecimal notation are

1. It is more compact than binary notation.
2. In most computers, binary data occupy some multiple of 4 bits, and hence some multiple of a single hexadecimal digit.
3. It is extremely easy to convert between binary and hexadecimal.

As an example of the last point, consider the binary string 110111100001. This is equivalent to

$$1101 \quad 1110 \quad 0001 = DE1_{16}$$
$$\quad D \qquad E \qquad 1$$

This process is performed so naturally that an experienced programmer can mentally convert visual representations of binary data to their hexadecimal equivalent without written effort. It is quite possible that you will never need this particular skill. Nevertheless, since you may encounter hexadecimal notation, this discussion has been included in the text.

# CHAPTER 9

# Instruction Sets: Characteristics and Functions

Much of what is discussed in this book is not readily apparent to the user or programmer of a computer. If a programmer is using a high-level language, such as Pascal or Ada, very little of the architecture of the underlying machine is visible.

One boundary where the computer designer and the computer programmer can view the same machine is the machine instruction set. From the designer's point of view, the machine instruction set provides the functional requirements for the CPU: implementing the CPU is a task that in large part involves implementing the machine instruction set. From the user's side, the user who chooses to program in machine language (actually, in assembly language; see Section 9.4) becomes aware of the register and memory structure, the types of data directly supported by the machine, and the functioning of the ALU.

A description of a computer's machine instruction set goes a long way toward explaining the computer's CPU. Accordingly, we focus on machine instructions in this and the next chapter, and then we turn to an examination of the structure and function of CPUs.

## 9.1

## MACHINE INSTRUCTION CHARACTERISTICS

The operation of the CPU is determined by the instructions it executes. These instructions are referred to as *machine instructions* or *computer instructions*. The CPU may perform a variety of functions, and these are reflected in the variety of instructions defined for the CPU. The collection of different instructions that the CPU can execute is referred to as the CPU's *instruction set*.

## Elements of a Machine Instruction

Each instruction must contain the information required by the CPU for execution. Figure 9.1, which repeats Figure 3.6, shows the steps involved in instruction execution and, by implication, defines the elements of a machine instruction. These elements are

- *Operation Code:* Specifies the operation to be performed (e.g., ADD, I/O). The operation is specified by a binary code, known as the *operation code,* or *opcode.*
- *Source Operand Reference:* The operation may involve one or more source operands, that is, operands that are inputs for the operation.
- *Result Operand Reference:* The operation may produce a result.
- *Next Instruction Reference:* This tells the CPU where to fetch the next instruction after the execution of this instruction is complete.

The next instruction to be fetched is located in main memory or, in the case of a virtual memory system, in either main memory or secondary memory (disk). In most cases, the next instruction to be fetched immediately follows the current instruction. In those cases, there is no explicit reference to the next instruction. When an explicit reference is needed, then the main memory or virtual memory address must be supplied. The form in which that address is supplied is discussed in Chapter 10.

Source and result operands can be in one of three areas:

- *Main or Virtual Memory:* As with next instruction references, the main or virtual memory address must be supplied.
- *CPU Register:* With rare exceptions, a CPU contains one or more registers that may be referenced by machine instructions. If only one register exists, reference to it may be implicit. If more than one register exists, then each register is assigned a unique number, and the instruction must contain the number of the desired register.

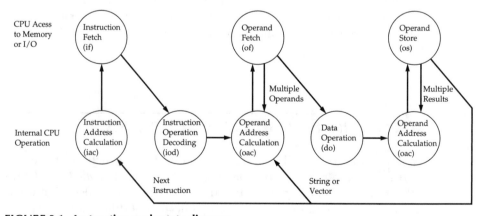

**FIGURE 9.1. Instruction cycle state diagram**

- *I/O Device:* The instruction must specify the I/O module and device for the operation. If memory-mapped I/O is used, this is just another main or virtual memory address.

## Instruction Representation

Within the computer, each instruction is represented by a sequence of bits. The instruction is divided into fields, corresponding to the constituent elements of the instruction. This layout of the instruction is known as the *instruction format*. A simple example is shown in Figure 9.2. As another example, the IAS instruction format is shown in Figure 2.2. With most instruction sets, more than one format is used. During instruction execution, an instruction is read into an instruction register (IR) in the CPU. The CPU must be able to extract the data from the various instruction fields to perform the required operation.

It is difficult for both the programmer and the reader of textbooks to deal with binary representations of machine instructions. Thus, it has become common practice to use a *symbolic representation* of machine instructions. An example of this was used for the IAS instruction set, in Table 2.1.

Opcodes are represented by abbreviations, called *mnemonics*, that indicate the operation. Common examples include

| | |
|---|---|
| ADD | Add |
| SUB | Subtract |
| MPY | Multiply |
| DIV | Divide |
| LOAD | Load data from memory |
| STOR | Store data to memory |

Operands are also represented symbolically. For example, the instruction

ADD    R, Y

may mean add the value contained in data location Y to the contents of register R. In this example, Y refers to the address of a location in memory, and R refers to a particular register. Note that the operation is performed on the contents of a location, not on its address.

Thus, it is possible to write a machine-language program in symbolic form. Each symbolic opcode has a fixed binary representation, and the programmer

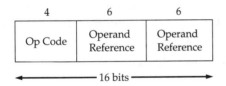

**FIGURE 9.2.  A simple instruction format**

specifies the location of each symbolic operand. For example, the programmer might begin with a list of definitions:

X = 513
Y = 514

and so on. A simple program would accept this symbolic input, convert opcodes and operand references to binary form, and construct binary machine instructions.

Machine-language programmers are rare to the point of nonexistence. Most programs today are written in a high-level language or, failing that, assembly language, which is discussed at the end of this chapter. However, symbolic machine language remains a useful tool for describing machine instructions, and we will use it for that purpose.

## Instruction Types

Consider a high-level language instruction that could be expressed in a language such as BASIC or FORTRAN. For example,

X = X + Y

This statement instructs the computer to add the value stored in Y to the value stored in X and put the result in X. How might this be accomplished with machine instructions? Let us assume that the variables X and Y correspond to locations 513 and 514. If we assume a simple set of machine instructions, this operation could be accomplished with three instructions:

1. Load a register with the contents of memory location 513.
2. Add the contents of memory location 514 to the register.
3. Store the contents of the register in memory location 513.

As can be seen, the single BASIC instruction may require three machine instructions. This is typical of the relationship between a high-level language and a machine language. A high-level language expresses operations in a concise algebraic form, using variables. A machine language expresses operations in a basic form involving the movement of data to or from registers.

With this simple example to guide us, let us consider the types of instructions that must be included in a practical computer. A computer should have a set of instructions that allows the user to formulate any data-processing task. Another way to view it is to consider the capabilities of a high-level programming language. Any program written in a high-level language must be translated into machine language in order to be executed. Thus, the set of machine instructions must be sufficient to express any of the instructions from a high-level language. With this in mind we can categorize instruction types as follows:

- *Data Processing:* Arithmetic and logic instructions
- *Data Storage:* Memory instructions
- *Data Movement:* I/O instructions
- *Control:* Test and branch instructions

*Arithmetic* instructions provide computational capabilities for processing numeric data. *Logic* (Boolean) instructions operate on the bits of a word as bits rather than as numbers; thus, they provide capabilities for processing any other type of data the user may wish to employ. These operations are performed primarily on data in CPU registers. Therefore, there must be *memory* instructions for moving data between memory and the registers. *I/O* instructions are needed to transfer programs and data into memory and the results of computations back out to the user. *Test* instructions are used to test the value of a data word or the status of a computation. *Branch* instructions are then used to branch to a different set of instructions depending on the decision made.

We will examine the various types of instructions in greater detail later in the chapter.

## Number of Addresses

One of the traditional ways of describing processor architecture is in terms of the number of addresses contained in each instruction. This dimension has become less significant with the increasing complexity of CPU design. Nevertheless, it is useful at this point to draw and analyze this distinction.

What is the maximum number of addresses one might need in an instruction? Evidently, arithmetic and logic instructions will require the most operands. Virtually all arithmetic and logic operations are either unary (one operand) or binary (two operands). Thus, we would need a maximum of two addresses to reference operands. The result of an operation must be stored, suggesting a third address. Finally, after completion of an instruction, the next instruction must be fetched, and its address is needed.

The above line of reasoning suggests that an instruction could plausibly be required to contain four address references: two operands, one result, and the address of the next instruction. In practice, four-address instructions are extremely rare. Most CPUs are of the one-, two-, or three-address variety, with the address of the next instruction being implicit (obtained from the program counter).

Figure 9.3 compares typical one-, two-, and three-address instructions that could be used to compute $Y = (A - B) \div (C + D * E)$. With three addresses, each instruction specifies two operand locations and a result location. Because we would like to not alter the value of any of the operand locations, a temporary location, T, is used to store some intermediate results. Note that there are four instructions and that the original expression had five operands.

Three-address instruction formats are not common, because they require a relatively long instruction format to hold the three address references. With two-address instructions, and for binary operations, one address must do double duty as both an operand and a result. Thus, the instruction SUB Y, B carries out the calculation Y - B and stores the result in Y. The two-address format reduces the space requirement but also introduces some awkwardness. To avoid altering the value of an operand, a MOVE instruction is used to move one of the values to a result or temporary location before performing the operation. Our sample program expands to six instructions.

| Instruction | | Comment |
|---|---|---|
| SUB | Y, A, B | Y ← A – B |
| MPY | T, D, E | T ← D × E |
| ADD | T, T, C | T ← T + C |
| DIV | Y, Y, T | Y ← Y ÷ T |

(a) Three-Address Instructions

| Instruction | | Comment |
|---|---|---|
| MOVE | Y, A | Y ← A |
| SUB | Y, B | Y ← Y – B |
| MOVE | T, D | T ← D |
| MPY | T, E | T ← T * E |
| ADD | T, C | T ← T + C |
| DIV | Y, T | Y ← Y ÷ T |

(b) Two-Address Instructions

| Instruction | | Comment |
|---|---|---|
| LOAD | D | AC ← D |
| MPY | E | AC ← AC * E |
| ADD | C | AC ← AC + C |
| STOR | Y | Y ← AC |
| LOAD | A | AC ← A |
| SUB | B | AC ← AC – B |
| DIV | Y | AC ← AC ÷ Y |
| STOR | Y | Y ← AC |

(c) One-Address Instructions

**FIGURE 9.3.  Programs to execute Y = (A – B) ÷ (C + D * E)**

Simpler yet is the one-address instruction. For this to work, a second address must be implicit. This was common in earlier machines, with the implied address being a CPU register known as the *accumulator,* or AC. The accumulator contains one of the operands and is used to store the result. In our example, eight instructions are needed to accomplish the task.

It is, in fact, possible to make do with zero addresses for some instructions. Zero-address instructions are applicable to a special memory organization, called a *stack.* A stack is a last-in-first-out set of locations. The stack is in a known location and, often, at least the top two elements are in CPU registers. Thus, zero-address instructions would reference the top two stack elements. Stacks are described in Appendix 9A. Their use is explored further later in this chapter and in Chapter 10.

Table 9.1 summarizes the interpretations to be placed on instructions with 0, 1, 2, or 3 addresses. In each case in the table, it is assumed that the address of the next instruction is implicit, and that one operation with two source operands and one result operand is to be performed.

The number of addresses per instruction is a basic design decision. Fewer addresses per instruction result in more-primitive instructions, which requires a

**TABLE 9.1** Utilization of Instruction Addresses (Nonbranching Instructions)

| Number of Addresses | Symbolic Representation | Interpretation |
|---|---|---|
| 3 | OP A, B, C | A←B OP C |
| 2 | OP A, B | A←A OP B |
| 1 | OP A | AC←AC OP A |
| 0 | OP | T←T OP (T–1) |

less complex CPU. It also results in instructions of shorter length. On the other hand, programs contain more total instructions, which in general results in longer execution times and longer, more complex programs. Also, there is an important threshold between one-address and multiple-address instructions. With one-address instructions, the programmer generally has available only one general-purpose register, the accumulator. With multiple-address instructions, it is common to have multiple general-purpose registers. This allows some operations to be performed solely on registers. Since register references are faster than memory references, this speeds up execution. For reasons of flexibility and ability to use multiple registers, most contemporary machines employ a mixture of two- and three-address instructions.

The design trade-offs involved in choosing the number of addresses per instruction are complicated by other factors. There is the issue of whether an address references a memory location or a register. Since there are fewer registers, fewer bits are needed for a register reference. Also, as we shall see in the next chapter, a machine may offer a variety of addressing modes, and the specification of mode takes one or more bits. The result is that most CPU designs involve a variety of instruction formats.

## Instruction Set Design

One of the most interesting, and most analyzed, aspects of computer design is instruction set design. The design of an instruction set is very complex, since it affects so many aspects of the computer system. The instruction set defines many of the functions performed by the CPU and thus has a significant effect on the implementation of the CPU. The instruction set is the programmer's means of controlling the CPU. Thus, programmer requirements must be considered in designing the instruction set.

It may surprise you to know that some of the most fundamental issues relating to the design of instruction sets remain in dispute. Indeed, in recent years, the level of disagreement concerning these fundamentals has actually grown. The most important of these fundamental design issues include

- *Operation Repertoire:* How many and which operations to provide, and how complex operations should be.
- *Data Types:* The various types of data upon which operations are performed.
- *Instruction Format:* Instruction length (in bits), number of addresses, size of various fields, and so on.

- *Registers:* Number of CPU registers that can be referenced by instructions, and their use.
- *Addressing:* The mode or modes by which the address of an operand is specified.

These issues are highly interrelated and must be considered together in designing an instruction set. This book, of course, must consider them in sequence, but an attempt is made to show the interrelationships.

Because of the importance of this topic, much of Part III is devoted to instruction set design. Following this overview section, this chapter examines data types and operation repertoire. Chapter 10 examines addressing modes (which includes a consideration of registers) and instruction formats. Chapter 12 examines an exciting recent development known as the reduced instruction set computer (RISC). RISC architecture calls into question many of the instruction set design decisions made in many contemporary commercial computers. One example of a RISC machine is the PowerPC. In this chapter and the next, we use this as one of our examples. However, the significance of the PowerPC design in the context of RISC is discussed in Chapter 12.

## 9.2

### TYPES OF OPERANDS

Machine instructions operate on data. The most important general categories of data are

- Addresses
- Numbers
- Characters
- Logical Data

We will see, in discussing modes in Chapter 10, that addresses are in fact a form of data. In many cases, some calculation must be performed on the operand reference in an instruction to determine the main or virtual memory address. In this context, addresses can be considered to be unsigned integers.

Other common data types are numbers, characters, and logical data, and each of these is briefly examined in this section. Beyond that, some machines define specialized data types or data structures. For example, there may be machine operators that operate directly on a list or a string of characters.

### Numbers

All machine languages include numeric data types. Even in nonnumeric data processing, there is a need for numbers to act as counters, field widths, and so forth. An important distinction between numbers used in ordinary mathematics and numbers stored in a computer is that the latter are limited. This is true in two senses. First, there is a limit to the magnitude of numbers representable on a machine and second, in the case of floating-point numbers, a limit to their precision. Thus, the programmer is faced with understanding the consequences of rounding, overflow, and underflow.

Three types of numerical data are common in computers:

- Integer or Fixed Point
- Floating Point
- Decimal

We examined the first two in some detail in Chapter 8. It remains to say a few words about decimal numbers.

Although all internal computer operations are binary in nature, the human users of the system deal with decimal numbers. Thus, there is a necessity to convert from decimal to binary on input and from binary to decimal on output. For applications in which there is a great deal of I/O and comparatively little, comparatively simple computation, it is preferable to store and operate on the numbers in decimal form. The most common representation for this purpose is packed decimal.

With packed decimal, each decimal digit is represented by a 4-bit code, in the obvious way. Thus, $0 = 0000$, $1 = 0001$, ..., $8 = 1000$, and $9 = 1001$. Note that this is a rather inefficient code since only 10 of a possible 16 4-bit values are used. To form numbers, 4-bit codes are strung together, usually in multiples of 8 bits. Thus, the code for 246 is 0000001001000110. This code is clearly less compact than a straight binary representation, but it avoids the conversion overhead. Negative numbers can be represented by including a 4-bit sign digit at either the left or right end of a string of packed decimal digits. For example, the code 1111 might stand for the minus sign.

Many machines provide arithmetic instructions for performing operations directly on packed decimal numbers. The algorithms are quite similar to those described in Section 8.3 but must take into account the decimal carry operation.

## Characters

A common form of data is text or character strings. While textual data are most convenient for human beings, they cannot, in character form, be easily stored or transmitted by data processing and communications systems. Such systems are designed for binary data. Thus, a number of codes have been devised by which characters are represented by a sequence of bits. Perhaps the earliest common example of this is the Morse code. Today, the most commonly used character code in the United States is the ASCII (American Standard Code for Information Interchange) code (Table 6.1) promulgated by the American National Standards Institute (ANSI). ASCII is also widely used outside the United States. Each character in this code is represented by a unique 7-bit pattern; thus, 128 different characters can be represented. This is a larger number than is necessary to represent printable characters, and some of the patterns represent *control* characters. Some of these control characters have to do with controlling the printing of characters on a page. Others are concerned with communications procedures. ASCII-encoded characters are almost always stored and transmitted using 8 bits per character. The eighth bit may be set to 0 or used as a parity bit for error detection. In the latter case, the bit is set such that the total number of binary 1s in each octet is always odd (odd parity) or always even (even parity).

Note that for the ASCII bit pattern 011XXXX, the digits 0 through 9 are represented by their binary equivalents, 0000 through 1001, in the rightmost 4 bits. This is the same code as packed decimal. This facilitates conversion between 7-bit ASCII and 4-bit packed decimal representation.

Another code used to encode characters is the Extended Binary Coded Decimal Interchange Code (EBCDIC). EBCDIC is used on IBM S/370 machines. It is an 8-bit code. As with ASCII, EBCDIC is compatible with packed decimal. In the case of EBCDIC, the codes 11110000 through 11111001 represent the digits 0 through 9.

## Logical Data

Normally, each word or other addressable unit (byte, halfword, and so on) is treated as a single unit of data. It is sometimes useful, however, to consider an $n$-bit unit as consisting of $n$ 1-bit items of data, each item having the value 0 or 1. When data are viewed this way, they are considered to be *logical* data.

There are two advantages to the bit-oriented view. First, we may sometimes wish to store an array of Boolean or binary data items, in which each item can take on only the values 1 (true) and 0 (false). With logical data, memory can be used most efficiently for this storage. Second, there are occasions when we wish to manipulate the bits of a data item. For example, if floating-point operations are implemented in software, we need to be able to shift significant bits in some operations. Another example: To convert from ASCII to packed decimal, we need to extract the rightmost 4 bits of each byte.

Note that, in the preceding examples, the same data are treated sometimes as logical and other times as numerical or text. The "type" of a unit of data is determined by the operation being performed on it. While this is not normally the case in high-level languages (e.g., Pascal), it is almost always the case with machine language.

## Pentium Data Types

The Pentium can deal with data types of 8 (byte), 16 (word), 32 (doubleword), and 64 (quadword) bits in length. To allow maximum flexibility in data structures and efficient memory utilization, words need not be aligned at even-numbered addresses; doublewords need not be aligned at addresses evenly divisible by four; and quadwords need not be aligned at addresses evenly divisible by eight. However, when data is accessed across a 32-bit bus, data transfers take place in units of doublewords, beginning at addresses divisible by four. The processor converts the request for misaligned values into a sequence of requests for the bus transfer. As with all of the Intel 80×86 machines, the Pentium uses the little-endian style; that is, the least-significant byte is stored in the lowest address (see Appendix 9B for a discussion of endianness).

The byte, word, doubleword, and quadword are referred to as general data types. In addition, the Pentium supports an impressive array of specific data types that are recognized and operated on by particular instructions. Table 9.2 summarizes these types.

**TABLE 9.2   Pentium Data Types**

| Data Type | Description |
|---|---|
| General | Byte, word (16 bits), doubleword (32 bits), and quadword (64 bits) locations with arbitrary binary contents. |
| Integer | A signed binary value contained in a byte, word, or doubleword, using two's complement representation. |
| Ordinal | An unsigned integer contained in a byte, word, or doubleword. |
| Unpacked Binary Coded Decimal (BCD) | A representation of a BCD digit in the range 0 through 9, with one digit in each byte. |
| Packed BCD | Packed byte representation of two BCD digits; value in the range 0 to 99. |
| Near Pointer | A 32-bit effective address that represents the offset within a segment. Used for all pointers in a nonsegmented memory and for references within a segment in a segmented memory. |
| Bit Field | A contiguous sequence of bits in which the position of each bit is considered as an independent unit. A bit string can begin at any bit position of any byte and can contain up to $2^{32}-1$ bits. |
| Byte String | A contiguous sequence of bytes, words, or doublewords, containing form zero to $2^{32}-1$ bytes. |
| Floating-Point | See Figure 9.4. |

The floating-point type actually refers to a set of types that are used by the floating-point unit and operated on by floating-point instructions. As Figure 9.4 illustrates, floating-point instructions can operate on integers and packed decimal integers as well as floating-point numbers. The integers are in two's complement representation and may be 16, 32, or 64 bits long. Packed decimal integers are stored in sign–magnitude representation with 18 digits in the range 0 through 9. The three floating-point representations conform to the IEEE 754 standard.

## PowerPC Data Types

The PowerPC can deal with data types of 8 (byte), 16 (halfword), 32 (word), and 64 (doubleword) bits in length. Some instructions require that memory operands be aligned on a 32-bit boundary. In general, however, alignment is not required. One interesting feature of the PowerPC is that it can use either the little-endian or big-endian style; that is, the least significant byte is stored in the lowest or highest address (see Appendix 9B for a discussion of endianness).

The byte, halfword, word, and doubleword are general data types. The processor interprets the contents of a given item of data depending on the instruction. The fixed-point processor recognizes the following data types:

- *Unsigned Byte:* Can be used for logical or integer arithmetic operations. It is loaded from memory into a general register by zero-extending on the left to the full register size.
- *Unsigned Halfword:* As above, for 16-bit quantities.
- *Signed Halfword:* Used for arithmetic operations; loaded into memory by sign-extending on the left to full register size (i.e., the sign bit is replicated in all vacant positions).

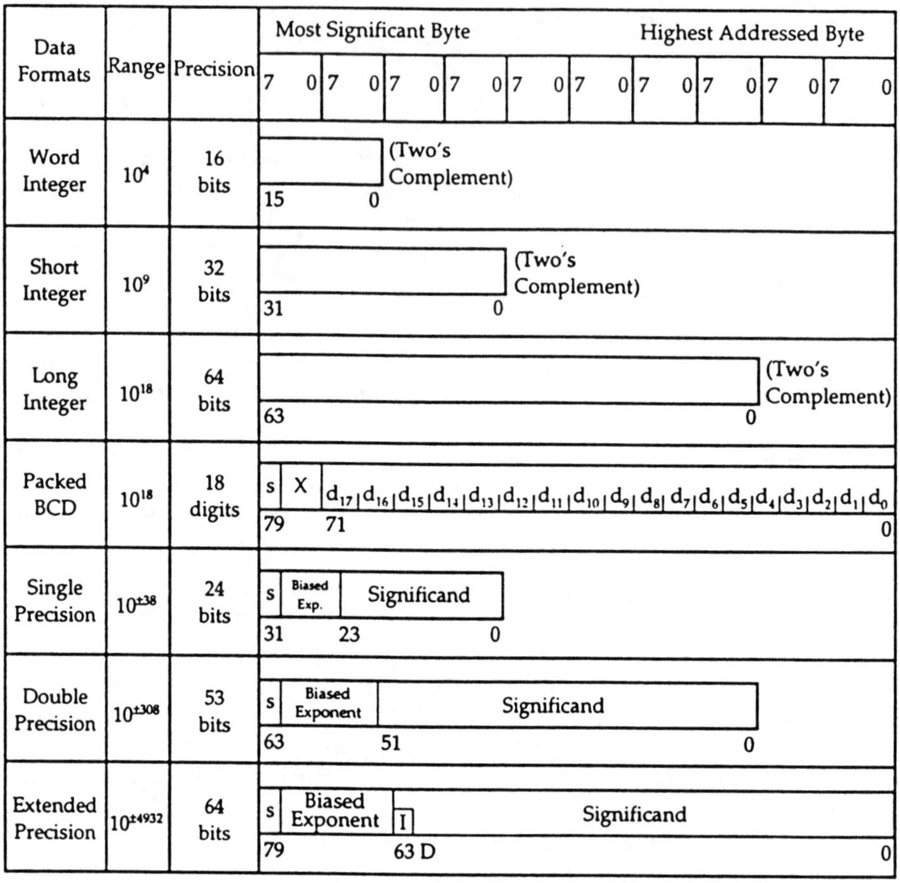

| Data Formats | Range | Precision | Most Significant Byte ... Highest Addressed Byte |
|---|---|---|---|
| Word Integer | $10^4$ | 16 bits | (Two's Complement) — 15 ... 0 |
| Short Integer | $10^9$ | 32 bits | (Two's Complement) — 31 ... 0 |
| Long Integer | $10^{18}$ | 64 bits | (Two's Complement) — 63 ... 0 |
| Packed BCD | $10^{18}$ | 18 digits | s X $d_{17}$|$d_{16}$|$d_{15}$|$d_{14}$|$d_{13}$|$d_{12}$|$d_{11}$|$d_{10}$|$d_9$|$d_8$|$d_7$|$d_6$|$d_5$|$d_4$|$d_3$|$d_2$|$d_1$|$d_0$ — 79 71 ... 0 |
| Single Precision | $10^{\pm38}$ | 24 bits | s Biased Exp. Significand — 31 23 ... 0 |
| Double Precision | $10^{\pm308}$ | 53 bits | s Biased Exponent Significand — 63 51 ... 0 |
| Extended Precision | $10^{\pm4932}$ | 64 bits | s Biased Exponent I Significand — 79 63 D ... 0 |

s = Sign Bit (0 = positive; 1= negative)
$d_n$ = Decimal Digit (two per byte)
X = Bits Have No Significance; Ignores when Loading, Zeros when Storing
D = Position of Implicit Binary Point
I = Integer Bit of Significand; Stored in Temporary Real, Implicit in Single and Double Precision

**FIGURE 9.4. Numerical Data Formats for Pentium Floating-Point Unit**

- *Unsigned Word:* Used for logical operations and as an address pointer.
- *Signed Word:* Used for arithmetic operations.
- *Unsigned Doubleword:* Used as an address pointer.
- *Byte String:* From 0 to 128 bytes in length.

In addition, the PowerPC supports the single- and double-precision floating-point data types defined in IEEE 754.

9.3

## TYPES OF OPERATIONS

The number of different opcodes varies widely from machine to machine. However, the same general types of operations are found on all machines. A useful and typical categorization is the following:

- Data Transfer
- Arithmetic
- Logical
- Conversion
- I/O
- System Control
- Transfer of Control

Table 9.3 (based on [HAYE88]) lists common instruction types in each category. This section provides a brief survey of these various types of operations, together with a brief discussion of the actions taken by the CPU to execute a particular type of operation (summarized in Table 9.4). The latter topic is examined in more detail in Chapter 11.

### Data Transfer

The most fundamental type of machine instruction is the data transfer instruction. The data transfer instruction must specify several things. First, the location of the source and destination operands must be specified. Each location could be memory, a register, or the top of the stack. Second, the length of data to be transferred must be indicated. Third, as with all instructions with operands, the mode of addressing for each operand must be specified. This latter point is discussed in Chapter 10.

The choice of data transfer instructions to include in an instruction set exemplifies the kinds of trade-offs the designer must make. For example, the general location (memory or register) of an operand can be indicated in either the specification of the opcode or the operand. Table 9.5 shows examples of the most common IBM S/370 data transfer instructions. Note that there are variants to indicate the amount of data to be transferred (8, 16, 32, or 64 bits). Also, there are different instructions for register to register, register to memory, and memory to register transfers. In contrast, the VAX has a move (MOV) instruction with variants for different amounts of data to be moved, but it specifies whether an operand is register or memory as part of the operand. The VAX approach is somewhat easier for the programmer, who has fewer mnemonics to deal with. However, it is also somewhat less compact than the IBM S/370 approach, since the location (register versus memory) of each operand must be specified separately in the instruction. We will return to this distinction when we discuss instruction formats, in the next chapter.

In terms of CPU action, data transfer operations are perhaps the simplest type. If both source and destination are registers, then the CPU simply causes data to be transferred from one register to another; this is an operation internal to the CPU. If

**TABLE 9.3    Common Instruction Set Operations**

| Type | Operation Name | Description |
|------|----------------|-------------|
| Data Transfer | Move (transfer) | Transfer word or block from source to destination |
|  | Store | Transfer word from processor to memory |
|  | Load (fetch) | Transfer word from memory to processor |
|  | Exchange | Swap contents of source and destination |
|  | Clear (reset) | Transfer word of 0s to destination |
|  | Set | Transfer word of 1s to destination |
|  | Push | Transfer word from source to top of stack |
|  | Pop | Transfer word from top of stack to destination |
| Arithmetic | Add | Computer sum of two operands |
|  | Subtract | Compute difference of two operands |
|  | Multiply | Compute product of two operands |
|  | Divide | Compute quotient of two operands |
|  | Absolute | Replace operand by its absolute value |
|  | Negate | Change sign of operand |
|  | Increment | Add 1 to operand |
|  | Decrement | Subtract 1 from operand |
| Logical | AND | ⎫ |
|  | OR |  |
|  | NOT (Complement) | Perform the specified logical operation bitwise |
|  | Exclusive-OR | ⎭ |
|  | Test | Test specified condition; set flag(s) based on outcome |
|  | Compare | Make logical or arithmetic comparison of two or more operands; set flag(s) based on outcome |
|  | Set Control Variables | Class or instructions to set controls for protection purposes, interrupt handling, timer control, etc. |
|  | Shift | Left (right) shift operand, introducing constants at end |
|  | Rotate | Left (right) shift operand, with wraparound end |
|  | Jump (branch) | Unconditional transfer; load PC with specified address |
|  | Jump Conditional | Test specified condition; either load PC with specified address or do nothing, based on condition |

one or both operands are in memory, then the CPU must perform some or all of the following actions:

1. Calculate the memory address, based on the address mode (discussed in Chapter 10).
2. If the address refers to virtual memory, translate from virtual to actual memory address.
3. Determine whether addressed item is in cache.
4. If not, issue command to memory module.

## Arithmetic

Most machines provide the basic arithmetic operations of add, subtract, multiply, and divide. These are invariably provided for signed integer (fixed-point) numbers. Often they are also provided for floating-point and packed decimal numbers.

**TABLE 9.3    (continued)**

| Type | Operation Name | Description |
|------|----------------|-------------|
| Transfer of Control | Jump to Subroutine | Place current program control information in known location; jump to specified address |
| | Return | Replace contents of PC and other register from known location |
| | Execute | Fetch operand from specified location and execute as instruction; do not modify PC |
| | Skip | Increment PC to skip next instruction |
| | Skip Conditional | Test specified condition; either skip or do nothing based on condition |
| | Halt | Stop program execution |
| | Wait (hold) | Stop program execution; test specified condition repeatedly; resume execution when condition is satisfied |
| | No operation | No operation is performed, but program execution is continued |
| Input/Output | Input (read) | Transfer data from specified I/O port or device to destination, e.g., main memory or processor register |
| | Output (write) | Transfer data from specified source to I/O port or device |
| | Start I/O | Transfer instructions to I/O processor to initiate I/O operation |
| | Test I/O | Transfer status information from I/O system to specified destination |
| Conversion | Translate | Translate values in a section of memory based on a table of correspondences |
| | Convert | Convert the contents of a word from one form to another (e.g., packed decimal to binary) |

Other possible operations include a variety of single-operand instructions; for example,

- *Absolute:* Take the absolute value of the operand.
- *Negate:* Negate the operand.
- *Increment:* Increment the operand by 1.
- *Decrement:* Decrement the operand by 1.

The execution of an arithmetic instruction may involve data transfer operations to position operands for input to the ALU, and to deliver the output of the ALU. Figure 3.5 illustrates the movements involved in both data transfer and arithmetic operations. In addition, of course, the ALU portion of the CPU performs the desired operation.

## Logical

Most machines also provide a variety of operations for manipulating individual bits of a word or other addressable units, often referred to as "bit twiddling." They are based upon Boolean operations (see appendix to this book).

**TABLE 9.4   CPU Actions For Various Types of Operations**

| | |
|---|---|
| Data Transfer | Transfer data from one location to another |
| | If memory is involved: |
| |     Determine memory address |
| |     Perform virtual-to-actual-memory address transformation |
| |     Check cache |
| |     Initiate memory read/write |
| Arithmetic | May involve data transfer, before and/or after |
| | Perform function in ALU |
| | Set condition codes and flags |
| Logical | Same as arithmetic |
| Conversion | Similar to arithmetic and logical. May involve special logic to perform conversion |
| Transfer of Control | Update program counter. For subroutine call/return, manage parameter passing and linkage |
| I/O | Issue command to I/O module |
| | If memory-mapped I/O, determine memory-mapped address |

Some of the basic logical operations that can be performed on Boolean or binary data are shown in Table 9.6. The NOT operation inverts a bit. AND, OR, and Exclusive OR (XOR) are the most common logical functions with two operands. EQUAL is a useful binary test.

These logical operations can be applied bitwise to $n$-bit logical data units. Thus, if two registers contain the data

**TABLE 9.5   Examples of IBM S/370 Data Transfer Operations**

| Operation Mnemonic | Name | Number of Bits Transferred | Description |
|---|---|---|---|
| L | Load | 32 | Transfer from memory to register |
| LH | Load Halfword | 16 | Transfer from memory to register |
| LR | Load | 32 | Transfer from register to register |
| LER | Load (Short) | 32 | Transfer from floating-point register to floating-point register |
| LE | Load (Short) | 32 | Transfer from memory to floating-point register |
| LDR | Load (Long) | 64 | Transfer from floating-point register to floating-point register |
| LD | Load (Long) | 64 | Transfer from memory to floating-point register |
| ST | Store | 32 | Transfer from register to memory |
| STH | Store Halfword | 16 | Transfer from register to memory |
| STC | Store Character | 8 | Transfer from register to memory |
| STE | Store (Short) | 32 | Transfer from floating-point register to memory |
| STD | Store (Long) | 64 | Transfer from floating-point register to memory |

**TABLE 9.6    Basic Logical Operations**

| P | Q | NOT P | NOT Q | P AND Q | P OR Q | P XOR Q | P=Q |
|---|---|-------|-------|---------|--------|---------|-----|
| 0 | 0 | 1 | 1 | 0 | 0 | 0 | 1 |
| 0 | 1 | 1 | 0 | 0 | 1 | 1 | 0 |
| 1 | 0 | 0 | 1 | 0 | 1 | 1 | 0 |
| 1 | 1 | 0 | 0 | 1 | 1 | 0 | 1 |

(R1) = 10100101

(R2) = 00001111

then

(R1) AND (R2) = 00000101

Thus, the AND operation can be used as a *mask* that selects certain bits in a word and zeros out the remaining bits. As another example, if two registers contain

(R1) = 10100101

(R2) = 11111111

then

(R1) XOR (R2) = 01011010

With one word set to all 1s, the XOR operation inverts all of the bits in the other word (one's complement).

In addition to bitwise logical operations, most machines provide a variety of shifting and rotating functions. The most basic operations are illustrated in Figure 9.5. With a *logical shift,* the bits of a word are shifted left or right. On one end, the bit shifted out is lost. On the other end, a 0 is shifted in. Logical shifts are useful primarily for isolating fields within a word. The 0s that are shifted into a word displace unwanted information that is shifted off the other end.

As an example, suppose we wish to transmit characters of data to an I/O device 1 character at a time. If each memory word is 16 bits in length and contains 2 characters, we must *unpack* the characters before they can be sent. To send the 2 characters in a word,

1. Load the word into a register.
2. AND with the value 1111111100000000. This masks out the character on the right.
3. Shift to the right eight times. This shifts the remaining character to the right half of the register.
4. Perform I/O. The I/O module will read the lower-order 8 bits from the data bus.

The preceding steps result in sending the left-hand character. To send the right-hand character,

1. Load the word again into the register.
2. AND with 0000000011111111.
3. Perform I/O.

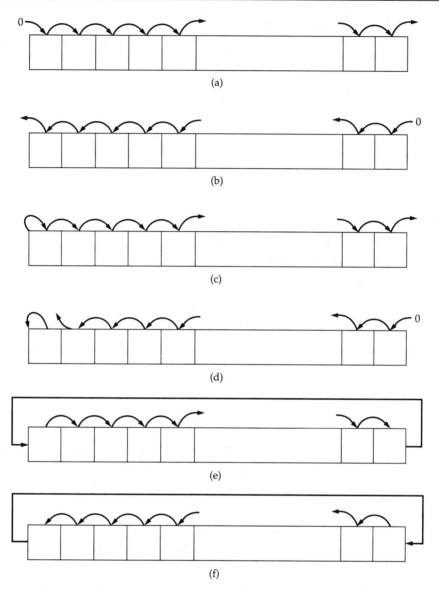

**FIGURE 9.5.  Shift and rotate operations: (a) logical right shift; (b) logical left shift;
(c) arithmetic right shift; (d) arithmetic left shift; (e) right rotate; (f) left rotate**

The *arithmetic shift* operation treats the data as a signed integer and does not shift
the sign bit. On a right arithmetic shift, the sign bit is normally replicated into the bit
position to its right. These operations can speed up certain arithmetic operations.
With numbers in two's complement notation, a left or right shift corresponds to multiplication or division by 2, respectively, provided there is no overflow or underflow.

*Rotate*, or cyclic shift, operations preserve all of the bits being operated on. One
possible use of a rotate is to bring each bit successively into the leftmost bit, where
it can be identified by testing the sign of the data (treated as a number).

As with arithmetic operations, logical operations involve ALU activity and may involve data transfer operations.

## Conversion

Conversion instructions are those which change the format or operate on the format of data. An example is converting from decimal to binary.

An example of a more complex editing instruction is the S/370 Translate (TR) instruction. This instruction can be used to convert from one 8-bit code to another, and it takes three operands:

TR R1, R2, L

The operand R2 contains the address of the start of a table of 8-bit codes. The L bytes starting at the address specified in R1 are translated, each byte being replaced by the contents of a table entry indexed by that byte. For example, to translate from EBCDIC to ASCII, we first create a 256-byte table in storage locations, say, 1000–10FF hexadecimal. The table contains the characters of the ASCII code in the sequence of the binary representation of the EBCDIC code; that is, the ASCII code is placed in the table at the relative location equal to the binary value of the EBCDIC code of the same character. Thus, locations 10F0 through 10F9 will contain the values 30 through 39, since F0 is the EBCDIC code for the digit 0, and 30 is the ASCII code for the digit 0, and so on through digit 9. Now suppose we have the EBCDIC for the digits 1984 starting at location 2100 and we wish to translate to ASCII. Assume the following:

Locations 2100–2103 contain F1 F9 F8 F4.
R1 contains 2100.
R2 contains 1000.

Then, if we execute

TR R1, R2, 4

locations 2100–2103 will contain 31 39 38 34.

## Input/Output

Input/Output instructions were discussed in some detail in Chapter 6. As we saw, there are a variety of approaches taken, including isolated programmed I/O, memory-mapped programmed I/O, DMA, and the use of an I/O processor. Many implementations provide only a few I/O instructions, with the specific actions specified by parameters, codes, or command words.

## System Control

System control instructions are generally privileged instructions that can be executed only while the processor is in a certain privileged state or is executing a program in a special privileged area of memory. Typically, these instructions are reserved for the use of the operating system.

Some examples of system control operations are as follows. A system control instruction may read or alter a control register; we will discuss control registers in Chapter 11. Another example is an instruction to read or modify a storage protection key, such as is used in the S/370 memory system. Another example is access to process control blocks in a multiprogramming system.

## Transfer of Control

For all of the operation types discussed so far, the instruction specifies the operation to be performed and the operands. Implicitly, the next instruction to be performed is the one that immediately follows, in memory, the current instruction. Thus, in the normal course of events, instructions are executed consecutively from memory. The CPU simply increments the program counter prior to fetching the next instruction.

However, a significant fraction of the instructions in any program have as their function changing the sequence of instruction execution. For these instructions, the operation performed by the CPU is to update the program counter to contain the address of some instruction in memory.

There are a number of reasons why transfer-of-control operations are required. Among the most important are

1. In the practical use of computers, it is essential to be able to execute each instruction more than once and perhaps many thousands of times. It may require thousands or perhaps millions of instructions to implement an application. This would be unthinkable if each instruction had to be written out separately. If a table or a list of items is to be processed, a program loop is needed. One sequence of instructions is executed repeatedly to process all the data.
2. Virtually all programs involve some decision making. We would like the computer to do one thing if one condition holds, and another thing if another condition holds. For example, a sequence of instructions computes the square root of a number. At the start of the sequence, the sign of the number is tested. If the number is negative, the computation is not performed, but an error condition is reported.
3. To correctly compose a large or even medium-size computer program is an exceedingly difficult task. It helps if there are mechanisms for breaking the task up into smaller pieces that can be worked on one at a time.

We now turn to a discussion of the most common transfer-of-control operations found in instruction sets:

- Branch
- Skip
- Subroutine Call

### Branch Instructions

A branch instruction, also called a jump instruction, has as one of its operands the address of the next instruction to be executed. Most often, the instruction is a *con-*

*ditional branch* instruction. That is, the branch is made (update program counter to equal address specified in operand) only if a certain condition is met. Otherwise, the next instruction in sequence is executed (increment program counter as usual).

There are two common ways of generating the condition to be tested in a conditional branch instruction. First, most machines provide a 1-bit or multiple-bit condition code that is set as the result of some operations. This code can be thought of as a short user-visible register. As an example, an arithmetic operation (ADD, SUBTRACT, and so on) could set a 2-bit condition code with one of the following four values: 0, positive, negative, overflow. On such a machine, there could be four different conditional branch instructions:

BRP X   Branch to location X if result is positive.
BRN X   Branch to location X if result is negative.
BRZ X   Branch to location X if result is zero.
BRO X   Branch to location X if overflow occurs.

In all of these cases, the result referred to is the result of the most recent operation that set the condition code.

Another approach that can be used with a three-address instruction format is to perform a comparison and specify a branch in the same instruction. For example,

BRE R1,R2,X     Branch to X if contents of R1 = contents of R2.

Figure 9.6 shows examples of these operations. Note that a branch can be either *forward* (an instruction with a higher address) or *backward* (lower address). The example shows how an unconditional and a conditional branch can be used to create a repeating loop of instructions. The instructions in locations 202 through 210 will be executed repeatedly until the result of subtracting Y from X is 0.

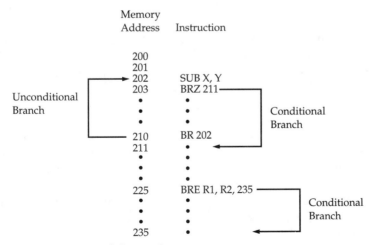

**FIGURE 9.6. Branch instructions**

## Skip Instructions

Another common form of transfer-of-control instruction is the skip instruction. The skip instruction includes an implied address. Typically, the skip implies that one instruction be skipped; thus, the implied address equals the address of the next instruction plus one instruction-length.

Because the skip instruction does not require a destination address field, it is free to do other things. A typical example is the increment-and-skip-if-zero (ISZ) instruction. Consider the following program fragment:

```
301
  .
  .
  .
  .
309    ISZ    R1
310    BR     301
311
```

In this fragment, the two transfer-of-control instructions are used to implement an iterative loop. R1 is set with the negative of the number of iterations to be performed. At the end of the loop, R1 is incremented. If it is not 0, the program branches back to the beginning of the loop. Otherwise, the branch is skipped, and the program continues with the next instruction after the end of the loop.

## Subroutine Call Instructions

Perhaps the most important innovation in the development of programming languages is the *subroutine*. A subroutine is a self-contained computer program that is incorporated into a larger program. At any point in the program the subroutine may be invoked, or *called.* That is, at that point, the computer is instructed to go and execute the entire subroutine and then return to the point from which the call took place.

The two principal reasons for the use of subroutines are economy and modularity. A subroutine allows the same piece of code to be used many times. This is important for economy in programming effort, and for making the most efficient use of storage space in the system (the program must be stored). Subroutines also allow large programming tasks to be subdivided into smaller units. This use of *modularity* greatly eases the programming task.

The subroutine mechanism involves two basic instructions: a call instruction that branches from the present location to the subroutine, and a return instruction that returns from the subroutine to the place from which it was called. Both of these are forms of branching instructions.

Figure 9.7 illustrates the use of subroutines to construct a program. In this example, there is a main program starting at location 4000. This program includes a call to subroutine SUB1, starting at location 4500. When this call instruction is encountered, the CPU suspends execution of the main program and begins execution of SUB1 by fetching the next instruction from location 4500. Within SUB1,

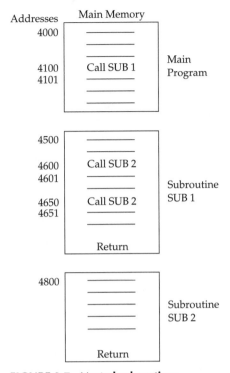

**FIGURE 9.7. Nested subroutines**

there are two calls to SUB2 at location 4800. In each case, the execution of SUB1 is suspended and SUB2 is executed. The RETURN statement causes the CPU to go back to the calling program and continue execution at the instruction after the corresponding CALL instruction. This behavior is illustrated in Figure 9.8.

Several points are worth noting:

1. A subroutine can be called from more than one location.
2. A subroutine call can appear in a subroutine. This allows the *nesting* of subroutines to an arbitrary depth.
3. Each subroutine call is matched by a return in the called program.

Since we would like to be able to call a subroutine from a variety of points, the CPU must somehow save the return address so that the return can take place appropriately. There are three common places for storing the return address:

• Register
• Start of Subroutine
• Top of Stack

Consider a machine-language instruction CALL X, which stands for *call subroutine at location X*. If the register approach is used, CALL X causes the following actions:

$$RN \leftarrow PC + \Delta$$
$$PC \leftarrow X$$

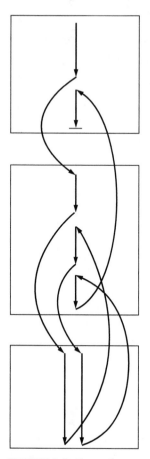

**FIGURE 9.8. Execution sequence for nested subroutines of Figure 9.7**

where RN is a register that is always used for this purpose, PC is the program counter, and $\Delta$ is the instruction length. The called subroutine can now save the contents of RN to be used for the later return.

A second possibility is to store the return address at the start of the subroutine. In this case, CALL X causes

$$X \leftarrow PC + \Delta$$
$$PC \leftarrow X + 1$$

This is quite handy. The return address has been stored safely away.

Both of the preceding approaches work and have been used. The only limitation of these approaches is that they prevent the use of *reentrant* subroutines [HIGM67, POHL81]. A reentrant subroutine is one in which it is possible to have several calls open to it at the same time. A recursive procedure is an example of the use of this feature [BARR68, BURG75].

A more general and powerful approach is to use a stack (see Appendix 9A for a definition of the stack). When the CPU executes a call, it places the return address

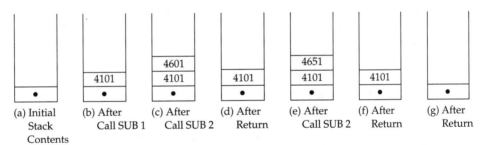

(a) Initial      (b) After       (c) After       (d) After       (e) After       (f) After       (g) After
    Stack         Call SUB 1      Call SUB 2       Return          Call SUB 2       Return          Return
    Contents

**FIGURE 9.9.  Use of stack to implement nested subroutines of Figure 9.7**

on the stack. When it executes a return, it uses the address on the stack. Figure 9.9 illustrates the use of the stack.

In addition to providing a return address, it is also often necessary to pass parameters with a subroutine call. These can be passed in registers. Another possibility is to store the parameters in memory just after the CALL instruction. In this case, the return must be to the location following the parameters. Again, both of these approaches have drawbacks. If registers are used, the called program and the calling program must be written to assure that the registers are used properly. The storing of parameters in memory makes it difficult to exchange a variable number of parameters. And both approaches prevent the use of reentrant subroutines.

A more flexible approach to parameter-passing is the stack. When the processor executes a call, it not only stacks the return address, it stacks parameters to be passed to the called procedure. The called procedure can access the parameters from the stack. Upon return, return parameters can also be placed on the stack, *under* the return address. The entire set of parameters, including return address, that is stored for a procedure invocation is referred to as a *stack frame.*

An example is provided in Figure 9.10. The example refers to procedure P in which the local variables x1 and x2 are declared, and procedure Q, which can be

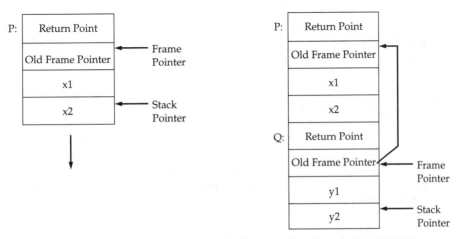

**FIGURE 9.10.  Stack frame growth using sample procedures P and Q [DEWA90]**

called by P and in which the local variables y1 and y2 are declared. In this figure, the return point for each procedure is the first item stored in the corresponding stack frame. Next is stored a pointer to the beginning of the previous frame. This is needed if the number or length of parameters to be stacked is variable.

## Pentium Operation Types

The Pentium provides a complex array of operation types, including a number of specialized instructions. The intent was to provide tools for the compiler writer to produce optimized machine language translation of high-level language programs. Table 9.7 lists the types and gives examples of each. Most of these are the conventional instructions found in most machine instruction sets, but several types of instructions are tailored to the 80x86/Pentium architecture and are of particular interest.

### Call/Return Instructions

The Pentium provides four instructions to support procedure call/return: CALL, ENTER, LEAVE, RETURN. It will be instructive to look at the support provided by these instructions.[1] Recall from Figure 9.10 that a common means of implementing the procedure call/return mechanism is via the use of stack frames. When a new procedure is called, the following must be performed upon entry to the new procedure:

- Push the return point on the stack.
- Push current frame pointer on stack.
- Copy stack pointer as new value of frame pointer.
- Adjust stack pointer to allocate frame.

The CALL instruction pushes the current instruction pointer value onto the stack and causes a jump to the entry point of the procedure by placing the address of the entry point in the instruction pointer. In the 8088 and 8086 machines, the typical procedure began with the sequence

```
PUSH     EBP
MOV      EBP, ESP
SUB      ESP, space_for_locals
```

where EBP is the frame pointer and ESP is the stack pointer. In the 80286 and later machines, the ENTER instruction performs all the above operations in a single instruction.

The ENTER instruction was added to the instruction set to provide direct support for the compiler. The instruction also includes a feature for support of what are called nested procedures in languages such as Pascal, COBOL, and Ada (not found in C or FORTRAN). It turns out that there are better ways of handling nested procedure calls for these languages. Furthermore, although the ENTER instruction

---

[1]This discussion is based on a treatment in [DEWA90], which should be consulted for a more detailed analysis.

**TABLE 9.7    Pentium Operation Types (with Examples of Typical Operations)**

| Instruction | Description |
|---|---|
| | *Data Movement* |
| MOV | Move operand, between registers or between register and memory. |
| PUSH | Push operand onto stack. |
| PUSHA | Push all registers on stack. |
| MOVSX | Move byte, word, dword, sign extended. Moves a byte to a word or a word to a doubleword with two's-complement sign extension. |
| LEA | Load effective address. Loads the offset of the source operand, rather than its value to the destination operand. |
| XLAT | Table lookup translation. Replaces a byte in AL with a byte from a user-coded translation table. When XLAT is executed, AL should have an unsigned index to the table. XLAT changes the contents of AL from the table index to the table entry. |
| IN, OUT | Input, output operand from I/O space. |
| | *Arithmetic* |
| ADD | Add operands. |
| SUB | Subtract operands. |
| MUL | Multiply double/single precision. |
| IDIV | Divide. |
| | *Logical* |
| AND | AND operands. |
| BTS | Bit test and set. Operates on a bit field operand. The instruction copies the current value of a bit to flag CF and sets the original bit to 1. |
| BSF | Bit scan forward. Scans a word or doubleword for a 1-bit and store the number of the first 1-bit into a register. |
| SHL/SHR | Shift logical left or right. |
| SAL/SAR | Shift arithmetic left or right. |
| ROL/ROR | Rotate left or right. |
| SETcc | Sets a byte to zero or one depending on any of the 16 conditions defined by status flags. |
| | *Control Transfer* |
| JMP | Unconditional jump. |
| CALL | Transfer control to another location. Before transfer, the address of the instruction following the CALL is placed on the stack. |
| JE/JZ | Jump if equal/zero. |
| LOOPE/LOOPZ | Loops if equal/zero. This is a conditional jump using a value stored in register ECX. The instruction first decrements ECX before testing ECX for the branch condition. |
| INT/INTO | Interrupt/Interrupt if overflow. Transfer control to an interrupt service routine. |

**TABLE 9.7    (continued)**

### String Operations

| | |
|---|---|
| MOVS | Move byte, word, dword string. The instruction operates on one element of a string, indexed by registers ESI and EDI. After each string operation, the registers are automatically incremented or decremented to point to the next element of the string. |
| LODS | Load byte, word, dword of string. |

### High-Level Language Support

| | |
|---|---|
| ENTER | Creates a stack frame that can be used to implement the rules of a block-structured high-level language. |
| LEAVE | Reverses the action of the previous ENTER. |
| BOUND | Check array bounds. Verifies that the value in operand 1 is within lower and upper limits. The limits are in two adjacent memory locations referenced by operand 2. An interrupt occurs if the value is out of bounds. This instruction is used to check an array index. |

### Flag Control

| | |
|---|---|
| STC | Set Carry flag. |
| LAHF | Load A register from flags. Copies SF, ZF, AF, PF, and CF bits into A register. |

### Segment Register

| | |
|---|---|
| LDS | Load pointer into D segment register. |

### System Control

| | |
|---|---|
| HLT | Halt. |
| LOCK | Asserts a hold on shared memory so that the Pentium has exclusive use of it during the instruction that immediately follows the LOCK. |
| ESC | Processor extension escape. An escape code that indicates the succeeding instructions are to be executed by a numeric coprocessor that supports high-precision integer and floating-point calculations. |
| WAIT | Wait until BUSY# negated. Suspends Pentium program execution until the processor detects that the BUSY pin in inactive, indicating that the numeric coprocessor has finished execution. |

### Protection

| | |
|---|---|
| SGDT | Store global descriptor table. |
| LSL | Load segment limit. Loads a user-specified register with a segment limit. |
| VERR/VERW | Verify segment for reading/writing. |

### Cache Management

| | |
|---|---|
| INVD | Flushes the internal cache memory. |
| WBINVD | Flushes the internal cache memory after writing dirty lines to memory. |
| INVLPG | Invalidates a translation lookaside buffer (TLB) entry. |

saves a few bytes of memory compared with the PUSH, MOV, SUB sequence (4 bytes versus 6 bytes), it actually takes longer to execute (11 clock cycles versus 1.5 clock cycles). Thus, although it may have seemed a good idea to the instruction set designers to add this feature, it complicates the implementation of the processor while providing little or no benefit. We will see in that, in contrast, a RISC approach to processor design would avoid complex instructions such as ENTER and might produce a more efficient implementation with a sequence of simpler instructions.

### Memory Management

Another set of specialized instructions deals with memory segmentation. These are privileged instructions that can be only executed from the operating system. They allow local and global segment tables (called descriptor tables) to be loaded and read, and for the privilege level of a segment to be checked and altered.

The special instructions for dealing with the on-chip cache were discussed in Chapter 5.

### Condition Codes

We have mentioned that condition codes are bits in special registers that may be set by certain operations and used in conditional branch instructions. These conditions are set by arithmetic and compare operations. The compare operation in most languages subtracts two operands, as does a subtract operation. The difference is that a compare operation only sets condition codes, whereas a subtract operation also stores the result of the subtraction in the destination operand.

Table 9.8 lists the condition codes used on the Pentium. Each condition, or combinations of these conditions, can be tested for a conditional jump. Table 9.9 shows the combinations of conditions for which conditional jump opcodes have been defined.

Several interesting observations can be made about this list. First, we may wish to test two operands to determine if one number is bigger than another. But this will depend on whether the numbers are signed or unsigned. For example, the 8-bit number 11111111 is bigger than 00000000 if the two numbers are interpreted as unsigned integers (255 > 0), but is less if they are considered as 8-bit two's complement numbers (-1 < 0). Many assembly languages therefore introduce two sets of terms to distinguish the two cases: If we are comparing two numbers as signed integers, we use the terms *less than* and *greater than*; if we are comparing them as unsigned integers, we use the terms *below* and *above*.

A second operation concerns the complexity of comparing signed integers. A signed result is greater than or equal to zero if (a) the sign bit is zero and there is no overflow (S = 0 AND O = 0), or (b) the sign bit is one and there is an overflow. A study of Figure 8.4 should convince you that the conditions tested for the various signed operations are appropriate (see Problem 9.14).

## PowerPC Operation Types

The PowerPC provides a large collection of operation types. Table 9.10 lists the types and gives examples of each. Several features are worth noting.

**TABLE 9.8   Pentium Condition Codes**

| Status Bit | Name | Description |
|---|---|---|
| C | Carry | Indicates carrying or borrowing into the leftmost bit position following an arithmetic operation. Also modified by some of the shift and rotate operations. |
| P | Parity | Parity of the result of an arithmetic or logic operation. 1 indicates even parity; 0 indicates odd parity. |
| A | Auxiliary Carry | Represents carrying or borrowing between half-bytes of an 8-bit arithmetic or logic operation using the AL register. |
| Z | Zero | Indicates that the result of an arithmetic or logic operation is 0. |
| S | Sign | Indicates the sign of the result of an arithmetic or logic operation. |
| O | Overflow | Indicates an arithmetic overflow after an addition or subtraction. |

## Branch-Oriented Instructions

The PowerPC supports the usual unconditional and conditional branch capabilities. Conditional branch instructions test a single bit of the condition register for true, false, or don't care and the contents of the count register for zero, nonzero, or don't care. Thus, there are nine separate conditions that can be defined for the conditional branch instruction. If the count register is tested for zero or nonzero, then it is decremented by 1 prior to the test. This is convenient for setting up iteration loops.

**TABLE 9.9   Pentium Conditions for Conditional Jump and SETcc Instructions**

| Symbol | Condition Tested | Comment |
|---|---|---|
| A, NBE | C=0 AND Z=0 | Above; Not below or equal (greater than, unsigned) |
| AE, NB, NC | C=0 | Above or equal; Not below (greater than or equal, unsigned); Not carry |
| B, NAE, C | C=1 | Below; Not above or equal (less than, unsigned); Carry set |
| BE, NA | C=1 OR Z=1 | Below or equal; Not above (less than or equal, unsigned) |
| E, Z | Z=1 | Equal; Zero (signed or unsigned) |
| G, NLE | [(S=1 AND O=1) OR (S=0 and O=0)] AND [Z=0] | Greater than; Not less than or equal (signed) |
| GE, NL | (S=1 AND O=1) OR (S=0 AND O=0) | Greater than or equal; Not less than (signed) |
| L, NGE | (S=1 AND O=0) OR (S=0 AND O=1) | Less than; Not greater than or equal (signed) |
| LE, NG | (S=1 AND O=0) OR (S=0 AND O=1) OR (Z=1) | Less than or equal; Not greater than (signed) |
| NE, NZ | Z=0 | Not equal; Not zero (signed or unsigned) |
| NO | O=0 | No overflow |
| NS | S=0 | Not sign (not negative) |
| NP, PO | P=0 | Not parity; Parity odd |
| O | O=1 | Overflow |
| P | P=1 | Parity; Parity even |
| S | S=1 | Sign (negative) |

## TABLE 9.10 PowerPC Operation Types (with Examples of Typical Operations)

| Instruction | Description |
|---|---|
| *Branch-Oriented* | |
| b | Unconditional branch |
| bl | Branch to target address and place effective address of instruction following the branch into the Link Register. |
| bc | Branch conditional on Count Register and/or on bit in Condition Register |
| sc | System call to invoke an operating system service |
| trap | Compare two operands and invoke system trap handler if specified conditions are met |
| *Load/Store* | |
| lwzu | Load word and zero extend to left; update source register |
| ld | Load doubleword |
| lmw | Load multiple word; load consecutive words into contiguous registers from the target register through general-purpose register 31 |
| lswx | Load a string of bytes into registers beginning with target register; four bytes per register; wrap around from register 31 to register 0 |
| *Integer Arithmetic* | |
| add | Add contents of two registers and place in third register |
| subf | Subtract contents of two registers and place in third register |
| mullw | Multiply low-order 32-bit contents of two registers and place 64-bit product in third register |
| divd | Divide 64-bit contents of two registers and place in quotient in third register |
| *Logical and Shift* | |
| cmp | Compare two operands and set four condition bits in the specified condition register field |
| crand | Condition register AND: two bits of the Condition Register are ANDed and the result placed in one of the two bit positions |
| and | AND contents of two registers and place in third register |
| cntlzd | Count number of consecutive 0 bits starting at bit zero in source register and place count in destination register |
| rldic | Rotate left doubleword register, AND with mask, and store in destination register |
| sld | Shift left bits in source register and store in destination register |
| *Floating-Point* | |
| lfs | Load 32-bit floating-point number from memory, convert to 64-bit format, and store in floating-point register |
| fadd | Add contents of two registers and place in third register |
| fmadd | Multiply contents of two registers, add the contents of a third, and place result in fourth register |
| fcmpu | Compare two floating-point operands and set condition bits |
| *Cache Management* | |
| dcbf | Data cache block flush; perform lookup in cache on specified target address and perform flushing operation |
| icbi | Instruction cache block invalidate |

Branch instructions can also indicate that the address of the location following the branch is to be placed in the link register, described in Chapter 13. This facilitates call/return processing.

### Load/Store Instructions

In the PowerPC architecture, only load and store instructions access memory locations; arithmetic and logical instructions are performed only on registers. This is characteristic of RISC design, and it is explored further in Chapter 12.

There are two features that characterize the different load/store instructions:

- *Data Size:* Data can be transferred in units of byte, halfword, word, or doubleword. Instructions are also available for loading or storing a string of bytes into or from multiple registers.
- *Sign Extension:* For halfword and word loads, the unused bits to the left in the 64-bit destination register are either filled with zeros or with the sign bit of the loaded quantity.

## 9.4

## ASSEMBLY LANGUAGE

A CPU can understand and execute machine instructions. Such instructions are simply binary numbers stored in the computer. If a programmer wished to program directly in machine language, then it would be necessary to enter the program as binary data.

Consider the simple BASIC statement

N = I + J + K

Suppose we wished to program this statement in machine language and to initialize I, J, and K to 2, 3, and 4, respectively. This is shown in Figure 9.11a. The program starts in location 101 (hexadecimal). Memory is reserved for the four variables starting at location 201. The program consists of four instructions:

1.  Load the contents of location 201 into the AC.
2.  Add the contents of location 202 to the AC.
3.  Add the contents of location 203 to the AC.
4.  Store the contents of the AC in location 204.

This is clearly a tedious and very error-prone process.

A slight improvement is to write the program in hexadecimal rather than binary notation (Figure 9.11b). We could write the program as a series of lines. Each line contains the address of a memory location and the hexadecimal code of the binary value to be stored in that location. Then we need a program that will accept this input, translate each line into a binary number, and store it in the specified location.

This is only a slight improvement. To do much better, we can make use of the symbolic name or mnemonic of each instruction. Let us use that instead of the

| Address | Contents |      |      |      |
| ------- | -------- | ---- | ---- | ---- |
| 101     | 0010     | 0010 | 0000 | 0001 |
| 102     | 0001     | 0010 | 0000 | 0010 |
| 103     | 0001     | 0010 | 0000 | 0011 |
| 104     | 0011     | 0010 | 0000 | 0100 |
|         |          |      |      |      |
| 201     | 0000     | 0000 | 0000 | 0010 |
| 202     | 0000     | 0000 | 0000 | 0011 |
| 203     | 0000     | 0000 | 0000 | 0100 |
| 204     | 0000     | 0000 | 0000 | 0000 |

(a) Binary Program

| 101 | LDA | 201 |
| --- | --- | --- |
| 102 | ADD | 202 |
| 103 | ADD | 203 |
| 104 | STA | 204 |
|     |     |     |
| 201 | DAT | 2   |
| 202 | DAT | 3   |
| 203 | DAT | 4   |
| 204 | DAT | 0   |

(c) Symbolic Program

| Address | Contents |
| ------- | -------- |
| 101     | 2201     |
| 102     | 1202     |
| 103     | 1203     |
| 104     | 3204     |
|         |          |
| 201     | 0002     |
| 202     | 0003     |
| 203     | 0004     |
| 204     | 0000     |

(b) Hexadecimal Program

| Label  | Operation | Opened |
| ------ | --------- | ------ |
| FORMUL | LDA       | I      |
|        | ADD       | J      |
|        | ADD       | K      |
|        | STA       | N      |
|        |           |        |
| I      | DATA      | 2      |
| J      | DATA      | 3      |
| K      | DATA      | 4      |
| N      | DATA      | 0      |

(d) Assembly Program

**FIGURE 9.11.  Computation of the formula N = I + J + K**

actual opcode. This results in the *symbolic program* shown in Figure 9.11c. Each line of input still represents one memory location. Each line consists of three fields, separated by spaces. The first field contains the address of a location. For an instruction, the second field contains the three-letter symbol for the opcode. If it is a memory-referencing instruction, then a third field contains the address. To store arbitrary data in a location, we invent a *pseudoinstruction* with the symbol DAT. This is merely an indication that the third field on the line contains a hexadecimal number to be stored in the location specified in the first field.

For this type of input we need a slightly more complex program. The program accepts each line of input, generates a binary number based on the second and third (if present) fields, and stores it in the location specified by the first field.

The use of a symbolic program makes life much easier but is still awkward. In particular, we must give an absolute address for each word. This means that the program and data can be loaded into only one place in memory, and we must know that place ahead of time. Worse, suppose we wish to change the program some day by adding or deleting a line. This will change the addresses of all subsequent words.

A much better system, and one commonly used, is to use symbolic addresses. This is illustrated in Figure 9.11d. Each line still consists of three fields. The first field is still for the address, but a symbol is used instead of an absolute numerical address. Some lines have no address, implying that the address of that line is one more than the address of the previous line. For memory-reference instructions, the third field also contains a symbolic address.

With this last refinement, we have invented an *assembly language*. Programs written in assembly language (assembly programs) are translated into machine language by an *assembler*. This program must not only do the symbolic translation discussed earlier, but also assign some form of memory addresses to symbolic addresses.

The development of assembly language was a major milestone in the evolution of computer technology. It was the first step to the high-level languages in use today. Although few programmers use assembly language, virtually all machines provide one. They are used, if at all, for systems programs such as compilers and I/O routines.

## 9.5

## RECOMMENDED READING

A number of textbooks provide good coverage of machine language and instruction set design, including [HENN90], [TANE90], and [HAYE88]. The Pentium instruction set is well covered by [BREY95] and [DEWA90]. The PowerPC instruction set is covered in [IBM94] and [WEIS94].

BREY95   Brey, B. *The Intel 32-Bit Microprocessors: 80386, 80486, and Pentium.* Englewood Cliffs, NJ: Prentice Hall, 1995.

DEWA90   Dewar, R., and Smosna, M. *Microprocessors: A Programmer's View.* New York: McGraw-Hill, 1990.

HAYE88   Hayes, J. *Computer Architecture and Organization, Second Edition.* New York: McGraw-Hill, 1988.

HENN90   Hennessy, J., and Patterson, D. *Computer Architecture: A Quantitative Approach.* San Mateo, CA: Morgan Kaufmann, 1990.

IBM94   International Business Machines, Inc. *The PowerPC Architecture: A Specification for a New Family of RISC Processors.* San Francisco, CA: Morgan-Kaufmann, 1994.

TANE90   Tanenbaum, A. *Structured Computer Organization.* Englewood Cliffs, NJ: Prentice-Hall, 1990.

WEIS94   Weiss, S., and Smith, J. *POWER and PowerPC.* San Francisco: Morgan Kaufmann, 1994.

## 9.6

## PROBLEMS

9.1   Many CPUs provide logic for performing arithmetic on packed decimal numbers. Although the rules for decimal arithmetic are similar to those for binary operations, the decimal results may require some corrections to the individual digits if binary logic is used.

Consider the decimal addition of two unsigned numbers. If each number consists of $N$ digits, then there are $4N$ bits in each number. The two numbers are to be added using a binary adder. Suggest a simple rule for correcting the result. Perform addition in this fashion on the numbers 1698 and 1786.

9.2 The ten's complement of the decimal number $X$ is defined to be $10^N - X$, where $N$ is the number of decimal digits in the number. Describe the use of ten's complement representation to perform decimal subtraction. Illustrate the procedure by subtracting $(0326)_{10}$ from $(0736)_{10}$.

9.3 It was stated that the instruction set defines many of the functions performed by the CPU. List some CPU functions not dependent on instruction set design.

9.4 Compare zero-, one-, two-, and three-address machines by writing programs to compute

$$X = (A + B \times C)/(D - E \times F)$$

for each of the four machines. The instructions available for use are

| 0 Address | 1 Address | 2 Address | 3 Address |
|---|---|---|---|
| PUSH M | LOAD M | MOV(X ← Y) | MOV(X ← Y) |
| POP M | STORE M | ADD(X ← X + Y) | ADD(X ← Y + Z) |
| ADD | ADD M | SUB(X ← X − Y) | SUB(X ← Y − Z) |
| SUB | SUB M | MUL(X ← X ∗ Y) | MUL(X ← Y ∗ Z) |
| MUL | MUL M | DIV(X ← X/Y) | DIV(X ← Y/Z) |
| DIV | DIV M | | |

9.5 Consider a hypothetical computer with an instruction set of only two $n$-bit instructions. The first bit specifies the opcode, and the remaining bits specify one of the $2^{n-1}$ $n$-bit words of main memory. The two instructions are

SUBS X    Subtract the contents of location X from the accumulator, and store the result in location X and in the accumulator.

JUMP X    Place address X in the program counter.

A word in main memory may contain either an instruction or a binary number in two's complement notation. Demonstrate that this instruction repertoire is reasonably complete by specifying how the following operations can be programmed:

(a) Data Transfer: Location X to accumulator, accumulator to location X
(b) Addition: Add contents of location X to accumulator
(c) Conditional Branching
(d) Logical OR
(e) I/O Operations

9.6 Many instruction sets contain the instruction NOOP, meaning no operation, which has no effect on the CPU state other than incrementing the program counter. Suggest some uses of this instruction.

9.7 Suppose a stack is to be used by the CPU to manage subroutine calls and returns. Can the program counter be eliminated by using the top of the stack as a program counter?

9.8 Appendix 9A points out that there are no stack-oriented instructions in an instruction set if the stack is to be used only by the CPU for such purposes as subroutine handling. How can the CPU use a stack for any purpose without stack-oriented instructions?

9.9 Convert the following formulas from reverse Polish to infix:
   (a) AB + C + D *
   (b) AB/CD/ +
   (c) ABCDE + * * /
   (d) ABCDE + F/ + G – H/ * +

9.10 Convert the following formulas from infix to reverse Polish:
   (a) A + B + C + D + E
   (b) (A + B) * (C + D) + E
   (c) (A * B) + (C * D) + E
   (d) (A – B) * ((((C – D * E)/F)/G) * H

9.11 Convert the expression A + B – C to postfix notation using Dijkstra's algorithm. Show the steps involved. Is the result equivalent to (A + B) – C or A + (B – C)? Does it matter?

9.12 In the IBM S/360 and S/370 architectures, each byte of main memory has a unique address. The original IBM S/360 architecture requires that the operands in memory be *boundary aligned*; that is, a 2-byte operand has to start at an address that is a multiple of 2, a 4-byte operand has to start at an address that is a multiple of 4, and an 8-byte operand has to start at an address that is a multiple of 8. Starting with the IBM 360/85 and continuing in the IBM 370 series, this alignment restriction was removed. Later, paging was introduced in the S/370 with page sizes of 2048 or 4096 bytes (aligned on 2K or 4K address boundaries). Discuss how nonaligned operands and page-fault checking interact to slow down *all* memory references on these later machines.

9.13 The Pentium architecture includes an instruction called Decimal Adjust after Addition (DAA). DAA performs the following sequence of instructions:

**if** ((AL AND 0FH) > 9) OR (AF + 1) **then**
   AL ← AL + 6;
   AF ← 1;
**else**
   AF ← 0;
**endif:**
**if** ((AL > 9FH) OR (CF = 1) **then**
   AL ← AL + 60H;
   CF ← 1;
**else**
   CF ← 0;
**endif:**

"H" indicates hexadecimal. AL is an 8-bit register that holds the result of addition of two unsigned 8-bit integers. AF is a flag set if there is a carry from bit 3 to bit 4 in the result of an addition. CF is a flag set if there is a carry from bit 7 to bit 8. Explain the function performed by the DAA instruction.

9.14 The Pentium Compare instruction (CMP) subtracts the source operand from the destination operand; it updates the status flags (C, P, A, Z, S, O) but does not alter either of the operands. The CMP instruction may be followed by a conditional Jump (Jcc) or Set Condition (SETcc) instruction, where cc refers to one of the 16 conditions listed in Table 9.9. Demonstrate that the conditions tested for a signed number comparison are correct.

9.15 Most microprocessor instruction sets include an instruction that tests a condition and sets a destination operand if the condition is true. Examples include the SETcc on the Pentium, the Scc on the Motorola MC68000, and the Scond on the National NS32000.

(a) There are a few differences among these instructions:
- SETcc and Scc operate only on a byte, whereas Scond operates on byte, word, and doubleword operands.
- SETcc and Scond set the operand to integer one if true and to zero if false. Scc sets the byte to all binary ones if true and all zeros if false.

What are the relative advantages and disadvantages of these differences?

(b) None of these instructions set any of the condition code flags, and thus an explicit test of the result of the instruction is required to determine its value. Discuss whether condition codes should be set as a result of this instruction.

(c) A simple IF statement such as IF a > b THEN can be implemented using a numerical representation method, that is, making the Boolean value manifest, as opposed to a *flow of control* method, which represents the value of a Boolean expression by a point reached in the program. A compiler might implement IF a > b THEN with the following 80×86 code:

```
         SUB    CX, CX      ;set register CX to 0
         MOV    AX, B       ;move contents of location B to register AX
         CMP    AX, A       ;compare contents of register AX and location A
         JLE    TEST        ;jump if A ≤ B
         INC    CX          ;add 1 to contents of register CX
TEST     JCXZ   OUT         ;jump if contents of CX equal 0
THEN

OUT
```

The result of (A > B) is a Boolean value held in a register and available later on, outside the context of the flow of code shown above. It is convenient to use register CX for this, because many of the branch and loop opcodes have a built-in test for CX.

Show an alternative implementation using the SETcc instruction that saves memory and execution time (Hint: no additional new 80x86 instructions are needed, other than the SETcc).

(d) Now consider the high-level language statement:

A: = (B > C) OR (D = F)

A compiler might generate the following code:

```
        MOV   EAX, B      ;move from location B to register EAX
        CMP   EAX, C
        MOV   BL, 0        ;0 represents false
        JLE   N1
        MOV   BL, 1        ;1 represents true
N1:     MOV   EAX, D
        CMP   EAX, F
        MOV   BH, 0
        JNE   N2
        MOV   BH, 1
N2:     OR    BL, BH
```

Show an alternative implementation using the SETcc instruction that saves memory and execution time.

9.16 Redraw the little-endian layout in Figure 9.18 so that the bytes appear as numbered in the big-endian layout. That is, show memory in 64-bit rows, with the bytes listed left-to-right, top-to-bottom.

9.17 For the following data structures, draw the big-endian and little-endian layouts, using the format of Figure 9.18, and comment on the results.

**(a)** struct {
    double i;   //0x1112131415161718
  } s1;
**(b)** struct {
    int i;      //0x11121314
    int j;      //0x15161718
  } s2;
**(c)** struct {
    short i;    //0x1112
    short j;    //0x1314
    short k;   //0x1516
    short l;    //0x1718
  } s3;

9.18 The PowerPC architecture specification does not dictate how a processor should implement little-endian mode. It specifies only the view of memory a processor must have when operating in little-endian mode. When converting a data structure from big-endian to little-endian, processors are free to implement a true byte-swapping mechanism or to use some sort of an address modification mechanism. Current PowerPC processors are all default big-endian machines and use address modification to treat data as little-endian.

Consider the structure s defined in Figure 9.18. The layout in the lower-right portion of the figure shows the structure s as seen by the processor. In fact, if structure s is compiled in little-endian mode, its layout in memory is shown in Figure 9.12. Explain the mapping that is involved, describe an easy way to implement the mapping, and discuss the effectiveness of this approach.

**Little-endian Address Mapping**

| Byte Address | | | | | | | | |
|---|---|---|---|---|---|---|---|---|
| | | | | | **11** | **12** | **13** | **14** |
| 00 | 00 | 01 | 02 | 03 | 04 | 05 | 06 | 07 |
| | **21** | **22** | **23** | **24** | **25** | **26** | **27** | **28** |
| 08 | 08 | 09 | 0A | 0B | 0C | 0D | 0E | 0F |
| | **'D'** | **'C'** | **'B'** | **'A'** | **31** | **32** | **33** | **34** |
| 10 | 10 | 11 | 12 | 13 | 14 | 15 | 16 | 17 |
| | | | **51** | **52** | | **'G'** | **'F'** | **'E'** |
| 18 | 18 | 19 | 1A | 1B | 1C | 1D | 1E | 1F |
| | | | | | **61** | **62** | **63** | **64** |
| 20 | 20 | 21 | 22 | 23 | 24 | 25 | 26 | 27 |

**FIGURE 9.12.  PowerPC Little-Endian Structures in Memory**

## APPENDIX 9A

### *Stacks*

A *stack* is an ordered set of elements, only one of which can be accessed at a time. The point of access is called the *top* of the stack. The number of elements in the stack, or *length* of the stack, is variable. Items may only be added to or deleted from the top of the stack. For this reason, a stack is also known as a *pushdown list* or a *last-in-first-out (LIFO) list.*

The simplest way of explaining stack structure and operation is by illustration. Figure 9.13 shows the basic operations that can be performed. We begin at some point in time when the stack contains some number of elements. A PUSH operation appends one new item to the top of the stack. A POP operation removes the top item from the stack. In both cases, the top of the stack moves accordingly. In addition, binary operations, which require two operands (e.g., multiply, divide, add, subtract), use the top two stack items as operands, pop both items, and push the result back onto the stack. Unary operations, which require only one operand (e.g., logical NOT), use the item on the top of the stack. All of these operations are summarized in Table 9.11.

### *9A.1  Stack Implementation*

The stack is a useful structure to provide as part of a CPU implementation. One use, discussed in Section 9.3, is to manage subroutine calls and returns. Stacks

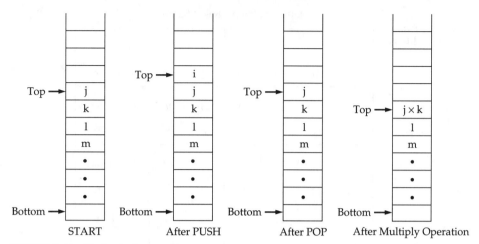

**FIGURE 9.13.  Basic stack operations**

may also be useful to the programmer. An example of this is expression evaluation, discussed later in this section.

The implementation of a stack depends in part on its potential uses. If it is desired to make stack operations available to the programmer, then the instruction set will include stack-oriented operations, including PUSH, POP, and operations that use the top one or two stack elements as operands. Since all of these operations refer to a unique location, namely the top of the stack, the address of the operand or operands is implicit and need not be included in the instruction. These are the zero-address instructions referred to in Section 9.1.

If the stack mechanism is to be used only by the CPU, for such purposes as subroutine handling, then there will not be explicit stack-oriented instructions in the instruction set. In either case, the implementation of a stack requires that there be some set of locations used to store the stack elements. A typical approach is illustrated in Figure 9.14a. A contiguous block of locations is reserved in main memory (or virtual memory) for the stack. Most of the time, the block is partially filled with stack elements and the remainder is available for stack growth. Three addresses are needed for proper operation, and these are often stored in CPU registers:

- *Stack Pointer:* Contains the address of the top of the stack. If an item is appended to or deleted from the stack, the pointer is incremented or decremented to contain the address of the new top of the stack.

**TABLE 9.11    Stack-Oriented Operations**

| | |
|---|---|
| PUSH | Append a new element on the top of the stack. |
| POP | Delete the top element of the stack. |
| Unary operation | Perform operation on top element of stack. Replace top element with result. |
| Binary operation | Perform operation on top two elements of stack. Delete top two elements of stack. Place result of operation on top of stack. |

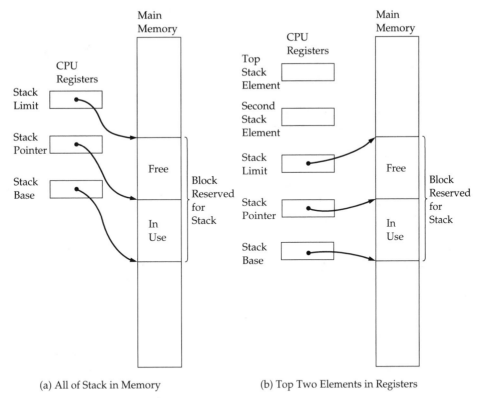

(a) All of Stack in Memory                     (b) Top Two Elements in Registers

**FIGURE 9.14. Typical stack organizations**

- *Stack Base:* Contains the address of the bottom location in the reserved block. If an attempt is made to POP when the stack is empty, an error is reported.
- *Stack Limit:* Contains the address of the other end of the reserved block. If an attempt is made to PUSH when the block is fully utilized for the stack, an error is reported.

To speed up stack operations, the top two stack elements are often stored in registers, as shown in Figure 9.14b. In this case, the stack pointer contains the address of the third element of the stack.

## 9A.2  *Expression Evaluation*

Mathematical formulas are usually expressed in what is known as *infix* notation. In this form, a binary operation appears between the operands (e.g., a + b). For complex expressions, parentheses are used to determine the order of evaluation of expressions. For example, a + (b × c) will yield a different result than (a + b) × c. To minimize the use of parentheses, operations have an implied precedence. Generally, multiplication takes precedence over addition, so that a + b × c is equivalent to a + (b × c).

An alternative technique is known as *reverse Polish,* or postfix, notation. In this notation, the operator follows its two operands. For example,

a + b          becomes   ab +
a + (b × c)    becomes   abc × +
(a + b) × c    becomes   ab + c ×

Note that, regardless of the complexity of an expression, no parentheses are required when using reverse Polish.

The advantage of postfix notation is that an expression in this form is easily evaluated using a stack. An expression in postfix notation is scanned from left to right. For each element of the expression, the following rules are applied.

1. If the element is a variable or constant, push it onto the stack.
2. If the element is an operator, pop the top two items of the stack, perform the operation, and push the result.

After the entire expression has been scanned, the result is on the top of the stack.

The simplicity of this algorithm makes it a convenient one for evaluating expressions. Accordingly, many compilers will take an expression in a high-level language, convert it to postfix notation, and then generate the machine instructions from that notation. Figure 9.15 shows the sequence of machine instructions for evaluating f = (a − b)/(c + d * e) using stack-oriented instructions. The figure also shows the use of one-address and two-address instructions. Note that, even though the stack-oriented rules were not used in the last two cases, the postfix notation served as a guide for generating the machine instructions. The sequence of events for the stack program is shown in Figure 9.16.

| | Stack | General Registers | Single Register |
|---|---|---|---|
| | Push a | Load G[1], a | Load d |
| | Push b | Subtract G[1], b | Multiply e |
| | Subtract | Load G[2], d | Add c |
| | Push c | Multiply G[2], e | Store f |
| | Push d | Add G[2], c | Load a |
| | Push e | Divide G[1], G[2] | Subtract b |
| | Multiply | Store G[1], f | Divide f |
| | Add | | Store f |
| | Divide | | |
| | Pop f | | |
| Number of Instructions | 10 | 7 | 8 |
| Memory Access | 10 op + 6 d | 7 op + 6 d | 8 op + 8 d |

**FIGURE 9.15. Comparison of three programs to calculate f = (a − b)/(c + d × e)**

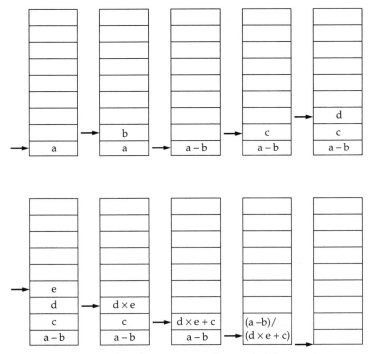

**FIGURE 9.16.  Use of stack to compute f = (a − b)/(d × e + c)**

The process of converting an infix expression to a postfix expression is itself most easily accomplished using a stack. The following algorithm is due to Dijkstra [DIJK63]. The infix expression is scanned from left to right, and the postfix expression is developed and output during the scan. The steps are as follows:

1. Examine the next element in the input.
2. If it is an operand, output it.
3. If it is an opening parenthesis, push it onto the stack.
4. If it is an operator, then

> If the top of the stack is an opening parenthesis, then push the operator.
> If it has higher priority than the top of the stack (multiply and divide have higher priority than add and subtract) then push the operator.
> Else, pop operation from stack to output, and repeat step 4.

5. If it is a closing parenthesis, pop operators to the output until an opening parenthesis is encountered. Pop and discard the opening parenthesis.
6. If there is more input, go to step 1.
7. If there is no more input, unstack the remaining operands.

Figure 9.17 illustrates the use of this algorithm. This example should give the reader some feel for the power of stack-based algorithms.

| Input | Output | Stack (top on right) |
|---|---|---|
| A + B * C + (D + E) * F | empty | empty |
| + B * C + (D + E) * F | A | empty |
| B * C + (D + E) * F | A | + |
| * C + (D + E) * F | A B | + |
| C + (D + E) * F | A B | + * |
| + (D + E) * F | A B C | + * |
| (D + E) * F | A B C * + | + |
| D + E) * F | A B C * + | + ( |
| + E) * F | A B C * + D | + ( |
| E) * F | A B C * + D | + ( + |
| ) * F | A B C * + D E | + ( + |
| * F | A B C * + D E + | + |
| F | A B C * + D E + | + * |
| empty | A B C * + D E + F | + * |
| empty | A B C * + D E + F * + | |

**FIGURE 9.17. Conversion of an expression from infix to postfix notation**

## APPENDIX 9B

## *Little-, Big-, and Bi-Endian*

An annoying and curious phenomenon relates to how the bytes within a word and the bits within a byte are both referenced and represented. We look first at the problem of byte ordering, then consider that of bits.

### *9B.1 Byte Ordering*

The concept of endianness was first discussed in the literature by Cohen [COHE81]. With respect to bytes, endianness has to do with the byte ordering of multibyte scalar values. The issue is best introduced with an example. Suppose that we have the 32-bit hexadecimal value 12345678 and that it is stored in a 32-bit word in byte-addressable memory at byte location 184. The value consists of four bytes, with the least significant byte containing the value 78 and the most significant byte containing the value 12. There are two ways to store this value:

| Address | Value |   | Address | Value |
|---|---|---|---|---|
| 184 | 12 |   | 184 | 78 |
| 185 | 34 |   | 185 | 56 |
| 186 | 56 |   | 186 | 34 |
| 187 | 78 |   | 187 | 12 |

The mapping on the left stores the most significant byte in the lowest numerical byte address; this is known as big-endian, and it is equivalent to the left-to-right order of writing in western-culture languages. The mapping on the right stores the least significant byte in the lowest numerical byte address; this is known as little-endian, and it is reminiscent of the right-to-left order of arithmetic operations in arithmetic units.[2] For a given multibyte scalar value, big-endian and little-endian are byte-reversed mappings of each other.

The concept of endianness arises when it is necessary to treat a multiple-byte entity as a single data item with a single address, even though it is composed of smaller addressable units. Some machines, such as the Intel 80x86, Pentium, and VAX, are little-endian machines, whereas others, such as the IBM System 370, the Motorola 680x0, and most RISC machines, are big-endian. This presents problems when data are transferred from a machine of one endian type to the other, and when a programmer attempts to manipulate individual bytes or bits within a multibyte scalar.

The property of endianness does not extend beyond an individual data unit. In any machine, aggregates such as files, data structures, and arrays are composed of multiple data units, each with endianness. Thus, conversion of a block of memory from one style of endianness to the other requires knowledge of the data structure.

Figure 9.18 illustrates how endianness determines addressing and byte order. The C structure at the top contains a number of data types. The memory layout in the lower left results from compilation of that structure for a big-endian machine, and that in the lower right for a little-endian machine. In each case, memory is depicted as a series of 64-bit rows. For the big-endian case, memory is laid out left-to-right, top-to-bottom, whereas for the little-endian case, memory is laid out right-to-left, top-to-bottom. Note that these layouts are arbitrary. Either scheme could use either left-to-right or right-to-left within a row; this is a matter of depiction, not memory assignment. In fact, in looking at programming manuals for a variety of machines, a bewildering collection of depictions is to be found, even within the same manual.

We can make several observations about this data structure:

- Each data item has the same address in both schemes. For example, the address of the doubleword with hexadecimal value 2122232425262728 is 08.
- Within any given multibyte scalar value, the ordering of bytes in the little-endian structure is the reverse of that in the big-endian structure.
- Endianness does not affect the ordering of data items within a structure. Thus, the four-character word c exhibits byte reversal, but the seven-character byte array d does not. Hence, the address of each individual element of d is the same in both structures.

The effect of endianness is perhaps more clearly demonstrated when we view memory as a vertical array of bytes, as shown in Figure 9.19.

There is no general consensus as to which is the superior style of endianness.[3] The following points favor the big-endian style:

---

[2]The terms *big-endian* and *little-endian* come from Part I, Chapter 4 of Jonathan Swift's *Gulliver's Travels*. They refer to a religious war between two groups, one that breaks eggs at the big end and the other that breaks eggs at the little end.

[3]The prophet revered by both groups in the Endian wars of *Gulliver's Travels* has this to say: "All true Believers shall break their Eggs at the convenient End." Not much help!

```
Struct {
    int     a ;       //0×1112_1314                      word
    int     pad ;
    double  b ;       //0×2122_2324_2526_2728            doubleword
    char*   c ;       //0×3132_3334                      word
    char    d [7] ;   //'A' , 'B' , 'C' , 'D' , 'E' , 'F' , 'G' byte array
    short   e ;       //0×5152                           halfword
    int     f ;       //0×6162_6364                      word
} s ;
```

**Big-endian Address Mapping**

| Byte Address | | | | | | | | |
|---|---|---|---|---|---|---|---|---|
| 00 | **11** | **12** | **13** | **14** | | | | |
| | 00 | 01 | 02 | 03 | 04 | 05 | 06 | 07 |
| 08 | **21** | **22** | **23** | **24** | **25** | **26** | **27** | **28** |
| | 08 | 09 | 0A | 0B | 0C | 0D | 0E | 0F |
| 10 | **31** | **32** | **33** | **34** | **'A'** | **'B'** | **'C'** | **'D'** |
| | 10 | 11 | 12 | 13 | 14 | 15 | 16 | 17 |
| 18 | **'E'** | **'F'** | **'G'** | | **51** | **52** | | |
| | 18 | 19 | 1A | 1B | 1C | 1D | 1E | 1F |
| 20 | **61** | **62** | **63** | **64** | | | | |
| | 20 | 21 | 22 | 23 | | | | |

**Little-endian Address Mapping**

| | | | | | | | | Byte Address |
|---|---|---|---|---|---|---|---|---|
| | | | | **11** | **12** | **13** | **14** | 00 |
| 07 | 06 | 05 | 04 | 03 | 02 | 01 | 00 | |
| **21** | **22** | **23** | **24** | **25** | **26** | **27** | **28** | 08 |
| 0F | 0E | 0D | 0C | 0B | 0A | 09 | 08 | |
| **'D'** | **'C'** | **'B'** | **'A'** | **31** | **32** | **33** | **34** | 10 |
| 17 | 16 | 15 | 14 | 13 | 12 | 11 | 10 | |
| | **51** | **52** | | **'G'** | **'F'** | **'E'** | | 18 |
| 1F | 1E | 1D | 1C | 1B | 1A | 19 | 18 | |
| | | | | **61** | **62** | **63** | **64** | 20 |
| | | | | 23 | 22 | 21 | 20 | |

FIGURE 9.18. Example C Data Structure and its Endian Maps [IBM94]

- *Character-String Sorting:* A big-endian processor is faster in comparing integer-aligned character strings; the integer ALU can compare multiple bytes in parallel.
- *Decimal/ASCII Dumps:* All values can be printed left to right without causing confusion.
- *Consistent Order:* Big-endian processors store their integers and character strings in the same order (most significant byte comes first).

The following points favor the little-endian style:

- *Integer Address Conversion:* A big-endian processor has to perform addition when it converts a 32-bit integer address to a 16-bit integer address, in order to use the least significant bytes.
- *Arithmetic:* It is easier to perform higher-precision arithmetic with the little-endian style; you don't have to find the least significant byte and move backwards.

The differences are minor, and the choice of endian style is often more a matter of accommodating previous machines than anything else.

The PowerPC is a bi-endian processor that supports both big-endian and little-endian modes. The bi-endian architecture enables software developers to choose either mode when migrating operating systems and applications from other machines. The operating system establishes the endian mode in which processes execute. Once a mode is selected, all subsequent memory loads and stores are determined by the memory-addressing model of that mode. To support this hardware feature, two bits are maintained in the machine state register (MSR) maintained by the operating system as part of the process state. One bit specifies the

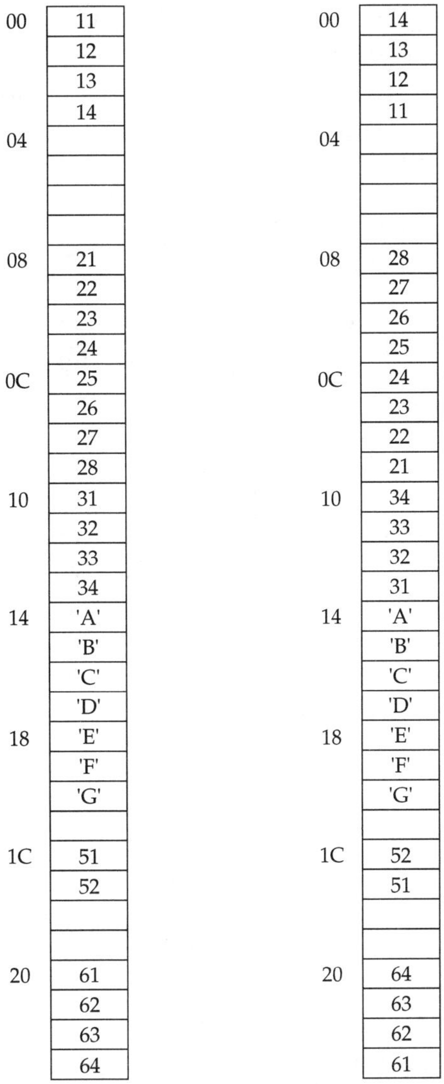

| (a) Big-endian | | (b) Little-endian | |
|---|---|---|---|
| 00 | 11 | 00 | 14 |
|  | 12 |  | 13 |
|  | 13 |  | 12 |
|  | 14 |  | 11 |
| 04 |  | 04 |  |
|  |  |  |  |
|  |  |  |  |
|  |  |  |  |
| 08 | 21 | 08 | 28 |
|  | 22 |  | 27 |
|  | 23 |  | 26 |
|  | 24 |  | 25 |
| 0C | 25 | 0C | 24 |
|  | 26 |  | 23 |
|  | 27 |  | 22 |
|  | 28 |  | 21 |
| 10 | 31 | 10 | 34 |
|  | 32 |  | 33 |
|  | 33 |  | 32 |
|  | 34 |  | 31 |
| 14 | 'A' | 14 | 'A' |
|  | 'B' |  | 'B' |
|  | 'C' |  | 'C' |
|  | 'D' |  | 'D' |
| 18 | 'E' | 18 | 'E' |
|  | 'F' |  | 'F' |
|  | 'G' |  | 'G' |
|  |  |  |  |
| 1C | 51 | 1C | 52 |
|  | 52 |  | 51 |
|  |  |  |  |
|  |  |  |  |
| 20 | 61 | 20 | 64 |
|  | 62 |  | 63 |
|  | 63 |  | 62 |
|  | 64 |  | 61 |

(a) Big-endian          (b) Little-endian

**FIGURE 9.19. Another View of Figure 9.18**

endian mode in which the kernel runs; the other specifies the processor's current operating mode. Thus, mode can be changed on a per-process basis.

## 9B.2  Bit Ordering

In ordering the bits within a byte, we are immediately faced with two questions:

1. Do you count the first bit as bit zero or as bit one?

2. Do you assign the lowest bit number to the byte's least significant bit (little-endian) or to the byte's most significant bit (big-endian)?

These questions are not answered in the same way on all machines. Indeed, on some machines, the answers are different in different circumstances. Furthermore, the choice of big- or little-endian bit ordering within a byte is not always consistent with big- or little-endian ordering of bytes within a multibyte scalar. The programmer needs to be concerned with these issues when manipulating individual bits.

Another area of concern is when data are transmitted over a bit-serial line. When an individual byte is transmitted, does the system transmit the most significant or the least significant bit first? The designer must make certain that incoming bits are handled properly. For a discussion of this issue, see [JAME90].

# CHAPTER 10

# Instruction Sets: Addressing Modes and Formats

In Chapter 9, we focused on *what* an instruction set does. Specifically, we examined the types of operands and operations that may be specified by machine instructions. This chapter turns to the question of *how* to specify the operands and operations of instructions. Two issues arise. First, how is the address of an operand specified, and second, how are the bits of an instruction organized to define the operand addresses and operation of that instruction.

## 10.1

### ADDRESSING

As we have mentioned, the address field or fields in a typical instruction format are quite limited. We would like to be able to reference a large range of locations in main memory or, for some systems, virtual memory. To achieve this objective, a variety of addressing techniques have been employed. They all involve some trade-off between address range and/or addressing flexibility on the one hand, and the number of memory references and/or the complexity of address calculation on the other. In this section, we examine the most common addressing techniques:

- Immediate
- Direct
- Indirect
- Register
- Register Indirect
- Displacement
- Stack

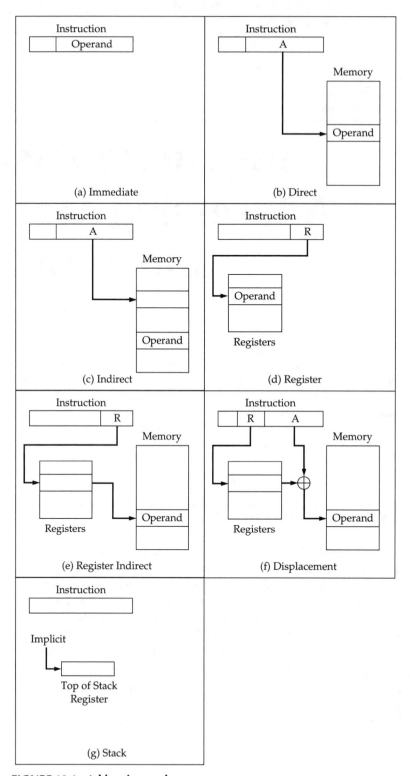

**FIGURE 10.1. Addressing modes**

These modes are illustrated in Figure 10.1. In this section, we use the following notation:

A = contents of the (an) address field in the instruction

EA = actual (effective) address of the location containing the

   referenced operand

(X) = contents of location X

Table 10.1 indicates the address calculation performed for each addressing mode.

Before beginning this discussion, two comments need to be made. First, virtually all computer architectures provide more than one of these addressing modes. The question arises as to how the control unit can determine which address mode is being used in a particular instruction. Several approaches are taken. Often, different opcodes will use different addressing modes. Also, one or more bits in the instruction format can be used as a *mode field*. The value of the mode field determines which addressing mode is to be used.

The second comment concerns the interpretation of the effective address (EA). In a system without virtual memory, the *effective address* will be either a main memory address or a register. In a virtual memory system, the effective address is a virtual address or a register. The actual mapping to a physical address is a function of the paging mechanism and is invisible to the programmer.

## Immediate Addressing

The simplest form of addressing is immediate addressing, in which the operand is actually present in the instruction:

OPERAND = A

This mode can be used to define and use constants or set initial values of variables. Typically, the number will be stored in two's complement form; the leftmost bit of the operand field is used as a sign bit. When the operand is loaded into a data register, the sign bit is extended to the left to the full data word size.

The advantage of immediate addressing is that no memory reference other than the instruction fetch is required to obtain the operand, thus saving one memory or

**TABLE 10.1    Basic Addressing Modes**

| Mode | Algorithm | Principal Advantage | Principal Disadvantage |
|------|-----------|---------------------|------------------------|
| Immediate | Operand = A | No memory reference | Limited operand magnitude |
| Direct | EA = A | Simple | Limited address space |
| Indirect | EA = (A) | Large address space | Multiple memory references |
| Register | EA = R | No memory reference | Limited address space |
| Register indirect | EA = (R) | Large address space | Extra memory reference |
| Displacement | EA = A + (R) | Flexibility | Complexity |
| Stack | EA = top of stack | No memory reference | Limited applicability |

cache cycle in the instruction cycle. The disadvantage is that the size of the number is restricted to the size of the address field, which, in most instruction sets, is small compared with the word length.

## Direct Addressing

A very simple form of addressing is direct addressing, in which the address field contains the effective address of the operand:

EA = A

The technique was common in earlier generations of computers and is still found on a number of small computer systems. It requires only one memory reference and no special calculation. The obvious limitation, mentioned earlier, is that it provides only a limited address space.

## Indirect Addressing

The problem with direct addressing is that the length of the address field is usually less than the word length, thus limiting the address range. One solution is to have the address field refer to the address of a word in memory, which in turn contains a full-length address of the operand. This is known as *indirect addressing:*

EA = (A)

(As defined earlier, the parentheses are to be interpreted as meaning *contents of.*) The obvious advantage of this approach is that for the word length of $N$, an address space of $2^N$ is now available. The disadvantage is that instruction execution requires two memory references to fetch the operand, one to get its address and a second to get its value.

You will note that although the number of words that can be addressed is now equal to $2^N$, the number of different effective addresses that may be referenced at any one time is limited to $2^K$, where $K$ is the length of the address field. Typically, this is not a burdensome restriction, and it can be an asset. In a virtual-memory environment, all the effective address locations can be confined to page 0 of any process. Since the address field of an instruction is small, it will naturally produce low-numbered direct addresses, which would appear in page 0. (The only restriction is that the page size must be greater than or equal to $2^K$.) When a process is active, there will be repeated references to page 0, causing it to remain in real memory. Thus, an indirect memory reference will involve, at most, one page fault rather than two.

A rarely used variant of indirect addressing is multilevel or cascaded indirect addressing:

EA = ( ... (A) ... )

In this case, one bit of a full-word address is an indirect flag (I). If the I bit is 0, then the word contains the EA. If the I bit is 1, then another level of indirection is invoked. There does not appear to be any particular advantage to this approach, and its disadvantage is that three or more memory references could be required to fetch an operand.

## Register Addressing

Register addressing is similar to direct addressing. The only difference is that the address field refers to a register rather than a main memory address:

EA = R

Typically, an address field that references registers will have 3 or 4 bits, so that a total of 8 or 16 general-purpose registers can be referenced.

The advantages of register addressing are that (1) only a small address field is needed in the instruction, and (2) no memory references are required. As was discussed in Chapter 4, the memory access time for a register internal to the CPU is much less than that for a main memory address. The disadvantage of register addressing is that the address space is very limited.

If register addressing is heavily used in an instruction set, this implies that the CPU registers will be heavily used. Because of the severely limited number of registers (compared with main memory locations), their use in this fashion makes sense only if they are employed efficiently. If every operand is brought into a register from main memory, operated on once, and then returned to main memory, then a wasteful intermediate step has been added. If, instead, the operand in a register remains in use for multiple operations, then a real savings is achieved. An example is the intermediate result in a calculation. In particular, suppose that the algorithm for two's complement multiplication were to be implemented in software. The location labeled A in the flowchart (Figure 8.11) is referenced many times and should be implemented in a register rather than a main memory location.

It is up to the programmer to decide which values should remain in registers and which should be stored in main memory. Most modern CPUs employ multiple general-purpose registers, placing a burden for efficient execution on the assembly-language programmer (e.g., compiler writer).

## Register Indirect Addressing

Just as register addressing is analogous to direct addressing, register indirect addressing is analogous to indirect addressing. In both cases, the only difference is whether the address field refers to a memory location or a register. Thus, for register indirect address,

EA = (R)

The advantages and limitations of register indirect addressing are basically the same as for indirect addressing. In both cases, the address space limitation (limited range of addresses) of the address field is overcome by having that field refer to a word-length location containing an address. In addition, register indirect addressing uses one less memory reference than indirect addressing.

## Displacement Addressing

A very powerful mode of addressing combines the capabilities of direct addressing and register indirect addressing. It is known by a variety of names depending upon the context of its use, but the basic mechanism is the same. We will refer to this as *displacement addressing:*

$$EA = A + (R)$$

Displacement addressing requires that the instruction have two address fields, at least one of which is explicit. The value contained in one address field (value = A) is used directly. The other address field, or an implicit reference based on opcode, refers to a register whose contents are added to A to produce the effective address.

We will describe three of the most common uses of displacement addressing:

- Relative Addressing
- Base-Register Addressing
- Indexing

### Relative Addressing

For relative addressing, the implicitly referenced register is the program counter (PC). That is, the current instruction address is added to the address field to produce the EA. Typically, the address field is treated as a two's complement number for this operation. Thus, the effective address is a displacement relative to the address of the instruction.

Relative addressing exploits the concept of locality that was discussed in Chapters 4 and 7. If most memory references are relatively near to the instruction being executed, then the use of relative addressing saves address bits in the instruction.

### Base-Register Addressing

For base-register addressing, the interpretation is the following: The referenced register contains a memory address, and the address field contains a displacement (usually an unsigned integer representation) from that address. The register reference may be explicit or implicit.

Base-register addressing also exploits the locality of memory references. It is a convenient means of implementing segmentation, which was discussed in Chapter 7. In some implementations, a single segment-base register is employed and is used implicitly. In others, the programmer may choose a register to hold the base address of a segment, and the instruction must reference it explicitly. In this latter case, if the length of the address field is $K$ and the number of possible registers is $N$, then one instruction can reference any one of $N$ areas of $2^K$ words.

### Indexing

For indexing, the interpretation is typically the following: The address field references a main memory address, and the referenced register contains a positive displacement from that address. Note that this usage is just the opposite of the interpretation for base-register addressing. Of course, it is more than just a matter of user interpretation. Because the address field is considered to be a memory address in indexing, it generally contains more bits than an address field in a comparable base-register instruction. Also, we shall see that there are some refinements to indexing that would not be as useful in the base-register context. Nevertheless, the method of calculating the EA is the same for both base-register addressing and indexing, and in both cases the register reference is sometimes explicit and sometimes implicit (for different CPU types).

An important use of indexing is to provide an efficient mechanism for performing iterative operations. Consider, for example, a list of numbers stored starting at location A. Suppose that we would like to add 1 to each element on the list. We need to fetch each value, add 1 to it, and store it back. The sequence of effective addresses that we need is A, A + 1, A + 2, . . ., up to the last location on the list. With indexing, this is easily done. The value A is stored in the instruction's address field, and the chosen register, called an *index register,* is initialized to 0. After each operation, the index register is incremented by 1.

Because index registers are commonly used for such iterative tasks, it is typical that there is a need to increment or decrement the index register after each reference to it. Since this is such a common operation, some systems will automatically do this as part of the same instruction cycle. This is known as *autoindexing.* If certain registers are devoted exclusively to indexing, then autoindexing can be invoked implicitly and automatically. If general-purpose registers are used, the autoindex operation may need to be signaled by a bit in the instruction. Autoindexing using increment can be depicted as follows.

$$EA = A + R$$
$$R \leftarrow (R) + 1$$

In some machines, both indirect addressing and indexing are provided, and it is possible to employ both in the same instruction. There are two possibilities: the indexing is performed either before or after the indirection.

If indexing is performed after the indirection, it is termed *postindexing:*

$$EA = (A) + (R)$$

First, the contents of the address field are used to access a memory location containing a direct address. This address is then indexed by the register value. This technique is useful for accessing one of a number of blocks of data of a fixed format. For example, it was described in Chapter 7 that the operating system needs to employ a process control block for each process. The operations performed are the same regardless of which block is being manipulated. Thus, the addresses in the instructions that reference the block could point to a location (value = A) containing a variable pointer to the start of a process control block. The index register contains the displacement within the block.

With *preindexing,* the indexing is performed before the indirection:

$$EA = (A + (R))$$

An address is calculated as with simple indexing. In this case, however, the calculated address contains not the operand, but the address of the operand. An example of the use of this technique is to construct a multiway branch table. At a particular point in a program, there may be a branch to one of a number of locations depending on conditions. A table of addresses can be set up starting at location A. By indexing into this table, the required location can be found.

Normally, an instruction set will not include both preindexing and postindexing.

## Stack Addressing

The final addressing mode that we consider is stack addressing. As defined in Appendix 9A, a stack is a linear array of locations. It is sometimes referred to as a *pushdown list* or *last-in-first-out queue*. The stack is a reserved block of locations. Items are appended to the top of the stack so that, at any given time, the block is partially filled. Associated with the stack is a pointer whose value is the address of the top of the stack. Alternatively, the top two elements of the stack may be in CPU registers, in which case the stack pointer references the third element of the stack (Figure 9.14b). The stack pointer is maintained in a register. Thus, references to stack locations in memory are in fact register indirect addresses.

The stack mode of addressing is a form of implied addressing. The machine instructions need not include a memory reference but implicitly operate on the top of the stack. Stacks have not been common traditionally but are becoming quite common in microprocessors.

## Pentium Addressing Modes

Recall from Figure 7.25 that the Pentium address translation mechanism produces an address, called a virtual or effective address, that is an offset into a segment. The sum of the starting address of the segment and the effective address produces a linear address. If paging is being used, this linear address must pass through a page-translation mechanism to produce a physical address. In what follows, we ignore this last step, since it is transparent to the instruction set and to the programmer.

The Pentium is equipped with a variety of addressing modes intended to allow the efficient execution of high-level languages such as C and FORTRAN. Figure 10.2 indicates the hardware involved. The segment that is the subject of the reference is determined by the segment register. There are six segment registers; the one being used for a particular reference depends on the context of execution and the instruction. Each segment register holds the starting address of the corresponding segment. Associated with each user-visible segment register is a segment descriptor register (not programmer-visible), which records the access rights for the segment, as well as the starting address and limit (length) of the segment. In addition, there are two registers that may be used in constructing an address: the base register and the index register.

Table 10.2 lists the 12 Pentium addressing modes. Let us consider each of these in turn.

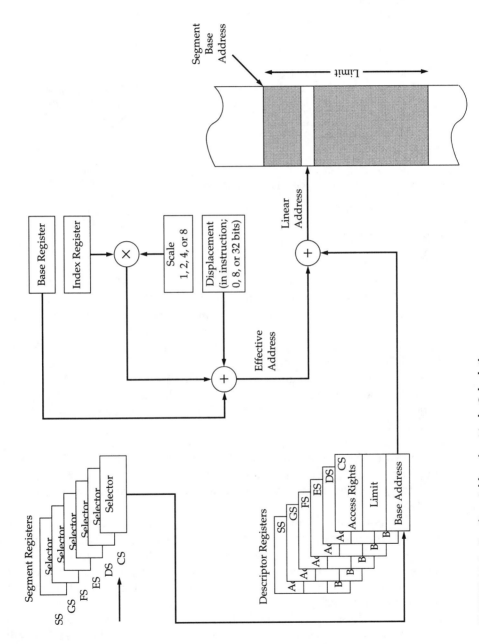

**FIGURE 10.2. Pentium Addressing Mode Calculation**

**TABLE 10.2    Pentium Addressing Modes**

| Mode | Algorithm |
|---|---|
| Immediate | Operand = A |
| Register | LA = R |
| Displacement | LA = (SR) + A |
| Base | LA = (SR) + (B) |
| Base with Displacement | LA = (SR) + (B) + A |
| Scaled Index with Displacement | LA = (SR) + (I) × S + A |
| Base with Index and Displacement | LA = (SR) + (B) + (I) + A |
| Base with Scaled Index and Displacement | LA = (SR) + (I) × S + (B) + A |
| Relative | LA = (PC) + A |

LA = linear address
(X) = contents of X
SR = segment register
PC = program counter
 A = contents of an address field in the instruction
 R = register
 B = base register
 I = index register
 S = scaling factor

For the **immediate mode,** the operand is included in the instruction. The operand can be a byte, word, or doubleword of data.

For **register operand mode,** the operand is located in a register. For general instructions, such as data transfer, arithmetic, and logical instructions, the operand can be one of the 32-bit general registers (EAX, EBX, ECX, EDX, ESI, EDI, ESP, EBP), one of the 16-bit general registers (AX, BX, CX, DX, SI, DI, SP, BP), or one of the 8-bit general registers (AH, BH, CH, DH, AL, BL, CL, DL). For floating-point operations, 64-bit operands are formed by using two 32-bit registers as a pair. There are also some instructions that reference the segment registers (CS, DS, ES, SS, FS, GS).

The remaining addressing modes reference locations in memory. The memory location must be specified in terms of the segment containing the location and the offset from the beginning of the segment. In some cases, a segment is specified explicitly; in others, the segment is specified by simple rules that assign a segment by default.

In the **displacement mode,** the operand's offset (the effective address of Figure 10.2) is contained as part of the instruction as an 8-, 16-, or 32-bit displacement. With segmentation, all addresses in instructions refer merely to an offset in a segment. The displacement addressing mode is found on few machines because, as mentioned earlier, it leads to long instructions. In the case of the Pentium, the displacement value can be as long as 32 bits, making for a 6-byte instruction. Displacement addressing can be useful for referencing global variables.

The remaining addressing modes are indirect, in the sense that the address portion of the instruction tells the processor where to look to find the address. The **base mode** specifies that one of the 8-, 16-, or 32-bit registers contains the effective address. This is equivalent to what we have referred to as register indirect addressing.

In the **base with displacement mode,** the instruction includes a displacement to be added to a base register, which may be any of the general-purpose registers. Examples of uses of this mode:

1. Used by a compiler to point to the start of a local variable area. For example, the base register could point to the beginning of a stack frame, which contains the local variables for the corresponding procedure.
2. Used to index into an array when the element size is not 2, 4, or 8 bytes and which therefore cannot be indexed using an index register. In this case, the displacement points to the beginning of the array, and the base register holds the results of a calculation to determine the offset to a specific element within the array.
3. Used to access a field of a record. The base register points to the beginning of the record, while the displacement is an offset to the field.

In the **scaled index with displacement mode,** the instruction includes a displacement to be added to a register, in this case called an index register. The index register may be any of the general-purpose registers except the one called ESP, which is generally used for stack processing. In calculating the effective address, the contents of the index register are multiplied by a scaling factor of 1, 2, 4, or 8, and then added to a displacement. This mode is very convenient for indexing arrays. A scaling factor of 2 can be used for an array of 16-bit integers. A scaling factor of 4 can be used for 32-bit integers or floating-point numbers. Finally, a scaling factor of 8 can be used for an array of double-precision floating-point numbers.

The **base with index and displacement mode** sums the contents of the base register, the index register, and a displacement to form the effective address. Again, the base register can be any general-purpose register and the index register can be any general-purpose register except ESP. As an example, this addressing mode could be used for accessing a local array on a stack frame. This mode can also be used to support a two-dimensional array; in this case, the displacement points to the beginning of the array, and each register handles one dimension of the array.

The **based scaled index with displacement mode** sums the contents of the index register multiplied by a scaling factor, the contents of the base register, and the displacement. This is useful if an array is stored in a stack frame; in this case, the array elements would be 2, 4, or 8 bytes each in length. This mode also provides efficient indexing of a two-dimensional array when the array elements are 2, 4, or 8 bytes in length.

Finally, **relative addressing** can be used in transfer-of-control instructions. A displacement is added to the value of the program counter, which points to the next instruction. In this case, the displacement is treated as a signed byte, word, or doubleword value, and that value either increases or decreases the address in the program counter.

## PowerPC Addressing Modes

In common with most RISC machines, and unlike the Pentium and most CISC machines, the PowerPC uses a simple and relatively straightforward set of addressing modes. As Table 10.3 indicates, these modes are conveniently classified with respect to the type of instruction.

## Load/Store Addressing

The PowerPC provides two alternative addressing modes for load/store instructions (Figure 10.3). With **indirect addressing,** the instruction includes a 16-bit displacement to be added to a base register, which may be any of the general-purpose registers. In addition, the instruction may specify that the newly computed effective address is to be fed back to the base register, updating the current contents. The update option is useful for progressive indexing of arrays in loops.

The other addressing technique of load/store instructions is **indirect indexed addressing.** In this case, the instruction references a base register and an index register, both of which may be any of the general-purpose registers. The effective address is the sum of the contents of these two registers. Again, the update option causes the base register to be updated to the new effective address.

## Branch Addressing

Three branch addressing modes are provided. When **absolute addressing** is used with unconditional branch instructions, the effective address of the next instruc-

**TABLE 10.3  PowerPC Addressing Modes**

| Mode | Algorithm |
| --- | --- |
| | *Load/Store Addressing* |
| Indirect | EA = (BR) + D |
| Indirect Indexed | EA = (BR) + (IR) |
| | *Branch Addressing* |
| Absolute | EA = I |
| Relative | EA = (PC) + I |
| Indirect | EA = (L/CR) |
| | *Fixed-Point Computation* |
| Register | EA = GPR |
| Immediate | Operand = I |
| | *Floating-Point Computation* |
| Register | EA = FPR |

$$
\begin{aligned}
\text{EA} &= \text{effective address} \\
\text{(X)} &= \text{contents of X} \\
\text{BR} &= \text{base register} \\
\text{IR} &= \text{index register} \\
\text{L/CR} &= \text{link or count register} \\
\text{GPR} &= \text{general-purpose register} \\
\text{FPR} &= \text{floating-point register} \\
\text{D} &= \text{displacement} \\
\text{I} &= \text{immediate value} \\
\text{PC} &= \text{program counter}
\end{aligned}
$$

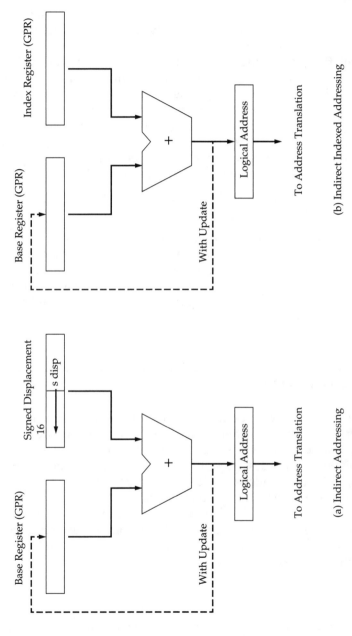

**FIGURE 10.3. PowerPC Memory Operand Addressing Modes [DIEF94a]**

373

tion is derived from a 24-bit immediate value within the instruction. The 24-bit value is extended to a 32-bit value by adding two zeros to its least significant end (this is permissible since all instructions must occur on 32-bit boundaries) and sign-extending. For conditional branch instructions, the effective address of the next instruction is derived from a 16-bit immediate value within the instruction. The 16-bit value is extended to a 32-bit value by adding two zeros to its least significant end and sign-extending.

With **relative addressing,** the 24-bit immediate value (unconditional branch instructions) or 14-bit immediate value (conditional branch instructions) is extended as before. The resulting value is then added to the program counter to define a location relative to the current instruction. The other conditional branch addressing mode is **indirect addressing.** This mode obtains the effective address of the next instruction from either the link register or the count register. Note that in this case the count register is used to hold the address for a branch instruction. This register may also be used to hold a count for looping, as explained earlier.

### Arithmetic Instructions

For integer arithmetic, all operands must be contained either in registers or as part of the instruction. With **register addressing,** a source or destination operand is specified as one of the general-purpose registers. With **immediate addressing,** a source operand appears as a 16-bit signed quantity in the instruction.

For floating-point arithmetic, all operands are in floating-point registers; that is, only register addressing is used.

## 10.2

## INSTRUCTION FORMATS

An instruction format defines the layout of the bits of an instruction, in terms of its constituent parts. An instruction format must include an opcode and, implicitly or explicitly, zero or more operands. Each explicit operand is referenced using one of the addressing modes described in Section 10.1. The format must, implicitly or explicitly, indicate the addressing mode for each operand. For most instruction sets, more than one instruction format is used.

The design of an instruction format is a complex art, and an amazing variety of designs have been implemented. In this section, we examine the key design issues, looking briefly at some designs to illustrate points, and then we examine the Pentium and PowerPC solutions in detail.

### Instruction Length

The most basic design issue to be faced is the instruction format length. This decision affects, and is affected by, memory size, memory organization, bus structure, CPU complexity, and CPU speed. This decision determines the richness and flexibility of the machine as seen by the assembly-language programmer.

The most obvious trade-off here is between the desire for a powerful instruction repertoire and a need to save space. Programmers want more opcodes, more operands, more addressing modes, and greater address range. More opcodes and more operands make life easier for the programmer, since shorter programs can be written to accomplish given tasks. Similarly, more addressing modes give the programmer greater flexibility in implementing certain functions, such as table manipulations and multiple-way branching. And, of course, with the increase in main memory size and the increasing use of virtual memory, programmers want to be able to address larger memory ranges. All of these things (opcodes, operands, addressing modes, address range) require bits and push in the direction of longer instruction lengths. But longer instruction length may be wasteful. A 32-bit instruction occupies twice the space of a 16-bit instruction but is probably much less than twice as useful.

Beyond this basic trade-off, there are other considerations. Either the instruction length should be equal to the memory-transfer length (in a bus system, data-bus length) or one should be a multiple of the other. Otherwise, we will not get an integral number of instructions during a fetch cycle. A related consideration is the memory transfer rate. This rate has not kept up with increases in processor speed. Accordingly, memory can become a bottleneck if the processor can execute instructions faster than it can fetch them. One solution to this problem is the use of cache memory (see Section 4.3); another is to use shorter instructions. Again, 16-bit instructions can be fetched at twice the rate of 32-bit instructions but probably can be executed less than twice as fast.

A seemingly mundane but nevertheless important feature is that the instruction length should be a multiple of the character length, which is usually 8 bits, and of the length of fixed-point numbers. To see this, we need to make use of that unfortunately ill-defined word, "word" [FRAI83]. The word length of memory is, in some sense, the "natural" unit of organization. The size of a word usually determines the size of fixed-point numbers (usually the two are equal). Word size is also typically equal to, or at least integrally related to, the memory transfer size. Since a common form of data is character data, we would like a word to store an integral number of characters. Otherwise, there are wasted bits in each word when storing multiple characters, or a character will have to straddle a word boundary. The importance of this point is such that IBM, when it introduced the System/360 and wanted to employ 8-bit characters, made the wrenching decision to move from the 36-bit architecture of the scientific members of the 700/7000 series to a 32-bit architecture.

## Allocation of Bits

We've looked at some of the factors that go into deciding the length of the instruction format. An equally difficult issue is how to allocate the bits in that format. The trade-offs here are complex.

For a given instruction length, there is clearly a trade-off between the number of opcodes and the power of the addressing capability. More opcodes obviously mean more bits in the opcode field. For an instruction format of a given length, this reduces the number of bits available for addressing. There is one interesting refinement to this trade-off, and that is the use of variable-length opcodes. In this approach, there is a minimum opcode length but, for some opcodes, additional operations may be specified for using additional bits in the instruction. For a fixed-length instruction, this leaves fewer bits for addressing. Thus, this feature is used for those instructions that require fewer operands and/or less powerful addressing. We will see examples of this strategy presently.

The following interrelated factors go into determining the use of the addressing bits.

- *Number of Addressing Modes:* Sometimes, an addressing mode can be indicated implicitly. For example, certain opcodes might always call for indexing. In other cases, the addressing modes must be explicit, and one or more mode bits will be needed.
- *Number of Operands:* We have seen that fewer addresses can make for longer, more awkward programs (e.g., Figure 9.3). Typical instructions on today's machines provide for two operands. Each operand address in the instruction might require its own mode indicator, or the use of a mode indicator could be limited to just one of the address fields.
- *Register vs. Memory:* A machine must have registers so that data can be brought into the CPU for processing. With a single user-visible register (usually called the *accumulator*), one operand address is implicit and consumes no instruction bits. However, single-register programming is awkward and requires many instructions. Even with multiple registers, only a few bits are needed to specify the register. The more that registers can be used for operand references, the fewer bits are needed. A number of studies indicate that a total of 8 to 32 user-visible registers is desirable [LUND77, HUCK83].
- *Number of Register Sets:* A number of machines have one set of general-purpose registers, with typically 8 or 16 registers in the set. These registers can be used to store data and can be used to store addresses for displacement addressing. The trend recently has been away from one bank of general-purpose registers and toward a collection of two or more specialized sets (such as data and displacement). This trend shows up everywhere from single-chip microprocessors to supercomputers. One advantage of this approach is that, for a fixed number of registers, a functional split requires fewer bits to be used in the instruction. For example, with two sets of eight registers, only 3 bits are required to identify a register; the opcode implicitly will determine which set of registers is being referenced. There seems to be little disadvantage to this approach [LUND77]. In systems such as the S/370, which has one set of general-purpose registers, programmers usually establish conventions that assign about half the registers to data and half to displacement and maintain a fixed assignment [MALL79].
- *Address Range:* For addresses that reference memory, the range of addresses that can be referenced is related to the number of address bits. Because this imposes a severe limitation, direct addressing is rarely used. With displacement addressing, the range is opened up to the length of the address register. Even so, it is still convenient to allow rather large displacements from the register address, which requires a relatively large number of address bits in the instruction.

- *Address Granularity:* For addresses that reference memory rather than registers, another factor is the granularity of addressing. In a system with 16- or 32-bit words, an address can reference a word or a byte at the designer's choice. Byte addressing is convenient for character manipulation but requires, for a fixed-size memory, more address bits.

Thus, the designer is faced with a host of factors to consider and balance. How critical the various choices are is not clear. As an example, we cite one study [CRAG79] that compared various instruction format approaches, including the use of a stack, general-purpose registers, an accumulator, and only memory-to-register approaches. Using a consistent set of assumptions, no significant difference in code space or execution time was observed.

Let us briefly look at how two machine designs balance these various factors.

## PDP-8

One of the simplest instruction designs for a general-purpose computer was for the PDP-8 [BELL78b]. The PDP-8 uses 12-bit instructions and operates on 12-bit words. There is a single general-purpose register, the accumulator.

Despite the limitations of this design, the addressing is quite flexible. Each memory reference consists of 7 bits plus 2 1-bit modifiers. The memory is divided into fixed-length pages of $2^7 = 128$ words each. Address calculation is based on references to page 0 or the current page (page containing this instruction) as determined by the page bit. The second modifier bit indicates whether direct or indirect addressing is to be used. These two modes can be used in combination, so that an indirect address is a 12-bit address contained in a word of page 0 or the current page. In addition, 8 dedicated words on page 0 are autoindex "registers." When an indirect reference is made to one of these locations, preindexing occurs.

Figure 10.4 shows the PDP-8 instruction format. There are a 3-bit opcode and 3 types of instructions. For opcodes 0 through 5, the format is a single-address memory reference instruction including a page bit and an indirect bit. Thus, there are only 6 basic operations. To enlarge the group of operations, opcode 7 defines a register reference or *microinstruction*. In this format, the remaining bits are used to encode additional operations. In general, each bit defines a specific operation (e.g., clear accumulator), and these bits can be combined in a single instruction. The microinstruction strategy was used as far back as the PDP-1 by DEC and is, in a sense, a forerunner of today's microprogrammed machines, to be discussed in Part IV. Opcode 6 is the I/O operation; 6 bits are used to select one of 64 devices, and 3 bits specify a particular I/O command.

The PDP-8 instruction format is remarkably efficient. It supports indirect addressing, displacement addressing, and indexing. With the use of the opcode extension, it supports a total of approximately 35 instructions. Given the constraints of a 12-bit instruction length, the designers could hardly have done better.

## PDP-10

A sharp contrast to the instruction set of the PDP-8 is that of the PDP-10. The PDP-10 was designed to be a large-scale time-shared system, with an emphasis on mak-

Memory Reference Instructions

| Op Code | D/I | Z/C | Displacement |
|---|---|---|---|
| 0          2 | 3 | 4 | 5                                     11 |

Input/Output Instructions

| 1   1   0 | Device | Op Code |
|---|---|---|
| 0              2 | 3                              8 | 9            11 |

Register Reference Instructions

*Group 1 Microinstructions*

| 1  1  1  0 | CLA | CLL | CMA | CML | RAR | RAL | BSW | IAC |
|---|---|---|---|---|---|---|---|---|
| 0  1  2  3 | 4 | 5 | 6 | 7 | 8 | 9 | 10 | 11 |

*Group 2 Microinstructions*

| 1  1  1  1 | CLA | SMA | SZA | SNL | RSS | OSR | HLT | 0 |
|---|---|---|---|---|---|---|---|---|
| 0  1  2  3 | 4 | 5 | 6 | 7 | 8 | 9 | 10 | 11 |

*Group 3 Microinstructions*

| 1  1  1  1 | CLA | MQA | 0 | MQL | 0 | 0 | 0 | 1 |
|---|---|---|---|---|---|---|---|---|
| 0  1  2  3 | 4 | 5 | 6 | 7 | 8 | 9 | 10 | 11 |

*Mnemonics*

| | |
|---|---|
| CLA = CLear Accumulator | SMA = Skip on Minus Accumulator |
| CLL = CLear Link | SZA = Skip on Zero Accumulator |
| CMA = CoMplement Accumulator | SNL = Skip on Nonzero Link |
| CML = CoMplement Link | RSS = Reverse Skip Sense |
| RAR = Rotate Accumulator Right | OSR = Or with Switch Register |
| RAL = Rotate Accumulator Left | HLT = HaLT |
| BSW = Byte SWap | MQA = Multiplier Quotient into Accumulator |
| IAC = Increment ACcumulator | MQL = Multiplier Quotient Load |

**FIGURE 10.4.  PDP-8 instruction formats**

ing the system easy to program, even if additional hardware expense was involved.

Among the design principles that were employed in designing the instruction set were [BELL78c].

- *Orthogonality:* Orthogonality is a principle by which two variables are independent of each other. In the context of an instruction set, the term indicates that other elements of an instruction are independent of (not determined by) the opcode. The PDP-10 designers use the term to describe the fact that an address is always computed in the same way, independent of the opcode. This is in contrast to many machines, where the address mode sometimes depends implicitly on the operator being used.

- *Completeness:* Each arithmetic data type (integer, fixed-point, real) should have a complete and identical set of operations.
- *Direct Addressing:* Base plus displacement addressing, which places a memory organization burden on the programmer, was avoided in favor of direct addressing.

Each of these principles advances the main goal of ease of programming.

The PDP-10 has a 36-bit word length and a 36-bit instruction length. The fixed instruction format is shown in Figure 10.5. The opcode occupies 9 bits, allowing up to 512 operations. In fact, a total of 365 different instructions are defined. Most instructions have two addresses, one of which is one of 16 general-purpose registers. Thus, this operand reference occupies 4 bits. The other operand reference starts with an 18-bit memory address field. This can be used as an immediate operand or a memory address. In the latter usage, both indexing and indirect addressing are allowed. The same general-purpose registers are also used as index registers.

A 36-bit instruction length is true luxury. There is no need to do clever things to get more opcodes; a 9-bit opcode field is more than adequate. Addressing is also straightforward. An 18-bit address field makes direct addressing desirable. For memory sizes greater than $2^{18}$, indirection is provided. For the ease of the programmer, indexing is provided for table manipulation and iterative programs. Also, with an 18-bit operand field, immediate addressing becomes attractive.

The PDP-10 instruction set design does accomplish the objectives listed earlier [LUND77]. It makes it comparatively easy for the programmer at the expense of an inefficient utilization of space. This was a conscious choice made by the designers and therefore cannot be faulted as poor design.

## Variable-Length Instructions

The examples we have looked at so far have used a single fixed instruction length, and we have implicitly discussed trade-offs in that context. But the designer may choose instead to provide a variety of instruction formats of different lengths. This tactic makes it easy to provide a large repertoire of opcodes, with different opcode lengths. Addressing can be more flexible, with various combinations of register

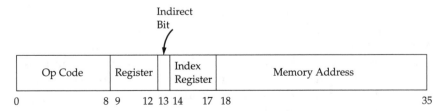

**FIGURE 10.5. PDP-10 instruction format**

and memory references plus addressing modes. With variable-length instructions, these many variations can be provided efficiently and compactly.

The principal price to pay for variable-length instructions is an increase in the complexity of the CPU. Falling hardware prices, the use of microprogramming (discussed in Part IV), and a general increase in understanding the principles of CPU design have all contributed to making this a small price to pay.

The use of variable-length instructions does not remove the desirability of making all of the instruction lengths integrally related to the word length. Since the CPU does not know the length of the next instruction to be fetched, a typical strategy is to fetch a number of bytes or words equal to at least the longest possible instruction. This means that sometimes multiple instructions are fetched. However, as we shall see in Chapter 11, this is a good strategy to follow in any case.

## *PDP-11*

The PDP-11 was designed to provide a powerful and flexible instruction set within the constraints of a 16-bit minicomputer [BELL70].

The PDP-11 employs a set of 8 16-bit general-purpose registers. Two of these registers have additional significance: one is used as a stack pointer for special-purpose stack operations, and one is used as the program counter, which contains the address of the next instruction.

Figure 10.6 shows the PDP-11 instruction formats. Thirteen different formats are used, encompassing zero-, one-, and two-address instruction types. The opcode can vary from 4 to 16 bits in length. Register references are 6 bits in length. Three bits identify the register, and the remaining 3 bits identify the addressing mode. The PDP-11 is endowed with a rich set of addressing modes. One advantage of linking the addressing mode to the operand rather than the opcode, as is sometimes done, is that any addressing mode can be used with any opcode. As was mentioned, this independence is referred to as *orthogonality*.

PDP-11 instructions are usually 1 word (16 bits) long. For some instructions, one or two memory addresses are appended, so that 32-bit and 48-bit instructions are part of the repertoire. This provides for further flexibility in addressing.

The PDP-11 instruction set and addressing capability are complex. This increases both hardware cost and programming complexity. The advantage is that more efficient or compact programs can be developed.

## Pentium Instruction Formats

The Pentium is equipped with a variety of instruction formats. Of the elements described below, only the opcode field is always present. Figure 10.7 illustrates the general instruction format. Instructions are made up of from zero to four optional instruction prefixes, a one- or two-byte opcode, an optional address specifier, which consists of the Mod r/m byte and the Scale Index byte, an optional displacement, and an optional immediate field.

Let us first consider the prefix bytes:

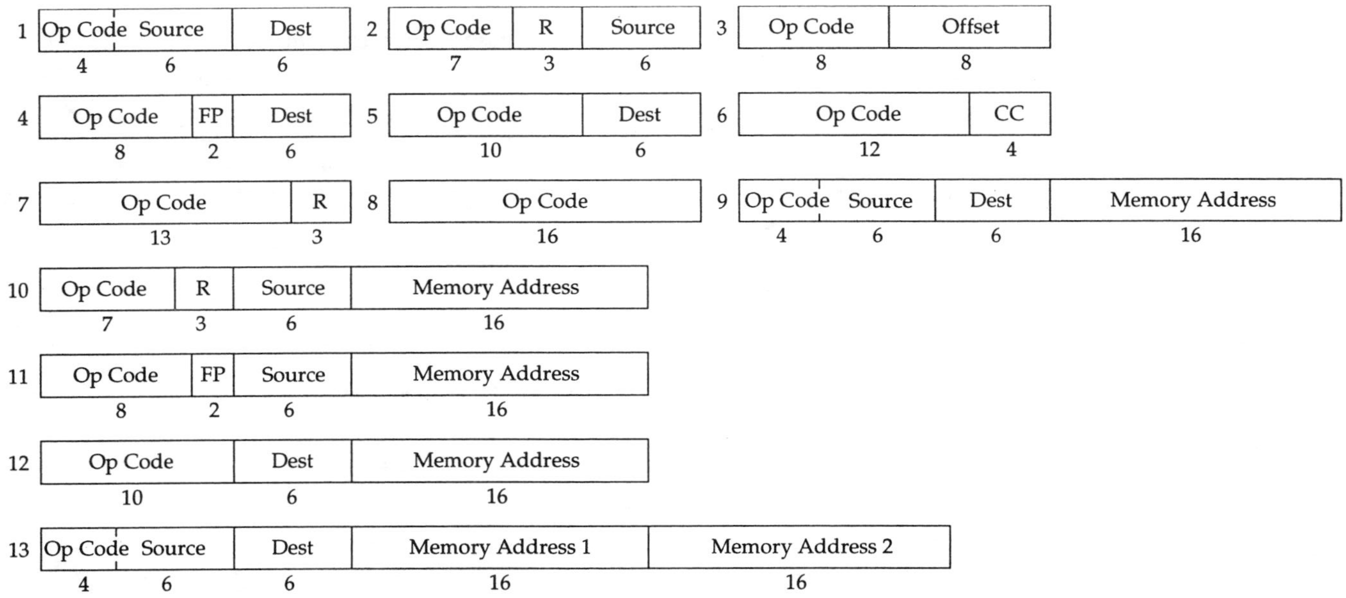

**FIGURE 10.6. Instruction formats used on the PDP-11; the numbers indicate the field lengths**

Source and dest each contain a 3-bit addressing mode field and a 3-bit register number;
FP is 1 of the floating point registers 0, 1, 2, or 3;
R is 1 of the general registers;
CC is the condition code field

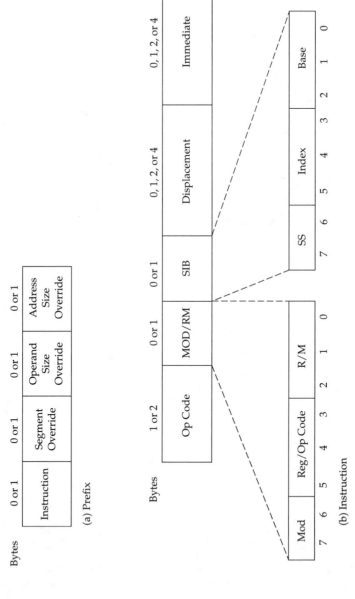

**FIGURE 10.7. Pentium Instruction Format**

- *Instruction Prefixes:* The instruction prefix, if present, consists of the LOCK prefix of one of the repeat prefixes. The LOCK prefix is used to ensure exclusive use of shared memory in multiprocessor environments. The repeat prefixes specify repeated operation of a string, which enables the Pentium to process strings much faster than with a regular software loop. There are five different repeat prefixes: REP, REPE, REPZ, REPNE, and REPNZ. When the absolute REP prefix is present, the operation specified in the instruction is executed repeatedly on successive elements of the string; the number of repetitions is specified in register CX. The conditional REP prefix causes the instruction to repeat until the count in CX goes to zero or until the condition is met.
- *Segment Override:* Explicitly specifies which segment register an instruction should use, overriding the default segment-register selection generated by the Pentium for that instruction.
- *Address Size:* The processor can address memory using either 16- or 32-bit addresses. The address size determines the displacement size in instructions and the size of address offsets generated during effective address calculation. One of these sizes is designated as default, and the address size prefix switches between 32-bit and 16-bit address generation.
- *Operand Size:* Similarly, an instruction has a default operand size of 16 or 32 bits, and the operand prefix switches between 32-bit and 16-bit operands.

The instruction itself includes the following fields:

- *Opcode:* one- or two-byte opcode. The opcode may also include bits that specify if data is byte- or full-size (16 or 32 bits depending on context), direction of data operation (to or from memory), and whether an immediate data field must be sign-extended.
- *Mod r/m:* This byte, and the next, provide addressing information. The Mod r/m byte specifies whether an operand is in a register or in memory; if it is in memory, then fields within the byte specify the addressing mode to be used. The Mod r/m byte consists of three fields: The Mod field (2 bits) combines with the r/m field to form 32 possible values: 8 registers and 24 indexing modes; the Reg/Opcode field (3 bits) specifies either a register number or three more bits of opcode information; the r/m field (3 bits) can specify a register as the location of an operand, or it can form part of the addressing-mode encoding in combination with the Mod field.
- *SIB:* Certain encoding of the Mod r/m byte specifies the inclusion of the SIB byte to fully specify the addressing mode. The SIB byte consists of three fields: The SS field (2 bits) specifies the scale factor for scaled indexing; the Index field (3 bits) specifies the index register; the Base field (3 bits) specifies the base register.
- *Displacement:* When the addressing-mode specifier indicates that a displacement is used, an 8-, 16-, or 32-bit signed integer displacement field is added.
- *Immediate:* Provides the value of an 8-, 16-, or 32-bit operand.

Several comparisons may be useful here. In the Pentium format, the addressing mode is provided as part of the opcode sequence rather than with each operand. Since only one operand can have address-mode information, only one memory operand can be referenced in an instruction. In contrast, the VAX carries the address-mode information with each operand, allowing memory-to-memory operations. The Pentium instructions are therefore more compact. However, if a memory-to-memory operation is required, the VAX can accomplish this in a single instruction.

The Pentium format allows the use of not only 1-byte, but 2-byte and 4-byte offsets for indexing. Although the use of the larger index offsets results in longer instructions, this feature provides needed flexibility. For example, it is useful in addressing large arrays or large stack frames. In contrast, the IBM S/370 instruction format allows offsets no greater than 4K bytes (12 bits of offset information), and the offset must be positive. When a location is not in reach of this offset, the compiler must generate extra code to generate the needed address. This problem is especially apparent in dealing with stack frames that have local variables occupying in excess of 4K bytes. As [DEWA90] puts it, "generating code for the 370 is so painful as a result of that restriction that there have even been compilers for the 370 that simply chose to limit the size of the stack frame to 4K bytes."

As can be seen, the encoding of the Pentium instruction set is very complex. This has to do partly with the need to be backward compatible with the 8086 machine and partly with a desire on the part of the designers to provide every possible assistance to the compiler writer in producing efficient code. It is a matter of some debate whether an instruction set as complex as this is preferable to the opposite extreme of the RISC instruction sets.

## PowerPC Instruction Formats

All instructions in the PowerPC are 32 bits long and follow a regular format. The first 6 bits of an instruction specify the operation to be performed. In some cases, there is an extension to the opcode elsewhere in the instruction that specifies a particular subcase of an operation. In Figure 10.8, opcode bits are represented by the shaded portion of each format.

Note the regular structure of the formats, which eases the job of the instruction execution units. For all load/store, arithmetic, and logical instructions, the opcode is followed by 2 5-bit register references, enabling 32 general-purpose registers to be used.

The branch instructions include a link (L) bit that indicates that the effective address of the instruction following the branch instruction is to be placed in the link register. Two forms of the instruction also include a bit (A) that indicates whether the addressing mode is absolute or PC relative. For the conditional branch instructions, the CR bit field specifies the bit to be tested in the condition register. The options field specifies the conditions under which the branch is to be taken. The following conditions may be specified:

- Branch always.
- Branch if count ≠ 0 and condition is false.
- Branch if count ≠ 0 and condition is true.
- Branch if count = 0 and condition is false.

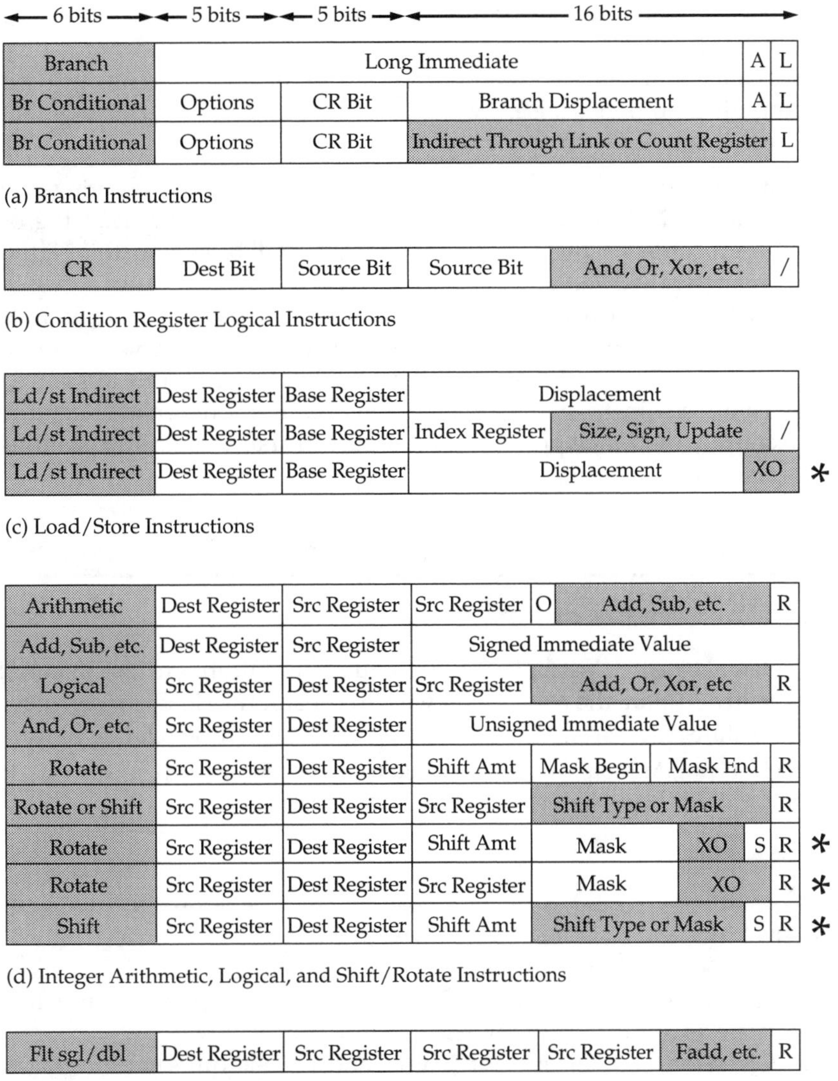

```
←—— 6 bits ——→←— 5 bits —→←— 5 bits —→←——————— 16 bits ———————→
```

| Branch | Long Immediate | | | A | L |
|---|---|---|---|---|---|
| Br Conditional | Options | CR Bit | Branch Displacement | A | L |
| Br Conditional | Options | CR Bit | Indirect Through Link or Count Register | | L |

(a) Branch Instructions

| CR | Dest Bit | Source Bit | Source Bit | And, Or, Xor, etc. | / |
|---|---|---|---|---|---|

(b) Condition Register Logical Instructions

| Ld/st Indirect | Dest Register | Base Register | Displacement | | |
|---|---|---|---|---|---|
| Ld/st Indirect | Dest Register | Base Register | Index Register | Size, Sign, Update | / |
| Ld/st Indirect | Dest Register | Base Register | Displacement | XO | ✶ |

(c) Load/Store Instructions

| Arithmetic | Dest Register | Src Register | Src Register | O | Add, Sub, etc. | | R | |
|---|---|---|---|---|---|---|---|---|
| Add, Sub, etc. | Dest Register | Src Register | Signed Immediate Value | | | | | |
| Logical | Src Register | Dest Register | Src Register | Add, Or, Xor, etc | | R | | |
| And, Or, etc. | Src Register | Dest Register | Unsigned Immediate Value | | | | | |
| Rotate | Src Register | Dest Register | Shift Amt | Mask Begin | Mask End | R | | |
| Rotate or Shift | Src Register | Dest Register | Src Register | Shift Type or Mask | | R | | |
| Rotate | Src Register | Dest Register | Shift Amt | Mask | XO | S | R | ✶ |
| Rotate | Src Register | Dest Register | Src Register | Mask | XO | R | | ✶ |
| Shift | Src Register | Dest Register | Shift Amt | Shift Type or Mask | S | R | | ✶ |

(d) Integer Arithmetic, Logical, and Shift/Rotate Instructions

| Flt sgl/dbl | Dest Register | Src Register | Src Register | Src Register | Fadd, etc. | R |
|---|---|---|---|---|---|---|

(e) Floating-Point Arithmetic Instructions

A = Absolute or PC Relative*     = 64-bit implementations only
L = Link to Subroutine
O = Record Overflow in XER
R = Record Conditions in CR1
XO = OpCode Extension
S = Part of Shift Amount Field

**FIGURE 10.8.  PowerPC Instruction Formats**

- Branch if count = 0 and condition is true.
- Branch if count ≠ 0.
- Branch if count = 0.
- Branch if condition is false.
- Branch if condition is true.

Most instructions that result in a computation (arithmetic, floating-point arithmetic, logical) include a bit that indicates whether the result of the operation should be recorded in the condition register. As will be shown, this feature is useful for branch prediction processing.

Floating-point instructions have fields for three source registers. In many cases, only two source registers are used. A few instructions involve multiplication of two source registers and then addition or subtraction of a third source register. These composite instructions are included because of the frequency of their use. For example, the inner product that is part of many matrix operations can be implemented using multiply-adds.

## 10.3

### RECOMMENDED READING

The references cited in Chapter 9 are equally applicable to the material of this chapter. In addition, the reader may wish to consult [FLYN85] for a discussion and analysis of instruction set design issues, particularly those relating to formats.

FLYN85  Flynn, M.; Johnson, J.; and Wakefield, S. "On Instruction Sets and Their Formats." *IEEE Transactions on Computers,* March 1985.

## 10.4

### PROBLEMS

10.1  Justify the assertion that a 32-bit instruction is probably much less than twice as useful as a 16-bit instruction.

10.2  Given the following memory values and a one-address machine with an accumulator, what values do the following instructions load into the accumulator?

- Word 20 contains 40.
- Word 30 contains 50.
- Word 40 contains 60.
- Word 50 contains 70.

(a) LOAD IMMEDIATE 20
(b) LOAD DIRECT 20
(c) LOAD INDIRECT 20
(d) LOAD IMMEDIATE 30
(e) LOAD DIRECT 30
(f) LOAD INDIRECT 30

10.3   Let the address stored in the program counter be designated by the symbol X1. The instruction stored in X1 has an address part (operand reference) X2. The operand needed to execute the instruction is stored in the memory word with address X3. An index register contains the value X4. What is the relationship between these various quantities if the addressing mode of the instruction is (a) direct; (b) indirect; (c) PC-relative; (d) indexed?

10.4   A PC-relative mode branch instruction is stored in memory at address $620_{10}$. The branch is made to location $530_{10}$. The address field in the instruction is 10 bits long. What is the binary value in the instruction?

10.5   How many times does the CPU need to refer to memory when it fetches and executes an indirect-address-mode instruction if the instruction is (a) a computation requiring a single operand; (b) a branch?

10.6   The IBM 370 does not provide indirect addressing. Assume that the address of an operand is in main memory. How would you access the operand?

10.7   Why was IBM's decision to move from 36 bits to 32 bits per word wrenching, and to whom?

10.8   In [COOK82], the author proposes that the PC-relative addressing modes be eliminated in favor of other modes, such as the use of a stack. What is the disadvantage of this proposal?

10.9   Assume an instruction set that uses a fixed 16-bit instruction length. Operand specifiers are 6 bits in length. There are $K$ two-operand instructions and $L$ zero-operand instructions. What is the maximum number of one-operand instructions that can be supported?

10.10  Design a variable-length opcode to allow all of the following to be encoded in a 36-bit instruction:

   7   instructions with two 15-bit addresses and one 3-bit register number
 500   instructions with one 15-bit address and one 3-bit register number
  50   instructions with no addresses or registers

10.11  Consider the results of Problem 9.4. Assume that M is a 16-bit memory address and that X, Y, and Z are either 16-bit addresses or 4-bit register numbers. The one-address machine uses an accumulator, and the two- and three-address machines have 16 registers and instructions operating on all combinations of memory locations and registers. Assuming 8-bit opcodes and instruction lengths that are multiples of 4 bits, how many bits does each machine need to compute X?

10.12  Is there any possible justification for an instruction with two opcodes?

10.13  The Pentium includes the following instruction:

IMUL op1, op2, immediate

This instruction multiplies op2, which may be either register or memory, by the immediate operand value, and places the result in op1, which must be a register. There is no other three-operand instruction of this sort in the instruction set. What is the possible use of such an instruction? Hint: consider indexing.

# CHAPTER 11

# CPU Structure and Function

This chapter discusses aspects of the processor not yet covered in Part III, and it sets the stage for the discussion of RISC and superscalar architecture in Chapters 12 and 13.

This chapter begins with a summary of processor organization. Registers, which form the internal memory of the processor, are then analyzed. We are then in a position to return to the discussion (begun in Section 3.2) of the instruction cycle. A description of the instruction cycle and a common technique known as instruction pipelining complete our description. The chapter concludes with an examination of some additional aspects of the Pentium and PowerPC organizations.

## 11.1

### PROCESSOR ORGANIZATION

To understand the organization of the CPU, let us consider the requirements placed on the CPU, the things that it must do:

- *Fetch Instructions:* The CPU must read instructions from memory.
- *Interpret Instructions:* The instruction must be decoded to determine what action is required.
- *Fetch Data:* The execution of an instruction may require reading data from memory or an I/O module.
- *Process Data:* The execution of an instruction may require performing some arithmetic or logical operation on data.
- *Write Data:* The results of an execution may require writing data to memory or an I/O module.

In order to be able to do these things, it should be clear that the CPU needs to temporarily store some data. It must remember the location of the last instruction so that it can know where to get the next instruction. It needs to store instructions and data temporarily while an instruction is being executed. In other words, the CPU needs a small internal memory.

Figure 11.1 is a simplified view of a CPU, indicating its connection to the rest of the system via the system bus. A similar interface would be needed for any of the interconnection structures described in Chapter 3. The reader will recall that the major components of the CPU are an *arithmetic and logic unit* (ALU) and a *control unit* (CU). The ALU does the actual computation or processing of data. The control unit controls the movement of data and instructions into and out of the CPU and controls the operation of the ALU. In addition, the figure shows a minimal internal memory, consisting of a set of storage locations, called *registers*.

Figure 11.2 is a slightly more detailed view of the CPU. The data transfer and logic control paths are indicated, including an element labeled *internal CPU bus*. This element is needed to transfer data between the various registers and the ALU, since the ALU in fact operates only on data in the internal CPU memory. The figure also shows typical basic elements of the ALU. Note the similarity between the internal structure of the computer as a whole and the internal structure of the CPU. In both cases, there is a small collection of major elements (computer: CPU, I/O, memory; CPU: control unit, ALU, registers) connected by data paths.

## 11.2

## REGISTER ORGANIZATION

As we discussed in Chapter 4, a computer system employs a memory hierarchy. At higher levels of the hierarchy, memory is faster, smaller, and more expensive (per bit). Within the CPU, there is a set of registers that function as a level of mem-

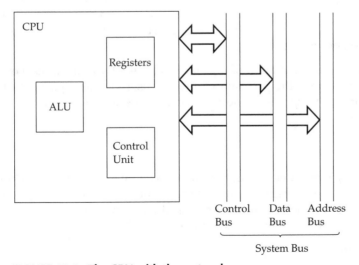

**FIGURE 11.1. The CPU with the system bus**

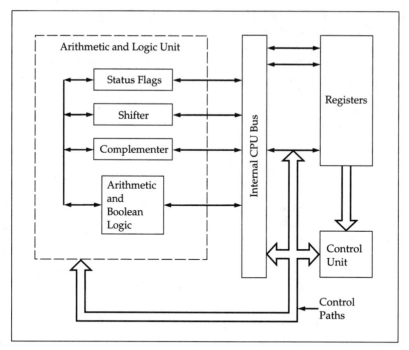

**FIGURE 11.2. Internal structure of the CPU**

ory above main memory and cache in the hierarchy. The registers in the CPU serve two functions:

- *User-Visible Registers:* These enable the machine- or assembly-language programmer to minimize main-memory references by optimizing use of registers.
- *Control and Status Registers:* These are used by the control unit to control the operation of the CPU and by privileged, operating-system programs to control the execution of programs.

There is not a clean separation of registers into these two categories. For example, on some machines the program counter is user-visible (e.g., VAX), but on many it is not. For purposes of the following discussion, however, we will use these categories.

## User-Visible Registers

A user-visible register is one that may be referenced by means of the machine language that the CPU executes. Virtually all contemporary CPU designs provide for a number of user-visible registers, as opposed to a single accumulator. We can characterize these in the following categories:

- General Purpose
- Data

- Address
- Condition Codes

*General-purpose registers* can be assigned to a variety of functions by the programmer. Sometimes, their use within the instruction set is orthogonal to the operation. That is, any general-purpose register can contain the operand for any opcode. This provides true general-purpose register use. Often, however, there are restrictions. For example, there may be dedicated registers for floating-point operations.

In some cases, general-purpose registers can be used for addressing functions (e.g., register indirect, displacement). In other cases, there is a partial or clean separation between data registers and address registers. *Data registers* may be used only to hold data and cannot be employed in the calculation of an operand address. *Address registers* may themselves be somewhat general-purpose, or they may be devoted to a particular addressing mode. Examples include

- *Segment Pointers:* In a machine with segmented addressing (see Section 7.3), a segment register holds the address of the base of the segment. There may be multiple registers: for example, one for the operating system and one for the current process.
- *Index Registers:* These are used for indexed addressing and may be autoindexed.
- *Stack Pointer:* If there is user-visible stack addressing, then typically the stack is in memory and there is a dedicated register that points to the top of the stack. This allows implicit addressing; that is, push, pop, and other stack instructions need not contain an explicit stack operand.

There are several design issues to be addressed here. An important one is whether to use completely general-purpose registers or to specialize their use. We have already touched on this issue in the preceding chapter, since it affects instruction set design. With the use of specialized registers, it can generally be implicit in the opcode which type of register a certain operand specifier refers to. The operand specifier must only identify one of a set of specialized registers rather than one out of all the registers, thus saving bits. On the other hand, this specialization limits the programmer's flexibility. There is no final and best solution to this design issue, but, as was mentioned, the trend seems to be toward the use of specialized registers.

Another design issue is the number of registers, either general-purpose or data plus address, to be provided. Again, this affects instruction set design since more registers require more operand specifier bits. As we previously discussed, somewhere between 8 and 32 registers appears optimum [LUND77]. Fewer registers result in more memory references; more registers do not noticeably reduce memory references (e.g., see [WILL90]). However, a new approach, which finds advantage in the use of hundreds of registers, is exhibited in some RISC systems and is discussed in Chapter 12.

Finally, there is the issue of register length. Registers that must hold addresses obviously must be at least long enough to hold the largest address. Data registers should be able to hold values of most data types. Some machines allow two contiguous registers to be used as one for holding double-length values.

A final category of registers, which is at least partially visible to the user, holds *condition codes* (also referred to as *flags*). Condition codes are bits set by the CPU hardware as the result of operations. For example, an arithmetic operation may produce a positive, negative, zero, or overflow result. In addition to the result itself being stored in a register or memory, a condition code is also set. The code may subsequently be tested as part of a conditional branch operation.

Condition code bits are collected into one or more registers. Usually, they form part of a control register. Generally, machine instructions allow these bits to be read by implicit reference, but they cannot be altered by the programmer.

In some machines, a subroutine call will result in the automatic saving of all user-visible registers, to be restored on return. The saving and restoring is performed by the CPU as part of the execution of call and return instructions. This allows each subroutine to use the user-visible registers independently. On other machines, it is the responsibility of the programmer to save the contents of the relevant user-visible registers prior to a subroutine call, by including instructions for this purpose in the program.

## Control and Status Registers

There are a variety of CPU registers that are employed to control the operation of the CPU. Most of these, on most machines, are not visible to the user. Some of them may be visible to machine instructions executed in a control or operating-system mode.

Of course, different machines will have different register organizations and use different terminology. We list here a reasonably complete list of register types, with a brief description.

Four registers are essential to instruction execution:

- *Program Counter (PC):* Contains the address of an instruction to be fetched.
- *Instruction Register (IR):* Contains the instruction most recently fetched.
- *Memory Address Register (MAR):* Contains the address of a location in memory.
- *Memory Buffer Register (MBR):* Contains a word of data to be written to memory or the word most recently read.

The program counter contains an instruction address. Typically, the program counter is updated by the CPU after each instruction fetch so that it always points to the next instruction to be executed. A branch or skip instruction will also modify the contents of the PC. The fetched instruction is loaded into an instruction register, where the opcode and operand specifiers are analyzed. Data are exchanged with memory using the MAR and MBR. In a bus-organized system, the MAR connects directly to the address bus, and the MBR connects directly to the data bus. User-visible registers, in turn, exchange data with the MBR.

The four registers just mentioned are used for the movement of data between the CPU and memory. Within the CPU, data must be presented to the ALU for processing. The ALU may have direct access to the MBR and user-visible registers. Alternatively, there may be additional buffering registers at the boundary to the ALU; these registers serve as input and output registers for the ALU and exchange data with the MBR and user-visible registers.

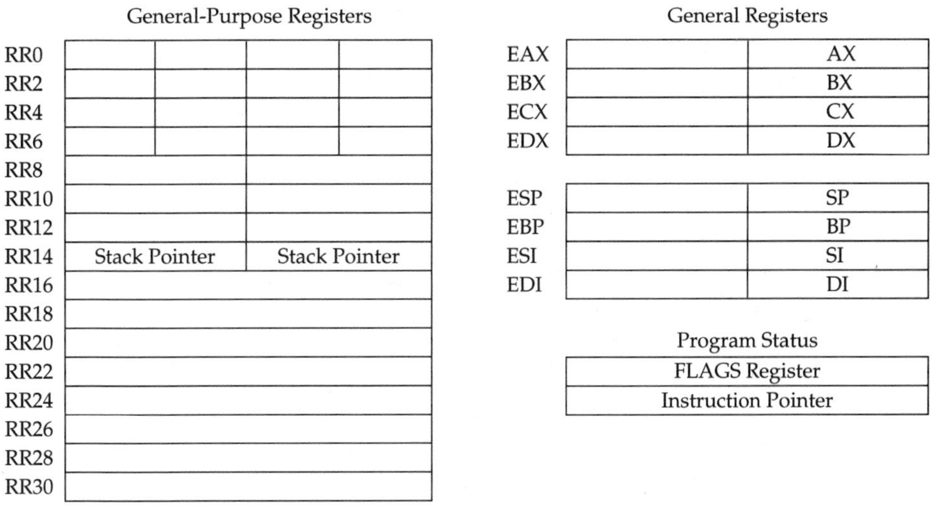

General-Purpose Registers

| | | | |
|------|---|---|---|
| RR0 | | | |
| RR2 | | | |
| RR4 | | | |
| RR6 | | | |
| RR8 | | | |
| RR10 | | | |
| RR12 | | | |
| RR14 | Stack Pointer | Stack Pointer | |
| RR16 | | | |
| RR18 | | | |
| RR20 | | | |
| RR22 | | | |
| RR24 | | | |
| RR26 | | | |
| RR28 | | | |
| RR30 | | | |

General Registers

| | | |
|------|---|----|
| EAX | | AX |
| EBX | | BX |
| ECX | | CX |
| EDX | | DX |
| ESP | | SP |
| EBP | | BP |
| ESI | | SI |
| EDI | | DI |

Program Status

| |
|---|
| FLAGS Register |
| Instruction Pointer |

(a) Z80,000      (b) 80386

**FIGURE 11.4.  Register organization extensions for 32-bit microprocessors**

eight data registers and nine address registers. The eight data registers are used primarily for data manipulation and are used in addressing only as index registers. The width of the registers allows 8-, 16-, and 32-bit data operations, determined by opcode. The address registers contain 32-bit (no segmentation) addresses; two of these registers are also used as stack pointers, one for users and one for the operating system, depending on the current execution mode. Both registers are numbered 7, since only one can be used at a time. The MC68000 also includes a 32-bit program counter and a 16-bit status register.

Like the Zilog designers, the Motorola team wanted a very regular instruction set, with no special-purpose registers. A concern for code efficiency led them to divide the registers into two functional components, saving one bit on each register specifier. This seems a reasonable compromise between complete generality and code compaction.

The point of this comparison should be clear. There is, as yet, no universally accepted philosophy concerning the best way to organize CPU registers [TOON81]. As with overall instruction set design and so many other CPU design issues, it is still a matter of judgment and taste.

A second instructive point concerning register organization design is illustrated in Figure 11.4. This figure shows the user-visible register organization for the Zilog 80,000 [PHIL85] and the Intel 80386 [ELAY85], which are 32-bit microprocessors designed as extensions of the Z8000 and 8086, respectively.[1] Both of these new processors use 32-bit registers. However, to provide upward compatibility for programs written on the earlier machines, both of the new processors retain the orig-

---

[1]Since the MC68000 already uses 32-bit registers, the MC68020 [MACG84], which is a full 32-bit extension, uses the same register organization.

inal register organization embedded in the new organization. Given this design constraint, the architects of the 32-bit processors had limited flexibility in designing the register organization.

## 11.3

### THE INSTRUCTION CYCLE

In Section 3.2, we described the CPU's instruction cycle. Figure 11.5 repeats one of the figures used in that description (Figure 3.9). To recall, an instruction cycle includes the following subcycles:

- *Fetch:* Read the next instruction from memory into the CPU.
- *Execute:* Interpret the opcode and perform the indicated operation.
- *Interrupt:* If interrupts are enabled and an interrupt has occurred, save the current process state and service the interrupt.

We are now in a position to elaborate somewhat on the instruction cycle. First, we must introduce one additional subcycle, known as the indirect cycle.

### The Indirect Cycle

We have seen, in Chapter 10, that the execution of an instruction may involve one or more operands in memory, each of which requires a memory access. Further, if indirect addressing is used, then additional memory accesses are required.

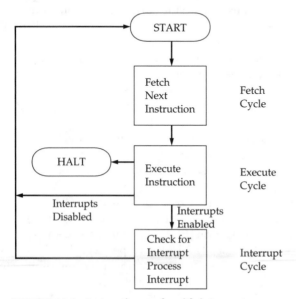

**FIGURE 11.5. Instruction cycle with interrupts**

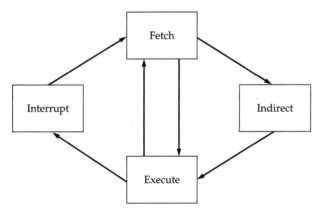

**FIGURE 11.6. The instruction cycle**

We can think of the fetching of indirect addresses as one more instruction sub-cycle. The result is shown in Figure 11.6. The main line of activity consists of alternating instruction fetch and instruction execution activities. After an instruction is fetched, it is examined to determine if any indirect addressing is involved. If so, the required operands are fetched using indirect addressing. Following execution, an interrupt may be processed before the next instruction fetch.

Another way to view this process is shown in Figure 11.7, which is a revised version of Figure 3.12. This illustrates more correctly the nature of the instruction cycle. Once an instruction is fetched, its operand specifiers must be identified. Each input operand in memory is then fetched, and this process may require indirect addressing. Register-based operands need not be fetched. Once the opcode is executed, a similar process may be needed to store the result in main memory.

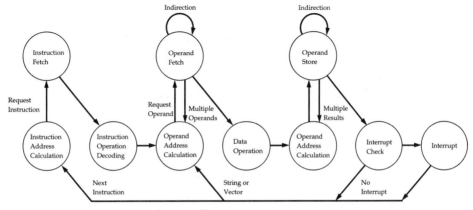

**FIGURE 11.7. Instruction cycle state diagram**

## Data Flow

The exact sequence of events during an instruction cycle depends on the design of the CPU. We can, however, indicate in general terms what must happen. Let us assume a CPU that employs a memory address register (MAR), a memory buffer register (MBR), a program counter (PC), and an instruction register (IR).

During the *fetch cycle,* an instruction is read from memory. Figure 11.8 shows the flow of data during this cycle. The PC contains the address of the next instruction to be fetched. This address is moved to the MAR and placed on the address bus. The control unit requests a memory read, and the result is placed on the data bus and copied into the MBR and then moved to the IR. Meanwhile, the PC is incremented by 1, preparatory for the next fetch.

Once the fetch cycle is over, the control unit examines the contents of the IR to determine if it contains an operand specifier using indirect addressing. If so, an *indirect cycle* is performed. As shown in Figure 11.9, this is a simple cycle. The rightmost N bits of the MBR, which contain the address reference, are transferred to the MAR. Then the control unit requests a memory read, to get the desired address of the operand into the MBR.

The fetch and indirect cycles are simple and predictable. The *instruction cycle* takes many forms since the form depends on which of the various machine instructions is in the IR. This cycle may involve transferring data among registers, read or write from memory or I/O, and/or the invocation of the ALU.

Like the fetch and indirect cycles, the *interrupt cycle* is simple and predictable (Figure 11.10). The current contents of the PC must be saved so that the CPU can resume normal activity after the interrupt. Thus, the contents of the PC are trans-

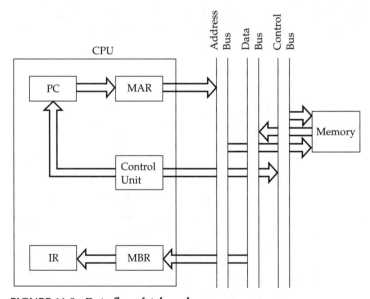

**FIGURE 11.8. Data flow, fetch cycle**

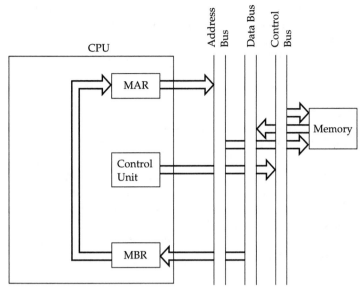

**FIGURE 11.9.  Data flow, indirect cycle**

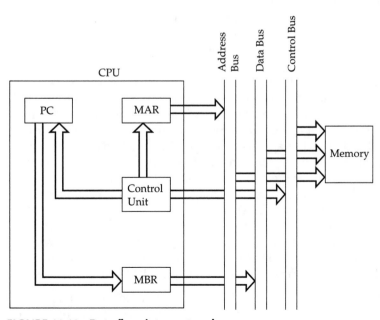

**FIGURE 11.10.  Data flow, interrupt cycle.**

ferred to the MBR to be written into memory. The special memory location reserved for this purpose is loaded into the MAR from the control unit. It might, for example, be a stack pointer. The PC is loaded with the address of the interrupt routine. As a result, the next instruction cycle will begin by fetching the appropriate instruction.

## 11.4

### INSTRUCTION PIPELINING

As computer systems evolve, greater performance can be achieved by taking advantage of improvements in technology, such as faster circuitry. In addition, organizational enhancements to the CPU can improve performance. We have already seen some examples of this, such as the use of multiple registers rather than a single accumulator, and the use of a cache memory. Another organizational approach, which is quite common, is instruction pipelining.

### Pipelining Strategy

Instruction pipelining is similar to the use of an assembly line in a manufacturing plant. An assembly line takes advantage of the fact that a product goes through various stages of production. By laying the production process out in an assembly line, products at various stages can be worked on simultaneously. This process is also referred to as *pipelining*, because, as in a pipeline, new inputs are accepted at one end before previously accepted inputs appear as outputs at the other end.

To apply this concept to instruction execution, we must recognize that, in fact, an instruction has a number of stages. Figure 11.7, for example, breaks the instruction cycle up into 10 tasks, which occur in sequence. Clearly, there should be some opportunity for pipelining.

As a simple approach, consider subdividing instruction processing into two stages: fetch instruction and execute instruction. There are times during the execution of an instruction when main memory is not being accessed. This time could be used to fetch the next instruction in parallel with the execution of the current one. Figure 11.11a depicts this approach. The pipeline has two independent stages. The first stage fetches an instruction and buffers it. When the second stage is free, the first stage passes it the buffered instruction. While the second stage is executing the instruction, the first stage takes advantage of any unused memory cycles to fetch and buffer the next instruction. This is called *instruction prefetch* or *fetch overlap*.

It should be clear that this process will speed up instruction execution. If the fetch and execute stages were of equal duration, the instruction cycle time would be halved. However, if we look more closely at this pipeline (Figure 11.11b), we will see that this doubling of execution rate is unlikely for two reasons:

1. The execution time will generally be longer than the fetch time. Execution will involve reading and storing operands and the performance of some operation. Thus, the fetch stage may have to wait for some time before it can empty its buffer.

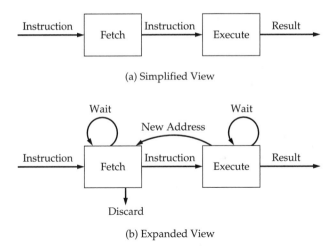

(a) Simplified View

(b) Expanded View

**FIGURE 11.11. Two-stage instruction pipeline**

2. A conditional branch instruction makes the address of the next instruction to be fetched unknown. Thus, the fetch stage must wait until it receives the next instruction address from the execute stage. The execute stage may then have to wait while the next instruction is fetched.

The time loss from the second reason can be reduced by guessing. A simple rule is the following: When a conditional branch instruction is passed on from the fetch to the execute stage, the fetch stage fetches the next instruction in memory after the branch instruction. Then, if the branch is not taken, no time is lost. If the branch is taken, the fetched instruction must be discarded and a new instruction fetched.

While these factors reduce the potential effectiveness of the two-stage pipeline, some speedup occurs. To gain further speedup, the pipeline must have more stages. Let us consider the following decomposition of the instruction processing.

- *Fetch Instruction (FI):* Read the next expected instruction into a buffer.
- *Decode Instruction (DI):* Determine the opcode and the operand specifiers.
- *Calculate Operands (CO):* Calculate the effective address of each source operand. This may involve displacement, register indirect, indirect, or other forms of address calculation.
- *Fetch Operands (FO):* Fetch each operand from memory. Operands in registers need not be fetched.
- *Execute Instruction (EI):* Perform the indicated operation and store the result, if any, in the specified destination operand location.
- *Write Operand (WO):* Store the result in memory.

With this decomposition, the various stages will be of more nearly equal duration. For the sake of illustration, let us assume equal duration. Then, Figure 11.12 shows that a six-stage pipeline can reduce the execution time for 9 instructions from 54 time units to 14 time units.

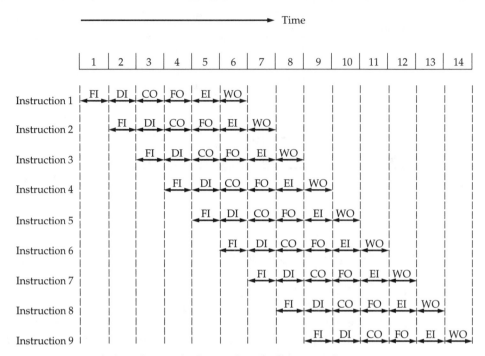

**FIGURE 11.12.  Timing Diagram for instruction pipeline operation**

Several comments: The diagram assumes that each instruction goes through all six stages of the pipeline. This will not always be the case. For example, a load instruction does not need the WO stage. However, to simplify the pipeline hardware, the timing is set up assuming that each instruction requires all six stages. Also, the diagram assumes that all of the stages can be performed in parallel. In particular, it is assumed that there are no memory conflicts. For example, the FI, FO, and WO stages involve a memory access. The diagram implies that all these accesses can occur simultaneously. Most memory systems will not permit that. However, the desired value may be in cache, or the FO or WO stage may be null. Thus, much of the time, memory conflicts will not slow down the pipeline.

Several other factors serve to limit the performance enhancement. If the six stages are not of equal duration, there will be some waiting involved at various pipeline stages, as discussed before for the two-stage pipeline. Another difficulty is the conditional branch instruction, which can invalidate several instruction fetches. A similar unpredictable event is an interrupt. Figure 11.13 illustrates the effects of the conditional branch, using the same program as Figure 11.12. Assume that instruction 3 is a conditional branch to instruction 15. Until the instruction is executed, there is no way of knowing which instruction will come next. The pipeline, in this example, simply loads the next instruction in sequence (instruction 4) and proceeds. In Figure 11.12, the branch is not taken, and we get the full performance benefit of the enhancement. In Figure 11.13, the branch is taken. This is not determined until the end of time unit 7. At this point, the pipeline must be cleared of instruc-

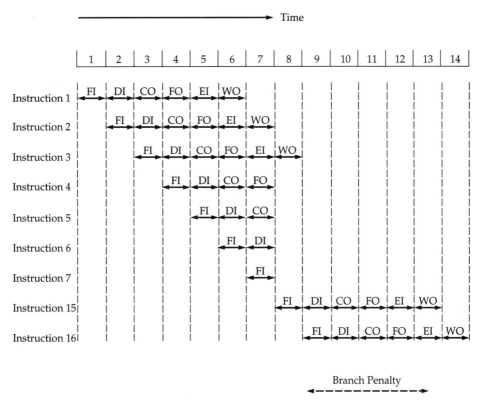

**FIGURE 11.13. The effect of a conditional branch on instruction pipeline operation**

tions that are not useful. During time unit 8, instruction 15 enters the pipeline. No instructions complete during time units 9 through 12; this is the performance penalty incurred because we could not anticipate the branch. Figure 11.14 indicates the logic needed for pipelining to account for branches and interrupts.

Other problems arise that did not appear in our simple two-stage organization. The CO stage may depend on the contents of a register that could be altered by a previous instruction that is still in the pipeline. Other such register and memory conflicts could occur. The system must contain logic to account for this type of conflict.

From the preceding discussion, it might appear that the greater the number of stages in the pipeline, the faster the execution rate. Some of the IBM S/360 designers pointed out two factors that frustrate this seemingly simple pattern for high-performance design [ANDE67], and they remain true today:

1. At each stage of the pipeline, there is some overhead involved in moving data from buffer to buffer and in performing various preparation and delivery functions. This overhead can appreciably lengthen the total execution time of a single instruction. This is significant when sequential instructions are logically dependent, either through heavy use of branching or through memory access dependencies.

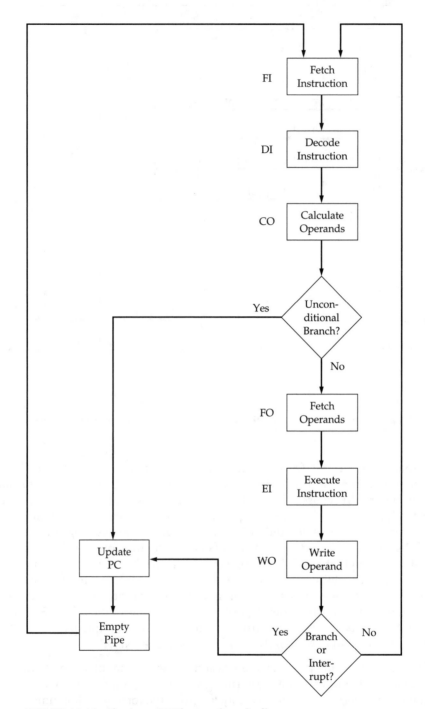

**FIGURE 11.14. Six-stage CPU instruction pipeline**

2. The amount of control logic required to handle memory and register dependencies and to optimize the use of the pipeline increases enormously with the number of stages. This can lead to a situation where the logic controlling the gating between stages is more complex than the stages being controlled.

Instruction pipelining is a powerful technique for enhancing performance but requires careful design to achieve optimum results with reasonable complexity.

## Dealing with Branches

One of the major problems in designing an instruction pipeline is assuring a steady flow of instructions to the initial stages of the pipeline. The primary impediment, as we have seen, is the conditional branch instruction. Until the instruction is actually executed, it is impossible to determine whether the branch will be taken or not.

A variety of approaches have been taken for dealing with conditional branches:

- Multiple Streams
- Prefetch Branch Target
- Loop Buffer
- Branch Prediction
- Delayed Branch

### Multiple Streams

A simple pipeline suffers a penalty for a branch instruction because it must choose one of two instructions to fetch next and may make the wrong choice. A brute-force approach is to replicate the initial portions of the pipeline and allow the pipeline to fetch both instructions, making use of two streams. There are several problems with this approach:

- With multiple pipelines there are contention delays for access to the registers and to memory.
- Additional branch instructions may enter the pipeline (either stream) before the original branch decision is resolved. Each such instruction needs an additional stream.

Despite these drawbacks, this strategy can improve performance. Examples of machines with two or more pipeline streams are the IBM 370/168 and the IBM 3033.

### Prefetch Branch Target

When a conditional branch is recognized, the target of the branch is prefetched, in addition to the instruction following the branch. This target is then saved until the branch instruction is executed. If the branch is taken, the target has already been prefetched.

The IBM 360/91 uses this approach.

## Loop Buffer

A loop buffer is a small, very-high-speed memory maintained by the instruction fetch stage of the pipeline, and containing the $n$ most recently fetched instructions, in sequence. If a branch is to be taken, the hardware first checks whether the branch target is within the buffer. If so, the next instruction is fetched from the buffer. The loop buffer has three benefits:

1. With the use of prefetching, the loop buffer will contain some instruction sequentially ahead of the current instruction fetch address. Thus, instructions fetched in sequence will be available without the usual memory access time.
2. If a branch occurs to a target just a few locations ahead of the address of the branch instruction, the target will already be in the buffer. This is useful for the rather common occurrence of IF–THEN and IF–THEN–ELSE sequences.
3. This strategy is particularly well suited to dealing with loops, or iterations, hence the name loop buffer. If the loop buffer is large enough to contain all the instructions in a loop, then those instructions need to be fetched from memory only once, for the first iteration. For subsequent iterations, all the needed instructions are already in the buffer.

The loop buffer is similar in principle to a cache dedicated to instructions. The differences are that the loop buffer only retains instructions in sequence and is much smaller in size and hence lower in cost.

Figure 11.15 gives an example of a loop buffer. If the buffer contains 256 bytes, and byte addressing is used, then the least significant 8 bits are used to index the buffer. The remaining most significant bits are checked to determine if the branch target lies within the environment captured by the buffer.

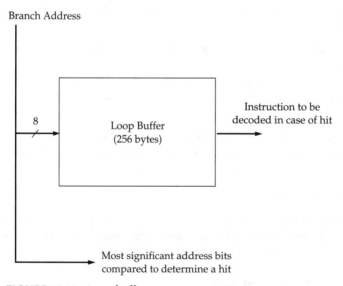

**FIGURE 11.15.  Loop buffer**

Among the machines using a loop buffer are some of the CDC machines (Star-100, 6600, 7600) and the CRAY-1. A specialized form of loop buffer is available on the Motorola 68010, for executing a three-instruction loop involving the DBcc (decrement and branch on condition) instruction (see Problem 11.8). A three-word buffer is maintained, and the processor executes these instructions repeatedly until the loop condition is satisfied.

### Branch Prediction

Various techniques can be used to predict whether a branch will be taken. Among the more common are the following:

- Predict Never Taken
- Predict Always Taken
- Predict by Opcode
- Taken/Not Taken Switch
- Branch History Table

The first three approaches are static: they do not depend on the execution history up to the time of the conditional branch instruction. The latter two approaches are dynamic: they depend on the execution history.

The first two approaches are the simplest. These either always assume that the branch will not be taken and continue to fetch instructions in sequence, or they always assume that the branch will be taken and always fetch from the branch target. The 68020 and the VAX 11/780 use the predict-never-taken approach. The VAX 11/780 also includes a feature to minimize the effect of a wrong decision. If the fetch of the instruction after the branch will cause a page fault or protection violation, the processor halts its prefetching until it is sure that the instruction should be fetched.

Studies analyzing program behavior have shown that conditional branches are taken more than 50 percent of the time [LILJ88], and so if the cost of prefetching from either path is the same, then always prefetching from the branch target address should give better performance than always prefetching from the sequential path. However, in a paged machine, prefetching the branch target is more likely to cause a page fault than prefetching the next instruction in sequence, and so this performance penalty should be taken into account. An avoidance mechanism may be employed to reduce this penalty.

The final static approach makes the decision based on the opcode of the branch instruction. The processor assumes that the branch will be taken for certain branch opcodes and not for others. [LILJ88] reports success rates of greater than 75 percent with this strategy.

Dynamic branch strategies attempt to improve the accuracy of prediction by recording the history of conditional branch instructions in a program. For example, one or more bits can be associated with each conditional branch instruction that reflect the recent history of the instruction. These bits are referred to as a taken/not taken switch that directs the processor to make a particular decision the next time the instruction is encountered. Typically, these history bits are not associated with the instruction in main memory. Rather, they are kept in temporary high-speed storage. One possibility is to associate these bits with any conditional branch instruction that is in a cache. When the instruction is replaced in the cache, its history is lost. Another possibility is to maintain a small table for recently executed branch instructions with one or more bits in each entry. The processor could access the table associatively, like a cache, or by using the low-order bits of the branch instruction's address.

With a single bit, all that can be recorded is whether the last execution of this instruction resulted in a branch or not. A shortcoming of using a single bit appears in the case of a conditional branch instruction that is almost always taken, such as a loop instruction. With only one bit of history, an error in prediction will occur twice for each use of the loop: once on entering the loop, and once on exiting.

If two bits are used, they can be used to record the result of the last two instances of the execution of the associated instruction, or to record a state in some other fashion. Figure 11.16 shows a typical approach (see Problem 11.6 for other possibilities). The decision process can be represented by a finite-state machine with four states. If the last two branches of the given instruction have taken the same path, the prediction is to take that path again. If the prediction is wrong, it remains the same the next time the instruction is encountered. If the prediction is wrong again, however, the next prediction will be to select the opposite path. Thus, the algorithm requires two consecutive wrong predictions to change the prediction decision. If a branch executes an unusual direction once, such as for a loop, the prediction will be wrong only once.

An example of a system that uses the taken/not taken switch approach is the IBM 3090/400.

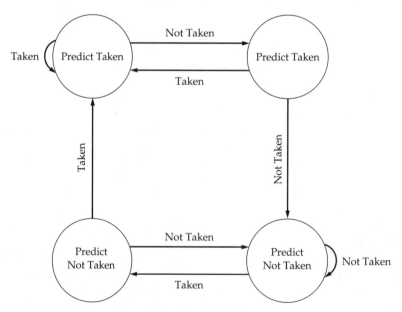

**FIGURE 11.16. Branch prediction state diagram**

The use of history bits, as just described, has one drawback: If the decision is made to take the branch, the target instruction cannot be fetched until the target address, which is an operand in the conditional branch instruction, is decoded. Greater efficiency could be achieved if the instruction fetch could be initiated as soon as the branch decision is made. For this purpose, more information must be saved, in what is known as a branch target buffer, or a branch history table.

The branch history table is a small cache memory associated with the instruction fetch stage of the pipeline. Each entry in the table consists of three elements: the address of a branch instruction, some number of history bits that record the state of use of that instruction, and information about the target instruction. In most proposals and implementations, this third field contains the address of the target instruction. Another possibility is for the third field to actually contain the target instruction. The trade-off is clear: Storing the target address yields a smaller table but a greater instruction fetch time compared with storing the target instruction.

Figure 11.17 contrasts this scheme with a predict never taken strategy. With the former strategy, the instruction fetch stage always fetches the next sequential address. If a branch is taken, some logic in the processor detects this and instructs that the next instruction be fetched from the target address (in addition to flushing the pipeline). The branch history table is treated as a cache. Each prefetch triggers a lookup in the branch history table. If no match is found, the next sequential address is used for the fetch. If a match is found, a prediction is made based on the state of the instruction: either the next sequential address or the branch target address is fed to the select logic.

When the branch instruction is executed, the execute stage signals the branch history table logic with the result. The state of the instruction is updated to reflect a correct or incorrect prediction. If the prediction is incorrect, the select logic is redirected to the correct address for the next fetch. When a conditional branch instruction is encountered that is not in the table, it is added to the table and one of the existing entries is discarded, using one of the cache replacement algorithms discussed in Chapter 4.

One example of an implementation of a branch history table is the Advanced Micro Device AMD29000 microprocessor.

### Delayed Branch

It is possible to improve pipeline performance by automatically rearranging instructions within a program, so that branch instructions occur later than actually desired. This intriguing approach is examined in Chapter 12.

## Intel 80486 Pipelining

The 80486 implements a five-stage pipeline with the following stages:

- *Fetch:* Instructions are fetched from the cache or from external memory and placed into one of the two 16-byte prefetch buffers. The objective of the fetch stage is to fill the prefetch buffers with new data as soon as the old data has been consumed by the instruction decoder. Since instructions are of variable length (from 1 to 11 bytes not counting prefixes), the status of the prefetcher relative to

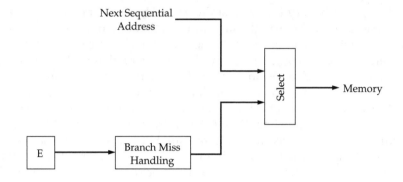

(a) Predict Never Taken Strategy

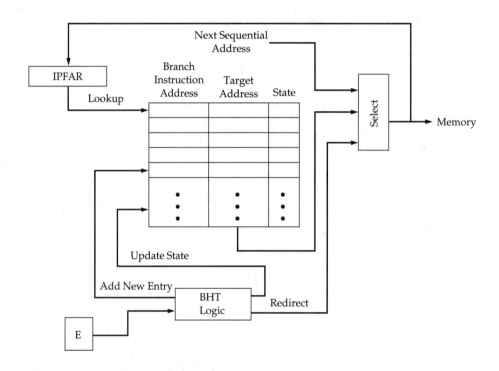

(b) Branch History Table Strategy

**FIGURE 11.17.  Dealing with branches**

the other pipeline stages varies from instruction to instruction. On average, about five instructions are fetched with each 16-byte load [CRAW90]. The fetch stage operates independently of the other stages to keep the prefetch buffers full.

- *Decode Stage 1:* All opcode and addressing-mode information is decoded in the D1 stage. The required information, as well as instruction-length information, is included in at most the first three bytes of the instruction. Hence, three bytes are passed to the D1 stage from the prefetch buffers. The D1 decoder can then direct the D2 stage to capture the rest of the instruction (displacement and immediate data), which is not involved in the D1 decoding.

- *Decode Stage 2:* The D2 stage expands each opcode into control signals for the ALU. It also controls the computation of the more complex addressing modes.
- *Execute:* This stage includes ALU operations, cache access, and register update.
- *Write Back:* This stage, if needed, updates registers and status flags modified during the preceding execute stage. If the current instruction updates memory, the computed value is sent to the cache and to the bus-interface write buffers at the same time.

With the use of two decode stages, the pipeline can sustain a throughput of close to one instruction per clock cycle. Complex instructions and conditional branches can slow this rate down.

Figure 11.18 shows examples of the operation of the pipeline. Part a shows that there is no delay introduced into the pipeline when a memory access is required.

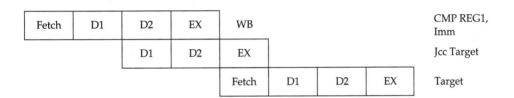

| Fetch | D1 | D2 | EX | WB | | | MOV Reg1, Mem1 |
| | | D1 | D2 | EX | WB | | MOV Reg1, Reg2 |
| | | | D1 | D2 | EX | WB | MOV Mem2, Reg1 |

(a) No Data Load Delay in the Pipeline

| Fetch | D1 | D2 | EX | WB | | MOV Reg1, Mem1 |
| | | D1 | 000 | D2 | EX | ADD Reg1, (Reg2) |

(b) A Pointer Load Delay

| Fetch | D1 | D2 | EX | WB | | | CMP REG1, Imm |
| | | D1 | D2 | EX | | | Jcc Target |
| | | | Fetch | D1 | D2 | EX | Target |

(c) Branch Instruction Timing

**FIGURE 11.18. 80486 instruction pipeline examples**

However, as part b shows, there can be a delay for values used to compute memory addresses. That is, if a value is loaded from memory into a register and that register is then used as a base register in the next instruction, the processor will stall for one cycle. In this example, the processor accesses the cache in the EX stage of the first instruction and stores the value retrieved in the register during the WB stage. However, the next instruction needs this register in its D2 stage. When the D2 stage lines up with the WB stage of the previous instruction, bypass signal paths allow the D2 stage to have access to the same data being used by the WB stage for writing, saving one pipeline stage.

Figure 11.18c illustrates the timing of a branch instruction, assuming that the branch is taken. The compare instruction updates condition codes in the WB stage, and bypass paths make this available to the EX stage of the jump instruction at the same time. In parallel, the processor runs a speculative fetch cycle to the target of the jump during the EX stage of the jump instruction. If the processor determines a false branch condition, it discards this prefetch and continues execution with the next sequential instruction (already fetched and decoded).

## 11.5

## THE PENTIUM PROCESSOR

An overview of the Pentium processor organization is depicted in Figure 4.24. In this section, we examine some of the details.

### Register Organization

The register organization includes the following types of registers (Table 11.1):

**TABLE 11.1    Pentium Processor Registers**

*(a) Integer Unit*

| Type | Number | Length (bits) | Purpose |
|---|---|---|---|
| General | 8 | 32 | General-purpose user registers |
| Segment | 6 | 16 | Contain segment selectors |
| Flags | 1 | 32 | Status and control bits |
| Instruction Pointer | 1 | 32 | Instruction pointer |

*(b) Floating-Point Unit*

| Type | Number | Length (bits) | Purpose |
|---|---|---|---|
| Numeric | 8 | 80 | Hold floating-point numbers |
| Control | 1 | 16 | Control bits |
| Status | 1 | 16 | Status bits |
| Tag Word | 1 | 16 | Specifies contents of numeric registers |
| Instruction Pointer | 1 | 48 | Points to instruction interrupted by exception |
| Data Pointer | 1 | 48 | Points to operand interrupted by exception |

- *General:* There are eight 32-bit general-purpose registers (see Figure 11.4b). These may be used for all types of Pentium instructions; they can also hold operands for address calculations. In addition, some of these registers also serve special purposes. For example, string instructions use the contents of the ECX, ESI, and EDI registers as operands without having to explicitly reference these registers in the instruction. As a result, a number of instructions can be encoded more compactly.
- *Segment:* The six 16-bit segment registers contain segment selectors, which index into segment tables, as discussed in Chapter 6. The code segment (CS) register references the segment containing the instruction being executed. The stack segment (SS) register references the segment containing a user-visible stack. The remaining segment registers (DS, ES, FS, GS) enable the user to reference up to four separate data segments at a time.
- *Flags:* The EFLAGS register contains condition codes and various mode bits.
- *Instruction Pointer:* Contains the address of the current instruction.

There are also registers specifically devoted to the floating-point unit:

- *Numeric:* Each register holds an extended-precision 80-bit floating-point number. There are eight registers that function as a stack, with push and pop operations available in the instruction set.
- *Control:* The 16-bit control register contains bits that control the operation of the floating-point unit, including the type of rounding control; single, double, or extended precision; and bits to enable or disable various exception conditions.
- *Status:* The 16-bit status register contains bits that reflect the current state of the floating-point unit, including a 3-bit pointer to the top of the stack; condition codes reporting the outcome of the last operation; and exception flags.
- *Tag Word:* This 16-bit register contains a 2-bit tag for each floating-point numeric register, which indicates the nature of the contents of the corresponding register. The four possible values are valid, zero, special (NaN, infinity, denormalized), and empty. These tags enable programs to check the contents of a numeric register without performing complex decoding of the actual data in the register.

The use of most of the above registers is easily understood. Let us elaborate briefly on several of the registers.

### EFLAGS Register

The EFLAGS register (Figure 11.19) indicates the condition of the processor and helps to control its operation. It includes the six condition codes defined in Table 9.8 (carry, parity, auxiliary, zero, sign, overflow), which report the results of an integer operation. In addition, there are bits in the register that may be referred to as control bits; these are

- *Trap Flag (TF):* When set, causes an interrupt after the execution of each instruction. This is used for debugging.
- *Interrupt Enable Flag (IF):* When set, the processor will recognize external interrupts.

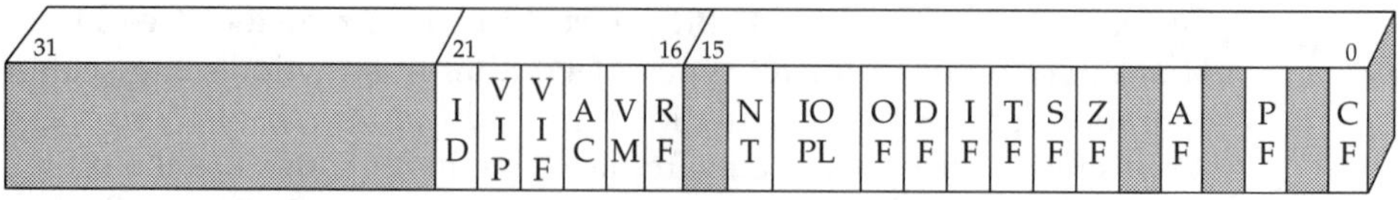

| 31 | | | | | | 21 | | 16 | 15 | | | | | | | | | | | 0 |

ID    =   Identification Flag                                DF   =   Direction Flag
VIP   =   Virtual Interrupt Pending                 IF    =   Interrupt Enable Flag
VIF   =   Virtual Interrupt Flag                          TF   =   Trap Flag
AC    =   Alignment Check                                   SF   =   Sign Flag
VM    =   Virtual 8086 Mode                             ZF   =   Zero Flag
RF    =   Resume Flag                                            AF   =   Auxiliary Carry Flag
NT    =   Nested Task Flag                                   PF   =   Parity Flag
IOPL =   I/O Privilege Level                               CF   =   Carry Flag
OF    =   Overflow Flag

**FIGURE 11.19. Pentium EFLAGS Register**

- *Direction Flag (DF):* Determines whether string processing instructions increment or decrement the 16-bit half-registers SI and DI (for 16-bit operations) or the 32-bit registers ESI and EDI (for 32-bit operations).
- *I/O Privilege Flag (IOPL):* When set, causes the processor to generate an exception on all accesses to I/O devices during protected-mode operation.
- *Resume Flag (RF):* Allows the programmer to disable debug exceptions so that the instruction can be restarted after a debug exception without immediately causing another debug exception.
- *Alignment Check (AC):* Activates if a word or doubleword is addressed on a nonword or nondoubleword boundary.
- *Identification Flag (ID):* If this bit can be set and cleared, that indicates that this processor supports the CPUID instruction. This instruction provides information about the vendor, family, and model.

In addition, there are four bits that relate to operating mode. The nested task (NT) flag indicates that the current task is nested within another task in protected-mode operation. The virtual mode (VM) bit allows the programmer to enable or disable virtual 8086 mode, which determines whether the processor runs as an 8086 machine. The virtual interrupt flag (VIF) and virtual interrupt pending (VIP) flag are used in a multitasking environment.

## Control Registers

The Pentium employs four 32-bit control registers (register CR1 is unused) to control various aspects of processor operation (Figure 11.20). The CR0 register contains system control flags, which control modes or indicate states that apply generally to the processor rather than to the execution of an individual task. The flags are

- *Protection Enable (PE):* Enable/disable protected mode of operation.
- *Monitor Coprocessor (MP):* Only of interest when running programs from earlier machines on the Pentium; it relates to the presence of an arithmetic coprocessor.

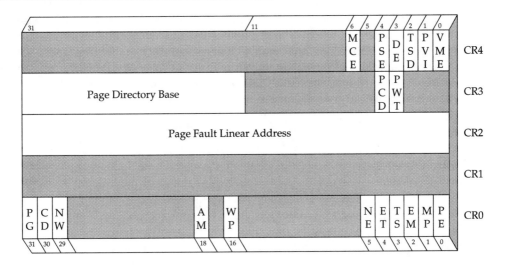

| MCE | = | Machine Check Enable | | NW | = | Not Write Through |
| PSE | = | Page Size Extensions | | AM | = | Alignment Mask |
| DE | = | Debugging Extensions | | WP | = | Write Protect |
| TSD | = | Time Stamp Disable | | NE | = | Numeric Error |
| PVI | = | Protected-Mode Virtual Interrupts | | ET | = | Extension Type |
| VME | = | Virtual-8086 Mode Extensions | | TS | = | Task Switched |
| PCD | = | Page-level Cache Disable | | EM | = | Emulation |
| PWT | = | Page-level Writes Transparent | | MP | = | Monitor Coprocessor |
| PG | = | Paging | | PE | = | Protection Enable |
| CD | = | Cache Disable | | | | |

**FIGURE 11.20. Pentium Control Registers**

- *Emulation (EM):* Set when the processor does not have a floating-point unit, and causes an interrupt when an attempt is made to execute floating-point instructions.
- *Task Switched (TS):* Indicates that the processor has switched tasks.
- *Extension Type (ET):* Not used on the Pentium; used to indicate support of math coprocessor instructions on earlier machines.
- *Numeric Error (NE):* Enables the standard mechanism for reporting floating-point errors on external bus lines.
- *Write Protect (WP):* When this bit is clear, read-only user-level pages can be written by a supervisor process. This feature is useful for supporting process creation in some operating systems.
- *Alignment Mask (AM):* Enables/disables alignment checking.
- *Not Write Through (NW):* Selects mode of operation of the data cache. When this bit is set, the data cache is inhibited from cache write-through operations.
- *Cache Disable (CD):* Enables/disables the internal cache fill mechanism.
- *Paging (PG):* Enables/disables paging.

When paging is enabled, the CR2 and CR3 registers are valid. The CR2 register holds the 32-bit linear address of the last page accessed before a page fault interrupt. The leftmost 20 bits of CR3 hold the 20 most significant bits of the base address of the page directory; the remainder of the address contains zeros. Two bits of CR3 are used to drive pins that control the operation of an external cache. The page-level cache disable (PCD) enables or disables the external cache, and the page-level writes transparent (PWT) bit controls write through in the external cache.

Six additional control bits are defined in CR4:

- *Virtual-8086 Mode Extension (VME):* Enables support for the virtual interrupt flag in virtual-8086 mode.
- *Protected-Mode Virtual Interrupts (PVI):* Enables support for the virtual interrupt flag in protected mode.
- *Time Stamp Disable (TSD):* Disables the read from time stamp counter (RDTSC) instruction, which is used for debugging purposes.
- *Debugging Extensions (DE):* Enables I/O breakpoints; this allows the processor to interrupt on I/O reads and writes.
- *Page Size Extensions (PSE):* Enables the use of 4-Mbyte pages.
- *Machine Check Enable (MCE):* Enables the machine check interrupt, which occurs when a data parity error occurs during a read bus cycle or when a bus cycle is not successfully completed.

## Interrupt Processing

Interrupt processing within a processor is a facility provided to support the operating system. It allows an application program to be suspended, in order that a variety of interrupt conditions can be serviced, and later resumed.

### Interrupts and Exceptions

Two classes of events cause the Pentium to suspend execution of the current instruction stream and respond to the event: interrupts and exceptions. In both cases, the processor saves the context of the current process and transfers to a predefined routine to service the condition. An *interrupt* is generated by a signal from hardware, and it may occur at random times during the execution of a program. An *exception* is generated from software, and it is provoked by the execution of an instruction. There are two sources of interrupts and two sources of exceptions:

1. Interrupts
   - *Maskable interrupts:* Received on the processor's INTR pin. The processor does not recognize a maskable interrupt unless the interrupt enable flag (IF) is set.
   - *Nonmaskable interrupts:* Received on the processor's NMI pin. Recognition of such interrupts cannot be prevented.
2. Exceptions
   - *Processor-detected exceptions:* Results when the processor encounters an error while attempting to execute an instruction.
   - *Programmed exceptions:* These are instructions that generate an exception (INT0, INT3, INT, and BOUND).

### Interrupt Vector Table

Interrupt processing on the Pentium uses the interrupt vector table. Every type of interrupt is assigned a number, and this number is used to index into the interrupt vector table. This table contains 256 32-bit interrupt vectors, which is the address (segment and offset) of the interrupt service routine for that interrupt number.

Table 11.2 shows the assignment of numbers in the interrupt vector table; shaded entries represent interrupts, while nonshaded entries are exceptions. The NMI hardware interrupt is type 2. INTR hardware interrupts are assigned numbers in the range 32–255; when an INTR interrupt is generated, it must be accompanied on the bus with the interrupt vector number for this interrupt. The remaining vector numbers are used for exceptions.

**TABLE 11.2   Pentium Exception and Interrupt Vector Table**

| Vector Number | Description |
|---|---|
| 0 | Divide error; division overflow or division by zero. |
| 1 | Debug exception; includes various faults and traps related to debugging. |
| 2 | NMI pin interrupt; signal on NMI pin. |
| 3 | Breakpoint; caused by INT 3 instruction, which is a one-byte instruction used for debugging. |
| 4 | INTO-detected overflow; occurs when the processor executes INTO with the OF flag set. |
| 5 | BOUND range exceeded; the BOUND instruction compares a register with boundaries stored in memory and generates an interrupt if the contents of the register is out of bounds. |
| 6 | Undefined op code. |
| 7 | Device not available; attempt to use ESC or WAIT instruction fails due to lack of external device. |
| 8 | Double fault; two interrupts occur during the same instruction, and cannot be handled serially. |
| 9 | Reserved. |
| 10 | Invalid task state segment; segment describing a requested task is not initialized or not valid. |
| 11 | Segment not present; required segment not present. |
| 12 | Stack fault; limit of stack segment exceeded or stack segment not present. |
| 13 | General protection; protection violation that does not cause another exception (e.g., writing to a read-only segment). |
| 14 | Page fault. |
| 15 | Reserved. |
| 16 | Floating-point error; generated by a floating-point arithmetic instruction. |
| 17 | Alignment check; access to a word stored at an odd byte address or a doubleword stored at an address not a multiple of four. |
| 18 | Machine check; model-specific |
| 19–31 | Reserved. |
| 32–255 | User interrupt vectors; provided when INTR signal is activated. |

Unshaded: exceptions; shaded: interrupts.

If more than one exception or interrupt is pending, the processor services them in a predictable order. The location of vector numbers within the table does not reflect priority. Instead, priority among exceptions and interrupts is organized into five classes. In descending order of priority, these are

- *Class 1:* Traps on the previous instruction (vector number 1).
- *Class 2:* External interrupts (2, 32–255).
- *Class 3:* Faults from fetching next instruction (3, 14).
- *Class 4:* Faults from decoding the next instruction (6, 7).
- *Class 5:* Faults on executing an instruction (0, 4, 5, 8, 10–14, 16, 17).

### Interrupt Handling

Just as with a transfer of execution using a CALL instruction, a transfer to an interrupt-handling routine uses the system stack to store the processor state. When an interrupt occurs and is recognized by the processor, a sequence of events takes place:

1. If the transfer involves a change of privilege level, then the current stack segment register and the current extended stack pointer (ESP) register are pushed onto the stack.
2. The current value of the EFLAGS register is pushed onto the stack.
3. Both the interrupt (IF) and trap (TF) flags are cleared. This disables INTR interrupts and the trap or single-step feature.
4. The current code segment (CS) pointer and the current instruction pointer (IP or EIP) are pushed onto the stack.
5. If the interrupt is accompanied by an error code, then the error code is pushed onto the stack.
6. The interrupt vector contents are fetched and loaded into the CS and IP or EIP registers. Execution continues from the interrupt service routine.

To return from an interrupt, the interrupt service routine executes an IRET instruction. This causes all of the values saved on the stack to be restored; execution resumes from the point of the interrupt.

## 11.6

## THE POWERPC PROCESSOR

An overview of the PowerPC processor organization is depicted in Figure 4.26. In this section, we examine some of the details of the 64-bit implementation.

### Register Organization

Figure 11.21 depicts the user-visible registers for the PowerPC. The fixed-point unit includes

- *General:* There are 32 64-bit general-purpose registers. These may be used to load, store, and manipulate data operands and may also be used for register

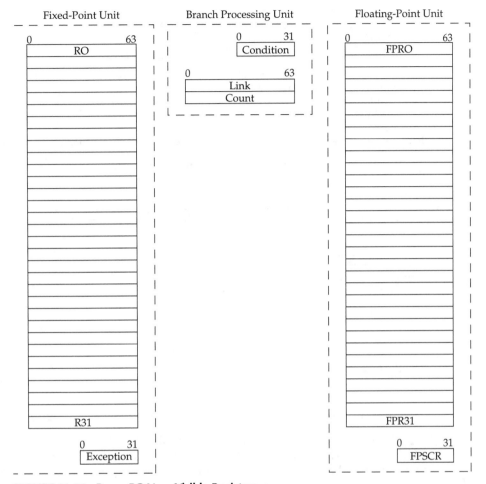

**FIGURE 11.21.  PowerPC User-Visible Registers**

indirect addressing. Register 0 is treated somewhat differently. For load and store operations and several of the add instructions, register 0 is treated as having a constant value zero regardless of its actual contents.

- *Exception Register (XER):* Includes three bits that report exceptions in integer arithmetic operations. This register also includes a byte count field that is used as an operand for some string instructions (Figure 11.22a).

The floating-point unit contains additional user-visible registers:

- *General:* There are 32 64-bit general-purpose registers, used for all floating-point operations.
- *Floating-Point Status and Control Register (FPSCR):* This 32-bit register contains bits that control the operation of the floating-point unit, and bits that record the status resulting from floating-point operations (Table 11.3).

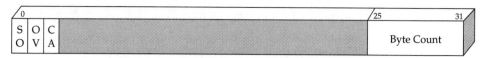

SO = Summary Overflow: set to 1 to indicate an overflow occurred during the execution of an instruction; remains 1 until reset by software

OV = Overflow: set to 1 to indicate an overflow occurred during the execution of an instruction; reset to 0 by next instruction if there is no overflow

CA = Carry: set to 1 to indicate carry out of bit 0 during the execution of an instruction

Byte Count = Specifies number of bytes to be transferred by Load/Store String indexed instruction

(a) Fixed-Point Exception Register (XER)

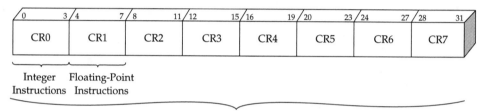

(b) Condition Register

**FIGURE 11.22. PowerPC Register Formats**

And the branch processing unit contains these user-visible registers:

- *Condition Register:* Consists of eight 4-bit condition code fields (Figure 11.22b).
- *Link Register:* The link register can be used in a conditional branch instruction for indirect addressing of the target address. This register is also used for call/return behavior. If the LK bit in a conditional branch instruction is set, then the address following the branch instruction is placed in the link register, and it can be used for a later return.
- *Count:* The count register can be used to control an iteration loop, as explained in Chapter 9; the count register is decremented each time it is tested in a conditional branch instruction. Another use for this register is indirect addressing of the target address in a branch instruction.

The fields of the condition register have a number of uses. The first four bits (CR0) are set for all integer arithmetic instructions for which the Rc bit is set. As Table 11.4 shows, the field indicates whether the result of the operation is positive, negative, or zero. The fourth bit is a copy of the summary overflow bit from the XER. The next field (CR1) is set for all floating-point arithmetic instructions for which the Rc bit is set. In this case, the four bits are set equal to the first four bits of the FPSCR (Table 11.3). Finally, the eight condition fields (CR0 through CR7) can be used with a compare instruction; in each case, the identity of the field is specified in the instruction itself. For both fixed-point and floating-point compare

**TABLE 11.3    PowerPC Floating-Point Status and Control Register**

| Bit | Definition |
| --- | --- |
| 0 | Exception summary. Set if any exception occurs; remains set until reset by software. |
| 1 | Enabled exception summary. Set if any enabled exception has occurred. |
| 2 | Invalid operation exception summary. Set if an invalid operation exception has occurred. |
| 3 | Overflow exception. Magnitude of result exceeds what can be represented. |
| 4 | Underflow exception. Result is too small to be normalized. |
| 5 | Zero divide exception. Divisor is zero and dividend is finite nonzero. |
| 6 | Inexact exception. Rounded result differs from intermediate result or an overflow occurs with overflow exception disabled. |
| 7:12 | Invalid operation exception. 7: signaling NaN; 8: ($\infty - \infty$); 9: ($\infty + \infty$); 10: $(0 + 0)$; 11: ($\infty \times 0$); 12: comparison involving NaN. |
| 13 | Fraction rounded. Rounding of the result incremented the fraction. |
| 14 | Fraction inexact. Rounded result changes fraction or an overflow occurs with overflow exception disabled. |
| 15:19 | Result flags. Five-bit code specifies less than, greater than, equal, unordered, quiet NaN, $\pm\infty$, $\pm$normalized, $\pm$denormalized, $\pm 0$. |
| 20 | Reserved. |
| 21:23 | Invalid operation exception. 21: software request; 22: square root of a negative number; 23: Integer conversion involving a large number, an infinity, or an NaN. |
| 24 | Invalid operation exception enable. |
| 25 | Overflow exception enable. |
| 26 | Underflow exception enable. |
| 27 | Zero divide exception enable. |
| 28 | Inexact exception enable. |
| 29 | Non-IEEE mode. |
| 30:31 | Rounding control. Two-bit code specifies to nearest, toward 0, toward $+\infty$, toward $-\infty$. |

Unshaded: status bits; shaded: control bits.

instructions, the first 3 bits of the designated condition field record whether the first operand is less than, greater than, or equal to the second operand. The fourth bit is the summary overflow bit for a fixed-point compare, and an unordered indicator for a floating-point compare.

## Interrupt Processing

As with any processor, the PowerPC includes a facility that enables the processor to interrupt the currently executing program to deal with an exception condition.

### Types of Interrupts

Interrupts on a PowerPC are classified as those caused by some system condition or event and those caused by the execution of an instruction. Table 11.5 lists the interrupts recognized by the PowerPC.

Most of the interrupts listed in the table are easily understood. A few warrant further comment. The system reset interrupt happens at power on and when the

**TABLE 11.4   Interpretation of Bits in Condition Register**

| Bit Position | CR0 (integer instruction with Rc = 1) | CR1 (floating-point instruction with Rc = 1) | CRi (fixed-point compare instruction) | CRi (floating-point compare instruction) |
|---|---|---|---|---|
| i | result < 0 | Exception summary | op1 < op2 | op1 < op2 |
| i+1 | result > 0 | Enabled exception summary | op1 > op2 | op1 > op2 |
| i+2 | result = 0 | Invalid operation exception summary | op1 = op2 | op1 = op2 |
| i+3 | Summary overflow | Overflow exception | Summary overflow | Unordered (one operand is a NaN) |

reset button on the system unit is pressed, and it causes the system to reboot. The machine check interrupt deals with certain anomalies, such as cache parity error and reference to a nonexistent memory location, and may cause the system to enter what is known as a checkstop state; this state suspends processor execution and freezes the contents of registers until a reboot. The floating-point assist enables the processor to invoke software routines to complete operations that cannot be handled directly by the floating-point unit, such as those involving denormalized numbers or unimplemented floating-point opcodes.

### Machine State Register (MSR)

Fundamental to the interruption of a program is the ability to recover the state of the processor at the time of the interrupt. This includes not only the contents of the various registers but also various control conditions relating to execution. These conditions are conveniently summarized in the MSR (Table 11.6). Again, several of the bits in this register warrant further comment.

When the privilege mode bit (bit 49) is set, the processor is operating at a user privilege level. Only a subset of the instruction set is available. When the bit is cleared, the processor operates at supervisor privilege level. This enables all of the instructions and provides access to certain system registers (such as the MSR) not accessible from the user privilege level.

The values of the two floating-point exception bits (bits 52 and 55) define the types of interrupts that the floating-point unit may generate. The interpretation is as follows:

| FE0 | FE1 | Interrupts that will be recognized |
|---|---|---|
| 0 | 0 | None |
| 0 | 1 | Imprecise non-recoverable |
| 1 | 0 | Imprecise recoverable |
| 1 | 1 | Precise |

When the single-step trace bit (bit 53) is set, the processor branches to the trace interrupt handler after the successful completion of each instruction. When the

**TABLE 11.5   PowerPC Interrupt Table**

| Entry Point | Interrupt Type | Description |
|---|---|---|
| 00000h | Reserved | |
| 00100h | System reset | Assertion of the processor's hard or soft reset input signals by external logic. |
| 00200h | Machine check | Assertion of TEA# to the processor when it is enabled to recognize machine checks. |
| 00300h | Data storage | Examples: data page fault; access rights violation on load/store. |
| 00400h | Instruction storage | Code page fault; attempted instruction fetch from I/O segment; access rights violation |
| 00500h | External | Assertion of the processor's external interrupt input signal by external logic when external interrupt recognition is enabled. |
| 00600h | Alignment | Unsuccessful attempt to access memory due to misaligned operand. |
| 00700h | Program | Floating-point interrupt; user attempts to execute privileged instruction; trap instruction executed with specified condition met; illegal instruction. |
| 00800h | Floating-point unavailable | Attempt to execute floating-point instruction with floating-point unit disabled. |
| 00900h | Decrementer | Exhaustion of the decrementer register when external interrupt recognition is enabled. |
| 00A00h | Reserved | |
| 00B00h | Reserved | |
| 00C00h | System call | Execution of a system call instruction. |
| 00D00h | Trace | Single-step or branch trace interrupt. |
| 00E00h | Floating-point assist | Attempt to execute relatively infrequent, complex floating-point operation (e.g., operation on denormalized number). |
| 00E10h through 00FFFh | Reserved | |
| 01000h through 02FFFh | Reserved (implementation specific) | |

Unshaded: interrupts caused by instruction execution; shaded: interrupts not caused by instruction execution.

branch trace bit (bit 54) is set, the processor branches to the branch trace interrupt handler after the successful completion of each branch instruction, whether or not the branch was taken.

The instruction address translation (bit 58) and data address translation (bit 59) determine whether real addressing is used or whether the memory management unit performs address translation.

**TABLE 11.6  PowerPC Machine State Register**

| Bit | Definition |
|---|---|
| 0 | Processor is in 32-bit/64-bit mode |
| 1:44 | Reserved |
| 45 | Power management enabled/disabled |
| 46 | Implementation-dependent |
| 47 | Defines whether interrupt handlers run in big-endian or little-endian mode |
| 48 | External interrupt enabled/disabled |
| 49 | Privileged/nonprivileged state |
| 50 | Floating-point unit available/unavailable |
| 51 | Machine check interrupts enabled/disabled |
| 52 | Floating-point exception mode 0 |
| 53 | Single-step trace enabled/disabled |
| 54 | Branch trace enabled/disabled |
| 55 | Floating-point exception mode 1 |
| 56 | Reserved |
| 57 | Most significant part of exception address is 000h/FFFh |
| 58 | Instruction address translation on/off |
| 59 | Data address translation on/off |
| 60:61 | Reserved |
| 62 | Interrupt is recoverable/nonrecoverable |
| 63 | Processor is in big-endian/little-endian mode |

Unshaded: copied to SRR1; shaded: not copied to SRR1.

## Interrupt Handling

When an interrupt occurs and is recognized by the processor, the following sequence of events takes place.

1. The processor places the address of the instruction to be executed next in the Save/Restore Register 0 (SRR0). This is the address of the currently executing instruction if the interrupt was caused by a failed attempt to execute that instruction; otherwise, it is the address of the next instruction to be executed after the current instruction.
2. The processor copies machine state information from the MSR to the Save/Restore Register 1 (SRR1). The bits that are depicted as unshaded in Table 11.6 are copied. The remaining bits of SRR1 are loaded with information specific to the interrupt type.
3. The MSR is set to a hardware-defined value specific to the interrupt type. For all interrupt types, address translation is turned off and external interrupts are disabled.
4. The processor then transfers control to the appropriate interrupt handler. The addresses of the interrupt handlers are stored in the Interrupt Table (Table 11.5). The base address of that table is determined by bit 57 of the MSR.

To return from an interrupt, the interrupt service routine executes an rfi instruction. This causes the bit values saved in SRR1 to be restored to the MSR. Execution resumes at the location stored in SRR0.

## 11.7

### RECOMMENDED READING

[HENN91] and [HAYE88] contain detailed discussions of pipelining. [SOHI90] provides an excellent, detailed discussion of the hardware design issues involved in an instruction pipeline. [CRAG92] is a detailed study of branch prediction in instruction pipelines. [DUBE91] and [LILJ88] examine various branch prediction strategies that can be used to enhance the performance of instruction pipelining. [KAEL91] examines the difficulty introduced into branch prediction by instructions whose target address is variable. The Intel 80486 instruction pipeline is described in [TABA91].

[BREY95] provides good coverage of interrupt processing on the Pentium, as does [SHAN94b] for the PowerPC.

BREY95   Brey, B. *The Intel 32-Bit Microprocessors: 80386, 80486, and Pentium.* Englewood Cliffs, NJ: Prentice Hall, 1995.

CRAG92   Cragon, H. *Branch Strategy Taxonomy and Performance Models.* Los Alamitos, CA: IEEE Computer Society Press, 1992.

DUBE91   Dubey, P., and Flynn, M. "Branch Strategies: Modeling and Optimization." *IEEE Transactions on Computers,* October 1991.

HAYE88   Hayes, J. *Computer Architecture and Organization, Second Edition.* New York: McGraw-Hill, 1988.

HENN91   Hennessy, J., and Jouppi, N. "Computer Technology and Architecture: An Evolving Interaction." *Computer,* September 1991.

KAEL91   Kaeli, D., and Emma, P., "Branch History Table Prediction of Moving Target Branches Due to Subroutine Returns." *Proceeding, 18th Annual International Symposium on Computer Architecture,* May 1991.

LILJ88   Lilja, D. "Reducing the Branch Penalty in Pipelined Processors." *Computer,* July 1988.

SHAN94b   Shanley, T. *PowerPC 601 System Architecture.* Richardson, TX: Mindshare Press, 1994.

SOHI90   Sohi, G. "Instruction Issue Logic for High-Performance Interruptable, Multiple Functional Unit, Pipelined Computers." *IEEE Transactions on Computers,* March 1990.

TABA91   Tabak, D. *Advanced Microprocessors.* New York: McGraw-Hill, 1991.

## 11.8

### PROBLEMS

11.1   **(a)** If the last operation performed on a computer with an 8-bit word was an addition in which the two operands were 2 and 3, what would be the value of the following flags?
- Carry
- Zero
- Overflow

- Sign
- Even Parity
- Half-Carry

**(b)** What if the operands were –1 (two's complement) and +1?

11.2  Consider the timing diagram of Figure 11.12. Assume that there is only a two-stage pipeline (fetch, execute). Redraw the diagram to show how many time units are now needed for four instructions.

11.3  One limitation of the multiple-stream approach to dealing with branches in a pipeline is that additional branches will be encountered before the first branch is resolved. Suggest two additional limitations or drawbacks.

11.4  What properties should be designed into the opcodes on a new system to allow future implementation of separate and pipelined, parallel circuitry for floating-point, fixed-point, and bit/byte string instructions?

11.5  Consider the state diagrams of Figure 11.23.

   **(a)** Describe the behavior of each.

   **(b)** Compare these with the branch prediction state diagram in Section 11.4. Discuss the relative merits of each of the three approaches to branch prediction.

11.6  The Motorola 680x0 machines include the instruction Decrement and Branch According to Condition, which has the following form:

DBcc Dn, displacement

where cc is one of the testable conditions, Dn is a general-purpose register, and displacement specifies the target address relative to the current address. The instruction can be defined as follows:

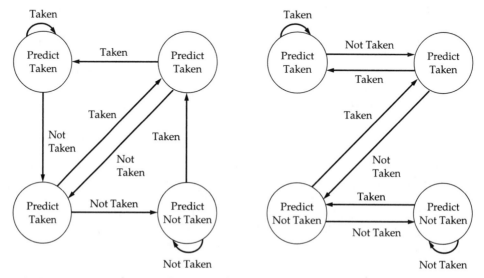

**FIGURE 11.23.  Branch Processing State Diagrams**

**if** (cc = False)
**then begin**
    Dn := (Dn) −1;
    **if** Dn ≠ −1 **then** PC := (PC) + displacement **end**
**else** PC := (PC) + 2;

When the instruction is executed, the condition is first tested to determine whether the termination condition for the loop is satisfied. If so, no operation is performed and execution continues at the next instruction in sequence. If the condition is false, the specified data register is decremented and checked to see if it is less than zero. If it is less than zero, the loop is terminated and execution continues at the next instruction in sequence. Otherwise, the program branches to the specified location.

Now consider the following assembly-language program fragment:

```
AGAIN    CMPM.L    (A0)+,(A1)+
         DBNE      D1,AGAIN
         NOP
```

Two strings addressed by A0 and A1 are compared for equality; the string pointers are incremented with each reference. D1 initially contains the number of longwords (4 bytes) to be compared.

**(a)** The initial contents of the registers are A0 = $00004000, A1 = $00005000, and D1 = $000000FF (the $ indicates hexadecimal notation). Memory between $4000 and $6000 is loaded with words $AAAA. If the program above is run, specify the number of times the DBNE loop is executed and the contents of the three registers when the NOP instruction is reached.

**(b)** Repeat (a), but now assume that memory between $4000 and $4FEE is loaded with $0000 and between $5000 and $6000 is loaded with $AAA.

11.7 Redraw Figure 11.18c assuming that the conditional branch is not taken.

# CHAPTER 12

# Reduced Instruction Set Computers

Since the development of the stored-program computer around 1950, there have been remarkably few true innovations in the areas of computer organization and architecture. The following, though not constituting a complete list, are some of the major advances since the birth of the computer.

- *The Family Concept:* Introduced by IBM with its System/360 in 1964, followed shortly thereafter by DEC, with its PDP-8. The family concept decouples the architecture of a machine from its implementation. A set of computers are offered, with different price/performance characteristics, that present the same architecture to the user. The differences in price and performance are due to different implementations of the same architecture.
- *Microprogrammed Control Unit:* Suggested by Wilkes in 1951, and introduced by IBM on the S/360 line in 1964. Microprogramming eases the task of designing and implementing the control unit and provides support for the family concept.
- *Cache Memory:* First introduced commercially on IBM S/360 Model 85 in 1968. The insertion of this element into the memory hierarchy dramatically improves performance.
- *Pipelining:* A means of introducing parallelism into the essentially sequential nature of a machine-instruction program. Examples are instruction pipelining and vector processing.
- *Multiple Processors:* This category covers a number of different organizations and objectives.

To this list must now be added one of the most interesting and, potentially, one of the most important innovations: reduced instruction set computer (RISC) architecture. The RISC architecture is a dramatic departure from the historical trend in CPU architecture and challenges the conventional wisdom expressed in words and deeds by most computer architects. An analysis of the RISC architecture brings into focus many of the important issues in computer organization and architecture.

Although RISC systems have been defined and designed in a variety of ways by different groups, the key elements shared by most (not all) designs are these:

- A limited and simple instruction set.
- A large number of general-purpose registers, or the use of compiler technology to optimize register usage.
- An emphasis on optimizing the instruction pipeline.

Table 12.1 compares several RISC and non-RISC systems.

We begin this chapter with a brief survey of some results on instruction sets, then examine each of the three topics just listed. This is followed by a description of two of the best-documented RISC designs.

## 12.1

## INSTRUCTION EXECUTION CHARACTERISTICS

One of the most visible forms of evolution associated with computers is that of programming languages. As the cost of hardware has dropped, the relative cost of software has risen. Along with that, a chronic shortage of programmers has driven up software costs in absolute terms. Thus, the major cost in the life cycle of a system is software, not hardware. Adding to the cost, and to the inconvenience, is the element of unreliability: it is common for programs, both system and application, to continue to exhibit new bugs after years of operation.

The response from researchers and industry has been to develop ever more powerful and complex high-level programming languages (compare FORTRAN with Ada). These high-level languages (HLL) allow the programmer to express algorithms more concisely, take care of much of the detail, and often support naturally the use of structured programming.

Alas, this solution gave rise to another problem, known as the *semantic gap*, the difference between the operations provided in HLLs and those provided in computer architecture. Symptoms of this gap are alleged to include execution inefficiency, excessive machine program size, and compiler complexity. Designers responded with architectures intended to close this gap. Key features include large instruction sets, dozens of addressing modes, and various HLL statements implemented in hardware. An example of the latter is the CASE machine instruction on the VAX. Such complex instruction sets are intended to

- Ease the task of the compiler writer.
- Improve execution efficiency, since complex sequences of operations can be implemented in microcode.
- Provide support for even more complex and sophisticated HLLs.

Meanwhile, a number of studies have been done over the years to determine the characteristics and patterns of execution of machine instructions generated from HLL programs. The results of these studies inspired some researchers to look for an altogether different approach: namely, to make the architecture that supports the HLL simpler, rather than more complex.

**TABLE 12.1**

**Characteristics of Some CISCs, RISCs, and Superscalar Processors**

| Characteristic | Complex Instruction Set Computer (CISC) | | | Reduced Instruction Set Computer (RISC) | | Superscalar | |
|---|---|---|---|---|---|---|---|
| | IBM 370/168 | VAX 11/780 | Intel 80486 | Motorola 88000 | MIPS R4000 | IBM RS/System 6000 | Intel 80960 |
| Year developed | 1973 | 1978 | 1989 | 1988 | 1991 | 1990 | 1989 |
| Number of instructions | 208 | 303 | 235 | 51 | 94 | 184 | 62 |
| Instruction size (bytes) | 2–6 | 2–57 | 1–11 | 4 | 32 | 4 | 4, 8 |
| Addressing modes | 4 | 22 | 11 | 3 | 1 | 2 | 11 |
| Number of general-purpose registers | 16 | 16 | 8 | 32 | 32 | 32 | 23–256 |
| Control memory size (Kbits) | 420 | 480 | 246 | — | — | — | — |
| Cache size (KBytes) | 64 | 64 | 8 | 16 | 128 | 32–64 | 0.5 |

So, to understand the line of reasoning of the RISC advocates, we begin with a brief review of instruction execution characteristics. The aspects of computation of interest are

- *Operations Performed:* These determine the functions to be performed by the CPU and its interaction with memory.
- *Operands Used:* The types of operands and the frequency of their use determine the memory organization for storing them and the addressing modes for accessing them.
- *Execution Sequencing:* This determines the control and pipeline organization.

In the remainder of this section, we summarize the results of a number of studies of high-level-language programs. All of the results are based on dynamic measurements. That is, measurements are collected by executing the program and counting the number of times some feature has appeared or a particular property has held true. In contrast, static measurements merely perform these counts on the source text of a program. They give no useful information on performance, because they are not weighted relative to the number of times each statement is executed.

## Operations

A variety of studies have been made to analyze the behavior of HLL programs. Table 4.8, discussed in Chapter 4, includes key results from a number of studies. There is quite good agreement in the results of this mixture of languages and applications. Assignment statements predominate, suggesting that the simple movement of data is of high importance. There is also a preponderance of conditional statements (IF, LOOP). These statements are implemented in machine language with some sort of compare and branch instruction. This suggests that the sequence control mechanism of the instruction set is important.

These results are instructive to the machine instruction set designer, indicating which types of statements occur most often and therefore should be supported in an "optimal" fashion. However, these results do not reveal which statements use the most time in the execution of a typical program. That is, given a compiled machine language program, which statements in the source language cause the execution of the most machine-language instructions?

To get at this underlying phenomenon, the Patterson programs [PATT82a] were compiled on the VAX, PDP-11, and Motorola 68000 to determine the average number of machine instructions and memory references per statement type. By multiplying the frequency of occurrence of each statement type by these averages, Table 12.2 is obtained. Columns 2 and 3 provide surrogate measures of the actual time spent executing the various statement types. The results suggest that the procedure call/return is the most time-consuming operation in typical HLL programs.

The reader should be clear on the significance of Table 12.2. This table indicates the relative significance of various statement types in an HLL, when that HLL is compiled for a typical contemporary instruction set architecture. Some other architecture could conceivably produce different results. However, this study produces results that are representative for contemporary complex instruction set

**TABLE 12.2    Weighted Relative Dynamic Frequency of HLL Operations [PATT82a]**

| | Dynamic Occurrence | | Machine-Instruction Weighted | | Memory-Reference Weighted | |
|---|---|---|---|---|---|---|
| | Pascal | C | Pascal | C | Pascal | C |
| ASSIGN | 45 | 38 | 13 | 13 | 14 | 15 |
| LOOP | 5 | 3 | 42 | 32 | 33 | 26 |
| CALL | 15 | 12 | 31 | 33 | 44 | 45 |
| IF | 29 | 43 | 11 | 21 | 7 | 13 |
| GOTO | — | 3 | — | — | — | — |
| OTHER | 6 | 1 | 3 | 1 | 2 | 1 |

computer (CISC) architectures. Thus, they can provide guidance to those looking for more efficient ways to support HLLs.

## Operands

Much less work has been done on the occurrence of types of operands, despite the importance of this topic. There are several aspects that are significant.

The Patterson study already referenced [PATT82a] also looked at the dynamic frequency of occurrence of classes of variables (Table 12.3). The results, consistent between Pascal and C programs, show that the majority of references are to simple scalar variables. Further, more than 80% of the scalars were local (to the procedure) variables. In addition, references to arrays/structures require a previous reference to their index or pointer, which again is usually a local scalar. Thus, there is a preponderance of references to scalars, and these are highly localized.

The Patterson study examined the dynamic behavior of HLL programs, independent of the underlying architecture. As discussed before, it is necessary to deal with actual architectures to examine program behavior more deeply. One study, [LUND77], examined DEC-10 instructions dynamically and found that each instruction on the average references 0.5 operand in memory and 1.4 registers. Similar results are reported in [HUCK83] for C, Pascal, and FORTRAN programs on S/370, PDP-11, and VAX. Of course, these figures depend highly on both the architecture and the compiler, but they do illustrate the frequency of operand accessing.

These latter studies suggest the importance of an architecture that lends itself to fast operand accessing, since this operation is performed so frequently. The Patterson study suggests that a prime candidate for optimization is the mechanism for storing and accessing local scalar variables.

**TABLE 12.3    Dynamic Percentage of Operands**

| | Pascal | C | Average |
|---|---|---|---|
| Integer Constant | 16 | 23 | 20 |
| Scalar Variable | 58 | 53 | 55 |
| Array/Structure | 26 | 24 | 25 |

## Procedure Calls

We have seen that procedure calls and returns are an important aspect of HLL programs. The evidence (Table 12.2) suggests that these are the most time-consuming operations in compiled HLL programs. Thus, it will be profitable to consider ways of implementing these operations efficiently. Two aspects are significant: the number of parameters and variables that a procedure deals with, and the depth of nesting.

In Tanenbaum's study [TANE78], he found that 98% of dynamically called procedures were passed fewer than six arguments, and that 92% of them used fewer than six local scalar variables. Similar results were reported by the Berkeley RISC team [KATE83], as shown in Table 12.4. These results show that the number of words required per procedure activation is not large. The studies reported earlier indicated that a high proportion of operand references are to local scalar variables. These studies show that those references are in fact confined to relatively few variables.

The same Berkeley group also looked at the pattern of procedure calls and returns in HLL programs. They found that it is rare to have a long uninterrupted sequence of procedure calls followed by the corresponding sequence of returns. Rather, they found that a program remains confined to a rather narrow window of procedure-invocation depth. This is illustrated in Figure 4.31, which was discussed in Chapter 4. These results reinforce the conclusion that operand references are highly localized.

## Implications

A number of groups have looked at results such as those just reported and have concluded that the attempt to make the instruction set architecture close to HLLs is not the most effective design strategy. Rather, the HLLs can best be supported by optimizing performance of the most time-consuming features of typical HLL programs.

Generalizing from the work of a number of researchers, three elements emerge that, by and large, characterize RISC architectures. First, use a large number of registers. This is intended to optimize operand referencing. The studies just discussed show that there are several references per HLL instruction, and that there is a high proportion of move (assignment) statements. This, coupled with the locality and predominance of scalar references, suggests that performance can be improved by reducing memory references at the expense of more register references. Because of the locality of these references, an expanded register set seems practical.

**TABLE 12.4   Procedure Arguments and Local Scalar Variables**

| Percentage of Executed Procedure Calls With | Compiler, Interpreter, and Typesetter | Small Nonnumeric Programs |
|---|---|---|
| >3 arguments | 0–7% | 0–5% |
| >5 arguments | 0–3% | 0% |
| >8 words of arguments and local scalars | 1–20% | 0–6% |
| >12 words of arguments and local scalars | 1–6% | 0–3% |

Second, careful attention needs to be paid to the design of instruction pipelines. Because of the high proportion of conditional branch and procedure call instructions, a straightforward instruction pipeline will be inefficient. This manifests itself as a high proportion of instructions that are prefetched but never executed.

Finally, a simplified (reduced) instruction set is indicated. This point is not as obvious as the others, but should become clearer in the ensuing discussion. In addition, we will see that the desire to implement an entire CPU on a single chip suggests a reduced instruction set solution.

## 12.2

## THE USE OF A LARGE REGISTER FILE

The results summarized in Section 12.1 point out the desirability of quick access to operands. We have seen that there is a large proportion of assignment statements in HLL programs, and many of these are of the simple form A = B. Also, there are a significant number of operand accesses per HLL statement. If we couple these results with the fact that most accesses are to local scalars, heavy reliance on register storage is suggested.

The reason that register storage is indicated is that it is the fastest available storage device, faster than both main memory and cache. The register file is physically small, generally on the same chip as the ALU and control unit, and employs much shorter addresses than addresses for cache and memory. Thus, a strategy is needed that will allow the most frequently accessed operands to be kept in registers and to minimize register-memory operations.

Two basic approaches are possible, one based on software and the other on hardware. The software approach is to rely on the compiler to maximize register usage. The compiler will attempt to allocate registers to those variables that will be used the most in a given time period. This approach requires the use of sophisticated program-analysis algorithms. The hardware approach is simply to use more registers so that more variables can be held in registers for longer periods of time.

In this section, we will discuss the hardware approach. This approach has been pioneered by the Berkeley RISC group [PATT82a] and is used in the first commercial RISC product, the Pyramid [RAGA83].

### Register Windows

On the face of it, the use of a large set of registers should decrease the need to access memory. The design task is to organize the registers in such a fashion that this goal is realized.

Since most operand references are to local scalars, the obvious approach is to store these in registers, with perhaps a few registers reserved for global variables. The problem is that the definition of *local* changes with each procedure call and return, operations that occur frequently. On every call, local variables must be saved from the registers into memory, so that the registers can be reused by the called program. Furthermore, parameters must be passed. On return, the variables of the parent program must be restored (loaded back into registers) and results must be passed back to the parent program.

The solution is based on two other results reported in Section 12.1. First, a typical procedure employs only a few passed parameters and local variables. Second, the depth of procedure activation fluctuates within a relatively narrow range (Figure 4.31). To exploit these properties, multiple small sets of registers are used, each assigned to a different procedure. A procedure call automatically switches the CPU to use a different fixed-size window of registers, rather than saving registers in memory. Windows for adjacent procedures are overlapped to allow parameter passing.

The concept is illustrated in Figure 12.1. At any time, only one window of registers is visible and is addressable as if it were the only set of registers (e.g., addresses 0 through $N - 1$). The window is divided into three fixed-size areas. Parameter registers hold parameters passed down from the procedure that called the current procedure and results to be passed back up. Local registers are used for local variables, as assigned by the compiler. Temporary registers are used to exchange parameters and results with the next lower level (procedure called by current procedure). The temporary registers at one level are physically the same as the parameter registers at the next lower level. This overlap permits parameters to be passed without the actual movement of data.

To handle any possible pattern of calls and returns, the number of register windows would have to be unbounded. Instead, the register windows can be used to hold the few most recent procedure activations. Older activations must be saved in memory and later restored when the nesting depth decreases. Thus, the actual organization of the register file is as a circular buffer of overlapping windows.

This organization is shown in Figure 12.2, which depicts a circular buffer of six windows. The buffer is filled to a depth of 4 (A called B; B called C; C called D) with procedure D active. The current-window pointer (CWP) points to the window of the currently active procedure. Register references by a machine instruction are offset by this pointer to determine the actual physical register. The saved-window pointer identifies the window most recently saved in memory. If procedure D now calls procedure E, arguments for E are placed in D's temporary registers (the overlap between w3 and w2) and the CWP is advanced by one window.

If procedure E then makes a call to procedure F, the call cannot be made with the current status of the buffer. This is because F's window overlaps A's window. If F begins to load its temporary registers, preparatory to a call, it will overwrite the

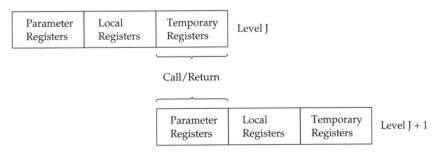

**FIGURE 12.1. Overlapping register windows**

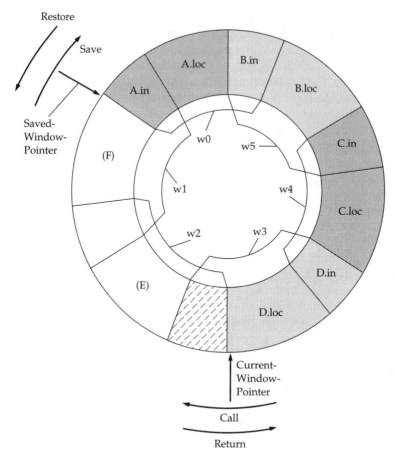

**FIGURE 12.2.  Circular-buffer organization of overlapped windows**

parameter registers of A (A.In). Thus, when CWP is incremented (modulo 6) so that it becomes equal to SWP, an interrupt occurs, and A's window is saved. Only the first two portions (A.In and A.loc) need be saved. Then, the SWP is incremented and the call to F proceeds. A similar interrupt can occur on returns. For example, subsequent to the activation of F, when B returns to A, CWP is decremented and becomes equal to SWP. This causes an interrupt that results in the restoration of A's window.

From the preceding, it can be seen that an $N$-window register file can hold only $N - 1$ procedure activations. The value of $N$ need not be large. As was mentioned earlier, one study [TAMI83] found that, with 8 windows, a save or restore is needed on only 1% of the calls or returns. The Berkeley RISC computers use 8 windows of 16 registers each. The Pyramid computer employs 16 windows of 32 registers each.

## Global Variables

The window scheme just described provides an efficient organization for storing local scalar variables in registers. However, this scheme does not address the need to store global variables, those accessed by more than one procedure (e.g., COMMON variables in FORTRAN). Two options suggest themselves. First, variables declared as global in an HLL can be assigned memory locations by the compiler, and all machine instructions that reference these variables will use memory-reference operands. This is straightforward, from both the hardware and software (compiler) points of view. However, for frequently accessed global variables, this scheme is inefficient.

An alternative is to incorporate a set of global registers in the CPU. These registers would be fixed in number and available to all procedures. A unified numbering scheme can be used to simplify the instruction format. For example, references to registers 0 through 7 could refer to unique global registers, and references to registers 8 through 31 could be offset to refer to physical registers in the current window. Thus, there is an increased hardware burden to accommodate the split in register addressing. In addition, the compiler must decide which global variables should be assigned to registers.

## Large Register File Versus Cache

The register file, organized into windows, acts as a small, fast buffer for holding a subset of all variables that are likely to be used the most heavily. From this point of view, the register file acts much like a cache memory. The question therefore arises as to whether it would be simpler and better to use a cache and a small traditional register file.

Table 12.5 compares characteristics of the two approaches. The window-based register file holds all the local scalar variables (except in the rare case of window overflow) of the most recent $N - 1$ procedure activations. The cache holds a selection of recently used scalar variables. The register file should save time, since all local scalar variables are retained. On the other hand, the cache may make more efficient use of space, since it is reacting to the situation dynamically. Furthermore, caches generally treat all memory references alike, including instructions and other types of data. Thus, savings in these other areas are possible with a cache and not a register file.

A register file may make inefficient use of space, since not all procedures will need the full window space allotted to them. On the other hand, the cache suffers from another sort of inefficiency: Data are read into the cache in blocks. Whereas the register file contains only those variables in use, the cache reads in a block of data, some or much of which will not be used.

**TABLE 12.5   Characteristics of Large-Register-File and Cache Organizations**

| Large Register File | Cache |
| --- | --- |
| All local scalars | Recently-used local scalars |
| Individual variables | Blocks of memory |
| Compiler-assigned global variables | Recently-used global variables |
| Save/Restore based on procedure nesting depth | Save/Restore based on cache replacement algorithm |
| Register addressing | Memory addressing |

The cache is capable of handling global as well as local variables. There are usually many global scalars, but only a few of them are heavily used [KATE83]. A cache will dynamically discover these variables and hold them. If the window-based register file is supplemented with global registers, it too can hold some global scalars. However, it is difficult for a compiler to determine which globals will be heavily used.

With the register file, the movement of data between registers and memory is determined by the procedure nesting depth. Since this depth usually fluctuates within a narrow range, the use of memory is relatively infrequent. Most cache memories are set associative with a small set size. Thus, there is the danger that other data or instructions will overwrite frequently used variables.

Based on the discussion so far, the choice between a large window-based register file and a cache is not clear-cut. There is one characteristic, however, in which the register approach is clearly superior and which suggests that a cache-based system will be noticeably slower. This distinction shows up in the amount of addressing overhead experienced by the two approaches.

Figure 12.3 illustrates the difference. To reference a local scalar in a window-based register file, a "virtual" register number and a window number are used.

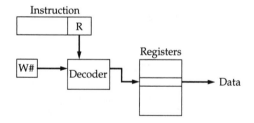

(a) Window-Based Register File

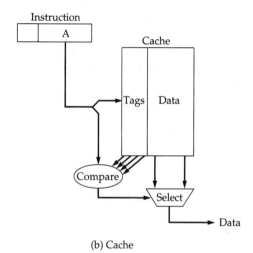

(b) Cache

**FIGURE 12.3. Referencing a local scalar**

These can pass through a relatively simple decoder to select one of the physical registers. To reference a memory location in cache, a full-width memory address must be generated. The complexity of this operation depends on the addressing mode. In a set associative cache, a portion of the address is used to read a number of words and tags equal to the set size. Another portion of the address is compared with the tags, and one of the words that were read is selected. It should be clear that even if the cache is as fast as the register file, the access time will be considerably longer. Thus, from the point of view of performance, the window-based register file is superior for local scalars. Further performance improvement could be achieved by the addition of a cache for instructions only.

## 12.3

### COMPILER-BASED REGISTER OPTIMIZATION

Let us assume now that only a small number (e.g., 16–32) of registers is available on the target RISC machine. In this case, optimized register usage is the responsibility of the compiler. A program written in a high-level language has, of course, no explicit references to registers. Rather, program quantities are referred to symbolically. The objective of the compiler is to keep the operands for as many computations as possible in registers rather than main memory, and to minimize load-and-store operations.

In general, the approach taken is as follows. Each program quantity that is a candidate for residing in a register is assigned to a symbolic or virtual register. The compiler then maps the unlimited number of symbolic registers into a fixed number of real registers. Symbolic registers whose usage does not overlap can share the same real register. If, in a particular portion of the program, there are more quantities to deal with than real registers, then some of the quantities are assigned to memory locations. Load-and-store instructions are used to temporarily position quantities in registers for computational operations.

The essence of the optimization task is to decide which quantities are to be assigned to registers at any given point in the program. The technique most commonly used in RISC compilers is known as graph coloring, which is a technique borrowed from the discipline of topology [CHAI82, CHOW86, COUT86, CHOW90].

The graph coloring problem is this. Given a graph consisting of nodes and edges, assign colors to nodes such that adjacent nodes have different colors, and do this in such a way as to minimize the number of different colors. This problem is adapted to the compiler problem in the following way. First, the program is analyzed to build a register interference graph. The nodes of the graph are the symbolic registers. If two symbolic registers are "live" during the same program fragment, then they are joined by an edge to depict interference. An attempt is then made to color the graph with $n$ colors, where $n$ is the number of registers. If this process does not fully succeed, then those nodes that cannot be colored must be placed in memory, and loads and stores must be used to make space for the affected quantities when they are needed.

Figure 12.4 is a simple example of the process. Assume a program with six symbolic registers to be compiled into three actual registers. Figure 12.4a shows the

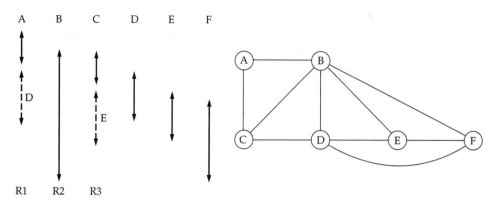

(a) Time Sequence of Active Use of Symbolic Registers          (b) Register Interference Graph

**FIGURE 12.4.  The graph coloring approach**

time sequence of active use of each symbolic register, and part b shows the register interference graph. A possible coloring with three colors is indicated. One symbolic register, F, is left uncolored and must be dealt with using loads and stores.

In general, there is a trade-off between the use of a large set of registers and compiler-based register optimization. For example, [BRAD91a] reports on a study that modeled a RISC architecture with features similar to the Motorola 88000 and the MIPS R2000. They varied the number of registers from 16 to 128, and they considered both the use of all general-purpose registers and registers split between integer and floating-point use. Their study showed that with even simple register optimization, there is little benefit to the use of more than 64 registers. With reasonably sophisticated register optimization techniques, there is only marginal performance improvement with more than 32 registers. Finally, they noted that with a small number of registers (e.g., 16), a machine with a shared register organization executes faster than one with a split organization. Similar conclusions can be drawn from [HUGU91], which reports on a study that is primarily concerned with optimizing the use of a small number of registers, rather than comparing the use of large register sets with optimization efforts.

## 12.4

# REDUCED INSTRUCTION SET ARCHITECTURE

In this section, we look at some of the general characteristics of and the motivation for a reduced instruction set architecture. Specific examples will be seen later in this chapter. We begin with a discussion of motivations for contemporary complex instruction set architectures.

## Why CISC

We have noted the trend to richer instruction sets, which include a larger number of instructions and more-complex instructions. Two principal reasons have motivated this trend: a desire to simplify compilers and a desire to improve performance. Underlying both of these reasons was the shift to high-level languages (HLL) on the part of programmers; architects attempted to design machines that provided better support for HLLs.

It is not the intent of this chapter to say that the CISC designers took the wrong direction. RISC technology is very new, and so the CISC versus RISC debate cannot now be settled. Indeed, because technology continues to evolve and because architectures exist along a spectrum rather than in two neat categories, a black-and-white assessment is unlikely ever to emerge. Thus, the comments that follow are simply meant to point out some of the potential pitfalls in the CISC approach and to provide some understanding of the motivation of the RISC adherents.

The first of the reasons cited, compiler simplification, seems obvious. The task of the compiler writer is to generate a sequence of machine instructions for each HLL statement. If there are machine instructions that resemble HLL statements, this task is simplified. This reasoning has been disputed by the RISC researchers ([HENN82], [RADI83], [PATT82b]). They have found that complex machine instructions are often hard to exploit since the compiler must find those cases that exactly fit the construct. The task of optimizing the generated code to minimize code size, reduce instruction execution count, and enhance pipelining is much more difficult with a complex instruction set. As evidence of this, studies cited earlier in this chapter indicate that most of the instructions in a compiled program are the relatively simple ones.

The other major reason cited is the expectation that a CISC will yield smaller, faster programs. Let us examine both aspects of this assertion: that programs will be smaller and that they will execute faster.

There are two advantages to smaller programs. First, because the program takes up less memory, there is a savings in that resource. With memory today being so inexpensive, this potential advantage is no longer compelling. More importantly, smaller programs should improve performance, and this will happen in two ways. First, fewer instructions means fewer instruction bytes to be fetched. And second, in a paging environment, smaller programs occupy fewer pages, reducing page faults.

The problem with this line of reasoning is that it is far from certain that a CISC program will be smaller than a corresponding RISC program. In many cases, the CISC program, expressed in symbolic machine language, may be *shorter* (i.e., fewer instructions), but the number of bits of memory occupied may not be noticeably *smaller*. Table 12.6 shows results from three studies that compared the size of compiled C programs on a variety of machines, including RISC I, which has a reduced instruction set architecture. Note that there is little or no savings using a CISC over a RISC. It is also interesting to note that the VAX, which has a much more complex instruction set than the PDP-11, achieves very little savings over the latter. These results were confirmed by IBM researchers [RADI83], who found that the IBM 801 (a RISC) produced code that was 0.9 times the size of code on an IBM S/370. The study used a set of PL/I programs.

There are several reasons for these rather surprising results. We have already noted that compilers on CISCs tend to favor simpler instructions, so that the conciseness of the complex instructions seldom comes into play. Also, since there are

**TABLE 12.6    Code Size Relative to RISC I**

|            | [PATT82a] 11 C Programs | [KATE83] 12 C Programs | [HEAT84] 5 C Programs |
|------------|:--------:|:--------:|:--------:|
| RISC I     | 1.0      | 1.0      | 1.0      |
| VAX-11/780 | 0.8      | 0.67     |          |
| M68000     | 0.9      |          | 0.9      |
| Z8002      | 1.2      |          | 1.12     |
| PDP-11/70  | 0.9      | 0.71     |          |

more instructions on a CISC, longer opcodes are required, producing longer instructions. Finally, RISCs tend to emphasize register rather than memory references, and the former require fewer bits. An example of this last effect is discussed presently (see Figure 12.5).

So, the expectation that a CISC will produce smaller programs, with the attendant advantages, may not be realized. The second motivating factor for increasingly complex instruction sets was that instruction execution would be faster. It seems to make sense that a complex HLL operation will execute more quickly as a single machine instruction rather than as a series of more-primitive instructions. However, because of the bias toward the use of those simpler instructions, this may not be so. The entire control unit must be made more complex, and/or the microprogram control store must be made larger, to accommodate a richer instruction set. Either factor increases the execution time of the simple instructions.

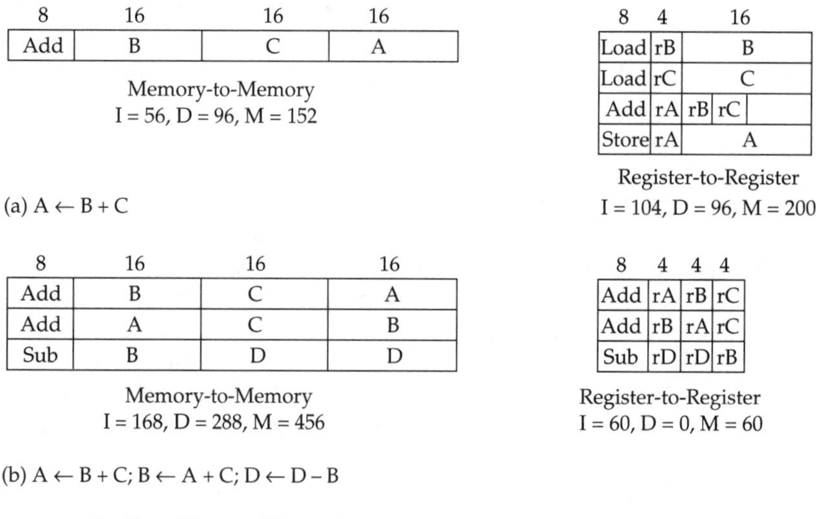

I = Size of Executed Instructions
D = Size of Executed Data
M = I + D = Total Memory Traffic

**FIGURE 12.5.  Two comparisons of register-to-register and memory-to-memory approaches**

In fact, some researchers have found that the speedup in the execution of complex functions is due not so much to the power of the complex machine instructions as to their residence in high-speed control store [RADI83]. In effect, the control store acts as an instruction cache. Thus, the hardware architect is in the position of trying to determine which subroutines or functions will be used most frequently and assigning those to the control store by implementing them in microcode. The results have been less than encouraging. Thus, on S/370 systems, instructions such as Translate and Extended-Precision-Floating-Point-Divide reside in high-speed storage, while the sequence involved in setting up procedure calls or initiating an interrupt handler are in slower main memory.

Thus, it is far from clear that the trend to increasingly complex instruction sets is appropriate. This has led a number of groups to pursue the opposite path.

## Characteristics of Reduced Instruction Set Architectures

Although a variety of different approaches to reduced instruction set architecture have been taken, certain characteristics are common to all of them. These characteristics are listed in Table 12.7 and described here. Specific examples are explored later in this chapter.

The first characteristic listed in Table 12.7 is that there is one machine instruction per machine cycle. A *machine cycle* is defined to be the time it takes to fetch two operands from registers, perform an ALU operation, and store the result in a register. Thus, RISC machine instructions should be no more complicated than, and execute about as fast as, microinstructions on CISC machines. With simple, one-cycle instructions, there is little or no need for microcode; the machine instructions can be hardwired. Such instructions should execute faster than comparable machine instructions on other machines, since it is not necessary to access a microprogram control store during instruction execution.

A second characteristic is that most operations should be register-to-register, with only simple LOAD and STORE operations accessing memory. This design feature simplifies the instruction set and therefore the control unit. For example, a RISC instruction set may include only one or two ADD instructions (e.g., integer add, add with carry); the VAX has 25 different ADD instructions. Another benefit is that such an architecture encourages the optimization of register use, so that frequently accessed operands remain in high-speed storage.

This emphasis on register-to-register operations is unique to RISC designs. Other contemporary machines provide such instructions but also include memory-to-memory and mixed register/memory operations. Attempts to compare these approaches were made in the 1970s, before the appearance of RISCs. Figure

**TABLE 12.7    Characteristics of Reduced Instruction Set Architectures**

One Instruction Per Cycle
Register-to-Register Operations
Simple Address Modes
Simple Instruction Formats

12.5a illustrates the approach taken. Hypothetical architectures were evaluated on program size and the number of bits of memory traffic. Results such as this one led one researcher to suggest that future architectures should contain no registers at all [MYER78]. One wonders what he would have thought, at the time, of the RISC machine marketed by Pyramid, which contains no less than 528 registers!

What was missing from those studies was a recognition of the frequent access to a small number of local scalars and that, with a large bank of registers or an optimizing compiler, most operands could be kept in registers for long periods of time. Thus, Figure 12.5b may be a fairer comparison.

Returning to Table 12.7, a third characteristic is the use of simple addressing modes. Almost all instructions use simple register addressing. Several additional modes, such as displacement and PC-relative, may be included. Other, more-complex modes can be synthesized in software from the simple ones. Again, this design feature simplifies the instruction set and the control unit.

A final common characteristic is the use of simple instruction formats. Generally, only one or a few formats are used. Instruction length is fixed and aligned on word boundaries. Field locations, especially the opcode, are fixed. This design feature has a number of benefits. With fixed fields, opcode decoding and register operand accessing can occur simultaneously. Simplified formats simplify the control unit. Instruction fetching is optimized since word-length units are fetched. This also means that a single instruction does not cross page boundaries.

Taken together, these characteristics can be assessed to determine the potential benefits of the RISC approach. These benefits fall into two main categories: those related to performance, and those related to VLSI implementation.

With respect to performance, a certain amount of "circumstantial evidence" can be presented. First, more-effective optimizing compilers can be developed. With more-primitive instructions, there are more opportunities for moving functions out of loops, reorganizing code for efficiency, maximizing register utilization, and so forth. It is even possible to compute parts of complex instructions at compile time. For example, the S/370 Move Characters (MVC) instruction moves a string of characters from one location to another. Each time it is executed, the move will depend on the length of the string, whether and in which direction the locations overlap, and what the alignment characteristics are. In most cases, these will all be known at compile time. Thus, the compiler could produce an optimized sequence of primitive instructions for this function.

A second point, already noted, is that most instructions generated by a compiler are relatively simple anyway. It would seem reasonable that a control unit built specifically for those instructions and using little or no microcode could execute them faster than a comparable CISC.

A third point relates to the use of instruction pipelining. RISC researchers feel that the instruction pipelining technique can be applied much more effectively with a reduced instruction set. We examine this point in some detail presently.

A final, and somewhat less significant, point is that RISC programs should be more responsive to interrupts since interrupts are checked between rather elementary operations. Architectures with complex instructions either restrict interrupts to instruction boundaries or must define specific interruptible points and implement mechanisms for restarting an instruction.

The case for improved performance for a reduced instruction set architecture is far from proven. A number of studies have been done but not on machines of comparable technology and power. Further, most studies have not attempted to separate the effects of a reduced instruction set and the effects of a large register file. The "circumstantial evidence," however, is suggestive.

The second area of potential benefit, which is more clear-cut, relates to VLSI implementation. When VLSI is used, the design and implementation of the CPU are fundamentally changed. Traditional CPUs, such as the IBM S/370 and the VAX, consist of one or more printed circuit boards containing standardized SSI and MSI packages. With the advent of LSI and VLSI, it is possible to put an entire CPU on a single chip. For a single-chip CPU, there are two motivations for following a RISC strategy. First, there is the issue of performance. On-chip delays are of much shorter duration than inter-chip delays. Thus, it makes sense to devote scarce chip real estate to those activities that occur frequently. We have seen that simple instructions and access to local scalars are, in fact, the most frequent activities. The Berkeley RISC chips were designed with this consideration in mind. Whereas a typical single-chip microprocessor dedicates about half of its area to the microcode control store, the RISC I chip devotes only about 6% of its area to the control unit [SHER84].

A second VLSI-related issue is design-and-implementation time. A VLSI processor is difficult to develop. Instead of relying on available SSI/MSI parts, the designer must perform circuit design, layout, and modeling at the device level. With a reduced instruction set architecture, this process is far easier, as evidenced by Table 12.8 [FITZ81]. If, in addition, the performance of the RISC chip is equivalent to comparable CISC microprocessors, then the advantages of the RISC approach become evident.

## CISC Versus RISC Characteristics

After the initial enthusiasm for RISC machines, there has been a growing realization that (1) RISC designs may benefit from the inclusion of some CISC features and that (2) CISC designs may benefit from the inclusion of some RISC features. The result is that the more recent RISC designs, notably the PowerPC, are no longer "pure" RISC and the more recent CISC designs, notably the Pentium, do incorporate some RISC characteristics.

An interesting comparison in [MASH94] provides some insight into this issue (Table 12.9). The table lists a number of processors and compares them across a

**TABLE 12.8   Design and Layout Effort For Some Microprocessors**

| CPU | Transistors (thousands) | Design (person-months) | Layout (person-months) |
|-----|-------------------------|------------------------|------------------------|
| RISC I | 44 | 15 | 12 |
| RISC II | 41 | 18 | 12 |
| M68000 | 68 | 100 | 70 |
| Z8000 | 18 | 60 | 70 |
| Intel iAPx-432 | 110 | 170 | 90 |

**TABLE 12.9  Characteristics of Some Processors**

| | Decode Complexity | | | Pipelining Difficulty | | | | | Compiler-Friendly | |
|---|---|---|---|---|---|---|---|---|---|---|
| Processor | Number of instruction sizes | Maximum instruction size in bytes | Number of addressing modes | Indirect addressing | Load/store with combined arithmetic | Maximum number of memory operands | Unaligned addressing allowed | Maximum number of MMU uses | Number of bits for integer register specifier | Number of bits for FP register specifier |
| AMD29000 | 1 | 4 | 1 | no | no | 1 | no | 1 | 8 | 3[a] |
| MIPS R2000 | 1 | 4 | 1 | no | no | 1 | no | 1 | 5 | 4 |
| SPARC | 1 | 4 | 2 | no | no | 1 | no | 1 | 5 | 4 |
| MC88000 | 1 | 4 | 3 | no | no | 1 | no | 1 | 5 | 4 |
| HP PA | 1 | 4 | 10[a] | no | no | 1 | no | 1 | 5 | 4 |
| IBM RT/PC | 2[a] | 4 | 1 | no | no | 1 | no | 1 | 4[a] | 3[a] |
| IBM RS/6000 | 1 | 4 | 4 | no | no | 1 | yes | 1 | 5 | 5 |
| Intel i860 | 1 | 4 | 4 | no | no | 1 | no | 1 | 5 | 4 |
| IBM 3090 | 4 | 8 | 2[b] | no[b] | yes | 2 | yes | 4 | 4 | 2 |
| Intel 80486 | 12 | 12 | 15 | no[b] | yes | 2 | yes | 4 | 3 | 3 |
| NSC 32016 | 21 | 21 | 23 | yes | yes | 2 | yes | 4 | 3 | 3 |
| MC68040 | 11 | 22 | 44 | yes | yes | 2 | yes | 8 | 4 | 3 |
| VAX | 56 | 56 | 22 | yes | yes | 6 | yes | 24 | 4 | 0 |
| Clipper | 4[a] | 8[a] | 9[a] | no | no | 1 | 0 | 2 | 4[a] | 3[a] |
| Intel 80960 | 2[a] | 8[a] | 9[a] | no | no | 1 | yes[a] | — | 5 | 3[a] |

[a] RISC that does not conform to this characteristic.
[b] CISC that does not conform to this characteristic.

number of characteristics. For purposes of this comparison, the following are considered typical of a RISC:

1. A single instruction size.
2. That size is typically 4 bytes.
3. A small number of data addressing modes, typically less than five. This parameter is difficult to pin down. In the table, register and literal modes are not counted and different formats with different offset sizes are counted separately.
4. No indirect addressing that requires you to make one memory access to get the address of another operand in memory.
5. No operations that combine load/store with arithmetic (e.g., add from memory, add to memory).
6. No more than one memory-addressed operand per instruction.
7. Does not support arbitrary alignment of data for load/store operations.
8. Maximum number of uses of the memory management unit (MMU) for a data address in an instruction.
9. Number of bits for integer register specifier equal to five or more. This means that at least 32 integer registers can be explicitly referenced at a time.
10. Number of bits for floating-point register specifier equal to four or more. This means that at least 16 floating-point registers can be explicitly referenced at a time.

Items 1 through 3 are an indication of instruction decode complexity. Items 4 through 8 suggest the ease or difficulty of pipelining, especially in the presence of virtual-memory requirements. Items 9 and 10 are related to the ability to take good advantage of compilers.

In the table, the first eight processors are clearly RISC architectures, the next five are clearly CISC, and the last two are processors often thought of as RISC that in fact have many CISC characteristics.

## 12.5

### RISC PIPELINING

#### Pipelining with Regular Instructions

As we discussed in Section 11.4, instruction pipelining is often used to enhance performance. Let us reconsider this in the context of a RISC architecture. Most instructions are register-to-register, and an instruction cycle has the following two phases:

- I: Instruction Fetch.
- E: Execute. Performs an ALU operation with register input and output.

For load and store operations, three phases are required:

- I: Instruction Fetch.
- E: Execute. Calculates memory address
- D: Memory. Register-to-memory or memory-to-register operation.

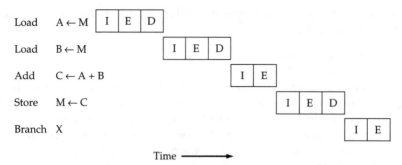

**FIGURE 12.6.  Timing of sequential execution**

Figure 12.6 depicts the timing of a sequence of instructions using no pipelining. Clearly, this is a wasteful process. Even very simple pipelining can substantially improve performance. Figure 12.7 shows a two-way pipelining scheme, in which the I and E phases of two different instructions are performed simultaneously. This scheme can yield up to twice the execution rate of a serial scheme. Two problems prevent the maximum speedup from being achieved. First, we assume that a single-port memory is used and that only one memory access is possible per phase. This requires the insertion of a wait state in some instructions. Second, a branch instruction interrupts the sequential flow of execution. To accommodate this with minimum circuitry, a NOOP instruction can be inserted into the instruction stream by the compiler or assembler.

Pipelining can be improved further by permitting two memory accesses per phase. This yields the sequence shown in Figure 12.8. Now, up to three instructions can be overlapped, and the improvement is as much as a factor of three. Again, branch instructions cause the speedup to fall short of the maximum possible. Also, note that data dependencies have an effect. If an instruction needs an operand that is altered by the preceding instruction, a delay is required. Again, this can be accomplished by a NOOP.

The pipelining discussed so far works best if the three phases are of approximately equal duration. Because the E phase usually involves an ALU operation, it may be longer. In this case, we can divide into two subphases:

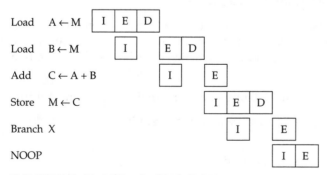

**FIGURE 12.7.  Two-way pipelined timing**

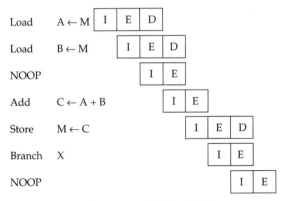

**FIGURE 12.8. Three-way pipelined timing**

- $E_1$: Register file read
- $E_2$: ALU operation and register write.

Because of the simplicity and regularity of the instruction set, the design of the phasing into three or four phases is easily accomplished. Figure 12.9 shows the result with a four-way pipeline. Up to four instructions at a time can be under way, and the maximum potential speedup is a factor of four. Note again the use of NOOPs to account for data and branch delays.

## Optimization of Pipelining

Because of the simple and regular nature of RISC instructions, pipelining schemes can be efficiently employed. There are few variations in instruction execution duration, and the pipeline can be tailored to reflect this. However, we have seen that data and branch dependencies reduce the overall execution rate.

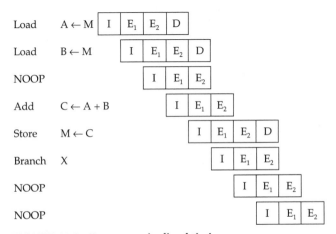

**FIGURE 12.9. Four-way pipelined timing**

**TABLE 12.10    Normal And Delayed Branch**

| Address | Normal Branch | | Delayed Branch | | Optimized Delayed Branch | |
|---|---|---|---|---|---|---|
| 100 | LOAD | X,A | LOAD | X,A | LOAD | X,A |
| 101 | ADD | 1,A | ADD | 1,A | JUMP | 105 |
| 102 | JUMP | 105 | JUMP | 106 | ADD | 1,A |
| 103 | ADD | A,B | NOOP | | ADD | A,B |
| 104 | SUB | C,B | ADD | A,B | SUB | C,B |
| 105 | STORE | A,Z | SUB | C,B | STORE | A,Z |
| 106 | | | STORE | A,Z | | |

To compensate for these dependencies, code reorganization techniques have been developed. First, let us consider branching instructions. *Delayed branch,* a way of increasing the efficiency of the pipeline, makes use of a branch that does not take effect until after the following instruction. This strange procedure is illustrated in Table 12.10. In the first column, we see a normal symbolic instruction machine-language program. After 102 is executed, the next instruction to be executed is 105. In order to regularize the pipeline, a NOOP is inserted after this branch. However, increased performance is achieved if the instructions at 101 and 102 are interchanged. Figure 12.10 shows the result. The JUMP instruction is fetched before the ADD instruction. Note, however, that the ADD instruction is

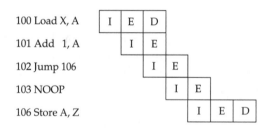

(a) Inserted NOOP

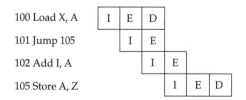

(b) Reversed Instructions

**FIGURE 12.10.  Use of the delayed branch**

fetched before the execution of the JUMP instruction has a chance to alter the program counter. Thus, the original semantics of the program are retained.

This interchange of instructions will work successfully for unconditional branches, calls, and returns. For conditional branches, this procedure cannot be blindly applied. If the condition that is tested for the branch can be altered by the immediately preceding instruction, then the compiler must refrain from doing the interchange and instead insert a NOOP. The experience with both the Berkeley RISC and IBM 801 systems is that the majority of conditional branch instructions can be optimized in this fashion ([PATT82a], [RADI83]).

A similar sort of tactic, called the delayed load, can be used on LOAD instructions. On LOAD instructions, the register that is to be the target of the load is locked by the CPU. The CPU then continues execution of the instruction stream until it reaches an instruction requiring that register, at which point it idles until the load is complete. If the compiler can rearrange instructions so that useful work can be done while the load is in the pipeline, efficiency is increased.

As a final note, we should point out that the design of the instruction pipeline should not be carried out in isolation from other optimization techniques applied to the system. For example, [BRAD91b] shows that the scheduling of instructions for the pipeline and the dynamic allocation of registers should be considered together to achieve the greatest efficiency.

## 12.6

### MOTOROLA 88000

The 88000 is the first RISC processor from Motorola. Although the part number might seem to indicate some relationship with the MC68000 family of CISCs, the differences are profound. The MC68000 is representative of recent CISCs, whereas the 88000 is a rather pure example of a RISC system.

### Instruction Set

Table 12.11 lists the instructions for the 88000, and Figure 12.11 shows the instruction formats. Like virtually all RISC systems, the 88000 employs a fixed 32-bit instruction length. The first 6 bits constitute the opcode for the instruction. In most instructions, the opcode is followed by two 5-bit register fields (result and first operand). The remaining 16 bits can contain an immediate operand or an offset for a conditional branch instruction. For instructions involving 3 registers (2 source and 1 result, or destination), 11 bits remain for an extension to the opcode to specify particular operations.

Note that in all of the formats, the positions of the key fields line up. Thus, the instruction decoder logic of the processor always accesses source and destination registers from the same relative location within the instruction. This speeds up instruction decoding and simplifies pipeline design.

Most of the instructions reference only register operands. Only a few simple load/store instructions reference memory. Bits in the subopcode indicate load and

**TABLE 12.11**

**Motorola 88000 Instruction Set**

| **Integer Arithmetic** | | **Bit-Field Instructions** | |
|---|---|---|---|
| ADD | Add | CLR | Clear Bit Field |
| ADDU | Add Unsigned | SET | Set Bit Field |
| SUB | Subtract | EXT | Extract Signed Bit Field |
| SUBU | Subtract Unsigned | EXTU | Extract Unsigned Bit Field |
| MUL | Multiply | MAKE | Make Bit Field |
| DIV | Divide | ROT | Rotate Bit Field |
| DIVU | Divide Unsigned | FF0 | Find First Bit Clear |
| CMP | Compare | FF1 | Find First Bit Set |

| **Floating-Point Arithmetic** | | **Flow Control Instructions** | |
|---|---|---|---|
| FADD | Floating-Point Add | BB0 | Branch on Bit Clear |
| FSUB | Floating-Point Subtract | BB1 | Branch on Bit Set |
| FMUL | Floating-Point Multiply | Bcnd | Conditional Branch |
| FDIV | Floating-Point Divide | BR | Unconditional Branch |
| FCMP | Floating-Point Compare | BSR | Branch to Subroutine |
| FLT | Convert Integer to Floating Point | JMP | Unconditional Jump |
| INT | Round Floating Point to Integer | JSR | Jump to Subroutine |
| NINT | Round Floating Point to Nearest Integer | TB0 | Trap on Bit Clear |
| | | TB1 | Trap on Bit Set |
| TRNC | Truncate Floating Point to Integer | TBND | Trap on Bounds Check |
| FLDCR | Load From Floating-Point Control Register | Tcnd | Conditional Trap |
| | | RTE | Return from Exception |
| FSTCR | Store to Floating-Point Control Register | | |
| FXCR | Exchange Floating-Point Control Register | **Load/Store/Exchange Instructions** | |
| | | LD | Load Register from Memory |
| | | LDA | Load Address |
| | | LDCR | Load from Control Register |
| **Logical Instructions** | | ST | Store Register to Memory |
| AND | And | STCR | Store to Control Register |
| MASK | Logical Mask Immediate | XMEM | Exchange Register with Memory |
| OR | Or | XCR | Exchange Control Register |
| XOR | Exclusive-Or | | |

store of word (32 bits), halfword, and byte. For the latter two cases, a load into a register can be treated as signed or unsigned. Signed numbers are sign-extended to fill out the 32-bit destination register in two's complement notation. Unsigned numbers are padded with 0s.

All memory references are formed by adding the contents of a base register to a second operand. To maintain the simplicity and uniformity of the instruction operations, the same logic that is provided for integer arithmetic instructions is reused for memory referencing. In the case of integer addition, the second operand can be either a 16-bit immediate quantity or a 32-bit register. The corresponding addressing modes are register indirect with unsigned immediate and

| 6 | 5 | 5 | 11 | 5 |
|---|---|---|---|---|
| Opcode | D | S1 | Subopcode | S2 |

(a) Register-Register Instructions

| 6 | 5 | 5 | 6 | 5 | 5 |
|---|---|---|---|---|---|
| Opcode | D | S1 | Subopcode | Width | Offset |

(b) Bit Mask Instructions

| 6 | 5 | 5 | 16 |
|---|---|---|---|
| Opcode | D | S1 | Subopcode |

(c) Immediate Instructions

| 6 | 5 | 5 | 16 |
|---|---|---|---|
| Opcode | M/B | S1 | Offset |

(d) Conditional Branch Instructions

| 6 | 26 |
|---|---|
| Opcode | Offset |

(e) Unconditional Branch Instructions

D = Destination Register
S1 = Source 1 Register
S2 = Source 2 Register
M/B = Mask or Bit

**FIGURE 12.11.  Motorola 88000 instruction formats**

register indirect with index. In addition, scaled indexing is provided to support the manipulation of arrays.[1]

One unique aspect of the instruction set is the inclusion of eight bit-field instructions, which are defined in Table 12.12. The fields on which these instructions operate can be of any width and located anywhere in the word. Bit-field hardware can clear, set, extract, and insert fields into registers. This hardware can essentially perform a single-cycle shift of any number of bits to a field of any width. The only limitation is that the amount of the shift plus the width of the affected field must be less than the width of the 32-bit register. This capability is handy for operations such as extracting the exponent from a floating-point number or Boolean data from a register that contains a set of flags.

[1]See the discussion of Pentium addressing modes in Chapter 10 for a description of scaled indexing.

**TABLE 12.12  Motorola 88000 Bit-Field Instructions**

| Name | Instruction | Function |
|------|-------------|----------|
| CLR | Clear bit field to zeros | D←S; D[(o + w − 1)...o]←0s |
| SET | Set bit field to ones | D←S; D[(o + w − 1)...o]←1s |
| EXT | Extract signed bit field | if (w = 0)<br>  then begin D[31...(32 − o)]←S[31]; D[(31 − o)...0]←S[31...o] end<br>  else begin D[31...w]←S[o + w − 1]; D[(w − 1)...0]←S[(o + w − 1)...o] end |
| EXTU | Extract unsigned bit field | if (w = 0)<br>  then begin D[31...(32 − o)]←0; D[(31 − o)...0]←S[31...o] end<br>  else begin D[31...w]←0; D[(w − 1)...0]←S[(o + w − 1)...o] end |
| MAK | Make a bit field | if (w = 0)<br>  then D←shiftL(S,o)<br>  else begin D←0; D[o + w − 1)...o]←S[(w − 1)...(0)] end |
| ROT | Rotate bit field right | D←rotateR(S,o) |
| FF0 | Find first zero-bit | i←31<br>  while (i≥0 and S2[i] = 1) do i←i−1;<br>  if (i<0) then D←32 else D←i; |
| FF1 | Find first one-bit | i←31<br>  while (i≥0 and S2[i] = 0) do i←i−1;<br>  if (i<0) then D←32 else D←i; |

D = destination register  o = offset
S = source register  w = width

## Architecture

Figure 12.12 shows the overall architecture of the 88000. The main processor chip consists of multiple independent function units connected to a multiported register file. The function units can operate independently and concurrently, providing a very efficient means of processing instructions.

- *Integer Unit:* Executes all integer arithmetic, bit field, Boolean, and control register accesses.
- *Floating-Point Unit:* Provides IEEE 754 functions. It consists of a five-stage adder pipeline and a separate six-stage multiplier pipeline. These pipelines allow for multiple floating-point operations to be performed concurrently.
- *Instruction Unit:* Responsible for fetching instructions and dispatching the decoded opcode via control signals to the appropriate execution units contained in the processor.
- *Data Memory Unit:* Responsible for loading and storing operands between the processor and external memory.

The memory bus (M bus) interfaces two cache memory management units to the memory system, one for data and one for instructions. This feature is implemented on a number of recent RISC systems. This architecture allows instructions to be fetched while transferring operands between the processor and memory, thus providing a speedup.[2]

## Register Management

The register file consists of 32 32-bit general-purpose registers. Register 0 is hardwired with the value 0. This is convenient for storing 0 in other registers or memory. The R1 register is used to automatically store the return address for a Branch or Jump to Subroutine instruction.

With the 88000 architecture, some means is needed to allow all of the function units to share the register file without destroying one another's register-based data. The mechanism used in the 88000 is known as register scoreboarding. The processor includes a scoreboard register, with one bit corresponding to each of the 31 registers (R0 is excluded since it cannot be updated). Any time that the instruction unit dispatches an instruction that takes more than one clock cycle to execute, the bit in the scoreboard register that corresponds to the destination register for that instruction is set. The bit is cleared when the result is stored in the destination register. All of the function units are free to access registers independently and proceed until they get to a point where they must fetch data from a register whose bit is set. At that point, the function unit must stall until the desired register is released.

## Instruction Unit Pipeline

Each of the function units in the 88000 has a pipelined architecture to provide as high a degree of parallelism as possible. Figure 12.13 shows the three-stage pipeline

---

[2]Manufacturers often refer to this configuration as a Harvard architecture. The original use of that term referred to the separation of instructions and data in main memory, not in caches.

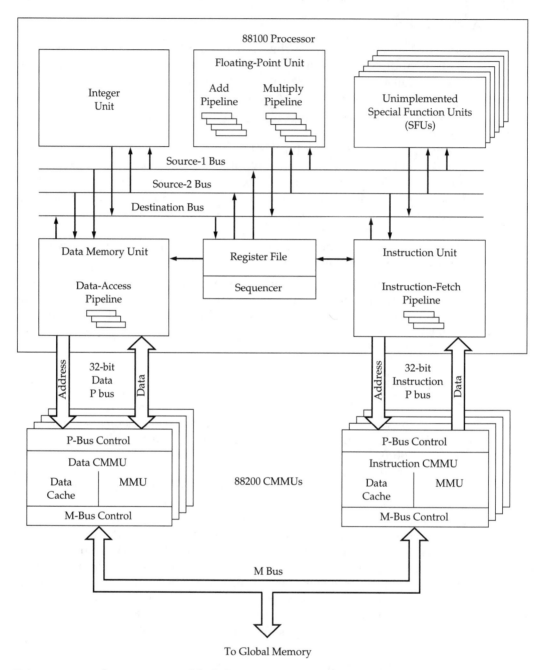

**FIGURE 12.12.  The 88000 system block diagram**

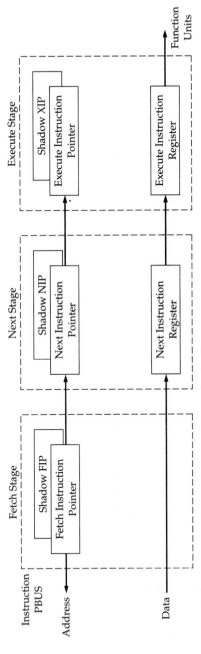

**FIGURE 12.13. Motorola 88000 Instruction Unit Pipeline**

in the instruction unit. The unit fetches instructions from the instruction cache via a bus referred to as the PBUS.

The fetch stage consists of a Fetch Instruction Pointer (FIP) register that contains the address of the instruction to be fetched. At the beginning of each clock cycle, if there are no pipeline stalls or memory wait states, the FIP issues an address to the instruction cache.

During the next stage, the address in the FIP is transferred to the Next Instruction Pointer (NIP) register, and the instruction is fetched from memory and placed in the Next Instruction register. During this stage, the instruction is partially decoded and any needed operands from the register file are prefetched and prepared for transfer to the appropriate function unit.

During the execute stage, the address in the NIP is transferred to the Execute Instruction Pointer (XIP) register, and the instruction is transferred to the Executing Instruction register. During this stage, the instruction is dispatched to the appropriate function unit.

For each of the instruction pointers, a shadow register is maintained. If an exception occurs during a cycle, the shadow registers are frozen to save the values at the time of the exception. These are restored after exception processing.

## 12.7

## MIPS R4000

One of the first commercially available chip sets was developed by MIPS Computer Systems. The system was inspired by an experimental system, also using the name MIPS, developed at Stanford [HENN84]. The most recent member of the MIPS family is the R4000. It has substantially the same architecture and instruction set of the earlier MIPS designs: the R2000, R3000, and R6000. The most significant difference is that the R4000 uses 64 rather than 32 bits for all internal and external data paths and for addresses, registers, and the ALU.

The use of 64 bits has a number of advantages over a 32-bit architecture. It allows a bigger address space—large enough for an operating system to map more than a terabyte of files directly into virtual memory for easy access. With 1-gigabyte and larger disk drives now common, the 4-gigabyte address space of a 32-bit machine becomes limiting. Also, the 64-bit capacity allows the R4000 to process data such as IEEE single-precision floating-point numbers and character strings up to 8 characters in a single action.

The R4000 processor chip is partitioned into two sections, one containing the CPU, and the other containing a coprocessor for memory management. The CPU has a very simple architecture. The intent was to design a system in which the instruction execution logic was as simple as possible, leaving space available for logic to enhance performance (e.g., the entire memory management unit).

The processor supports 32 64-bit registers. It also provides for up to 128 Kbytes of high-speed cache, half each for instructions and data. The relatively large cache (the IBM 3090 provides 128–256 Kbytes of cache) enables the system to keep large sets of program code and data local to the processor, off-loading the main memory bus and avoiding the need for a large register file with the accompanying windowing logic.

## Instruction Set

Table 12.13 lists the basic instruction set for all MIPS R series processors. Table 12.14 lists the additional instructions implemented in the R4000. All processor instructions are encoded in a single 32-bit word format. All data operations are register-to-register; the only memory references are pure load/store operations.

The R4000 makes no use of condition codes. If an instruction generates a condition, the corresponding flags are stored in a general-purpose register. This avoids the need for special logic to deal with condition codes as they affect the pipelining mechanism and the reordering of instructions by the compiler. Instead, the mechanisms already implemented to deal with register-value dependencies are employed. Further, conditions mapped onto the register files are subject to the same compile-time optimizations in allocation and reuse as other values stored in registers.

As with most RISC-based machines, the MIPS uses a single 32-bit instruction length. This single instruction length simplifies instruction fetch and decode, and it also simplifies the interaction of instruction fetch with the virtual memory management unit (i.e., instructions do not cross word or page boundaries). The three instruction formats (Figure 12.14) share common formatting of opcodes and register references, simplifying instruction decode. The effect of more complex instructions can be synthesized at compile time.

Only the simplest and most frequently used memory-addressing mode is implemented in hardware. All memory references consist of a 16-bit offset from a 32-bit register. For example, the "load word" instruction is of the form:

lw r2, 128(r3)    load word at address 128 offset from register 3 into register 2

Each of the 32 general-purpose registers can be used as the base register. One register, r0, always contains 0.

The compiler makes use of multiple machine instructions to synthesize typical addressing modes in conventional machines. Some examples are provided in Table 12.15 [CHOW87]. The table shows the use of the instruction **lui** (load upper immediate). This instruction loads the upper half of a register with a 16-bit immediate value, setting the lower half to zero.

## Instruction Pipeline

With its simplified instruction architecture, the MIPS can achieve very efficient pipelining. It is instructive to look at the evolution of the MIPS pipeline, as it illustrates the evolution of RISC pipelining in general.

The initial experimental RISC systems and the first generation of commercial RISC processors achieve execution speeds that approach one instruction per system clock cycle. To improve on this performance, two classes of processors have evolved to offer execution of multiple instructions per clock cycle: superscalar and superpipelined architectures. In essence, a **superscalar architecture** replicates each of the pipeline stages so that two or more instructions at the same stage of the pipeline can be processed simultaneously. A **superpipelined architecture** is one which makes use of more, and more fine-grained, pipeline stages. With more stages, more instructions can be in the pipeline at the same time, increasing parallelism.

**TABLE 12.13 MIPS R-Series Instruction Set**

| OP | Description | OP | Description |
|----|-------------|----|-------------|
| **Load/Store Instructions** | | **Multiply/Divide Instructions** | |
| LB | Load Byte | MULT | Multiply |
| LBU | Load Byte Unsigned | MULTU | Multiply Unsigned |
| LH | Load Halfword | DIV | Divide |
| LHU | Load Halfword Unsigned | DIVU | Divide Unsigned |
| LW | Load Word | MFHI | Move From HI |
| LWL | Load Word Left | MTHI | Move To HI |
| LWR | Load Word Right | MFLO | Move From LO |
| SB | Store Byte | MTLO | Move To LO |
| SH | Store Halfword | | |
| SW | Store Word | **Jump and Branch Instructions** | |
| SWL | Store Word Left | J | Jump |
| SWR | Store Word Right | JAL | Jump and Link |
| | | JR | Jump to Register |
| **Arithmetic Instructions (ALU Immediate)** | | JALR | Jump and Link Register |
| ADDI | Add Immediate | BEQ | Branch on Equal |
| ADDIU | Add Immediate Unsigned | BNE | Branch on Not Equal |
| SLTI | Set on Less Than Immediate | BLEZ | Branch on Less Than or Equal to Zero |
| SLTIU | Set on Less Than Immediate Unsigned | BGTZ | Branch on Greater Than Zero |
| ANDI | AND Immediate | BLTZ | Branch on Less Than Zero |
| ORI | OR Immediate | BGEZ | Branch on Greater Than or Equal to Zero |
| XORI | Exclusive-OR Immediate | | |
| LUI | Load Upper Immediate | BLTZAL | Branch on Less Than Zero And Link |
| | | BGEZAL | Branch on Greater Than or Equal to Zero And Link |
| **Arithmetic Instructions (3-operand, R-type)** | | | |
| ADD | Add | | |
| ADDU | Add Unsigned | **Coprocessor Instructions** | |
| SUB | Subtract | LWCz | Load Word to Coprocessor |
| SUBU | Subtract Unsigned | SWCz | Store Word to Coprocessor |
| SLT | Set on Less Than | MTCz | Move To Coprocessor |
| SLTU | Set on Less Than Unsigned | MFCz | Move From Coprocessor |
| AND | AND | CTCz | Move Control To Coprocessor |
| OR | OR | CFCz | Move Control From Coprocessor |
| XOR | Exclusive-OR | COPz | Coprocessor Operation |
| NOR | NOR | BCzT | Branch on Coprocessor z True |
| | | BCzF | Branch on Coprocessor z False |
| **Shift Instructions** | | | |
| SLL | Shift Left Logical | **Special Instructions** | |
| SRL | Shift Right Logical | SYSCALL | System Call |
| SRA | Shift Right Arithmetic | BREAK | Break |
| SLLV | Shift Left Logical Variable | | |
| SRLV | Shift Right Logical Variable | | |
| SRAV | Shift Right Arithmetic Variable | | |

**TABLE 12.14**

**Additional R4000 Instructions**

| OP | Description | OP | Description |
|---|---|---|---|
| **Load/Store Instructions** | | **Exception Instructions** | |
| LL | Load Linked | TGE | Trap if Greater Than or Equal |
| SC | Store Conditional | TGEU | Trap if Greater Than or Equal |
| SYNC | Sync | | Unsigned |
| | | TLT | Trap if Less Than |
| **Jump and Branch Instructions** | | TLTU | Trap if Less Than Unsigned |
| BEQL | Branch on Equal Likely | TEQ | Trap if Equal |
| BNEL | Branch on Not Equal Likely | TNE | Trap if Not Equal |
| BLEZL | Branch on Less Than or Equal to | TGEI | Trap if Greater Than or Equal |
| | Zero Likely | | Immediate |
| BGTZL | Branch on Greater Than Zero | TGEIU | Trap if Greater Than or Equal |
| | Likely | | Unsigned Immediate |
| BLTZL | Branch on Less Than Zero Likely | TLTI | Trap if Less Than Immediate |
| BGEZL | Branch on Greater Than or Equal | TLTIU | Trap if Less Than Unsigned |
| | to Zero Likely | | Immediate |
| BLTZALL | Branch on Less Than Zero And | TEQI | Trap if Equal Immediate |
| | Link Likely | TNEI | Trap if Not Equal Immediate |
| BGEZALL | Branch on Greater Than or Equal | | |
| | to Zero and Link Likely | **Coprocessor Instructions** | |
| BCzTL | Branch on Coprocessor z True | LDCz | Load Double Coprocessor |
| | Likely | SDCz | Store Double Coprocessor |
| CDzFL | Branch on Coprocessor z False | | |
| | Likely | | |

Both approaches have limitations. With superscalar pipelining, dependencies between instructions in different pipelines can slow down the system. Also, overhead logic is required to coordinate these dependencies. With superpipelining, there is overhead associated with transferring instructions from one stage to the next.

Chapter 13 is devoted to a study of superscalar architecture. The MIPS R4000 is a good example of a RISC-based superpipeline architecture.

Figure 12.15a shows the instruction pipelines of the R3000. In the R3000, the pipeline advances once per clock cycle. The MIPS compiler is able to reorder instructions to fill delay slots with code 70–90 percent of the time. All instructions follow the same sequence of five pipeline stages:

- Instruction fetch
- Source operand fetch from register file
- ALU operation or data operand address generation
- Data memory reference
- Write back into register file

As illustrated in Figure 12.15a, there is not only parallelism due to pipelining but also parallelism within the execution of a single instruction. The 60-ns clock cycle is divided into two 30-ns phases. The external instruction and data access operations to the cache each require 60 ns, as do the major internal operations (OP,

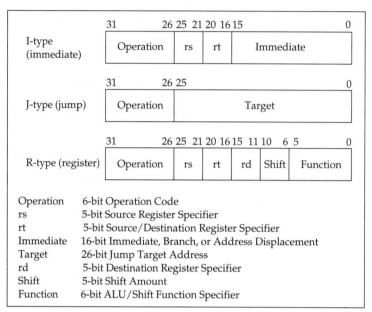

**FIGURE 12.14. MIPS instruction formats**

DA, IA). Instruction decode is a simpler operation, requiring only a single 30-ns phase, overlapped with register fetch in the same instruction. Calculation of an address for a branch instruction also overlaps instruction decode and register fetch, so that a branch at instruction $i$ can address the ICACHE access of instruction $i + 2$. Similarly, a load at instruction $i$ fetches data that are immediately used by the OP of instruction $i + 1$, while an ALU/shift result gets passed directly into instruction $i + 1$ with no delay. This tight coupling between instructions makes for a highly efficient pipeline.

In detail, then, each clock cycle is divided into separate phases, denoted as $\phi1$ and $\phi2$. The functions performed in each phase are summarized in Table 12.16.

The R4000 incorporates a number of technical advances over the R3000. The use of more advanced technology allows the clock cycle time to be cut in half, to 30 ns, and for the access time to the register file to be cut in half. In addition, there is greater density on the chip, which enables the instruction and data caches to be incorporated on the chip. Before looking at the final R4000 pipeline, let us consider how the R3000 pipeline can be modified to improve performance using R4000 technology.

**TABLE 12.15   Synthesizing Other Addressing Modes with the MIPS Addressing Mode**

| Apparent Instruction | Actual Instruction |
|---|---|
| lw r2, <16-bit offset> | lw r2, <16-bit offset> (r0) |
| lw r2, <32-bit offset> | lui r1, <high 16 bits of offset><br>lw r2, <low 16 bits of offset> (r1) |
| lw r2, <32-bit offset> (r4) | lui r1, <high 16 bits of offset><br>addu r1, r1, r4<br>lw r2, <low 16 bits of offset> (r1) |

**FIGURE**

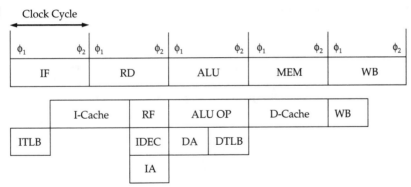

(a) Detailed R3000 Pipeline

IF = Instruction Fetch
RD = Read
MEM = Memory Access
WB = Write Back
I-Cache = Instruction Cache Acc
RF = Fetch Operand from F
D-Cache = Data Cache Access
ITLB = Instruction Address T
IDEC = Instruction Decode
IA = Compute Instruction .
DA = Calculate Data Virtual
DTLB = Data Address Transla
TC = Data Cache Tag Chec

| Cycle | Cycle | Cycle | Cycle | Cycle | Cycle |
|-------|-------|-------|-------|-------|-------|
| ITLB | I-Cache | RF | ALU | DTLB | D-Cache | WB |

(b) Modified R3000 Pipeline with Reduced Latencies

| Cycle | Cycle | Cycle | Cycle | Cycle |
|-------|-------|-------|-------|-------|
| I-Cache | RF | ALU | D-Cache | TC | WB |

(c) Optimized R3000 Pipeline with Parallel TLB and Cache Accesses

## 12.15. Enhancing the R3000 pipeline

Figure 12.15b shows a first step. Remember that the cycles in this figure are half as long as those in Figure 12.15a. Because they are on the same chip, the instruction and data cache stages take only half as long; so they still occupy only one clock cycle. Again, because of the speedup of the register file access, register read and write still occupy only half of a clock cycle.

Because the R4000 caches are on-chip, the virtual-to-physical address translation can delay the cache access. This delay is reduced by implementing virtually-indexed caches and going to a parallel cache access and address translation. Figure 12.15c shows the optimized R3000 pipeline with this improvement. Because of the compression of events, the data cache tag check is performed separately on the next cycle after cache access.

In a superpipelined system, existing hardware is used several times per cycle by inserting pipeline registers to split up each pipe stage. Essentially, each super-pipeline stage operates at a multiple of the base clock frequency, the multiple depending on the degree of superpipelining. The R4000 technology has the speed and density to permit superpipelining of degree 2. Figure 12.16a shows the opti-mized R3000 pipeline using this superpipelining. Note that this is essentially the same dynamic structure as Figure 12.15c.

**TABLE 12.16 R3000 Pipeline Stages**

| Pipeline Stage | Phase | Function |
|---|---|---|
| IF | $\phi 1$ | Using the TLB, translate an instruction virtual address to a physical address (after a branching decision). |
| IF | $\phi 2$ | Send the physical address to the instruction address. |
| RD | $\phi 1$ | Return instruction from instruction cache. Compare tags and validity of fetched instruction. |
| RD | $\phi 2$ | Decode instruction. Read register file. If branch, calculate branch target address. |
| ALU | $\phi 1 + \phi 2$ | If register-to-register operation, the arithmetic or logical operation is performed. |
| ALU | $\phi 1$ | If a branch, decide whether the branch is to be taken or not. If a memory reference (load or store), calculate data virtual address. |
| ALU | $\phi 2$ | If a memory reference, translate data virtual address to physical using TLB. |
| MEM | $\phi 1$ | If a memory reference, send physical address to data cache. |
| MEM | $\phi 2$ | If a memory reference, return data from data cache, and check tags. |
| WB | $\phi 1$ | Write to register file. |

Further improvements can be made. For the R4000, a much larger and specialized adder was designed. This makes it possible to execute ALU operations at twice the rate. Other improvements allow the execution of loads and stores at twice the rate. The resulting pipeline is shown in Figure 12.16b.

The R4000 has eight pipeline stages, meaning that as many as eight instructions can be in the pipeline at the same time. The pipeline advances at the rate of two stages per clock cycle. The eight pipeline stages are

- *Instruction Fetch First Half:* Virtual address is presented to the instruction cache and the translation lookaside buffer.
- *Instruction Fetch Second Half:* Instruction cache outputs the instruction and the TLB generates the physical address.
- *Register File:* Three activities occur in parallel:
    —instruction is decoded and check made for interlock conditions (i.e., this instruction depends on the result of a preceding instruction)
    —instruction cache tag check is made
    —operands are fetched from the register file
- *Instruction Execute:* One of three activities can occur:
    —if the instruction is a register-to-register operation, the ALU performs the arithmetic or logical operation
    —if the instruction is a load or store, the data virtual address is calculated
    —if the instruction is a branch, the branch target virtual address is calculated and branch conditions are checked
- *Data Cache First:* Virtual address is presented to the data cache and TLB.

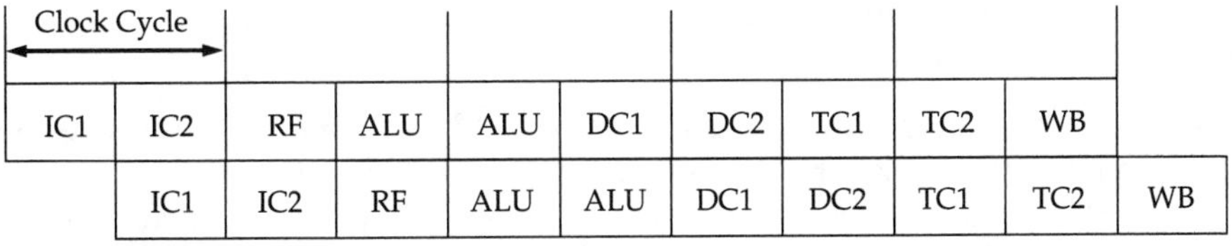

| Clock Cycle | | | | | | | | | | |
|------|------|------|------|------|------|------|------|------|------|------|
| IC1 | IC2 | RF | ALU | ALU | DC1 | DC2 | TC1 | TC2 | WB | |
| | IC1 | IC2 | RF | ALU | ALU | DC1 | DC2 | TC1 | TC2 | WB |

(a) Superpipelined Implementation of the Optimized R3000 Pipeline

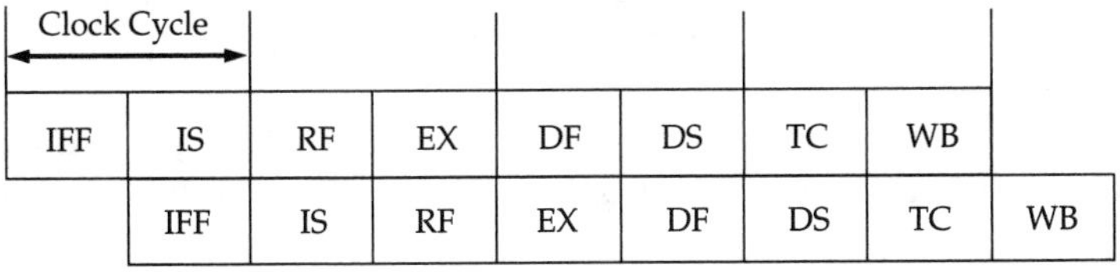

| Clock Cycle | | | | | | | | |
|------|------|------|------|------|------|------|------|------|
| IFF | IS | RF | EX | DF | DS | TC | WB | |
| | IFF | IS | RF | EX | DF | DS | TC | WB |

(b) R4000 Pipeline

IFF = Instruction Fetch First Half
IS = Instruction Fetch Second Half
RF = Fetch Operands from Register
EX = Instruction Execute
IC = Instruction Cache
DC = Data Cache
DF = Data Cache First Half
DS = Data Cache Second Half
TC = Tag Check

**FIGURE 12.16. Theoretical R3000 and actual R4000 superpipelines**

- *Data Cache Second:* Data cache outputs the instruction, and the TLB generates the physical address.
- *Tag Check:* Cache tag checks are performed for loads and stores.
- *Write Back:* Instruction result is written back to register file.

## 12.8

### THE RISC VERSUS CISC CONTROVERSY

For many years, the general trend in computer architecture and organization has been toward increasing CPU complexity: more instructions, more addressing modes, more specialized registers, and so on. The RISC movement represents a fundamental break with the philosophy behind that trend. Naturally, the appearance of RISC systems, and the publication of papers by its proponents extolling RISC virtues, has led to a reaction from what might be called the mainstream of computer architecture.

The work that has been done on assessing merits of the RISC approach can be grouped into two categories:

- *Quantitative:* Attempts to compare program size and execution speed of programs on RISC and CISC machines that use comparable technology.

- *Qualitative:* Examination of issues such as high-level language support and optimum use of VLSI real estate.

Most of the work on quantitative assessment has been done by those working on RISC systems [PATT82b, HEAT84, PATT84], and it has been, by and large, favorable to the RISC approach. Others have examined the issue and come away unconvinced [COLW85a, FLYN87, DAVI87]. There are several problems with attempting such comparisons [SERL86]:

- There is no pair of RISC and CISC machines that are comparable in life-cycle cost, level of technology, gate complexity, sophistication of compiler, operating-system support, and so on.
- No definitive test set of programs exists. Performance varies with the program.
- It is difficult to sort out hardware effects from effects due to skill in compiler writing.
- Most of the comparative analysis on RISC has been done on "toy" machines rather than commercial products. Furthermore, most commercially available machines advertised as RISC possess a mixture of RISC and CISC characteristics. Thus, a fair comparison with a commercial, "pure-play" CISC machine (e.g., VAX, Intel 80386) is difficult.

The qualitative assessment is, almost by definition, subjective. Several researchers have turned their attention to such an assessment [COLW85a, WALL85], but the results are, at best, ambiguous, and certainly subject to rebuttal [PATT85b] and, of course, counter-rebuttal [COLW85b].

The success of the RISC approach in the marketplace remains to be seen. As research, development, and product introduction continue, the assessment goes on.

In more recent years, the RISC versus CISC controversy has died down to a great extent. This is because there has been a gradual convergence of the technologies. As chip densities and raw hardware speeds increase, RISC systems have become more complex. At the same time, in an effort to squeeze out maximum performance, CISC designs have focused on issues traditionally associated with RISC, such as an increased number of general-purpose registers and increased emphasis on instruction pipeline design.

## 12.9

### RECOMMENDED READING

[FELD94], [TABA91], and [DEWA90] provide extensive coverage of RISC systems. Textbooks with good coverage of RISC concepts are [WARD90], [PATT94], and [HENN90].

The Motorola 88000 receives very detailed coverage in [ALSU90]. [TABA91] devotes a chapter to this microprocessor. [KANE92] covers the commercial MIPS machine in detail. [MIRA92] provides a good overview of the MIPS R4000. [BASH91] discusses the evolution from the R3000 pipeline to the R4000 super-pipeline.

ALSU90    Alsup, M. "The Motorola's 88000 Family Architecture." *IEEE Micro,* June 1990.

BASH91    Bashteen, A.; Lui, I.; and Mullan, J. "A Superpipeline Approach to the MIPS Architecture." *Proceedings, COMPCON Spring '91,* February 1991.

DEWA90    Dewar, R., and Smosna, M. *Microprocessors: A Programmer's View.* New York: McGraw-Hill, 1990.

FELD94    Feldman, J., and Retter, C. *Computer Architecture.* New York: McGraw-Hill, 1994.

HENN90    Hennessy, J., and Patterson, D. *Computer Architecture: A Quantitative Approach.* San Mateo, CA: Morgan Kaufmann, 1990.

KANE92    Kane, G., and Heinrich, J. *MIPS RISC Architecture.* Englewood Cliffs, NJ: Prentice Hall, 1992.

MIRA92    Mirapuri, S.; Woodacre, M.; and Vasseghi, N. "The MIPS R4000 Processor." *IEEE Micro,* April 1992.

PATT94    Patterson, D., and Hennessy, J. *Computer Organization and Design: The Hardware/ Software Interface.* San Mateo, CA: Morgan Kaufmann, 1994.

TABA91    Tabak, D. *Advanced Microprocessors.* New York: McGraw-Hill, 1991.

WARD90    Ward, S., and Halstead, R. *Computation Structures.* Cambridge, MA: MIT Press, 1990.

## 12.10

## PROBLEMS

12.1    Considering the call–return pattern in Figure 4.31, how many overflows and underflows (each of which causes a register save/restore) will occur with a window size of

(a) 5?

(b) 8?

(c) 16?

12.2    Assume an architecture in which 100 registers are to be used for a circular buffer of the type illustrated in Figure 12.2. In each window, five registers are used for parameters. Assume that the number of local variables used by a procedure obeys a uniform distribution from 5 to 14; that is, 10% use 5 variables, 10% use 6 variables, and so on. Finally, assume that the call–return pattern follows Figure 4.31. What combination of window size and number of windows is optimum?

12.3    In the discussion of Figure 12.2, it was stated that only the first two portions of a window are saved or restored. Why is it not necessary to save the temporary registers?

12.4    We wish to determine the execution time for a given program using the various pipelining schemes discussed in Section 12.5. Let

$N$ = number of executed instructions

$D$ = number of memory accesses

$J$ = number of jump instructions

For the simple sequential scheme (Figure 12.6), the execution time is $2N + D$ phases. Derive formulas for two-way, three-way, and four-way pipelining.

12.5 Redraw Figure 12.9, taking into account delayed branch load techniques.

12.6 For those Pentium addressing modes (Table 10.2) that can be synthesized in MIPS, show the MIPS equivalent.

12.7 In many cases, common machine instructions that are not listed as part of the MIPS instruction set can be synthesized with a single MIPS instruction. Show this for the following:

   (a) Register-to-Register Move
   (b) Increment, Decrement
   (c) Complement
   (d) Negate
   (e) Clear

12.8 Consider the following code fragment in a high-level language:

   **for I in** 1 ... 100 **loop**
       $S \leftarrow S + Q(I).VAL$
   **end loop;**

   Assume that Q is an array of 32-byte records and the VAL field is in the first 4 bytes of each record. Using 80x86 code, we can compile this program fragment as follows:

```
        MOV   ECX, 1          ;use register ECX to hold 1
LP:     IMUL  EAX, ECX, 32    ;get offset in EAX
        MOV   EBX, Q[EAX]     ;load VAL field
        ADD   S, EBX          ;add to S
        INC   ECX            ;increment I
        CMP   ECX, 100       ;test against limit
        JNE   LP             ;loop until I = 100
```

   This program makes use of the IMUL instruction, which multiplies the second operand by the immediate value in the third operand and places the result in the first operand (see Problem 10.18). A RISC advocate would like to demonstrate that a clever compiler can eliminate unnecessarily complex instructions such as IMUL. Provide the demonstration by rewriting the above 80x86 program without using the IMUL instruction.

12.9 The 88000 instruction set includes both a Branch to Subroutine instruction and a Jump to Subroutine instruction. Speculate on what might be the difference between the two and why both would be desired in an instruction set that is so limited.

12.10 In [ESPO92], the authors propose the use of Kiviat graphs to summarize some of the most relevant architectural parameters of RISC designs. Such graphs were used in [SIEW82] to depict performance characteristics of various machines. In this case, a Kiviat graph is used to assess the degree to which a processor exhibits RISC characteristics. As can be seen in Figure 12.17, eight variables are considered in the comparison of processors. These eight variables are laid out at regular angular intervals. The circle shows which point in each axis could be considered as a "typical" RISC value. The graph not only summarizes the major architectural characteristics but also graphically depicts the degree to which a system approaches a pure RISC design.

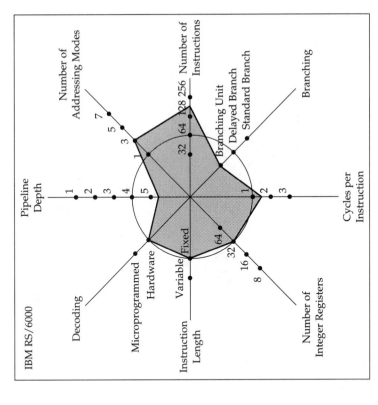

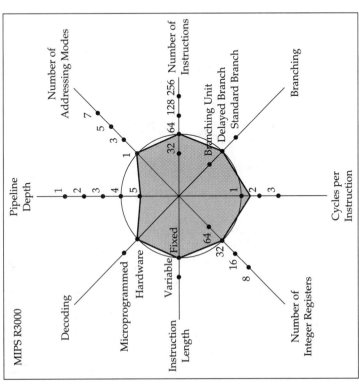

**FIGURE 12.17. Kiviat Graphs of Some Computers**

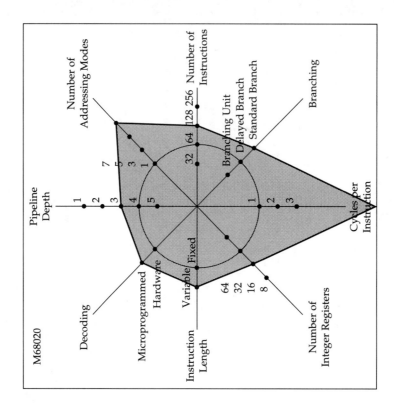

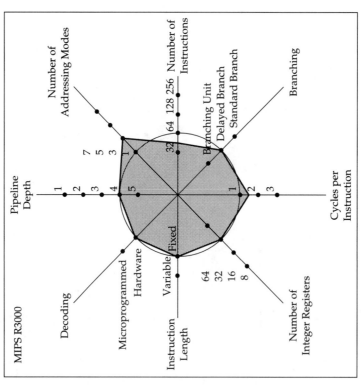

**FIGURE 12.17,** *Continued*

The figure includes graphs for the MIPS R3000 and Motorola 88000 processors, both of which exhibit a strong RISC flavor. Also shown is the IBM RS/6000, which is the precursor of the PowerPC architecture. This is a complex design with some strong RISC characteristics but with other characteristics that are more in the nature of a CISC design. Finally, the graph for the Motorola 68020 processor is shown. The CISC nature of this design is readily apparent.

Obtain the necessary information, draw Kiviat graphs for the following processors, and comment on the results.

**(a)** IBM S/370

**(b)** VAX

**(c)** Pentium

**(d)** PowerPC

12.11 Add entries for the following processors to Table 12.9:

**(a)** Pentium

**(b)** PowerPC

# CHAPTER 13

# Superscalar Processors

A superscalar implementation of a processor architecture is one in which common instructions—integer and floating-point arithmetic, loads, stores, and conditional branches—can be initiated simultaneously and executed independently. Such implementations raise a number of complex design issues related to the instruction pipeline.

Superscalar design arrives on the scene hard on the heels of RISC architecture. Although the simplified instruction set architecture of a RISC machine lends itself readily to superscalar techniques, the superscalar approach can be used on either a RISC or CISC architecture. However, virtually all of the superscalar implementations have been based on a RISC architecture.

Whereas the gestation period for the arrival of commercial RISC machines from the beginning of true RISC research with the IBM 801 and the Berkeley RISC I was seven or eight years, the first superscalar machines became commercially available within just a year or two of the coining of the term superscalar. Superscalar implementation, in conjunction with RISC or near-RISC architecture, looks to be one of the most exciting areas of research and development in computer organization and architecture over the next few years.

In this chapter, we begin with an overview of the superscalar approach, contrasting it with superpipelining. Next, the key design issues associated with superscalar implementation are presented. Finally, two of the most significant commercial superscalar processors are summarized.

## 13.1

### OVERVIEW

The term *superscalar*, first coined in 1987 [AGER87], refers to a machine that is designed to improve the performance of the execution of scalar instructions. The name contrasts the intent of this effort with vector processors, discussed in Chapter 16. In most applications, the bulk of the operations are on scalar quantities. Accordingly, the superscalar approach represents the next step in the evolution of high-performance general-purpose processors.

Many researchers have investigated superscalar-like processors, and their research indicates that some degree of performance improvement is possible. Table 13.1 presents the reported performance advantages. The differences in the results arise from differences both in the hardware of the simulated machine and in the applications being simulated.

## Superscalar Versus Superpipelined

An alternative approach to achieving greater performance is referred to as super-pipelining, a term first coined in 1988 [JOUP88]. Superpipelining exploits the fact that many pipeline stages perform tasks that require less than half a clock cycle. Thus, a doubled internal clock speed allows the performance of two tasks in one external clock cycle. We have seen one example of this approach with the MIPS R4000.

Figure 13.1 compares the two approaches. The upper part of the diagram illustrates an ordinary pipeline, used as a base for comparison. The base pipeline issues one instruction per clock cycle and can perform one pipeline stage per clock cycle. The pipeline has four stages: instruction fetch, operation decode, operation execution, and result write back. The execution stage is crosshatched for clarity. Note that although several instructions are executing concurrently, only one instruction is in its execution stage at any one time.

The next part of the diagram shows a superpipelined implementation that is capable of performing two pipeline stages per clock cycle. An alternative way of looking at this is that the functions performed in each stage can be split into two nonoverlapping parts and each can execute in half a clock cycle. A superpipeline implementation that behaves in this fashion is said to be of degree 2. Finally, the lowest part of the diagram shows a superscalar implementation capable of executing two instances of each stage in parallel. Higher-degree superpipeline and superscalar implementations are of course possible.

Both the superpipeline and the superscalar implementations depicted in Figure 13.1 have the same number of instructions executing at the same time in the steady state. The superpipelined processor falls behind the superscalar processor at the start of the program and at each branch target.

**TABLE 13.1   Reported Speedups of Superscalar-Like Machines**

| Reference | Speedup |
|-----------|---------|
| [TJAD70] | 1.8 |
| [KUCK72] | 8 |
| [WEIS84] | 1.58 |
| [ACOS86] | 2.7 |
| [SOHI87] | 1.8 |
| [SMIT89] | 2.3 |
| [JOUP89] | 2.2 |
| [LEE91] | 7 |

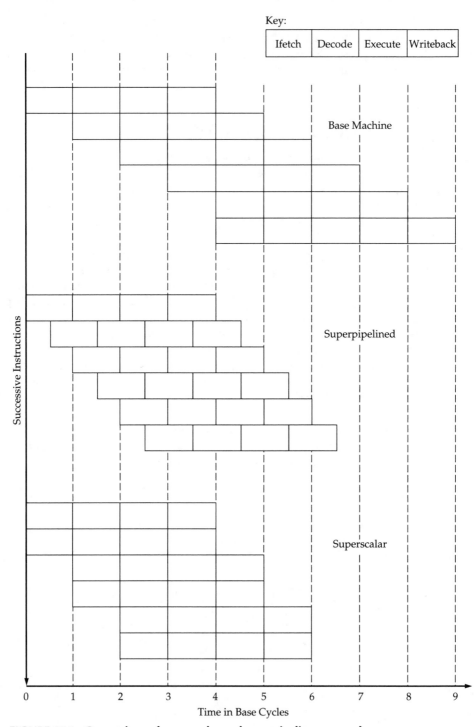

FIGURE 13.1.  Comparison of superscalar and superpipeline approaches

## Limitations

The superscalar approach depends on the ability to execute multiple instructions in parallel. The term **instruction-level parallelism** refers to the degree to which, on average, the instructions of a program can be executed in parallel. A combination of compiler-based optimization and hardware techniques can be used to maximize instruction-level parallelism. Before examining the design techniques used in superscalar machines to increase instruction-level parallelism, we need to look at the fundamental limitations to parallelism with which the system must cope. [JOHN91] lists five limitations:

- True Data Dependency
- Procedural Dependency
- Resource Conflicts
- Output Dependency
- Antidependency

We examine the first three of these limitations in the remainder of this section. A discussion of the last two must await some of the developments in the next section.

### *True Data Dependency*

Consider the following sequence:

```
add    r1, r2    ;load register r1 with the contents of r2 plus the contents of r1
move   r3, r1    ;load register r3 with the contents of r1
```

The second instruction can be fetched and decoded, but cannot execute until the first instruction executes. The reason is that the second instruction needs data produced by the first instruction. This situation is referred to as a true data dependency (also called **flow dependency** or **write–read dependency**).

Figure 13.2 illustrates this dependency in a superscalar machine of degree 2. With no dependency, two instructions can be fetched and executed in parallel. If there is a data dependency between the first and second instructions, then the second instruction is delayed as many clock cycles as required to remove the dependency. In general, any instruction must be delayed until all of its input values have been produced.

True data dependencies limit the performance of any type of pipeline. In a simple scalar pipeline, the above sequence of instructions would cause no delay. However, consider the following:

```
load   r1, eff   ;load register r1 with the contents of effective memory address eff
move   r3, r1    ;load register r3 with the contents of r1
```

A typical RISC processor takes two or more cycles to perform a load from memory, because of the delay of an off-chip memory or cache access. One way to compensate for this delay is for the compiler to reorder instructions so that one or more subsequent instructions that do not depend on the memory load can begin flowing through the pipeline. This scheme is less effective in the case of a super-

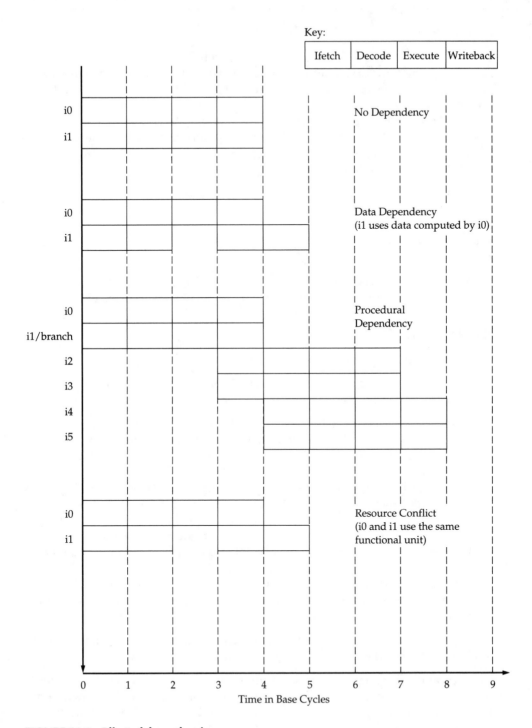

**FIGURE 13.2. Effect of dependencies**

scalar pipeline: The independent instructions executed during the load are likely to be executed on the first cycle of the load, leaving the processor with nothing to do until the load completes.

### Procedural Dependencies

As was discussed in Chapter 11, the presence of branches in an instruction sequence complicates the pipeline operation. The instructions following a branch (taken or not taken) have a procedural dependency on the branch and cannot be executed until the branch is executed. Figure 13.2 illustrates the effect of a branch on a superscalar pipeline of degree 2.

As we have seen, this type of procedural dependency also affects a scalar pipeline. Again, the consequence for a superscalar pipeline is more severe, since a greater magnitude of opportunity is lost with each delay.

If variable-length instructions are used, then another sort of procedural dependency arises. Because the length of any particular instruction is not known, it must be at least partially decoded before the following instruction can be fetched. This prevents the simultaneous fetching required in a superscalar pipeline. This is one of the reasons that superscalar techniques are more readily applicable to a RISC or RISC-like architecture, with its fixed instruction length.

### Resource Conflict

A resource conflict is a competition of two or more instructions for the same resource at the same time. Examples of resources include memories, caches, buses, register-file ports, and functional units (e.g., ALU adder).

In terms of the pipeline, a resource conflict exhibits similar behavior to a data dependency (Figure 13.2). There are some differences, however. For one thing, resource conflicts can be overcome by duplication of resources, whereas a true data dependency cannot be eliminated. Also, when an operation takes a long time to complete, resource conflicts can be minimized by pipelining the appropriate functional unit. For example, all of the functional units in the Motorola 88000 are pipelined.

## 13.2

## DESIGN ISSUES

### Instruction-Level Parallelism and Machine Parallelism

[JOUP89a] makes an important distinction between the two related concepts of instruction-level parallelism and machine parallelism. **Instruction-level parallelism** exists when instructions in a sequence are independent and thus can be executed in parallel by overlapping.

As an example of the concept of instruction-level parallelism, consider the following two code fragments [JOUP89b]:

| | | | |
|---|---|---|---|
| Load | R1 ← R2 | Add | R3 ← R3, "1" |
| Add | R3 ← R3, "1" | Add | R4 ← R3, R2 |
| Add | R4 ← R4, R2 | Store | [R4] ← R0 |
| (a) parallelism = 3 | | (b) parallelism = 1 | |

The three instructions in (a) are independent, and in theory all three could be executed in parallel. In contrast, the three instructions in (b) cannot be executed in parallel because the second instruction uses the result of the first, and the third instruction uses the result of the second.

Instruction-level parallelism is determined by the frequency of true data dependencies and procedural dependencies in the code. These factors, in turn, are dependent on the instruction set architecture and on the application. Instruction-level parallelism is also determined by what [JOUP89a] refers to as operation latency: the time until the result of an instruction is available for use as an operand in a subsequent instruction. The latency determines how much of a delay a data or procedural dependency will cause.

**Machine parallelism** is a measure of the ability of the processor to take advantage of instruction-level parallelism. Machine parallelism is determined by the number of instructions that can be fetched and executed at the same time (the number of parallel pipelines) and by the speed and sophistication of the mechanisms that the processor uses to find independent instructions.

Both instruction-level and machine parallelism are important factors in enhancing performance. A program may not have enough instruction-level parallelism to take full advantage of machine parallelism. The use of a fixed-length instruction set architecture, as in a RISC, enhances instruction-level parallelism. On the other hand, limited machine parallelism will limit performance no matter what the nature of the program.

## Instruction-Issue Policy

As was mentioned, machine parallelism is not simply a matter of having multiple instances of each pipeline stage. The processor must also be able to identify instruction-level parallelism and orchestrate the fetching, decoding, and execution of instructions in parallel. [JOHN91] uses the term **instruction issue** to refer to the process of initiating instruction execution in the processor's functional units and the term **instruction-issue policy** to refer to the protocol used to issue instructions.

In essence, the processor is trying to look ahead of the current point of execution to locate instructions that can be brought into the pipeline and executed. Three types of orderings are important in this regard:

- The order in which instructions are fetched.
- The order in which instructions are executed.
- The order in which instructions change register and memory locations.

The more sophisticated the processor, the less it is bound by a strict relationship between these orderings. To achieve maximum utilization of the various pipeline elements, the processor will need to alter one or more of the above orderings with respect to the ordering to be found in a strict sequential execution. The one constraint on the processor is that the result must be correct. Thus, the processor must accommodate the various dependencies and conflicts discussed earlier.

In general terms, we can group superscalar instruction issue policies into the following categories:

- In-order issue with in-order completion.
- In-order issue with out-of-order completion.
- Out-of-order issue with out-of-order completion.

### In-Order Issue with In-Order Completion

The simplest instruction-issue policy is to issue instructions in the exact order that would be achieved by sequential execution (in-order issue) and to write results in that same order (in-order completion). Not even scalar pipelines follow such a simple-minded policy. However, it is useful to consider this policy as a baseline for comparing more sophisticated approaches.

Figure 13.3a gives an example of this policy. We assume a superscalar pipeline capable of fetching and decoding two instructions at a time, having three separate functional units (e.g., integer arithmetic, floating-point arithmetic), and having two instances of the writeback pipeline stage. The example assumes the following constraints on a six-instruction code fragment:

- I1 requires two cycles to execute.
- I3 and I4 conflict for the same functional unit.
- I5 depends on the value produced by I4.
- I5 and I6 conflict for a functional unit.

Instructions are fetched two at a time and passed to the decode unit. Since instructions are fetched in pairs, the next two instructions must wait until the pair of decode pipeline stages has cleared. To guarantee in-order completion, instruction issuing stalls when there is a conflict for a functional unit or when a functional unit requires more than one cycle to generate a result.

In this example, the elapsed time from decoding the first instruction to writing the last results is eight cycles.

### In-Order Issue with Out-of-Order Completion

Out-of-order completion is used in scalar RISC processors to improve the performance of instructions that require multiple cycles. For example, floating-point operations on the Motorola 88000 are handled in this fashion.

Figure 13.3b illustrates its use on a superscalar processor. Instruction I2 is allowed to run to completion prior to I1. This allows I3 to be completed earlier, with the net result of a savings of one cycle.

| Decode | | Execute | | | Writeback | | Cycle |
|---|---|---|---|---|---|---|---|
| I1 | I2 | | | | | | 1 |
| I3 | I4 | I1 | I2 | | | | 2 |
| I3 | I4 | I1 | | | | | 3 |
| | I4 | | | I3 | I1 | I2 | 4 |
| I5 | I6 | | | I4 | | | 5 |
| | I6 | | I5 | | I3 | I4 | 6 |
| | | | I6 | | | | 7 |
| | | | | | I5 | I6 | 8 |

(a) In-Order Issue and In-Order Completion

| Decode | | Execute | | | Writeback | | Cycle |
|---|---|---|---|---|---|---|---|
| I1 | I2 | | | | | | 1 |
| I3 | I4 | I1 | I2 | | | | 2 |
| | I4 | I1 | | I3 | I2 | | 3 |
| I5 | I6 | | | I4 | I1 | I3 | 4 |
| | I6 | | I5 | | I4 | | 5 |
| | | | I6 | | I5 | | 6 |
| | | | | | I6 | | 7 |

(b) In-Order Issue and Out-of-Order Completion

| Decode | | Window | Execute | | | Writeback | | Cycle |
|---|---|---|---|---|---|---|---|---|
| I1 | I2 | | | | | | | 1 |
| I3 | I4 | I1, I2 | I1 | I2 | | | | 2 |
| I5 | I6 | I3, I4 | I1 | | I3 | I2 | | 3 |
| | | I4, I5, I6 | | I6 | I4 | I1 | I3 | 4 |
| | | I5 | | I5 | | I4 | I6 | 5 |
| | | | | | | I5 | | 6 |

(c) Out-of-Order Issue and Out-of-Order Completion

**FIGURE 13.3. Superscalar instruction issue and completion policies**

With out-of-order completion, any number of instructions may be in the execution stage at any one time, up to the maximum degree of machine parallelism across all functional units. Instruction issuing is stalled by a resource conflict, a data dependency, or a procedural dependency.

In addition to the above limitations, a new dependency, which we referred to earlier as an **output dependency** (also called **read–write dependency**), arises. The following code fragment illustrates this dependency (op represents any operation):

R3 := R3 op R5    (I1)
R4 := R3 + 1      (I2)
R3 := R5 + 1      (I3)
R7 := R3 op R4    (I4)

Instruction I2 cannot execute before instruction I1, because it needs the result in register R3 produced in I1; this is an example of a true data dependency, as described in Section 13.1. Similarly, I4 must wait for I3, because it uses a result produced by I3. What about the relationship between I1 and I3? There is no data dependency here, as we have defined it. However, if I3 executes to completion prior to I1, then the wrong value of the contents of R3 will be fetched for the execution of I4. Consequently, I3 must complete after I1 to produce the correct output values. To ensure this, the issuing of the third instruction must be stalled if its result might later be overwritten by an older instruction that takes longer to complete.

Out-of-order completion requires more complex instruction-issue logic than in-order completion. In addition, it is more difficult to deal with instruction interrupts and exceptions. When an interrupt occurs, instruction execution at the current point is suspended, to be resumed later. The processor must assure that the resumption takes into account that, at the time of interruption, instructions ahead of the instruction that caused the interrupt may already have completed.

### Out-of-Order Issue with Out-of-Order Completion

With in-order issue, the processor will only decode instructions up to the point of a dependency or conflict. No additional instructions are decoded until the conflict is resolved. As a result, the processor cannot look ahead of the point of conflict to subsequent instructions that may be independent of those already in the pipeline and that may be usefully introduced into the pipeline.

To allow out-of-order issue, it is necessary to decouple the decode and execute stages of the pipeline. This is done with a buffer referred to as an **instruction window.** With this organization, after a processor has finished decoding an instruction, it is placed in the instruction window. As long as this buffer is not full, the processor can continue to fetch and decode new instructions. When a functional unit becomes available in the execute stage, an instruction from the instruction window may be issued to the execute stage. Any instruction may be issued, provided that (a) it needs the particular functional unit that is available and (b) no conflicts or dependencies block this instruction.

The result of this organization is that the processor has a lookahead capability, allowing it to identify independent instructions that can be brought into the execute stage. Instructions are issued from the instruction window with little regard for their original program order. As before, the only constraint is that the program execution behaves correctly.

Figures 13.3c illustrates this policy. On each cycle, two instructions are fetched into the decode stage. On each cycle, subject to the constraint of the buffer size, two instructions move from the decode stage to the instruction window. In this example, it is possible to issue instruction I6 ahead of I5 (recall that I5 depends on I4, but I6 does not). Thus, one cycle is saved in both the execute and writeback stages, and the end-to-end savings, compared with Figure 13.3b, is one cycle.

The instruction window is depicted in Figure 13.3c to illustrate its role. However, this window is not an additional pipeline stage. An instruction being in the window simply implies that the processor has sufficient information about that instruction to decide when it can be issued.

The out-of-order issue, out-of-order completion policy is subject to the same constraints described earlier. An instruction cannot be issued if it violates a dependency or conflict. The difference is that more instructions are available for issuing, reducing the probability that a pipeline stage will have to stall. In addition, a new dependency, which we referred to earlier as an **antidependency** (also called **write–write dependency**), arises. The code fragment considered earlier illustrates this dependency:

R3 := R3 op R5    (I1)
R4 := R3 + 1      (I2)
R3 := R5 + 1      (I3)
R7 := R3 op R4    (I4)

Instruction I3 cannot complete execution before instruction I2 begins execution and had fetched its operands. This is so because I3 updates register R3, which is a source operand for I2. The term *antidependency* is used because the constraint is similar to that of a true data dependency, but reversed: instead of the first instruction producing a value that the second instruction uses, the second instruction destroys a value that the first instruction uses.

## Register Renaming

When out-of-order instruction issuing and/or out-of-order instruction completion are allowed, we have seen that this gives rise to the possibility of output dependencies and antidependencies. These dependencies differ from true data dependencies and resource conflicts, which reflect the flow of data through a program and the sequence of execution. Output dependencies and antidependencies, on the other hand, arise because the values in registers may no longer reflect the sequence of values dictated by the program flow.

When instructions are issued in sequence and complete in sequence, it is possible to specify the contents of each register at each point in the execution. When out-of-order techniques are used, the values in registers cannot be fully known at each point in time just from a consideration of the sequence of instructions dictated by the program. In effect, values are in conflict for the use of registers, and the processor must resolve those conflicts by occasionally stalling a pipeline stage.

Antidependencies and output dependencies are both examples of storage conflicts. Multiple instructions are competing for the use of the same register locations, generating pipeline constraints that retard performance. The problem is made more acute when register optimization techniques are used (as discussed in Chapter 12), because these compiler techniques attempt to maximize the use of registers, hence maximizing the number of storage conflicts.

One method for coping with these types of storage conflicts is based on a traditional resource-conflict solution: duplication of resources. In this context, the technique is referred to as **register renaming.** In essence, registers are allocated dynamically by the processor hardware, and they are associated with the values needed by instructions at various points in time. When a new register value is created (i.e., when an instruction executes that has a register as a destination operand), a new register is allocated for that value. Subsequent instructions that access that value as a source operand in that register must go through a renaming process: the register references in those instructions must be revised to refer to the register containing the needed value. Thus, the same original register reference in several different instructions may refer to different actual registers, if different values are intended.

Let us consider how register renaming could be used on the code fragment we have been examining:

$$R3_b := R3_a \text{ op } R5_a \quad (I1)$$
$$R4_b := R3_b + 1 \quad (I2)$$
$$R3_c := R5_a + 1 \quad (I3)$$
$$R7_b := R3_c \text{ op } R4_b \quad (I4)$$

The register reference without the subscript refers to the logical register reference found in the instruction. The register reference with the subscript refers to a hardware register allocated to hold a new value. When a new allocation is made for a particular logical register, subsequent instruction references to that logical register as a source operand are made to refer to the most recently allocated hardware register (recent in terms of the program sequence of instructions).

In this example, the creation of register $R3_c$ in instruction I3 avoids the antidependency on the second instruction and the output dependency on the first instruction, and it does not interfere with the correct value being accessed by I4. The result is that I3 can be issued immediately; without renaming, I3 cannot be issued until the first instruction is complete and the second instruction is issued.

## Machine Parallelism

In the preceding, we have looked at three hardware techniques that can be used in a superscalar processor to enhance performance: duplication of resources, out-of-order issue, and renaming. One study that illuminates the relationship among these techniques was reported in [SMIT89]. The study made use of a simulation that modeled a machine with the characteristics of the MIPS R2000, augmented with various superscalar features. A number of different program sequences were simulated.

Figure 13.4 shows the results. In each of the graphs, the vertical axis corresponds to the mean speedup of the superscalar machine over the scalar machine. The horizontal axis shows the results for four alternative processor organizations. The base machine does not duplicate any of the functional units, but it can issue instructions out of order. The second configuration duplicates the load/store functional unit that accesses a data cache. The third configuration duplicates the ALU, and the fourth configuration duplicates both load/store and ALU. In each graph, results are shown for instruction window sizes of 8, 16, and 32 instructions, which dictates the amount of lookahead the processor can do. The difference between the two graphs is that, in the second, register renaming is allowed. This is equivalent to saying that the first graph reflects a machine that is limited by all dependencies, whereas the second graph corresponds to a machine that is limited only by true dependencies.

The two graphs, combined, yield some important conclusions. The first is that it is probably not worthwhile to add functional units without register renaming.

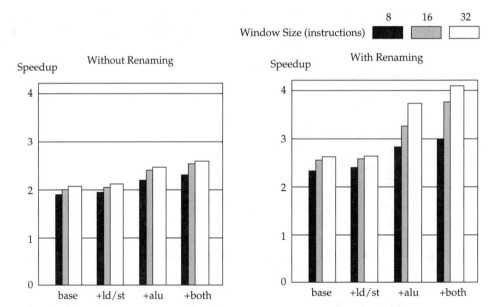

**FIGURE 13.4. Speedups of various machine organizations, without procedural dependencies**

There is some slight improvement in performance, but at the cost of increased hardware complexity. With register renaming, which eliminates antidependencies and output dependencies, noticeable gains are achieved by adding more functional units. Note, however, that there is a significant difference in the amount of gain achievable between using an instruction window of 8 versus a larger instruction window. This indicates that if the instruction window is too small, data dependencies will prevent effective utilization of the extra functional units; the processor must be able to look quite far ahead to find independent instructions in order to more fully utilize the hardware.

## Branch Prediction

Any high-performance pipelined machine must address the issue of dealing with branches. For example, the Intel 80486 addressed the problem by fetching both the next sequential instruction after a branch and speculatively fetching the branch target instruction. However, because there are two pipeline stages between prefetch and execution, this strategy incurs a two-cycle delay when the branch gets taken.

With the advent of RISC machines, the delayed branch strategy was explored. This allows the processor to calculate the result of conditional branch instructions before any unusable instructions have been prefetched. With this method, the processor always executes the single instruction that immediately follows the branch. This keeps the pipeline full while the processor fetches a new instruction stream.

With the development of superscalar machines, the delayed branch strategy has less appeal. The reason is that multiple instructions need to execute in the delay slot, raising several problems relating to instruction dependencies. Thus, superscalar machines have returned to pre-RISC techniques of branch prediction. Some, like the PowerPC 601, use a simple static branch prediction technique. More sophisticated processors, such as the PowerPC 620 and the Pentium, use dynamic branch prediction based on branch history analysis.

13.3

## POWERPC

The PowerPC architecture is a direct descendant of the IBM 801, the RT PC, and the RS/6000, the last also referred to as an implementation of the POWER architecture. All of these are RISC machines, but the first in the series to exhibit superscalar features was the RS/6000. The first implementation of the PowerPC architecture, the 601, has a superscalar design quite similar to that of the RS/6000. Subsequent PowerPC models carry the superscalar concept further. In this section, we focus on the 601, which provides a good example of a RISC-based superscalar design. At the end of the section, we briefly consider the 620.

### PowerPC 601

Figure 13.5 is a general view of the 601 organization. As with other superscalar machines, the 601 is broken up into independent functional units to enhance opportunities for overlapped execution. In particular, the core of the 601 consists of three independent pipelined execution units: integer, floating-point, and branch processing. Together, these units can execute three instructions at a time, yielding a superscalar design of degree three.

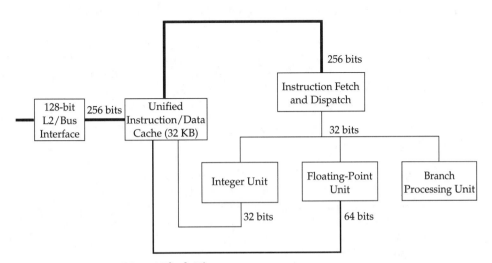

**FIGURE 13.5. PowerPC 601 Block Diagram**

Figure 13.6 shows a logical view of the 601 architecture, emphasizing the flow of instructions between functional units. The fetch unit can prefetch up to eight instructions at a time from the cache. The cache unit supports a combined instruction/data cache and is responsible for feeding instructions to the other units and data to the registers. Cache arbitration logic sends the address of the highest priority access to the cache.

### Dispatch Unit

The dispatch unit takes instructions from the cache and loads them into the dispatch queue, which can hold eight instructions at a time. It processes this stream of instructions to feed a steady flow of instructions to the branch processing, integer, and floating-point units. The upper half of the queue simply acts as a buffer to hold instructions until they move into the lower half. Its purpose is to ensure that the dispatch unit is not delayed waiting for instructions from the cache. In the lower half, instructions are dispatched according to the following scheme:

- *Branch Processing Unit:* Handles all branch instructions. The lowest such instruction in the bottom half of the dispatch queue is issued to the branch processing unit if that unit can accept it.
- *Floating-Point Unit:* Handles all floating-point instructions. The lowest such instruction in the bottom half of the dispatch queue is issued to the floating-point unit if the instruction pipeline in that unit is not full.
- *Integer Unit:* Handles integer instructions, load/stores between the register files and the cache, and integer compare instructions. An integer instruction is only issued after it has filtered to the bottom of the dispatch queue.

Allowing branch and floating-point instructions to be issued out of order from the dispatch queue helps keep the instruction pipelines in the branch processing and floating-point units full, and it moves instructions through the dispatch queue as rapidly as possible.

The dispatch unit also contains logic that enables it to calculate the prefetch address. It continues fetching instructions sequentially until a branch instruction moves into the lower half of the dispatch queue. When the branch processing unit processes an instruction, it may update the prefetch address so that succeeding instructions are fetched from the new address and entered into the dispatch queue.

## Instruction Pipelines

Figure 13.7 illustrates the instruction pipelines for the various units. There is a common fetch cycle for all instructions; this occurs before an instruction is dispatched to a particular unit. The second cycle begins with the dispatch of an instruction to a particular unit. This overlaps with other activities within the unit. During each clock cycle, the dispatch unit considers the bottom four entries of the instruction queue and dispatches up to three instructions.

For branch instructions, the second cycle involves decoding and executing instructions as well as predicting branches. The last activity is discussed next.

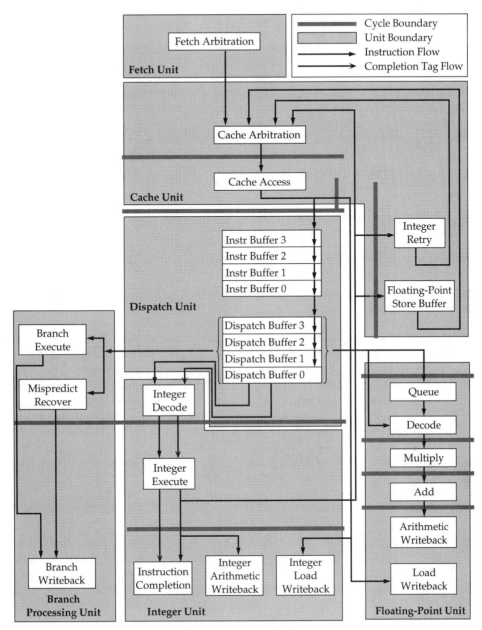

**FIGURE 13.6. PowerPC 601 Pipeline Structure [POTT94]**

The integer unit deals with instructions that cause a load/store operation with memory (including floating-point load/store), a register–register move, or an ALU operation. In the case of a load/store, there is an address generation cycle followed by sending the resulting address to the cache and, if necessary, a write-back cycle. For other instructions, the cache is not involved and there is an execute cycle followed by a write back to register.

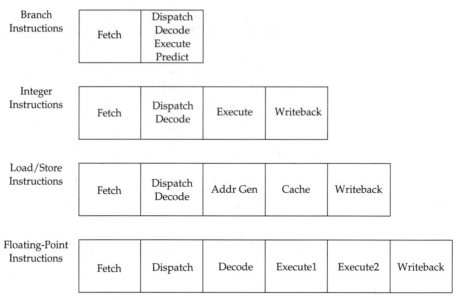

**FIGURE 13.7.  PowerPC 601 Pipeline**

Floating-point instructions follow a similar pipeline, but there are two execute cycles, reflecting the complexity of floating-point operations.

Several additional points are worth noting. The condition register contains eight independent 4-bit condition code fields. This allows multiple condition codes to be retained, which reduces the interlock or dependency between instructions. For example, the compiler can transform the sequence

 compare
 branch
 compare
 branch
  .
  .
  .

to the sequence

 compare
 compare
  .
  .
  .

 branch
 branch
  .
  .
  .

Since each functional unit can send its condition codes to different fields in the condition register, interlocks between instructions caused by sharing of condition codes can be avoided.

The presence of the Save and Restore registers (SRRs) in the branch processor allows it to handle simple interrupts and software interrupts without involving logic in the other functional units. Thus, simple operating-system services can be performed rapidly without complicated state manipulation or synchronization between the functional units.

Because the 601 can issue branch and floating-point instructions out of order, controls are needed to ensure proper execution. When a dependency exists (i.e., when an instruction needs an operand that has yet to be computed by a previous instruction), the pipeline in the corresponding unit stalls.

## Branch Processing

The key to the high performance of a RISC or superscalar machine is its ability to optimize the use of the pipeline. Typically, the most critical element in the design is how branches are handled. In the PowerPC, branch processing is the responsibility of the branch unit. The unit is designed so that in many cases, branches have no effect on the pace of execution in the other units; these type of branches are referred to as zero-cycle branches. To achieve zero-cycle branching, the following strategies are employed:

1. Logic is provided to scan through the dispatch buffer for branches. Branch target addresses are generated when a branch first appears in the lower half of the queue and no prior branches are pending execution.
2. An attempt is made to determine the outcome of conditional branches. If the condition code has been set sufficiently far in advance, this can be determined. In any case, as soon as a branch instruction is encountered, logic determines if the branch:
   a. Will be taken; this is the case for unconditional branches and for conditional branches whose condition code is known and indicates a branch.
   b. Will not be taken; this is the case for conditional branches whose condition code is known and indicates no branch.
   c. Outcome cannot yet be determined. In this case, the branch is guessed to be taken for backward branches (typical of loops) and guessed not to be taken for forward branches. Sequential instructions past the branch instruction are passed to the execution units in a conditional fashion. Once the condition code value is produced in the execution unit, the branch unit either cancels the instructions in the pipeline and proceeds with the fetched target if the branch is taken, or signals for the conditional instructions to be executed. The compiler can use a single bit in the instruction coding to reverse this default behavior.

The incorporation of a branch prediction strategy based on branch history was rejected because the designers felt that a minimal payoff would be achieved.

As an example of the branch prediction effect, consider the program of Figure 13.8 and assume that the branch processor predicts that the conditional branch

```
       if  (a > 0)
                    a = a + b + c + d + e;
       else
                    a = a – b – c – d – e;
```

(a) C Code

```
                                 #r1 points to a,
                                 #r1+4 points to b,
                                 #r1+8 points to c,
                                 #r1+12 points to d,
                                 #r1+16 points to e.
       lwz    r8=a (r1)          #load a
       lwz    r12=b (r1, 4)      #load b
       lwz    r9=c (r1, 8)       #load c
       lwz    r10=d (r1, 12)     #load d
       lwz    r11=e (r1,16)      #load e
       cmpi   cr0=r8, 0          #compare immediate
       bc     ELSE, cr0/gt=false #branch if bit false
IF:
       add    r12=r8, r12        #add
       add    r12=r12, r9        #add
       add    r12=r12, r10       #add
       add    r4=r12, r11        #add
       stw    a (r1) =r4         #store
       b      OUT                #unconditional branch
ELSE:
       subf   r12=r12, r8        #subtract
       subf   r12=r9, r12        #subtract
       subf   r12=r10, r12       #subtract
       subf   r4=r11, r12        #subtract
       stw    a (r1) =r4         #store
OUT:
```

(b) Assembly Code

**FIGURE 13.8.  Code Example with Conditional Branch [WEIS94]**

instruction is not taken (the default case for a forward branch). Figure 13.9a shows the effect on the pipeline if in fact the branch is not taken. In the first cycle, the dispatch queue is loaded with eight instructions. The first six instructions are integer instructions and are dispatched one per cycle to the integer unit. The conditional branch instruction cannot be dispatched until it progresses to the lower half of the dispatch queue, which happens in cycle 5. The branch unit predicts that this branch will not be taken, and so the next instruction in sequence is conditionally dispatched (indicated by a D'). The branch cannot be resolved until the compare instruction executes in cycle 8. At that time, the branch processor confirms that its prediction was correct, and execution continues. There are no delays, and the pipeline is kept full.

Note that no instructions are fetched during cycles 4 through 8. This is because the cache is busy during those cycles with the cache access stage of the five load

|  |  | 1 | 2 | 3 | 4 | 5 | 6 | 7 | 8 | 9 | 10 | 11 | 12 | 13 | 14 | 15 | 16 |
|---|---|---|---|---|---|---|---|---|---|---|---|---|---|---|---|---|---|
|  | lwz r8=a (r1) | F | D | E | C | W |  |  |  |  |  |  |  |  |  |  |  |
|  | lwz r12=b (r1, 4) | F |  | D | E | C | W |  |  |  |  |  |  |  |  |  |  |
|  | lwz r9=c (r1, 8) | F |  |  | D | E | C | W |  |  |  |  |  |  |  |  |  |
|  | lwz r10=d (r1, 12) | F |  |  |  | D | E | C | W |  |  |  |  |  |  |  |  |
|  | lwz r11=e (r1, 16) | F |  |  |  |  | D | E | C | W |  |  |  |  |  |  |  |
|  | cmpi cr0=r8, 0 | F |  |  |  |  |  | D | E |  |  |  |  |  |  |  |  |
|  | bc | F |  |  |  | S |  |  |  |  |  |  |  |  |  |  |  |
|  | ELSE, cr0/gt=false |  |  |  |  |  |  |  |  |  |  |  |  |  |  |  |  |
| IF: | add r12=r8, r12 | F |  |  |  |  |  |  | D' | E | W |  |  |  |  |  |  |
|  | add r12=r12, r9 |  | F |  |  |  |  |  |  | D | E | W |  |  |  |  |  |
|  | add r12=r12, r10 |  | F |  |  |  |  |  |  |  | D | E | W |  |  |  |  |
|  | add r4=r12, r11 |  |  | F |  |  |  |  |  |  |  | D | E | W |  |  |  |
|  | stw a (r1) =r4 |  |  | F |  |  |  |  |  |  |  |  | D | E | C |  |  |
|  | b OUT |  |  |  |  |  |  |  |  |  |  |  |  |  |  |  |  |
| ELSE: | subf r12=r8, r12 |  |  |  |  |  |  |  |  |  |  |  |  |  |  |  |  |
|  | subf r12=r12, r9 |  |  |  |  |  |  |  |  |  |  |  |  |  |  |  |  |
|  | subf r12=r12, r10 |  |  |  |  |  |  |  |  |  |  |  |  |  |  |  |  |
|  | subf r4=r12, r11 |  |  |  |  |  |  |  |  |  |  |  |  |  |  |  |  |
|  | stw a (r1) =r4 |  |  |  |  |  |  |  |  |  |  |  |  |  |  |  |  |
| OUT: |  |  |  |  |  |  |  |  |  |  |  |  |  |  |  |  |  |

**(a) Correct Prediction: Branch Was Not Taken**

|  |  | 1 | 2 | 3 | 4 | 5 | 6 | 7 | 8 | 9 | 10 | 11 | 12 | 13 | 14 | 15 | 16 |
|---|---|---|---|---|---|---|---|---|---|---|---|---|---|---|---|---|---|
|  | lwz r8=a (r1) | F | D | E | C | W |  |  |  |  |  |  |  |  |  |  |  |
|  | lwz r12=b (r1, 4) | F |  | D | E | C | W |  |  |  |  |  |  |  |  |  |  |
|  | lwz r9=c (r1, 8) | F |  |  | D | E | C | W |  |  |  |  |  |  |  |  |  |
|  | lwz r10=d (r1, 12) | F |  |  |  | D | E | C | W |  |  |  |  |  |  |  |  |
|  | lwz r11=e (r1, 16) | F |  |  |  |  | D | E | C | W |  |  |  |  |  |  |  |
|  | cmpi cr0=r8, 0 | F |  |  |  |  |  | D | E |  |  |  |  |  |  |  |  |
|  | bc | F |  |  |  | S |  |  |  |  |  |  |  |  |  |  |  |
|  | ELSE, cr0/gt=false |  |  |  |  |  |  |  |  |  |  |  |  |  |  |  |  |
| IF: | add r12=r8, r12 | F |  |  |  |  |  |  | D' |  |  |  |  |  |  |  |  |
|  | add r12=r12, r9 |  | F |  |  |  |  |  |  |  |  |  |  |  |  |  |  |
|  | add r12=r12, r10 |  | F |  |  |  |  |  |  |  |  |  |  |  |  |  |  |
|  | add r4=r12, r11 |  |  |  |  |  |  |  |  |  |  |  |  |  |  |  |  |
|  | stw a (r1) =r4 |  |  |  |  |  |  |  |  |  |  |  |  |  |  |  |  |
|  | b OUT |  |  |  |  |  |  |  |  |  |  |  |  |  |  |  |  |
| ELSE: | subf r12=r8, r12 |  |  |  |  |  |  |  | F | D | E | W |  |  |  |  |  |
|  | subf r12=r12, r9 |  |  |  |  |  |  |  | F |  | D | E | W |  |  |  |  |
|  | subf r12=r12, r10 |  |  |  |  |  |  |  | F |  |  | D | E | W |  |  |  |
|  | subf r4=r12, r11 |  |  |  |  |  |  |  | F |  |  |  | D | E | W |  |  |
|  | stw a (r1) =r4 |  |  |  |  |  |  |  | F |  |  |  |  | D | E | C |  |
| OUT: |  |  |  |  |  |  |  |  |  |  |  |  |  |  |  |  |  |

**(b) Incorrect Prediction: Branch Was Taken**

F = Fetch  
D = Dispatch/Decode  
E = Execute/Address  
C = Cache Access  
W = Writeback  
S = Dispatch  

**FIGURE 13.9. Branch Prediction: Not Taken [WEIS94]**

instructions. Even so, the instruction stream is not delayed, because the dispatch queue can hold eight instructions.

Figure 13.9b shows the result if the prediction is incorrect and the branch is taken. In this case, the three instructions starting at the IF must be flushed, and fetching resumes with instructions starting at ELSE. As a result, the execute stage of the integer pipeline is idle for cycles 9 and 10, resulting in a two-cycle loss because of the incorrect prediction.

## PowerPC 620

The 620 is the first 64-bit implementation of the PowerPC architecture. A general block diagram of this processor was shown in Figure 4.26. A notable feature of this implementation is that it includes six independent execution units:

- Instruction Unit
- Three Integer Units
- Load/Store Unit
- Floating-Point Unit

This organization enables the processor to dispatch up to four instructions simultaneously to the three integer units and one floating-point unit.

The 620 employs a high-performance branch prediction strategy that involves prediction logic, register rename buffers, and reservation stations inside the execution units. When an instruction is fetched, it is assigned a rename buffer to temporarily hold instruction results, such as register stores. Because of the use of rename buffers, it is possible for the processor to *speculatively execute* instructions based on branch prediction; if the prediction turns out to be incorrect, then the results of the speculative instructions can be flushed without damaging the register file. Once the outcome of a branch is confirmed, temporary results can be written out permanently.

Each unit has two or more reservation stations, which store dispatched instructions that must be held up for the results of other instructions. This feature clears these instructions out of the instruction unit, enabling it to continue dispatching instructions to other execution units.

The 620 can speculatively execute up to four unresolved branch instructions (versus one for the 601). Branch prediction is based on the use of a branch history table with 2048 entries. Simulations run by the PowerPC designers show that the branch prediction success rate is 90% [THOM94].

## 13.4

### PENTIUM

Although the concept of superscalar design is generally associated with the RISC architecture, the same superscalar principles can be applied to a CISC machine. Perhaps the most notable example of this is the Pentium. Compared with the most recent RISC designs, such as the PowerPC 620, the superscalar features on the

Pentium are fairly simple and straightforward. Nevertheless, they result in a substantial performance improvement.

A general block diagram of the Pentium was shown in Figure 4.24. Figure 13.10 provides more detail and focuses on those portions of the processor that are of interest in discussing instruction pipelining.

As with the 80486, the Pentium uses a five-stage integer pipeline:

- *Prefetch:* The processor prefetches instructions from the instruction cache. Instructions are of variable length and are stored in a buffer.
- *Decode Stage 1:* The processor decodes the instruction to determine opcode and addressing information. This stage also performs two functions examined below: checking for pairability and branch prediction.
- *Decode Stage 2:* This stage generates addresses for memory references.
- *Execute:* In this stage, the processor either accesses the data cache or calculates results in the ALU, barrel shifter, or other functional units in the data path.
- *Write Back:* This stage updates the registers and flags with the instruction's results.

From the point of view of instruction pipelining, the most significant difference between the Pentium and its predecessor, the 80486, is that the Pentium includes two separate integer execution units, designated U and V. Figure 13.11 compares the two.

## Instruction Pairing

The U and V units are capable of executing instructions in parallel. However, the processor must determine that there are not potential conflicts in such parallel execution. The first requirement is that two instructions must both be *simple* in order to execute in parallel. Simple instructions are those that are entirely hard-wired; they do not require any microcode control, and most execute in one clock cycle. The exceptions are the ALU register-to-memory and memory-to-register instructions, which require two or three clock cycles but which make use of sequencing hardware that enables them to be paired. Table 13.2 lists the instructions that can be paired.

The Pentium *Data Book* [INTE94a] defines the rules for pairing. Two successive instructions I1 and I2 can be dispatched in parallel to the U and V units according to the following rules:

1. Both instructions are simple.
2. There are no read-after-write or write-after-write dependencies. That is, the destination of I1 is not the source of I2 and the destination of I1 is not the destination of I2.
3. Neither instruction contains both a displacement and an immediate operand.
4. Only I1 may contain an instruction prefix.

Thus, the Pentium can achieve a superscalar degree of two. Benchmark results from several independent studies [POUN93] show that the Pentium performs almost exactly twice as fast as an equivalent 80486 on integer code. These results support the conclusion that the Pentium's twin superscalar pipelines are the processor's crucial architectural innovation.

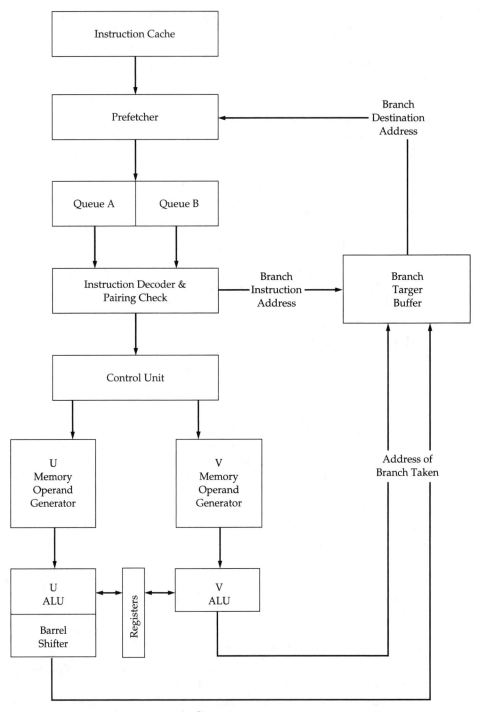

**FIGURE 13.10. Pentium Integer Pipeline Structure**

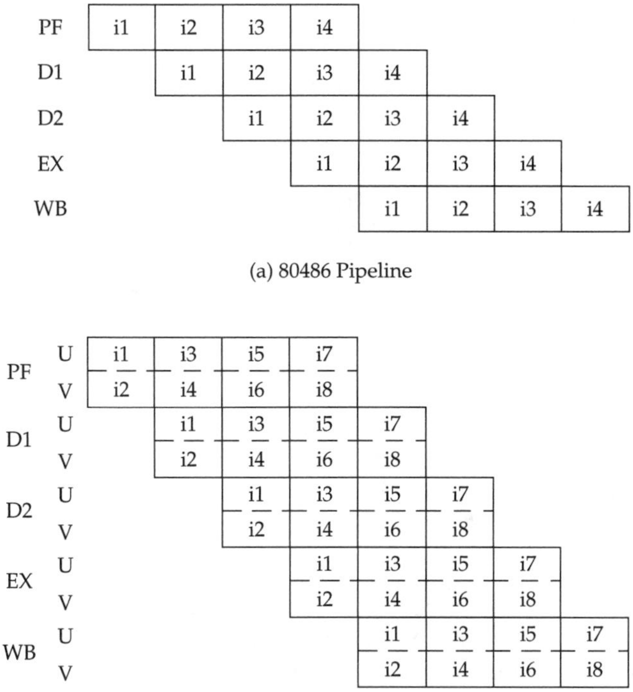

| PF | i1 | i2 | i3 | i4 |    |    |    |    |
|----|----|----|----|----|----|----|----|----|
| D1 |    | i1 | i2 | i3 | i4 |    |    |    |
| D2 |    |    | i1 | i2 | i3 | i4 |    |    |
| EX |    |    |    | i1 | i2 | i3 | i4 |    |
| WB |    |    |    |    | i1 | i2 | i3 | i4 |

(a) 80486 Pipeline

| | U/V | | | | | | | | |
|----|---|----|----|----|----|----|----|----|----|
| PF | U | i1 | i3 | i5 | i7 |    |    |    |    |
|    | V | i2 | i4 | i6 | i8 |    |    |    |    |
| D1 | U |    | i1 | i3 | i5 | i7 |    |    |    |
|    | V |    | i2 | i4 | i6 | i8 |    |    |    |
| D2 | U |    |    | i1 | i3 | i5 | i7 |    |    |
|    | V |    |    | i2 | i4 | i6 | i8 |    |    |
| EX | U |    |    |    | i1 | i3 | i5 | i7 |    |
|    | V |    |    |    | i2 | i4 | i6 | i8 |    |
| WB | U |    |    |    |    | i1 | i3 | i5 | i7 |
|    | V |    |    |    |    | i2 | i4 | i6 | i8 |

(b) Pentium Pipeline

**FIGURE 13.11. 80486 and Pentium Pipelines**

## Branch Prediction

The Pentium uses a dynamic branch prediction strategy based on the history of recent executions of branch instructions. Figure 13.12 illustrates the general flow involved. A branch target buffer (BTB) is maintained that caches information about recently encountered branch instructions. Whenever a branch instruction is encountered in the instruction stream, the BTB is checked. If an entry already exists in the BTB, then the instruction unit is guided by the history information for that entry in determining whether to predict that the branch is taken. If a branch is predicted, then the branch destination address associated with this entry is used for prefetching the branch target instruction.

Once the instruction is executed, the history portion of the appropriate entry is updated to reflect the result of the branch instruction. If this instruction is not represented in the BTB, then the address of this instruction is loaded into an entry in the BTB; if necessary, an older entry is deleted.

As instructions are prefetched, they are fed into one of two instruction queues. Only one queue is active at a time, and instructions are fed into and out of that queue. When a branch taken event is predicted, the currently active queue is frozen and the prefetcher begins to fetch instructions starting from the branch target address into the other queue. If the prediction is correct, then instruction

**TABLE 13.2    Simple Pentium Instructions**

| | | | |
|---|---|---|---|
| MOV | reg, reg | *shift* | reg, imm |
| MOV | reg, mem | *shift* | mem, imm |
| MOV | reg, imm | | |
| MOV | mem, reg | INC | reg |
| MOV | mem, imm | INC | mem |
| | | DEC | reg |
| *alu* | reg, reg | DEC | mem |
| *alu* | reg, mem | Pusit | reg |
| *alu* | reg, imm | POP | reg |
| *alu* | mem, reg | LEA | reg, mem |
| *alu* | mem, imm | JMP | near |
| | | CALL | near |
| *shift* | reg, 1 | Jcc | near |
| *shift* | mem, 1 | NOP | |

*alu* = ADD, ADC, AND, OR, XOR, SUB, SBB, CMP, TEST
*shift* = SAL, SAR, SHL, SHR, RCL, RCR, ROL, ROR
(RCL and RCR not pairable with immediate)

sequencing continues using the currently active queue. If the prediction is incorrect, then both pipelines are flushed and the processor incurs a three- or four-cycle delay while the correct target instruction is fetched.

The BTB is organized as a four-way set associative cache with 256 lines. Each entry (Figure 13.13) uses the address of the branch instruction as a tag. The entry also includes the branch destination address for the last time that this branch was taken and a two-bit history field. The four possible states of this field reflect the recent history of this instruction. A new entry is recorded with a history field of 11, and subsequent executions follow the state diagram of Figure 13.12. The processor predicts that the branch is taken unless the history value is 11.

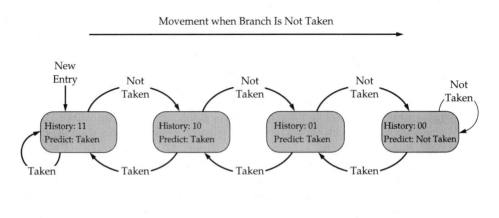

**FIGURE 13.12.  Branch Target Buffer State Diagram**

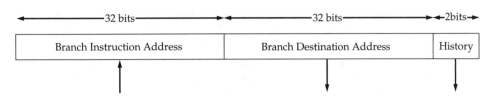

| ◄────────32 bits────────► | ◄────────32 bits────────► | ◄─2bits─► |
|---|---|---|
| Branch Instruction Address | Branch Destination Address | History |

**FIGURE 13.13. Pentium Branch Target Buffer Entry**

## 13.5

### RECOMMENDED READING

[JOHN91] is an excellent book-length treatment of superscalar design. [JOUP89a] examines instruction-level parallelism, looks at various techniques for maximizing parallelism, and compares superscalar and superpipelined approaches using simulation.

[POPE91] provides a detailed look at a proposed superscalar machine. It also provides an excellent tutorial on the design issues related to out-of-order instruction policies. Another look at a proposed system is found in [KUGA91]; this article raises and considers most of the important design issues for superscalar implementation. [LEE91] examines software techniques that can be used to enhance superscalar performance. [WALL91] is an interesting study of the extent to which instruction-level parallelism can be exploited in a superscalar processor. [WAYN92] provides an instructive comparison of the instruction pipelines of the Intel 80486, the MIPS R4000, and the IBM RS/6000. [WEIS93] provides an instructive analysis of the use of superscalar design to execute vector-oriented programs.

[POTT94] is a detailed examination of instruction pipelining on the PowerPC 601. Other articles with good coverage of 601 pipelining include [RYAN93] and [BECK93]. [WEIS94] also provides good coverage. The PowerPC 620 is described in [THOM94].

[ANDE93] contains a good description of instruction pipelining on the Pentium. [POUN93] critiques the superscalar design aspects of the Pentium, and [SCHM94] provides an interesting analysis of Pentium superscalar performance with different code fragments.

ANDE93   Anderson, D., and Shanley, T. *Pentium Processor System Architecture.* Richardson, TX: Mindshare Press, 1993.

BECK93   Becker, M., et al. "The PowerPC 601 Microprocessor." *IEEE Micro,* October 1993.

JOHN91   Johnson, M. *Superscalar Microprocessor Design.* Englewood Cliffs, NJ: Prentice-Hall, 1991.

JOUP89a  Jouppi, N., and Wall, D. "Available Instruction-Level Parallelism for Super-scalar and Superpipelined Machines." *Proceedings, Third International Conference on Architectural Support for Programming Languages and Operating Systems,* April 1989.

KUGA91   Kuga, M.; Murakami, K.; and Tomita, S. "DSNS (Dynamically-hazard resolved, Statically-code-scheduled, Nonuniform Superscalar): Yet Another Superscalar Processor Architecture." *Computer Architecture News,* June 1991.

LEE91   Lee, R.; Kwok, A.; and Briggs, F. "The Floating Point Performance of a Superscalar SPARC Processor." *Proceedings, Fourth International Conference on Architectural Support for Programming Languages and Operating Systems,* April 1991.

POPE91   Popescu, V., et al. "The Metaflow Architecture." *IEEE Micro,* June 1991.

POTT94   Potter, T., et al. "Resolution of Data and Control-Flow Dependencies in the PowerPC 601." *IEEE Micro,* October 1994.

POUN93   Pountain, D. "Pentium: More RISC than CISC." *Byte,* September 1993.

RYAN93   Ryan, B. "RISC Drives PowerPC." *Byte,* August 1993.

SCHM94   Schmit, M. "Optimizing Pentium Code." *Dr. Dobb's Journal,* January 1994.

THOM94   Thompson, T., and Ryan, B. "PowerPC 620 Soars." *Byte,* November 1994.

WALL91   Wall, D. "Limits of Instruction-Level Parallelism." *Proceedings, Fourth International Conference on Architectural Support for Programming Languages and Operating Systems,* April 1991.

WAYN92   Wayner, P. "Processor Pipelines." *Byte,* January 1992.

WEIS93   Weiss, S. "Optimizing a Superscalar Machine to Run Vector Code." *IEEE Parallel & Distributed Technology,* May 1993.

WEIS94   Weiss, S., and Smith, J. *POWER and PowerPC.* San Francisco: Morgan Kaufmann, 1994.

## 13.6

## PROBLEMS

13.1   When out-of-order completion is used in a superscalar processor, resumption of execution after interrupt processing is complicated, because the exceptional condition may have been detected as an instruction that produced its result out of order. The program cannot be restarted at the instruction following the exceptional instruction, because subsequent instructions have already completed, and doing so would cause these instructions to be executed twice. Suggest a mechanism or mechanisms for dealing with this situation.

13.2   Consider the following sequence of instructions, where the syntax consists of an opcode followed by the destination register followed by one or two source registers:

|     |      |          |
|-----|------|----------|
| 0   | ADD  | r3, r1, r2 |
| 1   | LOAD | r6, [r3] |
| 2   | AND  | r7, r5, 3 |
| 3   | ADD  | r1, r6, r0 |
| 4   | SRL  | r7, r0, 8 |
| 5   | OR   | r2, r4, r7 |
| 6   | SUB  | r5, r3, r4 |
| 7   | ADD  | r0, r1, 10 |
| 8   | LOAD | r6, [r5] |
| 9   | SUB  | r2, r1, r6 |
| 10  | AND  | r3, r7,15 |

Assume the use of a four-stage pipeline: fetch, decode/issue, execute, write back. Assume that all pipeline stages take one clock cycle except for the execute stage. For simple integer arithmetic and logical instructions, the execute stage takes one cycle, but for a LOAD from memory, five cycles are consumed in the execute stage.

If we have a simple scalar pipeline but allow out-of-order execution, we can construct the following table for the execution of the first seven instructions:

| Instruction | Fetch | Decode | Execute | Writeback |
|---|---|---|---|---|
| 0 | 0 | 1 | 2 | 3 |
| 1 | 1 | 2 | 4 | 9 |
| 2 | 2 | 3 | 5 | 6 |
| 3 | 3 | 4 | 10 | 11 |
| 4 | 4 | 5 | 6 | 7 |
| 5 | 5 | 6 | 8 | 10 |
| 6 | 6 | 7 | 9 | 12 |

The entries under the four pipeline stages indicate the clock cycle at which each instruction begins each phase. In this program, the second ADD instruction (instruction 3) depends on the LOAD instruction (instruction 1) for one of its operands, r6. Because the LOAD instruction takes five clock cycles, and the issue logic encounters the dependent ADD instruction after two clocks, the issue logic must delay the ADD instruction for three clock cycles. With an out-of-order capability, the processor can stall instruction 3 at clock cycle 4, and then move on to issue the following three independent instructions, which enter execution at clocks 6, 8, and 9. The LOAD finishes execution at clock 9, and so the dependent ADD can be launched into execution on clock 10.

(a) Complete the above table.

(b) Redo the table assuming no out-of-order capability. What is the savings using the capability?

(c) Redo the table assuming a superscalar implementation that can handle two instructions at a time at each stage.

13.3 In the instruction queue in the dispatch unit of the PowerPC 601, instructions may be dispatched out of order to the branch processing and floating-point units, but instructions intended for the integer unit must be dispatched only from the bottom of the queue. Why this limitation?

13.4 Produce a figure similar to Figure 13.9 for the following cases:

(a) Branch prediction: taken; correct prediction: branch was taken

(b) Branch prediction: taken; incorrect prediction: branch was not taken

13.5 Express the prediction rule implied by Figure 13.12 in words. Be succinct.

# PART IV

# THE CONTROL UNIT

The control unit is that portion of the CPU that actually causes things to happen. The control unit issues control signals external to the CPU to cause data exchange with memory and I/O modules. The control unit also issues control signals internal to the CPU to move data between registers, to cause the ALU to perform a specified function, and to regulate other internal operations. Input to the control unit consists of the instruction register, flags, and control signals from external sources (e.g., interrupt signals).

Chapter 14 examines the operation of the control unit, explaining in functional terms what the control unit does. It is seen that the basic responsibility of the control unit is to cause a sequence of elementary operations, called *micro-operations,* to occur during the course of an instruction cycle. Then, in Chapter 15, we see how the concept of micro-operation leads to an elegant and powerful approach to control unit implementation.

# CHAPTER 14

# Control Unit Operation

In Chapter 9, we pointed out that a machine instruction set goes a long way toward defining the CPU. If we know the machine instruction set, including an understanding of the effect of each op code and an understanding of the addressing modes, and if we know the set of user-visible registers, then we know the functions that the CPU must perform. This is not the complete picture. We must know the external interfaces, usually through a bus, and how interrupts are handled. With this line of reasoning, the following list of those things needed to specify the function of a CPU emerges:

1. Operations (opcodes)
2. Addressing Modes
3. Registers
4. I/O Module Interface
5. Memory Module Interface
6. Interrupt Processing Structure

This list, though general, is rather complete. Items 1 through 3 are defined by defining the instruction set. Items 4 and 5 are typically defined by defining the system bus. Item 6 is defined partially by the system bus and partially by the type of support the CPU offers to the operating system.

This list of six items might be termed the functional requirements for a CPU. They determine what a CPU must do. This is what occupied us in Parts II and III. Now, we turn to the question of how these functions are performed or, more specifically, how the various elements of the CPU are controlled to provide these functions. Thus, we turn to a discussion of the control unit, which controls the operation of the CPU.

## 14.1

### MICRO-OPERATIONS

The function of a computer is to execute programs. We have seen that the operation of a computer, in executing a program, consists of a sequence of instruction cycles, with one machine instruction per cycle. Of course, we must remember that this sequence of instruction cycles is not necessarily the same as the *written sequence* of instructions that make up the program, because of the existence of branching instructions. What we are referring to here is the execution *time sequence* of instructions.

We have further seen that each instruction cycle can be considered to be made up of a number of smaller units. One subdivision that we found convenient is fetch, indirect, execute, and interrupt, with only fetch and execute cycles always occurring.

To design a control unit, however, we need to break the description down further. In our discussion of pipelining in Chapter 11, we began to see that a further decomposition is possible. In fact, we will see that each of the smaller cycles involves a series of steps, each of which involves the CPU registers. We will refer to these steps as *micro-operations*. The prefix *micro* refers to the fact that each step is very simple and accomplishes very little. Figure 14.1 depicts the relationship among the various concepts we have been discussing. To summarize, the execution of a program consists of the sequential execution of instructions. Each instruction is executed during an instruction cycle made up of shorter subcycles (e.g., fetch, indirect, execute, interrupt). The performance of each subcycle involves one or more shorter operations, that is, micro-operations.

Micro-operations are the functional, or atomic, operations of a CPU. In this section, we will examine micro-operations, to gain an understanding of how the events of any instruction cycle can be described as a sequence of such micro-operations. A simple example, based on [MANO93], will be used. In the remainder of this chapter, we then show how the concept of micro-operations serves as a guide to the design of the control unit.

## The Fetch Cycle

We begin by looking at the fetch cycle, which occurs at the beginning of each instruction cycle and causes an instruction to be fetched from memory. For purposes of discussion, we assume the organization depicted in Figure 11.8. Four registers are involved:

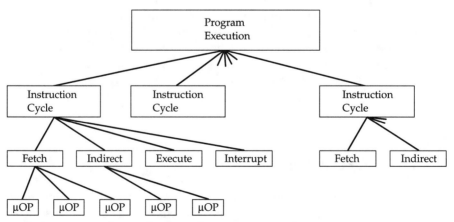

**FIGURE 14.1. Constituent elements of a program execution**

- *Memory Address Register (MAR):* Is connected to the address lines of the system bus. It specifies the address in memory for a read or write operation.
- *Memory Buffer Register (MBR):* Is connected to the data lines of the system bus. It contains the value to be stored in memory or the last value read from memory.
- *Program Counter (PC):* Holds the address of the next instruction to be fetched.
- *Instruction Register (IR):* Holds the last instruction fetched.

Let us look at the sequence of events for the fetch cycle from the point of view of its effect on the CPU registers. An example appears in Figure 14.2. At the beginning of the fetch cycle, the address of the next instruction to be executed is in the program counter (PC); in this case, the address is 1100100. The first step is to move that address to the memory address register (MAR), since this is the only register connected to the address lines of the system bus. The second step is to bring in the instruction. The desired address (in the MAR) is placed on the address bus, the control unit issues a READ command on the control bus, and the result appears on

| MAR | |
| --- | --- |
| MBR | |
| PC | 0 0 0 0 0 0 0 0 0 1 1 0 0 1 0 0 |
| IR | |
| AC | |

(a) Beginning

| MAR | 0 0 0 0 0 0 0 0 0 1 1 0 0 1 0 0 |
| --- | --- |
| MBR | |
| PC | 0 0 0 0 0 0 0 0 0 1 1 0 0 1 0 0 |
| IR | |
| AC | |

(b) First Step

| MAR | 0 0 0 0 0 0 0 0 0 1 1 0 0 1 0 0 |
| --- | --- |
| MBR | 0 0 0 1 0 0 0 0 0 0 1 0 0 0 0 0 |
| PC | 0 0 0 0 0 0 0 0 0 1 1 0 0 1 0 1 |
| IR | |
| AC | |

(c) Second Step

| MAR | 0 0 0 0 0 0 0 0 0 1 1 0 0 1 0 0 |
| --- | --- |
| MBR | 0 0 0 1 0 0 0 0 0 0 1 0 0 0 0 0 |
| PC | 0 0 0 0 0 0 0 0 0 1 1 0 0 1 0 1 |
| IR | 0 0 0 1 0 0 0 0 0 0 1 0 0 0 0 0 |
| AC | |

(d) Third Step

**FIGURE 14.2. Sequence of events, fetch style**

the data bus and is copied into the memory buffer register (MBR). We also need to increment the PC by 1 to get ready for the next instruction. Since these two actions (read word from memory, add 1 to PC) do not interfere with each other, we can do them simultaneously to save time. The third step is to move the contents of the MBR to the instruction register (IR). This frees up the MBR for use during a possible indirect cycle.

Thus, the simple fetch cycle actually consists of three steps and four micro-operations. Each micro-operation involves the movement of data into or out of a register. So long as these movements do not interfere with one another, several of them can take place during one step, saving time. Symbolically, we can write this sequence of events as follows:

$t_1$: MAR ← (PC)
$t_2$: MBR ← Memory
    PC    ← (PC) + 1
$t_3$: IR    ← (MBR)

We need to make several comments about this sequence. We assume that a clock is available for timing purposes, and that it emits regularly spaced clock pulses. Each clock pulse defines a time unit. Thus, all time units are of equal duration. Each micro-operation can be performed within the time of a single time unit. The notation $(t_1, t_2, t_3)$ represents successive time units. In words, we have

- *First time unit:* Move contents of PC to MAR.
- *Second time unit:* Move contents of memory location specified by MAR to MBR. Increment by 1 the contents of the PC.
- *Third time unit:* Move contents of MBR to IR.

Note that the second and third micro-operations both take place during the second time unit. The third micro-operation could have been grouped with the fourth without affecting the fetch operation:

$t_1$: MAR ← (PC)
$t_2$: MBR ← Memory
$t_3$: PC    ← (PC) + 1
    IR    ← (MBR)

The groupings of micro-operations must follow two simple rules:

1. The proper sequence of events must be followed. Thus (MAR ← (PC)) must precede (MBR ← Memory) since the memory read operation makes use of the address in the MAR.
2. Conflicts must be avoided. One should not attempt to read to and write from the same register in one time unit, since the results would be unpredictable. For example, the micro-operations (MBR ← Memory) and (IR ← MBR) should not occur during the same time unit.

A final point worth noting is that one of the micro-operations involves an addition. To avoid duplication of circuitry, this addition could be performed by the ALU. The use of the ALU may involve additional micro-operations, depending on the functionality of the ALU and the organization of the CPU. We defer a discussion of this point until later in this chapter.

It is useful to compare events described in this and the following subsections to Figure 3.5. Whereas micro-operations are ignored in that figure, this discussion shows the micro-operations needed to perform the subcycles of the instruction cycle.

## The Indirect Cycle

Once an instruction is fetched, the next step is to fetch source operands. Continuing our simple example, let us assume a one-address instruction format, with direct and indirect addressing allowed. If the instruction specifies an indirect address, then an indirect cycle must precede the execute cycle. The data flow is indicated in Figure 11.9 and includes the following micro-operations:

$t_1$: MAR ← (IR(Address))
$t_2$: MBR ← Memory
$t_3$: IR(Address) ← (MBR(Address))

The address field of the instruction is transferred to the MAR. This is then used to fetch the address of the operand. Finally, the address field of the IR is updated from the MBR, so that it now contains a direct rather than an indirect address.

The IR is now in the same state as if indirect addressing had not been used, and it is ready for the execute cycle. We skip that cycle for a moment, to consider the interrupt cycle.

## The Interrupt Cycle

At the completion of the execute cycle, a test is made to determine whether any enabled interrupts have occurred. If so, the interrupt cycle occurs. The nature of this cycle varies greatly from one machine to another. We present a very simple sequence of events, as illustrated in Figure 11.10. We have

$t_1$: MBR ← (PC)
$t_2$: MAR ← Save-address
    PC ← Routine-address
$t_3$: Memory ← (MBR)

In the first step, the contents of the PC are transferred to the MBR, so that they can be saved for return from the interrupt. Then the MAR is loaded with the address at which the contents of the PC are to be saved, and the PC is loaded with the address of the start of the interrupt-processing routine. These two actions may each be a single micro-operation. However, since most CPUs provide multiple types and/or levels of interrupts, it may take one or more additional micro-operations to obtain the save-address and the routine-address before they can be transferred to the MAR and PC, respectively. In any case, once this is done, the final step is to store the MBR, which contains the old value of the PC, into memory. The CPU is now ready to begin the next instruction cycle.

## The Execute Cycle

The fetch, indirect, and interrupt cycles are simple and predictable. Each involves a small, fixed sequence of micro-operations and, in each case, the same micro-operations are repeated each time around.

This is not true of the execute cycle. For a machine with $N$ different opcodes, there are $N$ different sequences of micro-operations that can occur. Let us consider several hypothetical examples.

First, consider an add instruction:

ADD R1, X

which adds the contents of the location X to register R1. The following sequence of micro-operations might occur:

$t_1$: MAR $\leftarrow$ (IR(address))
$t_2$: MBR $\leftarrow$ Memory
$t_3$: R1 $\leftarrow$ (R1) + (MBR)

We begin with the IR containing the ADD instruction. In the first step, the address portion of the IR is loaded into the MAR. Then, the referenced memory location is read. Finally, the contents of R1 and MBR are added by the ALU. Again, this is a simplified example. Additional micro-operations may be required to extract the register reference from the IR and perhaps to stage the ALU inputs or outputs in some intermediate registers.

Let us look at two more-complex examples. A common instruction is increment and skip if zero:

ISZ X

The content of location X is incremented by 1. If the result is 0, the next instruction is skipped. A possible sequence of micro-operations is

$t_1$: MAR $\leftarrow$ (IR(address))
$t_2$: MBR $\leftarrow$ Memory
$t_3$: MBR $\leftarrow$ (MBR) + 1
$t_4$: Memory $\leftarrow$ (MBR)
      If (MBR = 0) then (PC $\leftarrow$ (PC) + 1).

The new feature introduced here is the conditional action. The PC is incremented if MBR = 0. This test and action can be implemented as one micro-operation. Note also that this micro-operation can be performed during the same time unit during which the updated value in MBR is stored back to memory.

Finally, consider a subroutine call instruction. As an example, consider a branch-and-save-address instruction:

BSA X

The address of the instruction that follows the BSA instruction is saved in location X, and execution continues at location X + 1. The saved address will later be used for return. This is a straightforward technique for providing subroutine calls. The following micro-operations suffice:

$t_1$: MAR ← (IR(address))
    MBR ← (PC)
$t_2$: PC ← (IR(address))
    Memory ← (MBR)
$t_3$: PC ← (PC) + 1

The address in the PC at the start of the instruction is the address of the next instruction in sequence. This is saved at the address designated in the IR. The latter address is also incremented to provide the address of the instruction for the next instruction cycle.

## The Instruction Cycle

We have seen that each phase of the instruction cycle can be decomposed into a sequence of elementary micro-operations. In our example, there is one sequence each for the fetch, indirect, and interrupt cycles, and, for the execute cycle, there is one sequence of micro-operations for each opcode.

To complete the picture, we need to tie sequences of micro-operations together, and this is done in Figure 14.3. We assume a new 2-bit register called the *instruction cycle code* (ICC). The ICC designates the state of the CPU in terms of which portion of the cycle it is in:

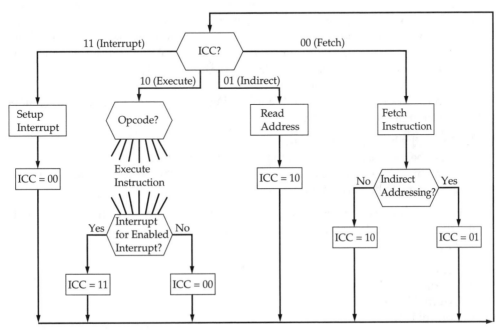

**FIGURE 14.3. Flowchart for instruction cycle**

00: Fetch
01: Indirect
10: Execute
11: Interrupt

At the end of each of the four cycles, the ICC is set appropriately. The indirect cycle is always followed by the execute cycle. The interrupt cycle is always followed by the fetch cycle (see Figure 11.6). For both the execute and fetch cycles, the next cycle depends upon the state of the system.

Thus, the flowchart of Figure 14.3 defines the complete sequence of micro-operations, depending only on the instruction sequence and the interrupt pattern. Of course, this is a simplified example. The flowchart for an actual CPU would be more complex. In any case, we have reached the point in our discussion in which the operation of the CPU is defined as the performance of a sequence of micro-operations. We can now consider how the control unit causes this sequence to occur.

## 14.2

## CONTROL OF THE CPU

### Functional Requirements

As a result of our analysis in the preceding section, we have decomposed the behavior or functioning of the CPU into elementary operations, called micro-operations. Our motivation is this: We want to determine the nature of the control unit. By reducing the operation of the CPU to its most fundamental level, we are able to define exactly what it is that the control unit must cause to happen. Thus, we can define the *functional requirements* for the control unit: those functions that the control unit must perform. A definition of these functional requirements is the basis for the design and implementation of the control unit.

With the information at hand, the following three-step process leads to a characterization of the control unit:

1. Define the basic elements of the CPU.
2. Describe the micro-operations that the CPU performs.
3. Determine the functions that the control unit must perform to cause the micro-operations to be performed.

We have already performed steps 1 and 2. Let us summarize the results. First, the basic functional elements of the CPU are the following:

- ALU
- Registers
- Internal Data Paths
- External Data Paths
- Control Unit

Some thought should convince the reader that this is a complete list. The ALU is the functional essence of the computer. Registers are used to store data internal to the CPU. Some registers contain status information needed to manage instruction sequencing (e.g., a program status word). Others contain data that go to or come from the ALU, memory, and I/O modules. Internal data paths are used to move data between registers and between register and ALU. External data paths link registers to memory and I/O modules, often by means of a system bus. The control unit causes operations to happen within the CPU.

The execution of a program consists of operations involving these CPU elements. As we have seen, these operations consist of a sequence of micro-operations. Upon review of Section 14.1, the reader should see that all micro-operations fall into one of the following categories:

- Transfer data from one register to another.
- Transfer data from a register to an external interface (e.g., system bus).
- Transfer data from an external interface to a register.
- Perform an arithmetic or logic operation, using registers for input and output.

All of the micro-operations needed to perform one instruction cycle, including all of the micro-operations to execute every instruction in the instruction set, fall into one of these categories.

We can now be somewhat more explicit about the way in which the control unit functions. The control unit performs two basic tasks:

- *Sequencing:* The control unit causes the CPU to step through a series of micro-operations in the proper sequence, based on the program being executed.
- *Execution:* The control unit causes each micro-operation to be performed.

The preceding is a functional description of what the control unit does. The key to how the control unit operates is the use of control signals.

## Control Signals

We have defined the elements that make up the CPU (ALU, registers, data paths) and the micro-operations that are performed. For the control unit to perform its function, it must have inputs that allow it to determine the state of the system and outputs that allow it to control the behavior of the system. These are the external specifications of the control unit. Internally, the control unit must have the logic required to perform its sequencing and execution functions. We defer a discussion of the internal operation of the control unit to Section 14.3 and Chapter 15. The remainder of this section is concerned with the interaction between the control unit and the other elements of the CPU.

Figure 14.4 is a general model of the control unit, showing all of its inputs and outputs. The inputs are

- *Clock:* This is how the control unit "keeps time." The control unit causes one micro-operation (or a set of simultaneous micro-operations) to be performed for

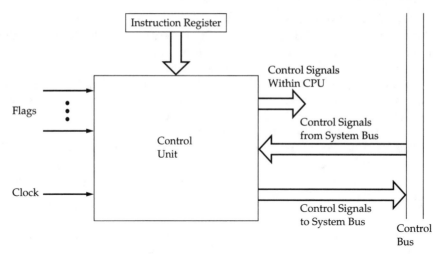

**FIGURE 14.4. Model of the control unit**

each clock pulse. This is sometimes referred to as the *processor cycle time,* or the *clock cycle time.*

- *Instruction Register:* The opcode of the current instruction is used to determine which micro-operations to perform during the execute cycle.
- *Flags:* These are needed by the control unit to determine the status of the CPU and the outcome of previous ALU operations. For example, for the increment-and-skip-if-zero (ISZ) instruction, the control unit will increment the PC if the zero flag is set.
- *Control Signals from Control Bus:* The control bus portion of the system bus provides signals to the control unit, such as interrupt signals and acknowledgments.

The outputs are

- *Control Signals Within the CPU:* These are two types: those that cause data to be moved from one register to another, and those that activate specific ALU functions.
- *Control Signals to Control Bus:* These are also of two types: control signals to memory, and control signals to the I/O modules.

The new element that has been introduced in this figure is the control signal. Three types of control signals are used: those that activate an ALU function, those that activate a data path, and those that are signals on the external system bus or other external interface. All of these signals are ultimately applied directly as binary inputs to individual logic gates.

Let us consider again the fetch cycle to see how the control unit maintains control. The control unit keeps track of where it is in the instruction cycle. At a given point, it knows that the fetch cycle is to be performed next. The first step is to transfer the contents of the PC to the MAR. The control unit does this by activating the control signal that opens the gates between the bits of the PC and the bits of the MAR. The next step is to read a word from memory into the MBR and increment the PC. The control unit does this by sending the following control signals simultaneously:

1. A control signal that opens gates allowing the contents of the MAR onto the address bus.
2. A memory read control signal on the control bus.
3. A control signal that opens the gates allowing the contents of the data bus to be stored in the MBR.
4. Control signals to logic that add 1 to the contents of the PC and store the result back to the PC.

Following this, the control unit sends a control signal that opens gates between the MBR and the IR.

This completes the fetch cycle except for one thing: The control unit must decide whether to perform an indirect cycle or an execute cycle next. To decide this, it examines the IR to see if an indirect memory reference is made.

The indirect and interrupt cycles work similarly. For the execute cycle, the control unit begins by examining the opcode and, on the basis of that, decides which sequence of micro-operations to perform for the execute cycle.

## A Control Signals Example

To illustrate the functioning of the control unit, let us examine a simple example, adapted from one in [ANDR80]. Figure 14.5 illustrates the example. This is a simple CPU with a single accumulator. The data paths between elements are indicated. The control paths for signals emanating from the control unit are not shown, but the terminations of control signals are labeled $C_i$ and indicated by a

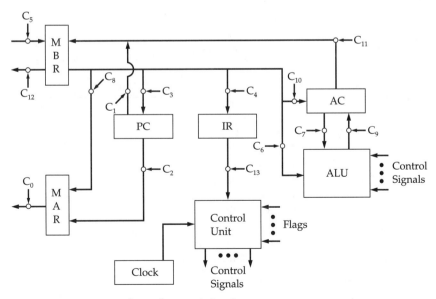

**FIGURE 14.5.  Data paths and control signals**

circle. The control unit receives inputs from the clock, the instruction register, and flags. With each clock cycle, the control unit reads all of its inputs and emits a set of control signals. Control signals go to three separate destinations:

- *Data Paths:* The control unit controls the internal flow of data. For example, on instruction fetch, the contents of the memory buffer register are transferred to the instruction register. For each path to be controlled, there is a gate (indicated by a circle in the figure). A control signal from the control unit temporarily opens the gate to let data pass.
- *ALU:* The control unit controls the operation of the ALU by a set of control signals. These signals activate various logic devices and gates within the ALU.
- *System Bus:* The control unit sends control signals out onto the control lines of the system bus (e.g., memory READ).

The control unit must maintain knowledge of where it is in the instruction cycle. Using this knowledge, and by reading all of its inputs, the control unit emits a sequence of control signals that causes micro-operations to occur. It uses the clock pulses to time the sequence of events, allowing time between events for signal levels to stabilize. Table 14.1 indicates the control signals that are needed for some of the micro-operation sequences described earlier. For simplicity, the data and control paths for incrementing the PC and for loading the fixed addresses into the PC and MAR are not shown.

It is worth pondering the minimal nature of the control unit. The control unit is the engine that runs the entire computer. It does this based only on knowing the instructions to be executed and the nature of the results of arithmetic and logical operations (e.g., positive, overflow, etc.). It never gets to see the data being processed or the actual results produced. And it controls everything with a few control signals to points within the CPU and a few control signals to the system bus.

**TABLE 14.1  Micro-operations and Control Signals**

| Micro-operations | | Active Control Signals |
|---|---|---|
| Fetch: | $t_1$: MAR $\leftarrow$ (PC) | $C_2$ |
| | $t_2$: MBR $\leftarrow$ Memory | $C_5, C_R$ |
| |     PC $\leftarrow$ (PC) + 1 | |
| | $t_3$: IR $\leftarrow$ (MBR) | $C_4$ |
| Indirect: | $t_1$: MAR $\leftarrow$ (IR(Address)) | $C_8$ |
| | $t_2$: MBR $\leftarrow$ Memory | $C_5, C_R$ |
| | $t_3$: IR(Address) $\leftarrow$ (MBR(Address)) | $C_4$ |
| Interrupt: | $t_1$: MBR $\leftarrow$ (PC) | $C_1$ |
| | $t_2$: MAR $\leftarrow$ Save-address | |
| |     PC $\leftarrow$ Routine-address | |
| | $t_3$: Memory $\leftarrow$ (MBR) | $C_{12}, C_W$ |

$C_R$ = Read control signal to system bus.
$C_W$ = Write control signal to system bus.

## Internal CPU Organization

Figure 14.5 indicates the use of a variety of data paths. The complexity of this type of organization should be clear. More typically, some sort of internal bus arrangement, as was suggested in Figure 11.2, will be used.

Using an internal CPU bus, Figure 14.5 can be rearranged as shown in Figure 14.6. The ALU and all CPU registers are connected by a single internal bus. Gates and control signals are provided for movement of data onto and off the bus from each register. Additional control signals control data transfer to and from the system (external) bus and the operation of the ALU.

Two new registers, labeled Y and Z, have been added to the organization. These are needed for the proper operation of the ALU. When an operation involving two

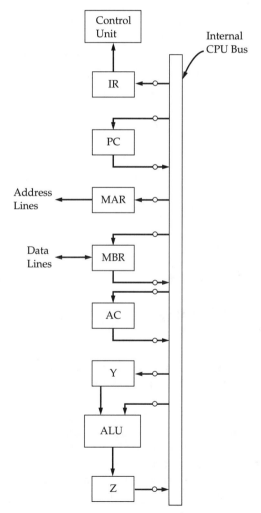

**FIGURE 14.6. CPU with internal bus**

operands is performed, one can be obtained from the internal bus, but the other must be obtained from another source. The AC could be used for this purpose, but this limits the flexibility of the system and would not work with a CPU with multiple general-purpose registers. Register Y provides temporary storage for the other input. The ALU is a combinatorial circuit (see the appendix to this book) with no internal storage. Thus, when control signals activate an ALU function, the input to the ALU is transformed to the output. Thus, the output of the ALU cannot be directly connected to the bus, since this output would feed back to the input. Register Z provides temporary output storage. With this arrangement, an operation to add a value from memory to the AC would have the following steps:

$t_1$: MAR ← (IR(address))
$t_2$: MBR ← Memory
$t_3$: Y ← (MBR)
$t_4$: Z ← (AC) + (Y)
$t_5$: AC ← (Z)

Other organizations are possible, but, in general, some sort of internal bus or set of internal buses is used. The use of common data paths simplifies the interconnection layout and the control of the CPU. Another practical reason for the use of an internal bus is to save space. Especially for microprocessors, which may occupy only a 1/4-inch square piece of silicon, space occupied by inter-register connections must be minimized.

## The Intel 8085

To illustrate some of the concepts introduced thus far in this chapter, let us consider the Intel 8085. Its organization is shown in Figure 14.7. Several key components that may not be self-explanatory are:

- *Incrementer/Decrementer Address Latch:* Logic that can add 1 to or subtract 1 from the contents of the stack pointer or program counter. This saves time by avoiding the use of the ALU for this purpose.
- *Interrupt Control:* This module handles multiple levels of interrupt signals.
- *Serial I/O Control:* This module interfaces to devices that communicate 1 bit at a time.

Table 14.2 describes the external signals into and out of the 8085. These are linked to the external system bus. These signals are the interface between the 8085 processor and the rest of the system (Figure 14.8).

The control unit is identified as having two components labeled (1) instruction decoder and machine cycle encoding and (2) timing and control. A discussion of the first component is deferred until the next section. The essence of the control unit is the timing and control module. This module includes a clock and accepts as inputs the current instruction and some external control signals. Its output consists of control signals to the other components of the CPU plus control signals to the external system bus.

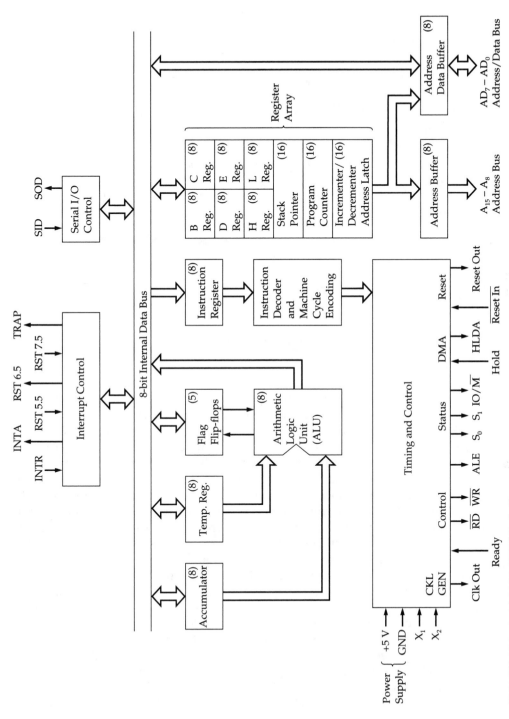

**FIGURE 14.7. Intel 8085 CPU block diagram**

517

**TABLE 14.2    Intel 8085 External Signals**

*Address and Data Signals*

**High Address ($A_{15}$–$A_8$)**
 The high-order 8 bits of a 16-bit address.
**Address/Data ($AD_7$–$AD_0$)**
 The lower-order 8 bits of a 16-bit address or 8 bits of data. This multiplexing saves on pins.
**Serial Input Data (SID)**
 A single-bit input to accommodate devices that transmit serially (one bit at a time).
**Serial Output Data (SOD)**
 A single-bit output to accommodate devices that receive serially.

*Timing and Control Signals*

**CLK (OUT)**
 The system clock. Each cycle represents one T state. The CLK signal goes to peripheral chips and synchronizes their timing.
**$X_1$, $X_2$**
 These signals come from an external crystal or other device to drive the internal clock generator.
**Address Latch Enabled (ALE)**
 Occurs during the first clock state of a machine cycle and causes peripheral chips to store the address lines. This allows the address module (e.g., memory, I/O) to recognize that it is being addressed.
**Status ($S_0$, $S_1$)**
 Control signals used to indicate whether a read or write operation is taking place.

The timing of CPU operations is synchronized by the clock and controlled by the control unit with control signals. Each instruction cycle is divided into from one to five *machine cycles;* each machine cycle is in turn divided into from three to five *states.* Each state lasts one clock cycle. During a state, the CPU performs one or a set of simultaneous micro-operations as determined by the control signals.

The number of machine cycles is fixed for a given instruction but varies from one instruction to another. Machine cycles are defined to be equivalent to bus accesses. Thus, the number of machine cycles for an instruction depends on the number of times the CPU must communicate with external devices. For example, if an instruction consists of two 8-bit portions, then two machine cycles are required to fetch the instruction. If that instruction involves a 1-byte memory or I/O operation, then a third machine cycle is required for execution.

Figure 14.9 gives an example of 8085 timing, showing the value of external control signals. Of course, at the same time, internal control signals are being generated by the control unit to control internal data transfers. The diagram shows the instruction cycle for an OUT instruction. Three machine cycles ($M_1$, $M_2$, $M_3$) are needed. During the first, the OUT instruction is fetched. The second machine cycle fetches the second half of the instruction, which contains the number of the I/O device selected for output. During the third cycle, the contents of the AC are written out to the selected device over the data bus.

The start of each machine cycle is signaled by the Address Latch Enabled (ALE) pulse from the control unit. The ALE pulse alerts external circuits. During timing

**TABLE 14.2    (continued)**

**IO/M**
Used to enable either I/O or memory modules for read and write operations.
**Read Control (RD)**
Indicates that the selected memory or I/O module is to be read and that the data bus is available for data transfer.
**Write Control (WR)**
Indicates that data on the data bus is to be written into the selected memory or I/O location.

*Memory and I/O Initiated Symbols*

**Hold**
Requests the CPU to relinquish control and use of the external system bus. The CPU will complete execution of the instruction presently in the IR and then enter a hold state, during which no signals are inserted by the CPU to the control, address, or data buses. During the hold state, the bus may be used for DMA operations.
**Hold Acknowledge (HOLDA)**
This control unit output signal acknowledges the HOLD signal and indicates that the bus is now available.
**READY**
Used to synchronize the CPU with slower memory or I/O devices. When an addressed device asserts READY, the CPU may proceed with an input (DBIN) or output (WR) operation. Ohterwise, the CPU enters a wait state until the device is ready.

*Interrupt-Related Signals*

**TRAP**
Restart Interrupts (RST 7.5, 6.5, 5.5)
**Interrupt Request (INTR)**
These five lines are used by an external device to interrupt the CPU. The CPU will not honor the request if it is in the hold state or if the interrupt is disabled. An interrupt is honored only at the completion of an instruction. The interrupts are in descending order of priority.
**Interrupt Acknowledge**
Acknowledges an interrupt.

*CPU Initialization*

**RESET IN**
Causes the contents of the PC to be set to zero. The CPU resumes execution at location zero.
**RESET OUT**
Acknowledges that the CPU has been reset. The signal can be used to reset the rest of the system.

*Voltage and Ground*

**$V_{CC}$**
+5 volt power supply
**$V_{SS}$**
Electrical ground.

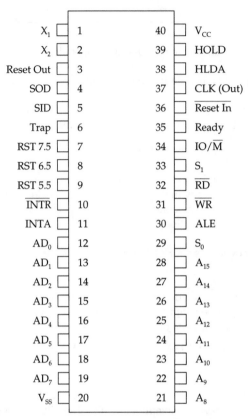

| | | | | |
|---|---|---|---|---|
| X$_1$ | 1 | 40 | V$_{CC}$ |
| X$_2$ | 2 | 39 | HOLD |
| Reset Out | 3 | 38 | HLDA |
| SOD | 4 | 37 | CLK (Out) |
| SID | 5 | 36 | $\overline{\text{Reset In}}$ |
| Trap | 6 | 35 | Ready |
| RST 7.5 | 7 | 34 | IO/$\overline{\text{M}}$ |
| RST 6.5 | 8 | 33 | S$_1$ |
| RST 5.5 | 9 | 32 | $\overline{\text{RD}}$ |
| $\overline{\text{INTR}}$ | 10 | 31 | $\overline{\text{WR}}$ |
| INTA | 11 | 30 | ALE |
| AD$_0$ | 12 | 29 | S$_0$ |
| AD$_1$ | 13 | 28 | A$_{15}$ |
| AD$_2$ | 14 | 27 | A$_{14}$ |
| AD$_3$ | 15 | 26 | A$_{13}$ |
| AD$_4$ | 16 | 25 | A$_{12}$ |
| AD$_5$ | 17 | 24 | A$_{11}$ |
| AD$_6$ | 18 | 23 | A$_{10}$ |
| AD$_7$ | 19 | 22 | A$_9$ |
| V$_{SS}$ | 20 | 21 | A$_8$ |

**FIGURE 14.8. Intel 8085 pin configuration**

state T$_1$ of machine cycle M$_1$, the control unit sets the IO/$\overline{\text{M}}$ signal to indicate that this is a memory operation. Also, the control unit causes the contents of the PC to be placed on the address bus (A$_{15}$ – A$_8$) and the address/data bus (AD$_7$ – AD$_0$). With the falling edge of the ALE pulse, the other modules on the bus store the address.

During timing state T$_2$, the addressed memory module places the contents of the addressed memory location on the address/data bus. The control unit sets the Read Control (RD) signal to indicate a read, but it waits until T$_3$ to copy the data from the bus. This gives the memory module time to put the data on the bus and for the signal levels to stabilize. The final state, T$_4$, is a *bus idle* state during which the CPU decodes the instruction. The remaining machine cycles proceed in a similar fashion.

## 14.3

## HARDWIRED IMPLEMENTATION

We have discussed the control unit in terms of its inputs, output, and functions. It is now time to turn to the topic of control unit implementation. A wide variety of techniques have been used. Most of these fall into one of two categories:

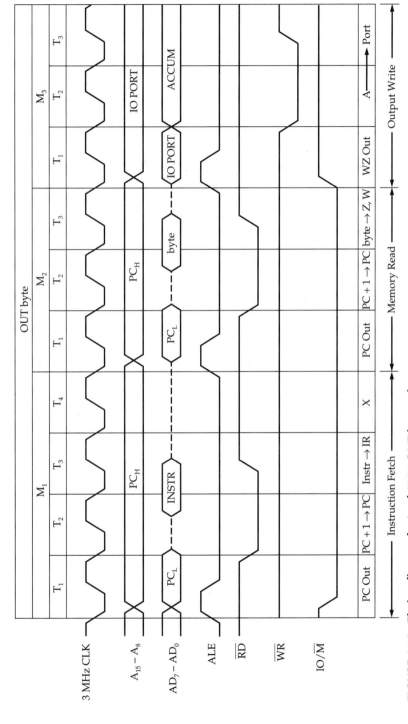

**FIGURE 14.9. Timing diagram for Intel 8085 OUT instruction**

521

- Hardwired Implementation
- Microprogrammed Implementation

In a hardwired implementation, the control unit is essentially a combinatorial circuit. Its input logic signals are transformed into a set of output logic signals, which are the control signals. This approach is examined in this section. Microprogrammed implementation is the subject of Chapter 15.

## Control Unit Inputs

Figure 14.4 depicts the control unit as we have so far discussed it. The key inputs are the instruction register, the clock, flags, and control bus signals. In the case of the flags and control bus signals, each individual bit typically has some meaning (e.g., overflow). The other two inputs, however, are not directly useful to the control unit.

First consider the instruction register. The control unit makes use of the opcode and will perform different actions (issue a different combination of control signals) for different instructions. To simplify the control unit logic, there should be a unique logic input for each opcode. This function can be performed by a *decoder*, which takes an encoded input and produces a single output. In general, a decoder will have $n$ binary inputs and $2^n$ binary outputs. Each of the $2^n$ different input patterns will activate a single unique output. Table 14.3 is an example. The decoder for a control unit will typically have to be more complex than that, to account for variable-length opcodes. An example of the digital logic used to implement a decoder is presented in Appendix A.

The clock portion of the control unit issues a repetitive sequence of pulses. This is useful for measuring the duration of micro-operations. Essentially, the period of the clock pulses must be long enough to allow the propagation of signals along data paths and through CPU circuitry. However, as we have seen, the control unit

**TABLE 14.3   A Decoder With Four Inputs and Sixteen Outputs**

| $I_1$ | $I_2$ | $I_3$ | $I_4$ | $O_1$ | $O_2$ | $O_3$ | $O_4$ | $O_5$ | $O_6$ | $O_7$ | $O_8$ | $O_9$ | $O_{10}$ | $O_{11}$ | $O_{12}$ | $O_{13}$ | $O_{14}$ | $O_{15}$ | $O_{16}$ |
|---|---|---|---|---|---|---|---|---|---|---|---|---|---|---|---|---|---|---|---|
| 0 | 0 | 0 | 0 | 0 | 0 | 0 | 0 | 0 | 0 | 0 | 0 | 0 | 0 | 0 | 0 | 0 | 0 | 0 | 1 |
| 0 | 0 | 0 | 1 | 0 | 0 | 0 | 0 | 0 | 0 | 0 | 0 | 0 | 0 | 0 | 0 | 0 | 0 | 1 | 0 |
| 0 | 0 | 1 | 0 | 0 | 0 | 0 | 0 | 0 | 0 | 0 | 0 | 0 | 0 | 0 | 0 | 0 | 1 | 0 | 0 |
| 0 | 0 | 1 | 1 | 0 | 0 | 0 | 0 | 0 | 0 | 0 | 0 | 0 | 0 | 0 | 0 | 1 | 0 | 0 | 0 |
| 0 | 1 | 0 | 0 | 0 | 0 | 0 | 0 | 0 | 0 | 0 | 0 | 0 | 0 | 0 | 1 | 0 | 0 | 0 | 0 |
| 0 | 1 | 0 | 1 | 0 | 0 | 0 | 0 | 0 | 0 | 0 | 0 | 0 | 0 | 1 | 0 | 0 | 0 | 0 | 0 |
| 0 | 1 | 1 | 0 | 0 | 0 | 0 | 0 | 0 | 0 | 0 | 0 | 0 | 1 | 0 | 0 | 0 | 0 | 0 | 0 |
| 0 | 1 | 1 | 1 | 0 | 0 | 0 | 0 | 0 | 0 | 0 | 0 | 1 | 0 | 0 | 0 | 0 | 0 | 0 | 0 |
| 1 | 0 | 0 | 0 | 0 | 0 | 0 | 0 | 0 | 0 | 0 | 1 | 0 | 0 | 0 | 0 | 0 | 0 | 0 | 0 |
| 1 | 0 | 0 | 1 | 0 | 0 | 0 | 0 | 0 | 0 | 1 | 0 | 0 | 0 | 0 | 0 | 0 | 0 | 0 | 0 |
| 1 | 0 | 1 | 0 | 0 | 0 | 0 | 0 | 0 | 1 | 0 | 0 | 0 | 0 | 0 | 0 | 0 | 0 | 0 | 0 |
| 1 | 0 | 1 | 1 | 0 | 0 | 0 | 0 | 1 | 0 | 0 | 0 | 0 | 0 | 0 | 0 | 0 | 0 | 0 | 0 |
| 1 | 1 | 0 | 0 | 0 | 0 | 0 | 1 | 0 | 0 | 0 | 0 | 0 | 0 | 0 | 0 | 0 | 0 | 0 | 0 |
| 1 | 1 | 0 | 1 | 0 | 0 | 1 | 0 | 0 | 0 | 0 | 0 | 0 | 0 | 0 | 0 | 0 | 0 | 0 | 0 |
| 1 | 1 | 1 | 0 | 0 | 1 | 0 | 0 | 0 | 0 | 0 | 0 | 0 | 0 | 0 | 0 | 0 | 0 | 0 | 0 |
| 1 | 1 | 1 | 1 | 1 | 0 | 0 | 0 | 0 | 0 | 0 | 0 | 0 | 0 | 0 | 0 | 0 | 0 | 0 | 0 |

emits different control signals at different time units within a single instruction cycle. Thus, we would like a counter as input to the control unit, with a different control signal being used for $T_1$, $T_2$, and so forth. At the end of an instruction cycle, the control unit must feed back to the counter to re-initialize it at $T_1$.

With these two refinements, the control unit can be depicted as in Figure 14.10.

## Control Unit Logic

To define the hardwired implementation of a control unit, all that remains is to discuss the internal logic of the control unit that produces output control signals as a function of its input signals.

Essentially, what must be done is, for each control signal, to derive a Boolean expression of that signal as a function of the inputs. This is best explained by example. Let us consider again our simple example illustrated in Figure 14.5. We saw in Table 14.1 the micro-operation sequences and control signals needed to control three of the four phases of the instruction cycle.

Let us consider a single control signal, $C_5$. This signal causes data to be read from the external data bus into the MBR. We can see that it is used twice in Table 14.1. Let us define two new control signals, P and Q, that have the following interpretation:

PQ = 00     Fetch Cycle
PQ = 01     Indirect Cycle
PQ = 10     Execute Cycle
PQ = 11     Interrupt Cycle

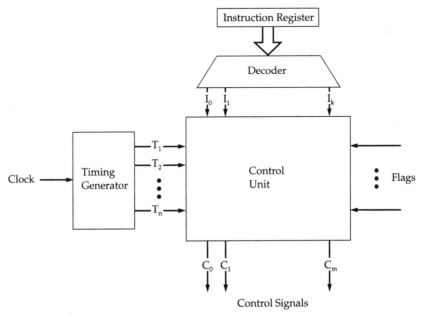

**FIGURE 14.10.  Control unit with decoded inputs**

Then the following Boolean expression defines $C_5$:

$$C_5 = \overline{P} \cdot \overline{Q} \cdot T_2 + \overline{P} \cdot Q \cdot T_2$$

That is, the control signal $C_5$ will be asserted during the second time unit of both the fetch and indirect cycles.

This expression is not complete. $C_5$ is also needed during the execute cycle. For our simple example, let us assume that there are only three instructions that read from memory: LDA, ADD, and AND. Now, we can define $C_5$ as

$$C_5 = \overline{P} \cdot \overline{Q} \cdot T_2 + \overline{P} \cdot Q \cdot T_2 + P \cdot \overline{Q} \cdot (LDA + ADD + AND) \cdot T_2$$

This same process could be repeated for every control signal generated by the CPU. The result would be a set of Boolean equations that define the behavior of the control unit and hence of the CPU.

To tie everything together, the control unit must control the state of the instruction cycle. As was mentioned, at the end of each subcycle (fetch, indirect, execute, interrupt), the control unit issues a signal that causes the timing generator to reinitialize and issue $T_1$. The control unit must also set the appropriate values of P and Q to define the next subcycle to be performed.

The reader should be able to appreciate that in a modern complex CPU, the number of Boolean equations needed to define the control unit is very large. The task of implementing a combinatorial circuit that satisfies all of these equations becomes extremely difficult. The result is that a far simpler approach, known as *microprogramming*, is usually used. This is the subject of the next chapter.

## 14.4

### RECOMMENDED READING

A number of textbooks treat the basic principles of control unit function, including [HENN91], [WARD90], [HAYE88], and [MANO93].

HAYE88    Hayes, J. *Computer Architecture and Organization, Second Edition.* New York: McGraw-Hill, 1988.

HENN91    Hennessy, J., and Jouppi, N. "Computer Technology and Architecture: An Evolving Interaction." *Computer,* September 1991.

MANO93    Mano, M. *Computer System Architecture.* Englewood Cliffs, NJ: Prentice Hall, 1993.

WARD90    Ward, S., and Halstead, R. *Computation Structures.* Cambridge, MA: MIT Press, 1990.

## 14.5

### PROBLEMS

14.1    Your ALU can add its two input registers, and it can logically complement the bits of either input register, but it cannot subtract. Numbers are to be stored in two's complement representation. List the micro-operations your control unit must perform to cause a subtraction.

14.2  Show the micro-operations and control signals in the same fashion as Table 14.1 for the CPU in Figure 14.5 for the following instructions:

- Load Accumulator
- Store Accumulator
- Add to Accumulator
- AND to Accumulator
- Jump
- Jump if AC = 0
- Complement Accumulator

14.3  Assume that propagation delay along the bus and through the ALU of Figure 14.6 are 20 and 100 ns, respectively. The time required for a register to copy data from the bus is 10 ns. What is the time that must be allowed for
     **(a)** transferring data from one register to another?
     **(b)** incrementing the program counter?

14.4  Write the sequence of micro-operations required for the bus structure of Figure 14.6 to add a number to the AC when the number is (a) an immediate operand, (b) a direct-address operand, and (c) an indirect-address operand.

14.5  Show diagrams similar to that of Figure 14.9 for the following 8085 instructions:
     **(a)**  MOV reg1, reg2       reg1 ← (reg2)
     **(b)**  MOV M, reg           M ← (reg)

14.6  Suggest an internal data path and control signal organization for the Intel 8085 register array.

14.7  A stack is implemented as shown in Figure 9.14. Show the sequence of micro-operations for (a) popping and (b) pushing the stack.

# CHAPTER 15

# Microprogrammed Control

The term *microprogram* was first coined by M. V. Wilkes in the early 1950s [WILK51]. Wilkes proposed an approach to control unit design that was organized and systematic and avoided the complexities of a hardwired implementation. The idea intrigued many researchers but appeared unworkable because it would require a fast, relatively inexpensive control memory.

The state of the microprogramming art was reviewed by *Datamation* in its February 1964 issue. No microprogrammed system was in wide use at that time, and one of the papers [HILL64] summarized the then-popular view that the future of microprogramming "is somewhat cloudy. None of the major manufacturers has evidenced interest in the technique, although presumably all have examined it."

This situation changed dramatically within a very few months. IBM's System/360 was announced in April, and all but the largest models were microprogrammed. Although the 360 series predated the availability of semiconducter ROM, the advantages of microprogramming were compelling enough for IBM to make this move. Since then, microprogramming has become an increasingly popular vehicle for a variety of applications, one of which is the use of microprogramming to implement the control unit of a CPU. That application is examined in this chapter.

## 15.1

### BASIC CONCEPTS

#### Microinstructions

The control unit, as just described, seems a reasonably simple device. Nevertheless, to implement a control unit as an interconnection of basic logic elements is no easy task. The design must include logic for sequencing through microoperations, for executing micro-operations, for interpreting opcodes, and for making decisions based on ALU flags. It is difficult to design and test such a piece of hardware. Furthermore, the design is relatively inflexible. For example, it is difficult to change the design if one wishes to add a new machine instruction.

There is an alternative, one that is quite common for computers made today, and that is to implement a microprogrammed control unit.

Consider again Table 14.1. In addition to the use of control signals, each micro-operation is described in symbolic notation. This notation looks suspiciously like a programming language! In fact it is a language, known as a *microprogramming language*. Each line describes a set of micro-operations occurring at one time and is known as a *microinstruction*. A sequence of instructions is known as a *microprogram*, or *firmware*. This latter term reflects the fact that a microprogram is midway between hardware and software. It is easier to design in firmware than hardware, but it is more difficult to write a firmware program than a software program.

How can we use the concept of microprogramming to implement a control unit? Consider that for each micro-operation, all that the control unit is allowed to do is generate a set of control signals. Thus, for any micro-operation, each control line emanating from the control unit is either on or off. This condition can, of course, be represented by a binary digit for each control line. So, we could construct a *control word* in which each bit represents one control line. Then, each micro-operation would be represented by a different pattern of 1s and 0s in the control word.

This begins to look promising. Suppose we string together a sequence of control words to represent the sequence of micro-operations performed by the control unit. Now we are almost there. Next, we must recognize that the sequence of micro-operations is not fixed. Sometimes we have an indirect cycle; sometimes we do not. So, let us put our control words in a memory, with each word having a unique address. Now, add an address field to each control word, indicating the location of the next control word to be executed if a certain condition is true (e.g., the indirect bit in a memory-reference instruction is 1). Also, add a few bits to specify the condition.

The result is known as a *horizontal microinstruction* and is shown in Figure 15.1a. The format of the microinstruction or control word is as follows. There are one bit for each internal CPU control line and one bit for each system bus control line. There is a condition field indicating the condition under which there should be a branch, and there is a field with the address of the microinstruction to be executed next when a branch is taken. Such a microinstruction is interpreted as follows:

1. To execute this microinstruction, turn on all the control lines indicated by a 1 bit; leave off all control lines indicated by a 0 bit. The resulting control signals will cause one or more micro-operations to be performed.
2. If the condition indicated by the condition bits is false, execute the next microinstruction in sequence.
3. If the condition indicated by the condition bits is true, the next microinstruction to be executed is indicated in the address field.

Figure 15.2 shows how these control words or microinstructions could be arranged in a *control memory*. The microinstructions in each routine are to be executed sequentially. Each routine ends with a branch or jump instruction indicating where to go next. There is a special execute cycle routine whose only purpose is to

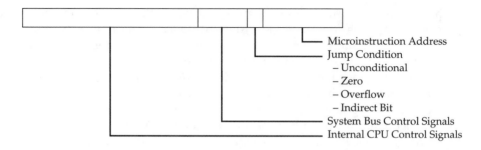

(a) Horizontal Microinstruction

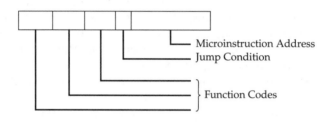

(b) Vertical Microinstruction

**FIGURE 15.1.  Typical microinstruction formats**

signify that one of the machine instruction routines (AND, ADD, and so on) is to be executed next, depending on the current opcode.

The control memory of Figure 15.2 is a concise description of the complete operation of the control unit. It defines the sequence of micro-operations to be performed during each cycle (fetch, indirect, execute, interrupt), and it specifies the sequencing of these cycles. If nothing else, this notation would be a useful device for documenting the functioning of a control unit for a particular computer. But it is more than that. It is also a way of implementing the control unit.

## Microprogrammed Control Unit

The control memory of Figure 15.2 contains a program that describes the behavior of the control unit. It follows that we could implement the control unit by simply executing that program.

Figure 15.3 shows the key elements of such an implementation. The set of microinstructions is stored in the *control memory*. The *control address register* contains the address of the next microinstruction to be read. When a microinstruction is read from the control memory, it is transferred to a *control buffer register*. The left-hand portion of that register (see Figure 15.1a) connects to the control lines emanating from the control unit. Thus, *reading* a microinstruction from the control

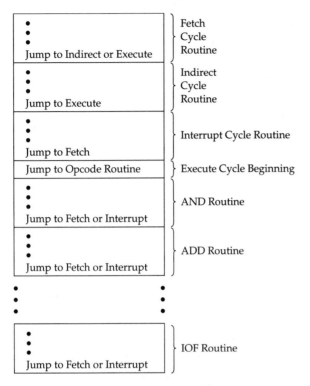

**FIGURE 15.2. Organization of control memory**

memory is the same as *executing* that microinstruction! The third element shown in the figure is a sequencing unit that loads the control address register and issues a read command.

Let us examine this structure in greater detail, as depicted in Figure 15.4. Comparing this with Figure 14.4, we see that the control unit still has the same inputs (IR, ALU flags, clock) and outputs (control signals). The control unit functions as follows:

1. To execute an instruction, the sequencing logic unit issues a READ command to the control memory.
2. The word whose address is specified in the control address register is read into the control buffer register.
3. The content of the control buffer register generates control signals and next-address information for the sequencing logic unit.
4. The sequencing logic unit loads a new address into the control address register based on the next-address information from the control buffer register and the ALU flags.

All this happens during one clock pulse.

The last step just listed needs elaboration. At the conclusion of each microinstruction, the sequencing logic unit loads a new address into the control address

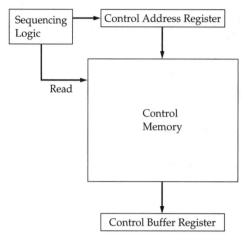

**FIGURE 15.3. Control unit microarchitecture**

register. Depending on the value of the ALU flags and the control buffer register, one of three decisions is made:

- *Get the next instruction:* Add 1 to the control address register.
- *Jump to a new routine based on a jump microinstruction:* Load the address field of the control buffer register into the control address register.
- *Jump to a machine instruction routine:* Load the control address register based on the opcode in the IR.

A final point: Figure 15.4 shows two modules labeled *decoder.* The upper decoder translates the opcode of the IR into a control memory address. The lower decoder is not used for horizontal microinstructions but is used for *vertical microinstructions* (Figure 15.1b). As was mentioned, in a horizontal microinstruction every bit in the control field attaches to a control line. In a vertical microinstruction, a code is used for each action to be performed, e.g., MAR ← (PC), and the decoder translates this code into individual control signals. The advantage of vertical microinstructions is that they are more compact (fewer bits) than horizontal microinstructions, at the expense of a small additional amount of logic and time delay.

## Wilkes Control

As was mentioned, Wilkes first proposed the use of a microprogrammed control unit in 1951 [WILK51]. This proposal was subsequently elaborated into a more detailed design [WILK53]. It is instructive to examine this seminal proposal.

Wilkes was concerned with developing a systematic approach to the design of a control unit. The configuration that he proposed is depicted in Figure 15.5. The heart of the system is a matrix partially filled with diodes. During a machine cycle, one row of the matrix is activated with a pulse. This generates signals at those

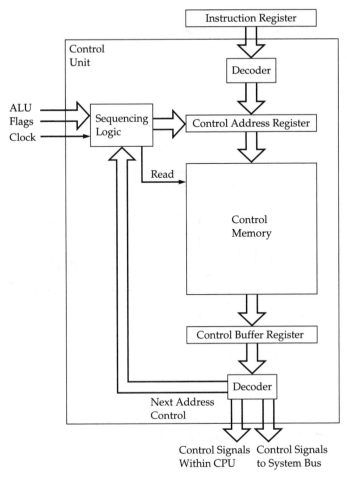

**FIGURE 15.4. Functioning of microprogrammed control unit**

points where a diode is present (indicated by a dot in the diagram). The first part of the row generates the control signals that control the operation of the CPU. The second part generates the address of the row to be pulsed in the next machine cycle. Thus, each row of the matrix is one microinstruction, and the layout of the matrix is the control memory.

At the beginning of the cycle, the address of the row to be pulsed is contained in Register I. This address is the input to the decoder, which, when activated by a clock pulse, activates one row of the matrix. Depending on the control signals, either the opcode in the instruction register or the second part of the pulsed row is passed into Register II during the cycle. Register II is then gated to Register I by a clock pulse. Alternating clock pulses are used to activate a row of the matrix and to transfer from Register II to Register I. The two-register arrangement is needed since the decoder is simply a combinatorial circuit; with only one register, the output would become the input during a cycle, causing an unstable condition.

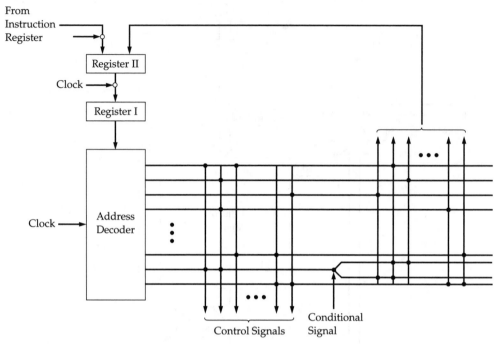

**FIGURE 15.5. Wilkes's microprogrammed control unit**

This scheme is very similar to the horizontal microprogramming approach described earlier (Figure 15.1a). The main difference is this: In the previous description, the control address register could be incremented by one to get the next address. In the Wilkes scheme, the next address is contained in the microinstruction. To permit branching, a row must contain two address parts, controlled by a conditional signal (e.g., flag), as shown in the figure.

Having proposed this scheme, Wilkes provides an example of its use to implement the control unit of a simple machine. This example, the first known design of a microprogrammed CPU, is worth repeating here because it illustrates many of the contemporary principles of microprogramming.

The CPU of the hypothetical machine includes the following registers:

A multiplicand
B accumulator (least-significant half)
C accumulator (most-significant half)
D shift register

In addition, there are three registers and two 1-bit flags accessible only to the control unit. The registers are

E serves as both a memory address register (MAR) and temporary storage
F program counter
G another temporary register, used for counting

Table 15.1 lists the machine instruction set for this example. Table 15.2 is the complete set of microinstructions, expressed in symbolic form, that implements the control unit. Thus, a total of 38 microinstructions is all that is required to completely define the system.

The first column gives the address (row number) of each microinstruction. Those addresses corresponding to opcodes are labeled. Thus, when the opcode for the add instruction (A) is encountered, the microinstruction at location 5 is executed. Columns 2 and 3 express the actions to be taken by the ALU and control unit, respectively. Each symbolic expression must be translated into a set of control signals (microinstruction bits). Columns 4 and 5 have to do with the setting and use of the two flags (flip-flops). Column 4 specifies the signal that sets the flag. For example, $(1)C_s$ means that flag number 1 is set by the sign bit of the number in register C. If column 5 contains a flag identifier, then columns 6 and 7 contain the two alternative microinstruction addresses to be used. Otherwise, column 6 specifies the address of the next microinstruction to be fetched.

Instructions 0 through 4 constitute the fetch cycle. Microinstruction 4 presents the opcode to a decoder, which generates the address of a microinstruction corresponding to the machine instruction to be fetched. The reader should be able to deduce the complete functioning of the control unit from a careful study of Table 15.2.

## Advantages and Disadvantages

The principal advantage of the use of microprogramming to implement a control unit is that it simplifies the design of the control unit. Thus, it is both cheaper and less error-prone to implement. A *hardwired* control unit must contain complex logic for sequencing through the many micro-operations of the instruction cycle.

### TABLE 15.1    Machine Instruction Set for Wilkes Example

Notation: $Acc$ = accumulator
$Acc_1$ = most significant half of accumulator
$Acc_2$ = least significant half of accumulator
$n$ = storage location $n$
$C(X)$ = contents of $X$ ($X$ = register or storage location)

| Order | Effect of Order |
|-------|-----------------|
| A $n$ | $C(Acc) + C(n)$ to $Acc_1$ |
| S $n$ | $C(Acc) - C(n)$ to $Acc_1$ |
| H $n$ | $C(n)$ to $Acc_2$ |
| V $n$ | $C(Acc_2) \cdot C(n)$ to $Acc$, where $C(n) \geq 0$ |
| T $n$ | $C(Acc_1)$ to $n$, 0 to $Acc$ |
| U $n$ | $C(Acc_1)$ to $n$ |
| R $n$ | $C(Acc) \cdot 2^{-(n+1)}$ to $Acc$ |
| L $n$ | $C(Acc) \cdot 2^{n+1}$ to $Acc$ |
| G $n$ | IF $C(Acc) < 0$, transfer control to $n$; if $C(Acc) \geq 0$, ignore (i.e., proceed serially) |
| I $n$ | Read next character on input mechanism into $n$ |
| O $n$ | Send $C(n)$ to output mechanism |

## TABLE 15.2   Microinstructions for Wilkes Example

Notation: A, B, C, ... stand for the various registers in the arithmetical and contol register units. 'C to D' indicates that the switching circuits connect the output of register C to the input register D; '(D + A) to C' indicates that the output register of A is connected to the one input of the adding unit (the output of D is permanently connected to the other input), and the output of the adder to register C.

A numerical symbol n in quotes (e.g., 'n') stands for the source whose output is the number n in units of the least significant digit.

| | | Arithmetical Unit | Control Register Unit | Conditional Flip-Flop Set | Conditional Flip-Flop Use | Next Micro-instruction 0 | Next Micro-instruction 1 |
|---|---|---|---|---|---|---|---|
| | 0 | | F to G and E | | | 1 | |
| | 1 | | (G to'1') to F | | | 2 | |
| | 2 | | Store to G | | | 3 | |
| | 3 | | G to E | | | 4 | |
| | 4 | | E to decoder | | | — | |
| A | 5 | C to D | | | | 16 | |
| S | 6 | C to D | | | | 17 | |
| H | 7 | Store to B | | | | 0 | |
| V | 8 | Store to A | | | | 27 | |
| T | 9 | C to Store | | | | 25 | |
| U | 10 | C to Store | | | | 0 | |
| R | 11 | B to D | E to G | | | 19 | |
| L | 12 | C to D | E to G | | | 22 | |
| G | 13 | | E to G | $(1)C_5$ | | 18 | |
| I | 14 | Input to Store | | | | 0 | |
| O | 15 | Store to Output | | | | 0 | |
| | 16 | (D + Store) to C | | | | 0 | |
| | 17 | (D − Store) to C | | | | 0 | |
| | 18 | | | | 1 | 0 | 1 |
| | 19 | D to B (R)* | (G − '1') to E | | | 20 | |
| | 20 | C to D | | $(1)E_5$ | | 21 | |
| | 21 | D to C (R) | | | 1 | 11 | 0 |
| | 22 | D to C (L)† | (G − '1') to E | | | 23 | |
| | 23 | B to D | | $(1)E_5$ | | 24 | |
| | 24 | D to B (L) | | | 1 | 12 | 0 |
| | 25 | '0' to B | | | | 26 | |
| | 26 | B to C | | | | 0 | |
| | 27 | '0' to C | '18' to E | | | 28 | |
| | 28 | B to D | E to G | $(1)B_1$ | | 29 | |
| | 29 | D to B (R) | (G − '1') to E | | | 30 | |
| | 30 | C to D (R) | | $(2)E_5$ | 1 | 31 | 32 |
| | 31 | D to C | | | 2 | 28 | 33 |
| | 32 | (D + A) to C | | | 2 | 28 | 33 |
| | 33 | B to D | | $(1)B_1$ | | 34 | |
| | 34 | D to B (R) | | | | 35 | |
| | 35 | C to D (R) | | | 1 | 36 | 37 |
| | 36 | D to C | | | | 0 | |
| | 37 | (D − A) to C | | | | 0 | |

*Right shift. The switching circuits in the arithmetic unit are arranged so that the least significant digit of the register C is placed in the most significant place of register B during right shift micro-operations, and the most significant digit of register C (sign digit) is repeated (thus making the correction for negative numbers).

†Left shift. The switching circuits are similarly arranged to pass the most significant digit of register B to the least significant place of register C during left shift micro-operations.

On the other hand, the decoders and sequencing logic unit of a microprogrammed control unit are very simple pieces of logic.

The principal disadvantage of a microprogrammed unit is that it will be somewhat slower than a hardwired unit of comparable technology. Despite this, microprogramming is the dominant technique for implementing control units in contemporary computers, due to its ease of implementation. We now examine the microprogrammed approach in greater detail.

## 15.2

### MICROINSTRUCTION SEQUENCING

The two basic tasks performed by a microprogrammed control unit are

- *Microinstruction Sequencing:* Get the next microinstruction from the control memory.
- *Microinstruction Execution:* Generate the control signals needed to execute the microinstruction.

In designing a control unit, these tasks must be considered together, since both affect the format of the microinstruction and the timing of the control unit. In this section, we will focus on sequencing and say as little as possible about format and timing issues. These issues are examined in more detail in the next section.

### Design Considerations

Two concerns are involved in the design of a microinstruction sequencing technique: the size of the microinstruction and the address-generation time. The first concern is obvious; minimizing the size of the control memory reduces the cost of that component. The second concern is simply a desire to execute microinstructions as fast as possible.

In executing a microprogram, the address of the next microinstruction to be executed is in one of these categories:

- Determined by Instruction Register
- Next Sequential Address
- Branch

The first category occurs only once per instruction cycle, just after an instruction is fetched. The second category is the most common in most designs. However, the design cannot be optimized just for sequential access. Branches, both conditional and unconditional, are a necessary part of a microprogram. Furthermore, microinstruction sequences tend to be short; one out of every three or four microinstructions could be a branch [SIEW82]. Thus, it is important to design compact, time-efficient techniques for microinstruction branching.

### Sequencing Techniques

Based on the current microinstruction, condition flags, and the contents of the instruction register, a control memory address must be generated for the next microinstruction. A wide variety of techniques have been used. We can group them into three general categories as illustrated in Figures 15.6 to 15.8 (based on [CLIN81]). These categories are based on the format of the address information in the microinstruction:

- Two Address Fields
- Single Address Field
- Variable Format

The simplest approach is to provide two address fields in each microinstruction. Figure 15.6 suggests how this information is to be used. A multiplexer is provided that serves as a destination for both address fields plus the instruction register. Based on an address-selection input, the multiplexer transmits either the opcode or one of the two addresses to the control address register (CAR). The CAR is subsequently decoded to produce the next microinstruction address. The address-selection signals are provided by a branch logic module whose input consists of control unit flags plus bits from the control portion of the microinstruction.

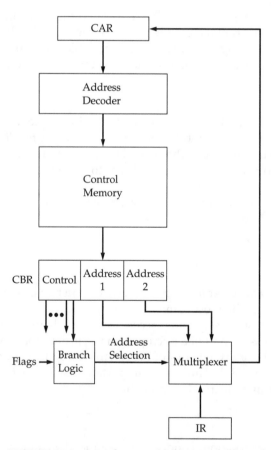

**FIGURE 15.6. Branch control logic, two address fields**

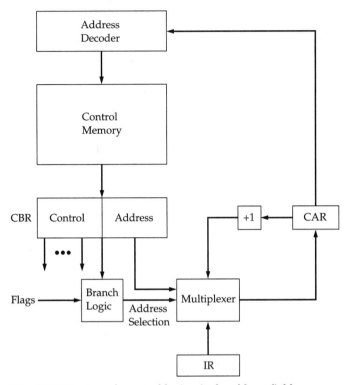

**FIGURE 15.7. Branch control logic, single address field**

Although the two-address approach is simple, it requires more bits in the microinstruction than other approaches. With some additional logic, savings can be achieved. A common approach is to have a single address field (Figure 15.7). With this approach, the options for next address are

- Address Field
- Instruction Register Code
- Next Sequential Address

The address-selection signals determine which option is selected. This approach reduces the number of address fields to one. Note, however, that the address field will often not be used. Thus, there is some inefficiency in the microinstruction coding scheme.

Another approach is to provide for two entirely different microinstruction formats (Figure 15.8). One bit designates which format is being used. In one format, the remaining bits are used to activate control signals. In the other format, some bits drive the branch logic module, and the remaining bits provide the address. With the first format, the next address is either the next sequential address or an address derived from the instruction register. With the second format, either a conditional or unconditional branch is being specified. One disadvantage of this

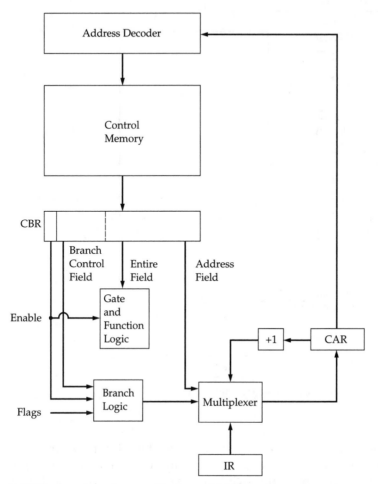

**FIGURE 15.8. Branch control logic, variable format**

approach, as just described, is that one entire cycle is consumed with each branch microinstruction. With the other approaches, address generation occurs as part of the same cycle as control signal generation, minimizing control memory accesses.

Of course, the approaches just described are general. Specific implementations will often involve a variation or combination of these techniques.

## Address Generation

We have looked at the sequencing problem from the point of view of format considerations and general logic requirements. Another viewpoint is to consider the various ways in which the next address can be derived or computed.

Table 15.3 lists the various address generation techniques. These can be divided into explicit techniques, in which the address is explicitly available in the microin-

**TABLE 15.3  Microinstruction Address Generation Techniques**

| Explicit | Implicit |
| --- | --- |
| Two-field | Mapping |
| Unconditional branch | Addition |
| Conditional branch | Residual control |

struction, and implicit techniques, which require additional logic to generate the address.

We have essentially dealt with the explicit techniques. With a two-field approach, two alternative addresses are available with each microinstruction. Using either a single address field or a variable format, various branch instructions can be implemented. A conditional branch instruction depends on the following types of information:

- ALU flags
- Part of the opcode or address mode fields of the machine instruction
- Parts of a selected register, such as the sign bit
- Status bits within the control unit

Several implicit techniques are also commonly used. One of these, mapping, is required with virtually all designs. The opcode portion of a machine instruction must be mapped into a microinstruction address. This occurs only once per instruction cycle.

A common implicit technique is one that involves combining or adding two portions of an address to form the complete address. This approach was taken for the IBM S/360 family [TUCK67] and used on many of the S/370 models. We will use the IBM 3033 as an example.

The control address register on the IBM 3033 is 13 bits long and is illustrated in Figure 15.9. Two parts of the address can be distinguished. The highest-order 8 bits (00–07) normally do not change from one microinstruction cycle to the next. During the execution of a microinstruction, these 8 bits are copied directly from an 8-bit field of the microinstruction (the BA field) into the highest-order 8 bits of the control address register. This defines a block of 32 microinstructions in control memory. The remaining 5 bits of the control address register are set to specify the

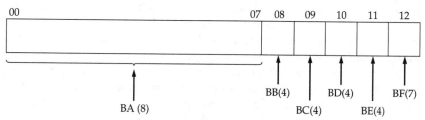

**FIGURE 15.9. IBM 3033 control address register**

specific address of the microinstruction to be fetched next. Each of these bits is determined by a 4-bit field (except one is a 7-bit field) in the current microinstruction; the field specifies the condition for setting the corresponding bit. For example, a bit in the control address register might be set to 1 or 0 depending on whether a carry occurred on the last ALU operation.

The final approach listed in Table 15.3 is termed *residual control*. This approach involves the use of a microinstruction address that has previously been saved in temporary storage within the control unit. For example, some microinstruction sets come equipped with a subroutine facility. An internal register or stack of registers is used to hold return addresses. An example of this approach is taken on the LSI-11, which we now examine.

## LSI-11 Microinstruction Sequencing

The LSI-11 is a microcomputer version of a PDP-11, with the main components of the system residing on a single board. The LSI-11 is implemented using a microprogrammed control unit [SEBE76, CLIN81].

The LSI-11 makes use of a 22-bit microinstruction and a control memory of 2K 22-bit words. The next microinstruction address is determined in one of five ways:

- *Next Sequential Address:* In the absence of other instructions, the control unit's control address register is incremented by 1.
- *Opcode Mapping:* At the beginning of each instruction cycle, the next microinstruction address is determined by the opcode.
- *Subroutine Facility:* Explained presently.
- *Interrupt Testing:* Certain microinstructions specify a test for interrupts. If an interrupt has occurred, this determines the next microinstruction address.
- *Branch:* Conditional and unconditional branch microinstructions are used.

A one-level subroutine facility is provided. One bit in every microinstruction is dedicated to this task. When the bit is set, an 11-bit return register is loaded with the updated contents of the control address register. A subsequent microinstruction that specifies a return will cause the control address register to be loaded from the return register.

The return is one form of unconditional branch instruction. Another form of unconditional branch causes the bits of the control address register to be loaded from 11 bits of the microinstruction. The conditional branch instruction makes use of a 4-bit test code within the microinstruction. This code specifies testing of various ALU condition codes to determine the branch decision. If the condition is not true, the next sequential address is selected. If it is true, the 8 lowest-order bits of the control address register are loaded from 8 bits of the microinstruction. This allows branching within a 256-word page of memory.

As can be seen, the LSI-11 includes a powerful address sequencing facility within the control unit. This allows the microprogrammer considerable flexibility and can ease the microprogramming task. On the other hand, this approach requires more control unit logic than simpler capabilities.

15.3

## MICROINSTRUCTION EXECUTION

The microinstruction cycle is the basic event on a microprogrammed CPU. Each cycle is made up of two parts: fetch and execute. The fetch portion is determined by the generation of a microinstruction address, and this was dealt with in the preceding section. This section deals with the execution of a microinstruction.

Let us recall what the execution of a microinstruction causes to happen. In essence, the effect of execution is to generate control signals. Some of these signals control points internal to the CPU. The remaining signals go to the external control bus or other external interface. As an incidental function, the address of the next microinstruction is determined.

The preceding description suggests the organization of a control unit shown in Figure 15.10. This slightly revised version of Figure 15.4 emphasizes the focus of this section. The major modules in this diagram should by now be clear. The sequencing logic module contains the logic to perform the functions discussed in the preceding section. It generates the address of the next microinstruction, using as inputs the instruction register, ALU flags, the control address register (for incrementing), and the control buffer register. The last may provide an actual address, control bits, or both. The module is driven by a clock that determines the timing of the microinstruction cycle.

The control logic module generates control signals as a function of some of the bits in the microinstruction. It should be clear that the format and content of the microinstruction will determine the complexity of the control logic module.

### A Taxonomy of Microinstructions

Microinstructions can be classified in a variety of ways. Distinctions that are commonly made in the literature include

- Vertical/Horizontal
- Packed/Unpacked
- Hard/Soft Microprogramming
- Direct/Indirect Encoding

All of these bear on the format of the microinstruction. None of these terms has been used in a consistent, precise way in the literature. However, an examination of these pairs of qualities serves to illuminate microinstruction design alternatives. In the following paragraphs, we first look at the key design issue underlying all of these pairs of characteristics, and then we look at the concepts suggested by each pair.

In the original proposal by Wilkes [WILK51], each bit of a microinstruction either directly produced a control signal or directly produced one bit of the next address. We have seen, in the preceding section, that more-complex address sequencing schemes, using fewer microinstruction bits, are possible. These schemes require a more-complex sequencing logic module. A similar sort of trade-off exists

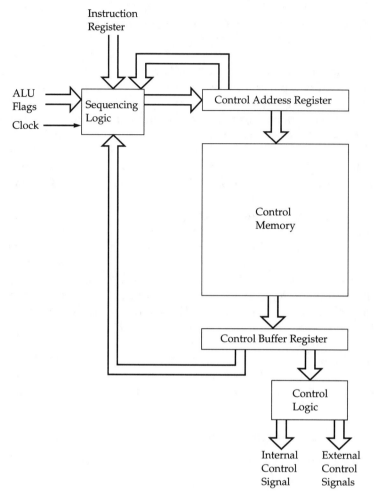

**FIGURE 15.10.  Control unit organization**

for the portion of the microinstruction concerned with control signals. By encoding control information, and subsequently decoding it to produce control signals, control word bits can be saved.

How can this encoding be done? To answer that, consider that there are a total of $K$ different internal and external control signals to be driven by the control unit. In Wilkes's scheme, $K$ bits of the microinstruction would be dedicated to this purpose. This allows all of the $2^K$ possible combinations of control signals to be generated during any instruction cycle. But we can do better than this if we observe that not all of the possible combinations will be used. Examples include the following:

- Two sources cannot be gated to the same destination (e.g., $C_2$ and $C_8$ in Figure 14.5).
- A register cannot be both source and destination (e.g., $C_5$ and $C_{12}$ in Figure 14.5).

- Only one pattern of control signals can be presented to the ALU at a time.
- Only one pattern of control signals can be presented to the external control bus at a time.

So, for a given CPU, all possible allowable combinations of control signals could be listed, giving some number $Q < 2^K$ possibilities. These could be encoded with $\log_2 Q$ bits, with $(\log_2 Q) < K$. This would be the tightest possible form of encoding that preserves all allowable combinations of control signals. In practice, this form of encoding is not used, for two reasons:

- It is as difficult to program as a pure decoded (Wilkes) scheme. This point is discussed further presently.
- It requires a complex and therefore slow control logic module.

Instead, some compromises are made. These are of two kinds:

- More bits than are strictly necessary are used to encode the possible combinations.
- Some combinations that are physically allowable are not possible to encode.

The latter kind of compromise has the effect of reducing the number of bits. The net result, however, is to use more than $\log_2 Q$ bits.

In the next subsection, we will discuss specific encoding techniques. The remainder of this subsection deals with the effects of encoding and the various terms used to describe it.

Based on the preceding, we can see that the control signal portion of the microinstruction format falls on a spectrum. At one extreme, there is one bit for each control signal; at the other extreme, a highly encoded format is used. Table 15.4 shows that other characteristics of a microprogrammed control unit also fall along a spectrum and that these spectra are, by and large, determined by the degree-of-encoding spectrum.

The second pair of items in the table is rather obvious. The pure Wilkes scheme will require the most bits. It should also be apparent that this extreme presents the

### TABLE 15.4 The Microinstruction Spectrum

| *Characteristics* | |
|---|---|
| Unencoded | Highly encoded |
| Many bits | Few bits |
| Detailed view of hardware | Aggregated view of hardware |
| Difficult to program | Easy to program |
| Concurrency fully exploited | Concurrency not fully exploited |
| Little or no control logic | Complex control logic |
| Fast execution | Slow execution |
| Optimize performance | Optimize programming |

| *Terminology* | |
|---|---|
| Unpacked | Packed |
| Horizontal | Vertical |
| Hard | Soft |

most detailed view of the hardware. Every control signal is individually controllable by the microprogrammer. Encoding is done in such a way as to aggregate functions or resources, so that the microprogrammer is viewing the CPU at a higher, less detailed level. Furthermore, the encoding is designed to ease the microprogramming burden. Again, it should be clear that the task of understanding and orchestrating the use of all the control signals is a difficult one. As was mentioned, one of the consequences of encoding, typically, is to prevent the use of certain otherwise allowable combinations.

The preceding paragraph discusses microinstruction design from the microprogrammer's point of view. But the degree of encoding also can be viewed from its hardware effects. With a pure unencoded format, little or no decode logic is needed; each bit generates a particular control signal. As more-compact and more-aggregated encoding schemes are used, more-complex decode logic is needed. This in turn may affect performance. More time is needed to propagate signals through the gates of the more-complex control logic module. Thus, the execution of encoded microinstructions takes longer than the execution of unencoded ones.

Thus, all of the characteristics listed in Table 15.4 fall along a spectrum of design strategies. In general, a design that falls toward the left end of the spectrum is intended to optimize the performance of the control unit. Designs toward the right end are more concerned with optimizing the process of microprogramming. Indeed, microinstruction sets near the right end of the spectrum look very much like machine instruction sets. A good example of this is the LSI-11 design, described later in this section. Typically, when the objective is simply to implement a control unit, the design will be near the left end of the spectrum. The IBM 3033 design, discussed presently, is in this category. As we shall discuss later, some systems permit a variety of users to construct different microprograms using the same microinstruction facility. In the latter cases, the design is likely to fall near the right end of the spectrum.

We can now deal with some of the terminology introduced earlier. Table 15.4 indicates how three of these pairs of terms relate to the microinstruction spectrum. In essence, all of these pairs describe the same thing but emphasize different design characteristics.

The degree of packing relates to the degree of identification between a given control task and specific microinstruction bits. As the bits become more *packed*, a given number of bits contains more information. Thus, packing connotes encoding. The terms *horizontal* and *vertical* relate to the relative width of microinstructions. [SIEW82] suggests as a rule of thumb that vertical microinstructions have lengths in the range of 16 to 40 bits, and that horizontal microinstructions have lengths in the range of 40 to 100 bits. The terms *hard* and *soft* microprogramming are used to suggest the degree of closeness to the underlying control signals and hardware layout. Hard microprograms are generally fixed and committed to read-only memory. Soft microprograms are more changeable and are suggestive of user microprogramming.

The other pair of terms mentioned at the beginning of this subsection refers to direct versus indirect encoding, a subject to which we now turn.

## Microinstruction Encoding

In practice, microprogrammed control units are not designed using a pure unencoded or horizontal microinstruction format. At least some degree of encoding is used to reduce control memory width and to simplify the task of microprogramming.

The basic technique for encoding is illustrated in Figure 15.11a. The microinstruction is organized as a set of fields. Each field contains a code, which, upon decoding, activates one or more control signals.

Let us consider the implications of this layout. When the microinstruction is executed, every field is decoded and generates control signals. Thus, with $N$ fields, $N$ simultaneous actions are specified. Each action results in the activation of one or more control signals. Generally, but not always, we will want to design the format

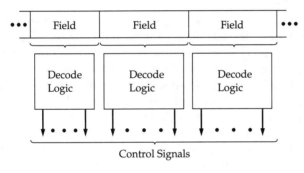

(a) Direct Encoding

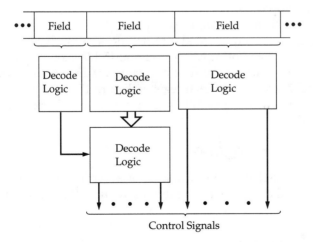

(b) Indirect Encoding

**FIGURE 15.11. Microinstruction encoding**

so that each control signal is activated by no more than one field. Clearly, however, it must be possible for each control signal to be activated by at least one field.

Now consider the individual field. A field consisting of $L$ bits can contain one of $2^L$ codes, each of which can be encoded to a different control signal pattern. Since only one code can appear in a field at a time, the codes are mutually exclusive, and, therefore, the actions they cause are mutually exclusive.

The design of an encoded microinstruction format can now be stated in simple terms:

- Organize the format into independent fields. That is, each field depicts a set of actions (pattern of control signals) such that actions from different fields can occur simultaneously.
- Define each field such that the alternative actions that can be specified by the field are mutually exclusive. That is, only one of the actions specified for a given field could occur at a time.

Two approaches can be taken to organizing the encoded microinstruction into fields: functional and resource. The *functional encoding* method identifies functions within the machine and designates fields by function type. For example, if various sources can be used for transferring data to the accumulator, one field can be designated for this purpose, with each code specifying a different source. *Resource encoding* views the machine as consisting of a set of independent resources and devotes one field to each (e.g., I/O, memory, ALU).

Another aspect of encoding is whether it is direct or indirect (Figure 15.11b). With indirect encoding, one field is used to determine the interpretation of another field. For example, consider an ALU that is capable of performing eight different arithmetic operations and eight different shift operations. A 1-bit field could be used to indicate whether a shift or arithmetic operation is to be used; a 3-bit field would indicate the operation. This technique generally implies two levels of decoding, increasing propagation delays.

Figure 15.12, from [RAUS80], is a simple example of these concepts. Assume a CPU with a single accumulator and several internal registers, such as a program counter and a temporary register for ALU input. Figure 15.12a shows a highly vertical format. The first 3 bits indicate the type of operation, the next 3 encode the operation, and the final 2 select an internal register. Figure 15.12b is a more horizontal approach, although encoding is still used. In this case, different functions appear in different fields.

## LSI-11 Microinstruction Execution

The LSI-11 [SEBE76, CLIN81] is a good example of a vertical microinstruction approach. We look first at the organization of the control unit, then at the microinstruction format.

### LSI-11 Control Unit Organization

The LSI-11 is the first member of the PDP-11 family that was offered as a single-board processor. The board contains three LSI chips, an internal bus known as the *microinstruction bus* (MIB), and some additional interfacing logic.

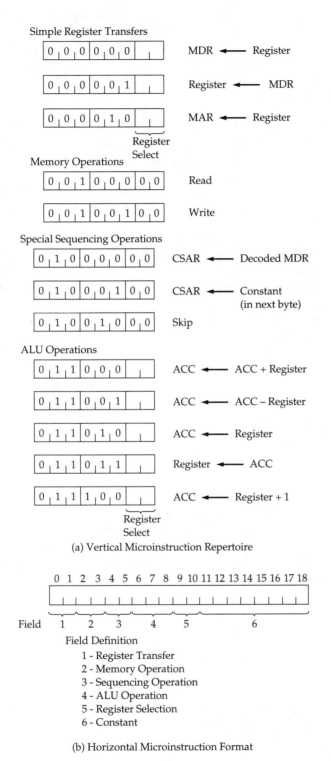

**FIGURE 15.12. Alternative microinstruction formats for a simple machine**

Figure 15.13 depicts, in simplified form, the organization of the LSI-11 CPU. The three chips are the data, control, and control store chips. The data chip contains an 8-bit ALU, 26 8-bit registers, and storage for several condition codes. Sixteen of the registers are used to implement the 8 16-bit general-purpose registers of the PDP-11. Others include a program status word, memory address register (MAR), and memory buffer register. Because the ALU deals with only 8 bits at a time, two passes through the ALU are required to implement a 16-bit PDP-11 arithmetic operation. This is controlled by the microprogram.

The control store chip or chips contain the 22-bit-wide control memory. The control chip contains the logic for sequencing and executing microinstructions. It contains the control address register, the control data register, and a copy of the machine instruction register.

The MIB ties all the components together. During microinstruction fetch, the control chip generates an 11-bit address onto the MIB. Control store is accessed, producing a 22-bit microinstruction, which is placed on the MIB. The low-order 16 bits go to the data chip, while the low-order 18 bits go to the control chip. The high-order 4 bits control special CPU board functions.

Figure 15.14 provides a still simplified but more detailed look at the LSI-11 control unit: the figure ignores individual chip boundaries. The address sequencing scheme described in Section 15.2 is implemented in two modules. Overall sequence control is provided by the microprogram sequence control module, which is capable of incrementing the microinstruction address register and per-

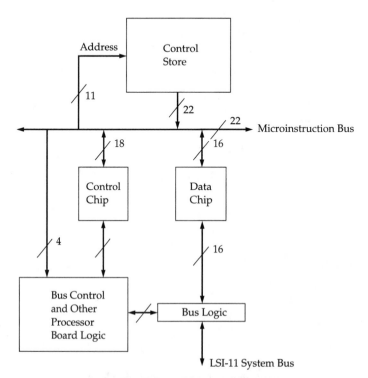

**FIGURE 15.13. Simplified block diagram of the LSI-11 processor**

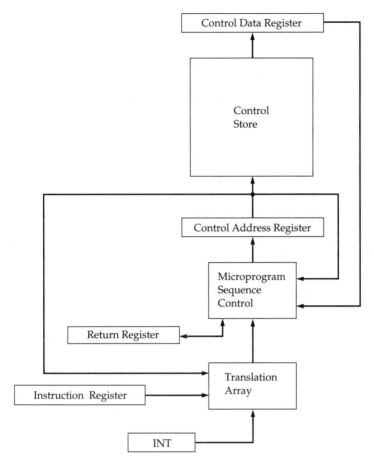

**FIGURE 15.14. Organization of the LSI-11 control unit**

forming unconditional branches. The other forms of address calculation are carried out by a separate translation array. This is a combinatorial circuit that generates an address based on the microinstruction, the machine instruction, the microinstruction program counter, and an interrupt register.

The translation array comes into play on the following occasions:

- The opcode is used to determine the start of a microroutine.
- At appropriate times, address mode bits of the microinstruction are tested to perform appropriate addressing.
- Interrupt conditions are periodically tested.
- Conditional branch microinstructions are evaluated.

### LSI-11 Microinstruction Format

The LSI-11 uses an extremely vertical microinstruction format, which is only 22 bits wide. The microinstruction set strongly resembles the PDP-11 machine instruction set that it implements. This design was intended to optimize the performance of the control unit within the constraint of a vertical, easily programmed design. Table 15.5 lists some of the LSI-11 microinstructions.

Figure 15.15 shows the 22-bit LSI-11 microinstruction format. The high-order 4 bits control special functions on the CPU board. The translate bit enables the translation array to check for pending interrupts. The load return register bit is used at the end of a microroutine to cause the next microinstruction address to be loaded from the return register.

The remaining 16 bits are used for highly encoded micro-operations. The format is much like a machine instruction, with a variable-length opcode and one or more operands.

### IBM 3033 Microinstruction Execution

The standard IBM 3033 control memory consists of 4K words. The first half of these (0000–07FF) contain 108-bit microinstructions, while the remainder (0800–0FFF) are used to store 126-bit microinstructions. The format is depicted in Figure 15.16. Although this is a rather horizontal format, encoding is still extensively used. The key fields of that format are summarized in Table 15.6.

The ALU operates on inputs from four dedicated, non-user-visible registers, A, B, C, and D. The microinstruction format contains fields for loading these registers from user-visible registers, performing an ALU function, and specifying a user-visible register for storing the result. There are also fields for loading and storing data between registers and memory.

The sequencing mechanism for the IBM 3033 was discussed in Section 15.2.

**TABLE 15.5    Some LSI-11 Microinstructions**

| **Arithmetic Operations** | Shift word (byte) right (left) with (without) |
| --- | --- |
| Add word (byte, literal) | carry |
| Test word (byte, literal) | Complement word (byte) |
| Increment word (byte) by 1 | **General Operations** |
| Increment word (byte) by 2 | MOV word (byte) |
| Negate word (byte) | Jump |
| Conditionally increment (decrement) byte | Return |
| Conditionally add word (byte) | Conditional jump |
| Add word (byte) with carry | Set (reset) flags |
| Conditionally add digits | Load G low |
| Subtract word (byte) | Conditionally MOV word (byte) |
| Compare word (byte, literal) | **Input/Output Operations** |
| Subtract word (byte) with carry | Input word (byte) |
| Decrement word (byte) by 1 | Input status word (byte) |
| **Logical Operations** | Read |
| And word (byte, literal) | Write |
| Test word (byte) | Read (write) and increment word (byte) by 1 |
| Or word (byte) | Read (write) and increment word (byte) by 2 |
| Exclusive-Or word (byte) | Read (write) acknowledge |
| Bit clear word (byte) | Output word (byte, status) |

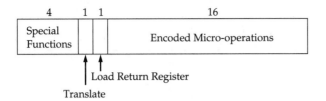

(a) Format of the Full LSI-11 Microinstruction

Unconditional Jump Microinstruction Format

Conditional Jump Microinstruction Format

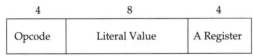

Literal Microinstruction Format

Register Microinstruction Format

(b) Format of the Encoded Part of the LSI-11 Microinstruction

**FIGURE 15.15. LSI-11 microinstruction format**

## 15.4

## TI 8800

The Texas Instruments 8800 Software Development Board (SDB) is a micropro-grammable 32-bit computer card. The system has a writable control store, imple-mented in RAM rather than ROM. Such a system does not achieve the speed or density of a microprogrammed system with a ROM control store. However, it is useful for developing prototypes and for educational purposes.

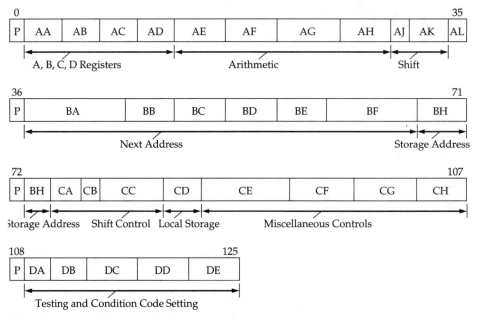

**FIGURE 15.16. IBM 3033 microinstruction format**

The 8800 SDB consists of the following components (Figure 15.17):

- Microcode Memory
- Microsequencer
- 32-bit ALU
- Floating-Point and Integer Processor
- Local Data Memory

Two buses link the internal components of the system. The DA bus provides data from the microinstruction data field to the ALU, the floating-point processor, or the microsequencer. In the latter case, the data consists of an address to be used for a branch instruction. The bus can also be used for the ALU or microsequencer to provide data to other components. The System Y bus connects the ALU and floating-point processor to local memory and to external modules via the PC interface.

The board fits into an IBM PC-compatible host computer. The host computer provides a suitable platform for microcode assembly and debug.

## Microinstruction Format

The microinstruction format for the 8800 consists of 128 bits broken down into 30 functional fields, as indicated in Table 15.7. Each field consists of one or more bits, and the fields are grouped into five major categories:

- Control of Board
- 8847 Floating-Point and Integer Processor Chip

### TABLE 15.6    IBM 3033 Microinstruction Control Fields

*ALU Control Fields*

| | |
|---|---|
| AA(3) | Load A register from one of data registers |
| AB(3) | Load B register from one of data registers |
| AC(3) | Load C register from one of data registers |
| AD93) | Load D register from one of data registers |
| AE(4) | Route specified A bits to ALU |
| AF(4) | Route specified B bits to ALU |
| AG(5) | Specifies ALU arithmetic operation on A input |
| AH(4) | Specifies ALU arithmetic operation on B input |
| AJ(1) | Specifies D or B input to ALU on B side |
| AK(4) | Route arithmetic output to shifter |
| CB(1) | Activate shifter |
| CC(5) | Specifies logical and carry functions |
| CE(7) | Specifies shift amount |
| CA(3) | Load F register |

*Sequencing and Branching Fields*

| | |
|---|---|
| AL(1) | End operation and perform branch |
| BA(8) | Set high-order bits (00–07) of control address register |
| BB(4) | Specifies condition for setting bit 8 of control address register |
| BC(4) | Specifies condition for setting bit 9 of control address register |
| BD(4) | Specifies condition for setting bit 10 of control address register |
| BE(4) | Specifies condition for setting bit 11 of control address register |
| BF(4) | Specifies condition for setting bit 12 of control address register |

- 8832 Registered ALU
- 8818 Microsequencer
- WCS Data Field

As indicated in Figure 15.17, the 32 bits of the WCS data field are fed into the DA bus to be provided as data to the ALU, floating-point processor, or microsequencer. The other 96 bits (fields 1–27) of the microinstruction are control signals that are fed directly to the appropriate module. For simplicity, these other connections are not shown in Figure 15.17.

The first six fields deal with operations that pertain to the control of the board, rather than controlling an individual component. Control operations include

1. Selection of condition codes for sequencer control. The first bit of field 1 indicates whether the condition flag is to be set to 1 or 0, and the remaining 4 bits indicate which flag is to be set.
2. Sending an I/O request to the PC/AT.
3. Enabling local data memory read/write operations.
4. Determination of the unit driving the system Y bus. One of the four devices attached to the bus (Figure 15.17) is selected.

The last 32 bits are the data field, which contain information specific to a particular microinstruction.

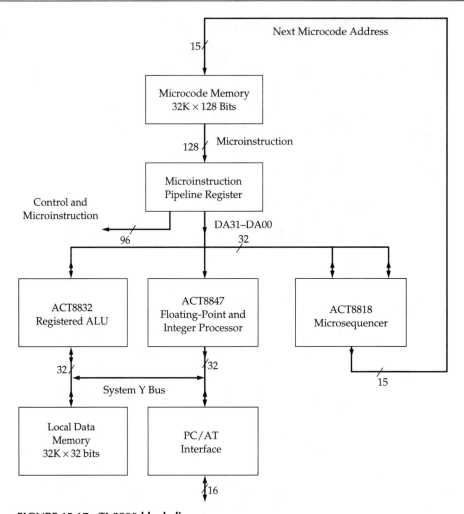

**FIGURE 15.17. TI 8800 block diagram**

The remaining fields of the microinstruction are best discussed in the context of the device that they control. In the remainder of this section, we discuss the microsequencer and the registered ALU. The floating-point unit introduces no new concepts and is skipped.

## Microsequencer

The principal function of the 8818 microsequencer is to generate the next microinstruction address for the microprogram. This 15-bit address is provided to the microcode memory (Figure 15.17).

The next address can be selected from one of five sources:

1. The microprogram counter (MPC) register, used for repeat (reuse same address) and continue (increment address by 1) instructions.

**TABLE 15.7    TI 8800 Microinstruction Format**

| Field Number | Number of Bits | Description |
|---|---|---|
| | | *Control of Board* |
| 1 | 5 | Select condition code input |
| 2 | 1 | Enable/disable external I/O request signal |
| 3 | 2 | Enable/disable local data memory read/write operations |
| 4 | 1 | Load status/do no load status |
| 5 | 2 | Determine unit driving Y bus |
| 6 | 2 | Determine unit driving DA bus |
| | | *8847 Floating Point and Integer Processing Chip* |
| 7 | 1 | C register control: clock, do not clock |
| 8 | 1 | Select most significant or least significant bits for Y bus |
| 9 | 1 | C register data source: ALU, multiplexer |
| 10 | 4 | Select IEEE or FAST mode for ALU and MUL |
| 11 | 8 | Select sources for data operands: RA registers, RB registers, P register, 5 register, C register |
| 12 | 1 | RB register control: clock, do not clock |
| 13 | 1 | RA register control: clock, do not clock |
| 14 | 2 | Data source confirmation |
| 15 | 2 | Enable/disable pipeline registers |
| 16 | 11 | 8847 ALU function |
| | | *8832 Registered ALU* |
| 17 | 2 | Write enable/disable data output to selected register: most significant half, least significant half |
| 18 | 2 | Select register file data source: DA bus, DB bus, ALU Y MUX output, system Y bus |
| 19 | 3 | Shift instruction modifier |
| 20 | 1 | Carry in: force, do not force |
| 21 | 2 | Set ALU configuration mode: 32, 16, or 8 bits |
| 22 | 2 | Select input to 5 multiplexer: register file, DB bus, MQ register |
| 23 | 1 | Select input to R multiplexer: register file, DA bus |
| 24 | 6 | Select register in file C for write |
| 25 | 6 | Select register in file B for read |
| 26 | 6 | Select register in file A for write |
| 27 | 8 | ALU function |
| | | *8818 Microsequencer* |
| 28 | 12 | Control input signals to the 8818 |
| | | *WCS Data Field* |
| 29 | 16 | Most significant bits of writable control store data field |
| 30 | 16 | Least significant bits of writable control store data field |

2. The stack, which supports microprogram subroutine calls as well as iterative loops and returns from interrupts.
3. The DRA and DRB ports, which provide two additional paths from external hardware by which microprogram addresses can be generated. These two ports are connected to the most significant and least significant 16 bits of the DA bus, respectively. This allows the microsequencer to obtain the next instruction address from the WCS data field of the current microinstruction or from a result calculated by the ALU.
4. Register counters RCA and RCB, which can be used for additional address storage.
5. An external input onto the bidirectional Y port to support external interrupts.

Figure 15.18 is a logical block diagram of the 8818. The device consists of the following principal functional groups:

- A 16-bit microprogram counter (MPC) consisting of a register and an incrementer.
- Two register counters, RCA and RCB, for counting loops and iterations, storing branch addresses, or driving external devices.
- A 65-word by 16-bit stack, which allows microprogram subroutine calls and interrupts.
- An interrupt return register and Y output enable for interrupt processing at the microinstruction level.
- A Y output multiplexer by which the next address can be selected from MPC, RCA, RCB, external buses DRA and DRB, or the stack.

### Registers/Counters

The registers RCA and RCB may be loaded from the DA bus, either from the current microinstruction or from the output of the ALU. The values may be used as counters to control the flow of execution and may be automatically decremented when accessed. The values may also be used as microinstruction addresses to be supplied to the Y output multiplexer. Independent control of both registers during a single microinstruction cycle is supported with the exception of simultaneous decrement of both registers.

### Stack

The stack allows multiple levels of nested calls or interrupts, and it can be used to support branching and looping. Keep in mind that these operations refer to the control unit, not the overall processor, and that the addresses involved are those of microinstructions in the control memory.

Six stack operations are possible:

1. Clear, which sets the stack pointer to zero, emptying the stack.
2. Pop, which decrements the stack pointer.
3. Push, which puts the contents of the MPC, interrupt return register, or DRA bus onto the stack and increments the stack pointer.
4. Read, which makes the address indicated by the read pointer available at the Y output multiplexer.

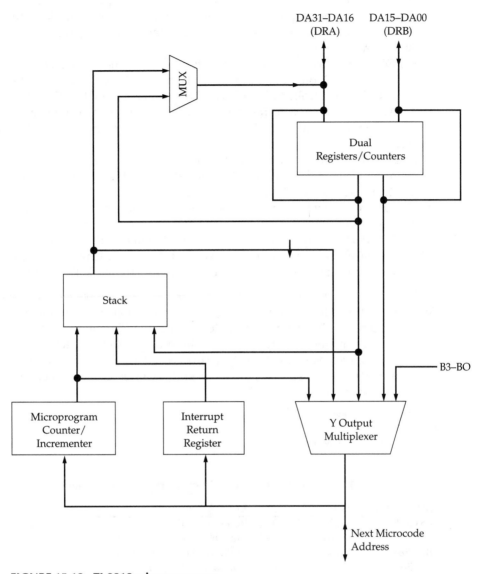

**FIGURE 15.18. TI 8818 microsequencer**

5. Hold, which causes the address of the stack pointer to remain unchanged.
6. Load stack pointer, which inputs the 7 least significant bits of DRA to the stack pointer.

## Control of Microsequencer

The microsequencer is controlled primarily by the 12-bit field of the current microinstruction, field 28 (Table 15.7). This field consists of the following subfields:

- OSEL (1 bit): Output select. Determines which value will be placed on the output of the multiplexer that feeds into the DRA bus (upper left-hand corner of

Figure 15.18). The output is selected to come from either the stack or from register RCA. DRA then serves as input to either the Y output multiplexer or to register RCA.

- SELDR (1 bit): Select DR bus. If set to 1, this bit selects the external DA bus as input to the DRA/DRB buses. If set to 0, selects the output of the DRA multiplexer to the DRA bus (controlled by OSEL) and the contents of RCB to the DRB bus.
- ZEROIN (1 bit): Used to indicate a conditional branch. The behavior of the microsequencer will then depend on the condition code selected in field 1 (Table 15.7).
- RC2–RC0 (3 bits): Register controls. These bits determine the change in the contents of registers RCA and RCB. Each register can either remain the same, decrement, or load from the DRA/DRB buses.
- S2–S0 (3 bits): Stack controls. These bits determine which stack operation is to be performed.
- MUX2–MUX0: Output controls. These bits, together with the condition code if used, control the Y output multiplexer and therefore the next microinstruction address. The multiplexer can select its output from the stack, DRA, DRB, or MPC.

These bits can be set individually by the programmer. However, this is typically not done. Rather, the programmer uses mnemonics that equate to the bit patterns that would normally be required. Table 15.8 lists the 15 mnemonics for field 28. A microcode assembler converts these into the appropriate bit patterns.

As an example, the instruction INC88181 is used to cause the next microinstruction in sequence to be selected, if the currently selected condition code is 1. From Table 15.8, we have

INC88181 = 000000111110

which decodes directly into

**TABLE 15.8   TI 8818 Microsequencer Microinstruction Bits (Field 28)**

| Mnemonic | Value | Description |
|---|---|---|
| RST8818 | 000000000110 | Reset Instruction |
| BRA88181 | 011000111000 | Branch to DRA Instruction |
| BRA88180 | 010000111110 | Branch to DRA Instruction |
| INC88181 | 000000111110 | Continue Instruction |
| INC88180 | 001000001000 | Continue Instruction |
| CAL88181 | 010000110000 | Jump to Subroutine at Address Specified by DRA |
| CAL88180 | 010000101110 | Jump to Subroutine at Address Specified by DRA |
| RET8818 | 000000011010 | Return from Subroutine |
| PUSH8818 | 000000110111 | Push Interrupt Return Address onto Stack |
| POP8818 | 100000010000 | Return from Interrupt |
| LOADDRA | 000010111110 | Load DRA Counter from DA Bus |
| LOADDRB | 000110111110 | Load DRB Counter from DA Bus |
| LOADDRAB | 000110111100 | Load DRA/DRB |
| DECRDRA | 010001111100 | Decrement DRA Counter and Branch if Not Zero |
| DECRDRB | 010101111100 | Decrement DRB Counter and Branch if Not Zero |

- OSEL = 0: Selects RCA as output from DRA output MUX; in this case the selection is irrelevant.
- SELDR = 0: As defined above; again, this is irrelevant for this instruction.
- ZEROIN = 0: Combined with the value for MUX, indicates no branch should be taken.
- R = 000: Retain current value of RA and RC.
- S = 111: Retain current state of stack.
- MUX = 110: Choose MPC when condition code = 1, DRA when condition code = 0.

## Registered ALU

The 8832 is a 32-bit ALU with 64 registers that can be configured to operate as four 8-bit ALUs, two 16-bit ALUs, or a single 32-bit ALU.

The 8832 is controlled by the 39 bits that make up fields 17 through 27 of the microinstruction (Table 15.7); these are supplied to the ALU as control signals. In addition, as indicated in Figure 15.17, the 8832 has external connections to the 32-bit DA bus and the 32-bit system Y bus. Inputs from the DA can be provided simultaneously as input data to the 64-word register file and to the ALU logic module. Input from the system Y bus is provided to the ALU logic module. Results of the ALU and shift operations are output to the DA bus or the system Y bus. Results can also be fed back to the internal register file.

Three 6-bit address ports allow a two-operand fetch and an operand write to be performed within the register file simultaneously. An MQ shifter and MQ register can also be configured to function independently to implement double-precision 8-bit, 16-bit, and 32-bit shift operations.

Fields 17 through 26 of each microinstruction control the way in which data flows within the 8832 and between the 8832 and the external environment. The fields are:

17. *Write enable.* These two bits specify write 32 bits, or 16 most significant bits, or 16 least significant bits, or do not write into register file. The destination register is defined by field 24.
18. *Select register file data source.* If a write is to occur to the register file, these two bits specify the source: DA bus, DB bus, ALU output, or system Y bus.
19. *Shift instruction modifier.* Specifies options concerning supplying end fill bits and reading bits that are shifted during shift instructions.
20. *Carry in.* This bit indicates whether a bit is carried into the ALU for this operation.
21. *ALU configuration mode.* The 8832 can be configured to operate as a single 32-bit ALU, two 16-bit ALUs, or four 8-bit ALUs.
22. *S input.* The ALU logic module inputs are provided by two internal multiplexers referred to as the S and R multiplexers. This field selects the input to be provided by the S multiplexer: register file, DB bus, or MQ register. The source register is defined by field 25.
23. *R input.* Selects input to be provided by the R multiplexer: register file or DA bus.
24. *Destination register.* Address of register in register file to be used for the destination operand.

25. *Source register.* Address of register in register file to be used for the source operand, provided by the S multiplexer.

26. *Source register.* Address of register in register file to be used for the source operand, provided by the R multiplexer.

Finally, field 27 is an 8-bit opcode that specifies the arithmetic or logical function to be performed by the ALU. Table 15.9 lists the different operations that can be performed.

As an example of the coding used to specify fields 17 through 27, consider the instruction to add the contents of register 1 to register 2 and place the result in register 3. The symbolic instruction is

CONT11 [17], WELH, SELRYFYMX, [24], R3, R2, R1, PASS+ADD

The assembler will translate this into the appropriate bit pattern. The individual components of the instruction can be described as follows:

- CONT11 is the basic NOP instruction.
- Field [17] is changed to WELH (write enable, low and high), so that a 32-bit register is written into
- Field [18] is changed to SELRFYMX to select the feedback from the ALU Y MUX output.
- Field [24] is changed to designate register R3 for the destination register.
- Field [25] is changed to designate register R2 for one of the source registers.
- Field [26] is changed to designate register R1 for one of the source registers.
- Field [27] is changed to specify an ALU operation of ADD. The ALU shifter instruction is PASS; therefore, the ALU output is not shifted by the shifter.

Several points can be made about the symbolic notation. It is not necessary to specify the field number for consecutive fields. That is,

CON11 [17], WELH, [18], SELRFYMX

can be written as

CONT11 [17], WELH, SELRFYMX

since SELRFYMX is in field 18.

ALU instructions from Group 1 of Table 15.9 must always be used in conjunction with Group 2. ALU instructions from Groups 3–5 must not be used with Group 2.

## 15.5

## APPLICATIONS OF MICROPROGRAMMING

Since the introduction of microprogramming, and especially since the late 1960s, the applications of microprogramming have become increasingly varied and widespread. As early as 1971, most if not all of the contemporary uses of microprogramming were in evidence [FLYN71, HAAV71]. More recent surveys discuss essentially the same set of applications [RAVS80]. The set of current applications for microprogramming includes

- Realization of Computers
- Emulation
- Operating-System Support
- Realization of Special-Purpose Devices
- High-Level Language Support
- Microdiagnostics
- User Tailoring

This chapter has been devoted to a discussion of *realization of computers*. The microprogrammed approach offers a systematic technique for control unit implementation. A related technique is *emulation* [MALL75]. Emulation refers to the use of a microprogram on one machine to execute programs originally written for another. The most common use of emulation is to aid users in migrating from one computer to another. This is frequently done by a vendor to make it easier for existing customers to trade in older machines for newer ones, thus making a switch to another vendor unattractive. Users are often surprised to find out how long this transition tool stays around. One observer [MALL83] noted that it was still possible in 1983 to find an IBM System/370 emulating an IBM 1401 that was physically replaced over a decade and a half earlier!

Another fruitful use of microprogramming is in the area of *operating-system support*. Microprograms can be used to implement primitives that replace important portions of operating system software. This technique can simplify the task of operating system implementation and improve operating system performance.

Microprogramming is useful as a vehicle for implementing *special-purpose devices* that may be incorporated into a host computer. A good example of this is a data communications board. The board will contain its own microprocessor. Since it is being used for a special purpose, it makes sense to implement some of its functions in firmware rather than software to enhance performance.

*High-level language support* is another fruitful area for the application of microprogramming techniques. Various functions and data types can be implemented directly in firmware. The result is that it is easier to compile the program into an efficient machine language form. In effect, the machine language is tailored to meet the needs of the high-level language (e.g., FORTRAN, COBOL, Ada).

Microprogramming can be used to support the monitoring, detection, isolation, and repair of system errors. These features are known as *microdiagnostics* and can significantly enhance the system maintenance facility. This approach allows the system to reconfigure itself when failure is detected; for example, if a high-speed multiplier is malfunctioning, a microprogrammed multiplier can take over.

A general category of application is *user tailoring*. A number of machines provide a *writable control store*, that is, a control memory implemented in RAM rather than ROM, and allow the user to write microprograms. Generally, a very vertical, easy-to-use microinstruction set is provided. This allows the user to tailor the machine to the desired application.

**TABLE 15.9   TI 8832 Registered ALU Instruction Field (Field 27)**

| Group 1 | | Function |
|---|---|---|
| ADD | H#01 | R + S + Cn |
| SUBR | H#02 | (NOT R) + S + Cn |
| SUBS | H#03 | R = (NOT S) + Cn |
| INSC | H#04 | S + Cn |
| INCNS | H#05 | (NOT S) + Cn |
| INCR | H#06 | R + Cn |
| INCNR | H#07 | (NOT R) + Cn |
| XOR | H#09 | R XOR S |
| AND | H#0A | R AND S |
| OR | H#0B | R OR S |
| NAND | H#0C | R NAND S |
| NOR | H#0D | R NOR S |
| ANDNR | H#0E | (NOT R) AND S |
| **Group 2** | | **Function** |
| SRA | H#00 | Arithmetic right single precision shift |
| SRAD | H#10 | Arithmetic right double precision shift |
| SRL | H#20 | Logical right single precision shift |
| SRLD | H#30 | Logical right double precision shift |
| SLA | H#40 | Arithmetic left single precision shift |
| SLAD | H#50 | Arithmetic left double precision shift |
| SLC | H#60 | Circular left single precision shift |
| SLCD | H#70 | Circular left double precision shift |
| SRC | H#80 | Circular right single precision shift |
| SRCD | H#90 | Circular right double precision shift |
| MQSRA | H#A0 | Arithmetic right shift MQ register |
| MQSRL | H#B0 | Logical right shift MQ register |
| MQSLL | H#C0 | Logical left shift MQ register |
| MQSLC | H#D0 | Circular left shift MQ register |
| LOADMQ | H#E0 | Load MQ register |
| PASS | H#F0 | Pass ALU to Y (no shift operation) |
| **Group 3** | | **Function** |
| SET1 | H#08 | Set bit 1 |
| Set0 | H#18 | Set bit 0 |
| TB1 | H#28 | Test bit 1 |
| TB0 | H#38 | Test bit 0 |
| ABS | H#48 | Absolute value |
| SMTC | H#58 | Sign magnitude/two's-complement |
| ADDI | H#68 | Add immediate |
| SUBI | H#78 | Subtract immediate |
| BADD | H#88 | Byte add R to S |
| BSUBS | H#98 | Byte subtract S from R |
| BSUBR | H#A8 | Byte subtract R from S |
| BINCS | H#B8 | Byte increment S |
| BINCNS | H#C8 | Byte increment negative S |
| BXOR | H#D8 | Byte XOR R and S |
| BAND | H#E8 | Byte AND R and S |
| BOR | H#F8 | Byte OR R and S |

**TABLE 15.9    (continued)**

| Group 4 | | Function |
|---|---|---|
| CRC | H#00 | Cyclic redundancy character accum. |
| SEL | H#10 | Select S or R |
| SNORM | H#20 | Single length normalize |
| DNORM | H#30 | Double length normalize |
| DIVRF | H#40 | Divide remainder fix |
| SDIVQF | H#50 | Signed divide quotient fix |
| SMULI | H#60 | Signed multiply iterate |
| SMULT | H#70 | Signed multiply terminate |
| SDIVIN | H#80 | Signed divide initialize |
| SDIVIS | H#90 | Signed divide start |
| SDIVI | H#A0 | Signed divide iterate |
| UDIVIS | H#B0 | Unsigned divide start |
| UDIVI | H#C0 | Unsigned divide iterate |
| UMULI | H#D0 | Unsigned multiply iterate |
| SDIVIT | H#E0 | Signed divide terminate |
| UDIVIT | H#F0 | Unsigned divide terminate |
| Group 5 | | Function |
| LOADFF | H#0F | Load divide/BCD flip-flops |
| CLR | H#1F | Clear |
| DUMPFF | H#5F | Output divide/BCD flip-flops |
| BCDBIN | H#7F | BCD to binary |
| EX3BC | H#8F | Excess −3 byte correction |
| EX3C | H#9F | Excess −3 word correction |
| SDIVO | H#AF | Signed divide overflow test |
| BINEX3 | H#DF | Binary to excess −3 |
| NOP32 | H#FF | No operation |

## 15.6

## RECOMMENDED READING

There are a number of books devoted to microprogramming. Perhaps the most comprehensive is [LYNC93]. [SEGE91] presents the fundamentals of microcoding and the design of microcoded systems by means of a step-by-step design of a simple 16-bit processor. [ANDR80] and [CLIN81] provide quite good coverage of control unit implementations. Other books that cover this topic as well as other applications of microprogramming are [BANE82] and [AGRA76]. [KRAF81] uses an AT&T-developed minicomputer as a detailed case study. [PARK89] and [TI90] provide a detailed description of the TI 8800 Software Development Board.

AGRA76    Agrawala, A., and Rauscher, T. *Foundations of Microprogramming: Architecture, Software, and Applications.* New York: Academic Press, 1976.

ANDR80    Andrews, M. *Principles of Firmware Engineering in Microprogram Control.* Silver Spring, MD: Computer Science Press, 1980.

BANE82    Banerji, D., and Raymond, J. *Elements of Microprogramming.* Englewood Cliffs, NJ: Prentice-Hall, 1982.

CLIN81    Cline, B. *Microprogramming Concepts and Techniques*. New York: Petrocelli, 1981.

KRAF81    Kraff, G., and Toy, W. *Microprogrammed Control and Reliable Design of Small Computers*. Englewood Cliffs, NJ: Prentice-Hall, 1981.

LYNC93    Lynch, M. *Microprogrammed State Machine Design*. Boca Raton, FL, 1993.

PARK89    Parker, A., and Hamblen, J. *An Introduction to Microprogramming with Exercises Designed for the Texas Instruments SN74ACT8800 Software Development Board*. Dallas, TX: Texas Instruments, 1989.

SEGE91    Segee, B., and Field, J. *Microprogramming and Computer Architecture*. New York: Wiley, 1991.

TI90    Texas Instruments Inc. *SN74ACT880 Family Data Manual*. SCSS006C, 1990.

## 15.7

## PROBLEMS

15.1    Describe the implementation of the multiply instruction in the hypothetical machine designed by Wilkes. Use narrative and a flowchart.

15.2    Assume a microinstruction set that includes a microinstruction with the following symbolic form:

$$I(AC_0 = 1) \text{ THEN CAR} \leftarrow (C_{0-6}) \text{ ELSE CAR} \leftarrow (CAR) + 1$$

where $AC_0$ is the sign bit of the accumulator and $C_{0-6}$ are the first seven bits of the microinstruction. Using this microinstruction, write a microprogram that implements a Branch Register Minus (BRM) machine instruction, which branches if the AC is negative. Assume that bits $C_1 - C_n$ of the microinstruction specify a parallel set of micro-operations. Express the program symbolically.

15.3    A simple CPU has four major phases to its instruction cycle: fetch, indirect, execute, and interrupt. Two 1-bit flags designate the current phase in a hard-wired implementation.
   **(a)** Why are these flags needed?
   **(b)** Why are they not needed in a microprogrammed control unit?

15.4    Consider the control unit of Figure 15.7. Assume that the control memory is 24 bits wide. The control portion of the microinstruction format is divided into two fields. A micro-operation field of 13 bits specifies the micro-operations to be performed. An address selection field specifies a condition, based on the flags, that will cause a microinstruction branch. There are eight flags.
   **(a)** How many bits are in the address selection field?
   **(b)** How many bits are in the address field?
   **(c)** What is the size of the control memory?

15.5    How can unconditional branching be done under the circumstances of the previous problem? How can branching be avoided; that is, describe a microinstruction that does not specify any branch, conditional or unconditional.

15.6    We wish to provide 8 control words for each machine instruction routine. Machine instruction opcodes have 5 bits, and control memory has 1024 words. Suggest a mapping from the instruction register to the control address register.

15.7 The machine instruction BPNZ causes a branch if the AC is positive and nonzero. The branch address may be expressed directly or indirectly, depending on an indirect (I) bit in the instruction. Suggest a microprogram routine, based on the organization of Figure 15.7, to implement this instruction.

15.8 An encoded microinstruction format is to be used. Show how a 9-bit micro-operation field can be divided into subfields to specify 46 different actions.

15.9 A CPU has 16 registers, an ALU with 16 logic and 16 arithmetic functions, and a shifter with 8 operations, all connected by an internal CPU bus. Design a microinstruction format to specify the various micro-operations for the CPU.

15.10 Analyze each of the microsequencer mnemonics in Table 15.9. Indicate why each bit is set to the indicated value, to achieve the desired function.

# PART V

## PARALLEL ORGANIZATION

The final part of the book looks at the increasingly important area of parallel organization. Chapter 16 looks at two of the most prominent and successful applications of parallel organization: multiple processor systems and vector organization. For multiple processors, the chapter examines the key design issue of cache coherence. The chapter also surveys the increasingly important area of parallel processors, which refers to the use of many processors in a multiple processor configuration. This organization presents new problems not associated with traditional multiple processor configurations simply because of the scale of the organization, which may include hundreds or even thousands of processors.

# CHAPTER 16

# Parallel Processing

Traditionally, the computer has been viewed as a sequential machine. Most computer programming languages require the programmer to specify algorithms as sequences of instructions. CPUs execute programs by executing machine instructions in a sequence and one at a time. Each instruction is executed in a sequence of operations (fetch instruction, fetch operands, perform operation, store results).

This view of the computer has never been entirely true. At the micro-operation level, multiple control signals are generated at the same time. Instruction pipelining, at least to the extent of overlapping fetch and execute operations, has been around for a long time. Both of these are examples of performing functions in parallel.

As computer technology has evolved, and as the cost of computer hardware has dropped, computer designers have sought more and more opportunities for parallelism, usually to improve performance and, in some cases, to improve reliability. In this chapter, we will look at three of the most prominent and successful approaches to parallel organization. First, the chapter examines multiprocessing, one of the earliest and still the most common example of parallel organization. Typically, multiprocessing involves the use of multiple CPUs sharing a common memory. Next, we look at hardware organizational approaches to vector computation. These approaches optimize the ALU for processing vectors or arrays of floating-point numbers. They have been used to implement the class of systems known as *supercomputers*. Finally, we look at the more general area referred to as parallel processor organization.

## 16.1

### MULTIPROCESSING

The use of multiple processors is motivated by considerations of performance and/or reliability. We can classify such systems as follows:

- *Loosely Coupled Multiprocessing:* Consists of a collection of relatively autonomous systems, each CPU having its own main memory and I/O channels. The term *multicomputer* is often used in this context.
- *Functionally Specialized Processors:* Such as an I/O processor. In this case, there is a master, general-purpose CPU, and specialized processors are controlled by the master CPU and provide services to it.

- *Tightly Coupled Multiprocessing:* Consists of a set of processors that share a common main memory and are under the integrated control of an operating system.
- *Parallel Processing:* Tightly coupled multiprocessors that can cooperatively work on one task or job in parallel.

As this book is concerned with the organization and architecture of a single computer system, the first category in the preceding list is beyond its scope; the interested reader can consult [STAL94]. We have already dealt with the concept of functionally specialized processors, primarily in Chapter 6. Parallel processing is primarily a software design problem and, although much research has been and is being done, is still beyond the state of practical application ([HABE85], [FOX87], [KARP87], [OBER88]). Thus, this section focuses on tightly coupled multiprocessing.

We begin by elaborating somewhat on the definition of a tightly coupled multiprocessing system, to which we refer as a *multiprocessor.* Following [ENSL77], the key characteristics of a multiprocessor are

1. It contains two or more similar general-purpose processors of comparable capability.
2. All processors share access to global (common) memory. Some local (private) memory may also be used.
3. All processors share access to I/O devices, either through the same channels or through different channels that provide paths to the same devices.
4. The system is controlled by an integrated operating system that provides interaction between processors and their programs at the job, task, file, and data element levels.

Points 1 to 3 should be self-explanatory. Point 4 illustrates one of the contrasts with a loosely coupled multiprocessing system. In the latter, the physical unit of interaction is usually the complete file. In a multiprocessor, individual data elements can constitute the level of interaction, and there can be a high degree of cooperation between processes.

## Organization

Figure 16.1 depicts in general terms the organization of a multiprocessor system. There are two or more CPUs. Each CPU is self-contained, including a control unit, ALU, registers, and, possibly, cache. Each CPU has access to a shared main memory and the I/O devices through some form of interconnection mechanism. The processors can communicate with each other through memory (messages and status information left in common data areas). It may also be possible for CPUs to directly exchange signals, as indicated by the dotted lines. The memory is often organized so that multiple simultaneous accesses to separate blocks of memory are possible. In some configurations, each CPU may also have its own private main memory and I/O channels in addition to the shared resources.

The organization of a multiprocessor system can be classified as follows:

- Time-Shared or Common Bus
- Multiport Memory
- Central Control Unit

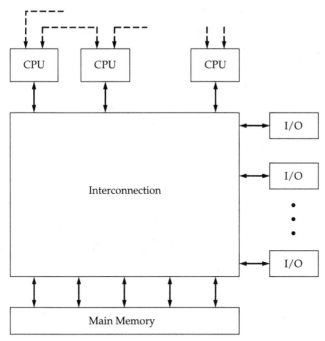

**FIGURE 16.1. Generic block diagram, tightly coupled multiprocessor system**

### Time-Shared Bus

The time-shared bus is the simplest mechanism for constructing a multiprocessor system (Figure 16.2a). The structure and interfaces are basically the same as for a single-processor system that uses a bus interconnection. The bus consists of control, address, and data lines. To facilitate DMA transfers from I/O processors, the following features are provided:

- *Addressing:* It must be possible to distinguish modules on the bus to determine the source and destination of data.
- *Arbitration:* Any I/O module can temporarily function as "master." A mechanism is provided to arbitrate competing requests for bus control, using some sort of priority scheme.
- *Time Sharing:* When one module is controlling the bus, other modules are locked out and must, if necessary, suspend operation until bus access is achieved.

These features are directly usable in a multiprocessor configuration. In this latter case, there are now multiple CPUs as well as multiple I/O processors all attempting to gain access to one or more memory modules via the bus.

The bus organization has several advantages compared with other approaches.

- *Simplicity:* This is the simplest approach to multiprocessor organization. The physical interface and the addressing, arbitration, and time-sharing logic of each processor remain the same as in a single-processor system.
- *Flexibility:* It is generally easy to expand the system by attaching more CPUs to the bus.

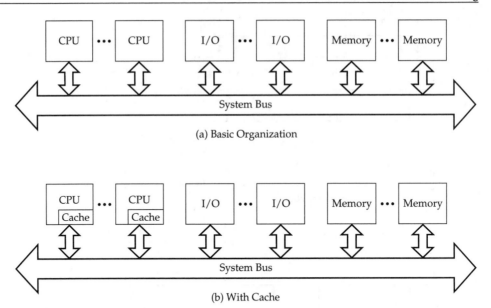

(a) Basic Organization

(b) With Cache

**FIGURE 16.2.  Time-shared bus**

- *Reliability:* The bus is essentially a passive medium, and the failure of any attached device should not cause failure of the whole system.

The main drawback to the bus organization is performance. All memory references pass through the common bus. Thus, the speed of the system is limited by the cycle time. To improve performance, it is desirable to equip each CPU with a cache memory (Figure 16.2b). This should reduce the number of bus accesses dramatically.

The use of caches introduces some new design considerations. Since each local cache contains an image of a portion of memory, if a word is altered in one cache, it could conceivably invalidate a word in another cache. To prevent this, the other CPUs must be alerted that an update has taken place. Section 16.2 addresses this issue.

### Multiport Memory

The multiport memory approach allows the direct, independent access of main memory modules by each CPU and I/O module (Figure 16.3). Logic associated with memory is required for resolving conflicts. The method often used to resolve conflicts is to assign permanently designated priorities to each memory port. Typically, the physical and electrical interface at each port is identical to what would be seen in a single-port memory module. Thus, little or no modification is needed for either CPU or I/O modules to accommodate multiport memory.

The multiport memory approach is more complex than the bus approach, requiring a fair amount of logic to be added to the memory system. It should, however, provide better performance since each processor has a dedicated path to

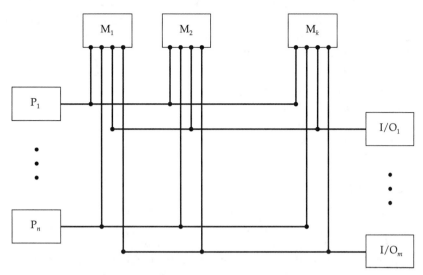

**FIGURE 16.3. Multiport memory**

each memory module. Another advantage of multiport is that it is possible to configure portions of memory as "private" to one or more CPUs and/or I/O modules. This feature allows for increasing security against unauthorized access and for the storage of recovery routines in areas of memory not susceptible to modification by other processors.

One other point: A write-through policy should be used for cache control since there is no other means to alert other processors to a memory update.

### Central Control Unit

The central control unit funnels separate data streams back and forth between independent modules: CPU, memory, I/O. The controller can buffer requests and perform arbitration and timing functions. It can also pass status and control messages between CPUs and perform cache update alerting.

Because all the logic for coordinating the multiprocessor configuration is concentrated in the central control unit, interfaces from I/O, memory, and CPU remain essentially undisturbed. This provides the flexibility and simplicity of interfacing of the bus approach. The key disadvantages of this approach are that the control unit is quite complex and that it is a potential performance bottleneck.

The central control unit structure is quite common for multiple processor mainframe systems, such as large-scale members of the IBM S/370 family.

## Multiprocessor Operating Systems

In a tightly coupled multiprocessor system, the user perceives a single operating system controlling system resources. In fact, such a configuration should appear as a single-processor multiprogramming system. In both cases, multiple jobs or processes may be active at one time, and it is the responsibility of the operating system to schedule their execution and to allocate resources.

Enslow [ENSL77] identifies the following seven functions for a multiprocessor operating system:

- Resource Allocation and Management
- Table and Data Protection
- Prevention of System Deadlock
- Abnormal Termination
- I/O Load Balancing
- Processor Load Balancing
- Reconfiguration

Only the last three are unique or substantially different for multiprocessing systems compared with uniprocessor, multiprogramming systems. It is the responsibility of the multiprocessor operating system to see that resources are used efficiently; otherwise, the investment in multiple CPUs is wasted. It must also reconfigure the system when a processor fails, to continue operation at a reduced performance level.

Tightly coupled multiprocessors can be characterized by the way in which jobs are scheduled. There are two dimensions to the scheduling function:

- Whether processes are dedicated to processors.
- How processes are scheduled on processors.

If a separate short-term queue (see Figure 7.14) is kept for each processor, then once a process is activated, it is permanently assigned to one processor until its completion. In this case, one processor can be idle, with an empty queue, while another processor has a backlog. To prevent this situation, a common queue can be used. All processes go into one queue and are scheduled to any available processor. Thus, over the life of a job, the job may be executed on different processors at different times.

Regardless of whether processes are dedicated to processors, some means is needed to assign processes to processors. Two approaches have been used: master/slave and peer. With a *master/slave* architecture, the operating system always runs on a particular processor. The other processors may only execute user programs. The master is responsible for scheduling jobs. Once a process is active, if the slave needs service (e.g., an I/O call), it must send a request to the master and wait for the service to be performed. This approach is quite simple and requires little enhancement to a uniprocessor multiprogramming operating system. Conflict resolution is simplified since one processor has control of all memory and I/O resources. The disadvantages of this approach are two: (1) a failure of the master brings down the whole system, and (2) the master can become a performance bottleneck.

In a *peer* architecture, the operating system can execute on any processor, and each processor does self-scheduling from the pool of available processes. This approach complicates the operating system. The operating system must ensure that two processors do not choose the same process, and that the processes are not somehow lost from the queue. Techniques must be employed to resolve and synchronize competing claims to resources.

## IBM System/370 Multiprocessing

The 370 architecture provides the capability for multiple CPUs to share main storage and to communicate with each other to coordinate activities. One copy of the operating system is shared by the CPUs, and the workload is dynamically balanced among them. Each CPU has its own set of I/O channels attached to it, but all CPUs have access to all I/O devices. If one CPU requires access to a device attached to another CPU, it asks the other CPU to execute the I/O operation for it.

Key characteristics of the S/370 multiprocessing capability are

- *Prefixing:* Used to share critical areas of main memory.
- *Signaling:* Used for processor-to-processor communication.
- *Synchronization:* Used to coordinate potentially conflicting CPU operations.

### Prefixing

Certain dedicated locations in main memory are used to store control and status information. In a single CPU system, the first 4K bytes of storage are reserved for this purpose. Clearly, this arrangement cannot work in a multiple processor configuration, since all CPUs would attempt to use the same locations.

To overcome this problem, a distinction is made between *real storage* and *absolute storage*. Real storage refers to a memory reference made by a CPU. In a multiprocessor configuration, real addresses are translated into absolute addresses by hardware. The effect is illustrated in Figure 16.4. Each CPU is equipped with a Prefix Value Register (PVR), which contains the starting address $P$ of a 4K-byte block

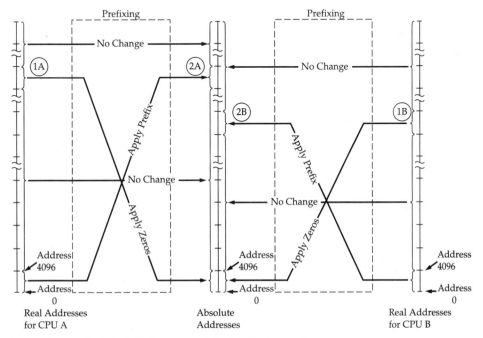

**FIGURE 16.4. Relationship between real and absolute addresses**

of memory. Thus, the lower-order 12 bits of the PVR are always 0. When a real address $R$ is generated by the CPU, an absolute address $A$ is constructed using the following rules:

1. If $R < 4K$, then $A = R + P$.
2. If $P < R < P + 4K$, then $A = R - P$.
3. Otherwise, $A = R$.

The result is that references to the first 4K bytes of memory are translated to another, predetermined 4K-byte block of memory. Each CPU is given a separate 4K-byte block to use as its dedicated area. The algorithm also maps real references to that dedicated area into absolute references to the first 4K-byte block of memory. This allows that first block to be used in coordinating the activities of the CPUs and provides an individual block for each CPU to use in controlling its own activities.

The prefixing function is peformed after the virtual memory function. The sequence of events is

1. A virtual address is converted to a real address by means of dynamic address translation, as explained in Section 7.3.
2. The real address is converted to an absolute address by means of prefixing.

### Signaling

Inter-CPU communication is provided by the Signal Processor Instruction (SIGP). This machine instruction has three operands: CPU address, order code, and status. The CPU address identifies the CPU to which the signal is being sent. The order code specifies the requested action, and the status operand specifies a register in which the status or result of the SIGP instruction is stored.

Table 16.1 lists some of the order codes used with the SIGP instruction. When the SIGP is executed on one CPU, the 2-bit condition code in the PSW indicates the result of the operation:

- Order Code Accepted
- Status Stored
- Busy
- Not Operational

**TABLE 16.1  IBM S/370 Interprocessor Orders**

**SENSE**
   The addressed CPU sends its status to the issuing CPU.
**START**
   The addressed CPU enters the Operating state if it is in the Stopped state.
**STOP**
   The addressed CPU enters the Stopped state if it is in the Operating state.
**STOP AND STORE STATUS**
   The addressed CPU enters the Stopped state and its status is saved in absolute locations 216 to 512. Status includes the PSW and general, control, and floating-point registers.
**EXTERNAL CALL**
   An external interrupt is sent by one CPU to another as a request to provide services.

The first two conditions indicate that the signal was successfully transmitted to the other CPU; some orders involve the return of status information, and others do not. A busy condition indicates that the access path to the other CPU is busy, or that the other CPU, though operational, cannot respond to the order code. Finally, the other CPU may not be operational.

The status bits indicate the response to the designated order. For example, the result of a successful STOP order is indicated by setting the appropriate status bit.

### Synchronization

The S/370 architecture provides a set of mechanisms to facilitate cooperation among processes and processors.

One means of cooperation is for multiple processes to be able to access the same common area of memory. This area can be used for the exchange of status information. Conventions are needed to avoid conflicts in reading and updating common areas. For this purpose, the S/370 supports what amounts to a software locking arrangement. One word of the common storage is designated as the lock. Each CPU checks the lockword before attempting to access the common data areas. If the lockword is 0, the CPU stores its identifier in the word, and other CPUs must wait until the first CPU is done and resets the lockword.

For this convention to work, it must be possible to examine and update the lockword without the possibility that another process will access the storage area between the examination and updating operations. The machine instruction for this is Compare and Swap (CS). CS takes three operands. The first and second operands are compared. If they are equal, the third operand is stored at the second-operand location. If they are not equal, the second operand is loaded into the first-operand location. To achieve the desired result, the first, second, and third operands should be 0, the lockword, and the CPU identifier, respectively. During the execution of the CS, no other CPU can access the specified location (second operand).

The architecture also specifies an interrupt mechanism and instructions for setting and synchronizing time-of-day (TOD) clocks in CPUs.

### IBM 3033 Multiprocessor Organization

The discussion so far has concerned the architecture of multiprocessing on the S/370 family. We now look briefly at the organization of multiprocessing on a specific machine, the IBM 3033 [CONN79].

The IBM 3033 can be configured with two tightly coupled CPUs. Each CPU has its own set of channels that can be switched from a failing processor to the functioning processor. The two CPUs are connected by a specialized hardware module called the *Multiprocessor Communications Unit* (MCU), as depicted in Figure 16.5. The MCU can communicate with each CPU and also has direct communication with the channels and cache of each CPU. The MCU performs the following functions for both processors:

- Prefixing
- Interprocessor Communication

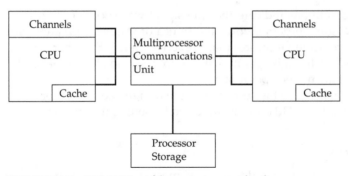

**FIGURE 16.5. IBM 3033 multiprocessor organization**

- Storage Access
- Broadcast of Storage Update

The first two functions have already been described. The MCU controls *storage access* to coordinate and resolve memory access conflicts between the two CPUs. Requests are buffered in the MCU and handled on a first-come-first-served basis when there is no conflict. When both CPUs attempt access to the same block of memory, a simple priority mechanism is used to resolve conflicts.

The IBM 3033 uses a write-through policy for its cache. That is, a write causes the corresponding word to be updated in both main memory and the cache. Since each CPU has its own cache, it is necessary for both caches to be updated. When a write takes place, the MCU automatically *broadcasts* this to the other processor, and, if that processor's cache contains the affected data, the data are automatically invalidated. I/O channel transfers are handled in the same way.

## 16.2

## CACHE COHERENCE AND THE MESI PROTOCOL

In contemporary multiprocessor systems, it is customary to have one or two levels of cache associated with each processor. This organization is essential to achieve reasonable performance. It does, however, create a problem known as the *cache coherence* problem. The essence of the problem is this: Multiple copies of the same data can exist in different caches simultaneously, and if processors are allowed to freely update their own copies, an inconsistent view of memory can result.

In this section, we will briefly survey various approaches to the cache coherence problem and then focus on the approach that is most widely used: the MESI protocol. A version of this protocol is used on both the Pentium and PowerPC implementations.

Cache coherence approaches have generally been divided into software and hardware approaches. Some implementations adopt a strategy that involves both software and hardware elements. Nevertheless, the classification into software and hardware approaches is still instructive and is commonly used in surveying cache coherence strategies.

## Software Solutions

Software cache coherence schemes attempt to avoid the need for additional hardware circuitry and logic by relying on the compiler and operating system to deal with the problem. Software approaches are attractive because the overhead of detecting potential problems is transferred from run time to compile time, and the design complexity is transferred from hardware to software. On the other hand, compile-time, software approaches generally must make conservative decisions, leading to inefficient cache utilization.

Compiler-based coherence mechanisms perform an analysis on the code to determine which data items may become unsafe for caching, and they mark those items accordingly. The operating system or hardware then prevents non-cachable items from being cached.

The simplest approach is to prevent any shared data variables from being cached. This is too conservative, since a shared data structure may be exclusively used during some periods and may be effectively read-only during other periods. It is only during periods when at least one process may update the variable and at least one other process may access the variable that cache coherence is an issue.

More efficient approaches analyze the code to determine safe periods for shared variables. The compiler then inserts instructions into the generated code to enforce cache coherence during the critical periods. A number of techniques have been developed for performing the analysis and for enforcing the results; see [LILJ93] and [STEN90] for surveys.

## Hardware Solutions

Hardware-based solutions are generally referred to as cache coherence protocols. These solutions provide dynamic recognition at run time of potential inconsistency conditions. Since the problem is only dealt with when it actually arises, there is more effective use of caches, leading to improved performance over a software approach. In addition, these approaches are transparent to the programmer and the compiler, reducing the software development burden.

Hardware schemes differ in a number of particulars, including where the state information about data blocks is held, how that information is organized, where coherence is enforced, and the enforcement mechanisms. In general, hardware schemes can be divided into two categories: directory protocols and snoopy protocols.

### Directory Protocols

Directory protocols collect and maintain information about where copies of blocks reside. Typically, there is a centralized controller that is part of the main memory controller, and a directory that is stored in main memory. The directory contains global state information about the contents of the various local caches. When an individual cache controller makes a request, the centralized controller checks and issues necessary commands for data transfer between memory and caches or between caches themselves. It is also responsible for keeping the state information up to date; therefore, every local action that can affect the global state of a block must be reported to the central controller.

Typically, the controller maintains information about which processors have a copy of which blocks. Before a processor can write to a local copy of a block, it must request exclusive access to the block from the controller. Before granting this exclusive access, the controller sends a message to all processors with a cached copy of this block forcing each processor to invalidate its copy. After receiving acknowledgments back from each such processor, the controller grants exclusive access to the requesting processor. When another processor tries to read a block that is exclusively granted to another processor, it will send a miss notification to the controller. The controller then issues a command to the processor holding that block that requires the processor to do a writeback to main memory. The block may now be shared for reading by the original processor and the requesting processor.

Directory schemes suffer from the drawbacks of a central bottleneck and the overhead of communication between the various cache controllers and the central controller. However, they are effective in large-scale systems that involve multiple buses or some other complex interconnection scheme.

### Snoopy Protocols

Snoopy protocols distribute the responsibility for maintaining cache coherence among all of the cache controllers in a multiprocessor. A cache must recognize when a block that it holds is shared with other caches. When an update action is performed on a shared cache block, it must be announced to all other caches by a broadcast mechanism. Each cache controller is able to "snoop" on the network to observe these broadcasted notifications, and react accordingly.

Snoopy protocols are ideally suited to a bus-based multiprocessor, since the shared bus provides a simple means for broadcasting and snooping. However, since one of the objectives of the use of local caches is to avoid bus accesses, care must be taken that the increased bus traffic required for broadcasting and snooping does not cancel out the gains from the use of local caches.

Two basic approaches to the snoopy protocol have been explored: write-invalidate and write-update (or write-broadcast). With a write-invalidate protocol, there can be multiple readers but only one writer at a time. Initially, a block may be shared among several caches for reading purposes. When one of the caches wants to perform a write to the block, it first issues a notice that invalidates that block in the other caches, making the block exclusive to the writing cache. Once the block is exclusive, the owning processor can make cheap local writes until some other processor requires the same block.

With a write-update protocol, there can be multiple writers as well as multiple readers. When a processor wishes to update a shared block, the word to be updated is distributed to all others, and caches containing that block can update it.

Neither of these two approaches is superior to the other under all circumstances. Performance depends on the number of local caches and the pattern of memory reads and writes. Some systems implement adaptive protocols that employ both write-invalidate and write-update mechanisms.

The write-invalidate approach is the most widely used in commercial multiprocessor systems, such as the Pentium and PowerPC. It marks the state of every cache line (using 2 extra bits in the cache tag) as modified, exclusive, shared, or invalid. For this reason, the write-invalidate protocol is called MESI. We have already looked at the MESI protocol in Chapter 4, in dealing with the coordination between level 1 and level 2 local caches. In the remainder of this section, we will look at its use among local caches across a multiprocessor. For simplicity in the presentation, we do not examine the mechanisms involved in coordinating among both level 1 and level 2 locally as well as at the same time coordinating across the distributed multiprocessor. This would not add any new principles but would greatly complicate the discussion.

## The MESI Protocol

Recall from Chapter 4 that, with the MESI protocol, the data cache includes 2 status bits per tag, so that each line can be in one of four states:

- *Modified:* The line in the cache has been modified (different from main memory) and is available only in this cache.
- *Exclusive:* The line in the cache is the same as that in main memory and is not present in any other cache.
- *Shared:* The line in the cache is the same as that in main memory and may be present in another cache.
- *Invalid:* The line in the cache does not contain valid data.

Figure 16.6 displays a state diagram for the MESI protocol. We describe each of the transitions in what follows.

### Read Miss

When a read miss occurs in the local cache, the processor initiates a memory read to read the block of main memory containing the missing address. The processor inserts a signal on the bus that alerts all other processor/cache units to snoop the transaction. There are a number of possible outcomes:

- If one other processor has a clean (unmodified since read from memory) copy of the block in the exclusive state, it returns a signal indicating that it shares this block. The responding processor then transitions the state of its copy from exclusive to shared, and the initiating processor reads the block and transitions the block in its cache from invalid to shared.
- If one or more processors have a clean copy of the block in the shared state, each of them signals that it shares the block. The initiating processor reads the block and transitions the block in its cache from invalid to shared.

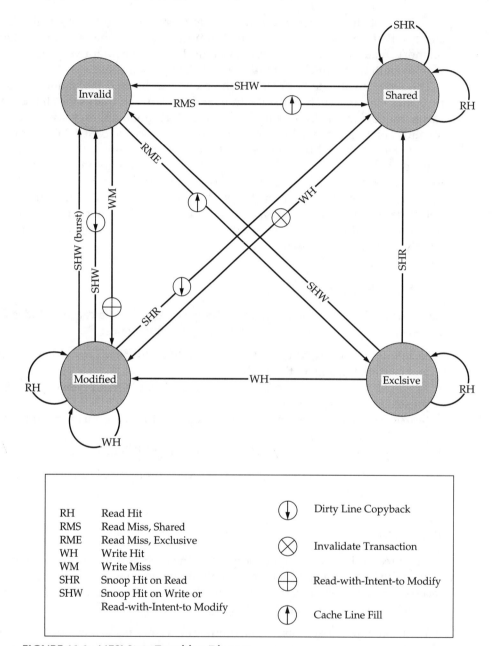

**FIGURE 16.6. MESI State Transition Diagram**

- If one other processor has a modified copy of the block, then it signals the initiating processor to retry. Meanwhile, the processor with the modified copy seizes the bus, writes the modified block back to main memory, and transitions the block in its cache from modified to shared. Subsequently, the requesting processor tries again and finds that one or more processors have a clean copy of the block in the shared state, as described in the preceding point.
- If no other cache has a copy of the block (clean or modified), then no signals are returned. The initiating processor reads the block and transitions the block in its cache from invalid to exclusive.

### Read Hit

When a read hit occurs on a block currently in the local cache, the processor simply reads the required item; there is no state change.

### Write Miss

When a write miss occurs in the local cache, the processor initiates a memory read to read the block of main memory containing the missing address. For this purpose, the processor issues a signal on the bus that means read-with-intent-to-modify (RWITM). When the block is loaded, it is immediately marked modified. With respect to other caches, two possible scenarios precede the loading of the block of data.

First, some other cache may have a modified copy of this block (state = modify). In this case, the alerted processor signals the initiating processor that another processor has a modified copy of the block. The initiating processor surrenders the bus and waits. The other processor gains access to the bus, writes the modified cache block back to main memory, and transitions the state of the cache block to invalid (since the initiating processor is going to modify this block). Subsequently, the initiating processor will again issue a signal to the bus of RWITM and then read the block back from main memory.

The second scenario is that no other cache has a modified copy of the requested block. In this case, no signal is returned, and the initiating processor proceeds to read in the block and modify it. Meanwhile, if one or more processors have a clean copy of the block in the shared state, each processor invalidates its copy of the block, and if one processor has a clean copy of the block in the exclusive state, it invalidates its copy of the block.

### Write Hit

When a write hit occurs on a block currently in the local cache, the effect depends on the current state of that block in the local cache:

- *Shared:* Before performing the update, the processor must gain exclusive ownership of the block. The processor signals its intent on the bus. Each processor that has a shared copy of the block in its cache transitions the sector from shared to invalid. The initiating processor then performs the update and transitions its copy of the block from shared to modified.

- *Exclusive:* The processor already has exclusive control of this block, and so it simply performs the update and transitions its copy of the block from exclusive to modified.
- *Modified:* The processor already has exclusive control of this block and has the block marked as modified, and so it simply performs the update.

## 16.3

### VECTOR COMPUTATION

Although the performance of mainframe general-purpose computers continues to improve relentlessly, there continue to be applications that are beyond the reach of the contemporary mainframe. There is a need for computers to solve mathematical problems of real processes, such as occur in disciplines including aerodynamics, seismology, meteorology, and atomic, nuclear, and plasma physics [WILS84].

Typically, these problems are characterized by the need for high precision and a program that repetitively performs floating-point arithmetic operations on large arrays of numbers. Most of these problems fall into the category known as *continuous-field simulation*. In essence, a physical situation can be described by a surface or region in three dimensions (e.g., the flow of air adjacent to the surface of a rocket). This surface is approximated by a grid of points. A set of differential equations defines the physical behavior of the surface at each point. The equations are represented as an array of values and coefficients, and the solution involves repeated arithmetic operations on the arrays of data.

To handle these types of problems, the supercomputer has been developed. These machines are typically capable of hundreds of millions of floating-point operations per second and cost in the 10 to 15 million dollar range. In contrast to mainframes, which are designed for multiprogramming and intensive I/O, the supercomputer is optimized for the type of numerical calculation just described.

The supercomputer has limited use and, because of its price tag, a limited market. Comparatively few of these machines are operational, mostly at research centers and some government agencies with scientific or engineering functions. As with other areas of computer technology, there is a constant demand to increase the performance of the supercomputer. In some current applications in aerodynamics and nuclear physics, as many as $10^{13}$ arithmetic operations, absorbing more than two days of computing time on a contemporary supercomputer, are needed for a single problem [LEVI82]. Thus, the technology and performance of the supercomputer continues to evolve.

There is another type of system that has been designed to address the need for vector computation, referred to as the *array processor*. Although a supercomputer is optimized for vector computation, it is a general-purpose computer, capable of handling scalar processing and general data processing tasks. Array processors do not include scalar processing; they are configured as peripheral devices by both mainframe and minicomputer users to run the vectorized portions of programs.

## Approaches to Vector Computation

The key to the design of a supercomputer or array processor is to recognize that the main task is to perform arithmetic operations on arrays or vectors of floating-point numbers. In a general-purpose computer, this will require iteration through each element of the array. For example, consider two vectors (one-dimensional arrays) of numbers, A and B. We would like to add these and place the result in C. In the example of Figure 16.7, this requires six separate additions. How could we speed up this computation? The answer is to introduce some form of parallelism.

Several approaches have been taken to achieving parallelism in vector computation. We illustrate this with an example based on one in [STON80]. Consider the vector multiplication $C = A \times B$, where A, B, and C are $N \times N$ matrices. The formula for each element of C is

$$c_{i,j} = \sum_{k=1}^{N} a_{i,k} \cdot b_{k,j}$$

where A, B, and C have elements $a_{i,j}$, $b_{i,j}$, and $c_{i,j}$, respectively. Figure 16.8a shows a FORTRAN program for this computation that can be run on an ordinary scalar CPU.

One approach to improving performance can be referred to as *vector processing*. This assumes that it is possible to operate on a one-dimensional vector of data. Figure 16.8b is a FORTRAN program with a new form of instruction that allows vector computation to be specified. The notation (J = 1, N) indicates that operations on all indices J in the given interval are to be carried out as a single operation. How this can be achieved is addressed shortly.

The program in Figure 16.8b indicates that all the elements of the *i*th row are to be computed in parallel. Each element in the row is a summation, and the summations (across K) are done serially rather than in parallel. Even so, only $N^2$ vector multiplications are required for this algorithm as compared with $N^3$ scalar multiplications for the scalar algorithm.

Another approach, *parallel processing*, is illustrated in Figure 16.8c. This approach assumes that we have N independent CPUs that can function in parallel. To utilize processors effectively, we must somehow parcel out the computation to the various processors. Two primitives are used. The primitive FORK *n* causes an independent process to be started at location *n*. In the meantime, the original

$$
\begin{bmatrix} 1.5 \\ 7.1 \\ 6.9 \\ 100.5 \\ 0 \\ 59.7 \end{bmatrix}
+
\begin{bmatrix} 2.0 \\ 39.7 \\ 1000.003 \\ 11 \\ 21.1 \\ 19.7 \end{bmatrix}
=
\begin{bmatrix} 3.5 \\ 46.8 \\ 1006.903 \\ 111.5 \\ 21.1 \\ 79.4 \end{bmatrix}
$$

$$A \quad + \quad B \quad = \quad C$$

**FIGURE 16.7. Example of vector addition**

```
            DO 100 I = 1, N
            DO 100 J = 1, N
            C(I, J) = 0.0
            DO 100 K = 1, N
            C(I, J) = C(I, J) + A(I, K) * B(K, J)
100         CONTINUE
```

(a) Scalar Processing

```
            DO 100 I = 1, N
            C(I, J) = 0.0 (J = 1, N)
            DO 100 K = 1, N
            C(I, J) = C(I, J) + A(I, K) * B(K, J) (J = 1, N)
100         CONTINUE
```

(b) Vector Processing

```
            DO 50 J = 1, N
            FORK 100
50          CONTINUE
            J = N
100         DO I = 1, N
            C(I, J) = 0.0
            DO 200 K = 1, N
            C(I, J) = C(I, J) + A(I, K) * B(K, J)
200         CONTINUE
            JOIN N
```

(c) Parallel Processing

**FIGURE 16.8. Matrix multiplication (C = A $\times$ B)**

process continues execution at the instruction immediately following the FORK. Every execution of a FORK spawns a new process. The JOIN instruction is essentially the inverse of the FORK. The statement JOIN N causes $N$ independent processes to be merged into one that continues execution at the instruction following the JOIN. The operating system must coordinate this merger, and so the execution does not continue until all $N$ processes have reached the JOIN instruction.

The program in Figure 16.8c is written to mimic the behavior of the vector processing program. In the parallel processing program, each column of $C$ is computed by a separate process. Thus, the elements in a given row of $C$ are computed in parallel.

The preceding discussion describes approaches to vector computation in logical or architectural terms. Let us turn now to a consideration of types of CPU organization that can be used to implement these approaches. A wide variety of organizations have been and are being pursued. Three main categories stand out:

- Pipelined ALU
- Parallel ALUs
- Parallel Processors

Figure 16.9 illustrates the first two of these approaches. We have already discussed pipelining in Chapter 11. Here the concept is extended to the operation of the ALU. Since floating-point operations are rather complex, there is opportunity for decomposing a floating-point operation into stages, so that different stages can operate on different sets of data concurrently. This is illustrated in Figure 16.10a. Floating-point addition is broken up into four stages (see Figure 8.21): compare, shift, add, and normalize. A vector of numbers is presented sequentially to the first stage. As the processing proceeds, four different sets of numbers will be operated on concurrently in the pipeline.

It should be clear that this organization is suitable for vector processing. To see this, consider the instruction pipelining described in Chapter 11. The CPU goes through a repetitive cycle of fetching and processing instructions. In the absence of branches, the CPU is continuously fetching instructions from sequential locations. Consequently, the pipeline is kept full and a savings in time is achieved. Similarly, a

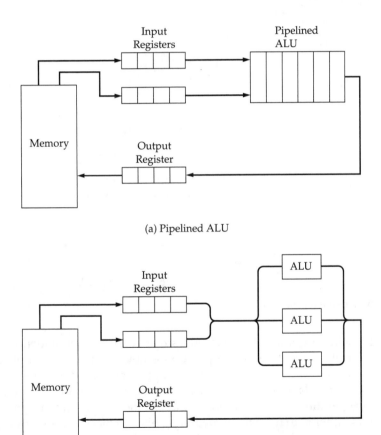

(a) Pipelined ALU

(b) Parallel ALUs

**FIGURE 16.9. Approaches to vector computation**

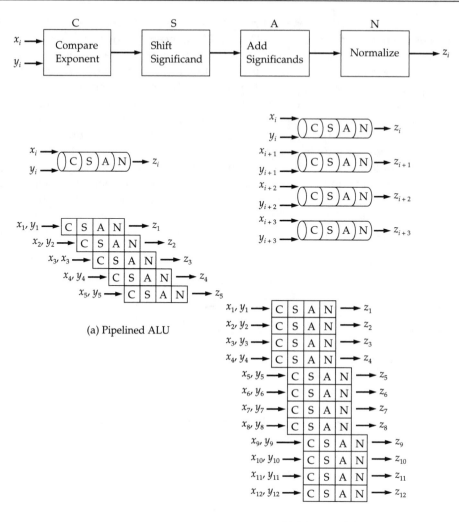

(a) Pipelined ALU

(b) Four Parallel ALUs

**FIGURE 16.10. Pipelined processing**

pipelined ALU will save time only if it is fed a stream of data from sequential locations. A single, isolated floating-point operation is not speeded up by a pipeline. The speedup is achieved when a vector of operands is presented to the ALU. The control unit cycles the data through the ALU until the entire vector is processed.

The pipeline operation can be further enhanced if the vector elements are available in registers rather than from main memory. This is in fact suggested by Figure 16.9a. The elements of each vector operand are loaded as a block into a **vector register,** which is simply a large bank of identical registers. The result is also placed in a vector register. Thus, most operations involve only the use of registers, and only load and store operations and the beginning and end of a vector operation require access to memory.

The mechanism illustrated in Figure 16.10 could be referred to as *pipelining within an operation*. That is, we have a single arithmetic operation (e.g., $C = A + B$) that is to be applied to vector operands, and pipelining allows multiple vector elements to be processed in parallel. This mechanism can be augmented with *pipelining across operations*. In this latter case, there is a sequence of arithmetic vector operations, and instruction pipelining is used to speed up processing. One approach to this, referred to as **chaining,** is found on the Cray supercomputers. The basic rule for chaining is this: A vector operation may start as soon as the first element of the operand vector(s) is available and the functional unit (e.g., add, subtract, multiply, divide) is free. Essentially, chaining causes results issuing from one functional unit to be fed immediately into another functional unit and so on. If vector registers are used, intermediate results do not have to be stored into memory and can be used even before the vector operation that created them runs to completion.

For example, when computing $C = (s \times A) + B$, where $A$, $B$, and $C$ are vectors and $s$ is a scalar, the Cray may execute three instructions at once. Elements fetched for a load immediately enter a pipelined multiplier, the products are sent to a pipelined adder, and the sums are placed in a vector register as soon as the adder completes them:

1. Vector Load          $A \rightarrow$ Vector Register (VR1)
2. Vector Load          $B \rightarrow$ VR2
3. Vector Multiply      $s \times$ VR1 $\rightarrow$ VR3
4. Vector Add           VR3 + VR2 $\rightarrow$ VR4
5. Vector Store         VR4 $\rightarrow$ C

Instructions 2 and 3 can be chained (pipelined) since they involve different memory locations and registers. Instruction 4 needs the results of instructions 2 and 3, but it can be chained with them as well. As soon as the first elements of vector registers 2 and 3 are available, the operation in instruction 4 can begin.

Another way to achieve vector processing is by the use of multiple ALUs in a single CPU, under the control of a single control unit. In this case, the control unit routes data to ALUs so that they can function in parallel. It is also possible to use pipelining on each of the parallel ALUs. This is illustrated in Figure 16.10b. The example shows a case in which four ALUs operate in parallel.

As with pipelined organization, a parallel ALU organization is suitable for vector processing. The control unit routes vector elements to ALUs in a round-robin fashion until all elements are processed. This type of organization is more complex than a single-ALU CPI.

Finally, vector processing can be achieved by using multiple parallel CPUs. In this case, it is necessary to break the task up into multiple processes to be executed in parallel. This organization is effective only if the software and hardware for effective coordination of parallel processors is available. This is still an active research area, although some products have appeared [GEHR88].

We can expand our taxonomy of Section 16.1 to reflect these new structures, as shown in Figure 16.11. Computer organizations can be distinguished by the presence of one or more control units. Multiple control units imply multiple proces-

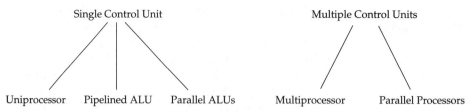

**FIGURE 16.11. A taxonomy of computer organizations**

sors. Following our previous discussion, if the multiple processors can function cooperatively on a given task, they are termed *parallel processors.*

The reader should be aware of some unfortunate terminology likely to be encountered in the literature. The term *vector processor* is often equated with a pipelined ALU organization, although a parallel ALU organization is also designed for vector processing, and, as we have discussed, a parallel processor organization may also be designed for vector processing. *Array processing* is sometimes used to refer to a parallel ALU, although, again, any of the three organizations is optimized for the processing of arrays. To make matters worse, *array processor* usually refers to an auxiliary processor attached to a general-purpose CPU and used to perform vector computation. An array processor may use either the pipelined or parallel ALU approach.

At present, the pipelined ALU organization dominates the marketplace [KOZD80, RIGA84]. Pipelined systems are less complex than the other two approaches. Their control unit and operating-system design are well developed to achieve efficient resource allocation and high performance. The remainder of this section is devoted to a more detailed examination of this approach, using a specific example.

## IBM 3090 Vector Facility

A good example of a pipelined ALU organization for vector processing is the vector facility developed for the IBM 370 architecture and implemented on the high-end 3090 series [PADE88, TUCK87]. This facility is an optional add-on to the basic system but is highly integrated with it. It resembles vector facilities found on supercomputers, such as the Cray family.

The IBM facility makes use of a number of vector registers. Each register is actually a bank of scalar registers. To compute the vector sum $C = A + B$, the vectors $A$ and $B$ are loaded into two vector registers. The data from these registers are passed through the ALU as fast as possible, and the results are stored in a third vector register. The computation overlap, and the loading of the input data into the registers in a block, results in a significant speeding up over an ordinary ALU operation.

### *Organization*

The IBM vector architecture, and similar pipelined vector ALUs, provides increased performance over loops of scalar arithmetic instructions in three ways:

- The fixed and predetermined structure of vector data permits housekeeping instructions inside the loop to be replaced by faster internal (hardware or microcoded) machine operations.
- Data-access and arithmetic operations on several successive vector elements can proceed concurrently by overlapping such operations in a pipelined design or by performing multiple-element operations in parallel.
- The use of vector registers for intermediate results avoids additional storage reference.

Figure 16.12 shows the general organization of the vector facility. Although the vector facility is seen to be a physically separate add-on to the CPU, its architecture is an extension of the System/370 architecture and is compatible with it. The vector facility is integrated into the System/370 architecture in the following ways:

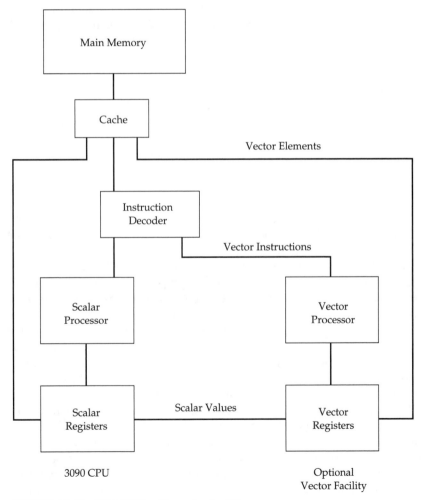

**FIGURE 16.12. IBM 3090 with vector facility**

- Existing System/370 instructions are used for all scalar operations.
- Arithmetic operations on individual vector elements produce exactly the same result as do corresponding System/370 scalar instructions. For example, one design decision concerned the definition of the result in a floating-point DIVIDE operation. Should the result be exact, as it is for scalar floating-point division, or should an approximation be allowed that would permit higher-speed implementation but could sometimes introduce an error in one or more low-order bit positions? The decision was made to uphold complete compatibility with the System/370 architecture at the expense of a minor performance degradation.
- Vector instructions are interruptible, and their execution can be resumed from the point of interruption after appropriate action has been taken, in a manner compatible with the System/370 program-interruption scheme.
- Arithmetic exceptions are the same as, or extensions of, exceptions for the scalar arithmetic instructions of the System/370, and similar fix-up routines can be used. To accommodate this, a vector interruption index is employed that indicates the location in a vector register that is affected by an exception (e.g., overflow). Thus, when execution of the vector instruction resumes, the proper place in a vector register is accessed.
- Vector data resides in virtual storage, with page faults being handled in a standard manner.

This level of integration provides a number of benefits. Existing operating systems can support the vector facility with minor extensions. Existing application programs, language compilers, and other software can be run unchanged. Software that could take advantage of the vector facility can be modified as desired.

## Registers

A key issue in the design of a vector facility is whether operands are located in registers or memory. The IBM organization is referred to as *register-to-register*, since the vector operands, both input and output, can be staged in vector registers. This approach is also used on the Cray supercomputer. An alternative approach, used on Control Data machines, is to obtain operands directly from memory. The main disadvantage of the use of vector registers is that the programmer or compiler must take them into account. For example, suppose that the length of the vector registers is $K$ and the length of the vectors to be processed is $N > K$. In this case, a vector loop must be performed, in which the operation is performed on $K$ elements at a time and the loop is repeated $N/K$ times. The main advantage of the vector register approach is that the operation is decoupled from slower main memory and instead takes place primarily with registers.

The speedup that can be achieved using registers is demonstrated in Figure 16.13 [PADE88]. The FORTRAN routine multiplies vector A by vector B to produce vector C, where each vector has a real part (AR, BR, CR) and an imaginary part (AI, BI, CI). The 3090 can perform one main-storage access per processor, or clock, cycle (either read or write), has registers that can sustain two accesses for reading and one for writing per cycle, and produces one result per cycle in its arithmetic unit. Let us assume the use of instructions that can specify two source

**FORTRAN ROUTINE:**

DO 100 J=1, 50
CR (J) = AR (J)*BR (J) – AI (J)*BI (J)
100    CI (J) = AR (J)*BI (J) – AI (J)*BR (J)

| Operation | Cycles |
|---|---|
| AR (J) *BR (J) → T1 (J) | 3 |
| AI (J) *BI (J) → T2 (J) | 3 |
| T1 (J)–T2 (J) → CR (J) | 3 |
| AR (J) *BI (J) → T3 (J) | 3 |
| AI (J) *BR (J) → T4 (J) | 3 |
| T3 (J)+T4 (J) → CI (J) | 3 |
| TOTAL | 18 |

(a) Storage to Storage

| Operation | Cycles |
|---|---|
| AR (J)            → V1 (J) | 1 |
| BR (J)            → V2 (J) | 1 |
| V1 (J) *V2 (J) → V3 (J) | 1 |
| AI (J)            → V4 (J) | 1 |
| B1 (J)            → V5 (J) | 1 |
| V4 (J) *V5 (J) → V6 (J) | 1 |
| V3 (J) –V6 (J) → V7 (J) | 1 |
| V7 (J)            → CR (J) | 1 |
| V1 (J) *V5 (J) → V8 (J) | 1 |
| V4 (J) *V2 (J) → V9 (J) | 1 |
| V8 (J) +V9 (J) → V0 (J) | 1 |
| V0 (J)            → C1 (J) | 1 |
| TOTAL | 12 |

(b) Register to Register

| Operation | Cycles |
|---|---|
| AR (J)            → V1 (J) | 1 |
| V1 (J) *BR (J) → V2 (J) | 1 |
| AI (J)            → V3 (J) | 1 |
| V3 (J) *BI (J) → V4 (J) | 1 |
| V2 (J) –V4 (J) → V5 (J) | 1 |
| V5 (J)            → CR (J) | 1 |
| V1 (J) *BI (J) → V6 (J) | 1 |
| V3 (J) *BR (J) → V7 (J) | 1 |
| V6 (J) +V7 (J) → V8 (J) | 1 |
| V8 (J)            → CI (J) | 1 |
| TOTAL | 10 |

(c) Storage to Register

Vi = Vector registers
AR, BR, AI, BI = operands in
    memory
Ti = temporary locations in
    memory

| Operation | Cycles |
|---|---|
| AR (J)                        → V1 (J) | 1 |
| V1 (J) *BR (J)            → V2 (J) | 1 |
| AI (J)                        → V3 (J) | 1 |
| V2 (J) –V3 (J) *B1 (J) → V2 (J) | 1 |
| V2 (J)                        → CR (J) | 1 |
| V1 (J) *BI  (J)           → V4 (J) | 1 |
| V4 (J) +V3 (J) *BR (J) → C4 (J) | 1 |
| V4 (J)                        CI  (J) | 1 |
| TOTAL | 8 |

(d) Compound Instructions

**FIGURE 16.13. Alternative programs for vector calculation**

operands and a result.[1] Part a of the figure shows that, with memory-to-memory instructions, each iteration of the computation requires a total of 18 cycles. With a pure register-to-register architecture (part b), this time is reduced to 12 cycles. Of course, with register-to-register operation, the vector quantities must be loaded into the vector registers prior to computation and stored in memory afterward. For large vectors, this fixed penalty is relatively small. Figure 16.13c shows that

---

[1]For the 370 architecture, the only three-operand instructions (register and storage instructions, RS) specify two operands in registers and one in memory. In part a of this example, we assume the existence of three-operand instructions in which all operands are in main memory. This is done for purposes of comparison and, in fact, such an instruction format could have been chosen for the vector architecture.

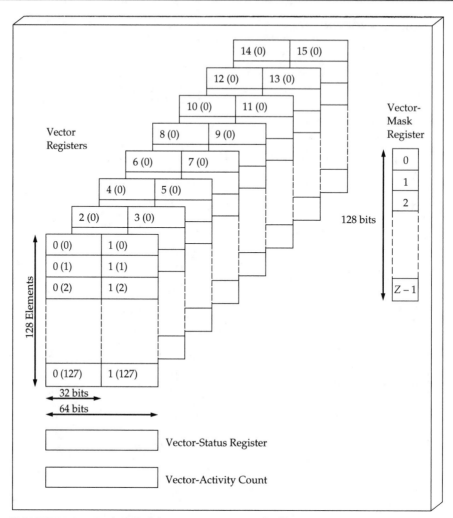

**FIGURE 16.14.  Registers of the IBM 3090 vector facility**

the ability to specify both storage and register operands in one instruction further reduces the time to 10 cycles per iteration. This latter type of instruction is included in the vector architecture.[2]

Figure 16.14 illustrates the registers that are part of the IBM 3090 vector facility. There are 16 32-bit vector registers. The vector registers can also be coupled to form 8 64-bit vector registers. Any register element can hold an integer or floating-point value. Thus, the vector registers may be used for 32-bit and 64-bit integer values, and 32-bit and 64-bit floating-point values.

The architecture specifies that each register contains from 8 to 512 scalar elements. The choice of actual length involves a design trade-off. The time to do a vector operation consists essentially of the overhead for pipeline startup and register filling plus one cycle per vector element. Thus, the use of a large number of

[2]Compound instructions, discussed below, afford a further reduction.

register elements reduces the relative start-up time for a computation. However, this efficiency must be balanced against the added time required for saving and restoring vector registers on a process switch and the practical cost and space limits. These considerations led to the use of 128 elements per register in the current 3090 implementation.

Three additional registers are needed by the vector facility. The vector-mask register contains mask bits that may be used to select which elements in the vector registers are to be processed for a particular operation. The vector-status register contains control fields, such as the vector count that determines how many elements in the vector registers are to be processed. The vector-activity count keeps track of the time spent executing vector instructions.

### Compound Instructions

As was discussed above, instruction execution can be overlapped using chaining to improve performance. The designers of the IBM vector facility chose not to include this capability for several reasons. The System/370 architecture would have to be extended to handle complex interruptions (including their effect on virtual memory management), and corresponding changes would be needed in the software. A more basic issue was the cost of including the additional controls and register access paths in the vector facility for generalized chaining.

Instead, three operations are provided that combine into one instruction (one opcode) the most common sequences in vector computation, namely multiplication followed by addition, subtraction, or summation. The storage-to-register MULTIPLY-AND-ADD instruction, for example, fetches a vector from storage, multiplies it by a vector from a register, and adds the product to a third vector in a register. By use of the compound instructions MULTIPLY-AND-ADD and MULTIPLY-AND-SUBTRACT in the example of Figure 16.13, the total time for the iteration is reduced from 10 to 8 cycles.

Unlike chaining, compound instructions do not require the use of additional registers for temporary storage of intermediate results, and they require one less register access. For example, consider the following chain:

$A \rightarrow VR1$
$VR1 + VR2 \rightarrow VR1$

In this case, two stores to the vector register VR1 are required. In the IBM architecture there is a storage-to-register ADD instruction. With this instruction, only the sum is placed in VR1. The compound instruction also avoids the need to reflect in the machine-state description the concurrent execution of a number of instructions, which simplifies status saving and restoring by the operating system and the handling of interrupts.

### The Instruction Set

Table 16.2 on the next page summarizes the arithmetic and logical operations that are defined for the vector architecture. In addition, there are memory-to-register load and register-to-memory store instructions. Note that many of the instructions

**TABLE 16.2  IBM 3090 Vector Facility: Arithmetic and Logical Instructions**

| Operation | Floating-Point Long | Floating-Point Short | Binary or Logical | Operand Locations | | | |
|---|---|---|---|---|---|---|---|
| Add | FL | FS | BI | V + V → V | V + S → V | Q + V → V | Q + S → V |
| Subtract | FL | FS | BI | V − V → V | V − S → V | Q − V → V | Q − S → V |
| Multiply | FL | FS | BI | V * V → V | V * S → V | Q * V → V | Q * S → V |
| Divide | FL | FS | — | V/V → V | V/S → V | Q/V → V | Q/S → V |
| Compare | FL | FS | BI | V · V → V | V · S → V | Q · V → V | Q · S → V |
| Multiply and Add | FL | FS | — | | V + V * S → V | V + Q * V → V | V + Q * S → V |
| Multiply and Subtract | FL | FS | — | | V − V * S → V | V − Q * V → V | V − Q * S → V |
| Multiply and Accumulate | FL | FS | — | P + · V → V | P + · S → V | | |
| Complement | FL | FS | BI | − V → V | | | |
| Positive Absolute | FL | FS | BI | \|V\| → V | | | |
| Negative Absolute | FL | FS | BI | −\|V\| → V | | | |
| Maximum | FL | FS | — | | · V → V | Q · V → Q | |
| Maximum Absolute | FL | FS | — | | · V → V | Q · V → Q | |
| Minimum | FL | FS | — | | · V → V | Q · V → Q | |
| Shift Left Logical | — | — | LO | · V → V | | | |
| Shift Right Logical | — | — | LO | · V → V | | | |
| And | — | — | LO | V & V → V | V & S → V | Q & V → V | Q & S → V |
| Or | — | — | LO | V\|V → V | V\|S → V | Q\|V → V | Q\|S → V |
| Exclusive-Or | — | — | LO | V ≠ V → V | V ≠ S → V | Q ≠ V → V | Q ≠ S → V |

*Explanation:*

Data Types
FL  Long floating-point
FS  Short floating-point
BI  Binary integer
LO  Logical

Operand Locations
V  Vector register
S  Storage
Q  Scalar (general or floating-point register)
P  Parital sums in vector register
·  Special operation

use a three-operand format. Also, many instructions have a number of variants, depending on the location of the operands. A source operand may be a vector register (V), storage (S), or a scalar register (Q). The target is always a vector register, except for comparison, the result of which goes into the vector-mask register. With all these variants, the total number of opcodes (distinct instructions) is 171. This rather large number, however, is not as expensive to implement as might be imagined. Once the machine provides the arithmetic units and the data paths to feed operands from storage, scalar registers, and vector registers to the vector pipelines, the major hardware cost has been incurred. The architecture can, with little difference in cost, provide a rich set of variants on the use of those registers and pipelines.

Most of the instructions in Table 16.2 are self-explanatory. The two summation instructions warrant further explanation. The accumulate operation adds together the elements of a single vector (ACCUMULATE) or the elements of the product of two vectors (MULTIPLY-AND-ACCUMULATE). These instructions present an interesting design problem. We would like to perform this operation as rapidly as possible, taking full advantage of the ALU pipeline. The difficulty is that the sum of two numbers put into the pipeline is not available until several cycles later. Thus, the third element in the vector cannot be added to the sum of the first two elements until those two elements have gone through the entire pipeline. To overcome this problem, the elements of the vector are added in such a way as to produce four partial sums. In particular, elements 0, 4, 8, 12, . . ., 124 are added in that order to produce partial sum 0; elements 1, 5, 9, 13, . . ., 125 to partial sum 1; elements 2, 6, 10, 14, . . ., 126 to partial sum 2; and elements 3, 7, 11, 15, . . ., 127 to partial sum 4. Each of these partial sums can proceed through the pipeline at top speed, since the delay in the pipeline is roughly four cycles. A separate vector register is used to hold the partial sums. When all elements of the original vector have been processed, the four partial sums are added together to produce the final result. The performance of this second phase is not critical, since only four vector elements are involved.

## 16.4

## PARALLEL PROCESSORS

The typical multiple processor system commercially available today involves only a few separate processors, ranging from two up to about a dozen. For years, there has been interest in developing multiple processor systems with massive numbers of processors—in the hundreds, thousands, or even tens of thousands. Such systems generally are referred to as parallel processor systems or, in the case of systems involving thousands of processors, massively parallel processor systems.

Until quite recently, there had been little in the way of commercial products to show for all the research in this area. Now, such products have begun to appear. The key factors that have led to the practical realization of parallel processors include

1. *The use of commodity RISC processors.* Inexpensive, high-performance RISC processors are now available off the shelf. In many systems, these commodity processors serve as the basic building block, relieving the parallel processor

system designer of the need to design the basic processor as well as the overall organization.

2. *Advances in processor-to-processor communication schemes.* With hundreds or thousands of processors working cooperatively, efficient and fail-safe methods of coordination and data exchange are vital.

3. *Performance demand.* Even with the stupendous gains made in performance with each successive generation of processor, application performance demands have grown even more rapidly. Parallel processing schemes provide a means of boosting performance using existing processor technology.

This last point is particularly important. Despite the rapidity with which new processor generations are produced, the software demands will always be one step ahead. This is not true just in the supercomputer realm, but on the desktop. Every time computer companies deliver more power in their latest product, invariably new applications come along that utilize the system to the maximum and then some. An Intel 80486 personal computer is clearly overkill for running a word processor under DOS, but only just adequate for running Windows. Pentium systems can handle Windows displays with ease, but they begin to buckle when trying to service multimedia functions (e.g., live-action video or videophone applications) or advanced technologies such as real-time voice recognition.

The subject of parallel processing is complex, involving issues relating to organization, interconnection structures, inter-processor communication, operating-system design, and application software techniques. The purpose of this section is to provide a brief overview of some of the important organizational concepts.

## Types of Parallel Processors

A parallel processor system is one in which multiple processors are interconnected and work cooperatively to execute application programs. The term is meant to refer to systems that support what might be referred to as high-level parallelism. These are systems that offer an explicit framework for developing system software and applications that exploit parallelism. Excluded are systems that employ only low-level parallelism but that are generally still viewed as having a single processor. Examples of low-level parallelism include

- *Instruction Pipelining:* Each instruction execution is divided into a sequence of stages, so that multiple instructions can be executed in parallel, each one in a different stage of execution.
- *Multiple Processor Functional Units:* Replication of ALU units enables a super-scalar approach, with multiple instructions executing in parallel, all at the same stage of execution.
- *Separate Specialized Processors:* The most common example is the use of I/O processors, which free the CPU from detailed I/O control responsibilities.

A taxonomy that highlights parallel processor systems first introduced by Flynn [FLYN72] is still the most common way of categorizing such systems. Flynn proposed the following categories of computer systems:

- *Single Instruction Single Data (SISD) stream:* A single processor interprets a single instruction stream to operate on data stored in a single memory. Some parallelism can be achieved using any of the techniques listed above.
- *Single Instruction Multiple Data (SIMD) stream:* A single machine instruction controls the simultaneous execution of a number of processing elements on a lockstep basis. Each processing element has an associated data memory, so that each instruction is executed on a different set of data by the different processors. Vector and array processors fall into this category.
- *Multiple Instruction Single Data (MISD) stream:* A sequence of data is transmitted to a set of processors, each of which executes a different instruction sequence. This structure has never been implemented.
- *Multiple Instruction Multiple Data (MIMD) stream:* A set of processors simultaneously execute different instruction sequences on different data sets.

With the MIMD organization, the processors are general-purpose, because they must be able to process all the instructions necessary to perform the appropriate data transformation. MIMDs can be further subdivided by the means in which the processors communicate (Figure 16.15). If the processors share a common memory, then each processor accesses programs and data stored in the shared memory, and processors communicate with each other via that memory; such a system is known as a **multiprocessor.** Multiprocessors were covered in Sections 16.1 and 16.2.

If the processors each have a dedicated memory, then each processing element is a self-contained computer. Communication among the computers is either via fixed paths or via some message-switching mechanism. Such a system is known as a **multicomputer.**

Practical parallel processing systems include SIMD, multiprocessors, and multicomputers. Figure 16.16 illustrates the general organization. First, as a baseline, Figure 16.16a illustrates the general organization of an SISD. There is some sort of control unit that provides an instruction stream (IS) to a processing unit. The processing unit operates on a single data stream (DS) from a memory unit. With an SIMD, there is still a single control unit, now feeding a single instruction stream to

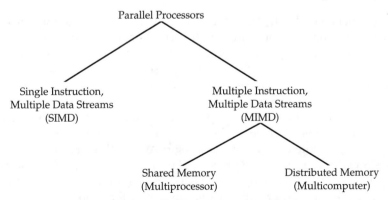

**FIGURE 16.15. Practical Parallel Processor Approaches**

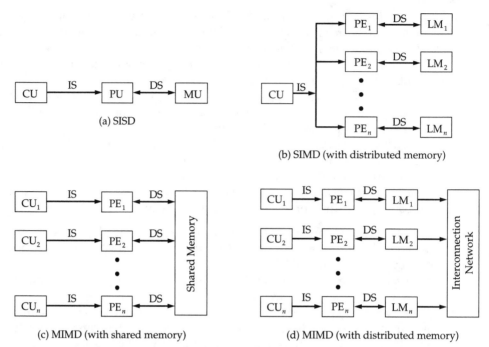

**FIGURE 16.16. Alternative Computer Organizations**

multiple processing elements. Each processing element may have its own dedicated memory (illustrated in Figure 16.16b), or there may be a shared memory. Finally, with the MIMD, there are multiple control units, each feeding a separate instruction stream to its own processing element. The MIMD may be a shared-memory multiprocessor (Figure 16.16c) or a distributed-memory multicomputer (Figure 16.16d).

## Multiprocessors

In a shared-memory MIMD, all of the processors have access to the same pool of main memory, usually via a shared high-speed bus. Communication among the processes is easy in principle. Each processor can leave a message or data results in a particular location and then tell another processor the address at which to find the data. This is typical of multiprocessing, as distinct from multiprocessors. With multiprocessing, as we have seen in Chapter 7, a computer system is running one or more applications that are broken up into a number of cooperating sequential processes. Such a scheme can be implemented on a single-processor system, but it is also easily implemented on a multiprocessor: At any time, each of the multiple processes is executing a separate process. The communication among processes is done by messages and flags that can be passed among processors via main memory.

In practice, performance requirements complicate the requirement for communication among processors. When you have many fast processors competing for access to the same memory across the same bus, contention can seriously degrade overall performance. The solution, as we have seen, is to add a local cache to each processor. This solution brings in the new problem of cache coherency, and a protocol such as MESI is needed to address this. The coordination among processors required to execute the MESI protocol in turn creates its own bottleneck in the shared bus. The result is that typical multiprocessor systems are limited to a few tens of processors. A shared-memory multiprocessor with thousands of processors does not appear to be practical.

## Multicomputers

In a distributed-memory MIMD, each processor has its own private memory space, which is not visible to other processors. Accordingly, results and coordination information must be passed between nodes over an interconnection network, usually in the form of formatted messages.

One of the principal motivations for the development of multicomputer organizations is to overcome the scale limitations of multiprocessors. The goal is to develop a *scalable* organization that can accommodate a wide range of numbers of processors.

Because the processors in a multicomputer must communicate by the exchange of messages, a key element in the design is the interconnection network, which must be made to operate as efficiently as possible. In general, there is a trade-off between the longest path between nodes and the number of physical connections required at each node. Various interconnection topologies have been explored to support scalability and to provide efficient performance. Figure 16.17 illustrates the following topologies:

- *Ring:* If communication is bidirectional along the ring, then the maximum distance between any two nodes in an $n$-node ring is $n/2$. Typically, fixed-size message packets are used that include the address of the intended destination. This topology is appropriate for a relatively small number of processors with minimal data communication.
- *Mesh:* The simplest form of mesh is a two-dimensional array in which each node is connected to four neighbors. The communications "diameter" for a simple mesh is $2(n-1)$. Wraparound connections at the edges reduce the diameter to $2(n/2)$. The mesh organization is well suited to dealing with matrix-oriented algorithms.
- *Tree:* Tree-topology networks have been investigated to support divide-and-conquer algorithms, such as searching and sorting. The figure illustrates a simple binary tree.
- *Hypercube:* A hypercube topology uses $N = 2^n$ processors arranged in an $n$-dimensional cube, where each node has $n = \log_2 N$ bidirectional links to adjacent nodes. The communication diameter of such a hypercube is $n$.

For a hardwired topology, the hypercube topology is perhaps the most attractive. As Table 16.3 indicates, the hypercube scales well: the diameter of the system rises slowly with the number of nodes, compared with the mesh.

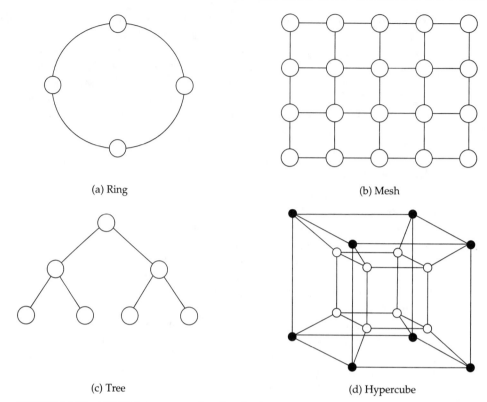

(a) Ring                                                  (b) Mesh

(c) Tree                                                  (d) Hypercube

**FIGURE 16.17.  MIMD Interconnection Topologies**

More recently, there has been increased interest in moving away from fixed topologies and toward user-selected topology controlled by a routing network. Instead of connecting all the processors directly together, they are connected to a fast-routing network that uses switches to make and break virtual connections, in much the same way as a packet-switching network. If the switches are designed to cause the minimum delay to messages, then communication latency will scale slowly as you add more nodes to the system. Another attractive feature is that each processor requires only a single bidirectional attachment to the switching network.

**TABLE 16.3    Worst-Case Communication**

| Number of Nodes | Mesh | Hypercube |
|---|---|---|
| 16 | 6 hops | 4 hops |
| 256 | 30 hops | 8 hops |
| 1,024 | 62 hops | 10 hops |
| 2,048 | 126 hops | 11 hops |
| 16,384 | 254 hops | 16 hops |

## 16.5

### RECOMMENDED READING

[CATA94] surveys the principles of multiprocessors and examines SPARC-based multiprocessors in detail. Multiprocessors are also covered in some detail in [MOLD93], [MORS94], and [STON93].

An excellent survey of the issues relating to cache coherence in multiprocessors is [LILJ93]. [TOMA93] contains reprints of many of the key papers on the subject.

Good discussions of vector computation can be found in [STON93] and [HWAN93].

CATA94  Catanzaro, B. *Multiprocessor System Architectures.* Mountain View, CA: Sunsoft Press, 1994.

HWAN93  Hwang, K. *Advanced Computer Architecture.* New York: McGraw-Hill, 1993.

LILJ93  Lilja, D. "Cache Coherence in Large-Scale Shared-Memory Multiprocessors: Issues and Comparisons." *ACM Computing Surveys,* September 1993.

MOLD93  Moldovan, D. *Parallel Processing: From Applications to Systems.* San Mateo, CA: Morgan Kaufmann, 1993.

MORS94  Morse, H. *Practical Parallel Computing.* Boston, MA: AP Professional, 1994.

STON93  Stone, H. *High-Performance Computer Architecture.* Reading, MA: Addison-Wesley, 1993.

TOMA93  Tomasevic, M., and Milutinovic, V. *The Cache Coherence Problem in Shared-Memory Multiprocessors: Hardware Solutions.* Los Alamitos, CA: IEEE Computer Society Press, 1993.

## 16.6

### PROBLEMS

16.1  In a multiprocessor IBM S/370 configuration, each CPU is assigned a separate 4K-byte block of absolute memory to hold its first 4K-byte block of real memory. Note that the prefixing mechanism does not prevent CPU X from writing into CPU Y's dedicated area. What other mechanism can be used to provide this protection?

16.2  Can you foresee any problem with the write-once cache approach on bus-based multiprocessors? If so, suggest a solution.

16.3  Produce a vectorized version of the following program:

```
      DO 20 I = 1, N
      B(I, 1) = 0
      DO 10 J = 1, M
      A(I) = A(I) + B(I, J) · C(I, J)
10 CONTINUE
      D(I) = E(I) + A(I)
20 CONTINUE
```

16.4   Consider the following method of sorting $N$ items:

Procedure QUICKSORT (LOW, HIGH, A);
Array A[1:N], integer LOW, HIGH;
begin integer PIVOTPOINT;
   comment QUICKSORT sorts the portion of A from A[LOW] to A[HIGH];
   call PARTITION (LOW, HIGH, A, PIVOTPOINT);
   comment PARTITION is a procedure that moves around the elements in
       A between A[LOW] and A[HIGH] so that for all I in the range
       LOW $\leq$ I < PIVOTPOINT, A[I] $\leq$ A[PIVOTPOINT], and for all J in
       the range PIVOTPOINT < J $\leq$ HIGH, A[PIVOTPOINT] $\leq$ A[J].
       PIVOTPOINT is an index selected by PARTITION and returned by
       PIVOTPOINT;
   if PIVOTPOINT > LOW + 1 then QUICKSORT (LOW, PIVOTPOINT – 1,
       A);
   if PIVOTPOINT < HIGH – 1 then QUICKSORT (PIVOTPOINT +1,
       HIGH, A);
end of QUICKSORT;

(a)  Give a brief explanation of QUICKSORT to indicate that you understand that it sorts A when called initially with the statement QUICKSORT (1, N, A).

(b)  Revise QUICKSORT by inserting FORK statements as necessary and corresponding JOIN statements. Indicate precisely what information has to be carried forth for each new branch of the fork from global data, and what information has to be handled in a private fashion for the fork.

(c)  Assume that the overhead of a FORK and a JOIN is about the same as the time it takes to QUICKSORT an array of length 7 on a serial computer. Estimate the relative running times for a sort of 1023 items for a serial computer, and for multiprocessors of 2, 3, 4, 8, and 16 processors. (Assume that, by some miracle, PARTITION always manages to find a PIVOTPOINT exactly in the middle of the range.) The time for PIVOTPOINT is proportional to HIGH – LOW.

(d)  Describe how to modify QUICKSORT so that it can interrogate to determine how many processors are in the total system and how many are idle via system calls, and then use this information to optimize its performance.

16.5   The inner loop of a matrix computation uses the statement

for J: = K step 1 until N do

A[I, J]: = A[I, J] $\times$ Q – A[K, J];

Assume that this statement is parceled out among the processors of a multiprocessor system so that each processor executes the statement for a different value of J. Assume also that the multiprocessor system has a central shared memory. When two different processors access the same memory module simultaneously, the module responds immediately to one processor, and the second processor has to wait one memory cycle, at which time it repeats its request.

**(a)** Assume that the array is stored by rows across the memories, so that at ascending addresses are elements with index pairs, $(1, 1)$, $(1, 2)$, . . ., $(1, N)$, $(2, 1)$, . . ., $(2, N)$, . . ., $(N, N)$, as ascending addresses cycle across the memories.

Diagram the cycle-by-cycle execution of the first five computation parcels under the assumption that all are initiated simultaneously, and that the number of memories is $N$.

**(b)** Now assume that the array is stored so that each row of A lies in a distinct memory module. Repeat part (a).

**(c)** Comment on the problem of data contention in this type of shared memory system, based on your observations.

# APPENDIX A

# Digital Logic

The operation of the digital computer is based on the storage and processing of binary data. Throughout this book, we have assumed the existence of storage elements that can exist in one of two stable states and of circuits than can operate on binary data under the control of control signals to implement the various computer functions. In this appendix, we suggest how these storage elements and circuits can be implemented in digital logic, specifically with combinational and sequential circuits. The appendix begins with a brief review of Boolean algebra, which is the mathematical foundation of digital logic. Next, the concept of a gate is introduced. Finally, combinational and sequential circuits, which are constructed from gates, are described.

## A.1

### BOOLEAN ALGEBRA

The digital circuitry in digital computers and other digital systems is designed, and its behavior is analyzed, with the use of a mathematical discipline known as *Boolean algebra*. The name is in honor of an English mathematician George Boole, who proposed the basic principles of this algebra in 1854 in his treatise, *An Investigation of the Laws of Thought on Which to Found the Mathematical Theories of Logic and Probabilities.* In 1938, Claude Shannon, a research assistant in the Electrical Engineering Department at M.I.T., suggested that Boolean algebra could be used to solve problems in relay-switching circuit design [SHAN38]. Shannon's techniques were subsequently used in the analysis and design of electronic digital circuits. Boolean algebra turns out to be a convenient tool in two areas:

- *Analysis:* It is an economical way of describing the function of digital circuitry.
- *Design:* Given a desired function, Boolean algebra can be applied to develop a simplified implementation of that function.

As with any algebra, Boolean algebra makes use of variables and operations. In this case, the variables and operations are logical variables and operations. Thus, a variable may take on the value 1 (TRUE) or 0 (FALSE). The basic logical operations are AND, OR, and NOT, which are symbolically represented by dot, plus sign, and overbar:

A AND B = A · B
A OR B = A + B
NOT A = $\overline{A}$

The operation AND yields true (binary value 1) if and only if both of its operands are true. The operation OR yields true if either or both of its operands are true. The unary operation NOT inverts the value of its operand. For example, consider the equation

D = A + ($\overline{B}$ · C)

D is equal to 1 if A is 1 or if both B = 0 and C = 1. Otherwise D is equal to 0.

Several points concerning the notation are needed. In the absence of parentheses, the AND operation takes precedence over the OR operation. Also, when no ambiguity will occur, the AND operation is represented by simple concatenation instead of the dot operator. Thus,

A + B · C = A + (B · C) = A + BC

all mean: Take the AND of B and C; then take the OR of the result and A.

Table A.1 defines the basic logical operations in a form known as a *truth table*, which simply lists the value of an operation for every possible combination of values of operands. The table also lists three other useful operators: XOR, NAND, and NOR. The exclusive-or (XOR) of two logical operands is 1 if and only if exactly one of the operands has the value 1. The NAND function is the complement (NOT) of the AND function, and the NOR is the complement of OR:

A NAND B = NOT(A AND B) = $\overline{AB}$
A NOR B = NOT(A OR B) = $\overline{A + B}$

As we shall see, these three new operations can be useful in implementing certain digital circuits.

Table A.2 summarizes key identities of Boolean algebra. The equations have been arranged in two columns to show the complementary, or dual, nature of the AND and OR operations. There are two classes of identities: basic rules (or *postulates*), which are stated without proof, and other identities that can be derived from the basic postulates. The postulates define the way in which Boolean expressions

**TABLE A.1   Boolean Operators**

| P | Q | NOT P | P AND Q | P OR Q | P XOR Q | P NAND Q | P NOR Q |
|---|---|-------|---------|--------|---------|----------|---------|
| 0 | 0 | 1 | 0 | 0 | 0 | 1 | 1 |
| 0 | 1 | 1 | 0 | 1 | 1 | 1 | 0 |
| 1 | 0 | 0 | 0 | 1 | 1 | 1 | 0 |
| 1 | 1 | 0 | 1 | 1 | 0 | 0 | 0 |

**TABLE A.2    Basic Identities of Boolean Algebra**

| | *Basic Postulates* | |
|---|---|---|
| $A \cdot B = B \cdot A$ | $A + B = B + A$ | Commutative Laws |
| $A \cdot (B + C) = (A \cdot B) + (A \cdot C)$ | $A + (B \cdot C) = (A + B) \cdot (A + C)$ | Distributive Laws |
| $1 \cdot \overline{A} = A$ | $0 + A = A$ | Identity Elements |
| $A \cdot \overline{A} = 0$ | $A + \overline{A} = 1$ | Inverse Elements |
| | *Other Identities* | |
| $0 \cdot A = 0$ | $1 + A = 1$ | |
| $A \cdot A = A$ | $A + A = A$ | |
| $A \cdot (B \cdot C) = (A \cdot B) \cdot C$ | $A + (B + C) = (A + B) + C$ | Associative Laws |
| $\overline{A \cdot B} = \overline{A} + \overline{B}$ | $\overline{A + B} = \overline{A} \cdot \overline{B}$ | DeMorgan's Theorem |

are interpreted. One of the two distributive laws is worth-noting because it differs from what we would find in ordinary algebra:

$$A + (B \cdot C) = (A + B) \cdot (A + C)$$

The two bottommost expressions are referred to as DeMorgan's theorem. We can restate them as follows:

$$A \text{ NOR } B = \overline{A} \text{ AND } \overline{B}$$
$$A \text{ NAND } B = \overline{A} \text{ OR } \overline{B}$$

The reader is invited to verify the expressions in Table A.2 by substituting actual values (1s and 0s) for the variables A, B, and C.

## A.2

## GATES

The fundamental building block of all digital logic circuits is the gate. Logical functions are implemented by the interconnection of gates.

A gate is an electronic circuit that produces an output signal that is a simple Boolean operation on its input signals. The basic gates used in digital logic are AND, OR, NOT, NAND, and NOR. Figure A.1 depicts these five gates. Each gate is defined in three ways: graphic symbol, algebraic notation, and truth table. The symbology used here and throughout the appendix is the IEEE standard, IEEE Std 91 [IEEE84]. Note that the inversion (NOT) operation is indicated by a circle.

Each gate has one or two inputs and one output. When the values at the input are changed, the correct output signal appears almost instantaneously, delayed only by the propagation time of signals through the gate (known as the *gate delay*). The significance of this is discussed in Section A.3.

In addition to the gates depicted in Figure A.1, gates with 3, 4, or more inputs can be used. Thus, $X + Y + Z$ can be implemented with a single OR gate with three inputs.

Typically, not all gate types are used in implementation. Design and fabrication are simpler if only one or two types of gates are used. Thus, it is important to identify *functionally complete* sets of gates. This means that any Boolean function can be implemented using only the gates in the set. The following are functionally complete sets:

| Name | Graphic Symbol | Algebraic Function | Truth Table |
|------|----------------|--------------------|-------------|
| AND | 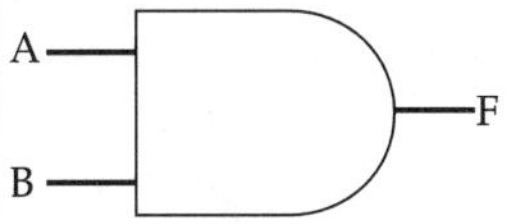 A ─┐⟩─ F  B ─┘ | F = A • B  or  F = AB | A B \| F<br>0 0 \| 0<br>0 1 \| 0<br>1 0 \| 0<br>1 1 \| 1 |
| OR | 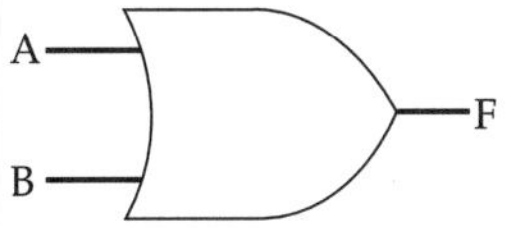 A ─┐⟩─ F  B ─┘ | F = A + B | A B \| F<br>0 0 \| 0<br>0 1 \| 1<br>1 0 \| 1<br>1 1 \| 1 |
| NOT | 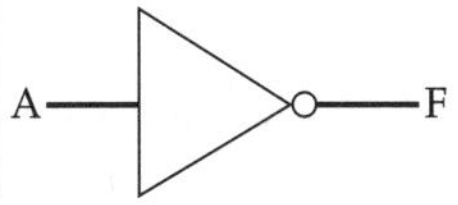 A ──▷o── F | F = $\overline{A}$  or  F = A′ | A \| F<br>0 \| 1<br>1 \| 0 |
| NAND | 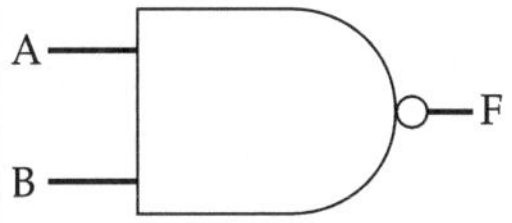 A ─┐⟩o─ F  B ─┘ | F = ($\overline{AB}$) | A B \| F<br>0 0 \| 1<br>0 1 \| 1<br>1 0 \| 1<br>1 1 \| 0 |
| NOR | 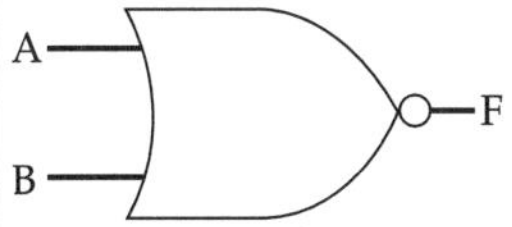 A ─┐⟩o─ F  B ─┘ | F = ($\overline{A + B}$) | A B \| F<br>0 0 \| 1<br>0 1 \| 0<br>1 0 \| 0<br>1 1 \| 0 |

**FIGURE A.1. Basic logic gates**

- AND, OR, NOT
- AND, NOT
- OR, NOT
- NAND
- NOR

It should be clear that AND, OR, and NOT gates constitute a functionally complete set, since they represent the three operations of Boolean algebra. For the AND and NOT gates to form a functionally complete set, there must be a way to synthesize the OR operation from the AND and NOT operations. This can be done by applying DeMorgan's theorem:

$A + B = \overline{\overline{A} \cdot \overline{B}}$

A OR B = NOT((NOT A) AND (NOT B))

Similarly, the OR and NOT operations are functionally complete because they can be used to synthesize the AND operation.

Figure A.2 shows how the AND, OR, and NOT functions can be implemented solely with NAND gates, and Figure A.3 shows the same thing for NOR gates. For this reason, digital circuits can be, and frequently are, implemented solely with NAND gates or solely with NOR gates.

With gates, we have reached the most primitive level of computer science and engineering. An examination of the transistor combinations used to construct gates departs from that realm and enters the realm of electrical engineering. For the interested reader, [CLAR80] is an entertaining yet informative description of these matters for the computer scientist. For our purposes, however, we are content to describe how gates can be used as building blocks to implement the essential logical circuits of a digital computer.

## COMBINATIONAL CIRCUITS

A combinational circuit is an interconnected set of gates whose output at any time is a function only of the input at that time. As with a single gate, the appearance of the input is followed almost immediately by the appearance of the output, with only gate delays.

In general terms, a combinational circuit consists of $n$ binary inputs and $m$ binary outputs. As with a gate, a combinational circuit can be defined in three ways:

- *Truth Table:* For each of the $2^n$ possible combinations of input signals, the binary value of each of the $m$ output signals is listed.
- *Graphical Symbols:* The interconnected layout of gates is depicted.

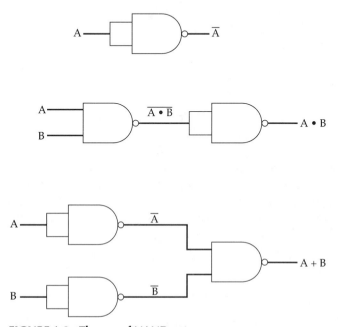

**FIGURE A.2. The use of NAND gates**

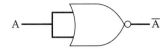

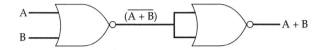

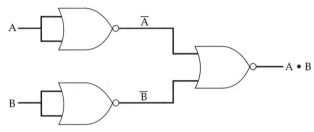

**FIGURE A.3.  The use of NOR gates**

- *Boolean Equations:* Each output signal is expressed as a Boolean function of its input signals.

## Implementation of Boolean Functions

Any Boolean function can be implemented in electronic form as a network of gates. For any given function, there are a number of alternative realizations. Consider the Boolean function represented by the truth table in Table A.3. We can express this function by simply itemizing the combinations of values of A, B, and C that cause F to be 1:

$$F = \overline{A}B\overline{C} + \overline{A}BC + AB\overline{C} \tag{A-1}$$

**TABLE A.3   A Boolean Function of Three Variables**

| A | B | C | F |
|---|---|---|---|
| 0 | 0 | 0 | 0 |
| 0 | 0 | 1 | 0 |
| 0 | 1 | 0 | 1 |
| 0 | 1 | 1 | 1 |
| 1 | 0 | 0 | 0 |
| 1 | 0 | 1 | 0 |
| 1 | 1 | 0 | 1 |
| 1 | 1 | 1 | 0 |

There are three combinations of input values that cause F to be 1, and if any one of these combinations occurs, the result is 1. This form of expression, for self-evident reasons, is known as the *sum of products* (SOP) form. Figure A.4 shows a straightforward implementation with AND, OR, and NOT gates.

Another form can also be derived from the truth table. The SOP form expresses that the output is 1 if any of the input combinations that produce 1 is true. We can also say that the output is 1 if none of the input combinations that produce 0 is true. Thus:

$$F = \overline{(\overline{A}\,\overline{B}\overline{C})} \cdot \overline{(\overline{A}\,\overline{B}C)} \cdot \overline{(A\overline{B}\overline{C})} \cdot \overline{(AB\overline{C})} \cdot \overline{(ABC)}$$

This can be rewritten using a generalization of deMorgan's theorem:

$$\overline{(X \cdot Y \cdot Z)} = \overline{X} + \overline{Y} + \overline{Z}$$

Thus,

$$
\begin{aligned}
F &= (\overline{\overline{A}} + \overline{\overline{B}} + \overline{\overline{C}}) \cdot (\overline{\overline{A}} + \overline{\overline{B}} + \overline{C}) \cdot (\overline{A} + \overline{\overline{B}} + \overline{\overline{C}}) \\
  &\quad \cdot (\overline{A} + \overline{\overline{B}} + \overline{C}) \cdot (\overline{A} + \overline{B} + \overline{C}) \\
  &= (A + B + C) \cdot (A + B + \overline{C}) \cdot (\overline{A} + B + C) \\
  &\quad \cdot (\overline{A} + B + \overline{C}) \cdot (\overline{A} + \overline{B} + \overline{C})
\end{aligned}
$$

(A-2)

This is in the *product of sums* (POS) form, which is illustrated in Figure A.5. For clarity, NOT gates are not shown. Rather, it is assumed that each input signal and its complement are available. This simplifies the logic diagram and makes the inputs to the gates more readily apparent.

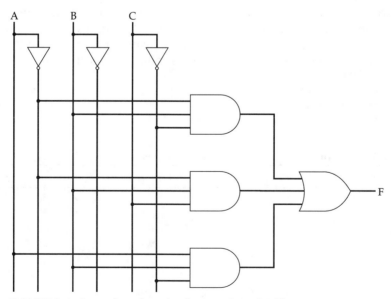

**FIGURE A.4. Sum-of-products implementation of Table A.3**

Thus, a Boolean function can be realized in either SOP or POS form. At this point, it would seem that the choice would depend on whether the truth table contains more 1s or 0s for the output function: The SOP has one term for each 1, and the POS has one term for each 0. However, there are other considerations:

- It is generally possible to derive a simpler Boolean expression from the truth table than either SOP or POS.
- It may be preferable to implement the function with a single gate type (NAND or NOR).

The significance of the first point is that, with a simpler Boolean expression, fewer gates will be needed to implement the function. Three methods that can be used to achieve simplification are

- Algebraic Simplification
- Karnaugh Maps
- Quine–McKluskey Tables

## *Algebraic Simplification*

Algebraic simplification involves the application of the identities of Table A.2 to reduce the Boolean expression to one with fewer elements. For example, consider

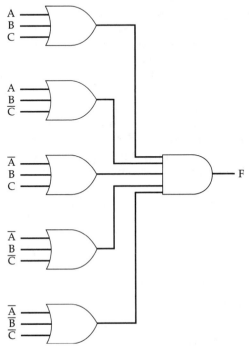

**FIGURE A.5. Product-of-sums implementation of Table A.3**

again Equation A–1. Some thought should convince the reader that an equivalent expression is

$$F = \overline{A}B + B\overline{C} \tag{A-3}$$

Or, even simpler,

$$F = B(\overline{A} + \overline{C})$$

This expression can be implemented as shown in Figure A.6. The simplification of Equation A–1 was done essentially by observation. For more complex expression, some more systematic approach is needed.

### Karnaugh Maps

For purposes of simplification, the Karnaugh map is a convenient way of representing a Boolean function of a small number (up to 4 to 6) of variables. The map is an array of $2^n$ squares, representing the possible combinations of values of $n$ binary variables. Figure A.7a shows the map of four squares for a function of two variables. It is convenient for later purposes to list the combinations in the order 00, 01, 11, 10. Since the squares corresponding to the combinations are to be used for recording information, the combinations are customarily written above the squares. In the case of three variables, the representation is an arrangement of 8 squares (Figure A.7b), with the values for one of the variables to the left and for the other two variables above the squares. For four variables, 16 squares are needed, with the arrangement indicated in Figure A.7c.

The map can be used to represent any Boolean function in the following way. Each square corresponds to a unique product in the sum-of-products form, with a 1 value corresponding to the variable and a 0 value corresponding to the NOT of that variable. Thus, the product $A\overline{B}$ corresponds to the fourth square in Figure A.7a. For each such product in the function, 1 is placed in the corresponding square. Thus, for the two-variable example, the map corresponds to $A\overline{B} + \overline{A}B$. Given the truth table of a Boolean function, it is an easy matter to construct the map: for each combination of values of variables that produce a result of 1 in the truth table, fill in the corresponding square of the map with 1. Figure A.7b shows the result for the truth table of Table A.3. To convert from a Boolean expression to a map, it is first necessary to put the expression into what is referred to as *canoni-*

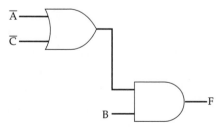

**FIGURE A.6. Simplified implementation of Table A.3**

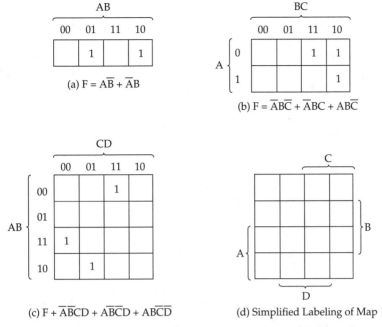

(a) $F = A\overline{B} + \overline{A}B$

(b) $F = \overline{A}B\overline{C} + \overline{A}BC + AB\overline{C}$

(c) $F + \overline{A}\overline{B}CD + A\overline{B}\overline{C}D + AB\overline{C}\overline{D}$

(d) Simplified Labeling of Map

**FIGURE A.7. The use of Karnaugh maps to represent Boolean functions**

*cal* form: each term in the expression must contain each variable. So, for example, if we have Equation A–3, we must first expand it into the full form of Equation A–1 and then convert this to a map.

The labeling used in Figure A.7d emphasizes the relationship between variables and the rows and columns of the map. Here the two rows embraced by the symbol A are those in which the variable A has the value 1; the rows not embraced by the symbol A are those in which A is 0. Similarly for B, C, and D.

Once the map of a function is created, we can often write a simple algebraic expression for it by noting the arrangement of the 1s on the map. The principle is as follows. Any two squares that are adjacent differ in only one of the variables. If two adjacent squares both have an entry of one, then the corresponding product terms differ in only one variable. In such a case, the two terms can be merged by eliminating that variable. For example, in Figure A.8a, the two adjacent squares correspond to the two terms $\overline{A}B\overline{C}D$ and $\overline{A}BCD$. Thus, the function expressed is

$$\overline{A}B\overline{C}D + \overline{A}BCD = \overline{A}BD$$

This process can be extended in several ways. First, the concept of adjacency can be extended to include wrapping around the edge of the map. Thus, the top square of a column is adjacent to the bottom square, and the leftmost square of a row is adjacent to the rightmost square. These conditions are illustrated in Figures A.8b and c. Second, we can group not just 2 squares but $2^n$ adjacent squares, that is, 4, 8, etc. The next three examples in Figure A.8 show groupings of 4 squares.

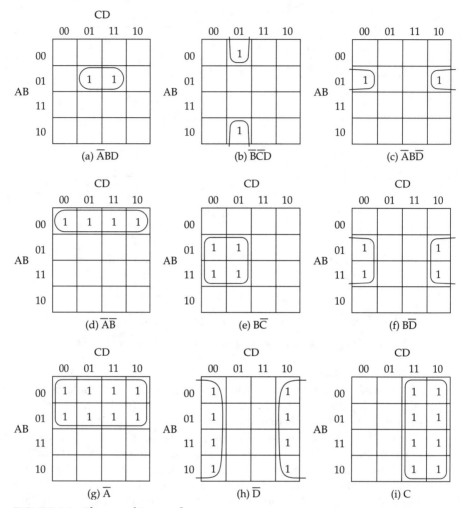

**FIGURE A.8.  The use of Karnaugh maps**

Note that in this case, two of the variables can be eliminated. The last three examples show groupings of 8 squares, which allow three variables to be eliminated.

In attempting to simplify, first look for the largest grouping possible (eight in a four-variable map). If any squares with a 1 remain uncircled, then look for successively smaller groupings. When you are circling groups, you are allowed to use the same 1 more than once. Figure A.9a, based on Table A.3, illustrates this. If any isolated 1s remain after the groupings, then each of these is circled as a group of 1s. Finally, before going from the map to a simplified Boolean expression, any group of 1s that is completely overlapped by other groups can be eliminated. This is shown in Figure A.9b. In this case, the horizontal group is redundant and may be ignored in creating the Boolean expression.

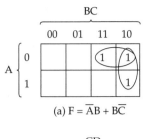

(a) $F = \overline{A}B + B\overline{C}$

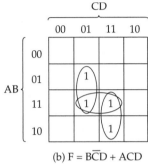

(b) $F = B\overline{C}D + ACD$

**FIGURE A.9.  Overlapping groups**

One additional feature of Karnaugh maps needs to be mentioned. In some cases, certain combinations of values of variables never occur, and therefore the corresponding output never occurs. These are referred to as "don't care" conditions. For each such condition, the letter "d" is entered into the corresponding square of the map. In doing the grouping and simplification, each "d" can be treated as a 1 or 0, whichever leads to the simplest expression.

An example, presented in [HAYE88], illustrates the points we have been discussing. We would like to develop the Boolean expressions for a circuit that adds 1 to a packed decimal digit. Recall from Section 9.2 that with packed decimal, each decimal digit is represented by a 4-bit code, in the obvious way. Thus, 0 = 0000, 1 = 0001, . . ., 8 = 1000, and 9 = 1001. The remaining 4-bit values, from 1010 to 1111, are not used. This code is also referred to as Binary Coded Decimal (BCD).

Table A.4 shows the truth table for producing a 4-bit result that is one more than a 4-bit BCD input. The addition is modulo 10. Thus, 9 + 1 = 0. Also, note that six of the input codes produce "don't care" results, since those are not valid BCD inputs. Figure A.10 shows the resulting Karnaugh maps for each of the output variables. The d squares are used to achieve the best possible groupings.

## The Quine–McKluskey Method

For more than four variables, the Karnaugh map method becomes increasingly cumbersome. With five variables, two $16 \times 16$ maps are needed, with one map considered to be on top of the other in three dimensions to achieve adjacency. Six variables requires the use of four $16 \times 16$ tables in four dimensions! An alternative

**TABLE A.4    Truth Table for the One-Digit Packed Decimal Incrementer**

| Number | Input A | B | C | D | Number | Output W | X | Y | Z |
|--------|---------|---|---|---|--------|----------|---|---|---|
| 0 | 0 | 0 | 0 | 0 | 1 | 0 | 0 | 0 | 1 |
| 1 | 0 | 0 | 0 | 1 | 2 | 0 | 0 | 1 | 0 |
| 2 | 0 | 0 | 1 | 0 | 3 | 0 | 0 | 1 | 1 |
| 3 | 0 | 0 | 1 | 1 | 4 | 0 | 1 | 0 | 0 |
| 4 | 0 | 1 | 0 | 0 | 5 | 0 | 1 | 0 | 1 |
| 5 | 0 | 1 | 0 | 1 | 6 | 0 | 1 | 1 | 0 |
| 6 | 0 | 1 | 1 | 0 | 7 | 0 | 1 | 1 | 1 |
| 7 | 0 | 1 | 1 | 1 | 8 | 1 | 0 | 0 | 0 |
| 8 | 1 | 0 | 0 | 0 | 9 | 1 | 0 | 0 | 1 |
| 9 | 1 | 0 | 0 | 1 | 0 | 0 | 0 | 0 | 0 |
| Don't care conditions | 1 | 0 | 1 | 0 | | d | d | d | d |
| | 1 | 0 | 1 | 1 | | d | d | d | d |
| | 1 | 1 | 0 | 0 | | d | d | d | d |
| | 1 | 1 | 0 | 1 | | d | d | d | d |
| | 1 | 1 | 1 | 0 | | d | d | d | d |
| | 1 | 1 | 1 | 1 | | d | d | d | d |

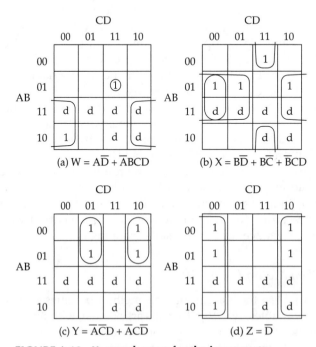

(a) $W = A\overline{D} + \overline{A}BCD$

(b) $X = B\overline{D} + B\overline{C} + \overline{B}CD$

(c) $Y = \overline{A}C\overline{D} + \overline{A}\overline{C}D$

(d) $Z = \overline{D}$

**FIGURE A.10.  Karnaugh maps for the incrementer**

approach is a tabular technique, referred to as the Quine–McKluskey method. The method is suitable for programming on a computer to give an automatic tool for producing minimized Boolean expressions.

The method is best explained by means of an example. Consider the following expression:

$$ABCD + AB\overline{C}D + AB\overline{C}\,\overline{D} + A\overline{B}CD + \overline{A}BCD + \overline{A}B\overline{C}D + \overline{A}B\overline{C}\,\overline{D} + \overline{A}\,\overline{B}\,\overline{C}D$$

Let us assume that this expression was derived from a truth table. We would like to produce a minimal expression suitable for implementation with gates.

The first step is to construct a table in which each row corresponds to one of the product terms of the expression. The terms are grouped according to the number of complemented variables. That is, we start with the term with no complements, if it exists, then all terms with one complement, and so on. Table A.5 shows the list for our example expression, with horizontal lines used to indicate the grouping. For clarity, each term is represented by a 1 for each uncomplemented variable and a 0 for each complemented variable. Thus, we group terms according to the number of 1s they contain. The index column is simply the decimal equivalent and is useful in what follows.

The next step is to find all pairs of terms that differ in only one variable, that is, all pairs of terms that are the same except that one variable is 0 in one of the terms and 1 in the other. Because of the way in which we have grouped the terms, we can do this by starting with the first group and comparing each term of the first group with every term of the second group. Then, compare each term of the second group with all of the terms of the third group, and so on. Whenever a match is found, place a check next to each term, combine the pair by eliminating the variable that differs in the two terms, and add that to a new list. Thus, for example, the terms $\overline{A}BC\overline{D}$ and $\overline{A}BCD$ are combined to produce $\overline{A}BC$. This process continues until the entire original table has been examined. The result is a new table with the following entries:

$\overline{A}\,\overline{C}D$

---

$AB\overline{C}$
$B\overline{C}D$ ✓
$\overline{A}BC$
$\overline{A}BD$ ✓

---

$ABD$ ✓
$ACD$
$BCD$ ✓

The new table is organized into groups, as indicated above, in the same fashion as the first table. The second table is then processed in the same manner as the first. That is, terms that differ in only one variable are checked and a new term produced for a third table. In this example, the third table that is produced contains only one term:

$BD$

**TABLE A.5   First Stage of Quine–McKluskey Method for F = ABCD + AB$\overline{\text{C}}$D + AB$\overline{\text{C}}$$\overline{\text{D}}$ + A$\overline{\text{B}}$CD + $\overline{\text{A}}$BCD + $\overline{\text{A}}$B$\overline{\text{C}}$D + $\overline{\text{A}}$B$\overline{\text{C}}$D + $\overline{\text{A}}$$\overline{\text{B}}$$\overline{\text{C}}$D**

| Product Term | Index | A | B | C | D | |
|---|---|---|---|---|---|---|
| $\overline{\text{A}}$$\overline{\text{B}}$$\overline{\text{C}}$D | 1 | 0 | 0 | 0 | 1 | ✓ |
| $\overline{\text{A}}$B$\overline{\text{C}}$D | 5 | 0 | 1 | 0 | 1 | ✓ |
| $\overline{\text{A}}$BC$\overline{\text{D}}$ | 6 | 0 | 1 | 1 | 0 | ✓ |
| AB$\overline{\text{C}}$$\overline{\text{D}}$ | 12 | 1 | 1 | 0 | 0 | ✓ |
| $\overline{\text{A}}$BCD | 7 | 0 | 1 | 1 | 1 | ✓ |
| A$\overline{\text{B}}$CD | 11 | 1 | 0 | 1 | 1 | ✓ |
| AB$\overline{\text{C}}$D | 13 | 1 | 1 | 0 | 1 | ✓ |
| ABCD | 15 | 1 | 1 | 1 | 1 | ✓ |

In general, the process would proceed through successive tables until a table with no matches was produced. In this case, this has involved three tables.

Once the process described above is completed, we have eliminated many of the possible terms of the expression. Those terms that have not been eliminated are used to construct a matrix, as illustrated in Table A.6. Each row of the matrix corresponds to one of the terms that has not been eliminated (has no check) in any of the tables used so far. Each column corresponds to one of the terms in the original expression. An X is placed at each intersection of a row and a column such that the row element is "compatible" with the column element. That is, the variables present in the row element have the same value as the variables present in the column element. Next, circle each X that is alone in a column. Then, place a square around each X in any row in which there is a circled X. If every column now has either a squared or a circled X, then we are done, and those row elements whose X's have been marked constitute the minimal expression. Thus, in our example, the final expression is

AB$\overline{\text{C}}$ + ACD + $\overline{\text{A}}$BC + $\overline{\text{A}}$$\overline{\text{C}}$D

In cases in which some columns have neither a circle nor a square, additional processing is required. Essentially, we keep adding row elements until all columns are covered.

Let us summarize the Quine–McKluskey method to try to justify intuitively why it works. The first phase of the operation is reasonably straightforward. The process eliminates unneeded variables in product terms. Thus, the expression

ABC + AB$\overline{\text{C}}$ is equivalent to AB, since

ABC + AB$\overline{\text{C}}$ = AB(C + $\overline{\text{C}}$) = AB1 = AB

After the elimination of variables, we are left with an expression that is clearly equivalent to the original expression. However, there may be redundant terms in this expression, just as we found redundant groupings in Karnaugh maps. The matrix layout assures that each term in the original expression is covered and does so in a way that minimizes the number of terms in the final expression.

**TABLE A.6   Last Stage of Quine–McKluskey Method for F = ABCD + AB$\overline{C}$D + AB$\overline{C}\overline{D}$ + A$\overline{B}$CD + $\overline{A}$BCD + $\overline{A}$B$\overline{C}\overline{D}$ + $\overline{A}\overline{B}$CD + $\overline{A}\overline{B}\overline{C}$D**

| | *ABCD* | *AB$\overline{C}$D* | *AB$\overline{C}\overline{D}$* | *A$\overline{B}$CD* | *$\overline{A}$BCD* | *$\overline{A}$B$\overline{C}\overline{D}$* | *$\overline{A}\overline{B}$CD* | *$\overline{A}\overline{B}\overline{C}$D* |
|---|---|---|---|---|---|---|---|---|
| BD | X | X | | | X | | X / [X] | (X) |
| $\overline{A}$CD | | | | | | | [X] | |
| $\overline{A}$BC | | | | | [X] | (X) | | |
| AB$\overline{C}$ | | | [X] | (X) | | | | |
| ACD | [X] | | | (X) | | | | |

## NAND and NOR Implementations

Another consideration in the implementation of Boolean functions concerns the types of gates used. It is often felt desirable to implement a Boolean function solely with NAND gates or solely with NOR gates. Although this may not be the minimum-gate implementation, it has the advantage of regularity, which can simplify the manufacturing process. Consider again Equation A–3:

$$F = B(\overline{A} + \overline{C})$$

Since the complement of the complement of a value is just the original value,

$$F = B(\overline{A} + \overline{C})$$
$$= \overline{\overline{(\overline{A}B) + (B\overline{C})}}$$

Applying DeMorgan's theorem,

$$F = \overline{(\overline{A}B)} \cdot \overline{(B\overline{C})}$$

which has three NAND forms, as illustrated in Figure A.11.

## Multiplexers

The multiplexer connects multiple inputs to a single output. At any time, one of the inputs is selected to be passed to the output. A general block diagram representation is shown in Figure A.12. This represents a 4-to-1 multiplexer. There are

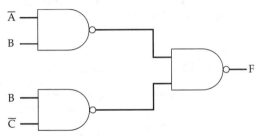

**FIGURE A.11.  NAND implementation of Table A–3**

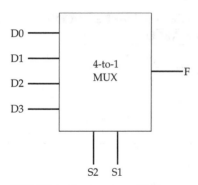

**FIGURE A.12. 4-to-1 multiplexer representation**

four input lines, labeled D0, D1, D2, and D3. One of these lines is selected to provide the output signal F. To select one of the four possible inputs, a 2-bit selection
code is needed, and this is implemented as two select lines labeled S1 and S2.

An example 4-to-1 multiplexer is defined by the truth table in Table A.7. This is
a simplified form of a truth table. Instead of showing all possible combinations of
input variables, it shows the output as data from line D0, D1, D2, or D3. Figure
A.13 shows an implementation using AND, OR, and NOT gates. S1 and S2 are
connected to the AND gates in such a way that, for any combination of S1 and S2,
three of the AND gates will output 0. The fourth AND gate will output the value
of the selected line, which is either 0 or 1. Thus, three of the inputs to the OR gate
are always 0, and the output of the OR gate will equal the value of the selected
input gate. Using this regular organization, it is easy to construct multiplexers of
size 8-to-1, 16-to-1, and so on.

Multiplexers are used in digital circuits to control signal and data routing. An
example is the loading of the program counter (PC). The value to be loaded into
the program counter may come from one of several different sources:

- A binary counter, if the PC is to be incremented for the next instruction.
- The instruction register, if a branch instruction using a direct address has just
  been executed.
- The output of the ALU, if the branch instruction specifies the address using a
  displacement mode.

These various inputs could be connected to the input lines of a multiplexer, with
the PC connected to the output line. The select lines determine which value is

**TABLE A.7   4-to-1 Multiplexer Truth Table**

| S2 | S1 | F |
|----|----|----|
| 0 | 0 | D0 |
| 0 | 1 | D1 |
| 1 | 0 | D2 |
| 1 | 1 | D3 |

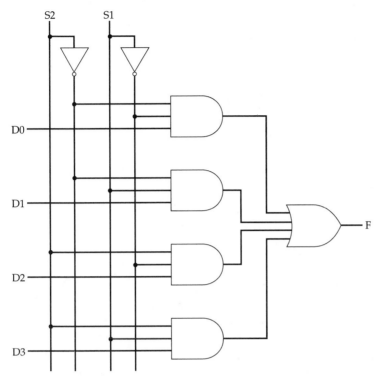

**FIGURE A.13. Multiplexer implementation**

loaded into the PC. Since the PC contains multiple bits, multiple multiplexers are used, one per bit. Figure A.14 illustrates this for 16-bit addresses.

## Decoders

A decoder is a combinational circuit with a number of output lines, only one of which is asserted at any time, dependent on the pattern of input lines. In general, a decoder has $n$ inputs and $2^n$ outputs. Figure A.15 shows a decoder with three inputs and eight outputs.

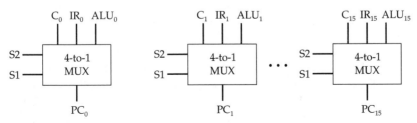

**FIGURE A.14. Multiplexer input to program counter**

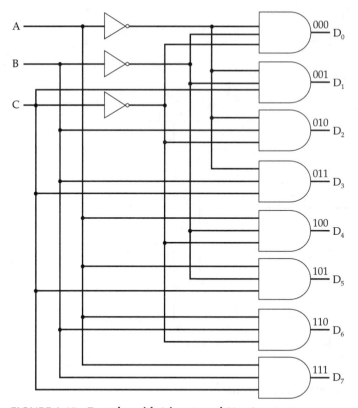

**FIGURE A.15.  Decoder with 3 inputs and $2^3 = 8$ outputs**

Decoders find many uses in digital computers. One example is address decoding. Suppose we wish to construct a 1K-byte memory using four $256 \times 8$–bit RAM chips. We want a single unified address space, which can be broken down as follows:

| Address | Chip |
|---------|------|
| 0000–00FF | 0 |
| 0100–01FF | 1 |
| 0200–02FF | 2 |
| 0300–03FF | 3 |

Each chip requires 8 address lines, and these are supplied by the lower-order 8 bits of the address. The higher-order 2 bits of the 10-bit address are used to select one of the four RAM chips. For this purpose, a 2-to-4 decoder is used whose output enables one of the four chips, as shown in Figure A.16.

With an additional input line, a decoder can be used as a demultiplexer. The demultiplexer performs the inverse function of a multiplexer; it connects a single input to one of several outputs. This is shown in Figure A.17. As before, $n$ inputs are decoded to produce a single one of $2^n$ outputs. All of the $2^n$ output lines are

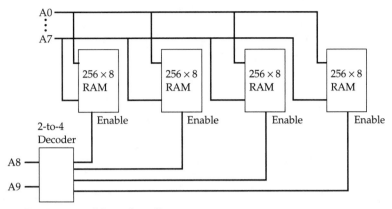

**FIGURE A.16. Address decoding**

ANDed with a data input line. Thus, the $n$ inputs act as an address to select a particular output line, and the value on the data input line (0 or 1) is routed to that output line.

The configuration in Figure A.17 can be viewed in another way. Change the label on the new line from *Data Input* to *Enable*. This allows for the control of the timing of the decoder. The decoded output appears only when the encoded input is present *and* the enable line has a value of 1.

## Programmable Logic Array (PLA)

Thus far, we have treated individual gates as building blocks, from which arbitrary functions can be realized. The designer could pursue a strategy of minimizing the number of gates to be used by manipulating the corresponding Boolean expressions.

As the level of integration provided by integrated circuits increases, other considerations apply. Early integrated circuits, using small-scale integration (SSI), provided from one to ten gates on a chip. Each gate is treated independently, in the building-block approach described so far. Figure A.18 is an example of some

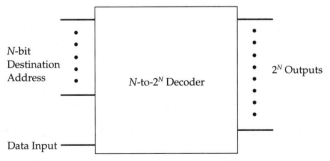

**FIGURE A.17. Implementation of a demultiplexer using a decoder**

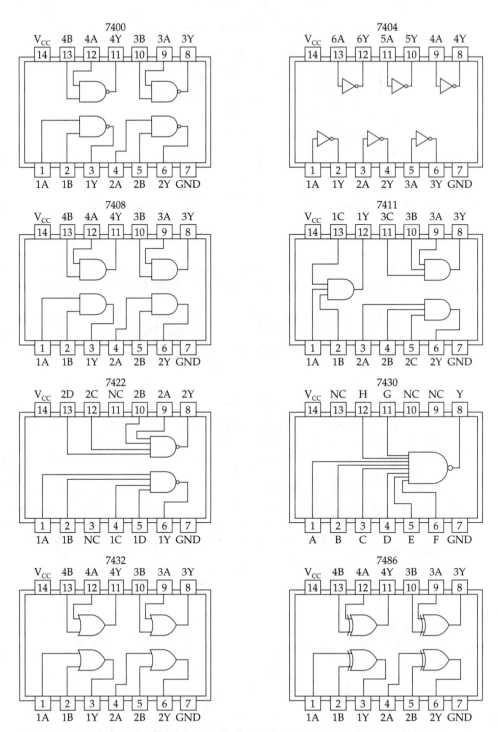

**FIGURE A.18.** Some SSI chips. Pin layouts from *The TTL Data Book for Design Engineers*, copyright © 1976 Texas Instruments Incorporated

SSI chips. To construct a logic function, a number of these chips are laid out on a printed-circuit board and the appropriate pin interconnections are made.

Increasing levels of integration made it possible to put more gates on a chip and to make gate interconnections on the chip as well. This yields the advantages of decreased cost, decreased size, and increased speed (since on-chip delays are of shorter duration than off-chip delays). A design problem arises, however. For each particular logic function or set of functions, the layout of gates and interconnections on the chip must be designed. The cost and time involved in such custom chip design is high. Thus, it becomes attractive to develop a general-purpose chip that can be readily adapted to specific purposes. This is the intent of the *programmable logic array* (PLA).

The PLA is based on the fact that any Boolean function (truth table) can be expressed in a sum-of-products (SOP) form, as we have seen. The PLA consists of a regular arrangement of NOT, AND, and OR gates on a chip. Each chip input is passed through a NOT gate so that each input and its complement are available to each AND gate. The output of each AND gate is available to each OR gate, and the output of each OR gate is a chip output. By making the appropriate connections, arbitrary SOP expressions can be implemented.

Figure A.19a shows a PLA with three inputs, eight gates, and two outputs. Most larger PLAs contain several hundred gates, 15 to 25 inputs, and 5 to 15 outputs. The connections from the inputs to the AND gates, and from the AND gates to the OR gates, are not specified.

PLAs are manufactured in two different ways to allow easy programming (making of connections). In the first, every possible connection is made through a fuse at every intersection point. The undesired connections can then be later removed by blowing the fuses. This type of PLA is referred to as a *field-programmable logic array*. Alternatively, the proper connections can be made during chip fabrication by using an appropriate mask supplied for a particular interconnection pattern. In either case, the PLA provides a flexible, inexpensive way of implementing digital logic functions.

Figure A.19b shows a design that realizes two Boolean expressions.

## Read-Only Memory (ROM)

Combinational circuits are often referred to as "memoryless" circuits, since their output depends only on their current input and no history of prior inputs is retained. However, there is one sort of memory that is implemented with combinational circuits, namely *read-only memory* (ROM).

Recall that a ROM is a memory unit that performs only the read operation. This implies that the binary information stored in a ROM is permanent and was created during the fabrication process. Thus, a given input to the ROM (address lines) always produces the same output (data lines). Because the outputs are a function only of the present inputs, the ROM is in fact a combinational circuit.

A ROM can be implemented with a decoder and a set of OR gates. As an example, consider Table A.8. This can be viewed as a truth table with four inputs and

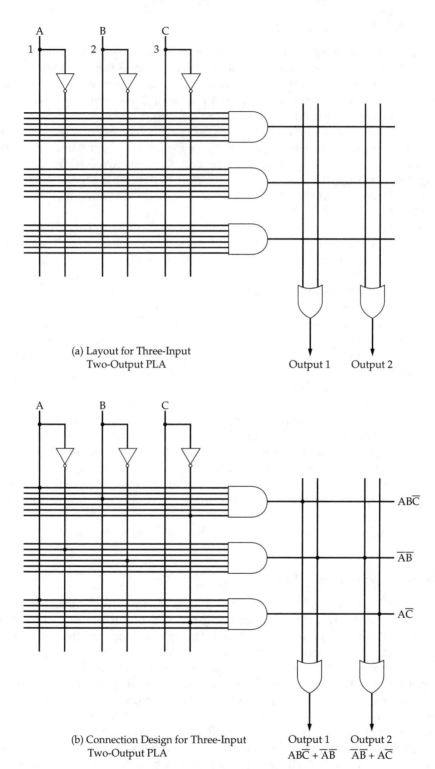

(a) Layout for Three-Input
    Two-Output PLA

Output 1    Output 2

(b) Connection Design for Three-Input
    Two-Output PLA

Output 1          Output 2
$AB\overline{C} + \overline{A}\,\overline{B}$          $\overline{A}\,\overline{B} + A\overline{C}$

**FIGURE A.19.  An example of a programmable logic array**

**TABLE A.8   Truth Table for a ROM**

| Input | | | | Output | | | |
|---|---|---|---|---|---|---|---|
| 0 | 0 | 0 | 0 | 0 | 0 | 0 | 0 |
| 0 | 0 | 0 | 1 | 0 | 0 | 0 | 1 |
| 0 | 0 | 1 | 0 | 0 | 0 | 1 | 1 |
| 0 | 0 | 1 | 1 | 0 | 0 | 1 | 0 |
| 0 | 1 | 0 | 0 | 0 | 1 | 1 | 0 |
| 0 | 1 | 0 | 1 | 0 | 1 | 1 | 1 |
| 0 | 1 | 1 | 0 | 0 | 1 | 0 | 1 |
| 0 | 1 | 1 | 1 | 0 | 1 | 0 | 0 |
| 1 | 0 | 0 | 0 | 1 | 1 | 0 | 0 |
| 1 | 0 | 0 | 1 | 1 | 1 | 0 | 1 |
| 1 | 0 | 1 | 0 | 1 | 1 | 1 | 1 |
| 1 | 0 | 1 | 1 | 1 | 1 | 1 | 0 |
| 1 | 1 | 0 | 0 | 1 | 0 | 1 | 0 |
| 1 | 1 | 0 | 1 | 1 | 0 | 1 | 1 |
| 1 | 1 | 1 | 0 | 1 | 0 | 0 | 1 |
| 1 | 1 | 1 | 1 | 1 | 0 | 0 | 0 |

four outputs. For each of the 16 possible input values, the corresponding set of values of the outputs is shown. It can also be viewed as defining the contents of a 64-bit ROM consisting of 16 words of 4 bits each. The four inputs specify an address, and the four outputs specify the contents of the location specified by the address. Figure A.20 shows how this memory could be implemented using a 4-to-

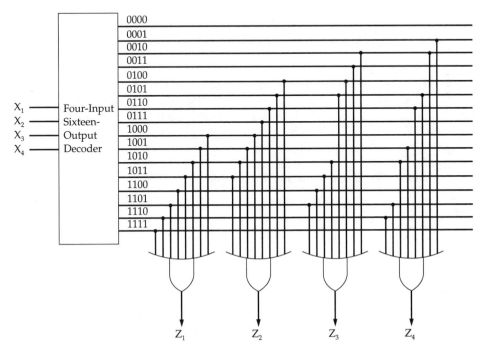

**FIGURE A.20. A 64-bit ROM**

16 decoder and four OR gates. As with the PLA, a regular organization is used, and the interconnections are made to reflect the desired result.

## Adders

So far, we have seen how interconnected gates can be used to implement such functions as the routing of signals, decoding, and ROM. One essential area not yet addressed is that of arithmetic. In this brief overview, we will content ourselves with looking at the addition function.

Binary addition differs from Boolean algebra in that the result includes a carry term. Thus,

$$
\begin{array}{cccc}
0 & 0 & 1 & 1 \\
+\ 0 & +\ 1 & +\ 0 & +\ 1 \\
\hline
0 & 1 & 1 & 10
\end{array}
$$

However, addition can still be dealt with in Boolean terms. In Table A.9a, we show the logic for adding 2 input bits to produce a 1-bit sum and a carry bit. This truth table could easily be implemented in digital logic. However, we are not interested in performing addition on just a single pair of bits. Rather, we wish to add two $n$-bit numbers. This can be done by putting together a set of adders so that the carry from one adder is provided as input to the next. A 4-bit adder is depicted in Figure A.21.

For a multiple-bit adder to work, each of the single-bit adders must have three inputs, including the carry from the next-lower-order adder. The revised truth table appears in Table A.9b. The two outputs can be expressed:

$$\text{Sum} = \overline{A}\,\overline{B}C + \overline{A}B\overline{C} + ABC + A\overline{B}\,\overline{C}$$
$$\text{Carry} = AB + AC + BC$$

Figure A.22 is an implementation using AND, OR, and NOT gates.

Thus we have the necessary logic to implement a multiple-bit adder such as shown in Figure A.23. Note that since the output from each adder depends on the

**TABLE A.9   Binary Addition Truth Tables**

| (a) Single-Bit Addition | | | | (b) Addition with Carry Input | | | | |
| --- | --- | --- | --- | --- | --- | --- | --- | --- |
| $A$ | $B$ | $Sum$ | $Carry$ | $C_{in}$ | $A$ | $B$ | $Sum$ | $C_{out}$ |
| 0 | 0 | 0 | 0 | 0 | 0 | 0 | 0 | 0 |
| 0 | 1 | 1 | 0 | 0 | 0 | 1 | 1 | 0 |
| 1 | 0 | 1 | 0 | 0 | 1 | 0 | 1 | 0 |
| 1 | 1 | 0 | 1 | 0 | 1 | 1 | 0 | 1 |
| | | | | 1 | 0 | 0 | 1 | 0 |
| | | | | 1 | 0 | 1 | 0 | 1 |
| | | | | 1 | 1 | 0 | 0 | 1 |
| | | | | 1 | 1 | 1 | 1 | 1 |

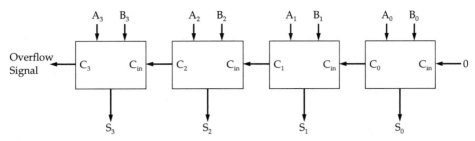

FIGURE A.21.  4-bit adder

carry from the previous adder, there is an increasing delay from the least signifi-cant to the most significant bit. Each single-bit adder experiences a certain amount of gate delay, and this gate delay accumulates. For larger adders, the accumulated delay can become unacceptably high.

If the carry values could be determined without having to ripple through all the previous stages, then each single-bit adder could function independently, and delay would not accumulate. This can be achieved with an approach known as *carry lookahead*. Let us look again at the 4-bit adder to explain this approach.

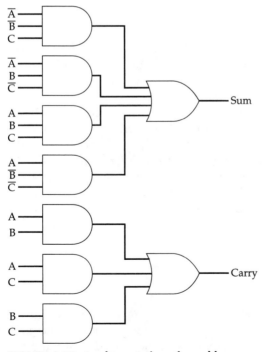

FIGURE A.22.  Implementation of an adder

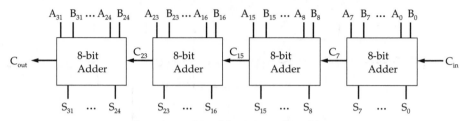

**FIGURE A.23. Construction of a 32-bit adder using 8-bit adders**

We would like to come up with an expression that specifies the carry input to any stage of the adder without reference to previous carry values. We have

$$C_0 = A_0 B_0 \tag{A-4}$$
$$C_1 = A_1 B_1 + (A_1 + B_1)C_0 \tag{A-5}$$

Substituting Equation A-4 into A-5,

$$C_1 = A_1 B_1 + A_1 A_0 B_0 + B_1 A_0 B_0$$

Following the same procedure, we get

$$C_2 = A_2 B_2 + A_2 A_1 B_1 + A_2 A_1 A_0 B_0 + A_2 B_1 A_0 B_0$$
$$+ B_2 A_1 B_1 + B_2 A_1 A_0 B_0 + B_2 B_1 A_0 B_0$$

This process can be repeated for arbitrarily long adders. Each carry term can be expressed in SOP form as a function only of the original inputs, with no dependence on the carries. Thus, only two levels of gate delay occur regardless of the length of the adder.

For long numbers, this approach becomes excessively complicated. Evaluating the expression for the most significant bit of an $n$-bit adder requires an OR gate with $n - 1$ inputs and $n$ AND gates with from 2 to $n + 1$ inputs. Accordingly, full carry lookahead is typically done only 4 to 8 bits at a time. Figure A.23 shows how a 32-bit adder can be constructed out of four 8-bit adders. In this case, the carry must ripple through the four 8-bit adders, but this will be substantially quicker than a ripple through 32 1-bit adders.

## A.4

### SEQUENTIAL CIRCUITS

Combinational circuits implement the essential functions of a digital computer. However, except for the special case of ROM, they provide no memory or state information, elements also essential to the operation of a digital computer. For the latter purposes, a more complex form of digital logic circuit is used: the sequential circuit. The current output of a sequential circuit depends not only on the current input, but also on the past history of inputs. Another and generally more useful way to view it is that the current output of a sequential circuit depends on the current input and the current state of that circuit.

In this section, we examine some simple but useful examples of sequential circuits. As will be seen, the sequential circuit makes use of combinational circuits.

## Flip-Flops

The simplest form of sequential circuit is the flip-flop. There are a variety of flip-flops, all of which share two properties:

- The flip-flop is a bistable device. It exists in one of two states and, in the absence of input, remains in that state. Thus, the flip-flop can function as a 1-bit memory.
- The flip-flop has two outputs, which are always the complements of each other. These are generally labeled $Q$ and $\overline{Q}$.

### The S–R Latch

Figure A.24 shows a common configuration known as the S–R flip-flop or *S–R latch*. The circuit has two inputs, $S$ (Set) and $R$ (Reset), and two outputs, $Q$ and $\overline{Q}$, and consists of two NOR gates hooked together in a feedback arrangement.

First, let us show that the circuit is bistable. Assume that both $S$ and $R$ are 0 and that $Q$ is 0. The inputs to the lower NOR gate are $Q = 0$ and $S = 0$. Thus, the output $\overline{Q} = 1$ means that the inputs to the upper NOR gate are $\overline{Q} = 1$ and $R = 0$, which has the output $Q = 0$. Thus, the state of the circuit is internally consistent and remains stable as long as $S = R = 0$. A similar line of reasoning shows that the state $Q = 1$, $\overline{Q} = 0$ is also stable for $R = S = 0$.

Thus, this circuit can function as a 1-bit memory. We can view the output $Q$ as the "value" of the bit. The inputs $S$ and $R$ serve to write the values 1 and 0, respectively, into memory. To see this, consider the state $Q = 0, \overline{Q} = 1, S = 0, R = 0$. Suppose that $S$ changes to the value 1. Now the inputs to the lower NOR gate are $S = 1, Q = 0$. After some time delay $\Delta t$, the output of the lower NOR gate will be $\overline{Q} = 0$

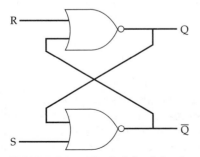

**FIGURE A.24. The S–R latch implemented with NOR gates**

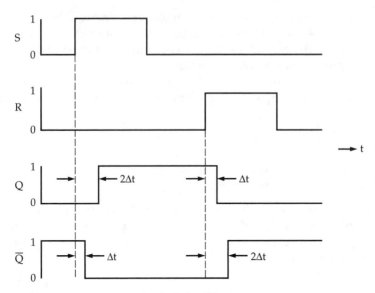

**FIGURE A.25. NOR S–R latch timing diagram**

(see Figure A.25). So, at this point in time, the inputs to the upper NOR gate become $R = 0$, $\overline{Q} = 0$. After another gate delay of $\Delta t$, the output $Q$ becomes 1. This is again a stable state. The inputs to the lower gate are now $S = 1$, $Q = 1$, which maintain the output $Q = 0$. As long as $S = 1$ and $R = 0$, the outputs will remain $Q = 1$, $\overline{Q} = 0$. Furthermore, if $S$ returns to 0, the outputs will remain unchanged.

The $R$ output performs the opposite function. When $R$ goes to 1, it forces $Q = 0$, $\overline{Q} = 1$ regardless of the previous state of $Q$ and $\overline{Q}$. Again, a time delay of $2\Delta t$ occurs before stability is re-established (Figure A.25).

The S–R latch can be defined with a table similar to a truth table, called a *characteristic table*, which shows the next state or states of a sequential circuit as a function of current states and inputs. In the case of the S–R latch, the state can be defined by the value of $Q$. Table A.10a shows the resulting characteristic table. Observe that the inputs $S = 1$, $R = 1$ are not allowed, since these would produce an inconsistent output (both $Q$ and $\overline{Q}$ equal 0). The table can be expressed more compactly, as in Table A.10b. An illustration of the behavior of the S–R latch is shown in Table A.10c.

## Clocked S–R Flip-Flop

The output of the S–R latch changes, after a brief time delay, in response to a change in the input. This is referred to as *asynchronous operation*. More typically, events in the digital computer are synchronized to a clock pulse, so that changes occur only when a clock pulse occurs. Figure A.26 shows this arrangement. This device is referred to as a *clocked S–R flip-flop*. Note that the $R$ and $S$ inputs are passed to the NOR gates only during the clock pulse.

**TABLE A.10   The S–R Latch**

| (a) Characteristic Table | | | (b) Simplified Characteristic Table | | |
|:---:|:---:|:---:|:---:|:---:|:---:|
| Current Inputs | Current State | Next State | $S$ | $R$ | $Q_{n+1}$ |
| SR | $Q_n$ | $Q_{n+1}$ | 0 | 0 | $Q_n$ |
| 00 | 0 | 0 | 0 | 1 | 0 |
| 00 | 1 | 1 | 1 | 0 | 1 |
| 01 | 0 | 0 | 1 | 1 | — |
| 01 | 1 | 0 | | | |
| 10 | 0 | 1 | | | |
| 10 | 1 | 1 | | | |
| 11 | 0 | — | | | |
| 11 | 1 | — | | | |

*(c) Response to Series of Inputs*

| t | 0 | 1 | 2 | 3 | 4 | 5 | 6 | 7 | 8 | 9 |
|:---:|:---:|:---:|:---:|:---:|:---:|:---:|:---:|:---:|:---:|:---:|
| S | 1 | 0 | 0 | 0 | 0 | 0 | 0 | 0 | 1 | 0 |
| R | 0 | 0 | 0 | 1 | 0 | 0 | 1 | 0 | 0 | 0 |
| $Q_{n+1}$ | 1 | 1 | 1 | 0 | 0 | 0 | 0 | 0 | 1 | 1 |

## *D Flip-Flop*

One problem with S–R flip-flop is that the condition $R = 1$, $S = 1$ must be avoided. One way to do this is to allow just a single input. The D flip-flop accomplishes this. Figure A.27 shows a gate implementation and the characteristic table of the D flip-flop. By using an inverter, the nonclock inputs to the two AND gates are guaranteed to be the opposite of each other.

The D flip-flop is sometimes referred to as the data flip-flop because it is, in effect, storage for one bit of data. The output of the D flip-flop is always equal to the most recent value applied to the input. Hence, it remembers and produces the last input. It is also referred to as the delay flip-flop, because it delays a 0 or 1 applied to its input for a single clock pulse.

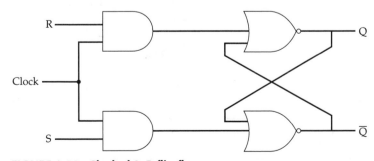

**FIGURE A.26.   Clocked S–R flip-flop**

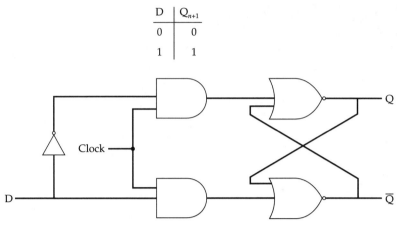

**FIGURE A.27. D flip-flop**

## J–K Flip-Flop

Another useful flip-flop is the J–K flip-flop. Like the S–R flip-flop, it has two inputs. However, in this case all possible combinations of input values are valid. Figure A.28 shows a gate implementation of the J–K flip-flop, and Figure A.29 shows its characteristic table (along with those for the S–R and D flip-flops). Note that the first three combinations are the same as for the S–R flip-flop. With no input, the output is stable. The J input alone performs a set function, causing the output to be 1; the K input alone performs a reset function, causing the output to be 0. When both J and K are 1, the function performed is referred to as the *toggle* function: the output is reversed. Thus, if Q is 1 and 1 is applied to J and K, then Q becomes 0. The reader should verify that the implementation of Figure A.28 produces this characteristic function.

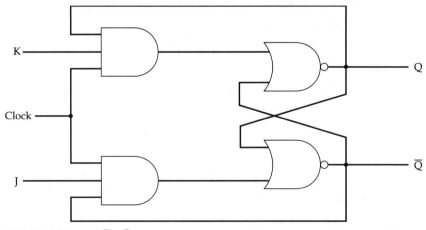

**FIGURE A.28. J–K flip-flop**

| Name | Graphic Symbol | Characteristic Table | | |
|------|----------------|---|---|---|

**S–R**

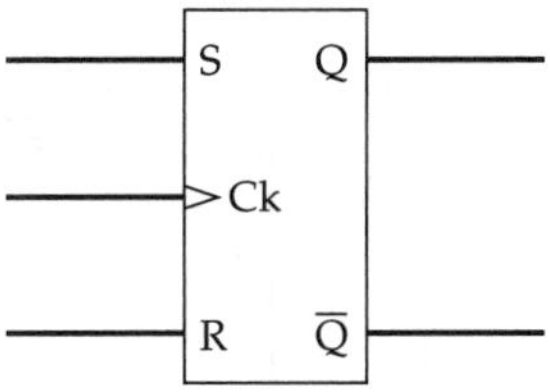

| S | R | $Q_{n+1}$ |
|---|---|---|
| 0 | 0 | $Q_n$ |
| 0 | 1 | 0 |
| 1 | 0 | 1 |
| 1 | 1 | – |

**J–K**

| 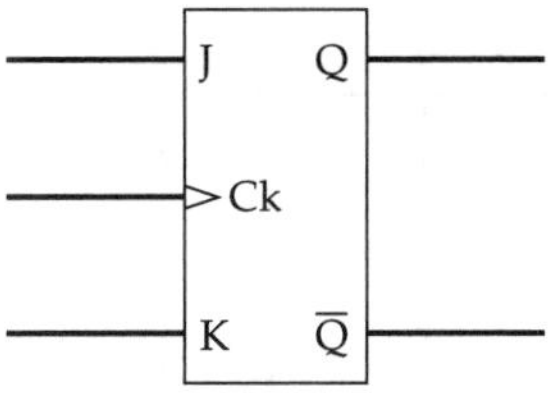 J | K | $Q_{n+1}$ |
|---|---|---|
| 0 | 0 | $Q_n$ |
| 0 | 1 | 0 |
| 1 | 0 | 1 |
| 1 | 1 | $\overline{Q_n}$ |

**D**

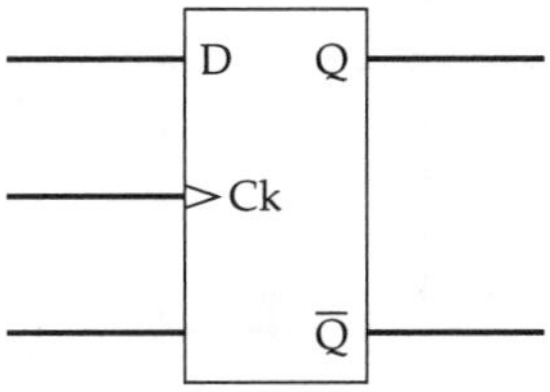

| D | $Q_{n+1}$ |
|---|---|
| 0 | 0 |
| 1 | 1 |

**FIGURE A.29.  Basic flip-flops**

## Registers

As an example of the use of flip-flops, let us first examine one of the essential elements of the CPU: the register. As we know, a register is a digital circuit used within the CPU to store one or more bits of data. Two basic types of registers are commonly used: parallel registers and shift registers.

### *Parallel Registers*

A parallel register consists of a set of 1-bit memories that can be read or written simultaneously. It is used to store data. The registers that we have discussed throughout this book are parallel registers.

The 8-bit register of Figure A.30 illustrates the operation of a parallel register. S–R latches are used. A control signal, labeled *input data strobe*, controls writing into

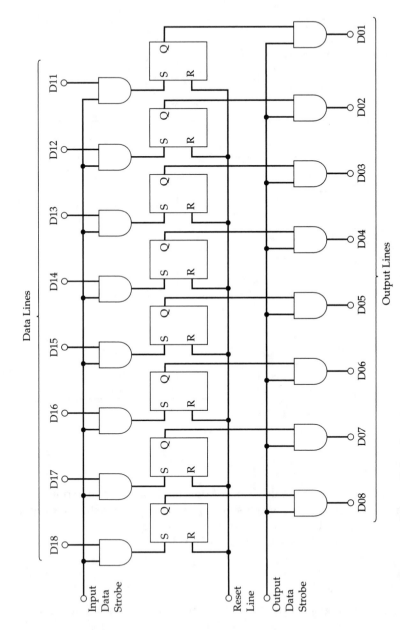

**FIGURE A.30.   8-bit parallel register**

the register from signal lines, D11 through D18. These lines might be the output of multiplexers, so that data from a variety of sources can be loaded into the register. Output is controlled in a similar fashion. As an extra feature, a reset line is available that allows the register to be easily set to 0. Note that this could not be accomplished as easily with a register constructed from D flip-flops.

## Shift Register

A shift register accepts and/or transfers information serially. Consider, for example, Figure A.31, which shows a 5-bit shift register constructed from clocked S–R flip-flops. Data are input only to the leftmost flip-flop. With each clock pulse, data are shifted to the right one position, and the rightmost bit is transferred out.

Shift registers can be used to interface to serial I/O devices. In addition, they can be used within the ALU to perform logical shift and rotate functions. In this latter capacity, they need to be equipped with parallel read/write circuitry as well as serial.

## Counters

Another useful category of sequential circuit is the counter. A counter is a register whose value is easily incremented by 1 modulo the capacity of the register. Thus, a register made up of $n$ flip-flops can count up to $2^n - 1$. When the counter is incremented beyond its maximum value, it is set to 0. An example of a counter in the CPU is the program counter.

Counters can be designated as asynchronous or synchronous, depending on the way in which they operate. Asynchronous counters are relatively slow since the output of one flip-flop triggers a change in the status of the next flip-flop. In a synchronous counter, all of the flip-flops change state at the same time. Because the latter type is much faster, it is the kind used in CPUs. However, it is useful to begin the discussion with a description of an asynchronous counter.

## Ripple Counter

An asynchronous counter is also referred to as a ripple counter, since the change that occurs in order to increment the counter starts at one end and "ripples" through to the other end. Figure A.32 shows an implementation of a 4-bit counter using J–K flip-flops, together with a timing diagram that illustrates its behavior. The timing diagram is idealized in that it does not show the propagation delay

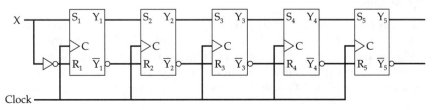

**FIGURE A.31. 5-bit shift register**

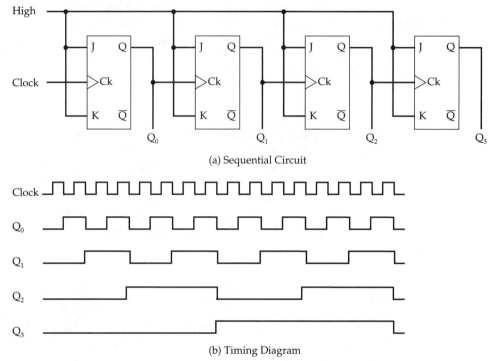

(a) Sequential Circuit

(b) Timing Diagram

**FIGURE A.32.  Ripple counter**

that occurs as the signals move down the series of flip-flops. The output of the leftmost flip-flop ($Q_0$) is the least significant bit. The design could clearly be extended to an arbitrary number of bits by cascading more flip-flops.

In the illustrated implementation, the counter is incremented with each clock pulse. The J and K inputs to each flip-flop are held at a constant 1. This means that, when there is a clock pulse, the output at Q will be inverted (1 to 0; 0 to 1). Note that the change in state is shown as occurring with the falling edge of the clock pulse; this is known as an edge-triggered flip-flop. Using flip-flops that respond to the transition in a clock pulse rather than the pulse itself provides better timing control in complex circuits. If one looks at patterns of output for this counter, it can be seen that it cycles through 0000, 0001, . . ., 1110, 1111, 0000, and so on.

### Synchronous Counters

The ripple counter has the disadvantage of the delay involved in changing value, which is proportional to the length of the counter. To overcome this disadvantage, CPUs make use of synchronous counters, in which all of the flip-flops of the counter change at the same time. In this subsection, we present a design for a 3-bit synchronous counter. In doing so, we illustrate some basic concepts in the design of a synchronous circuit.

For a 3-bit counter, three flip-flops will be needed. Let us use J–K flip-flops. Label the uncomplemented output of the three flip-flops A, B, C respectively, with C representing the least significant bit. The first step is to construct a truth table that relates the J–K inputs and outputs, to allow us to design the overall circuit. Such a truth table is shown in Figure A.33a. The first three columns show the possible combinations of outputs A, B, and C. They are listed in the order that they will appear as the counter is incremented. Each row lists the current value of A, B, C and the inputs to the three flip-flops that will be required to reach the next value of A, B, C.

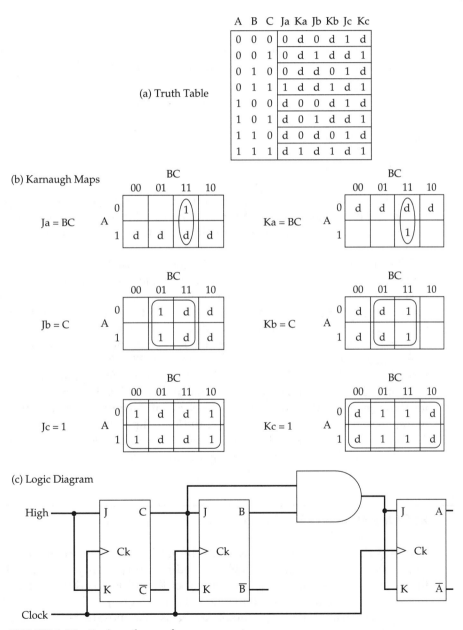

| A | B | C | Ja | Ka | Jb | Kb | Jc | Kc |
|---|---|---|----|----|----|----|----|----|
| 0 | 0 | 0 | 0 | d | 0 | d | 1 | d |
| 0 | 0 | 1 | 0 | d | 1 | d | d | 1 |
| 0 | 1 | 0 | 0 | d | d | 0 | 1 | d |
| 0 | 1 | 1 | 1 | d | d | 1 | d | 1 |
| 1 | 0 | 0 | d | 0 | 0 | d | 1 | d |
| 1 | 0 | 1 | d | 0 | 1 | d | d | 1 |
| 1 | 1 | 0 | d | 0 | d | 0 | 1 | d |
| 1 | 1 | 1 | d | 1 | d | 1 | d | 1 |

(a) Truth Table

(b) Karnaugh Maps

Ja = BC   Ka = BC

Jb = C   Kb = C

Jc = 1   Kc = 1

(c) Logic Diagram

**FIGURE A.33. Design of a synchronous counter**

To understand the way in which the truth table of Figure A.33a is constructed, it may be helpful to recast the characteristic table for the J–K flip-flop. Recall that this table was presented as follows:

| J | K | $Q_{n+1}$ |
|---|---|---|
| 0 | 0 | $Q_n$ |
| 0 | 1 | 0 |
| 1 | 0 | 1 |
| 1 | 1 | $\overline{Q}_n$ |

In this form, the table shows the effect that the J and K inputs have on the output. Now consider the following organization of the same information:

| $Q_n$ | J | K | $Q_{n+1}$ |
|---|---|---|---|
| 0 | 0 | d | 0 |
| 0 | 1 | d | 1 |
| 1 | d | 1 | 0 |
| 1 | d | 0 | 1 |

In this form, the table provides the value of the next output when the inputs and the present output are known. This is exactly the information needed to design the counter or, indeed, any sequential circuit. In this form, the table is referred to as an *excitation table*.

Let us return to Figure A.33a. Consider the first row. We want the value of A to remain 0, the value of B to remain 0, and the value of C to go from 0 to 1 with the next application of a clock pulse. The excitation table shows that to maintain an output of 0, we must have inputs of J = 0 and don't care for K. To effect a transition from 0 to 1, the inputs must be J = 1 and K = d. These values are shown in the first row of the table. By similar reasoning, the remainder of the table can be filled in.

Having constructed the truth table of Figure A.33a, we see that the table shows the required values of all of the J and K inputs as functions of the current values of A, B, and C. With the aid of Karnaugh maps, we can develop Boolean expressions for these six functions. This is shown in part b of the figure. For example, the Karnaugh map for the variable Ja (the J input to the flip-flop that produces the A output) yields the expression Ja = BC. When all six expressions are derived, it is a straightforward matter to design the actual circuit, as shown in part c of the figure.

## A.5

## RECOMMENDED READING

The literature in this area is vast, and the following recommendations are just samples of what is available. [FLOY90] and [REIS91] are both easy-to-follow yet thorough accounts that cover the material of this appendix. More rigorous treatments that can be highly recommended are [MANO93] and [WAKE90]. Another good text, with a somewhat different emphasis than most texts, is [UNGE89].

FLOY90   Floyd, T. *Digital Fundamentals.* New York: Merrill/Macmillan, 1990.

MANO93   Mano, M. *Computer System Architecture.* Englewood Cliffs, NJ: Prentice Hall, 1993.

REIS91   Reis, R. *Digital Electronics Through Project Analysis.* New York: Merrill/Macmillan, 1991.

UNGE89   Unger, S. *The Essence of Logic Circuits.* Englewood Cliffs, NJ: Prentice-Hall, 1989.

WAKE90   Wakerly, J. *Digital Design Principles and Practices.* Englewood Cliffs, NJ: Prentice-Hall, 1990.

## A.6

## PROBLEMS

A.1   Construct a truth table for the following Boolean expressions:

   **(a)** $ABC + \overline{AB}\,\overline{C}$       **(b)** $ACB + A\overline{B}\overline{C} + \overline{A}\,\overline{B}\overline{C}$

   **(c)** $A(\overline{B}\overline{C} + \overline{B}C)$     **(d)** $(A + B)(A + C)(\overline{A} + \overline{B})$

A.2   Simplify the following expressions according to the commutative law:
   **(a)** $A \cdot \overline{B} + \overline{B} \cdot A + C \cdot D \cdot E + \overline{C} \cdot D \cdot E + E \cdot \overline{C} \cdot D$
   **(b)** $A \cdot B + A \cdot C + B \cdot A$
   **(c)** $(L \cdot M \cdot N)(A \cdot B)(C \cdot D \cdot E)(M \cdot N \cdot L)$
   **(d)** $F \cdot (K + R) + S \cdot V + W \cdot \overline{X} + V \cdot S + \overline{X} \cdot W + (R + K) \cdot F$

A.3   Apply DeMorgan's theorem to the following equations:

   **(a)** $F = \overline{V + A + L}$

   **(b)** $F = \overline{A} + \overline{B} + \overline{C} + \overline{D}$

A.4   Simplify the following expressions:
   **(a)** $A = S \cdot T + V \cdot W + R \cdot S \cdot T$
   **(b)** $A = T \cdot U \cdot V + X \cdot Y + Y$
   **(c)** $A = F \cdot (E + F + G)$
   **(d)** $A = (P \cdot Q + R + S \cdot T)T \cdot S$
   **(e)** $A = \overline{\overline{\overline{D} \cdot \overline{D} \cdot E}}$
   **(f)** $A = Y \cdot (W + X + \overline{\overline{Y} + \overline{Z}}) \cdot Z$
   **(g)** $A = (B \cdot E + C + F) \cdot C$

A.5   Construct the operation XOR from the basic Boolean operations AND, OR, and NOT.

A.6   Given the following Boolean expression:

$$F = \overline{A}\overline{B}C + \overline{A}BC + A\overline{B}C$$

   **(a)** Develop an equivalent expression using only NAND operations, and draw the logic diagram.
   **(b)** Develop an equivalent expression using only NOR operations, and draw the logic diagram.

A.7.   Given a NOR gate and NOT gates, draw a logic diagram that will perform the 3-input AND function.

A.8   Write the Boolean expression for a 4-input NAND gate.

A.9 A combinational circuit is used to control a 7-segment display of decimal digits, as shown in Figure A.34. The circuit has four inputs, which provide the 4-bit code used in packed decimal representation ($0_{10}$ = 0000, ..., $9_{10}$ = 1001). The seven outputs define which segments will be activated to display a given decimal digit. Note that some combinations of inputs and outputs are not needed.

   **(a)** Develop a truth table for this circuit.
   **(b)** Express the truth table in SOP form.
   **(c)** Express the truth table in POS form.
   **(d)** Provide a simplified expression.

A.10 Design an 8-to-1 multiplexer.

A.11 Add an additional line to Figure A.15 so that it functions as a demultiplexer.

A.12 The Gray code is a binary code for integers. It differs from the ordinary binary representation in that there is just a single bit change between the representations of any two numbers. This is useful for applications such as counters or analog-to-digital converters where a sequence of numbers is generated. Because only one bit changes at a time, there is never any ambiguity due to slight timing differences. The first eight elements of the code are

| Binary Code | Gray Code |
|---|---|
| 000 | 000 |
| 001 | 001 |
| 010 | 011 |
| 011 | 010 |
| 100 | 110 |
| 101 | 111 |
| 110 | 101 |
| 111 | 100 |

Design a circuit that converts from binary to Gray code.

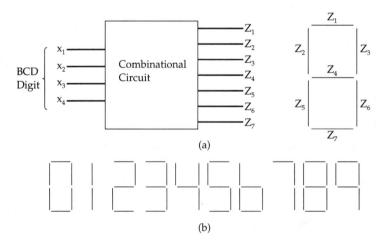

(a)

(b)

**FIGURE A.34. Seven-segment LED display example**

A.13 Design a $5 \times 32$ decoder using four $3 \times 8$ decoders (with enable inputs) and one $2 \times 4$ decoder.

A.14 Derive a PLA and a ROM implementation for the following set of combinational functions:

$$Z_1 = X_1 X_2 X_3 \overline{X}_4 + X_1 X_2 \overline{X}_3 \overline{X}_4 + X_1 \overline{X}_2 X_3 X_4 + \overline{X}_1 X_2 X_3 X_4$$
$$+ \overline{X}_1 \overline{X}_2 X_3 X_4 + \overline{X}_1 \overline{X}_2 \overline{X}_3 X_4 + \overline{X}_1 \overline{X}_2 \overline{X}_3 \overline{X}_4$$

$$Z_2 = X_1 X_2 X_3 X_4 + X_1 X_2 X_3 \overline{X}_4 + X_1 \overline{X}_2 X_3 \overline{X}_4 + \overline{X}_1 X_2 X_3 X_4$$
$$+ \overline{X}_1 \overline{X}_2 X_3 X_4$$

$$Z_3 = X_1 X_2 \overline{X}_3 X_4 + X_1 \overline{X}_2 X_3 X_4 + X_1 \overline{X}_2 X_3 \overline{X}_4$$
$$+ \overline{X}_1 \overline{X}_2 X_3 \overline{X}_4 + \overline{X}_1 \overline{X}_2 \overline{X}_3 \overline{X}_4$$

A.15 Implement the full adder of Figure A.22 with just five gates. (Hint: Some of the gates are XOR gates.)

A.16 Consider Figure A.22. Assume that each gate produces a delay of 10 ns. Thus, the sum output is valid after 30 ns and the carry output after 0 ns. What is the total add time for a 32-bit adder:
  **(a)** Implemented without carry lookahead, as in Figure A.21?
  **(b)** Implemented with carry lookahead and using 8-bit adders, as in Figure A.23?

A.17 Draw a realization of a D flip-flop using only NAND gates.

# Glossary

Some of the terms in this glossary are from the *American National Dictionary for Information Systems* [ANSI90]. These are indicated in the glossary by an asterisk.

**Absolute Address\*** An address in a computer language that identifies a storage location or a device without the use of any intermediate reference.

**Accumulator** The name of the CPU register in a single-address instruction format. The accumulator, or AC, is implicitly one of the two operands for the instruction.

**Address Bus** That portion of a system bus used for the transfer of an address. Typically, the address identifies a main memory location or an I/O device.

**Address Space** The range of addresses (memory, I/O) that can be referenced.

**Arithmetic and Logic Unit (ALU)\*** A part of a computer that performs arithmetic operations, logic operations, and related operations.

**ASCII** American Standard Code for Information Interchange. ASCII is a 7-bit code used to represent numeric, alphabetic, and special printable characters. It also includes codes for *control characters,* which are not printed or displayed but specify some control function.

**Assembly Language\*** A computer-oriented language whose instructions are usually in one-to-one correspondence with computer instructions and that may provide facilities such as the use of macroinstructions. Synonymous with *computer-dependent language.*

**Associative Memory\*** A memory whose storage locations are identified by their contents, or by a part of their contents, rather than by their names or positions.

**Asynchronous Timing** A technique in which the occurrence of one event on a bus follows and depends on the occurrence of a previous event.

**Autoindexing** A form of indexed addressing in which the index register is automatically incremented or decremented with each memory reference.

**Base(\*ANS)** In the numeration system commonly used in scientific papers, the number that is raised to the power denoted by the exponent and then multiplied by the mantissa to determine the real number represented (e.g., the number 6.25 in the expression $2.7 \times 6.25^{1.5} = 42.1875$).

**Base Address\*** A numeric value that is used as a reference in the calculation of addresses in the execution of a computer program.

**Binary Operator\*** An operator that represents an operation on two and only two operands.

**Bit\*** In the pure binary numeration system, either of the digits 0 and 1.

**Block Multiplexor Channel**   A multiplexer channel that interleaves blocks of data. See also *byte multiplexor channel.* Contrast with *selector channel.*

**Bubble Memory**   A solid-state magnetic memory device. Binary 1s and 0s are represented by the presence or absence of tiny magnetic domains, called *bubbles.*

**Buffer\***   Storage used to compensate for a difference in rate of flow of data, or time of occurrence of events, when transferring data from one device to another.

**Bus**   A shared communications path consisting of one or a collection of lines. In some computer systems, CPU, memory, and I/O components are connected by a common bus. Since the lines are shared by all components, only one component at a time can successfully transmit.

**Byte**   Eight bits. Also referred to as an *octet.*

**Byte Multiplexor Channel\***   A multiplexer channel that interleaves bytes of data. See also *block multiplexor channel.* Contrast with *selector channel.*

**Cache Memory\***   A special buffer storage, smaller and faster than main storage, that is used to hold a copy of instructions and data in main storage that are likely to be needed next by the processor, and that have been obtained automatically from main storage.

**CD-ROM**   Compact Disk Read-Only Memory. A nonerasable disk used for storing computer data. The standard system uses 12-cm disks and can hold more than 550 Mbytes.

**Central Processing Unit (CPU)**   That portion of a computer that fetches and executes instructions. It consists of an Arithmetic and Logic Unit (ALU), a control unit, and registers. Often simply referred to as a *processor.*

**Combinational Circuit\***   A logic device whose output values, at any given instant, depend only upon the input values at that time. A combinational circuit is a special case of a sequential circuit that does not have a storage capability. Synonymous with *combinatorial circuit.*

**Compact Disk (CD)**   A nonerasable disk that stores digitized audio information.

**Computer Instruction\***   An instruction that can be recognized by the processing unit of the computer for which it is designed. Synonymous with *machine instruction.*

**Computer Instruction Set\***   A complete set of the operators of the instructions of a computer together with a description of the types of meanings that can be attributed to their operands. Synonymous with *machine instruction set.*

**Conditional Jump\***   A jump that takes place only when the instruction that specifies it is executed and specified conditions are satisfied. Contrast with *unconditional jump.*

**Condition Code**   A code that reflects the result of a previous operation (e.g., arithmetic). A CPU may include one or more condition codes, which may be stored separately within the CPU or as part of a larger control register. Also known as a *flag.*

**Control Bus**   That portion of a system bus used for the transfer of control signals.

**Control Registers**   CPU registers employed to control CPU operation. Most of these registers are not user-visible.

**Control Storage**   A portion of storage that contains microcode.

**Control Unit**   That part of the CPU that controls CPU operations, including ALU operations, the movement of data within the CPU, and the exchange of data and control signals across external interfaces (e.g., the system bus).

**Daisy Chain\***   A method of device interconnection for determining interrupt priority by connecting the interrupt sources serially.

**Data Bus**   That portion of a system bus used for the transfer of data.

**Data Communication**   Data transfer between devices. The term generally excludes I/O.

**Decoder\***   A device that has a number of input lines of which any number may carry signals and a number of output lines of which not more than one may carry a signal, there being a one-to-one correspondence between the outputs and the combinations of input signals.

**Demand Paging\***   The transfer of a page from auxiliary storage to real storage at the moment of need.

**Direct Access\***   The capability to obtain data from a storage device or to enter data into a storage device in a sequence independent of their relative position, by means of addresses that indicate the physical location of the data.

**Direct Address\***   An address that designates the storage location of an item of data to be treated as operand. Synonymous with *one-level address.*

**Direct Memory Access (DMA)**   A form of I/O in which a special module, called a *DMA module,* controls the exchange of data between main memory and an I/O module. The CPU sends a request for the transfer of a block of data to the DMA module and is interrupted only after the entire block has been transferred.

**Disabled Interrupt**   A condition, usually created by the CPU, during which the CPU will ignore interrupt request signals of a specified class.

**Diskette\***   A flexible magnetic disk enclosed in a protective container. Synonymous with *flexible disk.*

**Disk Pack\***   An assembly of magnetic disks that can be removed as a whole from a disk drive, together with a container from which the assembly must be separated when operating.

**Disk Stripping**   A type of disk array mapping in which logically contiguous blocks of data, or strips, are mapped round-robin to consecutive array members. A set of logically consecutive strips that maps exactly one strip to each array member is referred to as a stripe.

**Dynamic RAM**   A RAM whose cells are implemented using capacitors. A dynamic RAM will gradually lose its data unless it is periodically refreshed.

**Emulation\***   The imitation of all or part of one system by another, primarily by hardware, so that the imitating system accepts the same data, executes the same programs, and achieves the same results as the imitated system.

**Enabled Interrupt**   A condition, usually created by the CPU, during which the CPU will respond to interrupt request signals of a specified class.

**Erasable Optical Disk**   A disk that uses optical technology but that can be easily erased and rewritten. Both 3.25-inch and 5.25-inch disks are in use. A typical capacity is 650 Mbytes.

**Error-Correcting Code\***   A code in which each character or signal conforms to specific rules of construction so that deviations from these rules indicate the presence of an error and in which some or all of the detected errors can be corrected automatically.

**Error-Detecting Code\*** A code in which each character or signal conforms to specific rules of construction so that deviations from these rules indicate the presence of an error.

**Execute Cycle** That portion of the instruction cycle during which the CPU performs the operation specified by the instruction opcode.

**Fetch Cycle** That portion of the instruction cycle during which the CPU fetches from memory the instruction to be executed.

**Firmware\*** Microcode stored in read-only memory.

**Fixed-Point Representation System\*** A radix numeration system in which the radix point is implicitly fixed in the series of digit places by some convention upon which agreement has been reached.

**Flip-Flop\*** A circuit or device containing active elements, capable of assuming either one of two stable states at a given time. Synonymous with *bistable circuit, toggle.*

**Floating-Point Representation System\*** A numeration system in which a real number is represented by a pair of distinct numerals, the real number being the product of the fixed-point part, one of the numerals, and a value obtained by raising the implicit floating-point base to a power denoted by the exponent in the floating-point representation, indicated by the second numeral.

**G** Prefix meaning *billion.*

**Gate** An electronic circuit that produces an output signal that is a simple Boolean operation on its input signals.

**General-Purpose Register\*** A register, usually explicitly addressable, within a set of registers, that can be used for different purposes, for example, as an accumulator, as an index register, or as a special handler of data.

**Global Variable** A variable defined in one portion of a computer program and used in at least one other portion of that computer program.

**Immediate Address\*** The contents of an address part that contains the value of an operand rather than an address. Synonymous with *zero-level address.*

**Indexed Address\*** An address that is modified by the content of an index register prior to or during the execution of a computer instruction.

**Indexing** A technique of address modification by means of index registers.

**Index Register\*** A register whose contents can be used to modify an operand address during the execution of computer instructions; it can also be used as a counter. An index register may be used to control the execution of a loop, to control the use of an array, as a switch, for table lookup, or as a pointer.

**Indirect Address\*** An address of a storage location that contains an address.

**Indirect Cycle** That portion of the instruction cycle during which the CPU performs a memory access to convert an indirect address into a direct address.

**Input-Output (I/O)** Pertaining to either input or output, or both. Refers to the movement of data between a computer and a directly attached peripheral.

**Instruction Address Register\*** A special-purpose register used to hold the address of the next instruction to be executed.

**Instruction Cycle** The processing performed by a CPU to execute a single instruction.

**Instruction Format**   The layout of a computer instruction as a sequence of bits. The format divides the instruction into fields, corresponding to the constituent elements of the instruction (e.g., opcode, operands).

**Instruction Register\***   A register that is used to hold an instruction for interpretation.

**Integrated Circuit (IC)**   A tiny piece of solid material, such as silicon, upon which is etched or imprinted a collection of electronic components and their interconnections.

**Interrupt\***   A suspension of a process, such as the execution of a computer program, caused by an event external to that process, and performed in such a way that the process can be resumed. Synonymous with *interruption.*

**Interrupt Cycle**   That portion of the instruction cycle during which the CPU checks for interrupts. If an enabled interrupt is pending, the CPU saves the current program state and resumes processing at an interrupt-handler routine.

**Interrupt-Driven I/O**   A form of I/O. The CPU issues an I/O command, continues to execute subsequent instructions, and is interrupted by the I/O module when the latter has completed its work.

**I/O Channel**   A relatively complex I/O module that relieves the CPU of the details of I/O operations. An I/O channel will execute a sequence of I/O commands from main memory without the need for CPU involvement.

**I/O Controller**   A relatively simple I/O module that requires detailed control from the CPU or an I/O channel. Synonymous with *device controller.*

**I/O Module**   One of the major component types of a computer. It is responsible for the control of one or more external devices (peripherals) and for the exchange of data between those devices and main memory and/or CPU registers.

**I/O Processor**   An I/O module with its own processor, capable of executing its own specialized I/O instructions or, in some cases, general-purpose machine instructions.

**Isolated I/O**   A method of addressing I/O modules and external devices. The I/O address space is treated separately from main memory address space. Specific I/O machine instructions must be used. Compare *memory-mapped* I/O.

**K**   Prefix meaning $2^{10} = 1024$. Thus, 2Kb = 2048 bits.

**Local Variable**   A variable that is defined and used only in one specified portion of a computer program.

**M**   Prefix meaning $2^{20} = 1,048,576$. Thus, 2Mb = $2 \times 2^{20}$ bits.

**Magnetic Disk\***   A flat circular plate with a magnetizable surface layer, on one or both sides of which data can be stored.

**Magnetic Tape\***   A tape with a magnetizable surface layer on which data can be stored by magnetic recording.

**Main Memory\***   Program-addressable storage from which instructions and other data can be loaded directly into registers for subsequent execution or processing.

**Memory Address Register (MAR)\***   A register, in a processing unit, that contains the address of the storage location being accessed.

**Memory Buffer Register (MBR)**   A register that contains data read from memory or data to be written to memory.

**Memory Cycle Time**   The inverse of the rate at which memory can be accessed. It is the minimum time between the response to one access request (read or write) and the response to the next access request.

**Memory-Mapped I/O**   A method of addressing I/O modules and external devices. A single address space is used for both main memory and I/O addresses, and the same machine instructions are used both for memory read/write and for I/O.

**Microcomputer***   A computer system whose processing unit is a microprocessor. A basic microcomputer includes a microprocessor, storage, and an input/output facility, which may or may not be on one chip.

**Microinstruction***   An instruction that controls data flow and sequencing in a processor at a more fundamental level than machine instructions. Individual machine instructions and perhaps other functions may be implemented by microprograms.

**Micro-Operation**   An elementary CPU operation, performed during one clock pulse.

**Microprocessor***   A processor whose elements have been miniaturized into one or a few integrated circuits.

**Microprogram***   A sequence of microinstructions that are in special storage where they can be dynamically accessed to perform various functions.

**Microprogrammed CPU**   A CPU whose control unit is implemented using microprogramming.

**Microprogramming Language**   An instruction set used to specify microprograms.

**Multiplexer**   A combinational circuit that connects multiple inputs to a single output. At any time, only one of the inputs is selected to be passed to the output.

**Multiplexor Channel**   A channel designed to operate with a number of I/O devices simultaneously. Several I/O devices can transfer records at the same time by interleaving items of data. See also *byte multiplexor channel, block multiplexor channel.*

**Multiprogramming***   A mode of operation that provides for the interleaved execution of two or more computer programs by a single processor.

**Nonvolatile Memory**   Memory whose contents are stable and do not require a constant power source.

**Nucleus**   That portion of an operating system that contains its basic and most frequently used functions. Often, the nucleus remains resident in main memory.

**One's Complement Representation**   Used to represent binary integers. A positive integer is represented as in sign–magnitude. A negative integer is represented by reversing each bit in the representation of a positive integer of the same magnitude.

**Opcode**   Abbreviated form for *operation code.*

**Operand***   An entity on which an operation is performed.

**Operating System***   Software that controls the execution of programs; and that provides services such as resource allocation, scheduling, input/output control, and data management.

**Operation Code***   A code used to represent the operations of a computer. Usually abbreviated to opcode.

**Orthogonality**   A principle by which two variables or dimensions are independent of one another. In the context of an instruction set, the term is generally used to indicate that other elements of an instruction (address mode, number of operands, length of operand) are independent of (not determined by) opcode.

**Page\*** In a virtual storage system, a fixed-length block that has a virtual address and that is transferred as a unit between real storage and auxiliary storage.

**Page Fault** Occurs when the page containing a referenced word is not in main memory. This causes an interrupt and requires the operating system to bring in the needed page.

**Page Frame\*** An area of main storage used to hold a page.

**Parity Bit\*** A binary digit appended to a group of binary digits to make the sum of all the digits either always odd (odd parity) or always even (even parity).

**Peripheral Equipment (IBM)** In a computer system, with respect to a particular processing unit, any equipment that provides the processing unit with out-side communication. Synonymous with *peripheral device.*

**Process** A program in execution. A process is controlled and scheduled by the operating system.

**Process Control Block** The manifestation of a process in an operating system. It is a data structure containing information about the characteristics and state of the process.

**Processor\*** In a computer, a functional unit that interprets and executes instruc-tions. A processor consists of at least an instruction control unit and an arith-metic unit.

**Processor Cycle Time** The time required for the shortest well-defined CPU micro-operation. It is the basic unit of time for measuring all CPU actions. Synonymous with *machine cycle time.*

**Program Counter** Instruction address register.

**Programmable Logic Array (PLA)\*** An array of gates whose interconnections can be programmed to perform a specific logical function.

**Programmable Read-Only Memory (PROM)** Semiconductor memory whose con-tents may be set only once. The writing process is performed electrically and may be performed by the user at a time later than original chip fabrication.

**Programmed I/O** A form of I/O in which the CPU issues an I/O command to an I/O module and must then wait for the operation to be complete before proceeding.

**Program Status Word (PSW)** An area in storage used to indicate the order in which instructions are executed, and to hold and indicate the status of the computer system. Synonymous with *processor status word.*

**Random-Access Memory (RAM)** Memory in which each addressable location has a unique addressing mechanism. The time to access a given location is inde-pendent of the sequence of prior access.

**Read-Only Memory (ROM)** Semiconductor memory whose contents cannot be altered, except by destroying the storage unit. Nonerasable memory.

**Redundant Array of Independent Disks (RAID)** A disk array in which part of the physical storage capacity is used to store redundant information about user data stored on the remainder of the storage capacity. The redundant informa-tion enables regeneration of user data in the event that one of the array's member disks or the access path to it fails.

**Registers** High-speed memory internal to the CPU. Some registers are user-visible, that is, available to the programmer via the machine instruction set. Other registers are used only by the CPU, for control purposes.

**Scalar\*** A quantity characterized by a single value.

**Secondary Memory** Memory located outside the computer system itself, including disk and tape.

**Selector Channel** An I/O channel designed to operate with only one I/O device at a time. Once the I/O device is selected, a complete record is transferred one byte at a time. Contrast with *block multiplexor channel, multiplexor channel.*

**Semiconductor** A solid crystalline substance, such as silicon or germanium, whose electrical conductivity is intermediate between insulators and good conductors. Used to fabricate transistors and solid-state components.

**Sequential Circuit** A digital logic circuit whose output depends on the current input plus the state of the circuit. Sequential circuits thus possess the attribute of memory.

**Sign–Magnitude Representation** Used to represent binary integers. In an $N$-bit word, the leftmost bit is the sign (0 = positive, 1 = negative) and the remaining $N - 1$ bits comprise the magnitude of the number.

**Solid-State Component\*** A component whose operation depends on the control of electric or magnetic phenomena in solids (e.g., transistor crystal diode, ferrite core).

**Stack\*** A list that is constructed and maintained so that the next item to be retrieved is the most recently stored item in the list, last-in-first-out (LIFO).

**Static RAM** A RAM whose cells are implemented using flip-flops. A static RAM will hold its data as long as power is supplied to it; no periodic refresh is required.

**Superpipelined Processor** A processor design in which the instruction pipeline consists of many very small stages, so that more than one pipeline stage can be executed during one clock cycle and so that a large number of instructions may be in the pipeline at the same time.

**Superscalar Processor** A processor design that includes multiple-instruction pipelines, so that more than one instruction can be executing in the same pipeline stage simultaneously.

**Synchronous Timing** A technique in which the occurrence of events on a bus is determined by a clock. The clock defines equal-width time slots, and events begin only at the beginning of a time slot.

**System Bus** A bus used to interconnect major computer components (CPU, memory, I/O).

**Truth Table\*** A table that describes a logic function by listing all possible combinations of input values and indicating, for each combination, the output value.

**Two's Complement Representation** Used to represent binary integers. A positive integer is represented as in sign–magnitude. A negative number is represented by adding one to the one's complement representation of the same number.

**Unary Operator\*** An operator that represents an operation on one and only one operand.

**Unconditional Jump\*** A jump that takes place whenever the instruction that specified it is executed.

**Uniprocessing** Sequential execution of instructions by a processing unit, or independent use of a processing unit in a multiprocessing system.

**User-Visible Registers**   CPU registers that may be referenced by the programmer. The instruction-set format allows one or more registers to be specified as operands or addresses of operands.

**Vector\***   A quantity usually characterized by an ordered set of scalars.

**Virtual Storage\***   The storage space that may be regarded as addressable main storage by the user of a computer system in which virtual addresses are mapped into real addresses. The size of virtual storage is limited by the addressing scheme of the computer system and by the amount of auxiliary storage available, and not by the actual number of main storage locations.

**Volatile Memory**   A memory in which a constant electrical power source is required to maintain the contents of memory. If the power is switched off, the stored information is lost.

**WORM**   Write-Once, Read-Many. A disk that is more easily written than CD-ROM, making single-copy disks commercially feasible. As with CD-ROM, after the write operation is performed, the disk is read-only. The most popular size is 5.25-in., which can hold from 200 to 800 Mbytes of data.

# References

**ABAD83**  Abadir, M., and Reghbati, H. "Functional Testing of Semiconductor Random Access Memories." *Computing Surveys*, September 1983.

**ACOS86**  Acosta, R.; Kjelstrup, J.; and Torng, H. "An Instruction Issuing Approach to Enhancing Performance in Multiple Functional Unit Processors." *IEEE Transactions on Computers*, September 1986.

**ADAM91**  Adamek, J. *Foundations of Coding.* New York: Wiley, 1991.

**AGAR89**  Agarwal, A. *Analysis of Cache Performance for Operating Systems and Multiprogramming.* Boston: Kluwer Academic Publishers, 1989.

**AGER87**  Agerwala, T., and Cocke, J. *High Performance Reduced Instruction Set Processors.* Technical Report RC12434 (#55845). Yorktown, NY: IBM Thomas J. Watson Research Center, January 1987.

**AGRA76**  Agrawala, A., and Rauscher, T. *Foundations of Microprogramming: Architecture, Software, and Applications.* New York: Academic Press, 1976.

**ALEX93**  Alexandridis, N. *Design of Microprocessor-Based Systems.* Englewood Cliffs, NJ: Prentice Hall, 1993.

**ALSU90**  Alsup, M. "The Motorola's 88000 Family Architecture." *IEEE Micro*, June 1990.

**ALTN79**  Altnether, J. *Error Detecting and Correcting Codes.* Intel Application Note AP-46, 1979.

**AMDA79**  Amdahl, G. "The Early Chapters of the PCM Story." *Datamation*, February 1979.

**ANDE67**  Anderson, D.; Sparacio, F.; and Tomasulo, F. "The IBM System/360 Model 91: Machine Philosophy and Instruction Handling." *IBM Journal of Research and Development*, January 1967.

**ANDE93**  Anderson, D., and Shanley, T. *Pentium Processor System Architecture.* Richardson, TX: Mindshare Press, 1993.

**ANDR80**  Andrews, M. *Principles of Firmware Engineering in Microprogram Control.* Silver Spring, MD: Computer Science Press, 1980.

**ANDR90**  Andrews, W. "Futurebus+ Spec Completed—Almost." *Computer Design*, February 1, 1990.

**ANDR91**  Andrews, W. "Enhancing the Performance of Standard Buses." *Computer Design*, September 1991.

**ANSI90**  American National Standards Institute. *American National Standard Dictionary for Information Systems.* ANSI X3.172-1990, 1990.

**ARDE80**  Arden, B. *What Can Be Automated?* Cambridge, MA: The MIT Press, 1980.

**AZIM92**  Azimi, M.; Prasad, B.; and Bhat, K. "Two Level Cache Architectures." *Proceedings COMPCON '92*, February 1992.

**BANE82**  Banerji, D., and Raymond, J. *Elements of Microprogramming.* Englewood Cliffs, NJ: Prentice-Hall, 1982.

**BARR68** Barron, D. *Recursive Techniques in Programming.* New York: American Elsevier, 1968.

**BART85** Bartee, T. *Digital Computer Fundamentals.* New York: McGraw-Hill, 1985.

**BASH81** Bashe, C.; Bucholtz, W.; Hawkins, G.; Ingram, J.; and Rochester, N. "The Architecture of IBM's Early Computers." *IBM Journal of Research and Development,* September 1981.

**BASH91** Bashteen, A.; Lui, I.; and Mullan, J. "A Superpipeline Approach to the MIPS Architecture." *Proceedings, COMPCON Spring '91,* February 1991.

**BECK93** Becker, M., et al. "The PowerPC 601 Microprocessor." *IEEE Micro,* October 1993.

**BELL70** Bell, C.; Cady, R.; McFarland, H.; Delagi, B.; O'Loughlin, J.; and Noonan, R. "A New Architecture for Minicomputers—The DEC PDP-11." *Proceedings, Spring Joint Computer Conference,* 1970.

**BELL71a** Bell, C., and Newell, A. *Computer Structures: Readings and Examples.* New York: McGraw-Hill, 1971.

**BELL71b** Bell, C., and Newell, A. "The IBM 1401." in [BELL71a].

**BELL78a** Bell, C.; Mudge, J.; and McNamara, J. *Computer Engineering: A DEC View of Hardware Systems Design.* Bedford, MA: Digital Press, 1978.

**BELL78b** Bell, C.; Newell, A.; and Siewiorek, D. "Structural Levels of the PDP-8." in [BELL78a].

**BELL78c** Bell, C.; Kotok, A.; Hastings, T.; and Hill, R. "The Evolution of the DEC System-10." *Communications of the ACM,* January 1978.

**BHAN79** Bhandarkar, D., and Rothman, S. "The VAX-11, DEC's 32-Bit Version of the PDP-11." *Datamation,* February 1979.

**BLAH83** Blahut, R. *Theory and Practice of Error Control Codes.* Reading, MA: Addison-Wesley, 1983.

**BOND83** Bond, R. "XA: The View from White Plains." *Datamation,* May 1983.

**BOND94** Bondurant, D. "Low Latency EDRAM Main Memory Subsystem for 66 Mhz Bus Operation." *Proceedings, COMPCON '94,* March 1994.

**BOOT51** Booth, A. "A Signed Binary Multiplication Technique." *Quarterly Journal of Mechanical and Applied Mathematics,* vol. 4, pt. 2, 1951.

**BRAD91a** Bradlee, D.; Eggers, S.; and Henry, R. "The Effect on RISC Performance of Register Set Size and Structure Versus Code Generation Strategy." *Proceedings, 18th Annual International Symposium on Computer Architecture,* May 1991.

**BRAD91b** Bradlee, D.; Eggers, S.; and Henry, R. "Integrating Register Allocation and Instruction Scheduling for RISCs." *Proceedings, Fourth International Conference on Architectural Support for Programming Languages and Operating Systems,* April 1991.

**BREY95** Brey, B. *The Intel 32-Bit Microprocessors: 80386, 80486, and Pentium.* Englewood Cliffs, NJ: Prentice Hall, 1995.

**BUCH86** Buchholz, W. "The IBM System/370 Vector Architecture." *IBM Systems Journal,* No. 1, 1986.

**BUDD87** Buddine, L., and Young, E. *The Brady Guide to CD-ROM.* New York: Prentice-Hall Press, 1987.

**BURG75** Burge, W. *Recursive Programming Techniques.* Reading, MA: Addison-Wesley, 1975.

**BURK46** Burks, A.; Goldstine, H.; and von Neumann, J. *Preliminary Discussion of the Logical Design of an Electronic Computer Instrument.* Report prepared for U.S. Army Ordnance Dept., 1946, reprinted in [BELL71a].

**CATA94** Catanzaro, B. *Multiprocessor System Architectures.* Mountain View, CA: Sunsoft Press, 1994.

**CHAI82**   Chaitin, G. "Register Allocation and Spilling via Graph Coloring." *Proceedings, SIGPLAN Symposium on Compiler Construction,* June 1982.

**CHEN94**   Chen, P.; Lee, E.; Gibson, G.; Katz, R.; and Patterson, D. "RAID: High-Performance, Reliable Secondary Storage." *ACM Computing Surveys,* June 1994.

**CHOW86**   Chow, F.; Himmelstein, M.; Killian, E.; and Weber, L. "Engineering a RISC Compiler System." *Proceedings, COMPCON Spring '86,* March 1986.

**CHOW87**   Chow, F.; Correll, S.; Himmelstein, M.; Killian, E.; and Weber, L. "How Many Addressing Modes Are Enough?" *Proceedings, Second International Conference on Architectural Support for Programming Languages and Operating Systems,* October 1987.

**CHOW90**   Chow, F., and Hennessy, J. "The Priority-Based Coloring Approach to Register Allocation." *ACM Transactions on Programming Languages,* October 1990.

**CLAR80**   Clark, W. "From Electron Mobility to Logical Structure: A View of Integrated Circuits." *Computing Surveys,* September 1980.

**CLAR82**   Clark, D., and Levy, H. "Measurement and Analysis of Instruction Use in the VAX-11/780." *Proceedings, Ninth Annual Symposium on Computer Architecture,* April 1982.

**CLAR83**   Clark, D. "Cache Performance in the VAX-11/780." *ACM Transactions on Computer Systems,* February 1983.

**CLAR85**   Clark, D., and Emer, J. "Performance of the VAX-11/780 Translation Buffer: Simulation and Measurement." *ACM Transactions on Computer Systems,* February 1985.

**CLIN81**   Cline, B. *Microprogramming Concepts and Techniques.* New York: Petrocelli, 1981.

**CODY84**   Cody, W., et al. "A Proposed Radix- and Word-Length-Independent Standard for Floating-Point Arithmetic." *IEEE Micro,* August 1984.

**COHE81**   Cohen, D. "On Holy Wars and a Plea for Peace." *Computer,* October 1981.

**COLW85a**   Colwell, R.; Hitchcock, C.; Jensen, E.; Brinkley-Sprunt, H.; and Kollar, C. "Computers, Complexity, and Controversy." *Computer,* September 1985.

**COLW85b**   Colwell, R.; Hitchcock, C.; Jensen, E.; and Sprunt, H. "More Controversy About 'Computers, Complexity, and Controversy.'" *Computer,* December 1985.

**COME92**   Come, R., and Watson, G., eds. "Memory Catches Up." *IEEE Spectrum,* October 1992.

**CONN79**   Connors, W.; Florkowski, J.; and Patton, S. "The IBM 3033: An Inside Look." *Datamation,* May 1979.

**CONW77**   Conway, J. "Approach to Unified Bus Architecture Sidestepping Inherent Drawbacks." *Computer Design,* January 1977.

**COOK82**   Cook, R., and Dande, N. "An Experiment to Improve Operand Addressing." *Proceedings, Symposium on Architecture Support for Programming Languages and Operating Systems,* March 1982.

**COON81**   Coonen J. "Underflow and Denormalized Numbers." *IEEE Computer,* March 1981.

**COUT86**   Coutant, D.; Hammond, C.; and Kelley, J. "Compilers for the New Generation of Hewlett-Packard Computers." *Proceedings, COMPCON Spring '86,* March 1986.

**CRAG79**   Cragon, H. "An Evaluation of Code Space Requirements and Performance of Various Architectures." *Computer Architecture News,* February 1979.

**CRAG92**   Cragon, H. *Branch Strategy Taxonomy and Performance Models.* Los Alamitos, CA: IEEE Computer Society Press, 1992.

**CRAW90**   Crawford, J. "The i486 CPU: Executing Instructions in One Clock Cycle." *IEEE Micro,* February 1990.

**DATT93**  Dattatreya, G. "A Systematic Approach to Teaching Binary Arithmetic in a First Course." *IEEE Transactions on Education,* February 1993.

**DAVI87**  Davidson, J., and Vaughan, R. "The Effect of Instruction Set Complexity on Program Size and Memory Performance." *Proceedings, Second International Conference on Architectural Support for Programming Languages and Operating Systems,* October 1987.

**DAWS86**  Dawson, W., and Dobinson, R. "A Framework for Computer Design." *IEEE Spectrum,* October 1986.

**DAWS87**  Dawson, W., and Dobinson, R. "Buses and Bus Standards." *Computer Standards and Interfaces,* June 1987.

**DEDE94**  Dedek, J. *Basics of SCSI.* Menlo Park, CA: Ancot Corp., 1994.

**DEIT90**  Deitel, H. *An Introduction to Operating Systems.* Reading, MA: Addison-Wesley, 1990.

**DENN68**  Denning, P. "The Working Set Model for Program Behavior." *Communications of the ACM,* May 1968.

**DEWA90**  Dewar, R., and Smosna, M. *Microprocessors: A Programmer's View.* New York: McGraw-Hill, 1990.

**DIEF94a**  Diefendorff, K.; Oehler, R.; and Hochsprung, R. "Evolution of the PowerPC Architecture." *IEEE Micro,* April 1994.

**DIEF94b**  Diefendorff, K., and Silha, E. "The PowerPC User Instruction Set Architecture." *IEEE Micro,* April 1994.

**DIJK63**  Dijkstra, E. "Making an ALGOL Translator for the X1." in *Annual Review of Automatic Programming, Volume 4,* Pergamon, 1963.

**DORA82**  Doran, R. "The Amdahl 470V/8 and the IBM 3033: A Comparison of Processor Designs." *Computer,* April 1982.

**DUBB78**  Dubbey, J. *The Mathematical Work of Charles Babbage.* Cambridge, England: Cambridge University Press, 1978.

**DUBE91**  Dubey, P., and Flynn, M. "Branch Strategies: Modeling and Optimization." *IEEE Transactions on Computers,* October 1991.

**DUGA83**  Dugan, R. "System/370 Extended Architecture: A Program View of the Channel Subsystem." *Proceedings, Tenth Annual International Symposium on Computer Architecture,* June, 1983.

**ECKE90**  Eckert, R. "Communication Between Computers and Peripheral Devices—An Analogy." *ACM SIGSCE Bulletin,* September 1990.

**EDEN83**  Eden, R.; Livingston, A.; and Welch, B. "Integrated Circuits: The Case for Gallium Arsenide." *IEEE Spectrum,* December 1983.

**ELAS84**  El-Asfouri, S.; Johnson, O.; and King, W. *Computer Organization and Programming: VAX-11.* Reading, MA: Addison-Wesley, 1984.

**ELAY79**  El-Ayat, K. "The Intel 8089: An Integrated I/O Processor." *Computer,* June 1979.

**ELAY85**  El-Ayat, K., and Agarwal, R. "The Intel 80386—Architecture and Implementation." *IEEE Micro,* December 1985.

**ENSL77**  Enslow, P. "Multiprocessor Organization—A Survey." *ACM Computing Surveys,* March 1977.

**ESPO92**  Esponda, M., and Rojas, R. "A Graphical Representation of RISC Processors." *Computer Architecture News,* September 1992.

**FELD94**  Feldman, J., and Retter, C. *Computer Architecture.* New York: McGraw-Hill, 1994.

**FITZ81**  Fitzpatrick, D., et al. "A RISCy Approach to VLSI." *VLSI Design,* 4th quarter, 1981. Reprinted in *Computer Architecture News,* March 1982.

**FLOY72**  Floyd, M. "Some Computer Organizations and Their Effectiveness." *IEEE Transactions on Computers,* September 1972.

**FLOY90**  Floyd, T. *Digital Fundamentals.* New York: Merrill/Macmillan, 1990.

**FLYN71**  Flynn, M., and Rosin, R. "Microprogramming: An Introduction and a Viewpoint." *IEEE Transactions on Computers,* July 1971.

**FLYN72**  Flynn, M. "Some Computer Organizations and Their Effectiveness." *IEEE Transactions on Computers,* September 1972.

**FLYN85**  Flynn, M.; Johnson, J.; and Wakefield, S. "On Instruction Sets and Their Formats." *IEEE Transactions on Computers,* March 1985.

**FLYN87**  Flynn, M.; Mitchell, C.; and Mulder, J. "And Now a Case for More Complex Instruction Sets." *Computer,* September 1987.

**FOSS85a**  Fossum, T.; McElroy, J.; and English, B. "New VAX Squeezes Mainframe Power into Mini Package." *Computer Design,* March 1985.

**FOSS85b**  Fossum, T.; Grundmann, W.; and Blaha, V. "Floating-Point Processor for the VAX 8600." *Proceedings, COMPCON Spring '85,* 1985.

**FOSS85c**  Fossum, T.; McElroy, J.; and English, W. "An Overview of the VAX 8600 System." *Digital Technical Journal,* August 1985.

**FOST67**  Foster, J. *List Processing.* New York: American Elsevier, 1967.

**FOX87**  Fox, G., and Messina, G. "Advanced Computer Architectures." *Scientific American,* October 1987.

**FRAI83**  Frailey, D. "Word Length of a Computer Architecture: Definitions and Applications." *Computer Architecture News,* June 1983.

**FREE88**  Freese, R. "Optical Disks Become Erasable." *IEEE Spectrum,* February 1988.

**FUJI84**  Fujitani, L. "Laser Optical Disk: The Coming Revolution in On-Line Storage." *Communications of the ACM,* June 1984.

**FURH87**  Furht, B., and Milutinovic, V. "A Survey of Microprocessor Architectures for Memory Management." *Computer,* March 1987.

**GARR94**  Garrett, B. "RDRAMs: A New Speed Paradigm." *Proceedings, COMPCON '94,* March 1994.

**GEHR88**  Gehringer, E.; Abullarade, J.; and Gulyn, M. "A Survey of Commercial Parallel Processors." *Computer Architecture News,* September 1988.

**GIBS88**  Gibson, S. "Hardware Roundup: Large and Medium-Scale Systems." *Computerworld,* September 19, 1988.

**GIFF87**  Gifford, D., and Spector, A. "Case Study: IBM's System/360-370 Architecture." *Communications of the ACM,* April 1987.

**GILL94**  Gillig, J. "Endian-Neutral Software." *Dr. Dobb's Journal,* October 1994.

**GJES92**  Gjessing, S., et al. "A RAM Link for High Speed." *IEEE Spectrum,* October 1992.

**GLAS91**  Glass, B. "The MIPS R4000." *Byte,* December 1991.

**GOLD91**  Goldberg, D. "What Every Computer Scientist Should Know About Floating-Point Arithmetic." *ACM Computing Surveys,* March 1991.

**GOOR89**  Goor, A. *Computer Architecture and Design.* Reading, MA: Addison-Wesley, 1989.

**GOSS89**  Goss, R. "Motorola's 88000: Integration, Performance and Applications." *Proceedings, COMPCOM Spring '89,* March 1989.

**GUST84**  Gustavson, D. "Computer Buses—A Tutorial." *IEEE Micro,* August 1984.

**GUTE88**  Guterl, F. "Compact Disc." *IEEE Spectrum,* November 1988.

**HAAV71**  Haavind, R. "The Many Faces of Microprogramming." *Computer Decisions*, September 1971.

**HABE85**  Haber, L. "Multiprocessor Technology Means More Muscle, Less Fat." *Mini-Micro Systems*, June 1985.

**HAND93**  Handy, J. *The Cache Memory Book*. San Diego: Academic Press, 1993.

**HAYE88**  Hayes, J. *Computer Architecture and Organization, Second Edition*. New York: McGraw-Hill, 1988.

**HEAT84**  Heath, J. "Re-evaluation of RISC I." *Computer Architecture News*, March 1984.

**HEGD92**  Hedge, A. "Detect/Correct Errors to Improve Data Reliability." *Electronic Design*, June 11, 1992.

**HENN82**  Hennessy, J., et al. "Hardware/Software Tradeoffs for Increased Performance." *Proceedings, Symposium on Architectural Support for Programming Languages and Operating Systems*, March 1982.

**HENN84**  Hennessy, J. "VLSI Processor Architecture." *IEEE Transactions on Computers*, December 1984.

**HENN90**  Hennessy, J., and Patterson, D. *Computer Architecture: A Quantitative Approach*. San Mateo, CA: Morgan Kaufmann, 1990.

**HENN91**  Hennessy, J., and Jouppi, N. "Computer Technology and Architecture: An Evolving Interaction." *Computer*, September 1991.

**HEYW83**  Heywood, S. "The 8086—An Architecture for the Future." *Byte*, June 1983.

**HIDA90**  Hidaka, H.; Matsuda, Y.; Asakura, M.; and Kazuyasu, F. "The Cache DRAM Architecture: A DRAM with an On-Chip Cache Memory." *IEEE Micro*, April 1990.

**HIGB83**  Higbie, L. "A Vector Processing Tutorial." *Datamation*, August 1983.

**HIGB90**  Higbie, L. "Quick and Easy Cache Performance Analysis." *Computer Architecture News*, June 1990.

**HIGM67**  Higman, B. *A Comparative Study of Programming Languages*. New York: American Elsevier, 1967.

**HILL64**  Hill, R. "Stored Logic Programming and Applications." *Datamation*, February 1964.

**HILL89**  Hill, M. "Evaluating Associativity in CPU Caches." *IEEE Transactions on Computers*, December 1989.

**HITC85**  Hitchcock, C., and Brinkley, H. "Analyzing Multiple Register Sets." *The 12th Annual International Symposium on Computer Architecture*, June 17–19, 1985.

**HOF95**  Hof, R. "Intel: Far Beyond the Pentium." *Business Week*, February 20, 1995.

**HOPK87**  Hopkins, M. "A Perspective on the 801/Reduced Instruction Set Computer." *IBM Systems Journal*, Vol. 26, No. 1, 1987.

**HUCK83**  Huck, T. *Comparative Analysis of Computer Architectures*. Stanford University Technical Report No. 83-243, May 1983.

**HUGU91**  Huguet, M., and Lang, T. "Architectural Support for Reduced Register Saving/Restoring in Single-Window Register Files." *ACM Transactions on Computer Systems*, February 1991.

**HWAN93**  Hwang, K. *Advanced Computer Architecture*. New York: McGraw-Hill, 1993.

**IBM94**  International Business Machines, Inc. *The PowerPC Architecture: A Specification for a New Family of RISC Processors*. San Francisco: CA: Morgan Kaufmann, 1994.

**IEEE84**  Institute of Electrical and Electronics Engineers. *IEEE Standard Graphic Symbols for Logic Functions*. ANSI/IEEE Std 91-1984, 1984.

**IEEE85** Institute of Electrical and Electronics Engineers. *IEEE Standard for Binary Floating-Point Arithmetic.* ANSI/IEEE Std 754-1985, 1985.

**INTE81** Intel Corp. "8085AH/8085AH-2/8085AH-1 3-Bit HMOS Microprocessor." 1981.

**INTE94a** Intel Corp. *Pentium Family User's Manual, Volume 1: Data Book.* Santa Clara, CA, 1994.

**INTE94b** Intel Corp. *Pentium Family User's Manual, Volume 3: Architecture and Programming Manual.* Santa Clara, CA, 1994.

**JAME90** James, D. "Multiplexed Buses: The Endian Wars Continue." *IEEE Micro,* June 1990.

**JEND83** Jendro, J. "Extending the Megabus." *Mini-Micro Systems,* September 1983.

**JOHN71** Johnson, A. "The Microdiagnostics for the IBM System/360 Model 30." *IEEE Transactions on Computers,* July, 1971.

**JOHN84** Johnson, J., and Kassel, S. *The Multibus Design Guidebook.* New York: McGraw-Hill, 1984.

**JOHN91** Johnson, M. *Superscalar Microprocessor Design.* Englewood Cliffs, NJ: Prentice-Hall, 1991.

**JONE91** Jones, S. "A Futurebus Interface from Off-the-Shelf Parts." *IEEE Micro,* February 1991.

**JOUP88** Jouppi, N. "Superscalar versus Superpipelined Machines." *Computer Architecture News,* June 1988.

**JOUP89a** Jouppi, N., and Wall, D. "Available Instruction-Level Parallelism for Superscalar and Superpipelined Machines." *Proceedings, Third International Conference on Architectural Support for Programming Languages and Operating Systems,* April 1989.

**JOUP89b** Jouppi, N. "The Nonuniform Distribution of Instruction-Level and Machine Parallelism and Its Effect on Performance." *IEEE Transactions on Computers,* December 1989.

**KAEL91** Kaeli, D., and Emma, P. "Branch History Table Prediction of Moving Target Branches Due to Subroutine Returns." *Proceedings, 18th Annual International Symposium on Computer Architecture,* May 1991.

**KANE92** Kane, G., and Heinrich, J. *MIPS RISC Architecture.* Englewood Cliffs, NJ: Prentice Hall, 1992.

**KARP87** Karp, A. "Programming for Parallelism." *Computer,* 1987.

**KATE83** Katevenis, M. *Reduced Instruction Set Computer Architectures for VLSI.* PhD dissertation, Computer Science Department, University of California at Berkeley, October 1983. Reprinted by MIT Press, Cambridge, MA, 1985.

**KNUT71** Knuth, D. "An Empirical Study of FORTRAN Programs." *Software Practice and Experience,* vol. 1, 1971.

**KNUT81** Knuth, D. *The Art of Computer Programming, Volume 2: Seminumerical Algorithms, Second Edition.* Reading, MA: Addison-Wesley, 1981.

**KOES78** Koestler, A. *Janus.* New York: Random House, 1978.

**KOP81** Kop, H. *Hard Disk Controller Design Using the Intel 8089.* Intel Application Note AP-122, 1981.

**KORN93** Koren, I. *Computer Arithmetic Algorithms.* Englewood Cliffs, NJ: Prentice Hall, 1993.

**KOZD80** Kozdrowicki, E., and Theis, D. "Second Generation of Vector Supercomputers." *Computer,* November 1980.

**KRAF81** Kraft, G., and Toy, W. *Microprogrammed Control and Reliable Design of Small Computers.* Englewood Cliffs, NJ: Prentice-Hall, 1981.

**KRUT88** Krutz, R. *Interfacing Techniques in Digital Design with Emphasis on Microprocessors.* New York, Wiley, 1988.

**KRYD86** Kryder, M., ed. "Special Section on Magnetic Information Storage Retrieval." *Proceedings of the IEEE,* November 1986.

**KRYD87** Kryder, M. "Data-Storage Technologies for Advanced Computing." *Scientific American,* October 1987.

**KUCK72** Kuck, D.; Muraoka, Y.; and Chen, S. "On the Number of Operations Simultaneously Executable in Fortran-like Programs and Their Resulting Speedup." *IEEE Transactions on Computers,* December 1972.

**KUGA91** Kuga, M.; Murakami, K.; and Tomita, S. "DSNS (Dynamically-hazard resolved, Statically-code-scheduled, Nonuniform Superscalar): Yet Another Superscalar Processor Architecture." *Computer Architecture News,* June 1991.

**LEE91** Lee, R.; Kwok, A.; and Briggs, F. "The Floating Point Performance of a Superscalar SPARC Processor." *Proceedings, Fourth International Conference on Architectural Support for Programming Languages and Operating Systems,* April 1991.

**LEVI82** Levine, R. "Supercomputers." *Scientific American,* January 1982.

**LEVY78** Levy, J. "Buses, the Skeleton of Computer Structures." in [BELL78a].

**LEVY89** Levy, H., and Eckhouse, R. *Computer Programming and Architecture: The VAX-11.* Bedford, MA: Digital Press, 1989.

**LILJ88** Lilja, D. "Reducing the Branch Penalty in Pipelined Processors." *Computer,* July 1988.

**LILJ93** Lilja, D. "Cache Coherence in Large-Scale Shared-Memory Multiprocessors: Issues and Comparisons." *ACM Computing Surveys,* September 1993.

**LUHN84** Luhn, R. "The Ups and Downs of Bubble Memory." *Computerworld,* December 3, 1984.

**LUND77** Lunde, A. "Empirical Evaluation of Some Features of Instruction Set Processor Architectures." *Communications of the ACM,* March 1977.

**LYNC93** Lynch, M. *Microprogrammed State Machine Design.* Boca Raton, FL, 1993.

**MACG84** MacGregor, D.; Mothersole, D.; and Moyer, B. "The Motorola MC68020." *IEEE Micro,* August 1984.

**MALL75** Mallach, E. "Emulation Architecture." *Computer,* August 1975.

**MALL79** Mallach, E. "The Evolution of an Architecture." *Datamation,* April 1979.

**MALL83** Mallach, E., and Sondak, N. *Advances in Microprogramming.* Dedham, MA: Artech House, 1983.

**MANO93** Mano, M. *Computer System Architecture.* Englewood Cliffs, NJ: Prentice Hall, 1993.

**MARC90** Marchant, A. *Optical Recording.* Reading, MA: Addison-Wesley, 1990.

**MASH94** Mashey, J. "CISC vs. RISC (or what is RISC really)." *USENET comp.arch newsgroup, article 22850,* January 1994.

**MASS94** Massiglia, P., ed. *The RAIDbook: A Sourcebook for Disk Array Technology.* St. Peter, MN: The Raid Advisory Board, 1994.

**MAY94** May, C.; Silha, E.; Simpson, R.; and Warren, H., eds. *The PowerPC Architecture.* San Francisco: Morgan Kaufmann, 1994.

**MAYB84** Mayberry, W., and Efland, G. "Cache Boosts Multiprocessor Performance." *Computer Design,* November 1984.

**MCEL85** McEliece, R. "The Reliability of Computer Memories." *Scientific American,* January 1985.

**MCGE90**  McGeady, S. "The i960CA Superscalar Implementation of the 80960 Architecture." *Proceedings, COMPCON Spring '90,* March 1990.

**MCGE91**  McGeady, S., et al. "Performance Enhancements in the Superscalar i960MM Embedded Microprocessor." *Proceedings, COMPCON Spring '91,* February 1991.

**MEIK86**  Meiklejohn, W. "Magnetooptics: A Thermomagnetic Recording Technology." *Proceedings of the IEEE,* November 1986.

**MEIN87**  Meindl, J. "Chips for Advanced Computing." *Scientific American,* October 1987.

**MELE89**  Melear, C. "The Design of the 88000 RISC Family." *IEEE Micro,* April 1989.

**MILE92**  Milenkovic, M. *Operating Systems: Concepts and Design.* New York: McGraw-Hill, 1992.

**MILU86**  Milutinovic, V. "GaAs Microprocessor Technology." *Computer,* October 1986.

**MIRA92**  Mirapuri, S.; Woodacre, M.; and Vasseghi, N. "The MIPS R4000 Processor." *IEEE Micro,* April 1992.

**MOKH84**  Mokhoff, N. "Magnetic Bubble Memories Making a Comeback." *Computer Design,* November 1984.

**MOLD93**  Moldovan, D. *Parallel Processing: From Applications to Systems.* San Mateo, CA: Morgan Kaufmann, 1993.

**MORG92**  Morgan, D. *Numerical Methods.* San Mateo, CA: M&T Books, 1992.

**MORS94**  Morse, H. *Practical Parallel Computing.* Boston, MA: AP Professional, 1994.

**MORS78**  Morse, S.; Pohlman, W.; and Ravenel, B. "The Intel 8086 Microprocessor: A 16-bit Evolution of the 8080." *Computer,* June 1978.

**MYER78**  Myers, G. "The Evaluation of Expressions in a Storage-to-Storage Architecture." *Computer Architecture News,* June 1978.

**NBS79**  National Bureau of Standards. *I/O Channel Interface.* FIPS PUB 60-1, August 27, 1979.

**NCR90**  NCR Corp. *SCSI: Understanding the Small Computer System Interface.* Englewood Cliffs, NJ: Prentice Hall, 1990.

**NOVI93**  Novitsky, J.; Azimi, M.; and Ghaznavi, R. "Optimizing Systems Performance Based on Pentium Processors." *Proceedings COMPCON '92,* February 1993.

**NUTT92**  Nutt, G. *Centralized and Distributed Operating Systems.* Englewood Cliffs, NJ: Prentice-Hall, 1992.

**OBER88**  Obermeier, K. "Side by Side." *Byte,* November 1988.

**OMON94**  Omondi, A. *Computer Arithmetic Systems: Algorithms, Architecture, and Implementations.* Englewood Cliffs, NJ: Prentice Hall, 1994.

**PADE81**  Padegs, A. "System/360 and Beyond." *IBM Journal of Research and Development,* September 1981.

**PADE88**  Padegs, A.; Moore, B.; Smith, R.; and Buchholz, W. "The IBM System/370 Vector Architecture: Design Considerations." *IEEE Transactions on Communications,* May 1988.

**PARK89**  Parker, A., and Hamblen, J. *An Introduction to Microprogramming with Exercises Designed for the Texas Instruments SN74ACT8800 Software Development Board.* Dallas, TX: Texas Instruments, 1989.

**PATT82a**  Patterson, D., and Sequin, C. "A VLSI RISC." *Computer,* September 1982.

**PATT82b**  Patterson, D., and Piepho, R. "Assessing RISCs in High-Level Language Support." *IEEE Micro,* November 1982.

**PATT84**  Patterson, D. "RISC Watch." *Computer Architecture News,* March 1984.

**PATT85a**  Patterson, D. "Reduced Instruction Set Computers." *Communications of the ACM.* January 1985.

**PATT85b**  Patterson, D., and Hennessy, J. "Response to 'Computers, Complexity, and Controversy.'" *Computer,* November 1985.

**PATT88**  Patterson, D.; Gibson, G.; and Katz, R. "A Case for Redundant Arrays of Inexpensive Disks (RAID)." *Proceedings, ACM SIGMOD Conference of Management of Data,* June 1988.

**PATT94**  Patterson, D., and Hennessy, J. *Computer Organization and Design: The Hardware/Software Interface.* San Mateo, CA: Morgan Kaufmann, 1994.

**PAYN80**  Payne, M., and Bhandarkar, D. "VAX Floating Point: A Solid Foundation for Numerical Computation." *Computer Architecture News,* June 1980.

**PEUT79**  Peuto, B. "Architecture of a New Microprocessor." *Computer,* February 1979.

**PHIL85**  Phillips, D. "The Z80000 Microprocessor." *IEEE Micro,* December 1985.

**PIER84**  Pierce, R. "Diskless Computers Emerge with Proper Mix of Firmware, Processor, and Bubble Memory." *Electronic Design,* October 13, 1984.

**POHL81**  Pohl, I., and Shaw, A. *The Nature of Computation: An Introduction to Computer Science.* Rockville, MD: Computer Science Press, 1981.

**POPE91**  Popescu, V., et al. "The Metaflow Architecture." *IEEE Micro,* June 1991.

**POTT94**  Potter, T., et al. "Resolution of Data and Control-Flow Dependencies in the PowerPC 601." *IEEE Micro,* October 1994.

**POUN93**  Pountain, D. "Pentium: More RISC than CISC." *Byte,* September 1993.

**PRIN91**  Prince, B. *Semiconductor Memories.* New York: Wiley, 1991.

**PRZY88**  Przybylski, S.; Horowitz, M.; and Hennessy, J. "Performance Trade-offs in Cache Design." *Proceedings, Fifteenth Annual International Symposium on Computer Architecture,* June 1988.

**PRZY90**  Przybylski, S. "The Performance Impact of Block Size and Fetch Strategies." *Proceedings, 17th Annual International Symposium on Computer Architecture,* May 1990.

**PRZY93a**  Przybylski, S. "New DRAMs Improve Bandwidth." *Microprocessor Report,* February 15, 1993.

**PRZY93b**  Przybylski, S. "DRAMs for New Memory Systems." *Microprocessor Report,* March 8, 1993.

**PRZY94**  Przybylski, S. *New DRAM Technologies.* Sebastapol, CA: MicroDesign Resources, 1994.

**RADI83**  Radin, G. "The 801 Minicomputer." *IBM Journal of Research and Development,* May 1983.

**RAGA83**  Ragan-Kelley, R., and Clark, R. "Applying RISC Theory to a Large Computer." *Computer Design,* November 1983.

**RAUS80**  Rauscher, T., and Adams, P. "Microprogramming: A Tutorial and Survey of Recent Developments." *IEEE Transactions on Computers,* January 1980.

**REIS91**  Reis, R. *Digital Electronics Through Project Analysis.* New York: Merrill/Macmillan, 1991.

**RIGA84**  Riganati, J., and Schneck, P. "Supercomputing." *Computer,* October 1984.

**ROSC94**  Rosch, W. *The Winn L. Rosch Hardware Bible.* Indianapolis, IN: Sams, 1994.

**RUSS78**  Russell, R. "The CRAY-1 Computer System." *Communications of the ACM,* January 1978.

**RYAN93**   Ryan, B. "RISC Drives PowerPC." *Byte,* August 1993.

**SATY81**   Satyanarayanan, M., and Bhandarkar, D. "Design Trade-Offs in VAX-11 Translation Buffer Organization." *Computer,* December 1981.

**SCHL89**   Schleicher, D., and Taylor, R. "Systems Overview of the Application System/400." *IBM Systems Journal,* No. 3, 1989.

**SCHM94**   Schmit, M. "Optimizing Pentium Code." *Dr. Dobb's Journal,* January 1994.

**SEBE76**   Sebern, M. "A Minicomputer-compatible Microcomputer System: The DEC LSI-11." *Proceedings of the IEEE,* June 1976.

**SEGE91**   Segee, B., and Field, J. *Microprogramming and Computer Architecture.* New York: Wiley, 1991.

**SERL86**   Serlin, O. "MIPS, Dhrystones, and Other Tales." *Datamation,* June 1, 1986.

**SHAN38**   Shannon, C. "Symbolic Analysis of Relay and Switching Circuits." *AIEE Transactions,* vol. 57, 1938.

**SHAN94a**   Shanley, T., and Anderson, D. *PCI Systems Architecture.* Richardson, TX: Mindshare Press, 1994.

**SHAN94b**   Shanley, T. *PowerPC 601 System Architecture.* Richardson, TX: Mindshare Press, 1994.

**SHER84**   Sherburne, R. *Processor Design Tradeoffs in VLSI.* PhD thesis, Report No. UCB/CSD 84/173, University of California at Berkeley, April 1984.

**SIER90**   Sierra, H. *An Introduction to Direct Access Storage Devices.* Boston, MA: Academic Press, 1990.

**SIEW82**   Siewiorek, D.; Bell, C.; and Newell, A. *Computer Structures: Principles and Examples.* New York: McGraw-Hill, 1982.

**SILB91**   Silberschatz, A.; Peterson, J.; and Galvin, P. *Operating System Concepts.* Reading, MA: Addison-Wesley, 1991.

**SILB94**   Silberschatz, A., and Galvin, P. *Operating System Concepts.* Reading, MA: Addison-Wesley, 1994.

**SIMO69**   Simon, H. *The Sciences of the Artificial.* Cambridge, MA: MIT Press, 1969.

**SIMP87**   Simpson, R., and Hester, P. "The IBM RT PC ROMP Processor and Memory Management Unit." *IBM Systems Journal,* Vol. 26, No. 4, 1987.

**SING94**   Singhal, M., and Shivaratri, N. *Advanced Concepts in Operating Systems.* New York: McGraw-Hill, 1994.

**SMIT82**   Smith, A. "Cache Memories." *ACM Computing Surveys,* September 1982.

**SMIT87a**   Smith, A. "Line (Block) Size Choice for CPU Cache Memories." *IEEE Transactions on Communications,* September 1987.

**SMIT87b**   Smith, A. "Cache Memory Design: An Evolving Art." *IEEE Spectrum,* December 1987.

**SMIT89**   Smith, M.; Johnson, M.; and Horowitz, M. "Limits on Multiple Instruction Issue." *Proceedings, Third International Conference on Architectural Support for Programming Languages and Operating Systems,* April 1989.

**SOHI90**   Sohi, G. "Instruction Issue Logic for High-Performance Interruptable, Multiple Functional Unit, Pipelined Computers." *IEEE Transactions on Computers,* March 1990.

**SOLA94**   Solari, E., and Willse, G. *PCI Hardware and Software: Architecture and Design.* San Diego, CA: Annabooks, 1994.

**STAL94**   Stallings, W. *Data and Computer Communications, Fourth Edition.* Englewood Cliffs, NJ: Prentice Hall, 1994.

**STAL95**   Stallings, W. *Operating Systems, Second Edition.* Englewood Cliffs, NJ: Prentice Hall, 1995.

**STEN90**   Stenstrom, P. "A Survey of Cache Coherence Schemes of Multiprocessors." *Computer,* June 1990.

**STEV64**   Stevens, W. "The Structure of System/360, Part II: System Implementation." *IBM Systems Journal,* Vol. 3, No. 2, 1964. Reprinted in [BELL71A] and [SIEW82].

**STON80**   Stone, H., editor. *Introduction to Computer Architecture.* Chicago: SRA, 1980.

**STON93**   Stone, H. *High-Performance Computer Architecture.* Reading, MA: Addison-Wesley, 1993.

**STRE78a**   Strecker, W. "Cache Memories for PDP-11 Family Computers." in [BELL78a].

**STRE78b**   Strecker, W. "VAX-11/780: A Virtual Address Extension to the DEC PDP-11 Family." *Proceedings, National Computer Conference,* 1978.

**STRE83**   Strecker, W. "Transient Behavior of Cache Memories." *ACM Transactions on Computer Systems,* November 1983.

**STRI79**   Stritter, E., and Gunter, T. "A Microprocessor Architecture for a Changing World: The Motorola 68000." *Computer,* February 1979.

**SWAR90**   Swartzlander, E., ed. *Computer Arithmetic, Volumes I and II.* Los Alamitos, CA: IEEE Computer Society Press, 1990.

**TABA87**   Tabak, D. *RISC Architecture.* New York: Wiley, 1987.

**TABA91**   Tabak, D. *Advanced Microprocessors.* New York: McGraw-Hill, 1991.

**TAMI83**   Tamir, Y., and Sequin, C. "Strategies for Managing the Register File in RISC." *IEEE Transactions on Computers,* November 1983.

**TANE78**   Tanenbaum, A. "Implications of Structured Programming for Machine Architecture." *Communications of the ACM,* March 1978.

**TANE90**   Tanenbaum, A. *Structured Computer Organization.* Englewood Cliffs, NJ: Prentice-Hall, 1990.

**TANE92**   Tanenbaum, A. *Modern Operating Systems.* Englewood Cliffs, NJ: Prentice-Hall, 1992.

**TEEN93**   Teener, M. "New Technology in the IEEE P1394 Serial Bus—Making it Fast, Cheap, and Easy to Use." *Proceedings, Hot Interconnects Symposium '93,* August 1993.

**TEJA85**   Teja, E. *The Designer's Guide to Disk Drives.* Reston, VA: Reston Publishing, 1985.

**THOM94**   Thompson, T., and Ryan, B. "PowerPC 620 Soars." *Byte,* November 1994.

**TI90**   Texas Instruments Inc. *SN74ACT880 Family Data Manual.* SCSS006C, 1990.

**TJAD70**   Tjaden, G., and Flynn, M. "Detection and Parallel Execution of Independent Instructions." *IEEE Transactions on Computers,* October 1970.

**TOMA93**   Tomasevic, M., and Milutinovic, V. *The Cache Coherence Problem in Shared-Memory Multiprocessors: Hardware Solutions.* Los Alamitos, CA: IEEE Computer Society Press, 1993.

**TOON81**   Toong, H., and Gupta, A. "An Architectural Comparison of Contemporary 16-Bit Microprocessors." *IEEE Micro,* May 1981.

**TUCK67**   Tucker, S. "Microprogram Control for System/360." *IBM Systems Journal,* No. 4, 1967. Also in [MALL83].

**TUCK87**   Tucker, S. "The IBM 3090 System Design with Emphasis on the Vector Facility." *Proceedings, COMPCON Spring '87,* February 1987.

**TURN86**   Turner, R. *Operating Systems: Design and Implementation.* New York: Macmillan, 1986.

**UNGE89**   Unger, S. *The Essence of Logic Circuits.* Englewood Cliffs, NJ: Prentice-Hall, 1989.

**VERN88**   Vernon, M., and Manber, U. "Distributed Round-Robin and First-Come-First-Serve Protocols and Their Application to Multiprocessor Bus Arbitration." *Proceedings, Fifteenth Annual International Symposium on Computer Architecture,* June 1988.

**VOEL88**   Voelker, J. "The PDP-8." *IEEE Spectrum,* November 1988.

**VOGL94**   Vogley, B. "800 Megabyte Per Second Systems Via Use of Synchronous DRAM." *Proceedings, COMPCON '94,* March 1994.

**VONN45**   Von Neumann, J. *First Draft of a Report on the EDVAC.* Moore School, University of Pennsylvania, 1945.

**VRAN80**   Vranesic, Z., and Thurber, K. "Teaching Computer Structures." *Computer,* June 1980.

**WAKE90**   Wakerly, J. *Digital Design Principles and Practices.* Englewood Cliffs, NJ: Prentice-Hall, 1990.

**WALL85**   Wallich, P. "Toward Simpler, Faster Computers." *IEEE Spectrum,* August 1985.

**WALL90**   Wallis, P. *Improving Floating-Point Programming.* New York: Wiley, 1992.

**WALL91**   Wall, D. "Limits of Instruction-Level Parallelism." *Proceedings, Fourth International Conference on Architectural Support for Programming Languages and Operating Systems,* April 1991.

**WARD90**   Ward, S., and Halstead, R. *Computation Structures.* Cambridge, MA: MIT Press, 1990.

**WATE86**   Waters, F., ed. *IBM RT Personal Computer Technology,* IBM Corp. SA23-1057, 1986.

**WAYN92**   Wayner, P. "Processor Pipelines." *Byte,* January 1992.

**WEBE67**   Weber, H. "A Microprogrammed Implementation of EULER on IBM System/360 Model 30." *Communications of the ACM,* September 1967.

**WEIN75**   Weinberg, G. *An Introduction to General Systems Thinking.* New York: Wiley, 1975.

**WEIS84**   Weiss, S., and Smith, J. "Instruction Issue Logic in Pipelined Supercomputers." *IEEE Transactions on Computers,* November 1984.

**WEIS93**   Weiss, S. "Optimizing a Superscalar Machine to Run Vector Code." *IEEE Parallel & Distributed Technology,* May 1993.

**WEIS94**   Weiss, S., and Smith, J. *POWER and PowerPC.* San Francisco: Morgan Kaufmann, 1994.

**WEIZ91**   Weizer, N., et al. *The Arthur D. Little Forecast on Information Technology and Productivity.* New York: Wiley, 1991.

**WIEC82**   Wiecek, L. "A Case Study of VAX-11 Instruction Set Usage for Compiler Execution." *Proceedings, Symposium on Architectural Support for Programming Languages and Operating Systems,* March 1982.

**WILK51**   Wilkes, M. "The Best Way to Design an Automatic Calculating Machine." *Proceedings, Manchester University Computer Inaugural Conference,* July 1951.

**WILK53**   Wilkes, M., and Stringer, J. "Microprogramming and the Design of the Control Circuits in an Electronic Digital Computer." *Proceedings of the Cambridge Philosophical Society,* April 1953. Also in [SIEW82].

**WILL90**   Williams, F., and Steven, G. "Address and Data Register Separation on the M68000 Family." *Computer Architecture News,* June 1990.

**WILS84**   Wilson, K. "Science, Industry, and the New Japanese Challenge." *Proceedings of the IEEE,* January 1984.

**WIND85**   Windsor, W. "IEEE Floating-Point Chips Implement DSP Architectures." *Computer Design,* January 1985.

**WONG80**   Wong, C. "Minimizing Expected Head Movement in One-Dimensional and Two-Dimensional Mass Storage Systems." *Computing Surveys,* June 1980.

**YEN85**   Yen, W.; Yen, D.; and Fu, K. "Data Coherence in a Multicache System." *IEEE Transactions on Computers,* January 1985.

**ZECH88**   Zech, R. "Systems, Applications, and Implications of Optical Storage." *Proceedings, COMPCON Spring '88,* March 1988.

# Index

## A

Access time, 102, 106*f*
  of magnetic disk, 160
Adders, 630–632
Addition
  in floating-point arithmetic, 295–297, 296*f*
  in integer arithmetic, 276–277, 277*f*
  vector, 585, 585*f*
Addressable unit, 101
Addresses, number of, in instructions, 317–319,
    318*f*, 319*t*
Addressing, 361–374
  base-register, 366
  direct, 362*f*, 363*t*, 364, 379
  displacement, 362*f*, 363*t*, 366–368
  effective, 363
  Futurebus+, 86
  immediate, 362*f*, 363*t*, 363–364
  indirect, 362*f*, 363*t*, 364–365
  modes of, 361–363, 362*f*, 363*t*
  Pentium, 368–371, 369*f*, 370*t*
  PowerPC, 371–374, 372*t*, 373*f*
  register, 362*f*, 363*t*, 365
  register indirect, 362*f*, 363*t*, 365
  relative, 366
  stack, 362*f*, 363*t*, 368
Address lines, 68
ALU. *See* Arithmetic and logic unit
American Standard Code for Information Inter-
    change (ASCII), 180–181, 181*t*–182*t*
Antidependency, 482
Apple, 43
Applications, 223
Arbiter, 72–73
Arbitrated message, definition of, 85*t*
Arbitration, 91, 206
  Futurebus+, 86–92, 88*f*, 89*f*
    centralized, 91–92, 92*f*
    distributed, 87–91

    phases of, 88–90, 89*f*
  PCI, 82–84, 83*f*
    between two masters, 83*f*, 83–84
  single pass, 90
Arbitration number, 90
  geographical address, 90, 90*f*
  priority, 90, 90*f*
  round-robin, 90, 90*f*, 91
Architecture, 3–4
  definition of, 3
  IBM System/370, 4
Arithmetic, 269–312. *See also* Vector computation
  floating-point, 292–304
    addition and subtraction in, 295–297, 296*f*
    division in, 297–299, 299*f*
    IEEE standard for, 302–304, 303*t*
    infinity in, 302
    multiplication in, 297–299, 298*f*
    NaNs in, 302, 303*t*
  integer, 270–275, 275–288
    addition in, 276–277, 277*f*
    conversion between different bit lengths,
      273–274
    division in, 286*f*, 286–288, 287*f*, 288*f*
    fixed-point, 274–275
    multiplication in, 277–286
    negation in, 275–277
    sign-magnitude, 270–271, 272*t*
    subtraction in, 277, 278*f*
    two's complement, 271–273, 272*t*
  machine instructions for, 326–327
  types of, 12
Arithmetic and logic unit (ALU), 8, 50*f*, 51, 269,
    270*f*, 389
  denormalized numbers in, 303*f*, 303–304
  guard bits in, 300, 300*f*
  NaNs in, 302, 303*t*
  overflow, 276–277, 290
  precision considerations in, 300–302

rounding in, 301–302
  TI 8800, 559–560, 562*t*–563*t*
    registers in, 559–560, 562*t*–563*t*
  underflow, 290–291, 295, 303
Arithmetic instructions, 317
Arithmetic shift, 282, 330, 330*f*
Array processor, 584
ASCII (American Standard Code for Information Interchange), 180–181, 181*t*–182*t*
Assembly language, 345*f*, 346
Associative mapping, in cache memory, 127–129, 128*f*, 129*f*, 130*f*, 131*f*
Associative memory, 102
Asynchronous transmission, 216, 217*f*
Autoindexing, 367


**B**

Base-register addressing, 366
Batch systems, 225, 226*t*
  efficiency of, 229–230, 233*f*
  multiprogramming in, 229–231, 230*f*, 231*t*, 234*t*
  simple, 226–229, 227*f*, 228*f*
  sophisticated, 229*f*, 229–231
Beat, definition of, 85*t*
Bell Labs, 23
Bi-endian, 356–360
Big-endian, 356–360, 358*f*, 359*f*
Binary numbers, 307–308, 308*t*
Bit-ordering, 359–360
Block data transfer, 75
Boolean algebra, 606–608, 611–623
Booth's algorithm, for integer multiplication, 282–286, 283*f*
Branching
  delayed, 409
    in RISCs, 450*t*, 450*f*, 450–451
  effect on instruction pipelines, 402–403, 403*f*, 405–409
Branch instructions, 317, 332–333, 333*f*
  PowerPC, 342–344
Branch prediction, 37
  in instruction pipelines, 407–409, 408*f*, 410*f*
  Pentium, 495–496, 496*f*, 497*f*
  in superscalar machines, 484–485
Branch processing, PowerPC, 489–492, 490*f*, 491*f*
Buffering, in I/O module, 184
Bus(es), 49–99. *See also* Peripheral component interconnect
  data. *See* Data bus
  data transfer type, 74–75*f*
  design elements, 71–75
  Futurebus+, 84–94

high-performance architecture, 70, 71*f*
  interconnection, 67–75, 68*f*
  multiple, 69–70
  operation of, 68–69
  P1394. *See* P1394 serial bus
  physical arrangement of, 69, 69*f*
  structure of, 33, 67–69
  timing, 73–74
  traditional architecture, 70, 71*f*
  types, 72
Bus controller, 72–73
Bus cycle, 73
Bus lines
  dedicated, 72
  multiplexed, 72
Bus priority in, 95
Bus priority out, 95
Bus tenure, definition of, 85*t*
Bus transaction, definition of, 85*t*
Byte ordering, 356–359


**C**

C (language), 432, 432*t*
Cache coherence, 578–584
  hardware approaches to, 579–581
  MESI protocol, 581–584
  snoopy protocols, 579–580
  software approaches to, 579
Cache dynamic random-access memory (CDRAM), 141
Cache memory
  block size in, 132–133
  design elements, 123–124, 124*t*
  mapping function in
    associative, 127–129, 128*f*, 129*f*, 130*f*, 131*f*
    direct, 124–127, 125*f*, 126*f*
  number of caches in, 133–134
  Pentium, 134–138, 135*f*, 136*f*, 138*f*
  PowerPC, 138–139, 139*t*, 139*f*, 140*f*
  principles of, 121–123, 122*f*, 123*f*
  replacement algorithms in, 129–130
  and RISCs, 437*t*, 437–439, 438*f*
  structure of, 122*f*
  and virtual memory, 249
  write policy in, 130–132
CCITT alphabet, 180, 181*t*–182*t*
CDRAM. *See* Cache dynamic random-access memory
CD-ROM
  organization of, 170–172, 171*f*, 172*t*, 173*f*
  performance characteristics of, 106*f*
Central processing unit (CPU), 8, 66

communication with I/O module, 184, 186*t*, 186–190, 188*f*, 189*f*
control of. *See* Control unit
functions of, 53, 388–389
instruction cycles in, 396*f*–399*f*, 396–400
instruction sets for. *See* Instruction sets
interaction with other components, 51
interconnection, 8
internal organization of, 515*f*, 515–516
and operating system, 224
register organization in, 389–396
examples of, 393–396, 394*f*, 395*f*
structure of, 8, 10*f*, 13, 389*f*, 390*f*
and system bus, 389, 389*f*
Chaining, 589
Chip(s), 28, 29*f*
memory
logic of, 112–113
packaging of, 113–115, 114*f*
Chip density, growth in, 30*f*
CISC. *See* Complex instruction set computers
Clock, and control unit, 511–512, 512*f*
Clock cycle, 73
Clock line, 99
Combinational circuits, 610–632
decoders, 621–623
Communication device, definition, 179
Compact disk read-only memory. *See* CD-ROM
Compaction, in memory management, 243
Compatibility, 31
Compelled data transfer protocol, definition of, 85*t*
Completeness, in instruction set design, 378
Complex instruction set computers (CISCs), 41, 430*t*, 431–432, 440–443
versus RISCs, 465–466
superscalar principles applied to, Pentium, 492–496
Computer(s), 8*f*
commercial, 21–22
compatibility of, 31
components of, 27, 27*f*
top-level view, 52*f*
evolution of, 15–45, 428–429
functions of, 4–9, 6*f*, 7*f*, 49, 52–65
generations of, 24*t*
hierarchic nature of, 4–5
history of, 15–36
structure of, 7–9
top-level, 8, 9*f*
Computer instructions. *See* Instructions
Computer modules, 66*f*
Computer system(s)
components of, 49–51
description of, 49

peripheral devices of, 178–181
Condition codes, Pentium, 341, 342*t*
Condition register, PowerPC, 420
Constant angular velocity (CAV), 171
Constant linear velocity (CLV), 171
Continuous-field simulation, 584
Control, 5, 28, 53, 316
of I/O module, 183
machine instructions for, 331–338
Control lines, 68
Control logic, 180
Control memory, 527
Control registers, 392–393
Pentium, 414–416, 415*f*
Control signals, 511–513
examples of, 513*f*, 513–514, 514*f*
Control unit (CU), 8, 10*f*, 11*f*, 389, 503–525
and clock, 511–512, 512*f*
flags and, 512, 512*f*
functional requirements, 510–511, 512*f*
hardwired implementation, 520–524
and instruction register, 512, 512*f*
Intel 8085, 516–520, 517*f*, 518*t*–519*t*, 520*f*
internal logic of, 523–524
LSI-11, 546–549, 548*f*, 549*f*
microprogramming in. *See* Micropro-
grammed control
organization of, 542*f*
Control word, 527
Conversion instructions, 331
Core, 33, 108
Counters, 639–642
Count register, PowerPC, 420
CPU. *See* Central processing unit
Cray supercomputers, 589
CU. *See* Control unit
Cycle stealing, 200

# D

Data buffering, in I/O module, 184
Data bus, 67
width of, 67, 74
Data channels, definition of, 24
Data flow analysis, 38
Data lines, 67–68
Data movement, 5–6, 28, 316
Data operation (do), 56*f*, 57
Data processing, 5, 28, 316
CPU, 53
Data storage, 5, 28, 316
Data transfer
Futurebus+, 92–93, 93*f*
machine instructions for, 325–326, 328*t*

Data types
    characters, 321–322
    logical data, 322
    numbers, 320–321
    Pentium, 322–323, 323*t*, 324*f*
    PowerPC, 323–324
DAT, performance characteristics of, 106*f*
DEC. *See* Digital Equipment Corporation
Decimal numbers, 306–307
Decoders, 621–623
Delayed branching, 409, 450*t*, 450*f*, 450–451
Demand paging, 245–246
Denormalized numbers, 303–304, 304*f*
Density, of magnetic disk, 156
D flip-flop, 635
Digital Equipment Corporation (DEC), 24
    PDP-8, 32–33
        block diagram of, 34*f*
        evolution of, 32*t*
Digital logic. *See* Logic
Direct access memory, 102
Direct addressing, 362*f*, 363*t*, 364, 379
Direct mapping, in cache memory, 124–127,
    125*f*, 126*f*
Direct memory access (DMA), 65, 199–201, 200*f*,
    201*f*
Directory protocols, 579–580
Disabled interrupt, 62–63
Discrete component, definition of, 26
Disk(s). *See* Magnetic disk memory
Disk cache, 108
Disk drive, as peripheral device, 181
Disk pack, 158
Displacement addressing, 362*f*, 363*t*, 366–368
Division
    in floating-point arithmetic, 297–299, 299*f*
    in integer arithmetic, 286*f*, 286–288, 287*f*, 288*f*
DMA. *See* Direct memory access
Double-precision numbers, 292
DRAM. *See* Dynamic random-access memory
Dynamic random-access memory (DRAM), 37,
    109–110, 112*f*, 112–114, 114*f*
    cache, 141
    enhanced, 141, 142*f*
    evolution of, 38*f*
    Rambus, 144
    RamLink, 144–146, 145*f*
    synchronous, 141–144, 143*f*
    trends in, 39, 39*f*

## E

Eckert, John Presper, 15–16, 21
Eckert-Mauchly Computer Corporation, 21

EDRAM. *See* Enhanced dynamic random-access
    memory
EEPROM. *See* Electrically erasable PROM
Effective addressing, 363
Efficiency
    and interrupts, 61
    of processor, 57–58
EFLAGS register, Pentium, 413–414, 414*f*
Electrically erasable PROM (EEPROM), 109*t*,
    110–111
Electronic Numerical Integrator And Computer.
    *See* ENIAC
Endian, 356–360
Enhanced dynamic random-access memory
    (EDRAM), 141, 142*f*
ENIAC, 15–16
EPROM. *See* Erasable PROM
Erasable optical disk, 173–174
Erasable PROM (EPROM), 109*t*, 110
Error correction, 117
    in semiconductor memory, 116–120, 117*f*
    and word length, 118*t*
Error detection, in I/O module, 185
Exception register, PowerPC, 419, 420*f*
Exceptions
    definition of, 416
    Pentium, 416
    PowerPC, 419
Execute cycle, 19, 20*f*, 52, 53*f*, 53–64, 508–509
Expanded storage, 108
Exponents. *See* Floating-point arithmetic; Float-
    ing-point representation
External devices. *See* Peripheral devices
External memory, 12

## F

Fairchild, 35
Fairness intervals, 216
Family of compatible computers, 31
Fetch cycle, 19, 20*f*, 52, 53*f*, 53–64, 398*f*, 398–400,
    504–507, 505*f*
Fetch overlap, 400
FIFO. *See* First-in-first-out algorithms
Firmware, 527
First-in-first-out (FIFO) algorithms, 130
Fixed-head magnetic disks, 158, 159*f*
Fixed-size partitioning, 242
Flags, and control unit, 512, 512*f*
Flip-flops, 633
Floating-point arithmetic, 292–304
    addition and subtraction in, 295–297, 296*f*
    division in, 297–299, 299*f*
    IEEE standard for, 302–304, 303*t*

infinity in, 302
limitations of, 584
multiplication in, 297–299, 298f
precision considerations in, 300–302
rounding in, 301–302
Floating-point representation, 289f, 289–293, 291f
IEEE standard for, 292f, 292–293, 293t, 294t
Floating-point status and control register (FPSCR), PowerPC, 419, 421t
Floppy disk, 158. *See also* Magnetic disk memory
performance characteristics of, 106f
FORTRAN, 432
FPSCR. *See* Floating-point status and control register
Frames, in memory paging, 244f, 244–245
Functional encoding, 546
Futurebus+, 84–94
data transfer, 92–93, 93f
requirements for, 84
signal lines, 86t–87t

**G**

Gaps, in magnetic disks, 155, 156f
Gate(s), 27, 27f, 28, 29f, 608–610
General-purpose arithmetic and logic, 50f, 51
General-purpose register, PowerPC, 419
Gigascale integration (GSI), 28–29
Global variables, 436–437
Gradual underflow, 304
Graph coloring, 439–440, 440f
GSI. *See* Gigascale integration
Guard bits, 300, 300f

**H**

Hamming code, 117, 117f, 121f
Hamming, Richard, 117
Hard disk, performance characteristics of, 106f
Hard failure, definition of, 116
Hardware failure interrupt, 57t
Hardware, programming in, 50f
Hardwired program, 50
Hardwiring, for control unit implementation, 520–524
Head, for magnetic disks, 155
Hexadecimal numbers, 54n, 310–312
Hierarchic system, 4–5
definition of, 5
High-level languages (HLL), 429–431, 432t
operands in, 432

procedure calls in, 433, 433t
HLL. *See* High-level languages
Human-readable, definition, 179
Hypercube topology, 601

**I**

IAS computer, 16–21
instructions, 20, 22t–23t
memory formats, 18, 18f
operation of, 18
structure of, 16, 17f
expanded, 19f
IBM, 21
701, 22
801, 42
7094, 24–26
configuration, 26t
3033, control address register in, 539, 539f
RISC System/6000, 43
RT PC, 43
700/7000 series, evolution of, 25t
System/360, 29–31
characteristics of, 31t
System/370
architecture, 4
data transfer in, 325, 328t
3090, vector computation in
compound instructions and, 595
instruction set for, 596t
registers in, 592–595, 593f, 594f
IBR. *See* Instruction Buffer Register
ICs, benefits of, 29
IEEE standard
for floating-point arithmetic, 302–304, 303t
for floating-point representation, 292f, 292–293, 293t, 294t
Immediate addressing, 362f, 363t, 363–364
Indexing, 366–368
Index registers, 391
Indirect addressing, 362f, 363t, 364–365
Indirect cycle, 507
Infinity, in floating-point arithmetic, 302
Infix notation, 353, 356f
In-order issue with in-order completion, 479, 480f
In-order issue with out-of-order completion, 479–481, 480f
Input/output, 8, 53, 64–65, 178–221
definition of, 5
direct memory access in, 199–201
evolution of, 202
interrupt-driven, 190–199, 191f
isolated, 189, 189f

machine instructions for, 331
memory-mapped, 189, 189*f*
programmed, 186*t*, 186–190, 188*f*, 189*f*
Input/output address register (I/OAR), interaction with other components, 51
Input/output buffer register, interaction with other components, 51
Input/output channels, 202–204, 203*f*
multiplexer, 203, 203*f*
selector, 203, 203*f*
Input/output components, 51
Input/output devices
bandwidth requirements for, 40*t*
operating system and, 224
queuing of, 239–240, 240*f*
Input/output instructions, 317
Input/output interrupt, 57*t*
Input/output modules, 12, 66, 179*f*
communication with CPU, 184, 186*t*, 186–190, 188*f*, 189*f*
external interfaces for. *See* Interface(s)
functions of, 182–185
interaction with other components, 51
structure of, 185*f*, 185–186
Input/output processors. *See* Input/output channels
Input/output queue, 239, 240
Instruction(s). *See also* Instruction sets
allocation of bits in, 375–379
arithmetic, 326–327
branch, 332–333, 342–344
conversion, 331
data transfer, 325–326, 328*t*
elements of, 314*f*, 314–315
format of, 315, 315*f*
input/output, 331
length of, 374–375
load/store, 344–346
logical, 327–331, 329*t*, 330*f*
number of addresses in, 317–319, 318*f*, 319*t*
operands of, 320–324
Pentium, 322
skip, 334
subroutine call, 334–338, 335*f*, 336*f*
symbolic representation of, 315*f*, 315–316
system control, 331–332
transfer of control, 332–338
types of, 316–317, 325, 326*t*, 327*t*
variable-length, 379–380
Instruction address calculation (iac), 56, 56*f*
Instruction Buffer Register (IBR), 18
Instruction cycle(s), 19, 52, 53*f*, 53–64, 396*f*–399*f*, 396–400, 509*f*, 509–510
fetch, 398*f*, 398–400
with indirect addressing, 396–397, 399*f*

interrupt, 398, 399*f*
interrupts and, 59–61, 60*f*
pipelining in, 400–412
states of, 56*f*, 56–57
with interrupts, 63*f*
Instruction fetch (if), 56, 56*f*
Instruction interpreter, 50*f*, 51
Instruction-issue policy, 478–482
in-order issue with in-order completion, 479, 480*f*
in-order issue with out-of-order completion, 479–481, 480*f*
out-of-order issue with out-of-order completion, 480*f*, 481–482
Instruction-level parallelism, 477–478
Instruction operation decoding (iod), 56, 56*f*
Instruction pairing, Pentium, 493, 496*t*
Instruction pipeline(s), 598
branch prediction in, 407–409, 408*f*, 410*f*
delayed branching in, 409
effect of branching on, 402–403, 403*f*, 405–409
Intel 80486, 409–412, 411*f*
loop buffer in, 406*f*, 406–407
MIPS R3000, 461, 463*f*, 464*t*
MIPS R4000, 459–465, 465*f*
Motorola 88000, 455–458, 457*f*
multiple-stream, 405
Pentium, 493, 494*f*, 495*f*
PowerPC, 486–489, 488*f*
prefetch branch target in, 405, 495–496, 496*f*, 497*f*
principles of, 400–405, 401*f*
in RISCs, 447–451, 448*f*–450*f*, 450*t*
six-stage, 401–405, 402*f*, 403*f*, 404*f*
superpipelined architecture, 459–465
timing diagram for, 402*f*
two-stage, 400–401, 401*f*
and vector multiplication, 587*f*, 587–589, 588*f*
Instruction register (IR), 18, 53
control unit and, 512, 512*f*
Instruction sets, 13, 313–360. *See also* Instructions
addressing of. *See* Addressing
completeness in, 379
complex. *See* Complex instruction set computers
design of, 319–320
formats for, 374–386
PDP-8, 377, 378*f*
PDP-10, 377–379, 379*f*
PDP-11, 380, 381*f*
Pentium, 380–384, 382*f*
PowerPC, 384–386, 385*f*
for MIPS R4000, 459, 460*t*, 461*t*, 462*f*
for Motorola 88000, 451–453, 452*t*, 453*f*, 454*f*

orthogonality in, 378
Pentium, 338–341, 339t–340t
PowerPC, 341–344, 343t
reduced. *See* Reduced instruction set
computers
Integer arithmetic, 275–288
addition in, 276–277, 277f
division in, 286f, 286–288, 287f, 288f
multiplication in, 277–286
negation in, 275–277
subtraction in, 277, 278f
Integers, representation of, 270–275
conversion between different bit lengths,
273–274
fixed-point, 274–275
sign-magnitude, 270–271, 272t
two's complement, 271–273, 272t
Integrated circuit(s), 26–33, 28, 29f
Intel
4004, 35
8008, 35, 36t
8080, 35–36, 36t, 41
8085
block diagram of, 517f
control unit in, 516–520, 517f, 518t–519t,
520f
8086, 36, 36t, 41
register organization in, 393–396, 394f
80286, 41, 41t
80386, 36, 36t, 41, 41t
register organization in, 395, 395f
80486, 36t, 41, 41t
instruction pipelines in, 409–412, 411f
8259A interrupt controller, 195, 196f
8255A programmable peripheral interface,
195–199, 197f, 198f
microprocessors, evolution of, 35, 41t, 41–42
P6, 41t, 42
P7, 41t, 42
Pentium. *See* Pentium
Interactive systems, 225, 226t
Interconnection structures, 65–66
Interconnection topologies, in multicomputer
design, 601–602
Interface(s)
parallel, 204, 204f
point-to-point, 205
between processor and main memory
developmental lag in, 38–39
improvements in, 39–40
serial, 204, 204f
small computer system (SCSI), 205–213
user/computer, operating system as, 223f,
223–224
Internal memory, 12, 100–154

International Business Machines. *See* IBM
Interrupt cycles, 60, 60f, 398, 399f, 507
Interrupt, disabled, 62–63
Interrupt-driven I/O, 190–199, 191f
design considerations, 194–195
examples of, 195–199, 196f, 197f, 198f
processing of, 191f, 191–194, 193f
Interrupt handling, 60, 418, 424
Interrupt processing
Pentium, 416–418
PowerPC, 421–424, 422t
Interrupt request, 59
Interrupts, 57–58
classes of, 57t
and instruction cycle, 59–61, 60f
multiple, 62–64
time sequence of, 65f
and transfer of control, 64
priorities for, 63–64
and program flow of control, 58, 58f
and transfer of control, 59f
types of, PowerPC, 421–423, 422t
Interrupt table
Pentium, 417t
PowerPC, 422t
I/O. *See* Input/output
I/OAR. *See* Input/output address register
IR. *See* Instruction register
Isochronous transmission, 216
Isolated I/O, 189, 189f

**J**

J-K flip flop, 636
Job control language, 228

**K**

Karnaugh maps, 614–620
Keyboards, 180–181

**L**

Languages, 429
high-level, 429–431, 432t
operands in, 432
procedure calls in, 433, 433t
Large-scale integration (LSI), 33, 103
Last-in-first-out (LIFO), 351
Latch. *See* Flip-flops
Leading edge, 98
Least-frequently used (LFU) algorithms, 130

Least-recently used (LRU) algorithms, 129
LFU. *See* Least-frequently used algorithms
LIFO. *See* Last-in-first-out
Link register, PowerPC, 420
Little-endian, 356–360, 358*f*, 359*f*
Load/store instructions, PowerPC, 344–346
Local area network(s), bandwidth requirements for, 40*t*
Locality of reference, 105
Locking, definition of, 85*t*
Logic, 606–644
  adders, 630–632
  Boolean, 606–608, 611–623
  combinational circuits, 610–632
    and Karnaugh maps, 614–620
    and multiplexers, 621–623
  gates, 608–610
  and ROM, 627–630
  sequential circuits, 632–642
    counters, 639–642
    flip-flops, 633
    and registers, 637–639
Logical instructions, 327–331, 329*t*, 330*f*
Logical shift, 329, 330*f*
Logic instructions, 317
Long-term queue, 238, 240
Loop buffer, in instruction pipelines, 406*f*, 406–407
LSI. *See* Large-scale integration
LSI-11
  control unit organization in, 546–549, 548*f*, 549*f*
  microinstruction execution in, 546–550
  microinstruction format in, 549–550, 550*t*, 551*t*
  microinstruction sequencing in, 540

## M

Machine instructions. *See* Instructions
Machine parallelism, 477–478, 483–484, 484*f*
Machine-readable, definition, 179
Machine state register (MSR), 423*t*, 423–424
Magnetic disk memory, 155–160
  access time, 160
  characteristics of, 158*t*, 158–159
  double-sided, 158
  fixed-head, 158
  formatting of, 155–158, 156*f*, 157*f*
  multiple-platter, 158, 160*f*
Magnetic-surface memory, 103
Magnetic tape memory
  organization of, 174*f*, 174–175
  performance characteristics of, 106*f*

Main memory, 8, 51
Mantissa, 290
MAR. *See* Memory Address Register
Master sync (MSYN) signal, 74
Mauchly, John, 15–16, 21
MBR. *See* Memory buffer register
MCU. *See* Multiprocessor communications unit
Memory, 12, 51
  access time, 102, 106*f*
  addressable unit, 101
  capacity, 101, 106*f*
  CD-ROM. *See* CD-ROM
  construction of, 33–35
  cost of, 107*f*
  CPU, 53
  design considerations, 103–104
  direct access, 102
  external, 12, 155–177
  internal, 12, 100–154
  location of, 100
  magnetic disk, 155–160
  magnetic-surface, 103
  performance characteristics of, 102, 105*f*, 149*t*, 149–154, 152*f*, 153*f*, 154*f*
  physical characteristics of, 103
  random-access. *See* Random-access memory
  read-only. *See* Read-only memory
  segmentation of, 249–252
    Pentium, 252–253, 254*f*
  semiconductor, 33–35
  sequential access, 101–102
  transfer rate, 102
  two-level, 104–108, 105*f*, 149*t*, 149–154, 152*f*
  unit of transfer, 101
  virtual, 245–246
Memory Address Register (MAR), 18
Memory address register (MAR), 398, 398*f*, 399*f*, 400
  interaction with other components, 51
Memory buffer register (MBR), 18, 398, 398*f*, 399*f*, 400
  interaction with other components, 51
Memory cells, 27, 27*f*, 111
Memory cycle time, 102
  definition of, 24
Memory hierarchy, 103–108, 104*f*
Memory instructions, 317
Memory management
  compaction in, 243
  in operating systems, 240–262
  paging in, 244*f*, 244–248, 247*f*, 248*f*
    Pentium, 253–256
  partitioning, 242*f*, 242–244, 243*f*
  partitioning in, 242–244
  Pentium, 252–256, 254*f*, 255*t*–256*t*, 257*f*, 341

PowerPC, 256–262, 258f–262f
swapping, 240–242, 241f
virtual memory in, 245–246
Memory-mapped I/O, 189, 189f
Memory module, 51, 65–66
Memory systems, characteristics of, 100–103, 101t
Mesh topology, 601
MESI (modified/exclusive/shared/invalid), 135–138, 137f
protocol for cache coherence, 581–584, 582f
Mezzanine architecture, 70, 71f
Microcomputers, architecture versus organization in, 4
Microelectronics, 27–29
Microinstructions, 526–528. *See also* Microprogrammed control
encoding of, 545f, 545–546
execution of, 541–550
LSI-11, 546–550
format of
LSI-11, 549–550, 550t, 551t
TI 8800, 551–554, 555t
horizontal, 527, 528f
IBM 3033, 550, 552t, 553t
sequencing of, 535–540
taxonomy of, 541–544, 543t
Micro-operations, 503–510, 504f
Microprocessor(s), 35–36
16-bit, 36
evolution of, 35–36, 36t
speed of, 37–38
Microprogrammed control, 526–565. *See also* Microinstructions
address generation in, 538–540, 539t, 539f
advantages and disadvantages of, 533–535
applications of, 560–561
branch control logic in, 535–538, 536f, 537f, 538f
LSI-11, 540, 546
memory organization in, 528–530, 529f
microinstruction sequencing in, 535–540
principles of, 526–535
Wilkes, 530–533, 532f, 534t
Microprogrammed implementation, 9
Microprogramming, 14
MIMD. *See* Multiple instruction multiple data stream
MIPS R4000, 458–465
instruction set for, 459, 460t, 461t
pipelining in, 459–465, 465f
MIPS R3000, pipelining in, 461, 463f, 464t
MISD. *See* Multiple instruction single data stream
Mnemonics, for machine instructions, 315

Mode field, 363
Monitor (batch system), 226–229, 227t
Monitors (display), 180–181
Moore's Law, 37
Motorola, 43
88000
pipelining in, 455–458, 457f
register management in, 455
MC68000, register organization in, 393–396, 394f
MSR. *See* Machine state register
Multibus I, distributed arbitration, 95f
Multicomputers, 599, 601–602, 602f
Multics, 233
Multiple instruction multiple data (MIMD) stream, 599, 600, 601, 602, 602f
Multiple instruction single data (MISD) stream, 599
Multiplexers, 621–623
definition of, 26
I/O channels, 203f, 204
Multiplication
in floating-point arithmetic, 297–299, 298f
in integer arithmetic, 277–286
Booth's algorithm for, 282–286, 283f
unsigned, 278–279, 279f, 280f, 281f
matrix, 585–586, 586f
Multiport memory, in multiprocessor, 572–573, 573f
Multiprocessor communications unit (MCU), 577, 578f
Multiprocessors, 8, 14, 569–578, 599
central control unit in, 573
IBM 3033, organization of, 577–578
IBM System/370, 575f, 575–578, 576t
prefixing in, 575f, 575–576
signaling in, 576t, 576–577
synchronization in, 577
multiport memory in, 572–573, 573f
operating systems in, 573–574
organization of, 570–573, 571f
tightly-coupled, 570, 571f
time-shared bus in, 571–572, 572f
Multiprogramming, 225, 229–231, 230f, 231t, 234t
scheduling in, 234–240, 235t
time sharing in, 231–232

# N

NaN. *See* Not a number
Negation, in integer arithmetic, 275–277
Nonremovable disks, 158
Not a Number (NaN), 293

Not a number (NaN), 293, 302, 303*t*
Nucleus, of operating system, 225
Numbers. *See also* Floating-point; Integers
    as data types, 320–321
    denormalized, 303–304, 304*f*
    double-precision, 292
    single-precision, 292
Number systems
    binary, 307–308, 308*t*
    converting between, 308–310, 310*f*, 311*f*
    decimal, 306–307
    hexadecimal, 310–312


# O

Opcodes. *See* Instructions
Operand(s). *See also* Data types
    and RISCs, 432, 432*f*
Operand address calculation (oac), 56*f*, 57
Operand fetch (of), 56*f*, 57
Operand store (os), 56*f*, 57
Operating systems, 222–266
    and CPU, 224
    evolution of, 226
    functions of, 222–225
    and I/O devices, 224
    memory management in, 240–262
    for multiprocessors, 573–574
    nucleus of, 225
    as resource manager, 224–225, 225*f*
    scheduling in, 234–240, 235*t*
        high-level, 235
        process states and, 236*f*, 236–237
        short-term, 235–240
        techniques for, 237–240, 238*f*, 240*f*
    types of, 225–234
    as user/computer interface, 223*f*, 223–224
Operation, 13
Optical disk, erasable, 173–174
Optical memory, 169–174, 170*t*. *See also* CD-
    ROM; WORM
Organization, definition of, 3–4
Orthogonality, in instruction set design, 378
Out-of-order issue with out-of-order comple-
    tion, 480*f*, 481–482
Overflow, 276–277, 290, 295


# P

Page table
    inverted, 248
    structure of, 246–248, 247*f*, 248*f*
Paging

    demand, 245–246
    in memory management, 244*f*, 244–248, 247*f*,
        248*f*
    Pentium, 253–256
Parallel contention arbitration, definition of, 85*t*
Parallel interface, 204, 204*f*
Parallelism
    instruction-level, 477–478
    machine, 477–478, 483–484, 484*f*
Parallel processors, 14, 569–605, 590, 597–602
    types of, 598–600, 599*f*, 600*f*
Parallel registers, 637–639
Parity bits, 118
Partitioning, 242–244.242*f*, 243*f*
    fixed-size, 242
    variable-size, 243
Pascal (language), 432, 432*t*
Patterson study, 432
PC. *See* Program Counter
PCI. *See* Peripheral component interconnect
PCI SIG, 76
PDP-8 instruction format, 377, 378*f*
PDP-10 instruction format, 377–379, 379*f*
PDP-11 instruction format, 380, 381*f*
Pentium, 40–42, 41*t*, 42
    addressing modes in, 368–371, 369*f*, 370*t*
    block diagram of, 135*f*
    branch prediction in, 495–496, 496*f*, 497*f*
    cache memory in, 134–138, 135*f*, 136*f*, 138*t*
    condition codes in, 341, 342*t*
    data types in, 322–323, 323*t*, 324*f*
    exceptions in, 416
    instruction pairing in, 493, 496*t*
    instruction set for, 338–341, 339*t*–340*t*,
        380–384, 382*f*
    interrupt processing in, 416–418
    interrupt vector table, 417*t*
    memory management in, 252–256, 254*f*,
        255*t*–256*t*, 257*f*, 341
    and PCI, 76
    pipelining in, 493, 494*f*, 495*f*
    register organization in, 412*t*, 412–416, 414*f*,
        415*f*
        control, 414–416, 415*f*
        EFLAFS, 413–414, 414*f*
    superscalar features of, 492–496, 494*f*, 495*f*
Performance
    designing for, 36–40
    of memory, 102, 105*f*, 149*t*, 149–154, 152*f*, 153*f*,
        154*f*
Performance balance, 38–40
Peripheral component interconnect (PCI), 75–84
    arbitration, 82–84, 83*f*
        between two masters, 83*f*, 83–84
        commands, 80–81

read, 81*t*
data transfer, 81–82
desktop system, 77*f*
mandatory signal lines, functional groups in, 76, 78*f*
optional signal lines, functional groups in, 76–77, 79*f*
read operation, timing of, 81, 82*f*
server system, 77*f*
structure of, 76–80
Peripheral, definition of, 5
Peripheral devices, 178–181, 180*f*, 184*t*
communication with I/O module, 184, 185
definition of, 179
interfaces for. *See* Interface(s)
Peripheral technologies, bandwidth requirements for, 40*t*
Physical dedication, 72
PLA. *See* Programmable logic array
Point-to-point interface, 205
Postfix notation, 354, 356*f*
Postindexing, 367
PowerPC, 40–44, 42–44, 43*f*
601, 43, 43*f*, 485*f*, 485–486, 487*f*, 488*f*
603, 43*f*, 44
604, 43*f*, 44
620, 43*f*, 44, 492
addressing modes in, 371–374, 372*t*, 373*f*
architecture, 43
bi-endian architecture of, 358
64-bit, 492
block diagram of, 139*f*
branch processing in, 489–492, 490*f*, 491*f*
cache memory in, 138–139, 139*t*, 139*f*, 140*f*
data types in, 323–324
dispatch unit of, 486
genealogy of, 42*f*
instruction set for, 341–344, 343*t*, 384–386, 385*f*
memory management in
32-bit, 256–258, 258*f*, 259*f*, 261*t*
64-bit, 256, 259–262, 260*f*, 261*t*, 262*f*
pipelining in, 486–489, 488*f*
register organization in, 418–421, 419*f*
superscalar architecture of, 485–492
Precision
double, 292
in floating-point arithmetic, 300–302
single, 292
Prefetch branch target, 405, 495–496, 496*f*, 497*f*
Procedure calls, in high-level languages, 433, 433*t*
Process control block, 236, 237*f*
Process, definition of, 234–235
Processing, interrupt, Pentium, 416–418

Processor(s). *See also* Central processing unit
speed of, evolution of, 38*f*
Process states, and short-term scheduling, 236*f*, 236–237
Program
hardwired, 50
symbolic, 345, 345*f*
Program counter (PC), 18, 53
Program execution, 52
example of, 54–55, 55*f*
Program interrupt, 57*t*
Programmable logic array (PLA), 625–627
Programmable ROM (PROM), 109*t*, 110
Programmed I/O, 186*t*, 186–190, 188*f*, 189*f*
Programmers, 223, 223*f*
Program status word (PSW), 393
PROM. *See* Programmable ROM
P1394 serial bus
configurations, 213–215, 214*f*, 215*f*
link layer of, 216–218, 217*f*
physical layer of, 215–216
PSW. *See* Program status word
Pyramid, 444

## Q

Queue(s), in operating system scheduling, 238–239, 240

## R

RAID. *See* Redundant array of independent disks
RAM. *See* Random-access memory
Rambus dynamic random-access memory (RDRAM), 144
RamLink dynamic random-access memory, 144–146, 145*f*
Random-access memory (RAM), 102
associative, 102
dynamic. *See* Dynamic random-access memory
organization of, 103
semiconductor, 109–111
static, 109–110
RDRAM. *See* Rambus dynamic random-access memory
Read-after write operation, 75
Read-modify-write operation, 74–75
Read-only memory (ROM), 103, 109*t*, 110, 627–630

Reduced instruction set computers (RISCs), 41, 428–471
architecture of, 440–447, 443t, 446t
common characteristics of, 443t, 443–445, 447
versus CISCs, 465–466
MIPS R4000, 458–465
instruction set for, 459, 460t, 461t
pipelining in, 459–465, 465f
Motorola 88000, 451–458
architecture of, 455, 456f
instruction set for, 451–453, 452t, 453f, 454f
pipelining in, 455–458, 457f
pipelining in
delayed branching in, 450t, 450f, 450–451
optimization of, 449–451
with regular instructions, 447–449, 448f, 449f
PowerPC, 485–492
register optimization in, compiler-based, 439–440, 440f
registers in, 434–439, 435f, 436f
Redundant array of independent disks (RAID), 161–169, 163t
level 0, 162–165, 163t, 164f, 166f
and data transfer capacity, 164
and I/O request rate, 165
level 1, 163t, 164f, 166–167
level 2, 163t, 164f, 167
level 3, 163t, 165f, 167–168
level 4, 163t, 165f, 168–169
level 5, 163t, 165f, 169
Reentrant subroutines, 336
Register(s), 8, 389, 637–639
control, 392–393
defined, 18
general-purpose, 391
index, 391
instruction, 392
memory address, 392
memory buffer, 392
Motorola 88000, 455
optimization of, in RISCs, 439–440, 440f
organization of, 393–396
program counter, 392
renaming, 482–483
RISCs, 434–439, 435f, 436f
segment pointers, 391
stack pointers, 391
user-visible, 390–392, 419f
Z8000, 393–396, 394f
Register addressing, 362f, 363t, 365
Register files, large, 437t, 437–439
Register indirect addressing, 362f, 363t, 365
Register organization

examples of, 393–396, 394f, 395f
Pentium, 412t, 412–416, 414f, 415f
PowerPC, 418–421, 419f, 420f
Register windows, 434–436, 435f, 436f, 438f
Relative addressing, 366
Removable disks, 158
Replacement algorithms, 129–130
Resource encoding, 546
Reverse Polish notation, 354, 356f
Ring topology, 601
Ripple counters, 639–640
RISC. See Reduced instruction set computers
ROM. See Read-only memory
Rotational latency, 160
Rounding, in floating-point arithmetic, 301–302

S

Scalable organization, 601
Scheduling, in operating systems, 234–240, 235t
high-level, 235
and process states, 236f, 236–237
short-term, 235–240
techniques for, 237–240, 238f, 240f
SCSI. See Small computer system interface
SDRAM. See Synchronous dynamic random-access memory
SEC. See Single-error-correcting code
SEC-DED. See Single-error-correcting, double-error-detecting code
Sectors, of magnetic disk, 156, 156f
Segmentation, of memory, 249–252
Pentium, 252–253, 254f
Segment pointers, 391
Selector I/O channels, 203, 203f
Semantic gap, 429
Semiconductor memory, 33–35, 103, 107f, 108–120
chip design for, 112–115, 114f
error correction in, 116–120, 117f
organization of, 111, 111f, 115f, 116f
types of, 109t, 109–111
Sequential access, 101, 175
Sequential circuits, 632–642
Serial interface, 204, 204f
Setup time, with early operating systems, 226
Shift registers, 639
Short-term queue, 239, 240
Significand, 290, 295
Sign-magnitude integer representation, 270–271, 272t
negation in, 275–277
SIMD. See Single instruction multiple data stream

Single-error-correcting (SEC) code, 120
Single-error-correcting, double-error-detecting (SEC-DED) code, 120, 121*f*
Single instruction multiple data (SIMD) stream, 599
Single instruction single data (SISD) stream, 599
Single-precision numbers, 292
SISD. *See* Single instruction single data stream
Skip instructions, 334
Small computer system interface (SCSI), 70
    commands, 211*f*, 211–213
    message formats, 210–211
    versus P1394, 214*f*
    signals and phases of, 206–207, 207*f*, 208*t*
    timing of, 207–210, 209*f*
    versions of, 205–206
Small-scale integration (SSI), 28
Snoopy protocols, 579–580
Soft error, definition of, 116
Software, 51
Solid-state device, 23
Speculative execution, 38
Sperry, 21
Sperry-Rand Corporation, UNIVAC division of, 21
Split transaction, definition of, 85*t*
S-R flip-flop, 633–634
SSI. *See* Small-scale integration
Stack(s), 351–355, 352*f*, 352*t*
    in formula evaluation, 353–355, 354*f*, 355*f*, 356*f*
    implementation of, 351–353
    for nested subroutine implementation, 336–337, 337*f*
Stack addressing, 362*f*, 363*t*, 368
Stack frame, 337
Stack pointers, 391
Starvation, definition of, 85*t*
States, process, and short-term scheduling, 236*f*, 236–237
Status registers, 392–393
Status signals, 180
Stored-program concept, 16
Subroutine call instructions, 334–338, 335*f*, 336*f*
Subroutines
    call instructions for, 334–338
    nested, 335*f*, 336*f*, 337*f*
    Pentium, 338–341
Subtraction
    in floating-point arithmetic, 295–297, 296*f*
    in integer arithmetic, 277, 278*f*
Superpipelined architecture, 459
    versus superscalar architecture, 473, 474*f*
Superscalar architecture, 430*t*, 459, 472–499
    branch prediction in, 484–485

    design issues in, 477–485
    instruction-issue policy in, 478–482, 480*f*
    limitations of, 475–477
    machine parallelism in, 483–484, 484*f*
    Pentium, 492–496, 494*f*, 495*f*
    procedural dependency in, 476*f*, 477
    register renaming in, 482–483
    resource conflict in, 476*f*, 477
    versus superpipelined architecture, 473, 474*f*
    true data dependency in, 475–477, 476*f*
Symbolic program, 345, 345*f*
SYNCH byte, 157*f*, 158
Synchronous counters, 640–642
Synchronous dynamic random-access memory (SDRAM), 141–144, 143*f*
Syndrome word, 118
System buses. *See* Bus(es)
System control, machine instructions for, 331–332
System interconnection, 8
System programs, 223. *See also* Utilities
System transaction, definition of, 85*t*

# T

Test instructions, 317
Texas instruments, TI 8800, 551–560
    block diagram of, 554*f*
    microinstruction format, 551–554, 555*t*
    microinstruction sequencing in, 554–559, 557*f*, 558*t*
Thrashing, 246
Time multiplexing, 72
Timer interrupt, 57*t*
Time-shared bus, in multiprocessor, 571–572, 572*f*
Time sharing, 231–232, 234*t*
Timing, 73–74
    asynchronous, 74
    of read operation, 73*f*
    synchronous, 74
Timing diagrams, 97–99, 98*f*
TLB. *See* Translation lookaside buffer
Topologies, in multicomputer design, 601–602
Tracks, on magnetic disk, 155
Trailing edge, 98
Transducers, 180
Transfer of control, machine instructions for, 332–338
Transfer rate, memory, 102
Transistor computers, 22–26
Transistor, development of, 26–28
Translation lookaside buffer (TLB), 249, 250*f*, 251*f*

Tree topology, 601
Two's complement integer representation, 271–273, 272*t*
  addition in, 276–277, 277*f*
  conversion to decimal, 273*t*
  multiplication in, 279–286, 283*f*
  subtraction in, 277, 278*f*

## U

Underflow, 290–291, 295, 303
  gradual, 304
Uniprogramming, 226, 232*t*
UNIVAC 1103, 21
UNIVACI, 21
UNIVACII, 21
UNIX, 233
Upward compatibility, 21
Utilities, 223
Utilization, of CPU, in batch systems, 229*t*, 229–231, 230*t*, 233*f*

## V

Vacuum-tube computers, 15–22
Variable-length instructions, 379–380
Variable-size partitioning, 243
VAX, data transfer in, 325
Vector computation, 584–597
  approaches to, 585*f*, 585–590, 586*f*, 587*f*
  IBM 3090, 590–597, 591*f*
    compound instructions in, 595
    instruction set for, 596*t*
    registers in, 592–595, 593*f*, 594*f*

    programs for, 593*f*
Vector multiplication, pipelining and, 587*f*, 587–589, 588*f*
Vector processing, 14
Very-large-scale integration (VLSI), 33, 103
Virtual memory, 245–246
VLSI. *See* Very-large-scale integration
von Neumann architecture, 49–50
von Neumann, John, 16, 49, 51
von Neumann Machine, 16–21. *See also* IAS computer

## W

Wafer, 28, 29*f*
Wilkes control, 530–533, 532*f*, 534*t*
Winchester disk track format, 157*f*, 159
Word, 101
  definition of, 18
Workstations, 37
WORM, 173
WORM disk, performance characteristics of, 106*f*
Write back, 1 31
Write-once read-many memory. *See* WORM
Write policy, in cache memory, 130–132
Write through, 131

## Z

Zilog
  Z8000, register organization in, 393–396, 394*f*
  Z80,000, register organization in, 395, 395*f*

# ACRONYMS

| | |
|---|---|
| **ALU** | Arithmetic and Logic Unit |
| **ASCII** | American Standard Code for Information Interchange |
| **ANSI** | American National Standards Institute |
| **BCD** | Binary Coded Decimal |
| **CD** | Compact Disk |
| **CD-ROM** | Compact Disk—Read Only Memory |
| **CPU** | Central Processing Unit |
| **CISC** | Complex Instruction Set Computer |
| **DRAM** | Dynamic Random Access Memory |
| **DMA** | Direct Memory Access |
| **EPROM** | Erasable Programmable Read-Only Memory |
| **EEPROM** | Electrically Erasable Programmable Read-Only Memory |
| **HLL** | High-Level Language |
| **I/O** | Input/Output |
| **IAR** | Instruction Address Register |
| **IC** | Integrated Circuit |
| **IEEE** | Institute of Electrical and Electronics Engineers |
| **IR** | Instruction Register |
| **LRU** | Least-Recently-Used |
| **LSI** | Large-Scale Integration |
| **MAR** | Memory Address Register |